Engineering Design and Creo Parametric

GUANGMING ZHANG

Department of Mechanical Engineering

The University of Maryland @ College Park

COLLEGE HOUSE ENTERPRISES, LLC
Knoxville, TN

The manuscript was prepared in Microsoft Word 2007 using 11 point Times New Roman font. The book was printed from camera ready copy by Publishing and Printing Inc, Knoxville, TN.

College House Enterprises, LLC.
5713 Glen Cove Drive
Knoxville, TN 37919-8611, U.S.A.
Phone: (865) 558 6111
FAX (865) 558 6111

ISBN 978-1-935673-05-7

To my wife Jinyu
my children Zumei and Haowei, and my
grandchildren Qianqian, Jiajia and Lele

who have always been with me especially at those difficult times. Their love and understanding have supported me in a journey for survival and success.

ABOUT THE AUTHOR

Guangming Zhang obtained a bachelor degree and a master degree both in mechanical engineering from Tianjin University, the People's Republic of China. He obtained a Master degree and a Ph. D. degree in mechanical engineering from the University of Illinois at Urbana-Champaign. He is currently an associate professor in the Department of Mechanical Engineering.

Professor Zhang worked at the Northwest Medical Surgical Instruments Factory in China where he served as a principal engineer to design surgical instruments and dental equipment. He also taught at the Beijing Institute of Printing and received the National Award for Outstanding Teaching from the Press and Publication Administration of the People's Republic of China in 1987. In 1992 he was selected by his peers at the University of Maryland to receive the Outstanding Systems Engineering Faculty Award. He was the recipient of the E. Robert Kent Outstanding Teaching Award of the College of Engineering in 1993, and the Poole and Kent Company Senior Faculty Teaching Award in 2004. He received the Professional Master of Engineering Program Award from the A. James Clark School of Engineering in 2006. He was a recipient of the 1992 Blackall Machine Tool & Gage Award of the American Society of Mechanical Engineering. In 1995, 1997, 1998 and 1999, he received the Award of Commendation, Award of Member of the Year, and the Award of Appreciation from the Society of Manufacturing Engineers, Region 3, for his outstanding service as the faculty advisor to the SME Student Chapter at College Park. In 2006, he was named as one of the 6 Keystone Professors, the Clark School of Academy of Distinguished Professors.

Professor Zhang actively participated in the NSF sponsored ECSEL grant between 1990 and 2000. He served as the principal investigator for this grant at the University of Maryland between 1997 and 2000, and coordinated the ECSEL sponsored projects on integration of design, on active learning and hands-on experiences, and on developing methods for team learning. He also participated in the NSF sponsored ENGAGE program. He has written 3 textbooks, co-authored 3 textbooks, about 70 technical papers, and holds one patent.

PREFACE

This book presents a comprehensive treatment of engineering design with focus on solutions that are based on information technology. With capabilities of computers expanding at an unthinkable pace, the importance of using advanced computer-aided design (CAD) systems in engineering design must be emphasized. Creo Parametric, a leading CAD system, is described to demonstrate the role of the computer in assisting engineers in the design process with efficiency and innovation. This book is written as an introductory textbook for undergraduate students in engineering in all specialty areas (e.g., mechanical, aerospace, civil, electrical, chemical, bioengineering, industrial, materials, and fire protection engineering). This book should also be useful to those engaged in the product design.

This book is organized into 10 chapters. The first three chapters provide a fundamental coverage of engineering design. They stress the need to follow national and international standards related to engineering graphics, dimensioning, and tolerances. Representative examples are provided to demonstrate industrial applications. A systematic description of the Creo Parametric design system is presented in Chapters 4-9. These chapters cover feature-based solid modeling, preparation of engineering drawings, concepts of virtual assembly, animation and mechanism. Chapter 10 presents applications of finite element analysis. Chapter 10 demonstrates the integration of a CAD system and a FEA simulation under the Creo Parametric design environment.

The material covered in this book is an outgrowth of several design and FEA courses taught by the author at the University of Maryland at College Park. The first edition was published at the beginning of 1998. To address the need due to the evolution of the Pro/ENGINEER design system, and now the Creo Parametric design system, several editions were also published. This new edition of this textbook is prepared for users, who are using Creo Parametric, a new edition to the previous Pro/ENGINEER design system.

The author wishes to acknowledge with special thanks the support from Mr. Alister Fraser and the staff members at the Education Program of the Parametric Technology Corporation.

It is a pleasure to extend grateful thanks to Dr. James W. Dally, President of the College House Enterprises, LLC. His support has been invaluable to the author, not only in the academic area, but also in many aspects of the author's life and career development.

Guangming Zhang
College Park, MD

CONTENTS

CHAPTER 4 CREO PARAMETRIC DESIGN SYSTEM

CHAPTER 5 FEATURE-BASED COMPONENT MODELING

CHAPTER 6 PREPARATION OF ENGINEERING DRAWINGS

CHAPTER 7 ASSEMBLY OF COMPONENTS

CHAPTER 1

COMPUTER AIDED DESIGN (CAD)

1.1 Introduction

We are now living in an information age. Use of computers has become part of our life no matter where we are, either in office or at school. When we use computers, we apply software tools to meet our needs or to deal with technical challenges. There is a revolution going on. It is called the digital revolution, which has already invaded the domain of engineering design. Nowadays engineers no longer use pens, pencils and rulers to design parts and prepare drawings. Communications among engineers have been in the digital format as we communicate with each other through the internet and the use of web tools. The concept of computer aided design has been developed in an unforeseeable manner.

Before getting on the subject of computer aided design, let us look back at the evolution of engineering design. During the industrial revolution, new machinery and manufacturing processes were introduced that significantly affected the society. The machinery and the processes not only reduced the time and labor to produce products and materials, but they also provided a richer lifestyle than previously existed. For example, the invention of the locomotive revolutionized the entire transportation system. Steam powered machinery replaced much of the physical power previously generated by humans or horses. Since the industrial revolution, we have worked continuously to invent and redesign machines so that the time and effort required for the society to produce goods and services can be further reduced. Besides, we also seek to create new ways to improve our standard of living.

Today, computers enable us to enhance our capabilities and provide a means for greatly increasing our productivity. The emergence of information technology has revolutionized the way we think, work, communicate, and live. In the engineering profession today, it is almost unthinkable to undertake a project without the use of computers. Applications of computers and information technology are a central element in all engineering disciplines. Among these applications, computer aided design (CAD), computer aided manufacturing (CAM) and computer aided engineering (CAE) have already gained wide acceptance in industry because they enable development teams to quickly generate new and innovative product designs, which meet the required specifications. As we enter the 21st century, industries are adopting new technologies in their product development process. Consequently, the developers of CAD systems are making sweeping changes in their products to support the emerging streamlined engineering processes. As a result, engineers in industry are now facing new challenges: they must select a CAD system from those commercially available in market. Upon the selection of one CAD system or another, the engineers have to adapt themselves to the new system, and find new personnel qualified to use the new system. Afterwards, all the engineers working in team design the product using the CAD system. They effectively share the design and manufacturing information, thus greatly facilitating the information and data exchange.

Over the past decades, CAD systems have become more intelligent and are more focused on system integration, such as assembly modeling, engineering analyses, and system simulation. Understanding the fundamentals of modern CAD systems and imparting the skills necessary to efficiently manage these systems represents a significant challenge in teaching CAD systems at universities. This book is written to support students attempting to become efficient with Creo Parametric (a new version of former Pro/ENGINEER), a major CAD system being used by industry. The three objectives that are addressed in this book are:

1. Understand the fundamentals of CAD systems.
2. Impart skills required in managing Creo Parametric.
3. Demonstrate application areas of using Creo Parametric.

1.2   Concept of Computer-Aided Design

Computer aided design involves the creation and preparation of an engineering documentation, which mainly consists of engineering drawings representing the design of components, subsystems or complete assemblies. A computer loaded with a CAD system assists the engineer or a design team in the product realization process. The computers' graphical capability and computing power allow designers to analyze their designs and test their ideas interactively in real time. In this regard, we must emphasize two equally important factors, the person and the computer. The computer is not used as a substitute for the person when the designer is most effective. On the other hand, the computer should be used in those tasks where the person is limited. The computer and the person are complementary. In fact, most good designs are produced with a multi-disciplinary approach. This includes an integrated development team and experienced personnel who are proficient with advanced CAD systems.

Traditionally, the main purpose of engineering design is to produce a clear definition of a component or a part, subsystem or a system to be manufactured. Producing engineering drawings of the component and/or the assembly usually makes the definition. These engineering drawings establish the physical configuration of the part or system. The uniqueness of computer-aided design is the creation of a solid model for the part (or solid models for the system) in the form of a geometric database. The drawings of the component and/or assembly are derived from this database. Engineering analyses of the designed part(s) or system can be performed. Communications for information and data exchange are thus greatly facilitated.

Major characteristics of CAD systems are presented below:

1. **A creative and innovative method of representing a design conceived by the engineer or the design team**. The judgment of an experienced designer is vital to the process. Moreover, the designer must control this process. This implies that the designer has the flexibility to work on various parts of the assembly at any time and in any sequence. By displaying component designs side by side and by comparing them, a better component or assembly of its components is produced. Computers with significant storage capability, rapid recall, and the ability to display complex three-dimensional images offer a superb environment in which the designer or the design team can work.
2. **An effective method of communicating design information**. Technology and design are becoming broad and complex. As a result, product and process developments rely on the work of teams much more than individual efforts. The team members share experiences, exchange information, and make assessments on a regular basis. Communications with the

computerized networking, such as the Internet and the web system, are new, effective and innovative. Today, these advanced technologies allow design engineers to communicate freely in "cyberspace" by gathering, exchanging, and utilizing information, which is related to the product design process, as illustrated in Figure 1-1.

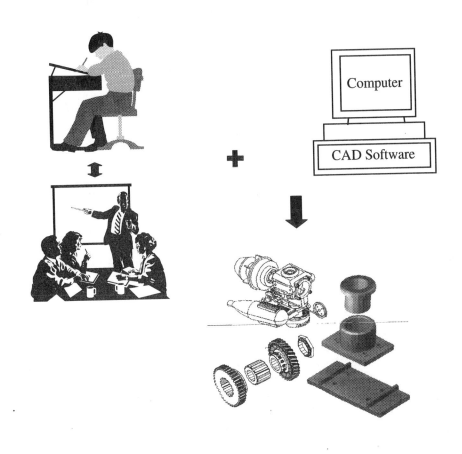

Figure 1-1 The Person, Team, Computer and Outputs with CAD

3. **Facilitate design modifications and redesign**. The design process requires several steps to refine ideas and concepts. Creative and innovative designs come from a process composed of thoughts, experience, and hard work. The ability to make modifications during the design phase of a component or assembly is essential. Under a computer based design environment, the geometric database stores information that can be retrieved at any time during the design process. More important is the fact that the computer software can be programmed to detect design redundancies and errors, thus reducing the need for design iterations. For example, a CAD program can compute the torque capacity of a shaft, while the designer may be limited to his/her experience and judgment to ascertain if the shaft is sized correctly. It is too much to expect a computer software system to automatically detect design errors and guide a process of correcting them.

4. **Execute long and complex engineering analyses**. A computer with the appropriate software is capable of performing complex numerical analysis. Individuals find these same

analyses time-consuming and tedious. In advanced CAD systems, the analysis tools are equipped with graphics tools. It is possible to conduct a finite element analysis and predict performance in the design stage. Today, it is common practice that much of the numerical analysis involved in the design is performed on computer, leaving the designer free to make decisions based on the output from these analyses and their knowledge-based judgment.

5. **Integrated design with other tasks, such as manufacturing**. Companies now use Computerized Numerically Controlled (CNC) machine tools and industrial robots as they seek to improve product quality, increase productivity, and reduce product cost. The geometric database generated by CAD systems is tailored to ensure compatibility of the data between CAD and CAM systems. As illustrated in Figure 1-2, the tools, which design engineers used in the past, have been replaced by computers and software systems.

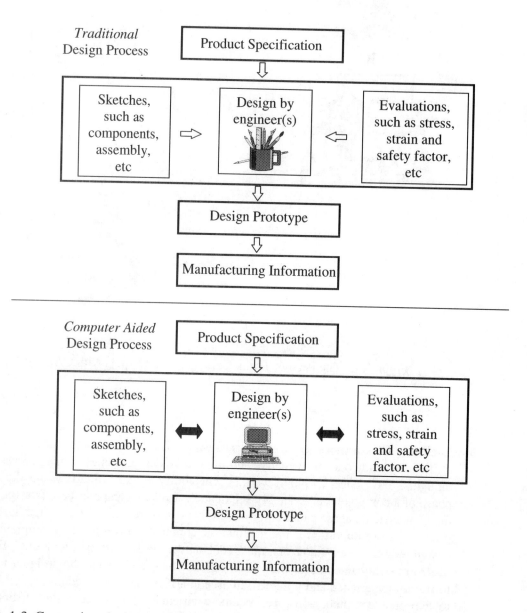

Figure 1-2 Comparison between the Traditional and Computer Aided Design Processes

The five characteristics discussed above illustrate the division between the functions of designer and the functions of computer software systems under a CAD system, as illustrated in Figure 1-3. The principle functions performed by the computer software systems are:

- To relieve the designer and/or design team from routine & repetitious tasks.
- To serve as an extension of the designer's memory.
- To provide a variety of communication tools for information exchange.
- To expand the analytical capabilities of the designer and/or design team.

The principle functions performed by the designer and/or the design team are:

- To apply creativity, ingenuity and experience in the design process.
- To make the fullest use of computer and information technology.
- To organize and manage the information during the design process.

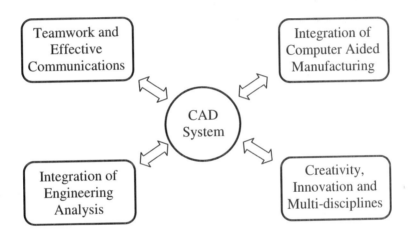

Figure 1-3 Characteristics of a CAD System

1.3   Process of Product Realization

As science and technology advance, the needs of our society change accordingly. Demands for new products are increasing at a rapid pace. To meet the new demands, the product realization process must incorporate:

1. **Customer-oriented design and production.** Managing a wide variety of options has become a business strategy. Being able to deliver a variety of versions of a standard product targeted toward niche markets has become a critical business objective of many corporations. The typical practice in developing a new product involves standard designs for about 80% of the output and customized designs for the remaining 20%. The automobile industry serves as a unique example. The industry has to provide a wide variety of new car models to attract its

customers. For example, the Honda Prelude is designed for the young generation, the Accord appeals to middle class households, and the Civic is targeted toward first car owners. The three Honda models share 40 - 60 % of their standardized parts. As a result, the three models change their appearances every year to attract new car buyers, as illustrated in Figure 1-4.

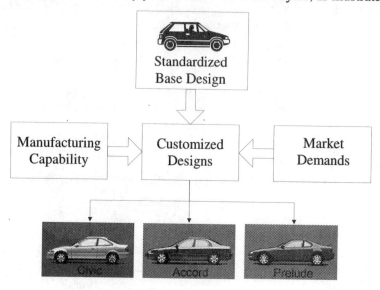

Figure 1-4   Customer Oriented Design and Production

2. **High quality and low cost.** The price of almost every product varies due to a variety of factors. Among them are the labor costs, the cost of raw materials, the market competition, etc. On the other hand, consumers pay much more attention to reliability and quality of the products they intend to purchase. In the meantime, they shop for the lowest prices possible. Quality assurance and pricing have become critical in competition among companies who make similar products. More important is the fact that this competition is global. Driving production costs lower without compromising quality is a goal for every company to compete successfully in the global marketplace.

3. **Globalization of marketing, suppliers, and competitors.** The availability of a great amount of information on products, the modern transportation system and the ability to quickly communicate with vendors in the world have opened the world market to all commodities and high-tech products. Today we do business on a worldwide scale. As an example, Asia and Latin America are two areas with a high population density, giving an opportunity for many companies to increase their customer base. In addition, the low cost of labor and availability of raw material in these areas offer great opportunities for companies to establish their production and supply base. Competition for the desirable markets and supplies is continuing on a global scale. Doing business in the world market is an endless challenge to product designers. As the time to market has become progressively shorter, and mass customization has become a reality, design engineers must accommodate more design changes in a shorter development cycle to capture and maintain their market shares.

4. **Environmental protection.** With increasing population throughout the world, pollution problems are becoming more severe. Society is becoming much more concerned with preserving the environment. Any product produced in the U. S. must meet regulations set by either federal or local environmental protection agencies. If a product development is viewed as a planning for manufacturing, design engineers have the responsibility of selecting the appropriate raw materials, ensuring environmentally conscious manufacturing processes, and

allowing for remanufacturing or recycling of the aging products. The concept of product life cycle management has emerged as a new design guideline for product and process development.

As a brief summary to the above discussion, the product realization process is complex. It plays a critical role in ensuring the production of reliable, profitable, and environmentally safe products that meet the needs of customers. The block diagram presented in Figure 1-5 depicts the central role of the product design process and the major factors that must be accommodated in the product realization process.

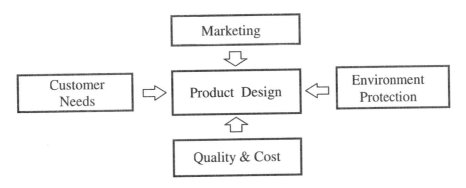

Figure 1-5 Product Realization, Product Design and Related Factors

1.4   The Design Process

Design is a process of creating a product or process that satisfies a clearly defined set of requirements. In general, a design problem has multiple solutions that are constrained by the available resources. In essentially all cases, the final design of a product must be completed within a budget and on schedule. With the rapid advancement in technology, and increased global pressure to be the first to market, a new concept known as concurrent (or simultaneous) engineering has been introduced. Concurrent engineering aims at shortening the product development cycle and enhancing the profit potential of the product by integrating process design with product design so as to reduce the product lead-time. It also provides a means for balancing the conflicting requirements between the design and the manufacturing processes. In general, the design process is viewed as an integration of four stages, namely, the conceptual design, preliminary design, detailed design, and product prototyping, as shown in Figure 1-6.

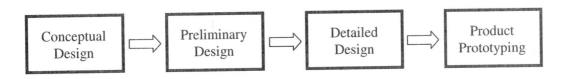

Figure 1-6 Four (4) Essential Stages in the Design Process

For the stage of conceptual design, it begins with the product specification, which is followed by the generation of design concepts, and the identification and analysis of critical product features. This first stage involves the definition of objectives, identification of alternative approaches, and the evaluation of the merits of each approach in terms of both technical and financial feasibility. If an approach does not meet the required specification, the approach should be modified or eliminated so as to come up with an approach, which best meets the design specifications. The flow of information that completes the conceptual design is illustrated in Figure 1-7

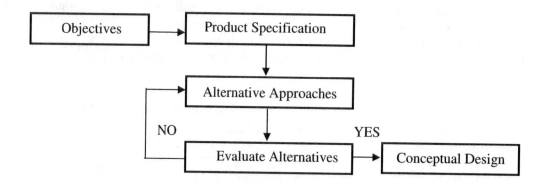

Figure 1-7 Information Flow in the Stage of Conceptual Design

Preliminary design is the second stage in the design process. At this stage, the structure necessary in implementing the conceptual design is visualized. Isometric drawings of the product are made to capture the major characteristics of the conceptual design and facilitate the review of the new product. Engineering drawings of the component are sketched to ensure spatial compatibility, and the material type for each component is selected. Finally, analyses and simplified tests are conducted to insure that the product will meet the product specifications. Information on resource availability and component cost is sought to estimate the cost of production of the product. In this stage, modifications to component designs are made routinely until the entire design team reaches an agreement to pursue detailed design.

The third stage in the process is "detailed design." In this stage, a complete engineering description of the product is developed. Detail design involves the specification of dimensional and geometric tolerances, the analytical evaluation of the system and components, the confirmation of the cost and quality of the manufacturing processes, and the examination of assembly and component drawings. Completion of the design documentation is the essential element in the detail design stage. It should be noted that computer-aided design and computer graphics provide exceptional capabilities for design and engineering documentation. When the detail design is complete, a conference is convened to "release" the design. Managerial and engineering personnel meet to conduct a thorough design review and to approve the design by signing the final documents.

Product prototyping represents the fourth stage in the design process. After the design release, production of the prototype representing the first article is initiated. It is necessary to build scaled or full-sized working models to verify performance and demonstrate the operations required in manufacturing and assembling the final product. Very often, the first prototype, often called the first article build, provides valuable information that identifies design deficiencies not detected prior to the release of the design. Corrections to the design, or design modifications, must be made and verified prior to initiating production. The time required to generate these working models is extremely important in controlling the time to bring a new product to market. A new technology called rapid prototyping has recently been introduced to reduce the time needed to fabricate prototypes of components. Most of the rapid prototyping equipment integrates laser and computer technologies to create a free form method of fabrication. Layers of polymer material are created by exposing a liquid to a focused laser beam that enables designer-directed construction of three-dimensional models. Testing the first article prototype represents a critical step in this stage of the design process. It determines if the design meets product specifications or if it is deficient. For example, the aerodynamic characteristics of an automobile can be evaluated by wind tunnel tests using the first article prototype. The design process ends when the building and the testing of the prototypes verify performance and manufacturability of the designed component(s). To meet such needs to prepare prototyping models, most CAD systems are capable of generating a computer file directly from the part file, for example, a STL file, which is specifically required for creating a layered structure of the prototyping model.

1.5   The Manufacturing Processes

Manufacturing starts upon completion of the design process. The first step in the manufacturing process is process planning. This is the principal activity of manufacturing in the product realization process. Process planning includes choosing the type and sequence of each production operation, the tooling requirements, the production equipment and systems, and estimating the overall cost of production based on these selections. If the product requires an assembly process, process planning includes determining an appropriate sequence of the steps, which assemble components together, and often the process planning requires the design of an assembly line or assembly cells. For production engineers, who are in charge of process planning, they have to understand the required production processes, the productivity capacity of the factory and the limitations imposed by available processing equipment. Components or subassemblies that cannot be produced in-house must be purchased from external suppliers. In some cases, components that can be produced internally may be purchased from outside suppliers for economic reasons. At the end of process planning, routing sheets are prepared to document the product realization process and specify the details of each step involved in the product realization process.

The use of computers in manufacturing, or computer-aided manufacturing (CAM), has grown in importance. Computer-aided process planning systems have been developed to automate process planning by employing computer hardware and software systems. For example, the computer files contain a standard process plan for a particular part to be manufactured. To develop a new process plan will be built on the existing standard process plan. Considerable efforts have been expanded in developing a link between the CAD and CAM systems for production efficiency and quality assurance. The basis of the link between the two systems is the data sharing and data exchange between the design and the manufacturing. For example, because of the shared database, numerical control (NC) codes for machining can be generated directly from the CAD files with additional information on tool selection and parameter settings, such as federate, depth of cut, etc.

When the planning process is complete, production of the components are started with manufacturing processes. In the manufacturing processes, quality inspections at various stages are required. Some of the inspected components may also be subjected to testing, or some of the finished products are subjected to testing even after packaging, as shown in Figure 1-8.

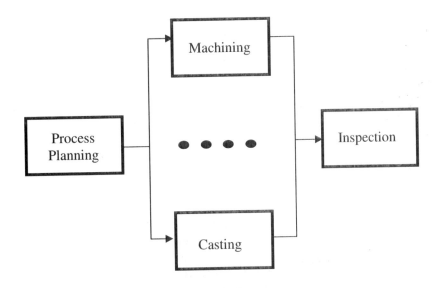

Figure 1-8 The Manufacturing Process

1.6   References

1. D. Banach, T. Jones and A. Kalameja, AutoDESK Inventor 10 Essentials Plus, Thomson, Delmar Learning, autodesk Press, 2006.
2. Ron K. C. C. Cheng, Using Autodesk Inventor, Thomson, Delmar Learning, autodesk Press, 2001.
3. S. Fingers, J. R. Dixon, A review of research in mechanical engineering design, Part II: Representations, analysis, and design for the life cycle, Research in Engineering Design, 1(2), 121-38, 1989.
4. Ellen Finkelstein, AutoCAD 2008 and AutoCAD LT 2008 Bible, Wiley Publishing, Inc., 2007.
5. Matt Lombard, SolidWorks 2007 Bible, Wiley Publishing, Inc., 2007.
6. P. Ingham, CAD System in Mechanical and Production Engineering, London, 1989.
7. R. L. Norton, Machine Design: An Integrated Approach, Prentice Hall, Upper Saddle River, New Jersey, 1996.
8. P. C. Smith and D. G. Reinersten, Developing Products in Half the Time, Van Nostrand Reinhold, New York, 1991.
9. N. P. Suh, The Principles of Design, Oxford University Press, New York, NY, 1990.
10. K. T. Ulrich and S. D. Eppinger, Product Design and Development, McGraw-Hill, New York, NY, 1995.
11. M. Valenti, Teaching Tomorrow's Engineers, Special Report, Mechanical Engineering, Vol. 118, No. 7, July 1996.
12. Gerard Voland, Engineering by Design, second edition, Pearson, Prentice Hall, 2004.
13. A. Yarwood, An Introduction to AutoCAD Release 14, Addison Wesley Longman Limited, 1998.

1.7   Exercises

1. Use your personal experience to describe the essential steps involved in engineering design. Make sure that the following information is presented.

    *   What was the product you designed?
    *   Was the design process a team effort or your own effort?
    *   What was the design objective(s)?

2. Based on your personal experience or observation, describe the importance of documentation in engineering design. Why do computers and information technology play an important role in today's engineering design community?

3. Present any experiences you have had using CAD software. What difficulties did you have in the process of creating your design while using the CAD software?

4. Have you made any engineering drawings? If yes, how did you prepare your engineering drawings? Did you prepare them using a computer and a software system, or using a pen or pencil by hand?

5. How to make an assessment on cost when using a CAD system to prepare an engineering document? Compare the cost of using CAD with the cost required for making the identical document without using computer.

6. What is your expectation from taking a course in CAD systems?

CHAPTER 2

ENGINEERING GRAPHICS

2.1 Introduction

When we play a basketball game, we must follow the rules, such as 5 people per team, no walk while holding the ball, etc. When we speak and write, we follow the grammatical rules, such as having a subject for the sentence, using prepositional phrases to indicate time and location of the action, etc. When we prepare engineering documents, specifically the engineering drawings, we also need to follow certain rules. As illustrated in Figure 2-1, a 3D view of a shaft is presented. The shape of the shaft is cylindrical. The size of the cylinder is 30 mm in diameter and 150 mm in length. Note that a symbol of ϕ is used for indicating the cylindrical shape. There is another dimension shown in Figure 2-1, which is marked as M20-2.5. The symbol of M is used for indicating the feature of thread. The pitch value of the thread is 2.5 mm. The reader may also note the presence of a centerline, characterizing the symmetrical nature of the cylindrical feature.

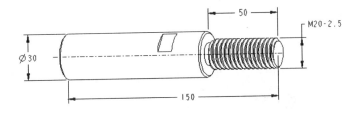

Figure 2-1 Dimensions of a Cylindrical Shaft

In the United States of America, the American National Standards Institute, or ANSI, is the organization to set up the standards, or the rules, used in preparing the engineering documents. In fact, ANSI administrates and coordinates the U.S. voluntary standardization and conformity assessment system. In the worldwide scale, the International Organization for Standardization, or ISO, is the organization to administrate and coordinate the standardization and conformity assessment system. The ISO is a network of national standards institutes from 154 countries. In order to implement the standards established for preparing the engineering documents, a scientific branch, called engineering graphics, has been developed. The subject of engineering graphics serves such a function to guide the communications in the process of design information exchange by following the standards set by ANSI and/or ISO. Consequently, in the field of engineering design, engineering graphics is the primary medium used in developing and communicating design concepts.

The primary mission in communication is the understanding among the parties involved. Engineering graphics accomplishes this mission by focusing on three-dimensional spatial visualization. It covers two major areas, namely descriptive geometry and documentation drawings. Descriptive geometry is the study of points, lines, and surfaces, and serves as the basis to represent objects in the three-dimensional space. Drawings for documentation involve the preparation of working documents or blueprints required to execute the design and to guide operations in production. All the CAD software systems follow these rules because the international community has adopted them. It is very important for CAD users to have a comprehensive understanding of engineering graphics while they are using a CAD system to carry out the design work.

2.2 Design Information and Visualization

Figure 2-2a presents a 3D view of the shaft shown in Figure 2-1. However, detailed information has not been provided in Figure 2-2a, such as the chamfers at the two ends of the shaft, and the dimension is 45° x 1, a slot cut near the middle of the shaft, and the size of the slot is 10 in width, 2 in depth (dimension 26).

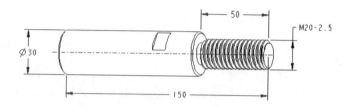

(a) A 3D View of the Cylindrical Shaft with Detailed Design Information

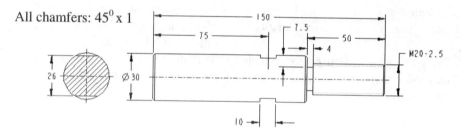

(b) A Front Projection View of the Cylindrical Shaft with Detailed Design Information

Figure 2-2 Comparisons between an Isometric View and a Projection View

Figure 2-2b presents 2 projection views of the same shaft as shown in Figure 2-2a. Although the characteristic of the cylindrical feature as a circular object does not appear in Figure 2-2b, the symbol of φ indicates that the shaft is cylindrical. When comparing the clarity in terms of the design information, and the amount of time and effort for preparing the drawing of the shaft, design engineers prefer the projection views to the 3D view. One of the major reasons is the reflection of true length of an individual feature. For example, the dimension of φ30 and the dimension of 150 characterize the total volume of this component. The dimension of M20 indicates a standard thread feature. The dimension of 26 and the dimension of 10 characterize the size of 2 flats, and the dimension of 75 indicates the position of these 2 flats. On the other hand, making a series of curves representing the thread is not an easy task, especially during those old days when there were no computers to assist engineers in the design process. Certainly, there are more reasons why the method of using the projection views has been adopted by industry. Readers will become clearer as the material covered in this book progresses. However, it should be admitted that the method of using the projection views lacks the power of visualization. It is natural for CAD software developers to provide tools, which combine project views and 3D view(s) so that the communications between design engineers will become not only much clearer, but also the visualization of the geometry will not be compromised.

2.3   Three-Dimensional (3D) Spatial Visualization

Because of the adoption of using the projection view method, the ability of visualizing an object in the three-dimensional (3D) space becomes critical for success in engineering design. Common sense also dictates that people learn new information most efficiently through visualization. The ability to visualize ideas is an extremely important talent that an engineer must develop if he or she is to function effectively. It is important to point out that the CAD software systems function as effective learning tools for users to gain the ability of spatial visualization. The author truly believes that a student, after taking a CAD course, will strengthen his/her ability of spatial visualization significantly.

Generally speaking, students acquire the ability of visualization through a development process as they grow up. For example, when we were children at home, we first learned topological spatial visualization. During those days we were able to discern the topological relationship of an object relative to other objects (i.e., how close are the subjects to one another? What is the object's location within a group of objects?). In the second stage of spatial visualization development, or when we attended elementary, middle and high schools, we learned the skill of projective representation. We were able to conceive the appearance of an object from different perspectives. In the third stage, as we become engineers, we learn to combine projective abilities with the concept of measurement.

A sample problem to learn 3D spatial ability is shown in Figure 2-3. On the top part, the orientation of an object called AA, is changed to a new orientation. On the bottom part, a new object is shown at a given orientation. Five (5) choices in terms of a new orientation are presented and a person is asked to identify one from the 5 choices so that the new orientation of the new object follows the same transformation pattern.

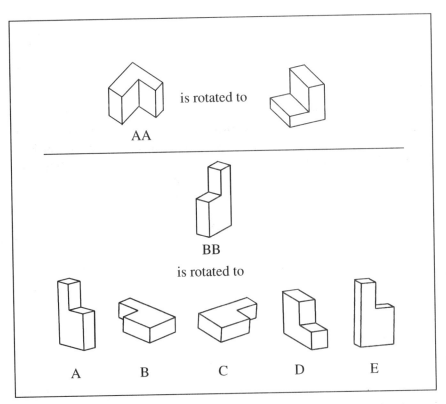

Figure 2-3 An Example of Learning Space Visualization

In order to facilitate the visualization process, we may introduce a Cartesian coordinate system having its origin associated with a corner of the object. By inspection, there are 2 rotations associated with the orientation variation. The first rotation is 90^0 about the X-axis in the clockwise direction. The second rotation is 90^0 about the Z-axis in the count-clockwise direction.

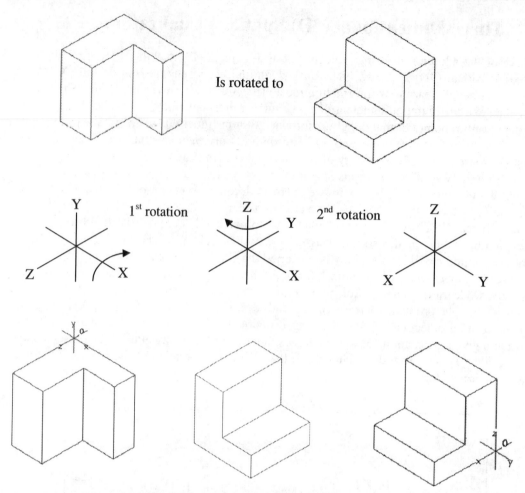

Is rotated to

Based on these observations, Choice B is the correct answer to this question. As illustrated, Object BB is rotated to the orientation shown by choice D through the 2 rotations. We leave the geometrical shape for the orientation after the first rotation to readers with hope that readers are able to fill in. In Exercise 2-9, similar examples are provided for readers to practice the skill of spatial visualization. We hope your visualization skills are sufficient to choose the correct answers.

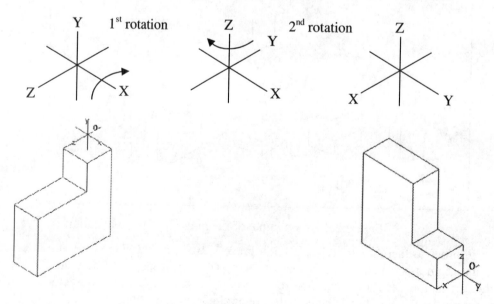

2.4 Product Design and Engineering Graphics

To illustrate the critical role that engineering graphics plays in the process of product design, we present a case study involving the design of a seesaw commonly found in a playground. The scenario is school administrators in a local area were requested that seesaws be built and installed for children attending kindergarten. A project sponsored by the school administrators was initiated. A group of five high school students formed a design team. Their responsibility was to design components of a seesaw, manufacture them, assemble them, install the assembled seesaw at the playground, and finally test it. The flow chart shown in Figure 2-4 outlines the three phases in the product design process the student team followed. It included design, manufacturing, and assembly. In each phase, specific tasks were planned. The team followed this plan, and the seesaw development process progressed from one phase to the next.

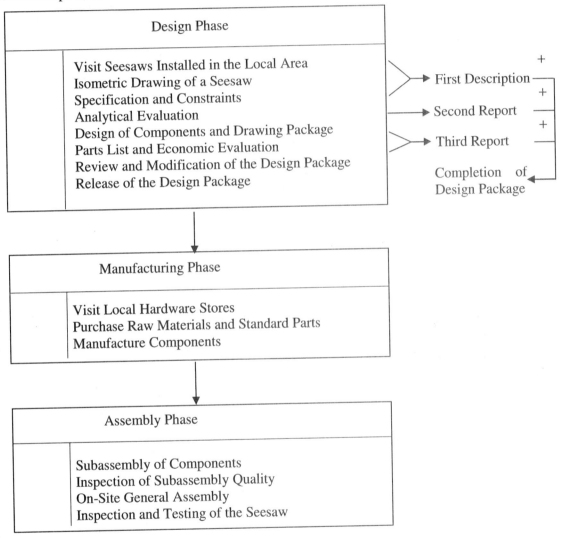

Figure 2-4 Three Phases of the Process of Designing a Seesaw

In Phase 1, the student team decided that wood would be the raw material for the seesaw because cutting wood to meet the required accuracy of components was manageable. Afterwards, the team prepared an isometric drawing of the seesaw the team wanted to have. The sketched isometric view is shown in Figure 2-5a. The sketched isometric view provided the team members with important information related to the design. As they counted the components one by one, they realized that at least 8 components were needed. Those components were the main board, the adjustable pivot, a connect to assemble the main board and the adjustable pivot together, the bottom support for housing the seesaw on the playground, 2 side supports for the component of the pivot shaft to sit on, and the connector to hold the pivot shaft onto the two side supports. In order to share the responsibility of manufacturing each of those components, they recognized the need to prepare an engineering drawing for each of those components. To make sure that all the components are fit together during the assembly process, they paid special attention to the dimensions, which functioned as interfaces connecting neighboring components. When looking at the need of such a great amount of effort, the student team used a CAD system to prepare the engineering drawings for each components as well as the engineering drawing for the seesaw assembly. Figure 2-5b presents the assembly drawing prepared by the student team. Note some changes to the product design completed in Phase 1. On the main board, two circular-shaped slots were added so that the extended portions of the main board could be eliminated. As a result, the process of manufacturing the main board could be facilitated. On the assembly drawing prepared by the use of a CAD system, 8 balloons were added to clearly depict the 8 components, and a table was prepared to name those components. When comparing the sketched one with the CAD created one, what a difference!

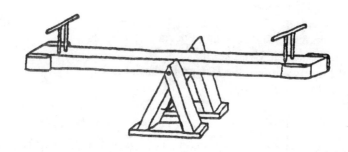

(a) An Isometric View of the Seesaw Product Made by Hand Sketch

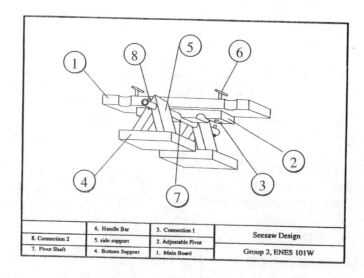

8. Connection 2	6. Handle Bar	3. Connection 1	Seesaw Design
7. Pivot Shaft	5. side support	2. Adjustable Pivot	
	4. Bottom Support	1. Main Board	Group 2, ENES 101W

(b) An Isometric View of the Seesaw Product Created Under the Use of a CAD system

Figure 2-6 Comparison between a Sketched and a CAD Creation of a Seesaw Product

2.5 Procedure of Preparing a Projection Engineering Drawing

Assume that you are given an object such as the one shown in Figure 2-7. Note that there are three maximum dimensions of an object in a three-dimensional space. The three maximum dimensions of the object shown in Figure 2-7 are (50+25) mm, 30 mm and 40 mm, respectively. Now you are given a piece of paper and a pencil, and asked to prepare an engineering drawing of it through the use of projections by sketching.

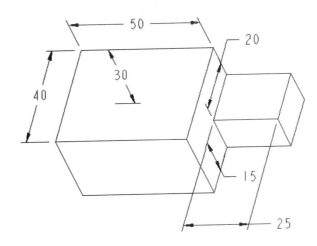

Figure 2-7 An Object with the Three Maximum Dimensions Equal to (50+25), 30, and 40 mm

Depending on the personal style or preference, the procedure of preparing an engineering drawing may vary. However, there are several steps, which are almost invariant because these steps serve as the key steps in sketching an engineering drawing by hand.

Step 1: draw 4 horizontal lines and 4 vertical lines, as shown in Figure 2-8. Pay great attention to the distances between 2 neighboring lines, assuring that the three maximum dimensions (75, 40 and 30) are maintained.

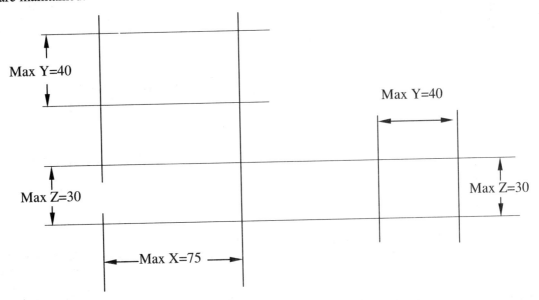

Figure 2-8 Draw Boundary Lines in both Horizontal and Vertical Directions

Step 2: prepare the front view. Sketch 2 rectangles, as shown in Figure 2-9. Note that the left side of the large rectangle and the right side of the small rectangle are aligned side by side or the 2 rectangles share a common line in the vertical direction. Also note that the maximum dimension in the x direction and the maximum dimension in the z direction control the sizes of the two rectangles. The maximum dimension of Y does not come into the picture in the process of preparing the Front View.

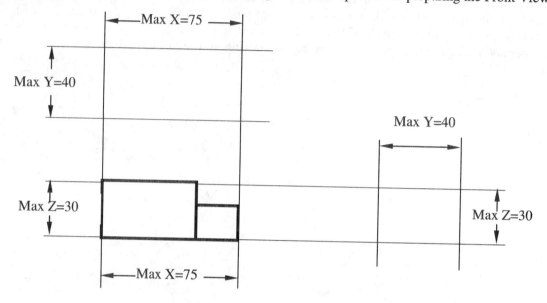

Figure 2-9 Prepare the Front View

Step 3: prepare the top view. Sketch 2 rectangles, as shown in Figure 2-10. Note that the left side of the large rectangle and the right side of the small rectangle are aligned side by side or the 2 rectangles share a common line in the horizontal direction. Also note that the maximum dimension in the x direction and the maximum dimension in the y direction control the sizes of the two rectangles. The maximum dimension of Z does not come into the picture in the process of preparing the Top View.

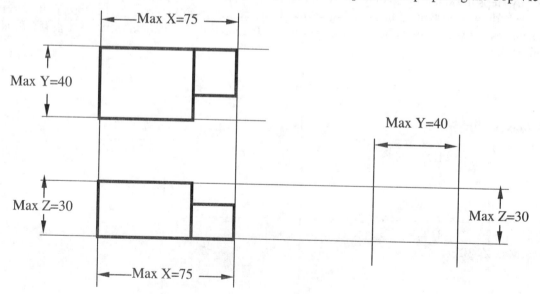

Figure 2-10 Prepare the Top View

Step 4: prepare the right-sided view or profile view. Sketch 2 rectangles, as shown in Figure 2-11. Note that the large rectangle and the small rectangle are aligned side by side or the 2 rectangles share a common line in the vertical direction. Also note that the maximum dimension in the y direction and the maximum dimension in the z direction control the sizes of the two rectangles. The maximum dimension of X does not come into the picture in the process of preparing the Right-Sided View.

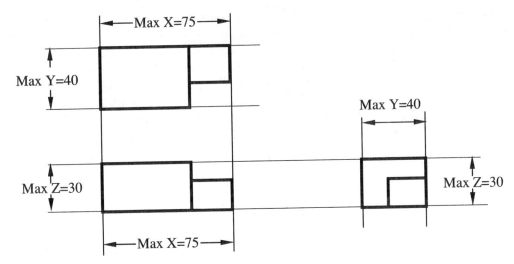

Figure 2-11 Prepare the Right-Sided View

The above layout for the three projection views, namely, the Front View, the Top View and the Right-Sided View (Profile View) is the standard adopted by ANSI for preparing an engineering drawing. The CAD software systems developed in the United States of America all follow this convention. It is true that creating such a layout under the environment of a CAD system is rather simple. However, it is important to note that the first view created, which is the Front View in the current study, is considered the Parent View. Both the Top View and the Right-Sided View are considered child views. Because of this standard or convention set forth for the layout of an engineering drawing, the Top View can only move vertically, and the Right-Sided View can only move horizontally when there is a need to relocate them, as illustrated in Figure 2-12.

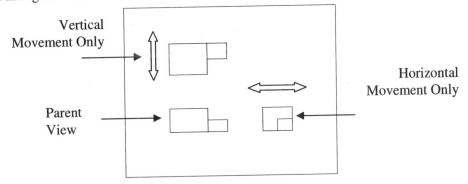

Figure 2-12 Restrictions on Moving the Child Views Created under the CAD Environment

2.6   Principles of Orthographic Drawings

Following the discussion on the procedure to prepare an engineering drawing in the previous section, a natural question to ask is "Why is the layout designed in such a way, not anything other than the standard one currently being used?" In reality, engineers deal with the design of machines and structures. In terms of their size and shape, these objects are characterized and measured in a three-dimensional space. In the engineering community, people communicate through the use of engineering drawings on paper. The effort to prepare those drawings for representation and construction is better completed in a two-dimensional space. This is especially true because of the importance on the clarity and accuracy in documentation. For a three-dimensional object to be defined and understood using a two-dimensional format, the method of orthographic projection is used.

This method is based on the assumption that the object remains fixed as the observer changes position to obtain different views of the object. Using the orthographic projection, drawings are prepared to document the shape and size of each component present in an assembly. Dimensions and tolerances are added to these drawings to complete the definition of a component.

The principle used by the orthographic projection is to draw perpendiculars for two or more sides of the object on a projection plane. To demonstrate the projection procedure, consider the object shown in Figure 2-7. The front view of this object based on the concept of orthographic projection is shown in Figure 2-13. As illustrated, a front plane is first introduced, and parallel lines are projected forward to locate the points necessary to draw the front view of the object with a small block attached to the right side of the big block. It is important to note that the front view does not completely specify the shape of the object. For example, the depths of those features projected are not given. For this reason, additional projections are required to completely describe the stepped block.

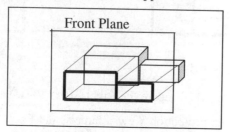

Figure 2-13 Creation of the Front View through Orthographic Projection

Figure 2-14 illustrates the process of creating the top view. First, a horizontal plane is introduced to imitate getting a piece of paper, which is horizontally oriented so that the top view can be displayed. Note that the front and horizontal planes are perpendicular to each other. The top view gives the appearance of the object as viewed from the top, and shows the dimensions from front to rear. In order to arrange the two views of the object on a two-dimensional plane, the horizontal plane is rotated through 90° to become co-planar with the frontal plane, as illustrated in Figure 2-15.

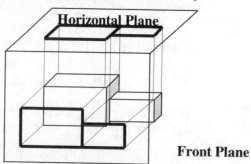

Figure 2-14 Creation of the Top View through Orthographic Projection

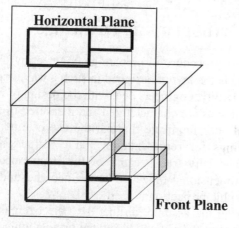

Figure 2-15 A 90° Rotation to Combine the Front and Top Views on a Single Plane

To generate the right-sided view, a third plane is introduced. It is the profile plane, which is on the right side, as shown in Fig. 2-16. The plane is perpendicular to both the frontal and the horizontal planes. The right-sided view is projected on the profile plane. This right-sided view shows the shape of the object when viewed from the side. It also shows the height and depth dimensions of the object. In order to arrange the three views of the object on the surface of a screen or paper, the profile plane is rotated 90° onto the frontal plane. As shown in Figure 2-17, a combination of the three views gives a presentation of the three-dimensional shape of the object.

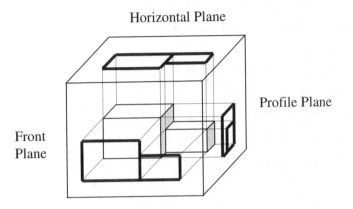

Figure 2-16 Creation of the Right-Sided View through Orthographic Projection

In an orthographic projection, the three picture planes first introduced are called "planes of projection", and the perpendiculars, "projecting lines" or "projectors." In examining these projections, or views, we should not think of them as flat surfaces on the transparent planes. Instead, imagine that you are examining the object through transparent planes.

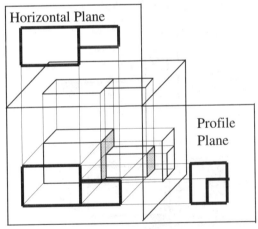

Figure 2-17 A 90° Rotation to Combine the Front, Top and Right-Sided Views on a Single Plane

The projection principles demonstrated in the above illustrations represent the convention widely adopted by design engineers in the United States and other countries with close economic ties to the U. S. On the other hand, the design engineers in Europe and much of Asia employ a different procedure. There are some significant differences between the two conventions. Examining Figure 2-18, four projection quadrants are shown. They are quadrant I, quadrant II, quadrant III and quadrant IV. Each of them is available for projecting a view of the object to a picture plane. As illustrated, a cubic object located in both quadrants I and III has been projected. The first difference in projecting these two cubes is the two squares formed by solid lines, as compared to the two squares formed by dashed lines. The second difference in using quadrant I for projection is that the front view of the object occurs above the horizontal plane, not below it as is the case when the cube is in quadrant III. Although the contents of this book are mainly based on using the third-angle projection (quadrant III placement of the object), the concept of the first-angle projection (quadrant I placement of the object) is important. In the international business world, we will from time to time be called upon to interpret engineering drawings made with the first-angle system. Being aware of both system conventions will assist you in reading engineering drawings correctly.

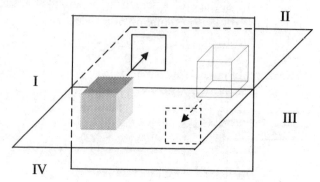

Figure 2-18 Placement of Cubes in Quadrants I and III to Illustrate Different Reference Systems

If the method of orthographic projection is extended, the maximum number of principal views that can be drawn is six (top, bottom, left, right, front, and back). As the viewer changes position at 90^0 intervals, the object is completely surrounded by a set of six projection planes. Four of the six principal projection planes are illustrated in Figure 2-19. In each view, two of the three dimensions of height, width, and depth are evident.

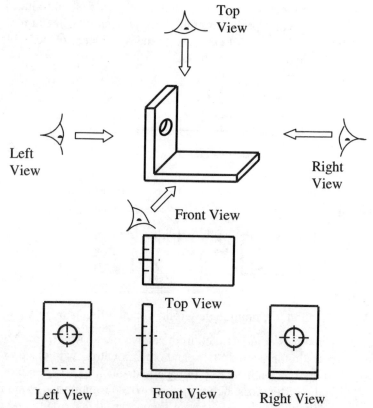

Figure 2-19 Four of the Six Principal Views of an Angle Bracket

Imagine the process of obtaining the six views as a person opens a six-sided box onto the surface of a pad of paper. Since the front plane has been selected for display on the plane of the paper, the front view automatically occurs on this plane. The other sides are hinged at the corners and rotated onto the surface of the paper. The projection onto the horizontal plane provides the top view. The projection onto the right profile plane gives the right side view. The projection onto the left profile plane is the left side view. By reversing the direction of observation, a bottom view is obtained instead of a top view, or a rear view instead of a front view. In some cases, a bottom view, rear view, or both may be required to show the detail of a complicated component.

In practice, three views usually are sufficient to represent the shape and dimensions of typical components. For objects with relatively simple geometric shapes, one or two views may be sufficient to completely define the shape and dimensions of the component. Figure 2-20 illustrates that a single view is sufficient to represent a simple cylindrical shaft.

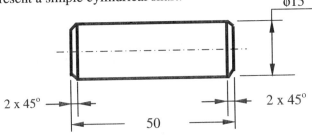

Figure 2-20 Using a Single Projection View for Representation

2.7 Descriptive Geometry

To assure the precision of a given component, relationships between its geometric features and the basic geometric elements must be established in an explicit and unique manner. Descriptive geometry is the study of these relationships, and it serves as the basis for algorithm development in all CAD systems.

2.7.1 Projection of Points

A point defines a position in space, and it is dimensionless by itself. Two or more points can be used to establish the length of a line, the area of a surface, and the volume of a three-dimensional shape. To uniquely define the position of a point in space, at least two adjacent orthographic views containing all three dimensions needed to position the point are required.

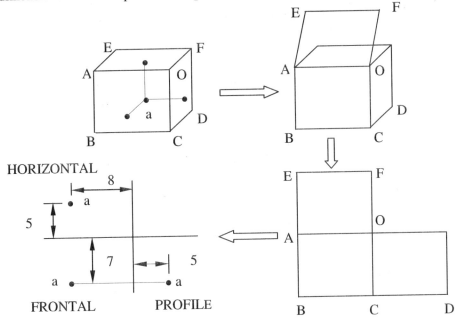

Figure 2-21 Point Projection onto the Horizontal, Frontal, and Profile Planes

In descriptive geometry, quantitative measurements are used to define the location of a point in space. We illustrate these measurements in Figure 2-21 where point (a), confined in a six-sided box, is shown. Three projections of the point onto the frontal, horizontal, and profile planes are indicated. We also illustrate the process of opening the box to arrange the three projection plans onto a single plane, i.e., the frontal plane. The corners of the box are labeled from A to F to aid in visualizing the hinge lines on the single plane representation. Finally, we show that point (a) is 8 units to the left of the profile plane, 7 units below the horizontal plane, and 5 units behind the front plane.

2.7.2 Projection of Lines

A line is the straight path between two points in the three-dimensional space. In drawings constructed using orthographic projection, a line may be viewed in its true length, foreshortened, or as a point. These three representations of a line are illustrated in Figure 2-22.

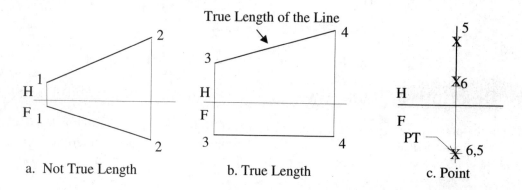

Figure 2-22 Concept of the True Length of a Line Shown in a Projection View

(a) A foreshortened line is not parallel or perpendicular to a principal projection plane.
(b) A true-length line is parallel to, at least, one of the principal projection planes. The three principal planes (horizontal, frontal, and profile) are shown in Figure 2-10. In Figure 2-10a, we show a horizontal line, which is parallel to the horizontal projection plane. It appears in true length in the horizontal projection plane that displays the top view.
(c) A line that projects as a point occurs when the line of sight is parallel to that line. In orthographic projection, a line that projects as a point is parallel to two principal planes. For example, a line that is projected, as a point in the front view is parallel to both the horizontal and profile planes.

The three standard orthographic views of an oblique line in the three-dimensional space are presented in Figure 2-23. The true length of the line is not reflected in any of the views. Under such a circumstance, we must calculate the true length of this oblique line.

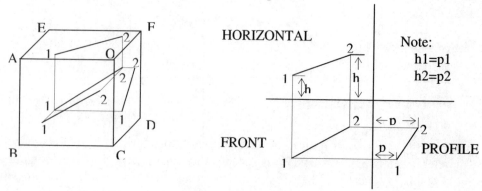

Figure 2-23 Three Orthographic Views of an Oblique Line in Space

2.7.3 Projection of Planes

A plane is a flat surface. Any two points on this surface may be connected by a straight line that lies entirely on the surface. The positions of planes in space may be designated by the positions of two intersecting lines, two parallel lines, a point and a line, or three points not in a line, as illustrated in Figure 2-24.

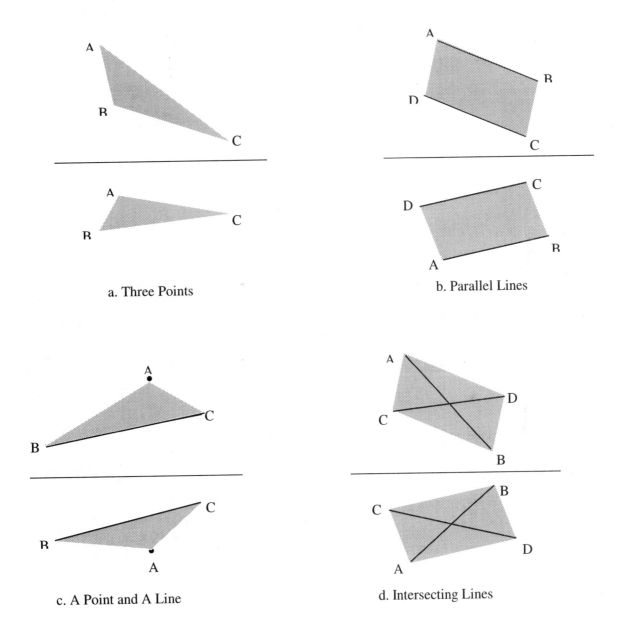

a. Three Points

b. Parallel Lines

c. A Point and A Line

d. Intersecting Lines

Figure 2-23 Defining Planes with Points, Lines and Combinations Thereof

If a plane is to appear as a line in a principal projection view, the line of observation for that view must be parallel to the plane. A plane must appear as an edge in any view in which a line on that plane appears as a point. A plane will be seen in its true shape and size in any view for which the line of observation is perpendicular to the plane.

2.7.4 Visibility

To draw a correct representation of a feature in an orthographic projection, it is necessary to indicate whether a line is visible or hidden. Any view of an object is bounded by visible lines, so visibility needs to be determined only for those lines that fall within the outline of the view. When nonintersecting lines cross in certain views, determining which line is above, or in front of, the other is referred to as establishing a line's visibility as shown in Figure 2 24.

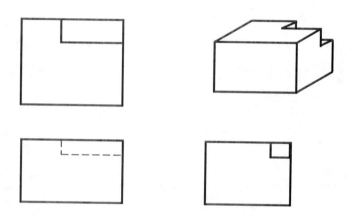

Figure 2-24 Concept of Visibility and Concept of Hidden Lines

Establishing line visibility is a requirement in preparing orthographic drawings representing many complex three-dimensional components. Fortunately, all CAD systems are capable of determining the visibility of the lines within the object's boundaries. In a computer aided design environment, the command "show hidden" is usually available on the design screen. Switching on "show hidden" results in the display of all hidden lines as dashed lines. Turning off "show hidden" eliminates all the dashed lines on the design screen.

2.7.5 Types of Lines Used in Engineering Drawings

Engineering drawings are made with lines and symbols. In general, there are 9 types of lines used in engineering drawings. They are shown in Figure 2-25. Each line is used for a distinct purpose.

Visible lines or object lines:	Solid, thick lines for outlines or visible edges of parts.
Hidden lines:	Dashed lines with medium width for edges that are not directly visible in a view.
Centerlines:	Thin lines composed of alternating long and short dashes used to represent the axes of symmetry.
Section lines:	Solid, thin lines used for sectional views at an angle with the outlines.
Dimension lines:	Same style as section lines, but used for dimensioning sizes of features.
Cutting plane lines:	Solid, thick lines used to locate a cross section.
Phantom lines:	Similar to centerlines except with double dots, used to represent adjacent parts.
Long break lines:	Similar to centerlines except with break signs to indicate the end of a partially illustrated feature.
Short break lines:	Drawn by hand to indicate the boundary of a small detail.

Engineering drawings make use of standard lines show the details associated with a part or parts. A CAD system may automatically select the proper line types for the user. However, it is important for a design engineer to understand proper line types when designing components.

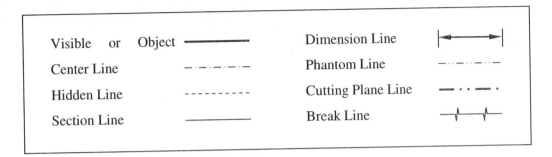

Figure 2-25 Types of Lines Used in Engineering Drawings

2.8 References

1. H. R. Buhl, Creative Engineering Design, Iowa State University Press, Ames, Iowa, 1960.
2. A. Burstall, A History of Mechanical Engineering, M.I.T. Press, Cambridge, MA, 1965.
3. B. L. Davids, A. J. Robotham and Yardwood A., Computer-aided Drawing and Design, London, 1991.
4. C. E. Douglass, and A. L. Hoag, Descriptive Geometry, Holt, Rinehart and Winston, Inc., 1962.
5. G. Farin, Curves and Surfaces for Computer-aided Geometric Design, New York, 1988.
6. C.S. Krishnamoorthy, Finite Element Analysis, Theory and Programming, 2nd Ed., 1995.
7. P. Ingham P. CAD System in Mechanical and Production Engineering, London, 1989.
8. N. P. Suh, The Principles of Design, Oxford University Press, New York, NY, 1990.
9. C. L. Svensen and W. E. Street, Engineering Graphics, Van Nostrand Company, 1962.

2.9 Exercises

1. What are the three engineering projections that are most commonly used?
2. Prepare the three projections for the object show below. You may sketch the projections by hand (unit: mm).

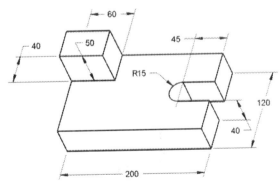

3. In what situations do you need more than three projections? In what situations do you only need 2 projections or one projection? Illustrate the principle that a minimum number of projections are preferred in engineering documentation.
4. Prepare an engineering drawing of an object where one projection is needed.
5. Prepare an engineering drawing of an object where two projections are needed.
6. Prepare an engineering drawing of an object where three projections are needed.
7. Prepare an engineering drawing of an object where more than three projections are needed.
8. Select the correct answers to the following 2 questions.

Question A

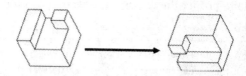

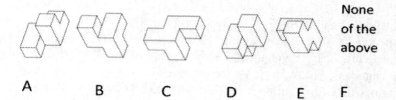

None of the above

A   B   C   D   E   F

Question B

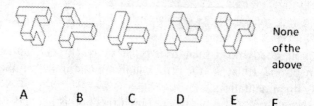

None of the above

A   B   C   D   E   F

CHAPTER 3

DIMENSIONING ENGINEERING DRAWINGS

3.1   Geometric Dimensioning

In the process of preparing an engineering drawing, the first step is to create a projection view or projection views, depending on the complexity of the object. When the projection view(s) is created, dimensions are needed to specify the sizes of the features. Figure 3-1 illustrates three dimensions used to specify the width, height and depth of a block. They are 150, 100 and 60, respectively. It is evident that an engineering drawing without dimensions only represents the geometric shape of an object. Such an engineering drawing is not a completed drawing.

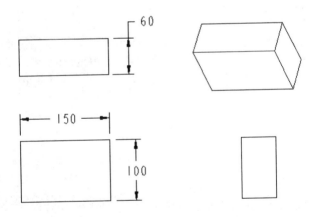

Figure 3-1 Three Dimensions to Specify the Size of a Block

Geometric dimensioning is the process of specifying the size and position of the features comprising a component, providing notes relevant to the manufacturing process, and providing information related to the product realization process, such as purchase, process planning, etc. With the addition of dimensions and notes, engineering drawings serve as part of the document to guide the product processes to follow, such as assembly, manufacturing, inspection, testing, etc. In fact, engineering drawings are often included as part of legal contracts. The process of dimensioning is so critical that the American National Standards Institute (ANSI) has established standards. These standards are referred to Y14.5M, a document entitled Dimensioning and Tolerancing for Engineering Drawings. The information on dimensioning and geometrical tolerancing is an important part of the communication of the design requirements to the manufacturing/quality departments within the company, to the customers of the company and to the outside suppliers.

3.1.1 Size and Position Dimensions

Generally speaking, there are two (2) types of dimensions. The first type of dimension is associated with the size of the feature. We call this type of dimension: *size dimension*. The three dimensions displayed on the drawing shown in Figure 3-1 are all size dimensions. The second type of dimension is to characterize the position of a feature with respect to another feature(s) or the reference(s) defined by the designer. We call this type of dimension: *position dimension*. To clarify these two types of dimensions, let us examine the five (5) dimensions shown in Figure 3-2. The component is a part made of sheet metal. The two dimensions of 150 and 100 specify the width and depth of the plate. The thickness of the plate is 6 mm, which is specified by a dimension in the form of a note. These three dimensions are all size dimensions because they characterize the size of the plate.

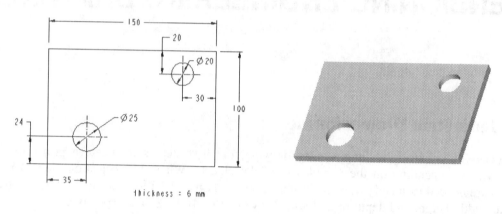

Figure 3-2 Concepts of Size Dimension and Position Dimension

The dimension of φ20 and the dimension of φ25 define the sizes of the two holes. Therefore, these two dimensions are also size dimensions. On the other hand, the two dimensions of 24 and 35 are not size dimensions. They are position dimensions because they define the location of the center of the hole with diameter equal to 25 mm. The two dimensions of 20 and 30 are also position dimensions because they define the location of the center of the hole with diameter equal to 20 mm. As illustrated in this example, those dimensions for positions are as important as the dimensions for sizes. Without these four (4) dimensions to define the 2 locations of the two holes, the design of this sheet metal part is not completed.

3.1.2 Use Reference(s) to Specify Dimensions

It is a common practice that design engineers use references when they specify dimensions. One of the major reasons is to facilitate the manufacturing and assembly processes, and to assure high quality. To understand the concept of using references, let us examine some of the dimensions shown in Figure 3-2. For example, the two position dimensions of 20 and 30 are used to define the center location of the hole with diameter equal to 20. From which place are these two dimensions measured? It is clear the right side and the topside are viewed as the two references to specify 30 mm and 20 mm, respectively. In the same way, the left side and bottom side of the plate are serving the two references to specify 35 mm and 24 mm, respectively. In the process of specifying the position dimensions, we need to select certain existing entities, such as the surfaces used in specifying those position dimensions just discussed, as the references.

The importance of selecting a reference before specifying a position dimension is illustrated through an example, which involves an assembly of three components. As shown in Figure 3-3, the sheet metal part is assembled with two other components. One is located at the upper right corner, and the other at the lower left corner, as shown in Figure 3-3a. The condition to ensure the accuracy of aligning those two components with the sheet metal part is to set the requirement so that the position dimensions for the two holes on the two contacting components share the same references, as shown in Figure 3-3b.

(a)   Two Components Are Assembled with the Sheet Metal Part in an Exploded View

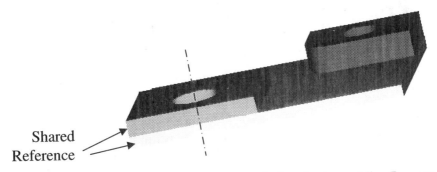

Shared
Reference

(b)   The Shared References between the components during the Assembling Process

Figure 3-3 Use of a Shared Reference to Align Two Components

Under a CAD environment, users should have a clear idea on selecting reference(s). To facilitate the selection process, most of the CAD systems utilize AI (artificial intelligence) technology, such as Intent Manager. The CAD software system automatically selects a minimum set of references, even without informing the designer when he or she is using the software system. Certainly, on the screen display, the reference information is usually indicated by dashed-lines. Those references selected by the system default may fit the need of the designer. However, sometimes or very often, the reference(s) selected by the system default does not meet the need of the designer. Under those circumstances, it is the responsibility of designer to redefine the reference(s).

Figure 3-4 presents an example to illustrate the use of both size dimensions and position dimensions in an engineering drawing. The object is a sheet metal part. As a result, the dimension of thickness, such as SD3, is needed. As shown in Figure 3-4, there are 7 size dimensions, marked as SD1, SD2, SD3, SD4, SD5, SD6 and SD7. There are also 5 position dimensions, marked as PD1, PD2, PD3, PD4 and PD5. Note that dimensions for positions are as important as dimensions for sizes. Without the five dimensions to define the positions, the part design would not be uniquely defined.

There are always a few alternatives in the process of dimensioning a certain component. The criterion for selecting an appropriate way to dimension is to make the size and position requirements clear to other people so that the manufacturing and assembly process, or purchase process, can be facilitated without confusing. Another important criterion for dimensioning is to characterize the requirement(s) for manufacturing processes. For example, to dimension the size of a hole, we should use the size of diameter, not the size of radius so that an operator can easily find a drill bit, which fits the need for drill the hole. It is evident that mastering the skills of dimensioning demands working experience in the product realization process, or the hands on experience in design and manufacturing. In fact, the ANSI standards embody the accumulation of design experience, and provide excellent guidelines for appropriate ways to specify dimensions. It is recommended that students in college should take opportunities to go to the shop floor and gain a comprehensive understanding of the product realization process.

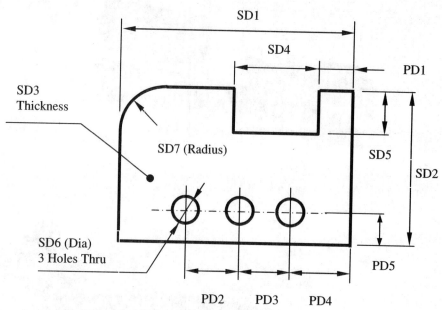

Figure 3-4 Size Dimensions and Position Dimensions

For those components, which contain a single feature, size dimensions are required, and position dimensions may not be needed. For example, the prism shown in Figure 3-5 can be viewed as having one feature. As a result, three size dimensions are needed with no position dimension.

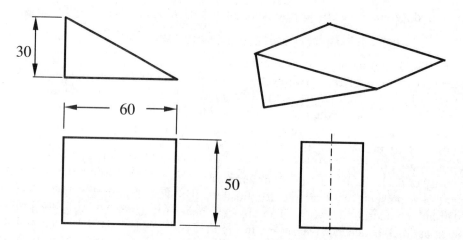

Figure 3-5 Size Dimensions Are Required and No Position Dimensions

3.1.3 Two Unit Systems

There are two units of measurement that are currently employed in dimensioning, the decimal inch in the U. S. customary system (English) and the millimeter in the SI system (metric), where SI stands for the International System of Units. Numerical values shown in engineering drawings are assumed to be in millimeters or inches unless a different unit is specified. The conversion factor between inch (in.) and millimeter (mm) is 25.4 mm = 1 inch. A comparison of units used to dimension a single view of a block is presented in Figure 3-6. It is very important to note that there is no need to write mm or inch on the engineering drawings. Engineers all over the world take it for granted that mm or inch is the unspecified unit for data and information exchange. Almost all the CAD software systems have a unit conversion function so that the conversion from the US customary system to the SI system and vise versa can be easily made.

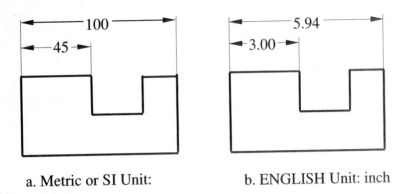

a. Metric or SI Unit: b. ENGLISH Unit: inch

Figure 3-6 Examples of dimensioning in SI and U. S. Customary units.

3.2   General Guidelines for Dimensioning

Although shop experience or hands-on experience is critical in specifying dimensions, there are several general guidelines in the process of specifying dimensions. In this section, we present 12 general guidelines. The first principle is "Specify all dimensions in one view if possible." This will minimize the number of projections needed to represent an object so that an operator can concentrate his or her effort on examining all the dimensions from a single projection in the process of manufacturing the part. As shown in Figure 3-7, using one view is sufficient to represent the shaft (rotation and axis-symmetry) component.

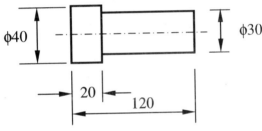

Figure 3-7 Show all Dimensions in a Single View for Convenience

Figure 3-8 shows a center-hollow cylinder and a plate with uniform thickness. The cylindrical component has two features. The first feature would be a solid cylinder with a diameter equal to 60 mm and 60 mm in length. The second feature would be a solid cylinder with a diameter equal to 20 mm and 60 mm in length. The total volume of the center-hollow cylinder is given by a subtraction. From the viewpoint of dimensioning, three dimensions are needed. Make sure that the symbol ϕ is used for presenting diameters. Partial cylinders, such as fillets and rounds, are dimensioned using the radius instead of the diameter, as illustrated in the plate component. Therefore, do not use symbol ϕ. The symbol for radius, R, should be used. A good general rule is to dimension complete circles with the diameter and circular arcs (partial circles) with the radius.

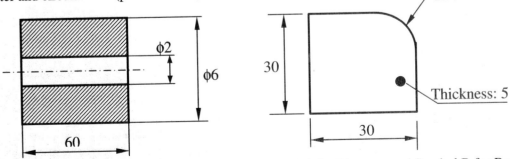

Figure 3-8 Use of a Single View and Use of Symbol ϕ for Diameter and Symbol R for Radius

The second principle is "Specify the three maximum dimensions". This principle is extremely important for a shop operator, who needs to prepare raw material for manufacturing. When the three maximum dimensions are specified, such as 75, 60 and 25, as shown in Figure 3-9, the operator does not need to add several numerical numbers to get the size of raw material in the process of preparing the stock for the component to be produced.

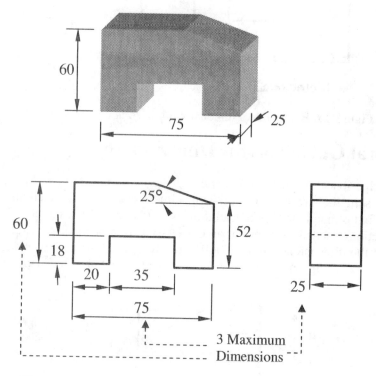

Figure 3-9 Three Maximum Dimensions Are Required

Sometimes a design engineer may specify a maximum dimension through a summation of two dimensions, as shown in Figure 3-10. Note that there is an arc or a circle involved in defining the maximum dimension. As illustrated, the maximum dimensions are specified through summing a size dimension and a position dimension. For example, the total height of the object on the left side is given by (50+20/2), and the total width is given by (70+20/2). The total height of the object on the right side is given by (35+10).

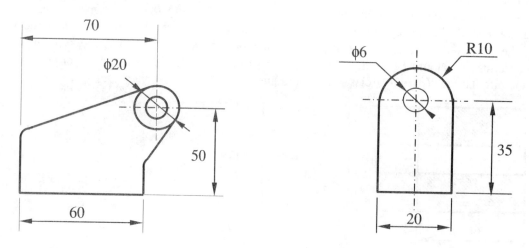

Figure 3-10 Maximum Dimensions with an Arc or a Circle

The third principle is "Consider the manufacturing process when dimensioning". For example, an end mill is used to machine a key-way, as shown in Figure 3-11. The diameter of the end mill is 20 mm. The travel length of the end mill is 40 mm. The starting point of machining is a distance of 30 mm from the left end. Therefore, the plane on the left end is used as a reference for the position dimension.

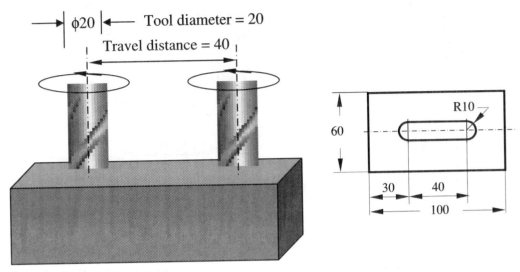

Figure 3-11 Method to Dimension a Key-Way Based on the Manufacturing Process

The fourth principle is "Use section views to show those hidden features before dimensioning". Figure 3-12 illustrates that a through-hole of $\phi 10$ is best described when a section view is prepared. The two diameters of $\phi 18$ and $\phi 10$ are specified in the section-view together with the two depths of 5 mm and 15 mm. Such a way presents a clear picture of the designer's intention and directs the manufacturing process to make a through-hole of $\phi 10$ and a hole of $\phi 18$ with a depth of 5 mm. Without the use of a section view, dashed lines have to be used to represent the two hole-features. Generally speaking, design engineers want to reduce the number of dashed lines to represent hidden features when preparing engineering drawings, thus enhancing the clarity and readability of engineering drawings.

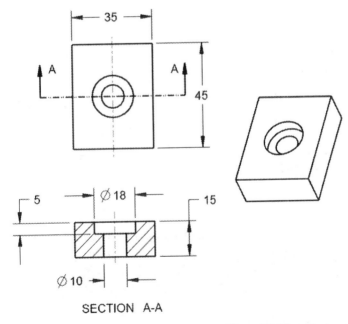

SECTION A-A

Figure 3-12 Using a Section-view to Show Hidden Features

The fifth principle is "Use centerlines for symmetrical features". Figure 3-13 presents two different ways to dimension an identical object. The drawing displayed on the left side has a centerline, and the drawing displayed on the right side does not have a centerline. Examining these two drawings, using a centerline reduces the number of dimensions needed. More important is the fact that the presence of a centerline is a strong indication of the requirement to keep the right portion the same as the left portion in terms of the size and shape.

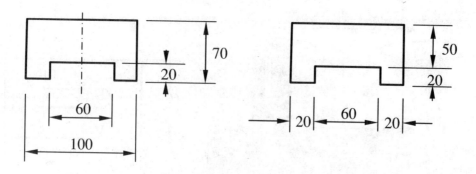

Figure 3-13 A Symmetrical Part Is always Preferred

Suppose that two parts were made with the 3 dimensions in the horizontal direction listed below:

Part 1: 20.1   59.9   19.6   Part 2: 20.1   59.9   20.2

If you were asked to select one to be preferred by design engineers, who one would you choose? It is likely that your choice would be Part 2, because Part 2 is better in terms of symmetry. In our daily life, when people go shopping and look at products, such as cars, TV sets, vases and frames, people pay attention to symmetry in appearance on the product. Symmetric features are generally preferred.

The sixth principle is "Do not close a dimension loop." In practice, redundant and unnecessary dimensions often occur when all individual dimensions are specified together with the overall dimension, as illustrated in Figure 3-14.

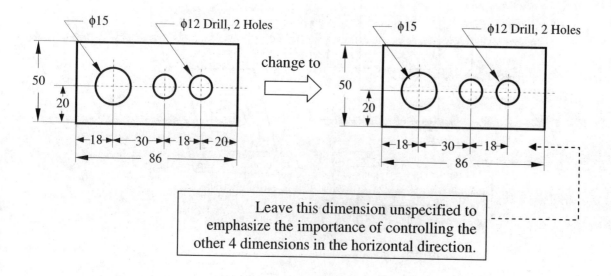

Figure 3-14 Removal of an Unnecessary Dimension to Avoid Forming a Closed Loop

Figure 3-15 presents an engineering drawing of a block that can be found in toy boxes. There are two dimension loops. One is in the horizontal direction, and the other is in the vertical directions. The two dimension loops are not closed to ensure that there is no redundancy, and the emphasis on keeping the dimensional accuracy is implicitly stressed.

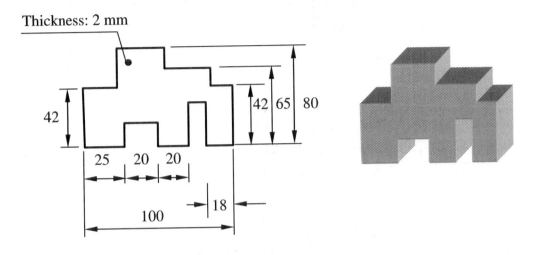

Figure 3-15 Two Open Dimension Loops

The seventh principle is "Consider reference(s) when specifying position dimensions". Selecting dimensions for position usually requires more consideration than selecting dimensions of size, because there are usually several options for specifying a position. In general, a datum reference should be determined before positional dimensions are specified. Candidates for a datum reference can finish surfaces, centerlines, or a combination thereof, as illustrated in Figure 3-16.

The importance of specifying position dimensions is also shown in Figure 3-17 where a section view is used to explore the hidden feature – four holes. The position dimension of 15 mm defines the position where the section view is taken.

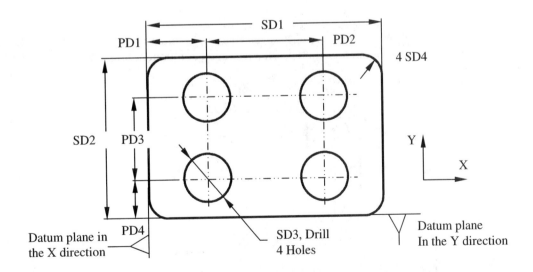

Figure 3-16 Use References to Specify Size and Position Dimensions (S = size and P = position)

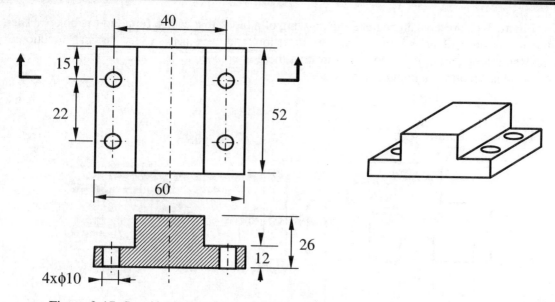

Figure 3-17 Specify the Location of the Plane Used to Create the Section View

The eighth principle is "Avoid intersections between dimension lines". Figure 3-18 presents two cases to demonstrate the concept of an intersection of dimension lines, and how to avoid such an occurrence. The principle is simple by placing dimension lines associated with small dimensions close to the projection. However, it is not uncommon to observe that unnecessary intersections between dimension lines are shown on engineering drawings.

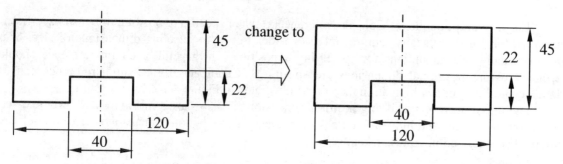

Figure 3-18 Avoid Intersections between Dimension Lines

The ninth principle is "Use national and international standards when specifying dimensions". Figure 3-19 presents the specification of threads on a designed component and a bolt where M stands for

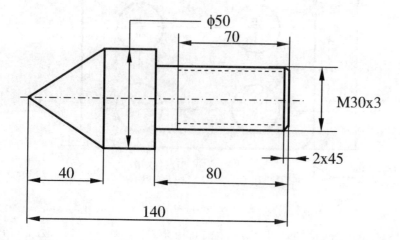

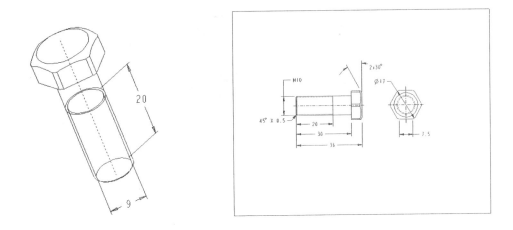

Figure 3-19 Use Dashed Lines to Represent Threads

metric thread, followed by the basic major diameter and then the pitch in millimeters. Engineers do not draw the actual shape of threads on engineering drawings. Dashed lines are used to indicate the portion where threads are present.

Most CAD systems in the market follow national and international standards when dimensions are generated in the process of creating drawings. Figure 3-20 presents some of the notations adopted by the American National Standards Institute in the documentation called Y14.5M.

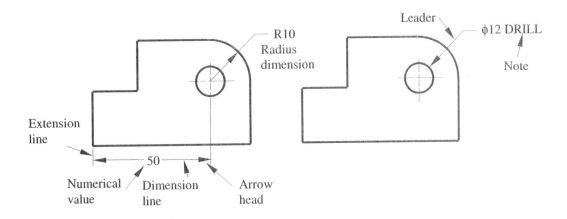

Figure 3-20 Notations on Dimensioning in Y14.5 Adopted by ANSI

In designing electronic products, another type of dimension, called ordinate dimensions, has been widely used. Instead of using two arrow heads at both ends in linear dimensions, ordinate dimensions use a single line. The numerical value of the dimension is placed on the top or right or left side of the dimensional lines, as illustrated in Figure 3-21. Most CAD systems have the built-in function, which converts linear dimensions to ordinate dimensions, and vise versa. It is important to note that ordinate dimensions are only used for position dimensions. They are not used for size dimensions. For example, a designer will not be able to mark the diameter value of a hole using an ordinate dimension. More important is the fact that a common base for a set of linear dimensions has to be available when converting the set of linear dimensions to a set of ordinate dimensions. As a result, before converting a set of linear dimensions to a set of ordinate dimensions, a check for the common basis is important.

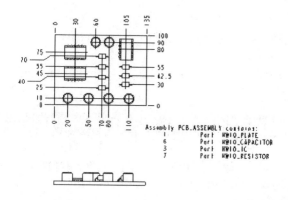

Figure 3-21 Use Ordinate Dimensions for Position Dimensions

Another important note about the conversion from linear dimensions to ordinate dimensions is that before the conversion, all the linear dimensions have to be arranged in such a way that in each direction there exists a unique base line from which all the linear dimensions are measured. Figure 3-22 illustrates such a requirement just before converting the linear dimensions to their corresponding ordinate dimensions.

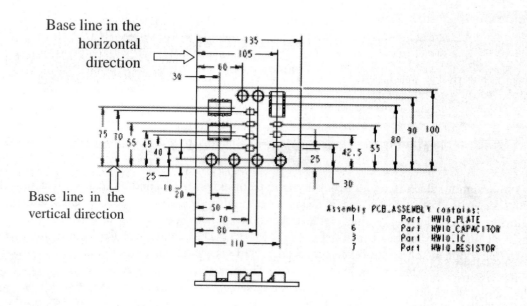

Figure 3-22 Special Arrangements for Converting Linear Dimensions to Ordinate Dimensions

The tenth principle is "Add a chamfer or a round to a sharp corner". As illustrated in the following figure, a large chamfer (4x45°) is mainly for facilitating an assembly process. A roundness (R3) is used to reduce the stress concentration at the step corner. Two (2) small chamfers (2x45°) are used to eliminating 2 sharp corners so that operators can easily pick up the component without hurting their hands.

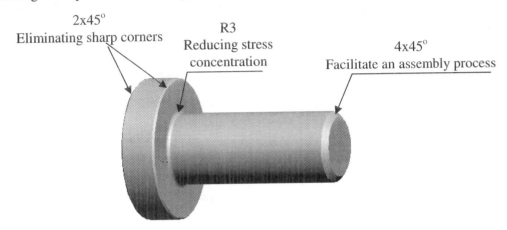

The eleventh principle is "Add a draft to a surface or add drafts to surfaces in the process of designing the component and designing the upper and lower portions of a mold." For those manufacturing processes, such as casting and forging, a parting surface is usually required. As illustrated in the following figure, the upper portion and the lower portion of a mold are needed with respect to the parting surface. In order to facilitate the pull out the component after being manufactured, draft surfaces should be added in the direction perpendicular to the parting surface.

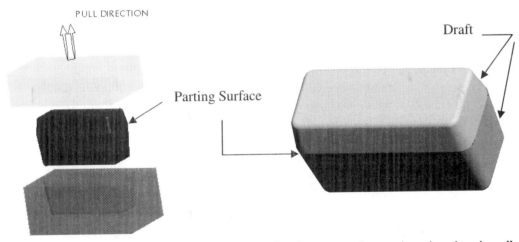

The twelfth principle is "Appropriate use of scale when preparing engineering drawings." When a designer or a design team prepares engineering drawings, they are preparing official documents that will be used in the process of product realization. Other people, such as production engineers, quality inspectors, and people at the purchase department, will read and use the engineering drawings in carrying out daily operations. A scale of an engineering drawing should be selected in such a way that projections are clearly depicted, and dimensions, tolerances, and notes are easily readable.

In reality, a part may be drawn to any scale convenient to the designer or design team. However, the scale must be indicated on the working drawing, often in the title block. It is important to realize that the dimensions placed on the drawing are always dimensions of the actual size of the component. The value of the dimension for a given length never changes, regardless of the scale used to prepare the drawing. For example, if a length is 50 mm on the component, the value 50 will appear on the drawing regardless of the scale used in representing the component.

3.3   Selecting the Front View, Datum or Reference

The ten principles used to guide the process of dimensioning are important because they ensure the clarity in delivering the design intents and the accuracy of the geometric shape and size of the part or component. When using a CAD system to prepare an engineering drawing, the first step is to create a first projection from the 3D solid model, which has been developed. The first project is often positioned in the front view location. Very often, the front view becomes the parent, from which other projections are created. Selection of the best view for the front view is important. Figure 3-23 presents an object, and three possible views as candidates for being the front view. Which view should be selected as the front view?

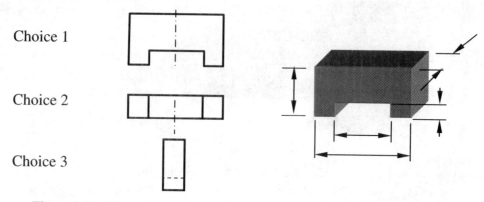

Figure 3-23 Illustration of How to Select the Best View as the Front View

The best choice should be Choice 1 because it captures the characteristics of the object in terms of the geometric shape, and is capable of displaying 4 dimensions out of the 5 shown dimensions.

Datum points, lines, and edges of surfaces are all component features that are assumed to be exact for purposes of computation or reference. As such they are preferred features from which the positions of other features are established. For example, in Figure 3-24, the pair of two centerlines of the central hole serves as the datum lines for the 2 size dimensions as well. When the positions of one feature are specified by dimensions from a datum, other features are also positioned from the same datum, and not with respect to one another.

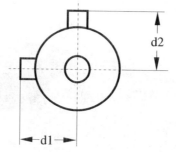

Figure 3-24 The Pair of Centerlines Serves as the Datum Lines to Specify the 2 Size Dimensions

A feature selected to function as a datum must be clearly identified and readily recognizable. The datum surfaces must be accessible during manufacturing so that difficulties will not be encountered in measuring the dimensions. Figures 3-25a, 3-25b and 3-26c present a case study that employs the design of a manufacturing process sequence to follow the two references specified in the engineering drawing.

The first reference is the reference used to specify the dimensions along the X direction. The reference is a vertical plane. As shown in Figure 3-25a, the 2 dimensions of 25 and 55 are measured from this reference plane. The second reference is the centerline of the part because the part is a cylindrical component. As shown in Figure 3-25a, the 3 dimensions of 20, 50 and 65 in diameters are measured with respect to the centerline.

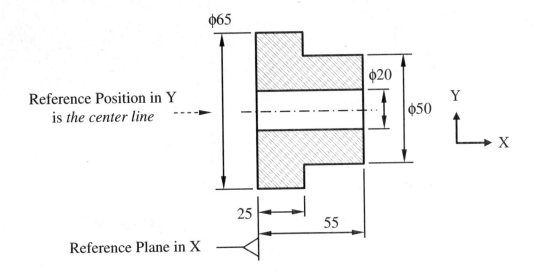

Figure 3-25a Engineering Drawing of a Cylindrical Shaped Shaft

Because of these reasons, a lathe is supposed to be used to manufacture this component. As shown in Figure 3-25b, a cylindrical bar is used as the form of the stock material. The bar diameter before machining is sufficiently larger than 50 mm. The first set of operations includes: to turn the vertical plane to make sure the reference is accurate enough so that variations on any specifications, such as flatness and surface finish, are within the tolerance specified. It is required that the through-hole should be made immediately after the machining of the vertical surface is completed so that the perpendicularity between the centerline and the vertical plane is assured. After making the through-hole, the outer surface should be turned to the dimension of 50 mm in diameter. The fourth operation is to cut off the work piece from the cylindrical bar.

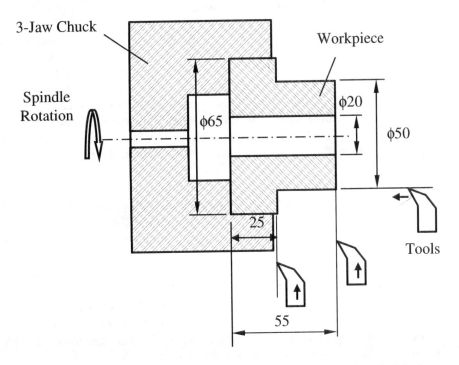

Figure 3-25b The First Set of Operations to Ensure the 2 Specified References

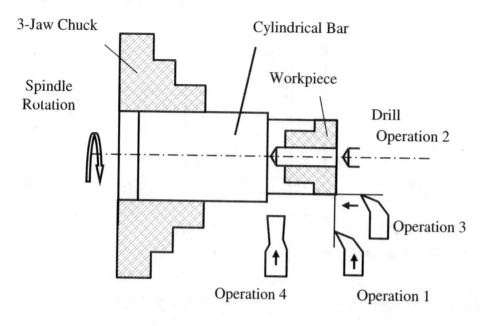

(c) Turning Operations of a Cylindrical Shaped Shaft

Figure 3-25 Selection of References and the Sequence of Manufacturing Processes

The second set of operations requires a new setup, as shown in Figure 3-25c. Operation 1 is to turn the outer diameter to 20 mm. Operation 2 is to turn the vertical surface that is parallel to the reference plane, or perpendicular to the centerline, and ensure the dimension 55. This case study clearly indicates that the selection of references has great impact on how the designed part is manufactured.

3.4   Dimensioning Assembly Drawings

When components are made or available, an assembly process puts the components together to produce a product that provides certain desirable functions. An assembly drawing is a document that describes how the components are related to each other in order to accomplish the required functions.

There is a significant difference in dimensioning between component drawings and assembly drawings. There is no need to present dimensions of each component in the assembly drawing. In fact, it is not realistic to show the size dimensions and the position dimension of each component on the assembly drawing. On the other hand, certain dimensions are required when preparing an assembly drawing. A case study is present to illustrate those principles to guide the process of dimensioning an assembly drawing.

Figure 3-26 presents an assembly drawing. There are 7 dimensions shown. Dimensions 156 and 60 indicate the dimensions of the locations of the 4 holes used to place this assembled product on the ground. These 2 dimensions provide the information with the users of this product so that the users may drill 4 holes and place 4 bolts on the ground, to which the product can be held. Dimension ϕ12 indicates that the diameter of the shaft, supposed to be connected with another component, say an electrical motor, to drive this assembled system. Dimension 84 indicates the distance of the centerline of the shaft with respect to the ground. This information is important for the users to set the centerline of the electrical motor at this height level so that both the shaft and electrical motor can be connected without difficulty. Dimension ϕ100 indicates one of the maximum dimensions of the assembly. This dimension also indicates the height of the assembly when adding the dimension of 84. The dimensions of 176 and 80 also indicate the maximum dimensions of the assembly on the ground so that the space requirement for the assembly shop can be estimated.

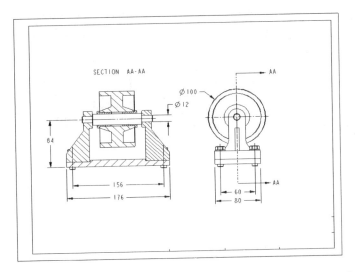

Figure 3-26 Critical Dimensions Needed for an Assembly Drawing

To present a detailed discussion on preparing an assembly drawing, a case study is present to illustrate the procedure. Assume that an assembled product consists of three components. They are Part 1, Part 2 and Part 3, as shown in Figure 3-27a where the size dimensions and position dimensions for each part are detailed. Figure 3-27b presents an assembly drawing that consists of the three parts shown in Figure 3-27a. By examining the assembly drawing, the following characteristics can be identified:

1. The maximum dimensions of the assembled product, such as the maximum diameter of $\phi 300$ and the maximum length of the assembly, 480 mm, have to be specified.
2. Orientations of the hatched lines of parts should be varied in such a way that individual parts can be easily distinguished from other parts.
3. A table is needed to list all the components with Index, Part Number, Part Name, QTY, Material, and Notes. Such a table is called Bill of Material, or BOM table, as shown in Figure 3-27b.
4. Balloons are used to label the three parts, based on the Index information listed in the table.
5. It is important to note that dimensions of each part should not be shown on the assembly drawing.

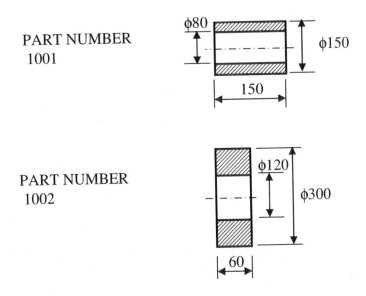

PART NUMBER
1001

PART NUMBER
1002

PART NUMBER
1003

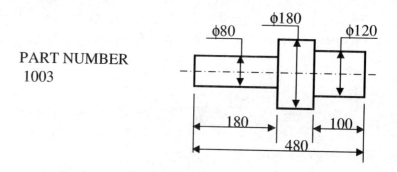

(a) Engineering Drawings of the Three Components

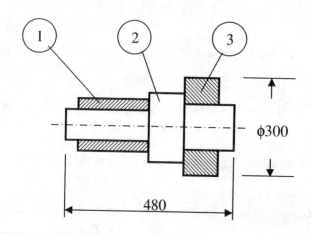

3	PRT-1002	GEAR	1	1040	PURCHASE
2	PRT-1003	SHAFT	1	1030	HEAT TREAT
1	PRT-1001	SLEEVE	1	ALUMINUM	ANEALING
INDEX	PART NUMBER	PART NAME	QTY	MATERIAL	NOTES

(b) An Assembly Drawing of the Three Parts Shown in Figure 3-27a

Figure 3-27 Procedure to Prepare an Assembly Drawing

3.5   Tolerancing

In engineering practice, tolerance is defined as the maximum deviation from a nominal specification within which the component is still acceptable for its intended purpose. According to the American Society of Mechanical Engineers, tolerance is the total amount, by which a specific dimension is permitted to vary. The numerical value of a tolerance is the difference between the maximum and minimum limits.

For practical considerations, tight tolerances tend to increase the cost of production, while components with large tolerances are easy to manufacture and cost less. However, those components with large tolerances may pose difficulties in controlling functional performance, as large deviations usually induce errors. As a result, a balance between precision and cost has to be made for design engineers.

Products we use on a daily basis are designed to operate at particular performance levels. To operate at these levels, products are made with various degrees of precision. Take as an example two very different products, each with a feature that performs a similar function --- a wheel on an axle.

Suppose the wheel and axle assembly is installed on a child's wagon and another on a Boeing 737 airplane. In both cases the purpose of the wheel and axle assembly is to allow the vehicle to roll. Obviously, the performance levels are quite different for these two applications, and the degree of precision needed for each assembly differs greatly. The need for precision and careful machining in manufacturing the components is far greater for the airplane than for the child's wagon.

Technology and business today require that parts be specified with increasingly exact dimensions. Many parts made by different companies at widely separated locations must be interchangeable. This requirement demands precise size specifications and achieving these exact dimensions in production. The technique of dimensioning parts within a required range of variation to ensure interchangeability requires the designers to be knowledgeable in tolerancing.

3.5.1 Tolerance of a Component

Tolerances are the allowable deviations from a specified dimension. For example, the tolerance of a certain length of a component with a dimension specified as 120 mm can be defined as 120 ± 1 mm. This means that a component is acceptable provided that the measurement of this dimension is within the range from 119 mm to 121 mm. Certainly, tolerancing is directly related to the manufacturing process involved in producing the component. In general, manufacturing costs increase as tolerances become smaller, and it is prudent to specify tolerances as large as possible to minimize production costs without interfering with the function of the component.

Tolerances associated with their components allow the designer to control the dimensions, namely the maximum and minimum sizes of features and their positions relatively to each other. The component shown in Figure 3-28 has a hole with two deviations with respect to the hole diameter. The hole diameter may vary from 50.50 mm to 50.00 mm. The range of allowed variation, 0.50 mm, is the numerical value of this tolerance.

Tolerance = Maximum Dimension – Minimum Dimension

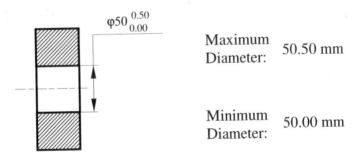

Figure 3-28 Interpretation of Tolerance for a Hole of a Component

The tolerance of a dimension, either in size, position and geometrical shape of a feature, can affect the tooling selected to produce the component. Manufacturing components with numerically higher tolerances can be accomplished by using less precise tooling than lower ones. The hole shown in Figure 3-28 could be made with a sharp drill, but if the tolerance is reduced to 0.05 mm, higher cost processes, such as reaming or grinding, may be required.

3.5.2 Fitting of a Pair of Contact Parts in Mass Production

The interaction between two contacting components during an assembly process is called a fit. A typical example would be an assembly of a hole and a shaft, as shown in Figure 3-29 The interaction between two contacting components is called a fit. A typical example would be an assembly of a hole and a shaft, as shown in Figure 3-29. The fit of a shaft in a hole is very common in a wide range of products. Wheels rolling on shafts and pistons sliding in cylinders are just two examples. The performance of these contacting systems is primarily dependent on the fit of the contacting components. There are three classifications used to specify different types of fit. These fits are clearance fit, interference fit and transition fit.. The fit of a shaft in a hole is very common in a wide range of products. Wheels rolling on shafts and pistons sliding in cylinders are just two examples. The performance of these contacting systems is primarily dependent on the fit of the contacting components. There are three classifications used to specify different types of fit. These fits are clearance fit, interference fit and transition fit.

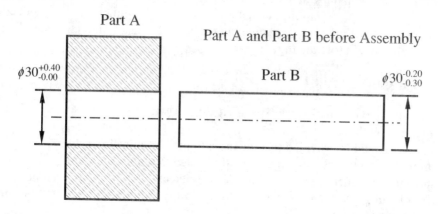

Figure 3-29 Part A and Part B before Being Assembled

Clearance Fit

Assume that there are thousands of shaft-components and thousands of hole-components that are ready for assembling them together. This assumption means that we are dealing with a mass production process. When you take a shaft from the pile of shaft-components and a hole from the pile of hole-components. In a clearance fit, the diameter of the shaft is always smaller than the diameter of the hole. This means that the shaft "clears" the hole, leaving an annular gap. The amount of clearance varies with the tolerance value placed on the hole and shaft.

The example presented in Figure 3-29 indicates that the actual dimension of a shaft component after manufacturing may vary from 29.70 mm to 29.80 mm. On the other side, the hole diameter may vary from 30.00 mm to 30.40 mm. The tolerances are 0.10 mm on the shaft and 0.40 mm in on the hole, respectively. The maximum clearance is determined by subtracting the smallest shaft diameter from the largest hole diameter, and the minimum clearance is determined by subtracting the largest shaft diameter from the smallest hole diameter as follows:

$$\text{Maximum Clearance} = A_{max} - B_{min} = 30.40 - 29.70 = 0.70 \text{ mm}$$
$$\text{Minimum Clearance} = A_{min} - B_{max} = 30.00 - 29.80 = 0.20 \text{ mm}$$

$$\text{Tolerance of Assembly for the Clearance Fit} = 0.70 - 0.20 = 0.50 \text{ mm}$$

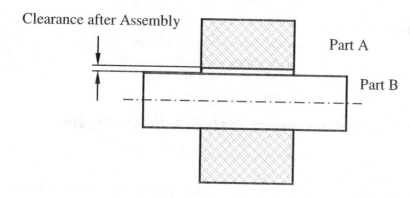

Figure 3-30 Part A and Part B before Being Assembled

It is important to note that the level of the clearance after assembly varies depending on the actual sizes of the shaft and the hole components taken from the two piles of shaft and components, respectively.

Interference Fit

Interference fit occurs when the shaft diameter is larger than the hole diameter prior to assembly. Interference fits are also known as force fits since the shaft is forced into the hole during an assembly operation. A simple tap of a shaft into a hole may be sufficient to assemble a light force fit, but a heavy force fit often requires the shaft to be cooled and/or the hole to be heated to facilitate assembly. Once assembled, interference fit provides a permanent coupling of the two components. Disassembly occurs only if the shaft is forced out of the hole. In severe cases, the housing containing the hole may have to be cut to permit the shaft to be withdrawn. Interference fits are an excellent way to assemble parts, which are to remain fixed in position relative to each other. A bearing at a fixed location on an axle is an example.

A drawing of a shaft and a disk, presented in Figure 3-31, illustrates interference fit. The shaft diameter is always larger than the hole diameter. In this instance, the tolerances are 0.10 mm on the shaft diameter and 0.20 mm on the hole diameter, respectively. The maximum clearance for the interference fit is determined using the same approach employed for the clearance fit as follows:

Maximum Interference = $A_{min} - B_{max}$ = 30.00 -30.35 = -0.35 mm

Minimum Interference = $A_{max} - B_{min}$ = 30.20 - 30.25 = -0.05 mm

Tolerance of Assembly for Interference Fit = -0.35 – (-0.05) = -0.30 mm

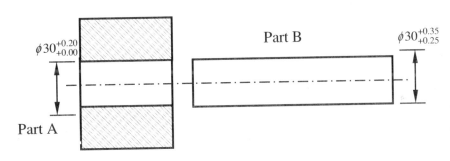

a. Part A and Part B before Assembly

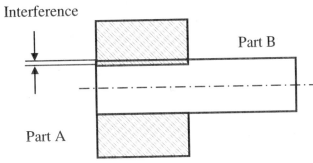

b. Interference after Assembling Part A and Part B together

Figure 3-31 Interference Fit during Assembling

Note the minus sign. The sign implies a negative clearance, which is in fact the amount of interference. For the maximum interference, the largest shaft diameter is subtracted from the smallest hole diameter. For the minimum interference, the smallest shaft diameter is subtracted from the largest hole diameter. Again, the tolerance is a negative value indicating the amount of interference.

Transition Fit

Transition fit exists when the maximum clearance is positive and the minimum clearance is negative. Therefore, the shaft may clear the hole with an annular gap or it may have to be forced into the hole, all depending on the actual dimensions of the shaft and hole components picked from the 2 piles of shaft and components, respectively. Transition fits are used only for locating a shaft relative to a hole, where accuracy is important, but either large clearance or large interference is permitted. An example of a transition fit is presented in Figure 3-32. The tolerances are 0.20 mm on the shaft diameter, and 0.20 mm on the hole diameter, respectively.

Maximum Clearance = $A_{max} - B_{min}$ = 30.20 - 30.15 = 0.05 mm

Maximum Interference = $A_{min} - B_{max}$ = 30.00 - 30.35 = -0.35 mm

Tolerance of Assembly for Transition Fit = 0.05 − (-0.35) = 0.40 mm

The maximum clearance is 0.05mm, a positive value indicating clearance. The maximum interference is −0.35 mm, a negative value indicating interference.

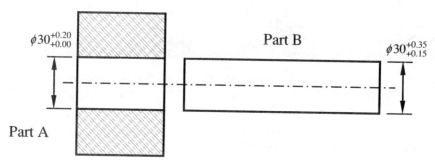

a. Part A and Part B before Assembly

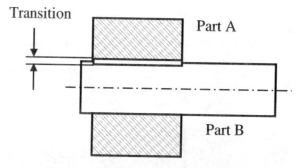

b. Clearance and Interference after Assembling Part A and Part B together

Figure 3-32 Transition Fit during Assembling

3.5.3 Basic Hole System vs Basic Shaft System

A comparison of the three types of fit during the assembling process in mass production is presented in Figure 3-33. It is important to note that the tolerance of the hole dimension remains unchanged while the tolerance of the shaft dimensions vary so as to obtain the three different types of fit during the assembling process. Such a system is called Basic Hole System, as defined by ANSI.

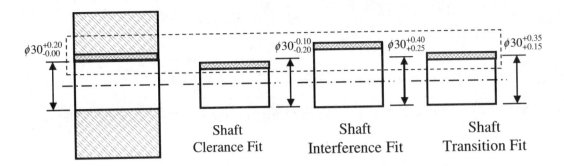

Figure 3-33 Concept of a Basic Hole System

The basic hole system is a system, in which the basic size appears as one of the limit dimensions (usually the minimum dimension) of the hole, but not of the shaft. This means that a designer keeps the maximum and minimum dimensions of a hole unchanged and varies the maximum and minimum dimensions of the mating shaft to achieve different fittings, such as clearance fit, transition fit and interference fit. A graphic representation of the basic hole system is presented in Figure 3-34. As an example, for a basic size of 20 mm, the maximum and minimum dimensions of a hole are 20.021 and 20.000, respectively. For the shaft, which is to fit into the hole as a clearance fit, the maximum and minimum dimensions are (20-0.007) and (20-0.020), respectively. For an interference fit, the maximum and minimum dimensions are (20+0.048) and (20+0.035), respectively. For a transition fit, the maximum and minimum dimensions are (20+0.015) and (20+0.002), respectively.

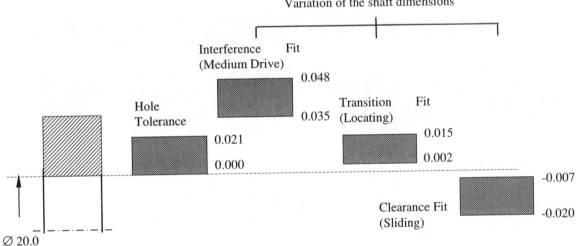

Figure 3-34 Graphic Representation of the Basic Hole System

A natural question to ask is "Is there a Basic Shaft System?" The answer is YES. Based on the definition given by ANSI, the basic shaft system is a system, in which the basic diameter appears as one of the limit dimensions (usually the maximum diameter) of the shaft, not the hole. This means that a designer keeps the maximum and minimum dimensions of a shaft unchanged and varies the maximum and minimum dimensions of the mating hole to achieve different fittings, such as clearance fit, transition fit and interference fit. A graphic representation of the basic shaft system is presented in Figure 3-35. As an example, for a basic size of 20 mm, the maximum and minimum dimensions of a shaft are 20.000 and 19.987, respectively. For the hole, which is assembled with the shaft as a clearance fit, the maximum and minimum dimensions are (20+0.028) and (20+0.007), respectively. For an interference fit, the 2 dimensions are (20-0.027) and (20-0.048), respectively. For a transition fit, the 2 dimensions are (20+0.006) and (20-0.015), respectively.

Basic Shaft System

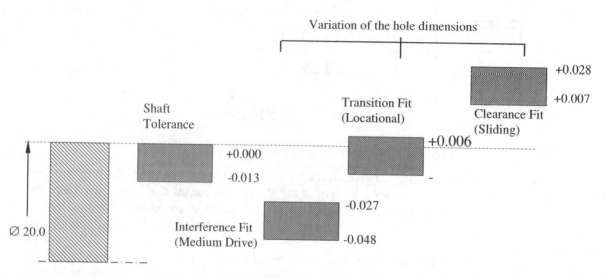

Figure 3-35 Graphic Representation of the Basic Shaft System

Both the basic hole system and the basic shaft system are important. They are widely used in engineering practice. For example, as illustrated in Figure 3-36, the tolerance of the inner diameter of a bearing purchased from a bearing manufacturer is controlled by the bearing manufacturer. A designer has no control on the tolerance of the inner diameter. In order to achieve a clearance fit, or an interference fit, the designer has to change the deviations of the maximum diameter and the minimum diameter of the shaft about its nominal size. Under such a circumstance, the basic hole system should be applied. On the other hand, the outer diameter of a bearing purchased from a bearing manufacturer is also controlled by the bearing manufacturer. A designer has no control on the tolerance of the outer diameter. In order to achieve a clearance fit or an interference fit, the designer has to change the deviation of the maximum diameter and the minimum diameter of the hole about its nominal size. Under such a circumstance, the basic shaft system should be applied.

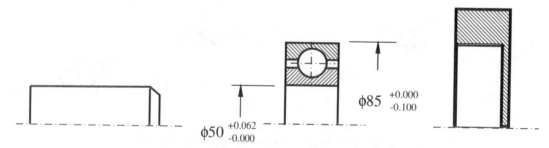

Figure 3-36 Applications of the Basic Shaft System and the Basic Shaft System

It is important that under certain circumstances, a designer may have a choice of either selecting a basic hole system or selecting a basic shaft system. When those circumstances occur, it is advisable for the designer to select the basic hole system over the basic shaft system. One of the major reasons is that applications of a basic hole system are generally associated with low cost in terms of tooling and machines. For example, when using a lathe to turn a shaft, control of the diameter dimension of the shaft only requires an adjustment of a cutting tool with respect to the shaft. However, control of the diameter of the hole component requires special tooling, such as a special drill bit with the required diameter, or a boring process to control the size of the hole. Therefore, the basic hole system is more widely adopted by industry as compared with the basic shaft system.

3.5.4 Examples of Determining Tolerances for Various Fits

How do we determine the tolerances when we design a complex machine with clearance, transition and interference fits? Standards for tolerances have been established to guide the selection process. Design engineers are required to use those standards at the time the numerical values of tolerances are needed. In this way, interchangeability for parts can be rigorously sustained.

   Example 3-1   Suppose you are given instructions to specify tolerances on two holes with diameters of 20 and 50 mm. The tolerances are to be selected from the IT table (International Tolerance Grades --- ANSI B4.2). If the tolerance grades are IT7, IT9, and IT11, determine the tolerances for each hole and for each grade.
   1. For a hole 20 mm in diameter with an IT7 tolerance, we find IT7 = 0.021 mm.
   2. For a hole 20 mm in diameter with an IT9 tolerance, we find IT9 = 0.052 mm.
   3. For a hole 20 mm in diameter with an IT11 tolerance, we find IT11 = 0.130 mm.
   4. For a hole 50 mm in diameter with an IT7 tolerance, we find IT7 = 0.025 mm.
   5. For a hole 50 mm in diameter with an IT9 tolerance, we find IT9 = 0.062 mm.
   6. For a hole 50 mm in diameter with an IT11 tolerance, we find IT11 = 0.160 mm.

   This example presents a concept that the range of tolerance is determined by the tolerance grade selected and the dimension of the component under design. In the international standard, there are 16 grades. Grade 1 represents the highest grade associated with the smallest tolerance range.

   Example 3-2   Suppose that we are dealing with a basic hole system as illustrated in Figure 3-37. The basic diameter of the hole is 20 mm, its tolerance grade is H7, and it is to be used in an assembly involving a medium drive interference fit. Determine the maximum and minimum diameter of the hole.

   Readers may refer to relevant document, and find D_{MAX} = 20.021 mm and D_{MIN} = 20.00 mm. Next, consider a basic shaft system as illustrated in Figure 3-31. The basic diameter of the shaft is 20 mm, and for a medium drive fit a tolerance grade of s6 is specified. Find the maximum and minimum diameter of the shaft. Finally, find D_{MAX} = 20.048 mm and D_{MIN} = 20.035 mm.

   This example demonstrates that, for tolerance design, there could be two choices, the basic hole system and the basic shaft system, for a designer to choose from. Which one is better? In general, design engineers prefer the basic hole system to the basic shaft system if he or she is given both choices to choose from. The reason is varying the dimension of a shaft is easily achievable. As a result, the basic hole system comes up with a relative low level of cost. However, the basic shaft system has its unique applications. For example, the outside diameter of a bearing is determined by its manufacturer. In order to achieve different fitting conditions, one has to vary the diameter of the mating hole. Under such circumstances, the designer has no choice but to use the basic shaft system to accomplish the design job.

   Example 3-3:   The following drawing shows that there is a bearing purchased from a bearing manufacturer. We need to insert the shaft to the bearing with a transition fit. We have to use the hole basis system to define the tolerance of the shaft dimension d1. We also need to insert the bearing to its support. We have to use the shaft basis system to define the tolerance of the support dimension D1.

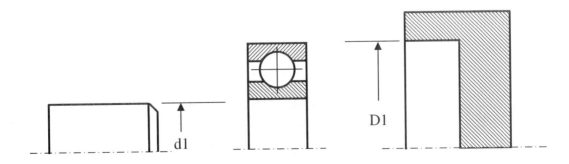

3.6 Assembly Tolerances

In this section, we discuss the maximum-minimum method for determining the tolerance associated with the assembly of two or more parts. Specifying assembly tolerances is extremely important. When you walk into a department to buy an oil filter for your car, you expect that the purchased filter will fit on your car. Such confidence comes from using the maximum-minimum method to ensure 100% interchangeability of two mating parts. A series of four examples will be used to illustrate the procedure to analyze the tolerancing issue related to an assembly consisting of several components.

3.6.1 Tolerancing for 100% Interchangeability

Example 3-4: As illustrated in the following figure, the dimensions and tolerances of Part A and Part B are 15 ± 0.05 mm and $45^{+0.30}_{-0.00}$ mm, respectively. If Parts A and B are assembled together, determine the maximum and minimum dimensions of the assembly.

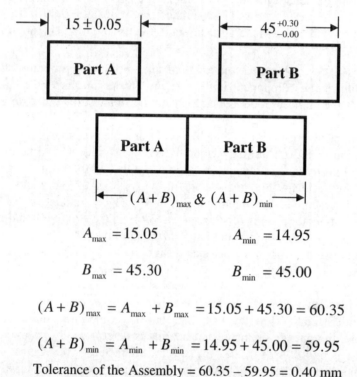

$$A_{max} = 15.05 \qquad\qquad A_{min} = 14.95$$

$$B_{max} = 45.30 \qquad\qquad B_{min} = 45.00$$

$$(A+B)_{max} = A_{max} + B_{max} = 15.05 + 45.30 = 60.35$$

$$(A+B)_{min} = A_{min} + B_{min} = 14.95 + 45.00 = 59.95$$

Tolerance of the Assembly = 60.35 − 59.95 = 0.40 mm

Note that the tolerance of Part A is 0.10 mm and Part B is 0.30 mm. The tolerance of the assembly is 0.40 mm. Therefore, this example demonstrates a concept that the tolerance range of the assembly is equal to the sum of the tolerance ranges of the two components.

Tolerance of the Assembly = Tolerance of Part A + Tolerance of Part B = 0.10+ 0.30 = 0.40 mm

The interpretation of this example is shown below where Part A is a shaft component and Part B is a hole component. (Part A + Part B) represents the dimension obtained after the assembly.

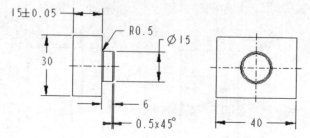

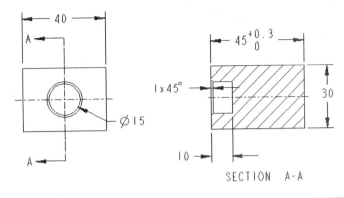

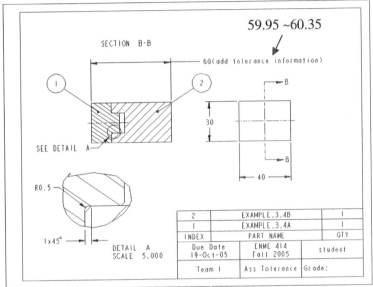

Example 3-5: Suppose that Company XYZ produces a product that consists of two components to be assembled together. The maximum and minimum dimensions of the assembly are shown as $85^{+0.80}_{-0.00}$ mm in the following figure. The company is capable of manufacturing Part A with an acceptable profit margin. The maximum and minimum dimensions of Part A are shown as 25 ± 0.15 in the following figure. The company plans to purchase components of Part B from an outside manufacturer to sustain the profit margin from selling the products. Determine the maximum and minimum dimensions of Part B for the purchase department.

$$A_{max} = 25.15 \qquad A_{min} = 24.85$$

$$(A+B)_{max} = 85.80 \qquad (A+B)_{min} = 85.00$$
$$B_{max} = (A+B)_{max} - A_{max} = 85.80 - 25.15 = 60.65$$

$$B_{min} = (A+B)_{min} - A_{min} = 85.00 - 24.85 = 60.15$$

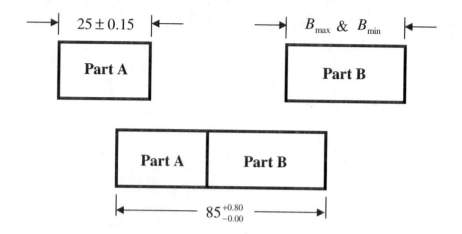

In this example, the tolerance of Part A is 0.30 mm. The tolerance of Part B is 0.50 mm. The tolerance of the assembly is 0.80 mm. Therefore, this example further illustrates the concept that the tolerance range of the assembly is equal to the sum of the tolerance ranges of the two components.

Example 3-6: A company is manufacturing boxes to be used for carrying computer diskettes. The specification of the width of the diskette is 90 ± 0.10 mm. To insure that disks can be inserted into the box easily, the minimum clearance should be kept, at least, 0.1 mm. To avoid excessive motion of the disks within the box, the maximum clearance between the inner wall of the container and a disk should be kept at no more than 0.4 mm. Determine the maximum and minimum dimensions of the interior of the box to meet the specification for the clearance, which is between 0.1 mm and 0.4 mm.
Solution:

Box_{min} - 90.10 = 0.10 $\qquad\qquad$ Box_{max} − 89.9 = 0.40

Box_{min} = 90.10+0.10 = 90.20 mm $\qquad\qquad$ Box_{max}= 89.9 +0.4 = 90.30 mm

Tolerance of the Box = Box_{max} - Box_{min} = 90.30 −90.20 = 0.10 mm

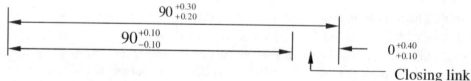

The tolerance of the closing link C_L is given by:

$$C_L = \sum_{i=1}^{2} \text{Tolerance of individual dimension composing link}_i$$

$$C_L = (0.30\text{-}0.20) + [+0.10\text{-}(\text{-}0.10)] = 0.10 + 0.20 = 0.30 \text{ mm}$$

In this example, we have introduced a new concept called the closing link. The closing link C_L is a variable dimension formed during the assembly process. Since C_L is a variable dimension it has a tolerance that is equal to the sum of the tolerances of all individual parts that make up the assembly.

Example 3-7: An assembly is shown below. Part B and Part C are inserted into Part A. Part D is used to keep Part B and Part C in their assembled positions. The company manufactures components of Part D. In order to ensure that Part D be assembled with ease, the minimum clearance and maximum clearance are specified as 0.10 and 0.50 mm, respectively. Determine the maximum and minimum dimensions of Part D.

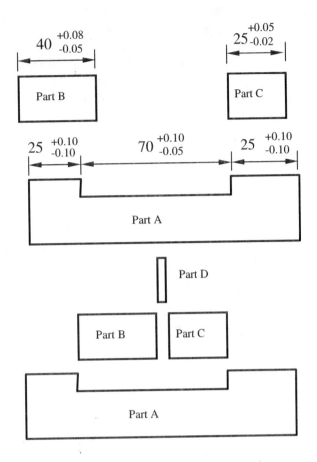

Solution:

It is important to identify the closing link in this assembly. The four dimensions of Part A, Part B, Part C and Part D should be viewed as given before the assembly. The dimension formed during assembly is the clearance with its maximum value of 0.50 mm and minimum 0.10 mm. Therefore, the closing link is the clearance after the assembly.

$$Clearance_{max} = 0.50 = (70+0.10) - (40-0.05) - (25-0.02) - D_{min}$$

$$Clearance_{min} = 0.10 = (70-0.05) - (40+0.08) - (25+0.05) - D_{max}$$

$$D_{max} = 4.72 \text{ mm and } D_{min} = 4.67 \text{ mm}$$

Verification: Tolerance of the Clerance after Assembly:

$$(0.50-0.10) = 0.40 = 0.15+ 0.13 + 0.07 + 0.05$$

The maximum-minimum method for determining dimensions and clearances described in this section is known as tolerancing for 100% interchangeability. The tolerance of the closing link C_L, or an assembly tolerance, is based on the worst-case scenario. The worst case occurs when all the minimum dimensions or the maximum dimensions, are encountered in the assembly for each of the components involved. The worst-case scenario truly ensures 100% interchangeability, a concept which is extremely important in our daily life For example, when changing an oil filter for a car, you went to a local store to buy a new filter, you had never experienced the new filter you had just purchased did not fit because the concept of 100% interchangeability was built in the design and production process. It is clear that the maximum-minimum method to determine assembly tolerances ensures a proper assembly

However, in reality, it is not likely to occur that all the minimum dimensions or the maximum dimensions are encountered in the assembly for each of the components. When such circumstances do occur on the shop floor, operators may just pick up another component(s) as replacement(s). Therefore, the maximum-minimum method overly constrains the allowable tolerances by over-estimating difficulties that may be encountered during the assembly process. Because of this reason, the constraint condition on the tolerance of assembly can be somehow relaxed if a new method can be developed.

3.6.2 A Statistical Approach for Determining Assembly Tolerances

Another method used to determine assembly tolerances is based on statistical interchangeability. This approach is based on a scenario that a large percentage of the available parts should be interchangeable. As a result, this approach results in larger allowable tolerances at the expense of having a small percentage of mating parts that cannot be assembled during the first attempt. Assembly problems that arise with this approach may be minimized until they are of no importance. Two examples are presented to demonstrate the application of the method of statistical interchangeability.

Example 3-9:   As illustrated in the following figure, the dimensions and tolerances of a hole and a shaft are 20±0.15 and 19.85±0.09 mm, respectively. The hole and the shaft are to be assembled together to provide a "clearance fit". Determine the range of the clearance between the hole and the shaft after assembly, using the method of statistical interchangeability.

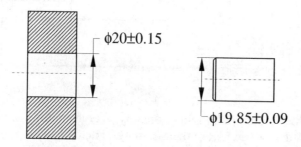

There are three assumptions when using the statistical method. These assumptions are:

1. The actual dimension measured from a component taken from a big batch is a random variable. This random variable obeys a normal distribution, as shown in the following figure.
2. Characteristics of a normal distribution are

    - The distribution is symmetric about its mean value.
    - The mean value represents the central location, and the standard deviation represents the level of variation about the mean.
    - The probability density function indicates that ranges of

    $[\mu-\sigma, \mu+\sigma]$ covers 68% of the all possible outcomes;
    $[\mu-2\sigma, \mu+2\sigma]$ covers 95% of the all possible outcomes; and
    $[\mu-3\sigma, \mu+3\sigma]$ covers 99.74% of all the possible outcomes.

3. The tolerance range is equal to $[\mu-3\sigma, \mu+3\sigma]$, or the range of dimension variation is equal to 6σ.

Based on the 3 assumptions, let us examine the characteristics of the normal distribution representing the variation of the hole dimensions. The maximum dimension and minimum dimension of the hole are 20.15 and 19.85 mm, respectively. Therefore the tolerance is equal to 0.30 mm. Based on these three assumptions, the mean and standard deviation of the normal distribution are given by

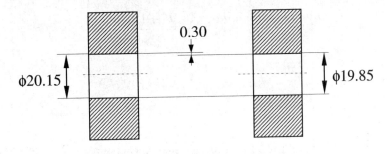

$$\mu_{hole} = \frac{Maximum + Minimum}{2} = \frac{20.15 + 19.85}{2} = 20.00$$

$$\sigma_{hole} = \frac{Maximum - Minimum}{6} = \frac{20.15 - 19.85}{6} = 0.05$$

The graphical representation of this normal distribution representing the variation of the hole dimension is shown in Figure 3-37.

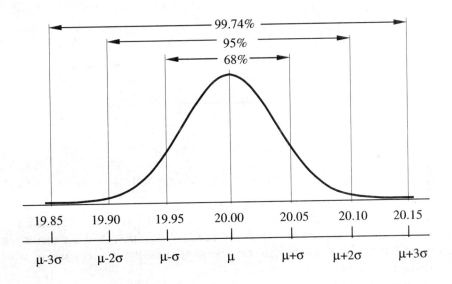

Figure 3-37 Normal Distribution of the Variation of the Hole Dimensions

Following the same procedure, we characterize the statistical distribution for the variation of the dimensions representing the shaft diameters. As illustrated below, the maximum and minimum dimensions of the shaft diameter are 19.94 and 19.76, respectively, and the tolerance of the shaft diameter is 0.18 mm.

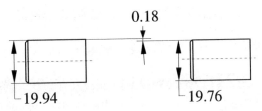

$$\mu_{shaft} = \frac{Maximum + Minimum}{2} = \frac{19.94 + 19.76}{2} = 19.85$$

$$\sigma_{shaft} = \frac{Maximum - Minimum}{6} = \frac{19.94 - 19.76}{6} = 0.03$$

The graphical representation of this normal distribution representing the variation of the shaft dimension is shown in Figure 3-38.

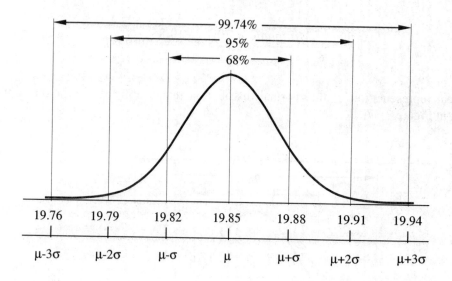

Figure 3-38 Normal Distribution of the Variaton of the Shaft Dimensions

In this case study, the assembly of a hole and a shaft will result in a clearance fit. Because the dimension of a hole and the dimension of a shaft are random variables, the clearance obtained from the assembly is also a random variable, which also obeys a normal distribution. The mean, or central position of this normal distribution is given by:

$$\mu_{clearance} = \mu_{hole} - \mu_{shaft} = 20.00 - 19.85 = 0.15$$

The standard deviation of the clearance distribution is given by:

$$\sigma_{clerance} = \sqrt{\sigma_{hole}^2 + \sigma_{shaft}^2} = \sqrt{(0.05)^2 + (0.03)^2} = 0.058$$

The normal distribution characterizing the clearance distribution after the assembly, which inserts a randomly selected shaft into a randomly selected hole, is shown in Figure 3-39.

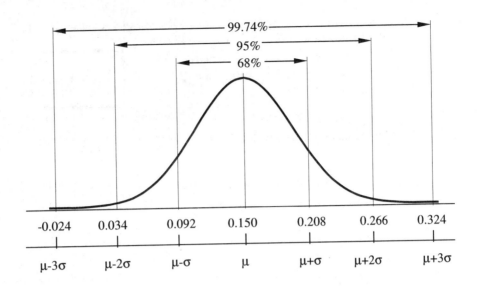

Figure 3-39 Normal Distribution of the Variation of the Clerance after Assembly

The data listed in Table 3.1 gives an interpretation of the clearances after the assembly. 67% of the assemblies will have a clearance between 0.092 and 0.208 mm (± 1σ). 95% of the assemblies will have a clearance between 0.034 and 0.266 mm (± 2σ). 99.75% of the assemblies will have a clearance between –0.024 and 0.266 mm (± 3σ).

Table 3-1 Probability of the Occurance of Various Clearances after Assembly

The Variation of the Clearances after Assembly	Probability (%)
0.092 – 0.208	68%
0.034 – 0.266	95%
-0.024 – 0.324	99.74%

It is critical that the meaning of a negative value for the clearance be clearly understood. A negative clearance means that the shaft diameter is greater than the hole diameter. This situation indicates that interference (not clearance) will occur in the assembly of a few of the components. When this circumstance occurs, a selection of either a different shaft or a different hole may be sufficient to overcome the assembly problem. Recall that the diameter of the hole and the shaft are random variables, and for this reason another selection is likely to assure a clearance fit in assembly. "Is it possible that interference will occur again after another selection of components?" It is very unlikely to select a second combination of shaft and hole that will produce an interference fit because the probability of this interference occurring on the first selection was only 5%. The probability of two consecutive selections producing interference is only (5%)(5%) = 0.25%. It is clear that a clearance fit can be assured without significant difficulty if the tolerances of the shaft and the hole are established at ± 3σ. This example demonstrates the importance of using the statistical method to determine the distribution of clearances and predicting the consequences of random selection of components when assembly occurs on the production line.

Example 3-10: Let us next revisit Example 3-4. Let us use the statistical method for the analysis of the tolerances. For the length dimension of Part A, the mean and standard deviation are calculated as follows:

$$\mu_{partA} = \frac{Maximum + Minimum}{2} = \frac{15.05 + 14.95}{2} = 15.00$$

$$15 \pm 0.05$$

Part A

$$\sigma_{partA} = \frac{Maximum - Minimum}{6} = \frac{15.05 - 14.95}{6} = 0.017$$

$\mu = 15.00$
$\sigma = 0.017$

For the length dimension of Part A, the mean and standard deviation are calculated as follows:

$$\mu_{partB} = \frac{Maximum + Minimum}{2} = \frac{45.30 + 45.00}{2} = 45.15$$

$$45^{+0.30}_{-0.00}$$

Part B

$$\sigma_{partB} = \frac{Maximum - Minimum}{6} = \frac{45.30 - 45.00}{6} = 0.050$$

$\mu = 45.15$
$\sigma = 0.050$

For the length dimension of the assembly, namely, (Part A + Part B), the mean and standard deviation are calculated as follows:

Part A | **Part B**

$$\mu_{(A+B)} = \mu_{partA} + \mu_{partB} = 15.00 + 45.15 = 60.15$$

$$(A+B)_{max} \,\&\, (A+B)_{min}$$

$$\sigma_{(A+B)} = \sqrt{\sigma^2_{partA} + \sigma^2_{partB}} = \sqrt{(0.017)^2 + (0.05)^2} = 0.053$$

$\mu = 15.00$
$\sigma = 0.017$

The normal distribution characterizing the length after assembling Parts A and Part B is shown in Figure 3-40. Note that the bell shaped curve is centered at 60.15 mm. In examining the extremes of this curve, we can conclude that 99.74% of the assemblies will be between 59.991 and 60.309 mm in length. More specifically speaking, 68% of the assemblies will be between 60.097 and 60.203 mm in length, and 95% of the assemblies will be between 60.044 and 60.256 mm in length. The tolerance for the assembled length dimension is given by:

Tolerance of the Assembled Length = 60.309 − 59.991 = 0.168 mm

When comparing this value with the tolerance calculated in Example 3-4, which was 0.40 mm using the maximum and minimum method, the magnitude of the tolerance value is significantly reduced.

Such a reduction indicates, on the shop floor, what actually happened when assembling Part A and Part B together would be between 59.991 and 60.309 mm in length.

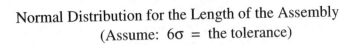
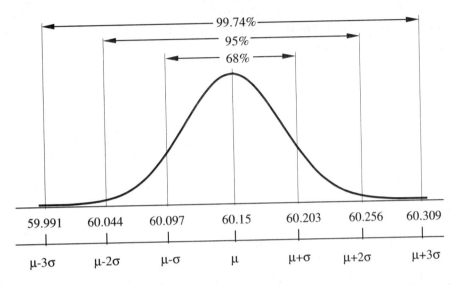

Figure 3-40 Normal Distribution of the Variation of the Assembled Length Dimensions

3.7   Geometric Tolerancing

Figure 3-41 illustrates a part sliding over a shaft that is supported at both ends. In order to ensure a smooth sliding motion and reduce the friction between the moving part and the support shaft, not only does the clearance between them need to be well controlled, but also the straightness of the support shaft needs to be well controlled. Any bending of the shaft component will disturb the sliding motion of the part. As illustrated in Figure 3-41, not only a tolerance on the variation of the diameter dimension is specified, but also a tolerance on straightness of 0.06 mm is specified, limiting any possible bending to a value below 0.06 mm. This tolerance of ensuring the straightness is called a geometric tolerance.

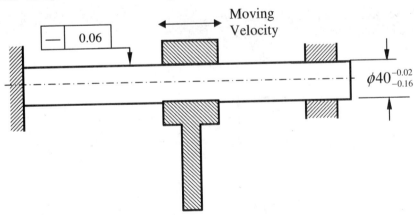

Figure 3-41 Concept of the Geometric Tolerance on Straightness

As illustrated in Figure 3-41, a rectangular box is used to specify the numerical value and the symbol of a geometric tolerance. Geometric tolerances, such as the straightness illustrated above, specify the maximum variation that can be allowed in form or position from true geometry. Actually, a geometrical tolerance is either the width or diameter of a tolerance zone. Within the tolerance zone, a surface or axis of a hole or cylinder can lie with the resulting part satisfying the necessary standards of accuracy for proper functioning and interchangeability. Figure 3-42 illustrates the tolerance specification for perpendicularity. It indicates that a datum plane is needed to specify the geometric tolerance of perpendicularity. In this case, the datum plane is the bottom plane, marked as A. The cylindrical surface of the hole should be perpendicular to the bottom plane with tolerance equal to 0.01 mm. In fact, the perpendicularity tolerance specifies a cylindrical tolerance zone perpendicular to the datum plane A, within which the axis of the hole must lie.

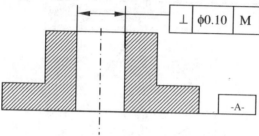

Figure 3-42 Concept of the Geometric Tolerance on Perpendicularity

Based on the ANSI standards, geometric tolerances consist of two groups. They are Form Tolerances and Position Tolerances. Form Tolerances include, for single features, straightness, flatness, roundness, and cylindricity. For related features, Form Tolerances are perpendicularity, parallelism, angularity, and runout. Position Tolerances include true position, concentricity, and symmetry. In a computer aided design environment, geometric characteristic symbols of Form Tolerances and Position Tolerances are tabulated. Users can easily access them during the design process.

3.8   Definitions Used in Tolerances

(1) <u>Nominal size</u>: The size used for a general description. Example: 10 mm diameter.
(2) <u>Tolerance</u>: The total variation permitted in the size of a feature. It can be specified in three ways:

<u>Unilateral tolerances:</u> dimensions vary in only one direction from the basic size (either larger or smaller).
<u>Bilateral tolerances:</u> dimensions vary in both directions from the basic size (larger and smaller).
<u>Limit tolerances:</u> dimensions representing the largest and smallest sizes permitted for a feature.

The following figure presents these three forms of specifying tolerances on dimensions. They are unilateral form, bilateral form and limit form.

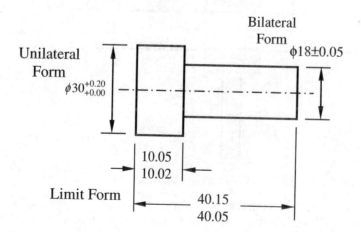

3.9   References

1.   American National Standards Institute, Y14 series of standards: e.g. Y14.1 Drawing Sheet Size and Format; Y14.2 line Converting and Lettering; Y14.3 Multi and Sectional View Drawing; Y14.5 Dimensioning and Tolerancing.

2.   P. E. Allaire, <u>Basics of the Finite Element Method, Solid Mechanics, Heat Transfer, and Fluid Mechanics</u>, University of Virginia , 1985.

3.   R. E. Barnhill, <u>IEEE Computer-Graphics and Applications</u>, 3(7), 9-16, 1983.

4.   C. A. Born, W, J, Rasdorf, and R. E. Fulton, Engineering Data Management: <u>The Technology for Integration</u>, Boston MA, 1990.

5.   J. W. Dally and T. Regan, Introduction to Engineering Design, Book1: Solar Desalination, College House Enterprise, Knoxville, TN, 1996.

6.   J. W. Dally and T. Regan, Introduction to Engineering Design, Book2: Weighing Machines, College House Enterprise, Knoxville, TN, 1997.

7.   J. W. Dally and G. M. Zhang, "A Freshman Engineering Design Course," Journal of Engineering Education, 83-91, April, 1993.

8.   B. L. Davids, A. J. Robotham and Yardwood A., <u>Computer-aided Drawing and Design</u>, London, 1991.

9.   J. Encarnacao, E. G. Schlechtendahl, <u>Computer-aided Design: Fundamentals and System Architectures</u>, Springer-Verlag, New York, 1983.

10.   G. Farin, <u>Curves and Surfaces for Computer-aided Geometric Design</u>, New York, 1988.

11.   S. Fingers, J. R. Dixon, A review of research in mechanical engineering design, Part I: Descriptive, prescriptive and computer-based models of design processes, <u>Research in Engineering Design</u>, 1(1), 51-68, 1989.

12.   S. Fingers, J. R. Dixon, A review of research in mechanical engineering design, Part II: Representations, analysis, and design for the life cycle, <u>Research in Engineering Design</u>, 1(2), 121-38, 1989.

13.   M. P. Groover and E. W. Zimmers, <u>Computer-aided Design and Manufacturing</u>, Englewood Cliffs, NJ, 1984.

14.   D. Hearn, M. P. Baker, Computer Graphics, Englewood Cliffs, NJ, 1986.

15.   P. Ingham P. <u>CAD System in Mechanical and Production Engineering</u>, London, 1989.

16.   E. B. Magrab, <u>Integrated Product and Process Design and Development: The Product Realization Process</u>, CRC Press, Boca Raton, NY, 1997.

17.   R. L. Norton, <u>Machine Design: An Integrated Approach</u>, Prentice Hall, Upper Saddle River, New Jersey, 1996.

18.   N. P. Suh, <u>The Principles of Design</u>, Oxford University Press, New York, NY, 1990.

3.10   EXERCISES

1.   Tolerances can be specified in three formats depending on their nature. They are unilateral format, bilateral format, and limit format. For each of the tolerances listed below, write the other two forms.

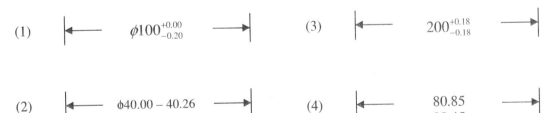

(1) $\phi 100^{+0.00}_{-0.20}$ (3) $200^{+0.18}_{-0.18}$

(2) $\phi 40.00 - 40.26$ (4)   80.85
                                    80.45

2.   A product manufactured by a company consists of three components. They are Part A, Part B, and Part C, as shown below. The company is capable of manufacturing Part A and Part C. Part B is available to the company through purchase. The requirement of the assembly is to maintain a minimum clearance of 0.05 mm and a maximum clearance of 0.70 mm after inserting Part A and Part B into Part C. What are the maximum dimension, minimum dimension and tolerance of Part B that meet the assembly specification?

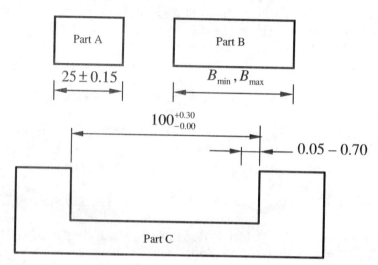

3.   The following assembly consists of 8 components. Note that there are 3 ring components, which are identical.

The engineering drawings for Shaft, Gear_1, Gear_2, Gear_3, Key and Ring are shown below.
Engineering drawing of Shaft

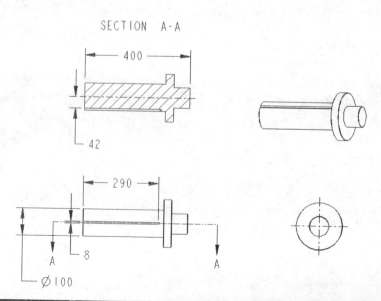

Engineering drawing of Gear_1

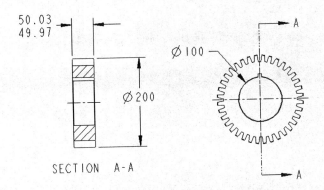

Engineering drawing of Gear_2

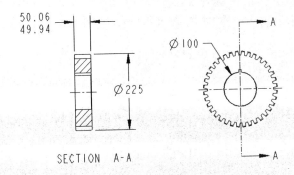

Engineering drawing of Key

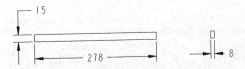

Engineering drawing of Ring

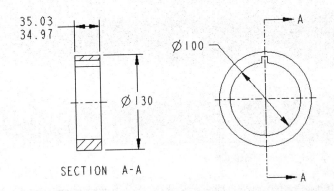

Based on the information provided in the 6 engineering drawings, determine the maximum length and minimum length of the assembly as shown below:

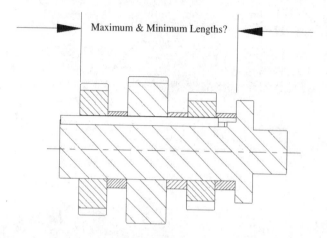

(1) Use the maximum-minimum method.

(2) Use the statistical method, assuming that the difference between the maximum dimension and the minimum dimension is equal to 6σ where parameter σ is the standard deviation of the production process.

(3) Compare the results obtained from (1) and (2).

4. As illustrated in the following figure, the dimensions and tolerances for parts A and B are $50^{+0.12}_{-0.06}$ mm and $75^{+0.20}_{-0.04}$ mm, respectively. Parts A and B will be assembled into part C, which is a container. The maximum and minimum clearances between the assembly and the container are 0.50 and 0.02 mm, respectively. Determine the maximum and minimum dimensions of the container's width.

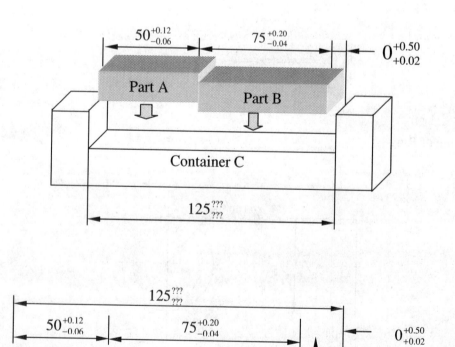

5.   Company XYZ has a product requiring a shaft component and a component with a hole. The
     company is capable of manufacturing the shaft components with an acceptable profit margin.
     The company purchases the components with a hole from an outside provider. The maximum
     and minimum dimensions of the shaft component and the hole component are shown below. The
     assembly process is characterized by clearance fit.

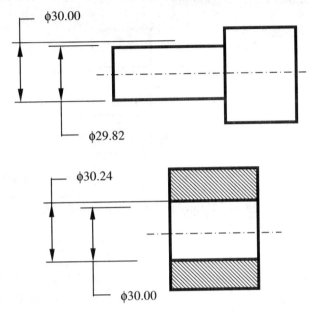

(1) Use the statistical method to determine:

     The mean value and standard deviation value of the clearance fit.
     Mean Value: _____
     Standard Deviation Value: _____

(2) Use the statistical method to determine three ranges:
     After the assembly, 68% of the assembly parts will have a clearance range from _____ to _____.
     After the assembly, 95% of the assembly parts will have a clearance range from _____ to _____.
     After the assembly, 99.74% of the assembly parts will have a clearance range from_____ to_____.

6. Part A and Part B are assembled as shown below. Determine the positive and negative deviations
    about the nominal dimension of 90 mm, as shown.

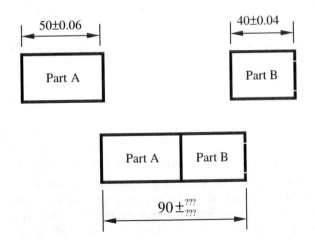

7.   A shaft component and a hole component are assembled together. The required minimum and maximum clearances are 0.02 and 0.09 mm, respectively. The maximum and minimum dimensions of the hole component are given and shown in the following figure. What are the minimum and maximum dimensions of the shaft component to achieve the required minimum and maximum clearances after assembling?

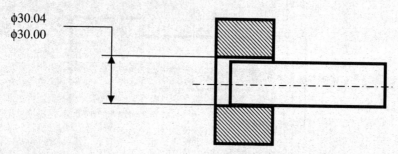

$\phi 30.04$
$\phi 30.00$

8.   Thousands of bearings have been purchased. Determine the maximum and minimum diameters of shafts, which will be assembled with the bearings shown below. The nominal dimension of the inner diameter of the bearing is 50 mm, and the nominal dimension of the outer diameter is 85 mm.

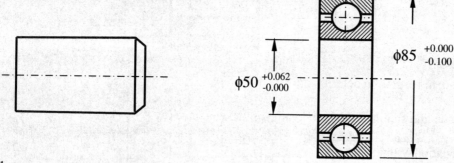

$\phi 50 \begin{smallmatrix} +0.062 \\ -0.000 \end{smallmatrix}$ $\phi 85 \begin{smallmatrix} +0.000 \\ -0.100 \end{smallmatrix}$

Case 1:
For clearance fit, the maximum clearance is 0.302 mm and the minimum clearance is 0.008 mm.
The maximum diameter is _____ mm.
The minimum diameter is _____ mm.

Case 2:
For transition fit, the maximum interference is 0.091 mm and the maximum clearance is 0.006 mm.
The maximum diameter is _____ mm.
The minimum diameter is _____ mm.

Case 3:
For interference fit, the maximum interference is 0.105 mm and the minimum interference is 0.014 mm.
The maximum diameter is _____ mm.
The minimum diameter is _____ mm.

9.   An assembly consists of 3 components, as shown below. They are a bearing component, a shaft component and a support component. For mass production, the bearing components are purchased. The company produces both the support and shaft components. A transition fit is used to insert the shaft component to the inner ring of the bearing component. An interference fit is used to insert the bearing component to the large hole feature of the support component.
      (a) The hole basis system should be used to specify the tolerance (the deviations from the nominal dimension of 50) of the shaft component, and the shaft basis system should be used

to specify the tolerance (the deviations from the nominal dimension of 85) of the support component.

(b) The shaft basis system should be used to specify the tolerance (the deviations from the nominal dimension of 50) of the shaft component, and the hole basis system should be used to specify the tolerance (the deviations from the nominal dimension of 85) of the support component.

(c) The hole basis system should be used to specify the tolerance (the deviations from the nominal dimension of 50) of the shaft component, and the hole basis system should be used to specify the tolerance (the deviations from the nominal dimension of 85) of the support component.

(d) The shaft basis system should be used to specify the tolerance (the deviations from the nominal dimension of 50) of the shaft component, and the shaft basis system should be used to specify the tolerance (the deviations from the nominal dimension of 85) of the support component.

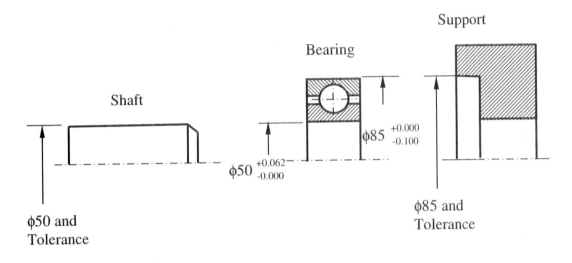

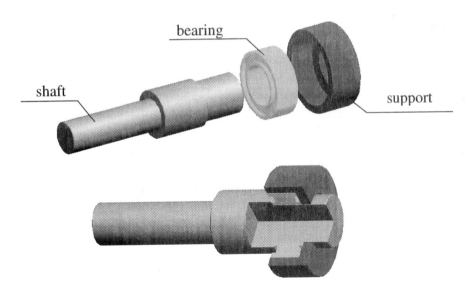

10. An assembly consists of five components. They are Container, Part1, Part2, Part3, Insert1, and Insert2. The assembly process belongs to "clearance fit." The range of the clearance in the horizontal direction after the assembly is between 0.03 and 0.30 mm. The range of the clearance in the vertical direction after the assembly is between 0.02 and 0.22 mm.

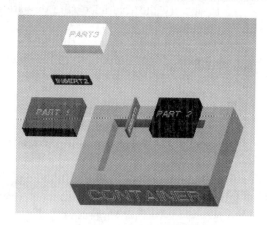

The dimensions and tolerances of Container, Part1, Part2 and Part 3 are given. They are shown below.

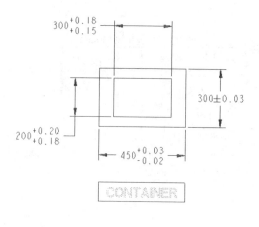

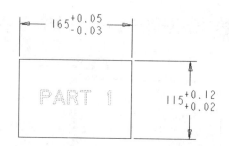

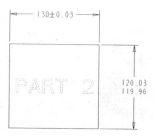

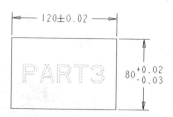

What are the maximum and minimum dimensions of Insert1, which is used to control the clearance in the horizontal direction during this assembly process? What are the maximum and minimum dimensions of Insert 2, which is used to control the clearance in the vertical direction during this assembly process?

CHAPTER 4

Creo PARAMETRIC DESIGN SYSTEM

4.1 Introduction to the Creo Parametric Design System

This chapter is an introduction to the fundamentals of Creo Parametric design system. Just as babies must learn to crawl before they can walk, and walk before they run, a designer must first understand the design requirements and conduct the design through a procedure, in which features are created step by step. With the material presented in this textbook, the concept of feature-based design is demonstrated with examples and illustrations. Afterwards, creations of the mechanical components, such as shafts, supports, springs and gears, are also introduced. Now let us start the crawling process and begin to understand the capabilities of Creo Parametric Design System. Take it easy!

4.2 Feature-Based Design

The principle of using computers to aid engineering designers in the process of product development is to utilize the computing power and graphical capabilities of software systems so that computing and visualization of geometry can be accomplished with manageable efforts. As the computer science advances, the concept of feature-based modeling in the 3D space matures as well.

The following figure presents two typical features used in the process of geometric interpretation and reasoning. The first feature is a rectangular-shaped block and the second feature is a cylinder. It is evident that features used in computer-aided design are in their geometric sense, namely shapes such as blocks, cylinders, holes, ribs, key-ways, threads, ribs, and many others. In addition to their geometric meanings, features also have engineering meanings. Making a hole requires a drilling process, and making a key-way may use an end-milling process. In summary, a feature is a perceived or functional entity of a designed part. These entities are useful in understanding the function and performance of the designed part.

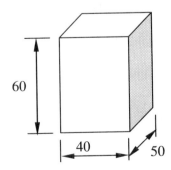
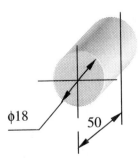

4.2.1 Geometric Interpretation Using Features

Assume that a design engineer has designed a part, called Part I, which is shown in Figure 4-1. In terms of geometric interpretation using features, the designed part can be viewed as having two features. The first feature is a block, and the second feature is a cylinder. From the mathematical viewpoint of reasoning, the designed part can be viewed as a union of these two features at a specific location. The location is characterized by the use of two dimensions. They are 20 mm and 30 mm on the front surface of the block, respectively.

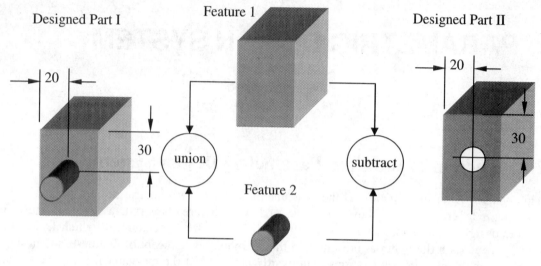

Figure 4-1 Geometric Interpretation Using Features

The operation of union represents an interaction between the two features, characterized by the term "extrusion" in engineering. Figure 4-1 also presents a designed part, called Part II. It is viewed as subtracting the cylinder from the block. The operation of subtraction is to remove the material or mass from the block feature, an operation similar to cutting a portion of material from the block. The method of developing a design model through the use of features is called feature-based modeling. The method requires the creation of a first feature. After the completion of the first feature, a second feature can be added or subtracted from the first feature, thus keeping the design process ongoing, until the design is fully completed. In fact, Creo Parametric characterizes the approach of feature-based modeling with the embedded parametric and associate capabilities.

4.2.2 Launch the Creo Parametric Design System

This section introduces the basic steps employed in designing a part under the Creo Parametric design environment. The command to start Creo Parametric depends on the computer system you are using. (i.e., a desktop PC, a laptop PC, or a Sun workstation) However, the following procedure is applicable to initiate the design process regardless of the computer system used to run Creo Parametric.

Figure 4-2 presents the window appearance when launching Creo Parametric. The window which appears offers the following functions:

1. Provide a Main Toolbar, from which a new file can be opened for initiating the design process, such as creating a new object.
2. Provide tutorial materials on Creo Parametric.
3. Provide a Folder Tree for file management.
4. Provide the guidelines for getting help from the PTC website.

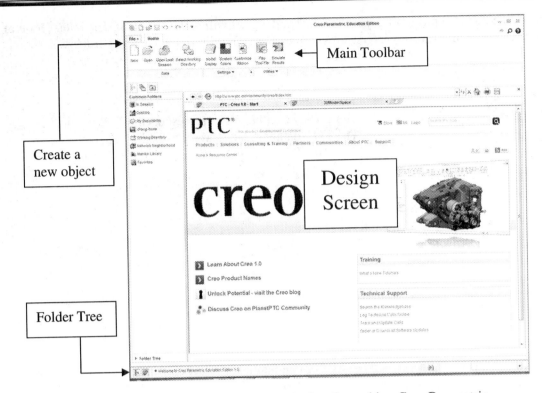

Figure 4-2 Window Appeared when Launching Creo Parametric

To start the design process, click the icon, called "**Create a new file**", which is displayed on the File menu. Make sure "**Part**" is selected. Type the name of the file, or accept the default name, such as prt0001 shown on display. Click the button of **OK**. The design screen appears, as shown.

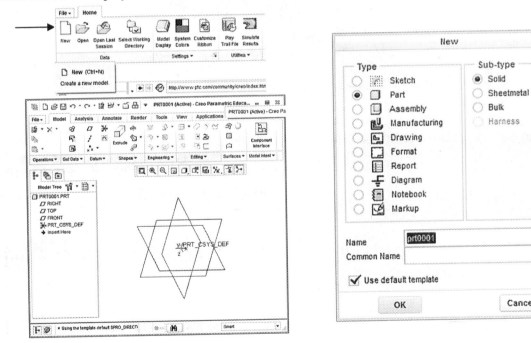

4.2.3 Feature Creation under Creo Parametric

Before creating the first feature in the design process, let us first examine the three datum planes listed in the model tree and hidden from display. These three datum planes are called the **FRONT** datum plane, the **TOP** datum plane and the **RIGHT** datum plane. These three planes are orthogonal to each other, and they function as the three (3) pieces of paper, on which a designer will make a sketch. The intersection of these three planes is a point. It is this intersecting point where the origin of a default coordinate system is established. The orientation of the default coordinate system is shown in the following figures.

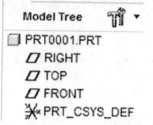

The **FRONT** datum plane represents the XOY plane.
The **TOP** datum plane represents the XOZ plane.
The **RIGHT** datum plane represents the YOZ plane.

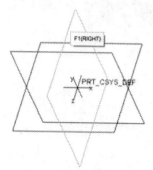 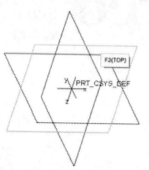 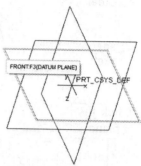

Assume that a part to be designed consists of one feature only. As illustrated below, the part is a rectangular-shaped block. The three dimensions are 10, 6 and 4 inches, respectively.

Example 4-1: Create a rectangular-shaped block with the dimensions: 10 x 6 x 4 inches.

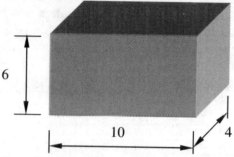

Click the icon of **New** from the main toolbar or menu toolbar. This brings up a window called **New**, as shown below. Make sure that the **Part** module is selected. Type the file name, say *block* as in the current case. Click the button of **OK**. This will bring up the design window.

Select the Part Mode

Type the file name

Click the button of OK

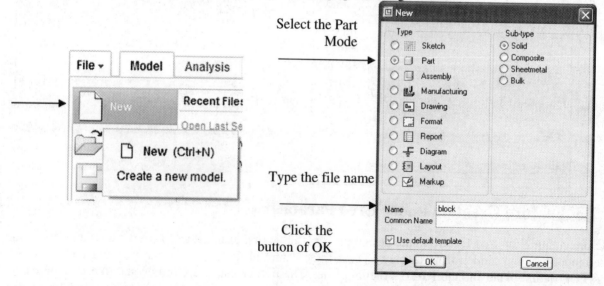

From the Model tab, select the icon of **Extrude.** Specify 4 as the depth value of extrusion.

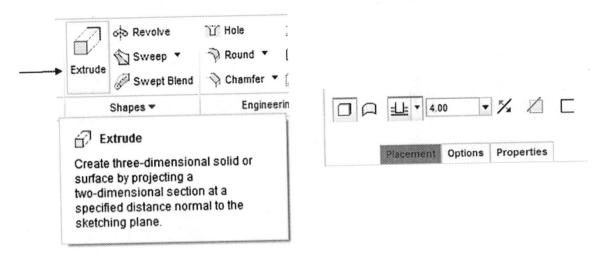

Click the **FRONT** datum plane displayed in the Model Tree. We use this datum plane as the sketching plane. Click the icon of **Sketch View** to orient the sketching plane parallel to the screen.

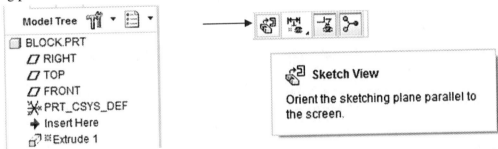

There are 2 dashed lines on display. One dashed line is in the vertical direction and the other is in the horizontal direction. These 2 dashed lines are "selected references for making sketch". Actually, these 2 dashed lines represent the locations of the **Top** datum plane and the **Right** datum plane. The Creo Parametric design software system, by default, has selected them as 2 references for making sketch.

Click the icon of **Rectangle**, and left-click the origin or the intersction of the 2 dashed lines, and left click at a location, as shown. To modify the 2 dimensions, click the icon of **Select** or **One by One**. Afterwards, double click the displayed numbers and change the 2 dimensions to 10 and 6, respectively.

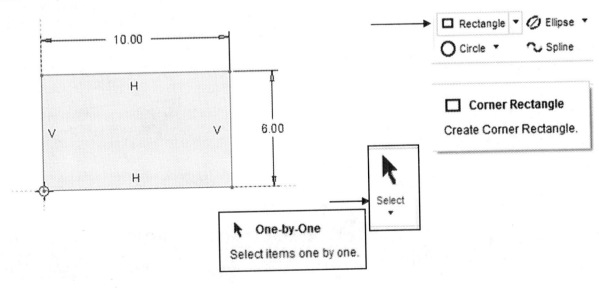

Upon completing this sketch, click the icon of **OK** and click the icon of **Apply and Save** to complete the creation of the block feature.

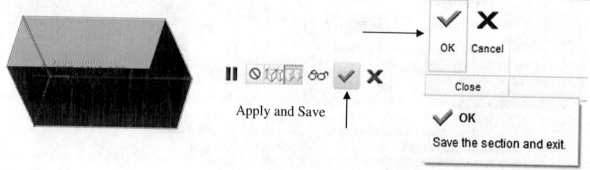

When the creation of a 3D solid model is completed, users are able to view the 3D solid model from different settings of the viewing angle. Click the icon of **Named Views**, as shown > select **Stardard Orientation** to have a 3D view of the created 3D model on display.

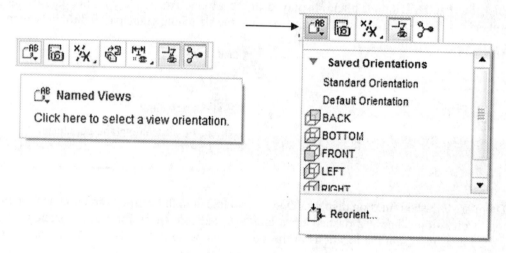

Users may also use the buttons of mouse to spin, turn, zoom and pan the 3D solid model. For example, holding down the middle button and moving the pointer will spin the 3D solid model. Information on the mouse controls is listed below.

Spin the model by holding down the middle mouse button and moving the pointer.

Turn the model by moving your mouse from left to right while holding down the CTRL key and the middle mouse button.

Zooming takes advantage of the roll wheel, which pulls in the model or pushes it away. You can also zoom by moving your mouse up and down while holding down the CTRL key and middle mouse button.

Panning also complies with the new roll wheel standard by using the SHIFT key and the middle mouse button.

Users may select the icon of **Shade** from the menu bar. The block component displayed on the computer screen will turn the created 3D model to a shaded object. The user may also try other icons shown on the tool bar, such as viewing the object with no hidden line, with hidden line or under wireframe, etc.

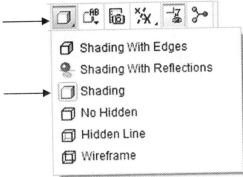

At the time, a 3D model has been successfully completed. Let us save the block design. Click **Save > OK**.

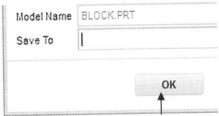

4.3 Preparation of an Engineering Drawing

Traditionally, a designer uses pencils, rulers, T-squares, rubber, and other instruments to prepare the front view, top view and right-side view, a subject we discussed in Chapter 2. Under a computer aided design environment, the designer is mainly responsible for creating a solid model of the part under design. The software system is capable of generating both orthogonal projections and 3D views, such as isometric view or trimetric view. The designer has a full control of the layout of engineering drawings.

The following figure presents an engineering drawing for the object of the block just created. The drawing consists of three projection views, a 3D view, and three dimensions. In the following, we present the procedure to create such an engineering drawing.

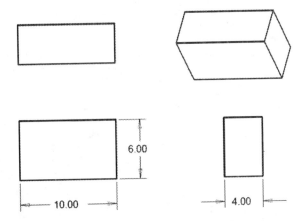

To prepare an engineering drawing based on the 3D solid model, we need to create a drawing file. First, we click the icon of **New**, or "Create a new model".

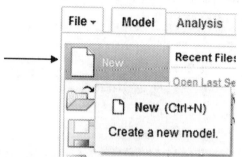

A **New** window appears, as illustrated below. This is the same step we used to open a new file when creating the 3D solid model of *block*. However, this time, "**Drawing**" mode, instead of "**Part**" mode, should be selected. Type *block* as the name of the file.. Clear the box of **Use default template** because we do not want to use the default setting for the drawing work. Afterwards, click **OK**. In the window of **New Drawing**, make sure that the file of the 3D solid model called *block* is shown. Otherwise, use "**Browse**" to locate it. Select **Empty** under Specify Template, and select the paper size to be **A**. Afterwards, click **OK**.

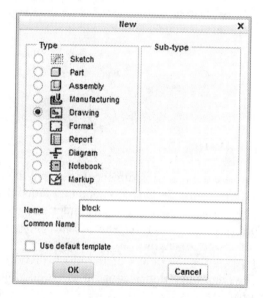 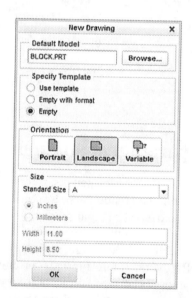

This brings up the drawing screen. Click the icon of **Layout**. Click the icon of **General.** In the **Select Combined State** window, click OK to accept **No Combined State**.

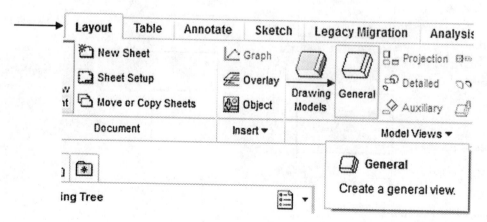

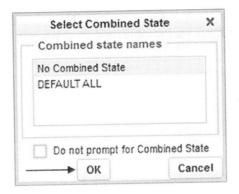

Select a location on the drawing screen as the center point for the **General View**. A general view appears on the screen.

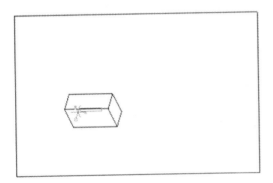

In the pop-up Drawing View window, select **FRONT > Apply > Close**, the construction of the **Front View** is completed.

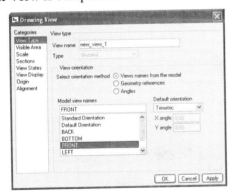

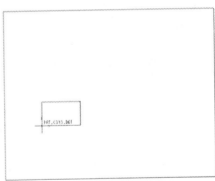

To insert the right side view, pick the **FRONT** View just created so that the Front View is activated, click the icon of Projection and make a left click at the right side of the Front View.

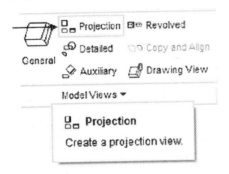

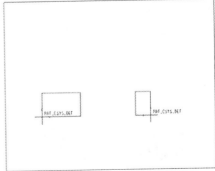

An alternative method to create a projection on the right side is to click the Front View for activation. Afterwards, make a right-click and hold, and then select **Insert Projection View** > move the cursor to the right side and click the left button of mouse. The construction of the right side view is completed.

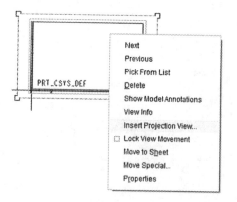
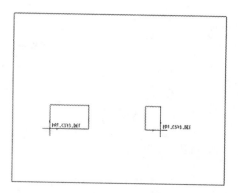

Follow the same procedure to create the top view, as shown below.

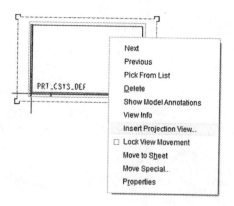
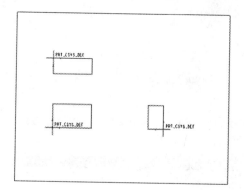

Click the icon of **General.** In the **Select Combined State** window, click OK to accept **No Combined State.** Select a location on the drawing screen as the center point for the 3D View (click the left button of mouse). A general view appears on the screen. In the pop-up Drawing View window, select **Standard Orientation > Apply > Close**, the construction of the 3D View is completed.

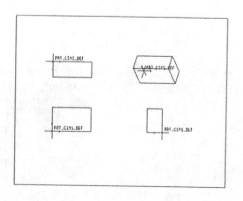
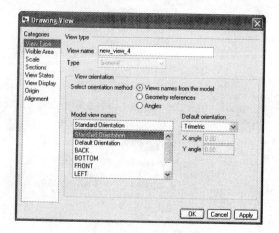

Users may notice that the names of the default coordinate system, such as PRT_CSYS_DEF appears. To clean the drawing screen, click the icon of **Datun Display Filter**.

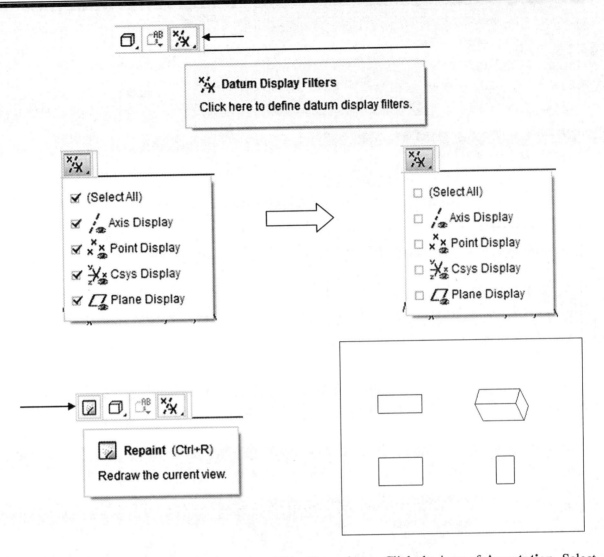

Upon completing the layout, we start adding dimensions. Click the icon of **Annotation**. Select the icon of **Show Model Annotation.**

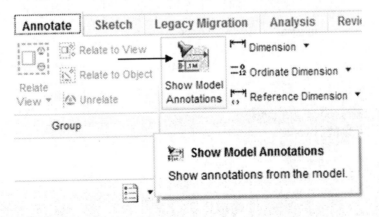

In the pop-up window, select the icon of **Dimensions.** To show the dimension of Extrude 1, click Extrude 1 listed in the model tree. Click Accept and OK. The 3 dimensions of 10, 6 and 4 are shown. Click the box of **Accept All > OK**.

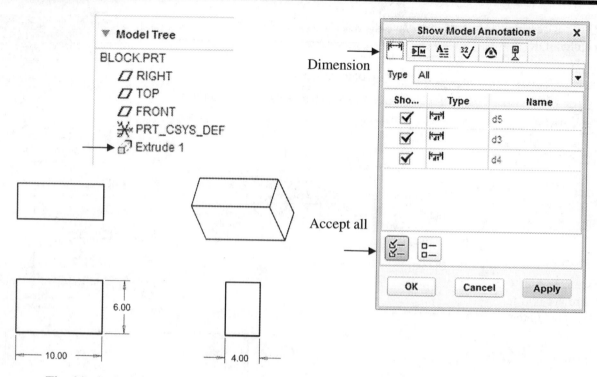

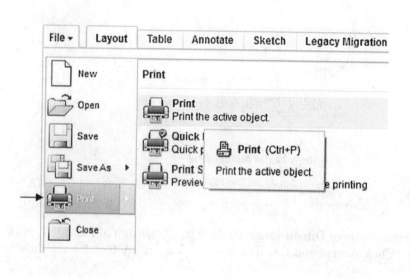

The block design is completed and remember to save all of your work with the engineering drawing. You select **Save** from the main toolbar > **OK**.

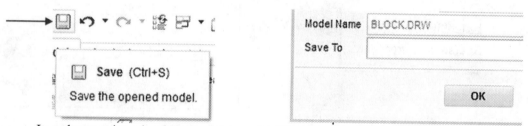

In order to print a hard copy of the engineering drawing, click File > Print > Print. As illustrated in the following figure, select **OK** from the print window to get a hard copy.

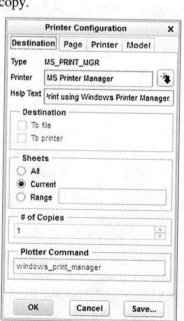

Users may select **PDF** to save the drawing file. Click **File > Save As** and select **PDF** as the type and click OK.

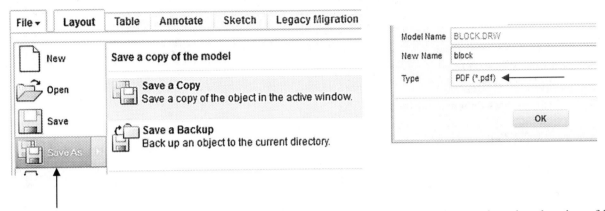

Example 4-2: Create a 3D solid model for the following object, and prepare an engineering drawing of it. There are two features. The first feature is a block, and its size is 12x8x5 inch. The second feature is a hole. The diameter of the hole is 5 inch, and the depth of the hole is 4 inch.

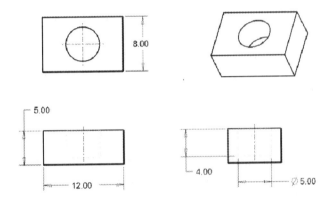

Click the icon of **New** from the main toolbar or menu toolbar. This brings up a window called **New**, as shown below. Make sure that the **Part** module is selected. Type the file name, say *block_hole* as in the current case. Click the button of **OK**. This will bring up the design window.

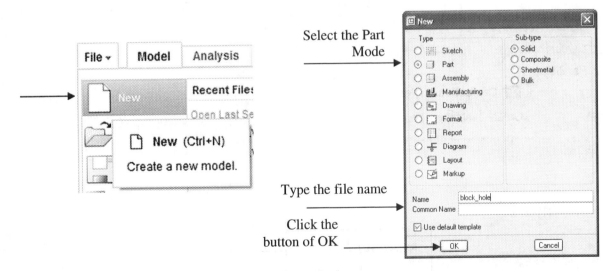

From the Model tab, click **Extrude,** and specify 5 as the height value of extrusion.

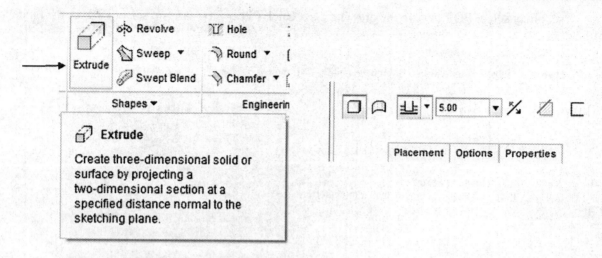

From the **Model Tree**, pick the **TOP** datum plane as the scketching plane. Click the icon of Sketch View to orient the sketching plane parallel to the screen.

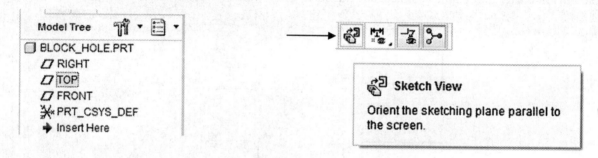

Click the icon of **Rectangle**, and select **Center Rectangle**. Sketch a rectangle, which is symmetric about the vertcial and horizontal axes. Click the icon of Select to modify the 2 dimensions to 12 and 8, respectively.

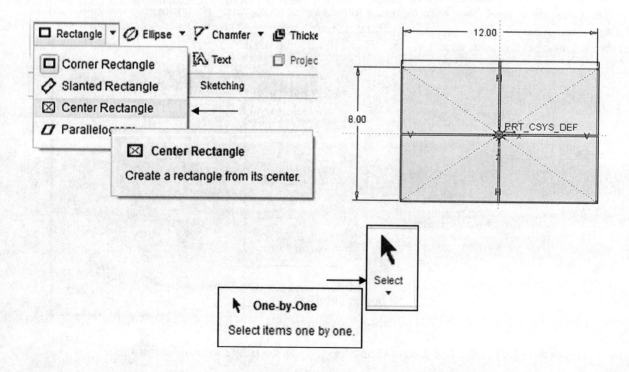

Upon completing this sketch, click the icon of **OK** and click the icon of **Apply and Save** to complete the creation of the block feature.

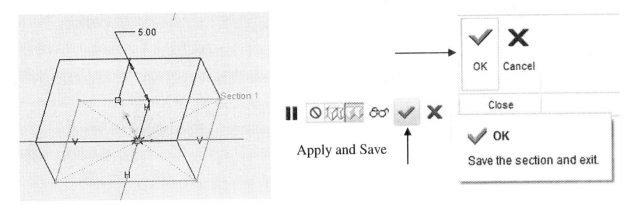

The second feature is a hole. Click the icon of **Hole**. Specify *5* as the diameter value and specify *4* as the depth of the hole, as shown below:

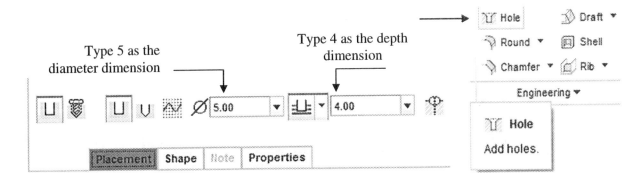

Click **Placement**, click or activate the box under **Placement**, and select the top surface of the block as the primary surface, and select **Linear**.

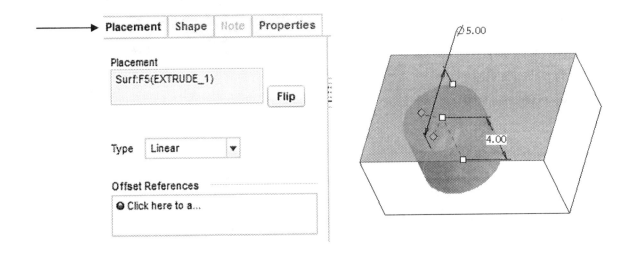

To define the center location of the hole, click or activate the box under **Offset References**, and select **FRONT**, then hold down the **Ctrl** key, select **RIGHT**. Specify the values of offsets to be 0.00, thus completing the creation of the hole feature.

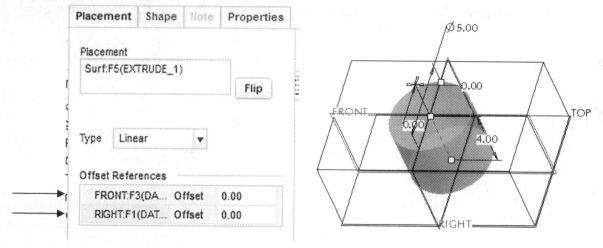

Note that users may change **Offset** to **Align** to position the center of this hole, as shown below:

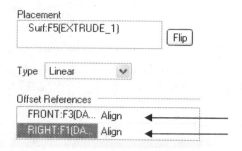

Click icon of **Apply and Save** to complete the creation of the hole feature, as shown below:

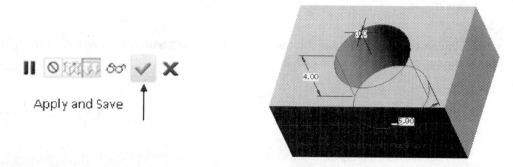

At the time, a 3D model has been successfully completed. Let us save the block-hole design. Click **Save > OK**.

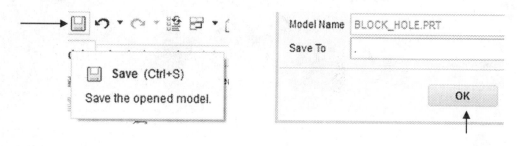

To prepare an engineering drawing, we select the icon of **New** displayed on the main toolbar. A **New** window appears.

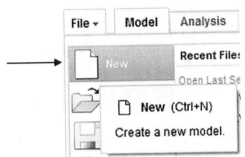

Click **Drawing**, instead of **Part**, Type block_hole as the name of the file. Clear the box of **Use default template** because we do not want to use the default setting for the drawing work. Afterwards, click **OK**.

This brings up a new window called "New Drawing". Make sure that the file of the 3D solid model is shown. Otherwise, use the "**Browse**" option to locate it. Select **Empty** under Specify Template, and select the paper size **A**. Afterwards, click **OK**.

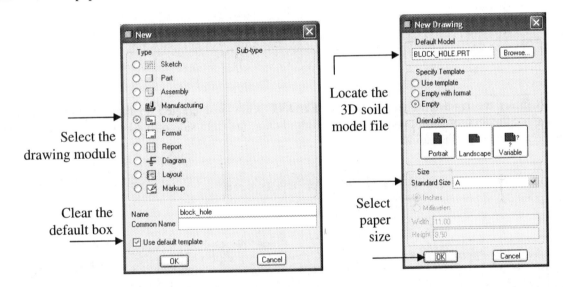

This brings up the drawing screen. Click the icon of **Layout**. Click the icon of **General.** In the **Select Combined State** window, click **OK** to accept **No Combined State.**

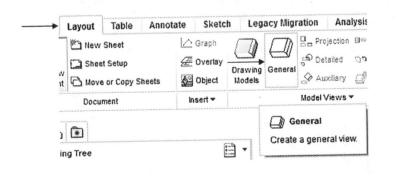

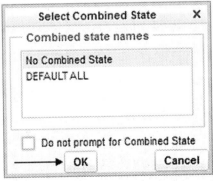

Select a location on the drawing screen as the center point for the **General View**. A general view appears on the screen.

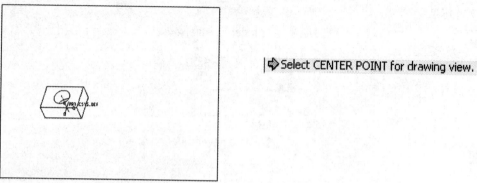

In the pop-up Drawing View window, select **FRONT > Apply > Close**, the construction of the **Front View** is completed.

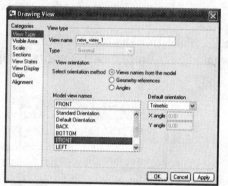

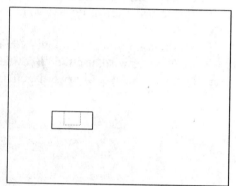

To insert the right side view, pick the **FRONT** View just created so that the Front View is activated, click the icon of Projection and make a left click at the right side of the Front View. Follow the same procedure to create the top view.

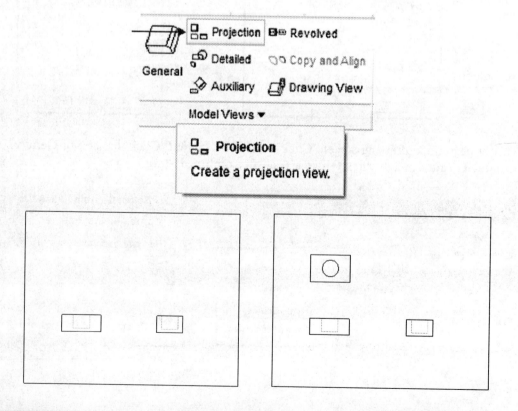

Click the icon of **General.** In the **Select Combined State** window, click OK to accept **No Combined State**. Select a location on the drawing screen as the center point for the 3D View (click the left button of mouse).   A general view appears on the screen. In the pop-up Drawing View window, select **Standard Orientation > Apply > Close**, the construction of the 3D View is completed.

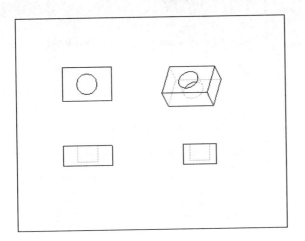 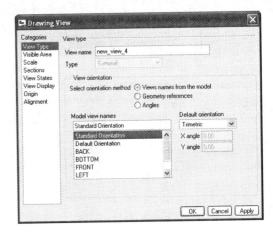

Sometimes there is a need to move the position of a projection view or the 3D view. For example, the user wants to move the 3D view to a new location. First click the 3D view > right-click and click Lock View Movement if it is checked. When Lock View Movement is not checked, the user is able to relocate the 3D view to a new location he or she desires.

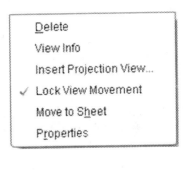

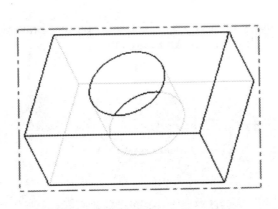

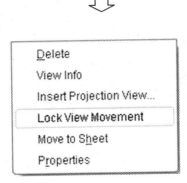

In general, a 3D view should have no dashed lines. How to eliminate the dashed line displayed on the 3D view while keeping the dashed lines on the projection views? Click the 3D view first > right-click and hold, select **Properties**. In the **Drawing View** window, select **View Display.** Change **Follow Environment** to **No hidden > OK**.

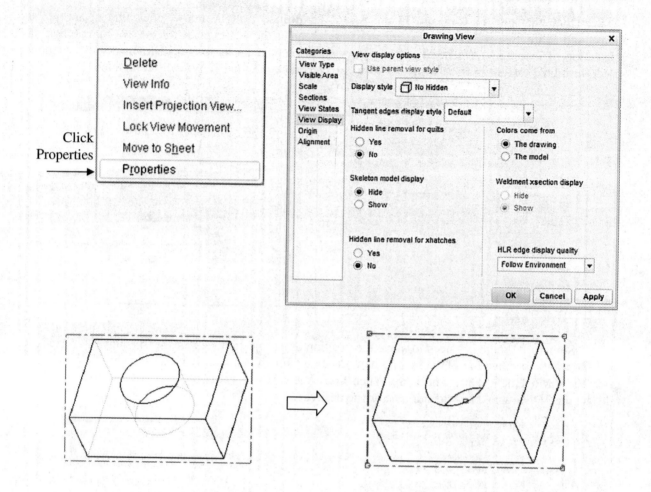

Click
Properties →

Upon completing the layout, we start adding dimensions. Click the icon of **Annotation**. Select the icon of **Show Model Annotation**, which is displayed in the **Annotate** tab.

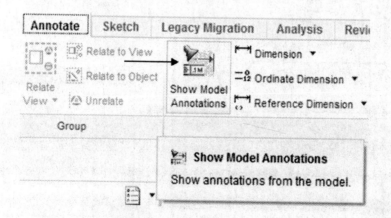

In the pop-up window, select the icon of **Dimensions**, and click the Front View. The two dimensions of 12 and 5 associated with the Front View are shown. Click the box of **Accept All > Apply**.

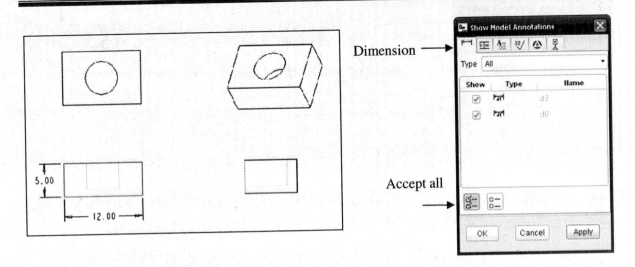

In the pop-up window, click the Top View. The dimension of 5 associated with the Top View is shown. Click the button of **Accept All > Apply.**

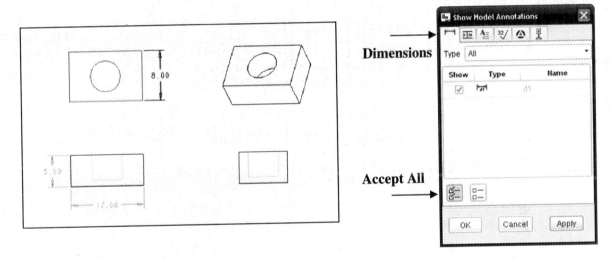

To add the dimensions associated with the hole feature, click the Hole 1 listed in the model tree, the two dimensions of Ø5 and 4 are on display. Click **Accept All > Apply.**

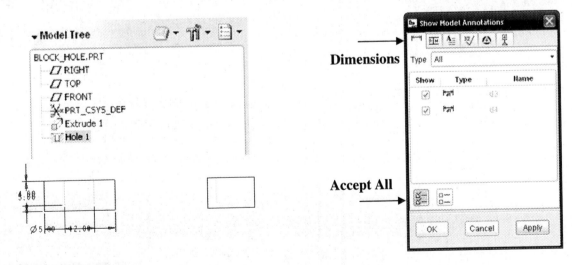

However, the 2 displayed dimensions are overlapped with the other displayed dimensions. Let us move these 2 dimensions from the Front View to the Right-Sided View. Let us move the dimension of Ø5 first. Click the dimension of Ø5 > right-click and hold, click **Move Item to View** > click the Right-Sided View. The dimension of Ø5 is displayed on the Right-Sided View, as shown.

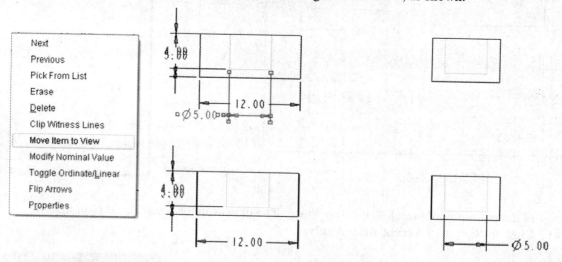

Now let us the dimension of 4. Click the dimension of 4 > right-click and hold, click **Move Item to View** > click the Right-Sided View. The dimension of 4 is displayed on the Right-Sided View, as shown.

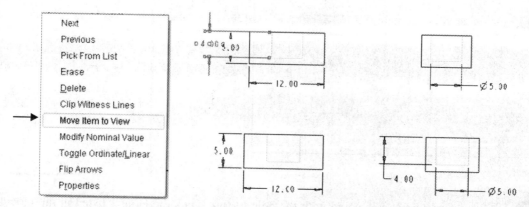

Now let us add centerlines to the drawing. In the pop-up window, select the box of centerlines. Click the hole feature listed in the model tree. All the centerlines are shown. Click **Accept All > OK.**

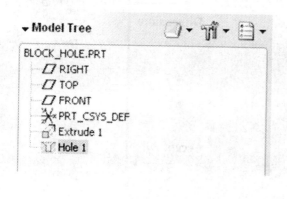
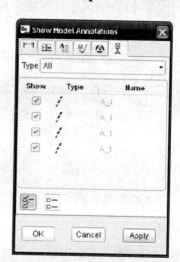

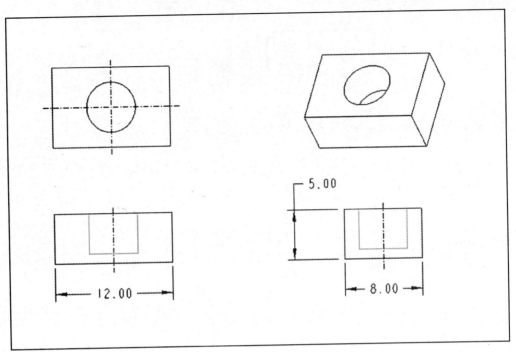

In general, there is no need to display centerlines on a 3D view. To delete the displayed centerline on the 3D view, click the centerline first. Afterwards, click **Delete** from the Annotation menu.

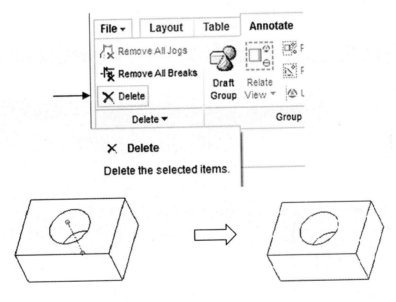

At the time you have successfully completed the block-hole design, remember to save all of your work with the engineering drawing. You select **Save** from the main toolbar > **OK**.

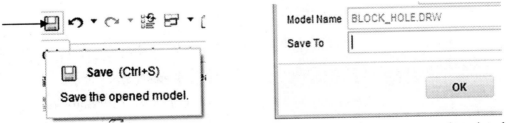

Example 4-3: Create a 3D solid model for the following object, and prepare an engineering drawing of it.

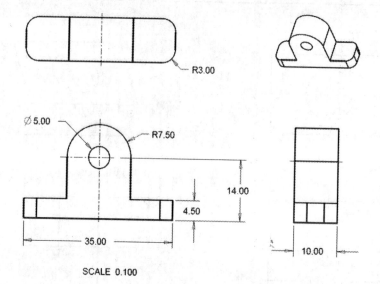

SCALE 0.100

Click the icon of **New** from the tool bar. From the **New** window, select the **Part** mode. Type *support* as the file name. Click the box of **OK**.

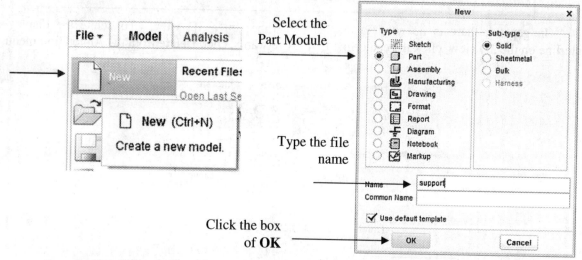

From the **Model** tab, select the icon of **Extrude**. Specify 10 as the extrusion distance.

From the Model Tree, pick the **FRONT** datum plane as the sketching plane. Click the icon of **Sketch View** to orient the sketching plane parallel to the screen.

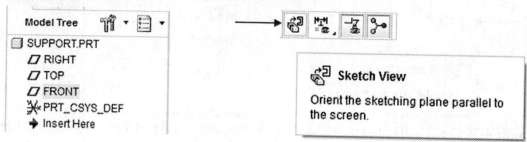

Let us create a vertical centerline. Click the icon of **Centerline**, or right click on the screen and select **Construction Centerline**.from the pop up menu, to scketch a vertical centerline.

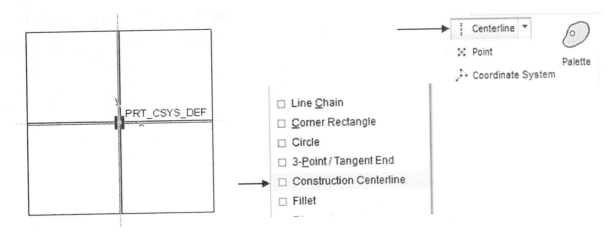

Click the icon of **Line** or **Line Chain**. Sketch a horizontal line symmetric about the vertical centerline. Modify the dimension to 35.

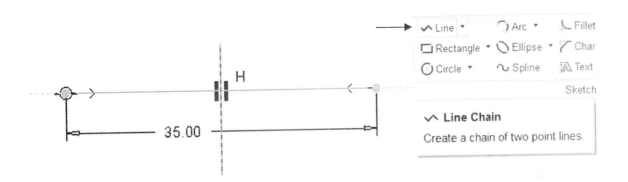

Click the icon of **Line** or **Line Chain**. Sketch 3 line segments, as shown. Make sure that there is no equal length among the 3 line segments.

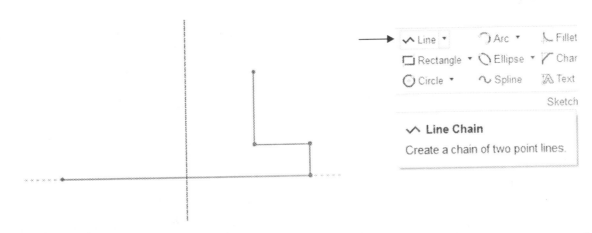

Click the icon of **Arc** to sketch an $180°$ arc and make sure that the arc center is on the vertical axis.

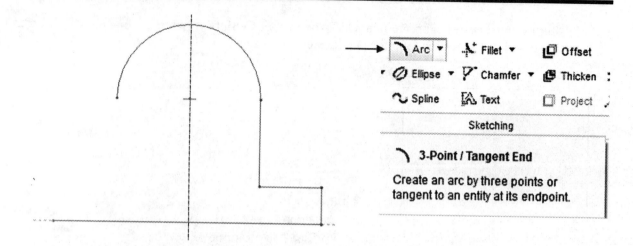

Click the icon of **Line** or **Line Chain**. Sketch 3 line segments, as shown. Make sure that there are 2 equal constraints added in the sketching process. Modify the 3 dimensions to 7.5, 9.5 and 4.5, respectively..

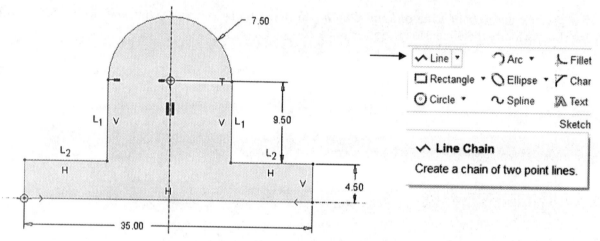

Click the icon of **Circle** to sketch a circle centered at the arc center. The diameter value is 5, as shwon.

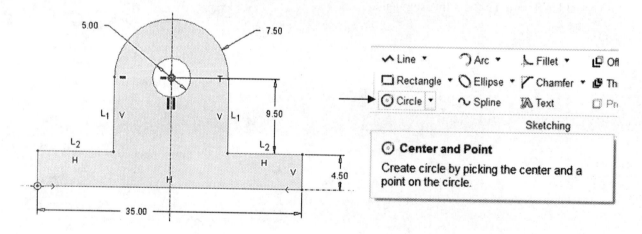

Upon completing this sketch, click the icon of **OK** and click the icon of **Apply and Save** to complete the creation of the support feature.

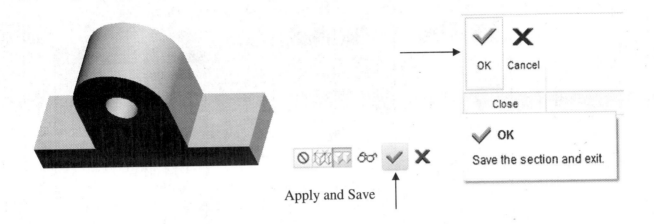

Apply and Save

After creating the support feature, let us create 4 rounds. Select the icon of **Round**. Specify *3* as the radius value and pick the 4 vertical edges while holding down the **Ctrl** key. Click the icon of **Apply and Save** to complete the creation of the round feature.

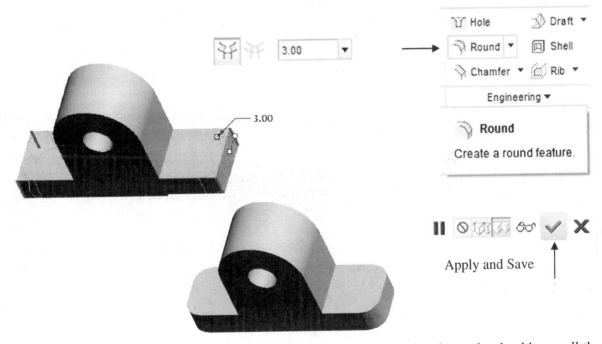

Apply and Save

At this time the user has successfully completed the support design, he or she should save all the work with the 3D solid model. Select **Save** from the main toolbar > **OK**.

To prepare an engineering drawing, we select the icon of **New** displayed on the main toolbar. Select the "**Drawing**" mode. Type *support* as the file name and clear the box of **Use default template**.

Afterwards, click the box of **OK**. This leads to the New Drawing window. Select **Empty** under Specify Template, and select the paper size to be **A**. Afterwards, click the button of **OK**.

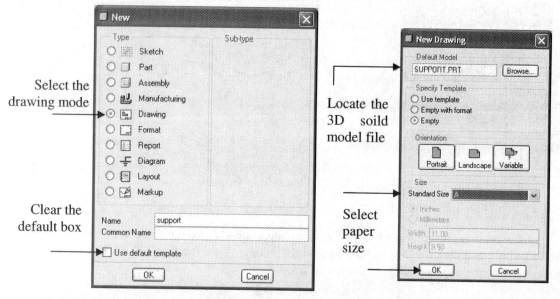

This brings up the drawing screen. Click the icon of **Layout**. Click the icon of **General.** In the **Select Combined State** window, click **OK** to accept **No Combined State**.

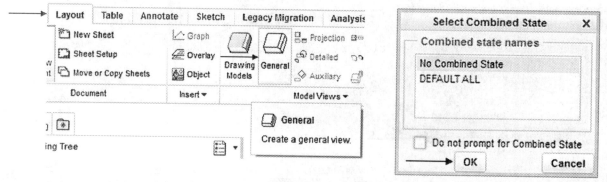

Select a location on the drawing screen as the center point for the **General View**. A general view appears on the screen.

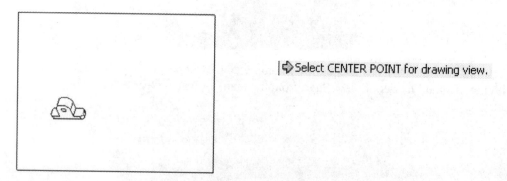

In the pop-up Drawing View window, select **FRONT > Apply**, the insertion of the front projection is completed. Click **Scale > Custom scale** to adjust the projection size. The current scale value is set to 0.1 > **Close**.

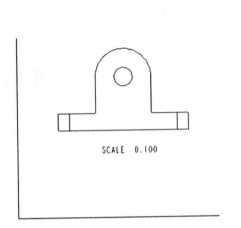
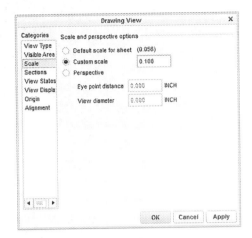

Afterwards, define the projection on the top, the projection on the right side, and a 3D view, as shown.

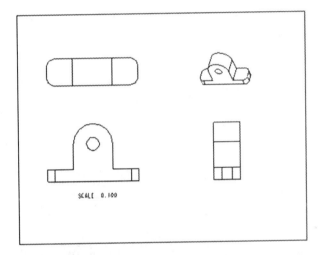

Upon completing the layout, we start adding dimensions. Click the icon of **Annotation**. Select the icon of **Dimension – New References**, which is displayed on the toolbar.

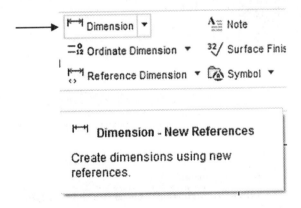

To add the 3 maximum dimensions, click the base lines using the left button of mouse > click the middle button of mouse to position the dimension at an appropriate location. The dimension of 35 is shown. Repeat this process to add the dimension of 10, as shown.

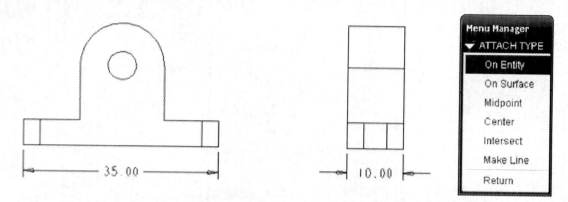

To specify the maximum dimension in the vertical direction, we need 2 dimensions to accomplish this task. From the **Attach Type** window, select **Center** > click the circle to locate the center position > use the left buttom to click the base > use the middle buttom to position the dimension value, which is 14.

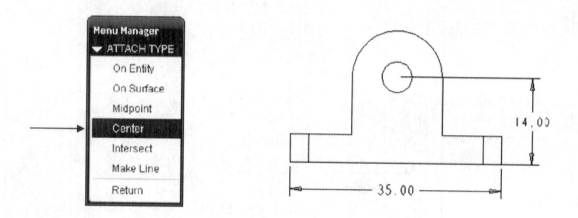

Afterwards, from the **Attach Type** window, select **On Entity** > click the arc once, using the left buttom, and use the middle-buttom to position the raidus valuel, which is 7.5 > **Return**.

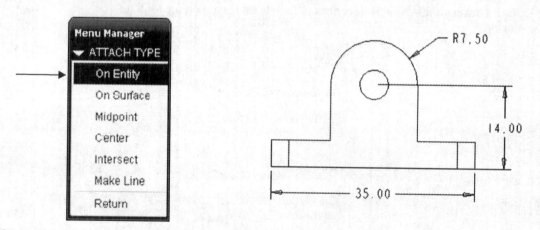

Users are asked to add the other dimensions, such as the diameter of the hole and radius value of the rounds, to complete the dimensioning task.

To add centerlines, click **Annotation** > **Show Model Annotion**. In the pop-up window, select the box of centerlines. Click the hole feature on display. Whenever a centerline is shown. Click the box of **Accept All** > **Apply or OK**.

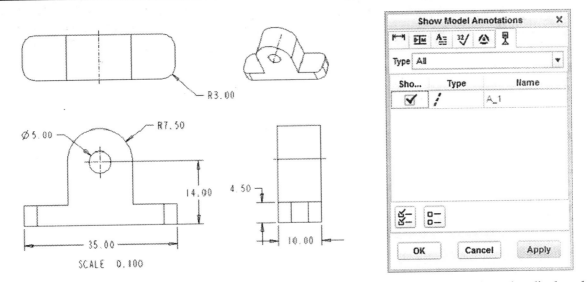

In general, there is no need to display centerlines on a 3D view. To delete the displayed centerline on the 3D view, click the centerline first. Afterwards, click **Delete** from the Annotation menu.

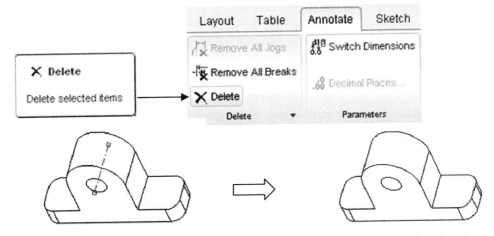

At this time you have successfully completed the engineering drawing for the support design, remember to save all of your work with the engineering drawing. You select **Save** from the main toolbar > **OK**.

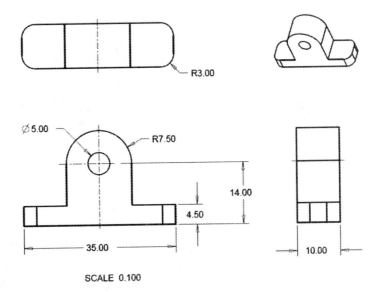

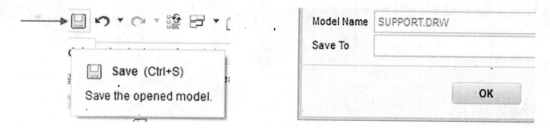

Example 4-4: Create a 3D solid model for the following object, and prepare an engineering drawing of it.

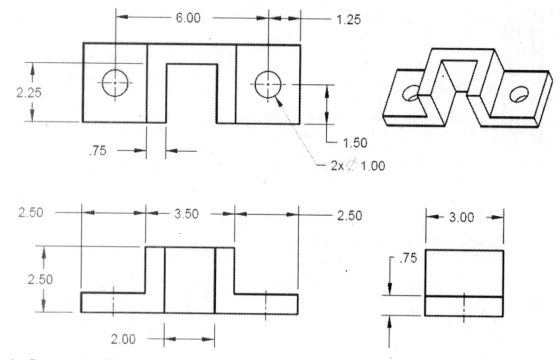

Step 1: Create a new file for the 3D solid model.

Select the icon of **New** from the toolbar. In the **New** window, select the **Part** module. Type *block_slot_hole* as the file name. Click the box of **OK**. This will bring up the design window.

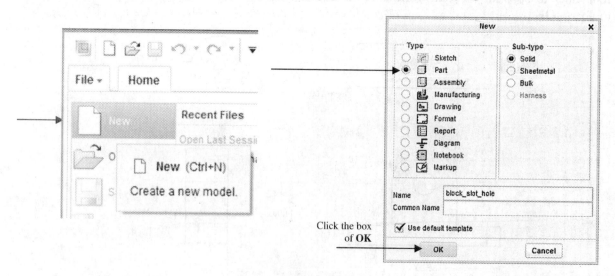

Step 2: Create the first feature, which is a block and the 3 dimensions are 3.5 x 3.0 x 2.5 inches.

Click the icon of **Extrude** from the Model tab. Specify 2.5 as the height of the block feature.

From the Model Tree, pick the **TOP** datum plane as the sketching plane. Click the icon of **Sketch View** to orient the sketching plane parallel to the screen.

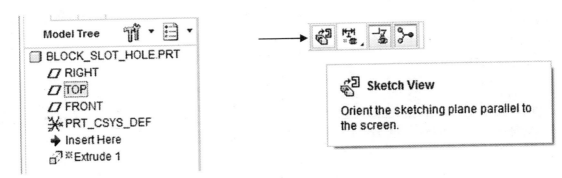

Let us create a vertical centerline. Click the icon of **Centerline**, or right click on the screen and select **Construction Centerline**.from the pop up menu, to scketch a vertical centerline.

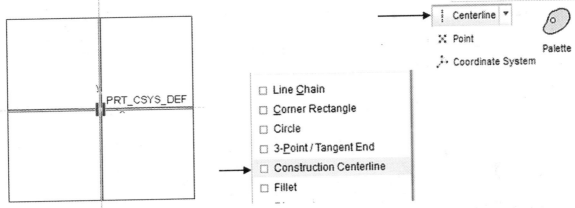

To create a rectangle, click the icon of **Rectangle**, and start the sketch by picking one point on the left side of the horizontal axis, and the other point on the other side. Before making the second click, set the rectangle symmetric about the vertical axis. A pair of arrows is displayed, indicating the symmetry, as shown below.   To modify the 2 dimensions, click the icon of **Select** or **One by One**. Afterwards, double click the displayed numbers and change the 2 dimensions to 3.5 and 3, respectively.

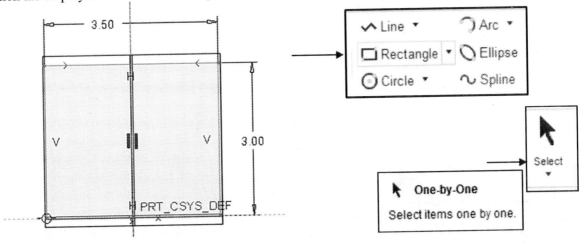

Upon completing this sketch, click the icon of **OK** and click the icon of **Apply and Save** to complete the creation of the block feature.

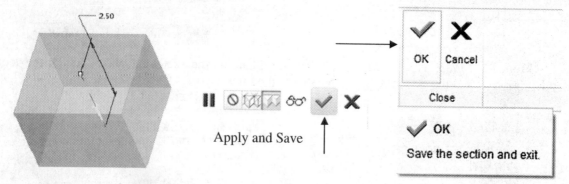

Step 3: Create the second feature, which is a slot and the 3 dimensions are 2 x 2.25 x 2.5 inch.

Click the icon of **Extrude** from the Model tab. Select **Cut** because we are going to remove the material from the created block. Specify 2.5 as the depth of cut.

Select the top surface of the block feature as the sketching plane. Click the icon of **Sketch View** to orient the sketching plane parallel to the screen.

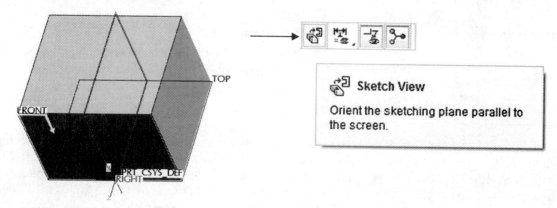

Let us create a vertical centerline. Click the icon of **Centerline**, or right click on the screen and select **Construction Centerline**.from the pop up menu, to scketch a vertical centerline.

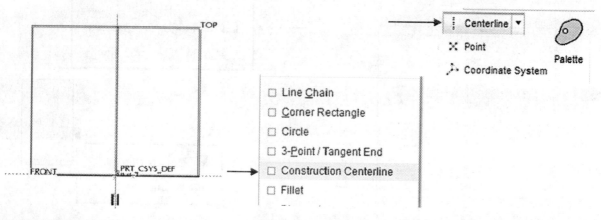

To create a rectangle, click the icon of **Rectangle**, and start the sketch by picking one point on the left side of the horizontal axis, and the other point on the other side. Before making the second click, set the rectangle symmetric about the vertical axis. A pair of arrows is displayed, indicating the symmetry, as shown below. Afterwards, double click the displayed numbers and change the 2 dimensions to 2.25 and 2, respectively.

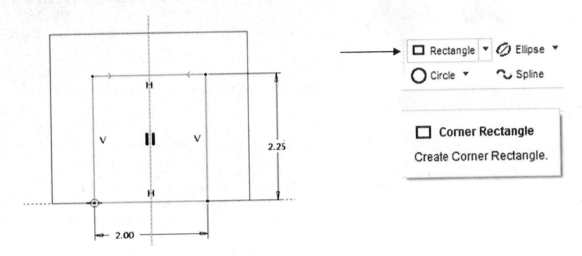

Upon completing this sketch, click the icon of **OK** and click the icon of **Apply and Save** to complete the creation of the block cut feature.

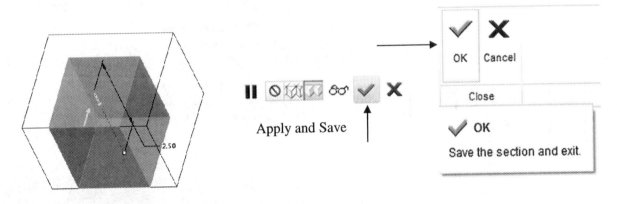

Step 4: Create a plate before creating the required hole feature. The plate size is 2.5 x 0.75 x 3 inch. Click the icon of **Extrude** from the Model tab. Specify 3 as the depth of extrusion.

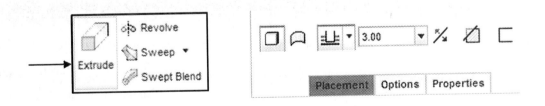

Select the front surface of the block feature as the sketching plane. Click the icon of **Sketch View** to orient the sketching plane parallel to the screen.

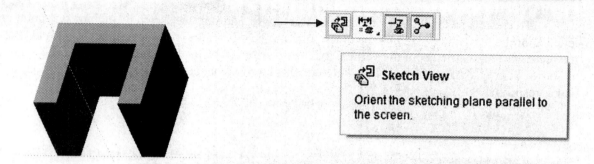

Click the icon of **References**. Click the surface on the right side of the block, as shown. After defining this new reference, click **Close**.

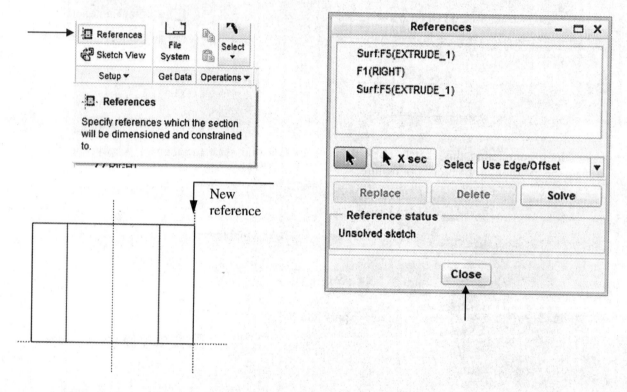

Click the icon of **Rectangle**, and sketch a rectangle as shown below. The 2 size dimensions are 2.5 and 0.75, respectively.

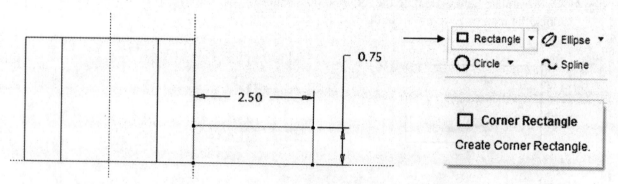

Upon completing the sketch, click the icon of **OK.** Pay attention to the direction of extrusion. Users may click the arrow to reverse the direction of extrusion. Click the icon of **Apply and Save**.

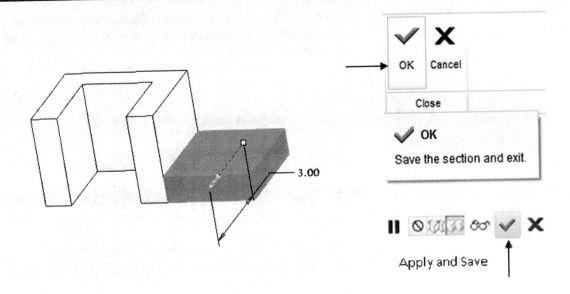

Step 5: Create the required hole feature. The diameter dimension is 1 inch and the 2 position dimensions are 1.5 and 1.25, respectively.

Click the icon of **Hole** displayed on the toolbar. Specify 1 as the diameter value and use **Thru All** as the depth choice (a through hole). Specify Thru All, as shown below.

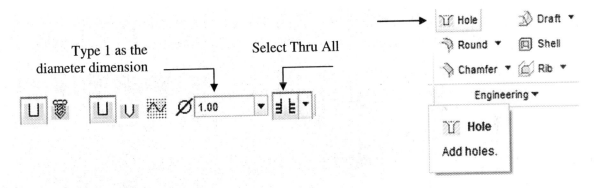

Click **Placement**, click or activate the box under **Placement**, and select the top surface of the plate as the primary surface, and select **Linear**.

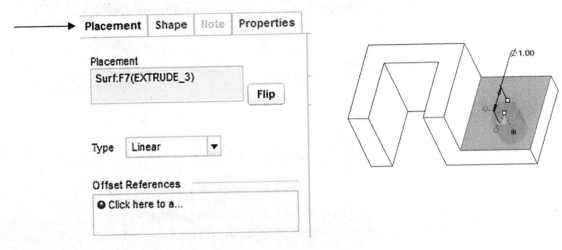

To define the center location of the hole, click or activate the box under **Offset References**, and select the front surface of the block and the surface on the left side of the block while holding down the **Ctrl** key. Specify the values of offsets to be 1.5 and 1.25, respectively.

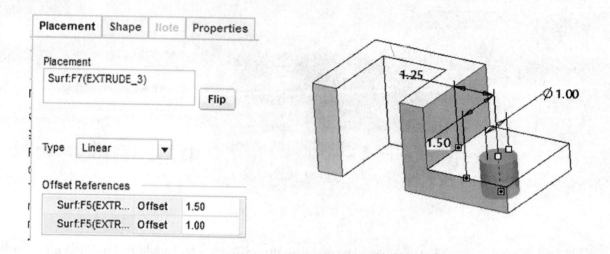

Click the icon of **Apply and Save** to complete the creation of the hole feature, as shown below:

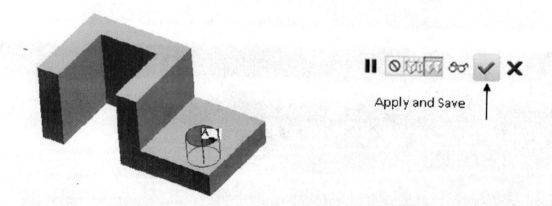

Apply and Save

Step 6: Use Mirror to create the plate with hole on the left side.

In the model tree, highlight Extrude 3 and Hole 1 features while holding down the **Ctrl** key. Click Mirror, and pick the RIGHT datum plane. Click the icon of **Apply and Save**.

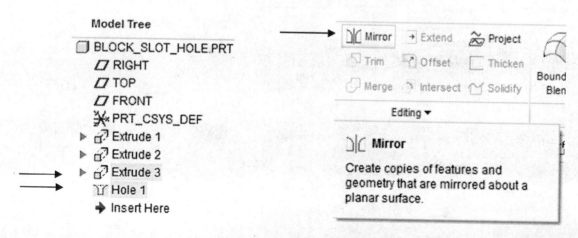

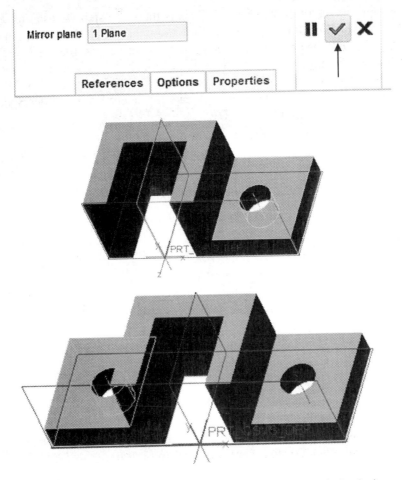

At the time you have successfully completed the block_slot_hole design, remember to save all of your work with the 3D solid model. You select **Save** from the main toolbar > **OK**.

To prepare an engineering drawing based on the 3D solid model, we need to create a drawing file. First, we click the icon of **New**, or "Create a new model".

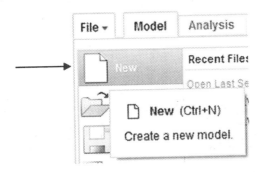

A **New** window appears, as illustrated below. This is the same step we used to open a new file when creating the 3D solid model of *block_slot_hole*. However, this time, "**Drawing**" mode, instead of "**Part**" mode, should be selected. Type *block_slot_hole* as the name of the file.. Clear the box of **Use default template** because we do not want to use the default setting for the drawing work. Afterwards, click **OK**. In the window of **New Drawing**, make sure that the file of the 3D solid model called *block_slot_hole* is shown. Otherwise, use "**Browse**" to locate it. Select **Empty** under Specify Template, and select the paper size to be **A**. Afterwards, click **OK**.

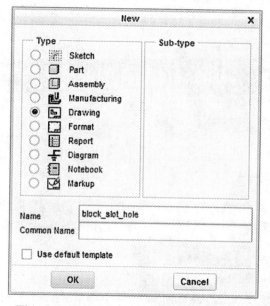 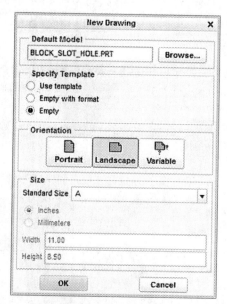

This brings up the drawing screen. Click the icon of **Layout**. Click the icon of **General.** In the **Select Combined State** window, click OK to accept **No Combined State**.

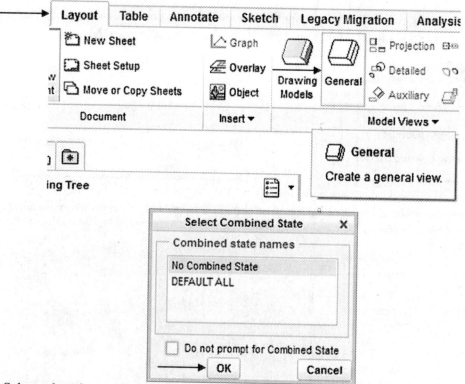

Select a location on the drawing screen as the center point for the **General View**. A general view appears on the screen.

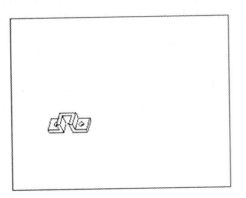

⇨ Select CENTER POINT for drawing view.

In the pop-up Drawing View window, select **FRONT > Apply > Close**, the construction of the **Front View** is completed.

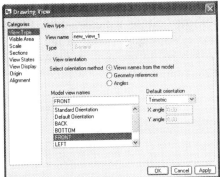

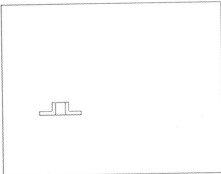

To insert the right side view, pick the **FRONT** View just created so that the Front View is activated, click the icon of Projection and make a left click at the right side of the Front View.

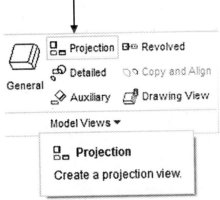

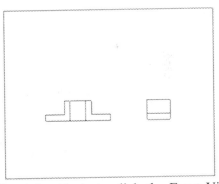

An alternative method to create a projection on the right side is to click the Front View for activation. Afterwards, make a right-click and hold, and then select **Insert Projection View** > move the cursor to the right side and click the left button of mouse. The construction of the right side view is completed.

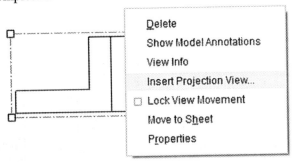

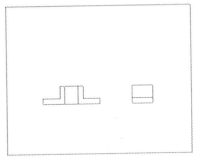

Follow the same procedure to create the top view, as shown below.

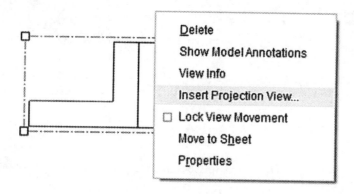

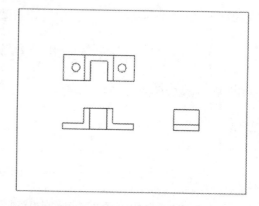

Click the icon of **General.** In the **Select Combined State** window, click OK to accept **No Combined State.** Select a location on the drawing screen as the center point for the 3D View (click the left button of mouse). A general view appears on the screen. In the pop-up Drawing View window, select **Standard Orientation > Apply > Close**, the construction of the 3D View is completed.

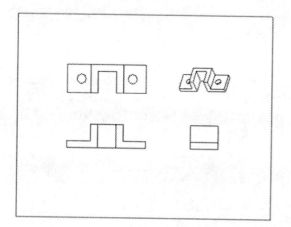

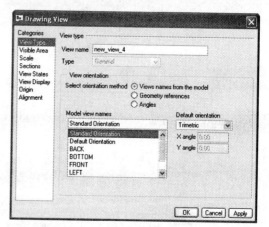

Sometimes, users may notice that the names of the datum planes, such as FRONT, RIGHT and TOP, appear on the drawing. The name of coordinate system, such as PRT_CSYS_DEF, also appears. To clean the drawing screen, click the icon of Datun Display Filter.

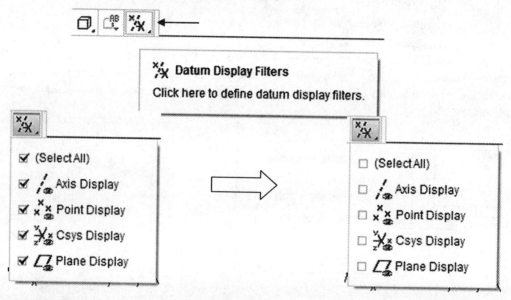

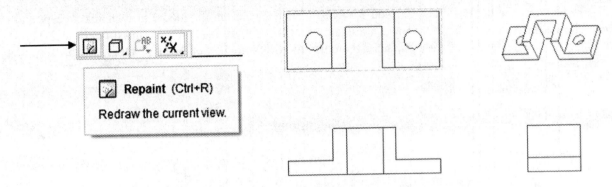

Upon completing the layout, we start adding dimensions. Click the icon of **Annotation**. Select the icon of **Show Model Annotation.**

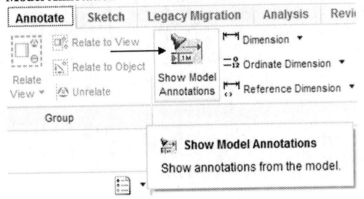

In the pop-up window, select the icon of **Dimensions.** To show the dimension of Extrude 1, click Extrude 1 listed in the model tree. Click Accept and OK. The 3 dimensions of 2.5, 3.5 and 3.0 are shown. Click the box of **Accept All > OK**.

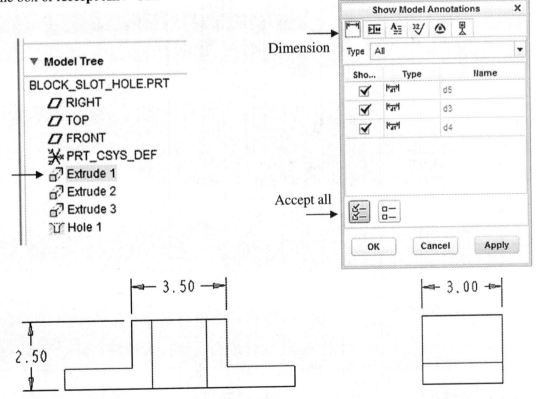

To show the dimension of Extrude 2, click Extrude 2 listed in the model tree. Click Accept and OK. The 3 dimensions of 2.25, 2.0 and 2.5 are shown. Click the dimension 2.25 and dimension 2.0 and do not click dimension 2.5 because there is 2.5 on display. Click the box of **Apply > OK**.

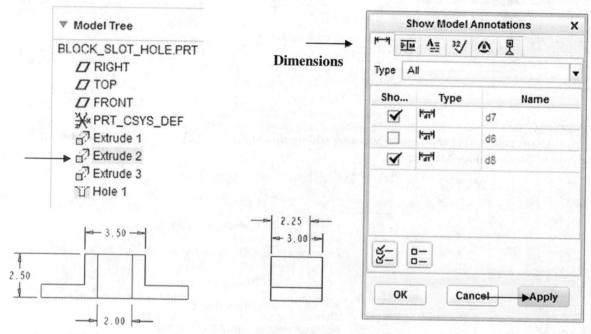

Users may use the left button of mouse to pick up a dimension and draw it for moving to an appropriate location. For example, the dimension of 2.0 is repositioned.

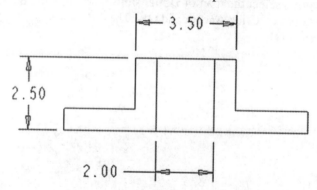

Users may move the dimension of 2.25 from the right-sided view to the top view. First pick the dimension of 2.25 and right-click to pick **Move Item to View**. Click the top view.

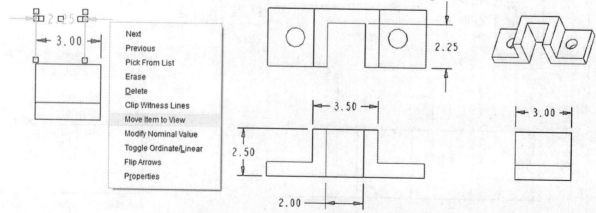

To show the dimensions, for example of Extrude 3, an alternative way is to click the icon of **Dimension** - **New References** > **On Entity** > Pick the relevant lines using the left clicks on the mouse > click the middle button of the mouse to position the dimension at an appropriate location.

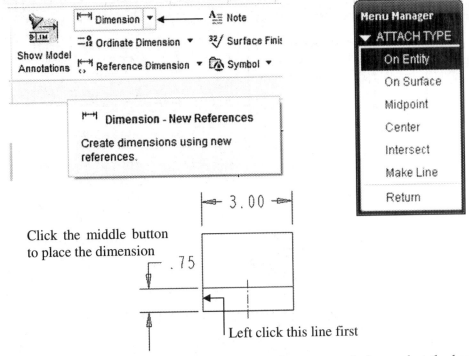

Click the middle button to place the dimension

Left click this line first

Now let us add centerlines to the drawing. In the pop-up window, select the box of centerlines. Click the hole feature listed in the model tree. All the centerlines are shown. Click **Accept All** > **OK.**

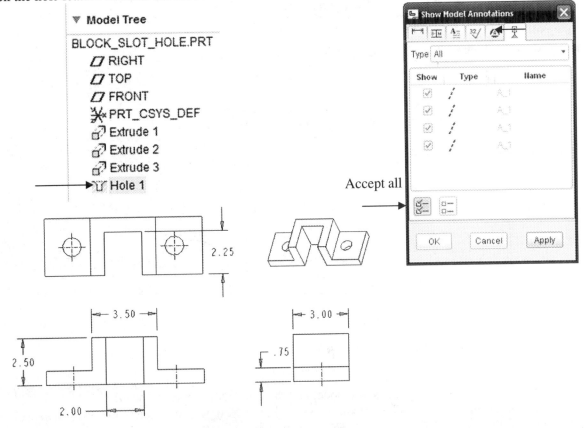

Users may add the required dimensions on their own. At this time the user has successfully completed the engineering drawing of the designed BLOCK_SLOT_HOLE part. Select **Save** from the main toolbar > **OK**.

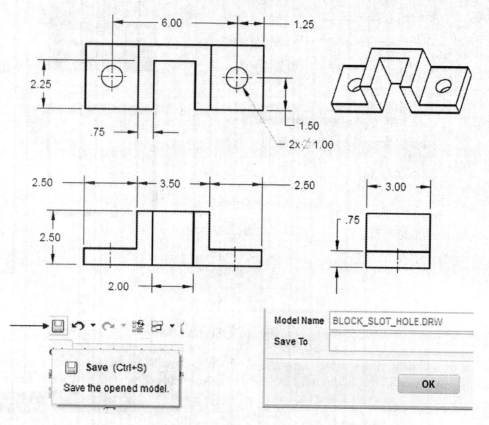

Example 4-5: Create a 3D solid model for the wrench component and prepare an engineering drawing.

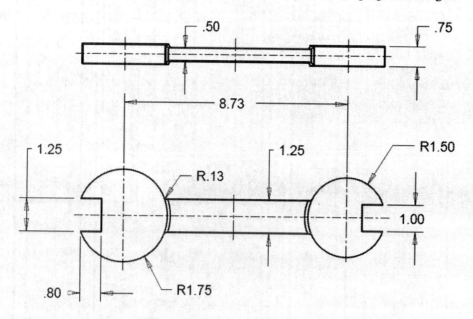

Step 1: Create a new file for the 3D solid model and the first feature (wrench head)

From the File menu, click the icon of **New**. In the **New** window, select the **Part** module. Type *wrench* as the file name. Click the box of **OK**. This will bring up the design window.

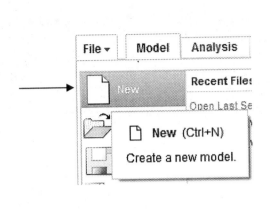

Click the icon of **Extrude** from the Model tab. Select Symmetry and specify 0.75 as the thickness value of the head.

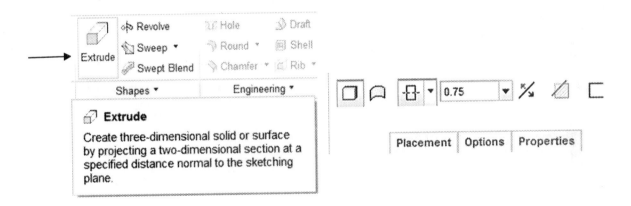

In the model tree, double click **TOP** (sketching plane). Click the icon of **Sketch View** so that the sketching plane is oriented parallel to the screen.

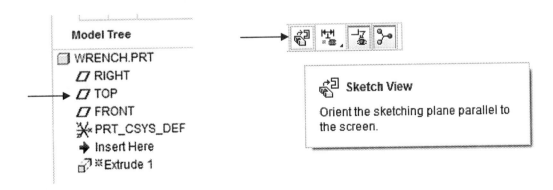

Click the icon of **Circle** to sketch a circle, as shown. Click the icon of **Line** to sketch 3 lines to form the shape of wrench head.

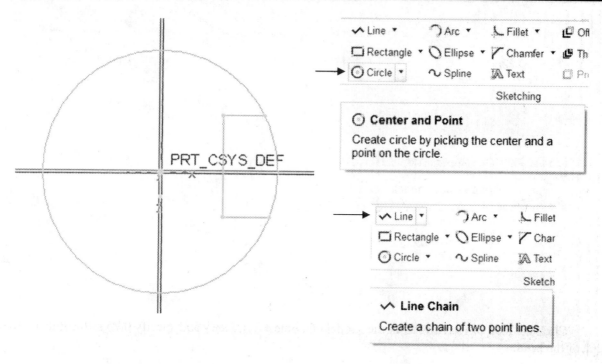

Click the icon of Delete to remove part of the circle, as shown.

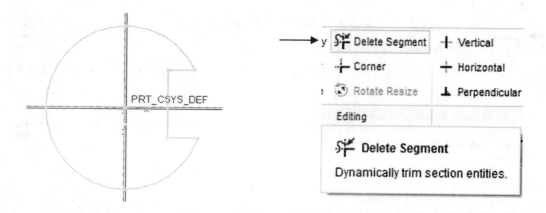

Click the icon of Equal constraint to set the 2 horizontal lines equal in length.

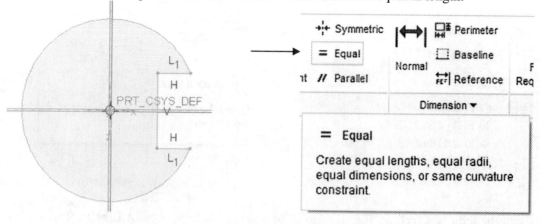

Click the icon of Select or One by One and modify the dimensions to 1.5, 1.0 and 0.80, as shown.

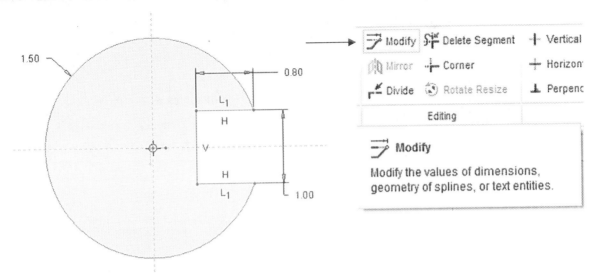

Click the icon of **OK** and the icon of **Apply and Save.**

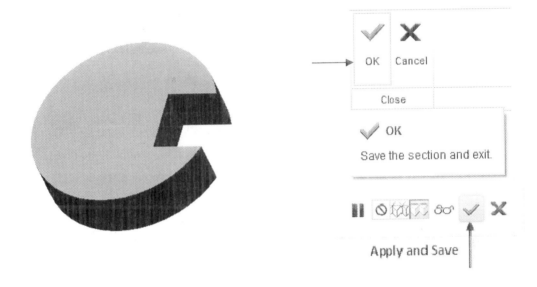

Step 2: Create the wrench handle or the second feature.
Click the icon of **Extrude** from the **Model** tab. Select **Symmetry** and specify 0.5 as the thickness value of the head.

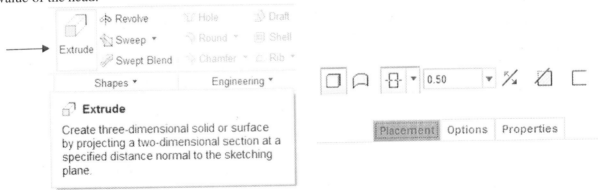

In the model tree, double click **TOP** (sketching plane). Click the icon of **Sketch View** so that the sketching plane is oriented parallel to the screen.

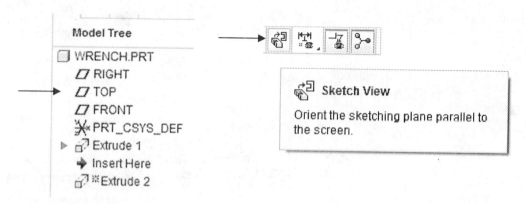

In the Sketch tab, click the icon of References. Pick the outside circle as a new reference > **Close**. Click the icon of Rectangle.

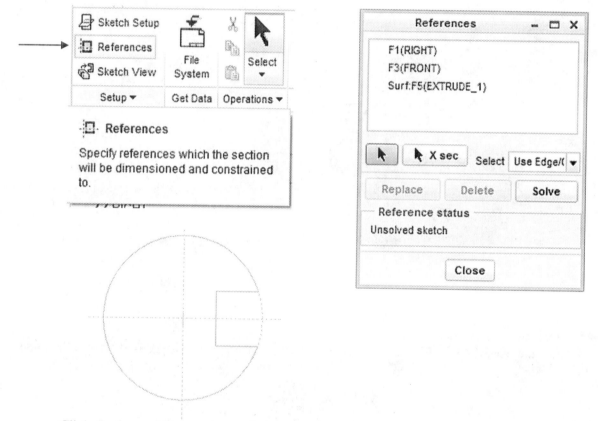

Click the icon of Rectangle., and sketch a rectangle with 2 dimensions equal to 3.0 and 1.25, respectively.

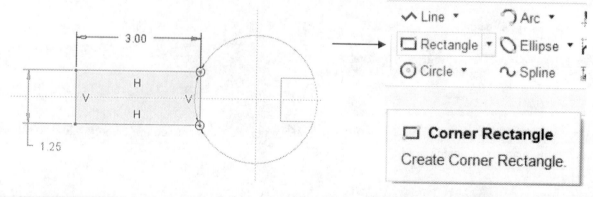

Click the icon of **OK** and the icon of **Apply and Save** to complete the feature creation.

In **the Datum** group, click the icon of **Axis.** While holding down the Ctrl, pick the end surface and FRONT > OK. An axis is created.

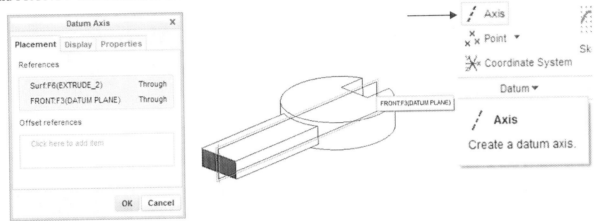

In the Operation group, click **Feature Operations**.
Copy > Move > Select > Independent > Done.
In the model tree, pick Extrude 1 and Extrude 2 while holding down the **Ctrl** key. > **OK**.

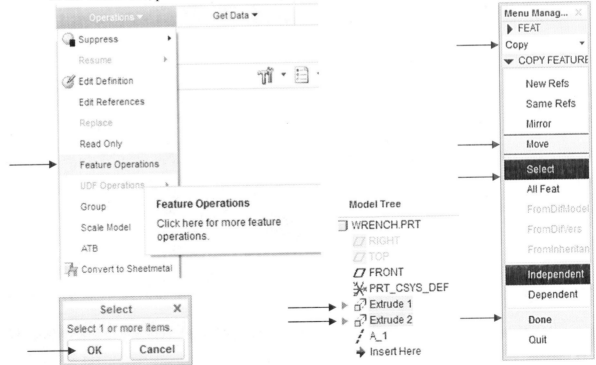

Rotate > Crv/Edg/Axis. Pick the created axis > **Okay** to accept the rotation direction > type 180 as the amount to rotate and press **Enter** > **Done Move**.

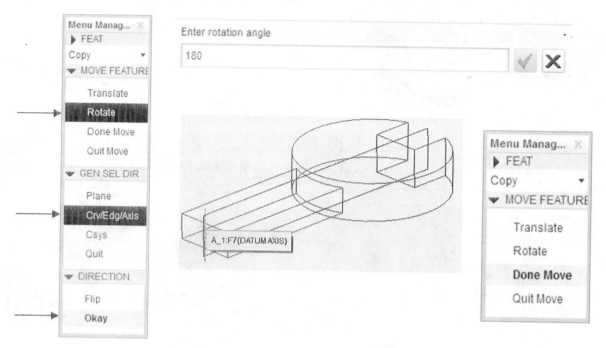

In order to modify the head dimensions using **Copy**, check **Dim 2** (R1.5) and **Dim 4** (1.0) > **Done**. Change 1.5 to 1.75 and press **Enter**. Change 1.0 to 1.25 and press **Enter**.

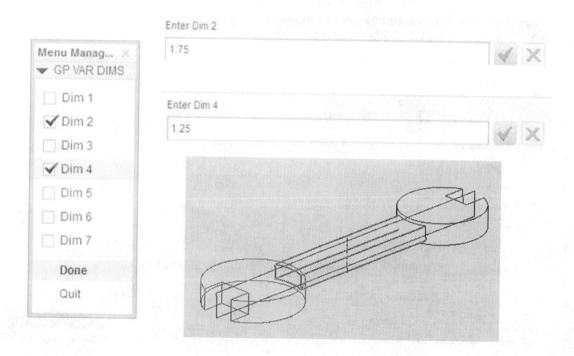

Click **OK** in the **Group Elements** window, thus completing the creation of the wrench head on the left side, as shown.

Now let us add rounds to the edges. Click the icon of **Round** and specify 0.125 as the radius value. While holding down the **Ctrl** key, pick the edges shown below. Click the icon of **Apply and Save**.

Click **Save > OK** to save the created 3D model for the wrench component.

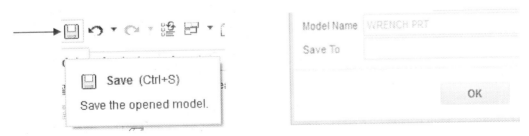

Users are asked to prepare an engineering drawing for this wrench component. Users may refer to the engineering drawing shown at the beginning of this case study.

Example 4-6: Create a 3D solid model for a jewelry box shown below, and prepare an engineering drawing of it. There are four (4) features. The first feature is a block, and its size is 12.25 x 10.25 x 6 inch. The second feature is a shell operation to set the thickness value to 0.2 inch. The third feature is thin wall plate with thickness value equal to 0.2 inch. The fourth feature is pattern to create another 2 idential thin wall plate.

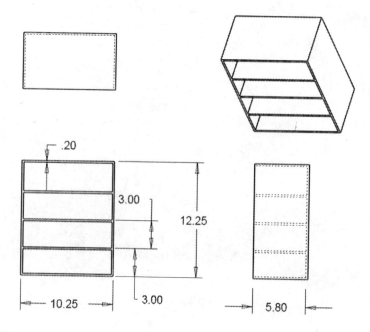

From the **File** menu, click the icon of **New**. From the **New** window, select the **Part** module. Type *jewelry_box* as the file name. Click the box of **OK**.

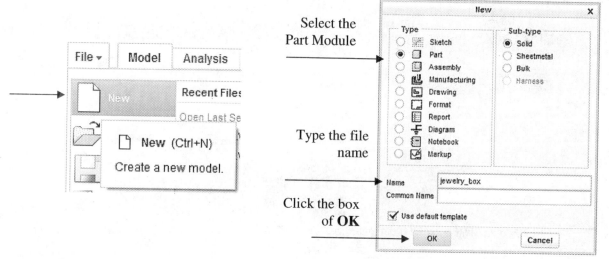

Click the icon of **Extrude** from the **Model** tab. Specify 6 as the depth value of the box.

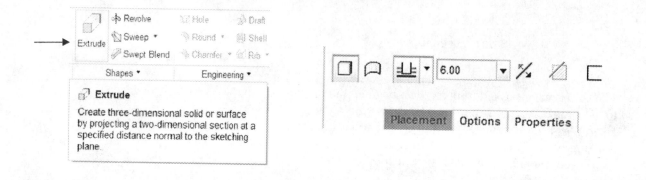

In the model tree, double click **FRONT** (sketching plane). Click the icon of **Sketch View** so that the sketching plane is oriented parallel to the screen.

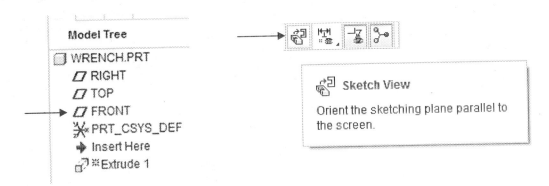

Click the icon of **Rectangle** to sketch a corner rectangle. Click the icon of Select or One-by-One, and modify the 2 dimensions to 12.25 and 10.25, respectively.

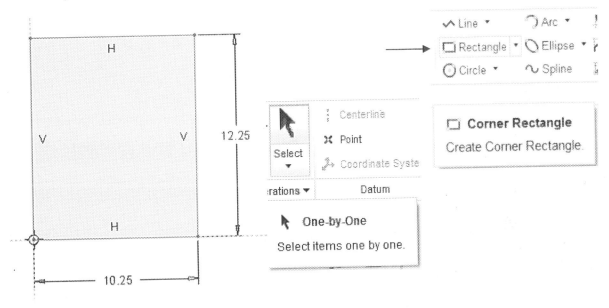

Click the icon of **OK** and the icon of **Apply and Save** to complete the feature creation.

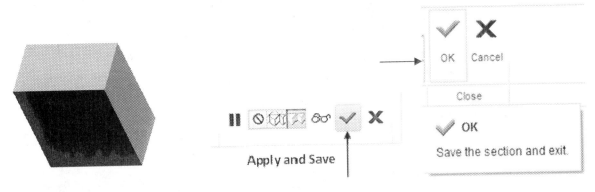

To create the second feature, click the icon of **Shell** under the Model tag.. Specify 0.2 as the thickness value and pick the front surface of the block as the removed surface. Click the icon of Apply and Save.

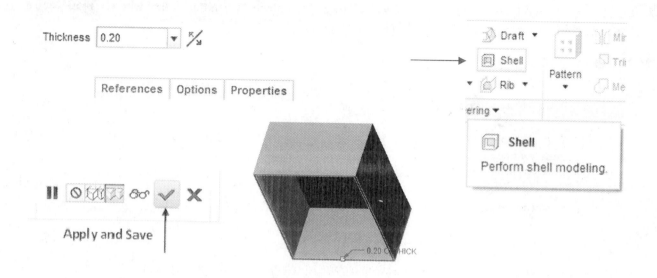

To create the third feature click the icon of **Extrude**, click the icon of **Thicken Sketch**, and specify 0.2 as the thickness value. Specify 5.8 as the depth value.

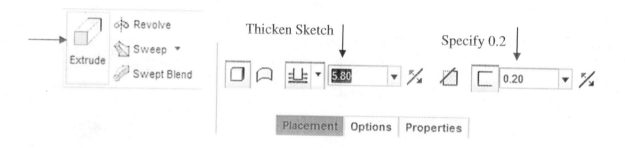

Double click the inner surface (sketching plane). Click the icon of Sketch View to set the sketching plane parrallel to the screen.

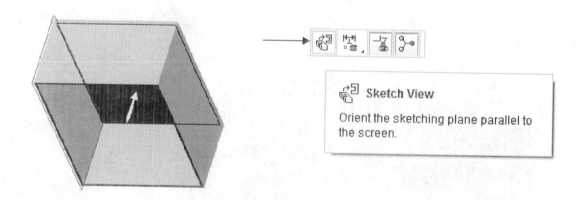

Before sketching, let us click **References** in the Sketch group, and add 2 new references. Click the 2 vertical lines or the inner surfaces of the box, as shown. After defining thess new references, click **Close**.

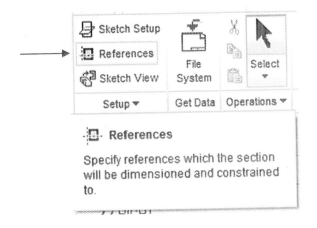

New references

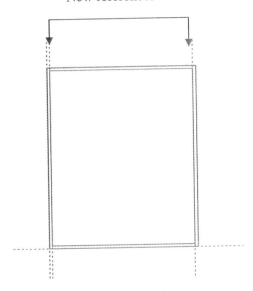

Click the icon of **Line** and sketch a horizontal line, as shown. Click the icon of Select or One-by-One. Specify 3 as the distance from the base line.

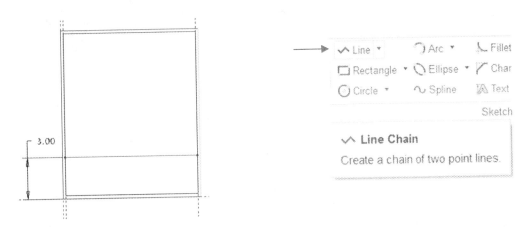

Click the icon of **OK** and the icon of **Apply and Save** to complete the creation of the first drawwr.

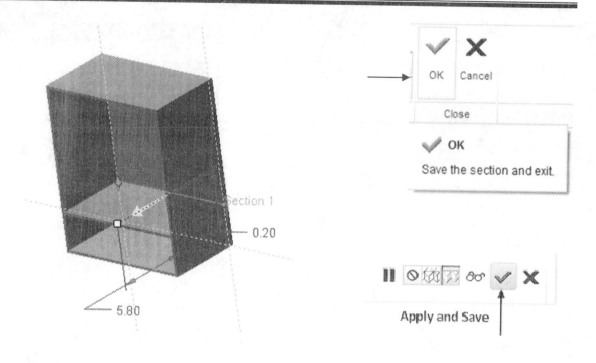

In the model tree, highlight Extrude 2, right-click to select **Pattern**.

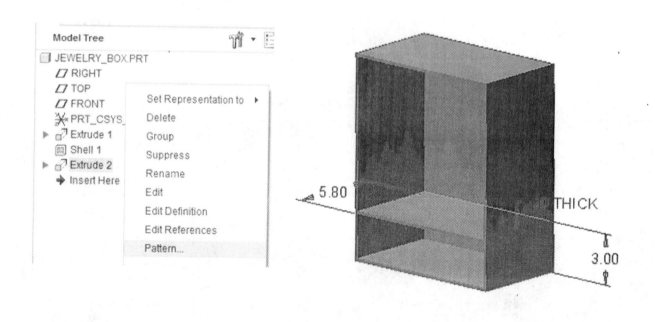

In the pattern window, pick the dimension of 3 under **Direction 1**, and change the value of copies to 3, as shown. Click the icon of **Apply and Save**.

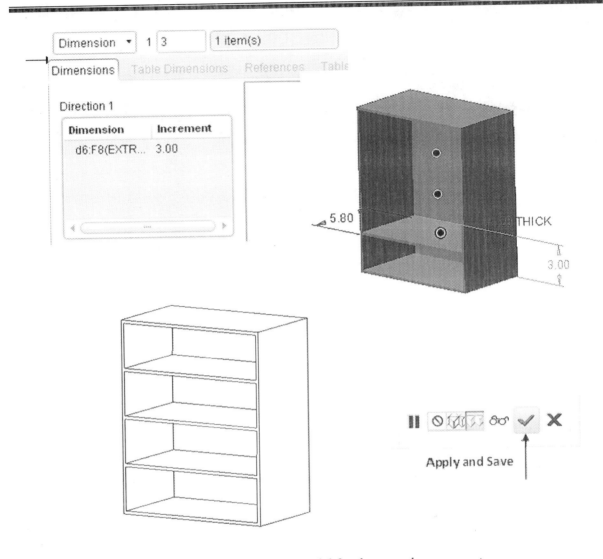

Click **Save** > **OK** to save the created 3D model for the wrench component.

Users are asked to prepare an engineering drawing for this wrench component. Users may refer to the engineering drawing shown at the beginning of this case study.

4.4 Modification and Re-design Using Edit and Edit Definition

It is not uncommon that a designer or a design team make modifications to the design, which has been made. To further improve quality of the product, the process of revisiting the existing design and making modifications is often required. In this section, we present 3 methods, which are commonly used to make modifications to an existing design.

The first example is to change the 3 dimensions of the block component created in Example 1 where the 3 dimensions are 10 x 6 x 4 inches. Assume that we want to change the 3 dimensions to 10 x 6 x 8 inches. In the model tree, highlight the feature called Extrude 1, right-click and pick **Edit**. The 3 dimensions appear on the screen.

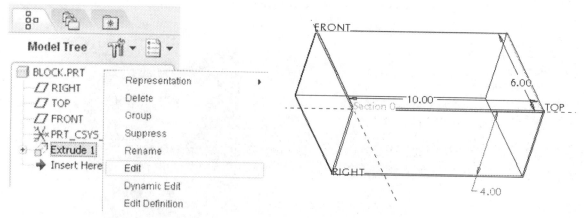

Double click the dimension marked as 4. Type 8 and presss the **Enter** key. From the main toolbar, click the icon of Regenerate to finalize the modification.

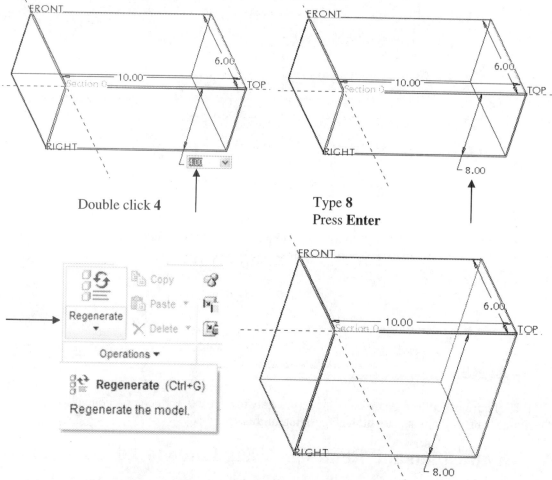

Double click **4**

Type **8**
Press **Enter**

Regenerate (Ctrl+G)

Regenerate the model.

In fact, users may just make double clicks on the screen. The regeneration process will be automatically executed.

To demonstrate the second method to make modifications, assume the new dimensions should be 30 x 15 x 5 inches. In the model tree, highlight the feature called **Extrude** 1, right-click and pick **Edit Definition**. This action bring back to the process of creating a new feature.

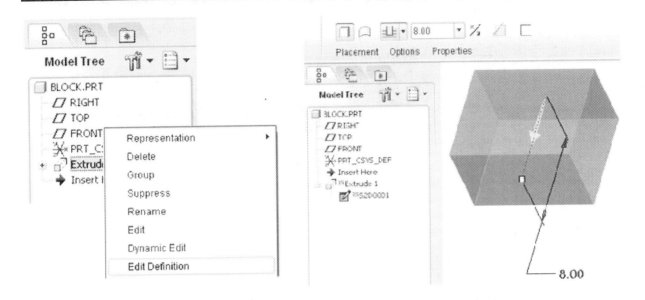

On the dashboard, change the depth value from 8 to 5.

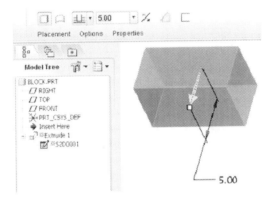

Click **Placement > Edit**. This action brings back to the sketch process. The previously sketched rectangule is on display with the 2 dimensions equal to 10 and 6.

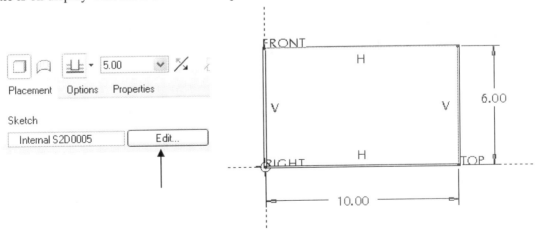

Double click each of these 2 dimensions and change their values to 30 and 15, respectively > click the icon of **Done** and click the icon of **Apply and Save** from the feature control panle. The 3D soild model is automatically regerated and alll the 3 modifications are confirmed. There is no need to click the icon of Regenerator.

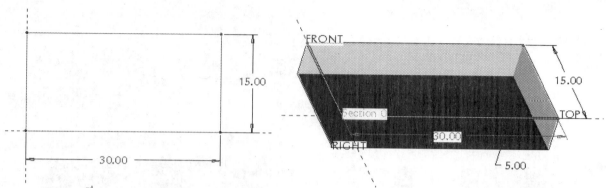

The 3rd method to make a modification is to change the selection of the sketch plane. For example, the current sketch plane is the **FRONT** datum plane and we want to use the TOP datum plane as the sketch plane so that the standard view of the 3D solid model will be reset to a new orientation.

In the model tree, highlight the feature called **Extrude** 1, right-click and pick **Edit Definition**. This action bring back to the process of creating a new feature. Click **Placement** > **Edit**. This action brings back to the sketch process. The previously sketched rectangle is on display with the 2 dimensions equal to 30 and 15.

Ckick the **Sketch** tab > **Sketch Setup** > Pick the **TOP** datum plane as the sketch plane > **Sketch**.

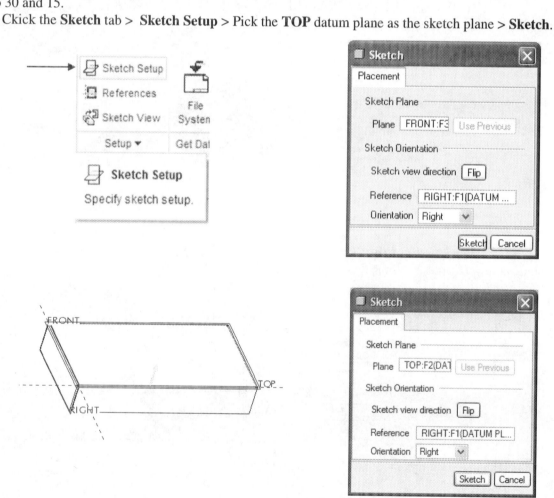

In the References window, highlight the Failed reference and click **Delete**. Afterwards, select FRONT as the new reference > click **Close** to close the References window.

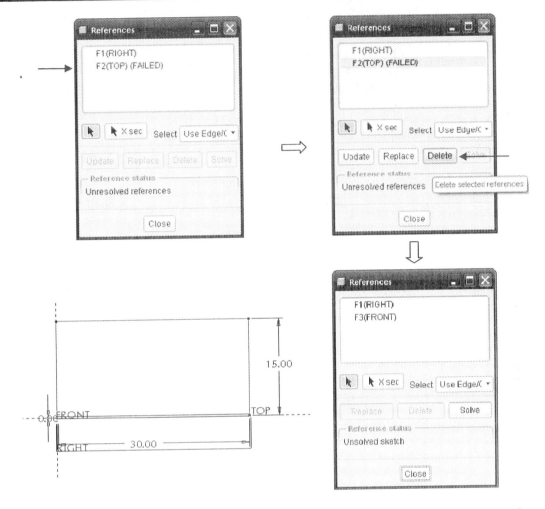

Click the icon of **OK** and the icon of **Apply and Save** from the feature control panel, thus completing the modification process. The new orientation for the standard view is shown below.

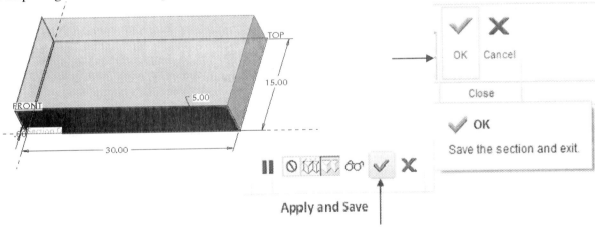

4.5   References

1.   F. L. Amirouche, <u>Computer-aided Design and Manufacturing</u>, Prentice Hall, Englewood Cliffs, New Jersey, 1993.
2.   D. D. Bedworth, M. R. Henderson, and P. M. Wolfe, <u>Computer-Integrated Design and Manufacturing</u>, McGraw-Hill, New York, NY, 1991.

3.   B. L. Davids, A. J. Robotham and Yardwood A., <u>Computer-aided Drawing and Design</u>, London, 1991.

5.   J. Encarnacao, E. G. Schlechtendahl, <u>Computer-aided Design: Fundamentals and System Architectures</u>, Springer-Verlag, New York, 1983.

7.   S. Fingers, J. R. Dixon, A review of research in mechanical engineering design, Part II: Representations, analysis, and design for the life cycle, <u>Research in Engineering Design</u>, 1(2), 121-38, 1989.

8.   J. D. Foley, A. Van Dam, Feiner S. and J. Hughes, <u>Computer Graphics, Principles and Practice</u>, 2nd edition, 1990.

9.   J. D. Foley, A. D. VanDam, <u>Fundamentals of Interactive Computer Graphics</u>, Addision-Wesley, San Francisco, 1982.

10. J. G. Griffiths, A bibliography of hidden-line and hidden-surface algorithms, <u>Computer-aided Design</u>, 10(3), 203-6. 1978.

11. C. McMahon and J. Browne, <u>CADCAM: from Principles to Practice</u>, Addison Wesley, Workingham, England, 1993.

4.6   Exercises

1.   An object is shown in a three dimensional space below. If you are asked to use Pro/ENGINEER to create a three-dimensional solid model of it, how many features are there?

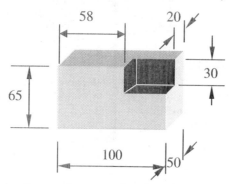

If you were a production engineer on the shop floor, how would you plan to make this designed part? List the manufacturing operations required? Do you expect any difficulties in making this part? If yes, how should the design be modified so that the process of manufacturing this part can be facilitated?

2.   For a given part that has been designed, there could be more than one feature interpretation of the designed part.
   • List, at least, two feature interpretations of the designed part shown below.
   • For each of the feature interpretation, state the corresponding process to manufacturing the designed part.
   • Compare the two feature interpretations and the two manufacturing processes, which one would you prefer? List the reason(s).

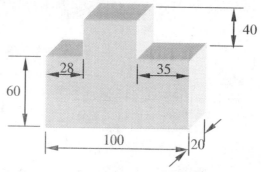

3.   Create a 3D solid model for the following object, and prepare an engineering drawing with the dimensions as shown.

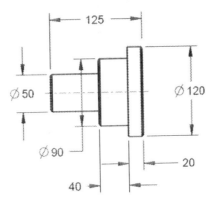

Chamfer Dimensions = 2x45°

4.   Create a 3D solid model for the following object, and prepare an engineering drawing with the dimensions as shown.

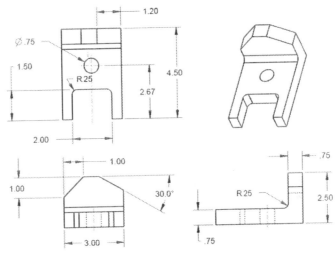

5.   Create a 3D solid model for the following object, and prepare an engineering drawing with the dimensions as shown.

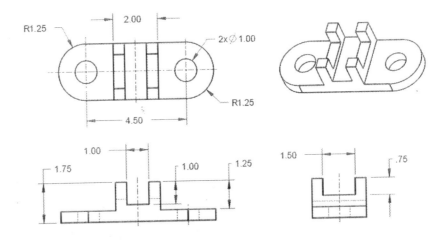

CHAPTER 5

FEATURE-BASED COMPONENT MODELING

5.1 Design by Features

As discussed in Chapter 4, under a computer aided design environment, a part is viewed as a combination of features, such as blocks, cylinders, holes, slots, chamfers, rounds, etc. A model is developed to represent the component being designed using these features, which comprise the geometric shape and size of the part. The Creo Parametric design environment offers the design engineer or the design team a unique and powerful tool to visualize the design intent and idea(s) and facilitates creativeness in the design process using feature-based component modeling. The modeling process is characterized by:

1. The procedure to model a part in Creo Parametric follows the process used in producing the part in a manufacturing environment. Figure 5-1a illustrates a block component with dimensions. The block has a through hole located in its central location, as shown. The process of manufacturing this block components consists of four steps:

    a. An operator goes to a storeroom to select a bar stock that best fits the requirements, i.e., not too big and not too small. As illustrated in Figure 5-1b, the dimensions of bar stock available are 1.5 x 1.0 x 4.

    b. A cutting blade is used to cut a block from the bar stock with the length required for manufacturing the part. As illustrated in Figure 5-1c, the dimension of length of the bar stock after the cutting operation is 2, which meets the design specification.

    c. Finally, a drill bit and a drilling machine are used to drill the hole at the central position in the block. The diameter of the drill bit selected is 0.5, which follows the design specification.

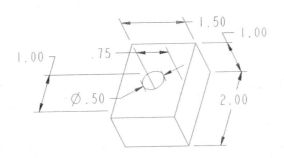

(a) A Component to Be Produced

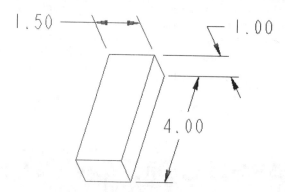

(b) Find the Raw Material Stock that Best Fits the Need in Terms of Size and Shape

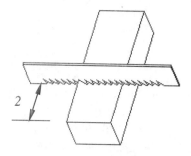

(c) Obtain a Portion of the Stock by Cutting

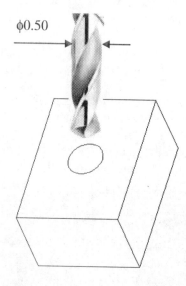

(d) Drill the hole at the central Location

Figure 5-1 Procedure to Manufacture a Component, Namely, a Block with a Central Hole

Now let us examine the process of creating the design for such a block with a central hole. As it will become evident, the modeling procedure under the Creo Parametric design environment closely follows the process of manufacturing the part being designed. The basic steps in the modeling process under the Creo Parametric design environment are listed below and illustrated in Figure 5-2 for the purpose of making comparison with the procedure of manufacturing, as described in Figure 5-1. The feature-based model procedure begins with

a) Sketch a 2D rectangle with the 2 dimensions equal to those of the cross sectional area of the bar stock.

b) Extend the 2D sketch in the third direction. The depth value is 2, which is equal to the length of the bar stock to be cut by the saw.

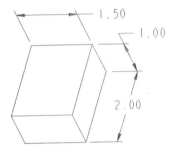

c) Create a hole feature at the central location of the block, which is equivalent to drilling a hole at the same location.

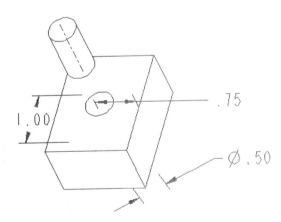

Figure 5-2 Procedure of Feature-Based Model Follows the Sequence of Manufacturing Processes

The procedure described above is called 3D solid modeling, which is the foundation of a CAD software system. The uniqueness of using the solid modeling methodology, such as Creo Parametric, is to facilitate the design process, to integrate the manufacturing processes to the design process and to lay a fundamental work for carrying out engineering analysis, such as finite element analysis. The database established under a CAD system offers unique opportunities for system integration, such as analysis, manufacturing, purchasing, marketing and even quality inspection. The streamline characteristics in the process of product development will provide the best product to customers with the lowest cost possible.

5.2 Solid Modeling of an Object in the 3D Space

In this section, we present several examples to show the process of feature-based design. In the meantime, the procedure of preparing an engineering drawing with section views is also discussed

5.2.1 Example 5-1: Construction of a LEGO Component

Figure 5-3 presents an object, which is a LEGO component. A 3D view of the object and an engineering drawing of the component are shown below.

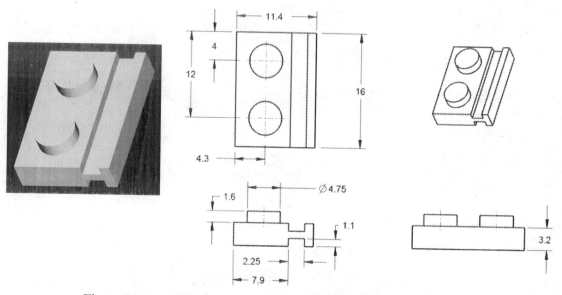

Figure 5-3 A LEGO Component with an Engineering Drawing

Figure 5-4 presents 3 key steps in creating a 3D solid model. The first step is to create a simple block with dimensions equal to 11.4 x 3.2 x 16 mm. Afterwards, create 2 slots with dimensions equal to 2.25 x 1.10 mm. Finally, add 2 identical cylinders. The diameter value is 4.75 mm. The height value is 1.6 mm.

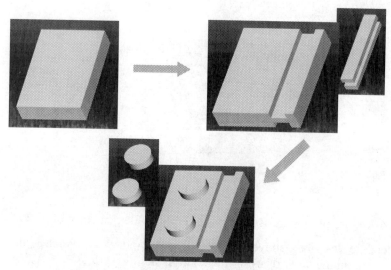

Figure 5-4 Feature-Based Modeling Approach

To begin with the modeling process, from the **File** menu, select the icon of **New**. In the **New** window, select the **Part** mode is selected. Type *lego_part1* as the file name. Click the box of **OK**.

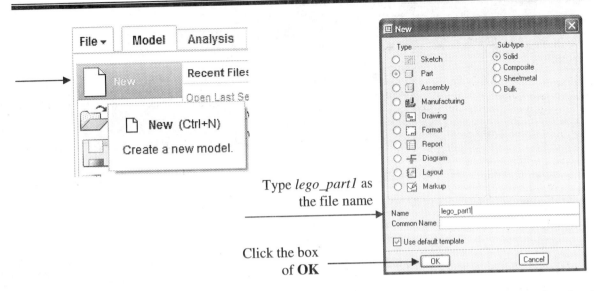

Type *lego_part1* as
the file name

Click the box
of **OK**

Click the icon of **Extrude** from the **Model** tab on the Ribbon Toolbar. Specify *16* as the depth value.

In the model tree, click **FRONT** (sketching plane). Click the icon of **Sketch View** to orient the sketching plane parallel to the screen.

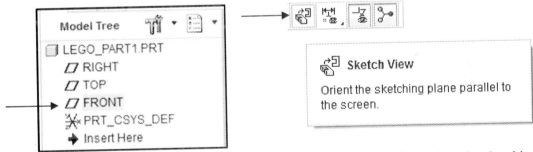

This approach is equivalent to selecting **FRONT,** and click **Sketch** to orient the sketching plane, as illustrated below:

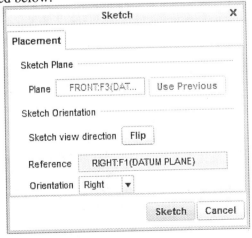

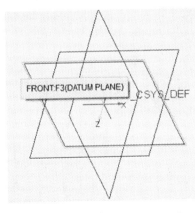

Click the icon of **Rectangle** from the Sketch tab on the Ribbon toolbar. Sketch a rectangle from the origin, as shown. Click the icon of **Select** or **One-by-One**. Modify the 2 dimensions to 11.4 and 3.2, respectively.

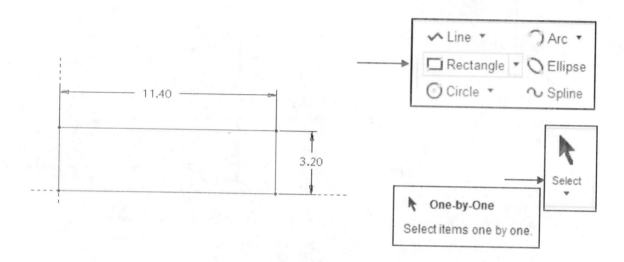

Upon completing the sketch, pick the icon of **Done.** Click the icon of **Apply and Save.**

After completing the creation of the first feature, let us get on creating the second feature, namely, 2 identical slots. Click the icon of **Extrude** displayed on the toolbar of feature creation. Make sure that the icon of **Cut** is selected because we will take material away from the 3D solid model. Select **Through All** as the choice of depth of cut.

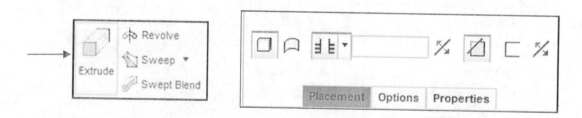

Click the front surface of the block (note: do not select the **FRONT** datum plane). The front surface of the block will be used as the sketching plane. Click the icon of **Sketch View** to orient the sketching plane parallel to the screen.

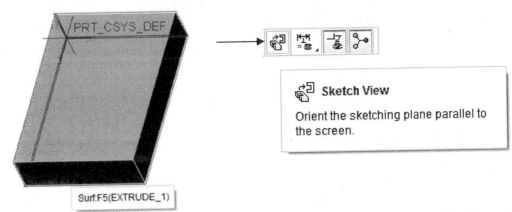

Click the icon of **Rectangle**, and sketch a rectangle as shown below. The 2 size dimensions are 2.25 and 1.10, respectively. The dimension of 7.90 is a position dimension required to specify the location of the rectangle in the horizontal direction.

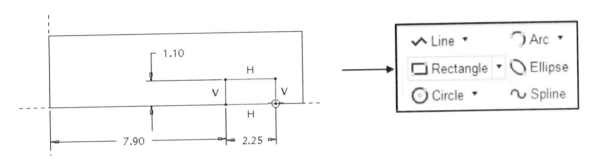

Before sketching the second rectangle, click the icon of **References** from the Sketch tab. Click the top surface of the block, as shown. After defining this new reference, click **Close**.

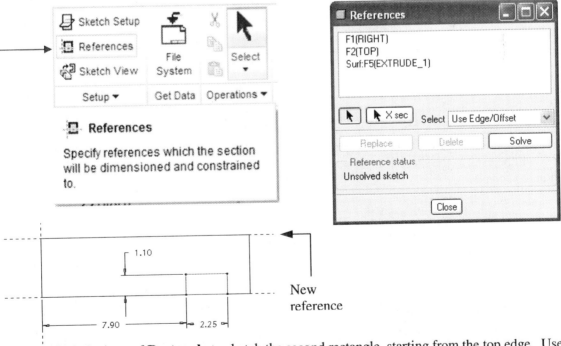

New reference

Click the icon of **Rectangle** to sketch the second rectangle, starting from the top edge. Users may use a coincident constraint and 2 equal constraints, as shown below, so that no dimension is needed for the second rectangle.

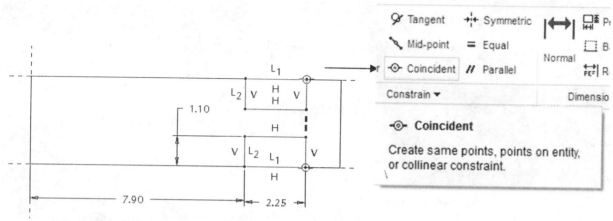

Upon completing the sketch, click the icon of **OK**, and click the icon of **Apply and Save.**

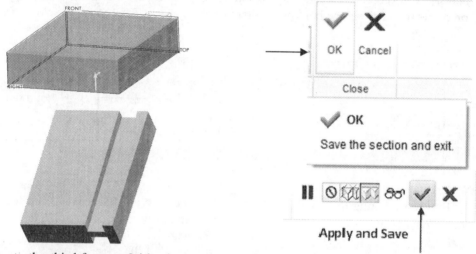

Let us create the third feature, 2 identical cylinders. Click the icon of **Extrude**. Specify 1.6 as the height value.

Click the top surface of the block (note: do not select the **TOP** datum plane). The top surface of the block will be used as the sketching plane. Click the icon of **Sketch View** to orient the sketching plane parallel to the screen.

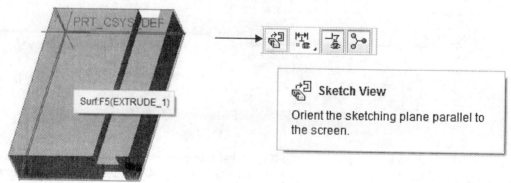

Click the icon of **Circle**, and sketch 2 circles as shown. The diameter dimension is 4.75. There are 3 position dimensions. They are 4, 4.3 and 12, respectively. To change the value of a dimension, just double click on the dimension displayed on screen, type the required value, and press the **Enter** key.

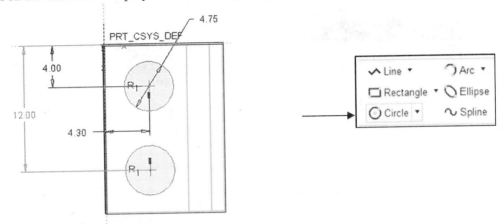

Upon completing the sketch, click the icon of **OK**. Click the icon of **Apply and Save**.

It is important to note that the unit of the dimensions used to create this 3D solid model should be mm. However, the default unit of **Creo Parametric** is inch. Therefore, a conversion from the inch unit system to the mm unit system is needed.

From the File menu, click **Prepare > Model Properties**. A pop up window called **Model Properties** appears, indicating that the current unit system is **Inch lbm Second (Pro/E Default).**

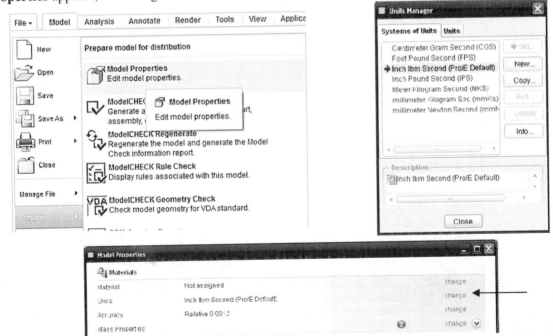

To convert the current Inch lbm Second (Pro/E Default) to millimeter Newton Second (mmNs), select millimeter Newton Second (mmNs) from the Units Manager window > **Set** > another pop up window called Changing Model Units appears, select Interpret dimensions (for example 1" becomes 1 mm) and **OK > Close**.

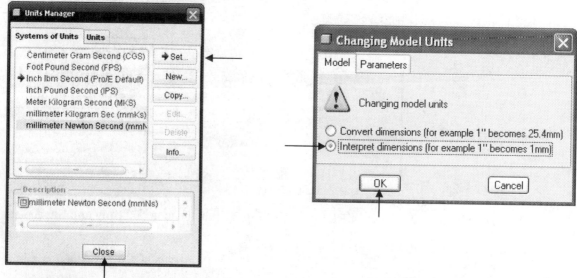

At this time the user has successfully completed the design of a LEGO part, he or she should save all the work with the 3D solid model. Click **Save** from the top toolbar, or Ribbon toolbar > **OK**.

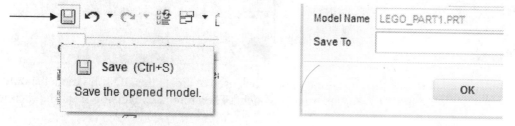

To prepare an engineering drawing, the icon of **New** from the File menu. Select **Drawing.** Type *lego_part1* as the name of the file. Clear the box of **Use default template** because we do not want to use the default setting for the drawing work. Afterwards, click **OK**.

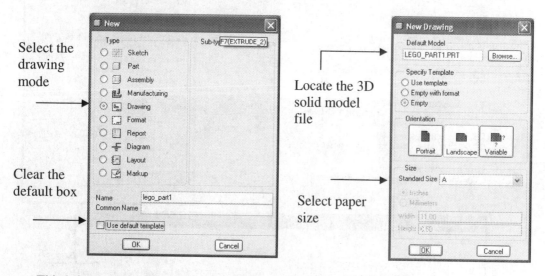

This brings up the drawing screen. Click the **Layout** tab. Click the icon of **General.** In the **Select Combined State** window, click **OK** to accept **No Combined State.**

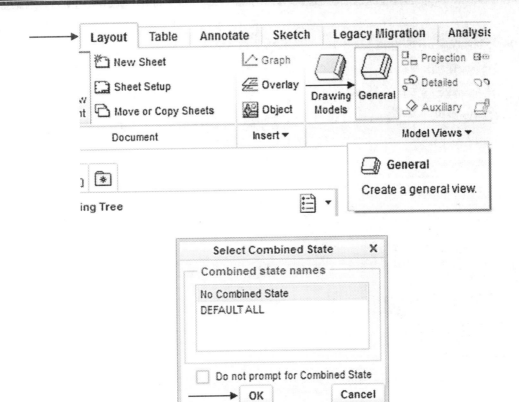

Select a location on the drawing screen as the center point for the **General View**. A general view appears on the screen.

In the pop-up Drawing View window, select **FRONT > Apply > Close**, the construction of the **Front View** is completed.

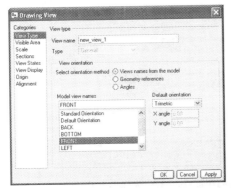

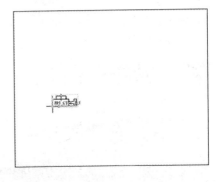

To insert the right side view, pick the **FRONT** View just created so that the Front View is activated, click the icon of Projection and make a left click at the right side of the Front View.

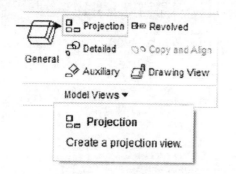

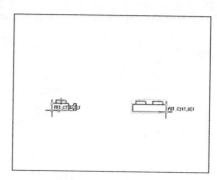

Follow the same procedure to create the top view, as shown below.

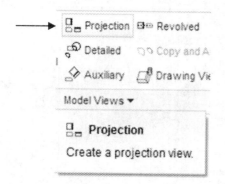

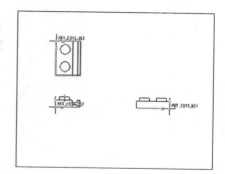

Click the icon of **General.** In the **Select Combined State** window, click OK to accept **No Combined State**. Select a location on the drawing screen as the center point for the 3D View (click the left button of mouse). A general view appears on the screen. In the pop-up Drawing View window, select **Standard Orientation > Apply > Close**, the construction of the 3D View is completed.

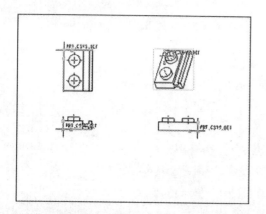

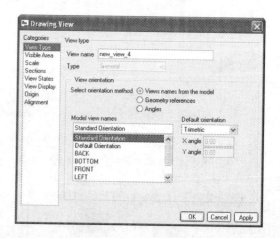

Users may notice that the names of the default coordinate system, such as PRT_CSYS_DEF appears. To clean the drawing screen, click the icon of **Datum Display Filter**.

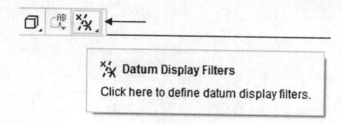

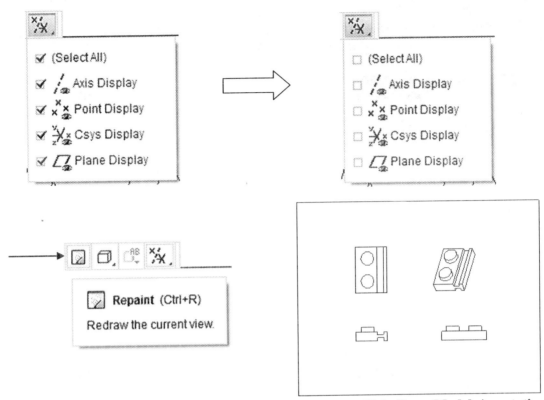

Upon completing the layout, we start adding dimensions. Click **Show Model Annotations** > select the icon of **Dimensions**. From the model tree, click Extrude 1. Three dimensions of 16, 11.4 and 3.2 associated with Extrude 1 are shown. Click the box of **Accept All** > **Apply**.

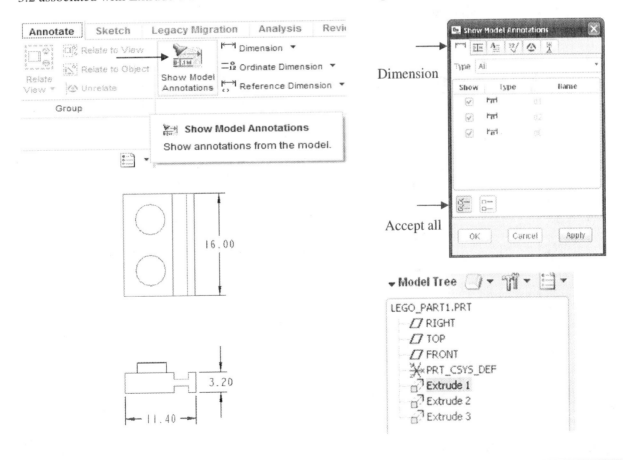

From the model tree, click Extrude 2. Three dimensions of 7.9, 2.25 and 1.1 associated with Extrude 2 are shown. Click the box of **Accept All > Apply**.

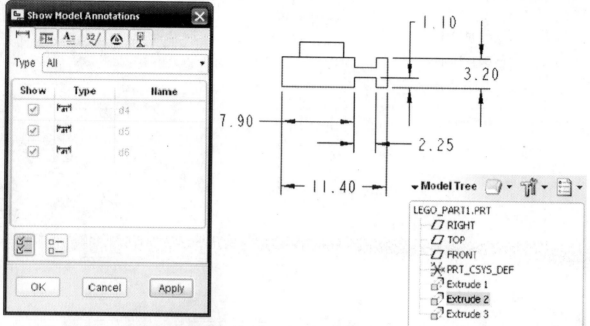

From the model tree, click Extrude 3. Five dimensions of 12, Ø4.75, 4.3, 4 and 1.6 associated with Extrude 3 are shown. Click the box of **Accept All > Apply**.

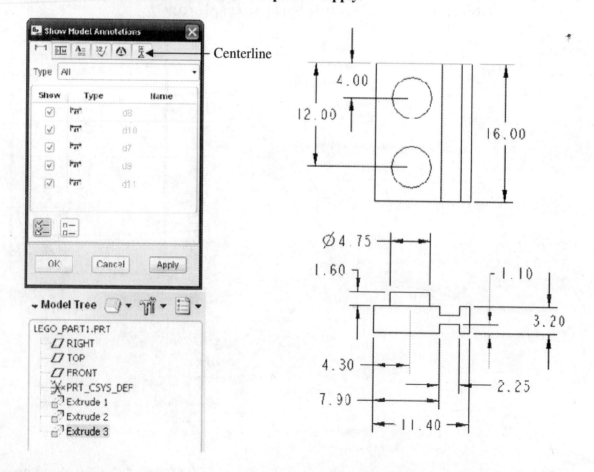

To add centerlines, select the box of centerlines. Click Extrude 3 listed in the model tree. Three (3) centerlines are on display > click the box of **Accept All > OK.**

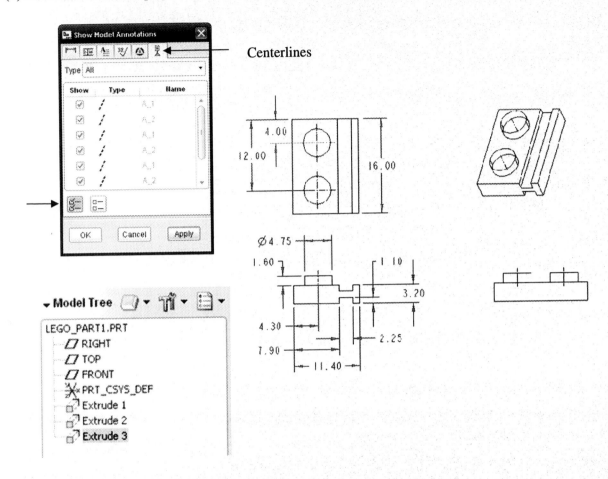

In general, there is no need to display centerlines on a 3D view. To delete the displayed 2 centerlines on the 3D view, click those 2 centerlines first. Afterwards, click **Delete** from the Annotation menu.

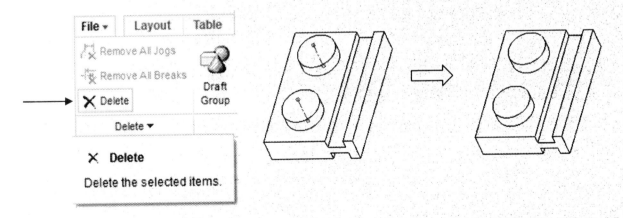

Users may move some of the dimensions displayed on Front View to the Right-Sided View. For example, let us move the diameter dimension of Ø4.75. First, pick the diameter dimension of Ø4.75 > right click and hold, select **Move Item to View**.

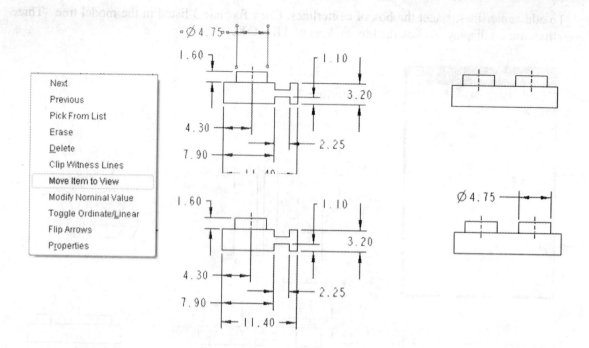

At this time the user has successfully completed the engineering drawing of the designed LEGO part. Click **Save** from the top toolbar, or Ribbon toolbar > **OK**.

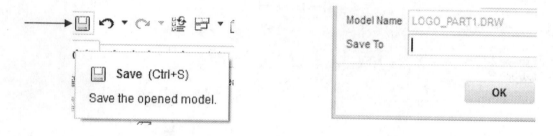

Example 5-2: Create a crankshaft component.

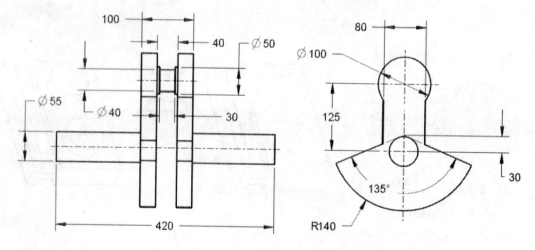

Note that the unit used in this example is mm. In Example 5-1, the unit system should be mm. However, we started our work with the unit default setting, which is inch. Because of that reason, we made a conversion from the inch unit system to the mm unit system. To avoid such a conversion process, let us get on this example by setting the unit system to mm before creating the first feature.

Step 1: Create a file for the 3D solid model and set the unit system to mm.
From the **File** menu click **New > Part.** Type *crankshaft* as the file name and clear the icon of **Use default template**.
Select **mmns_part_solid** (units: Millimeter, Newton, Second) and type *crankshaft* in **DESCRIPTION**, and *student* in **MODELED_BY**, then **OK.**

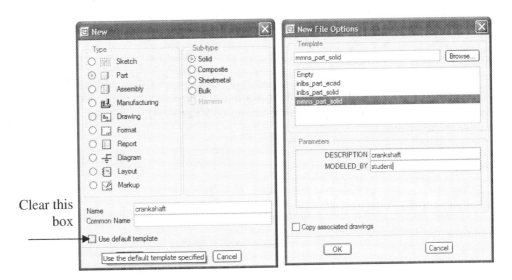

Step 2: Create the first feature.
Select the icon of **Extrude** from the **Model** tab. Select the icon of **Symmetry**. Specify *100* as the extrusion distance.

In the model tree, click **RIGHT** (sketching plane). Click the icon of **Sketch View** to orient the sketching plane parallel to the screen.

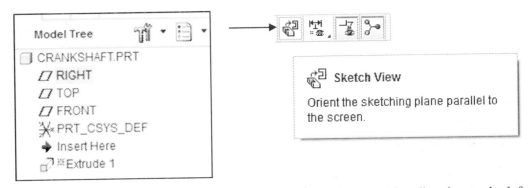

It is important to note that the default orientation is set the y positive direction to the left and z positive direction downward.

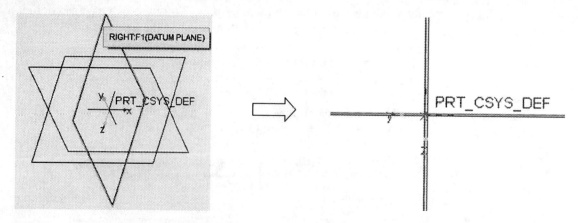

In order to orient the y positive direction upward and z positive direction to the left, make a right-click. Pick **Select Orientation** from the pop up menu and pick **Set vertical reference**. Click the y axis to re-orient the coordinate system.

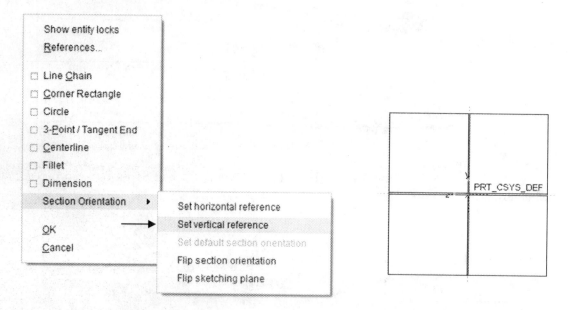

Click the icon of Point, and define a point on the y axis. Specify 30 as the distance from the origin.

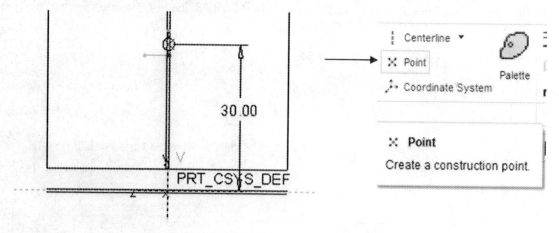

Right click and pick **Centerline**. Sketch a vertical centerline.

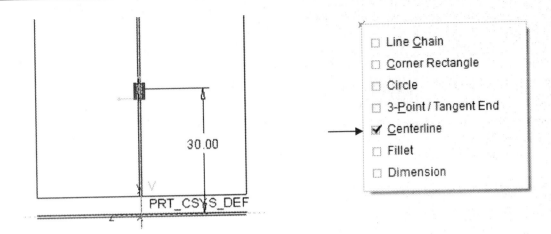

Click the icon of **Line** and sketch an inclined line starting from the defined point.

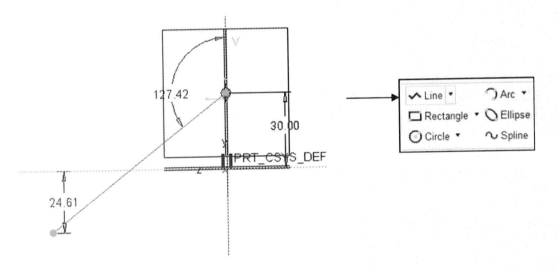

Click the icon of **Mirror** and click the vertical centerline to obtain a new line symmetric about the vertical centerline. Specify 135 degrees between these 2 inclined lines.

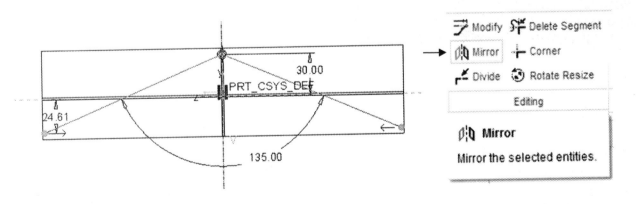

Click the icon of Arc and sketch an arc with the center of the arc located at the defined point. Specify the radius value equal to 140.

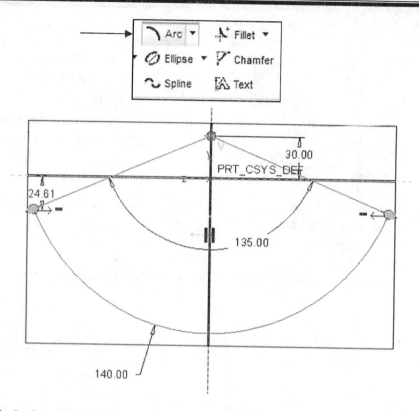

Click the icon of **Circle** and sketch a second circle, as shown below. The distance value is 125 and the diameter value is 100.

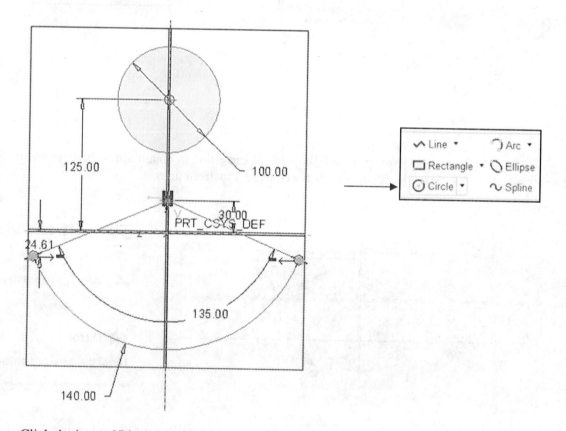

Click the icon of **Line** and sketch a vertical line, as shown below.

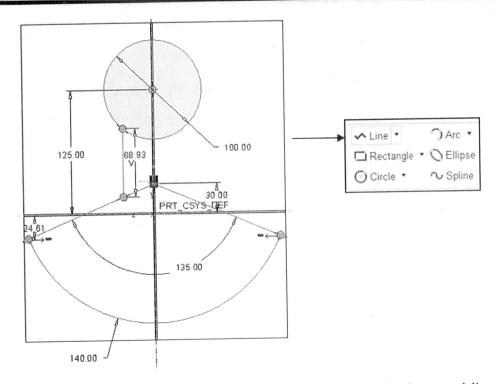

Click the icon of **Mirror**. Click the vertical centerline to obtain the second line, as shown. Specify 80 as the distance between these 2 lines.

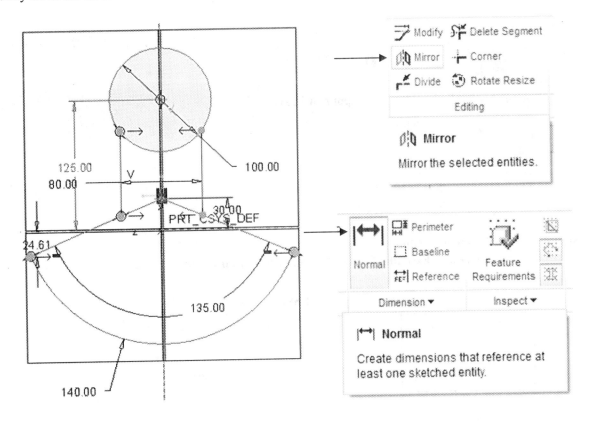

Select the icon of **Delete** to remove those line segments and arcs, which are not part of this required sketch. Add the dimension of 80 and the angular dimension of 135 if they are not on display.

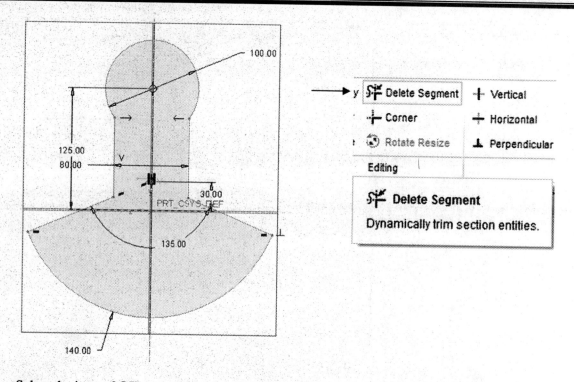

Select the icon of **OK** to complete the 2D sketch. Click the icon of **Apply and Save**.

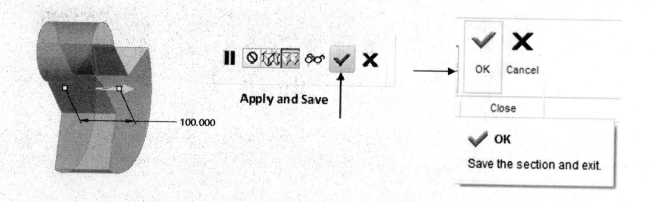

Step 3: Create the second feature.
Select the icon of **Extrude.** Select the icon of **Symmetry**, and set the distance value to *420*.

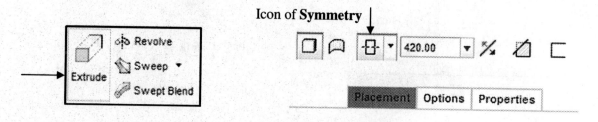

In the model tree, click **RIGHT** (sketching plane). Click the icon of **Sketch View** to orient the sketching plane parallel to the screen.

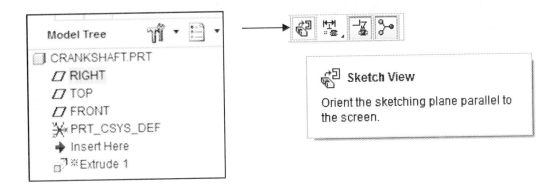

Click the icon of **Circle** and sketch a circle, as shown below. The diameter value is 55.

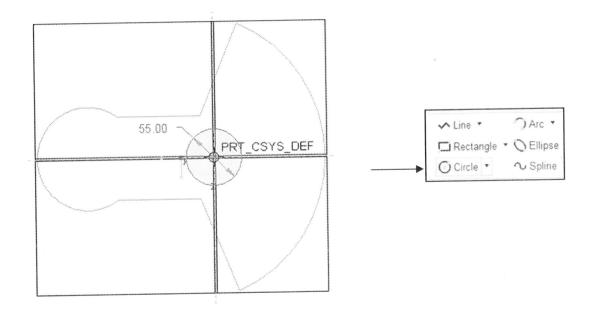

Select the icon of **OK** to complete the 2D sketch. Click the icon of **Apply and Save**.

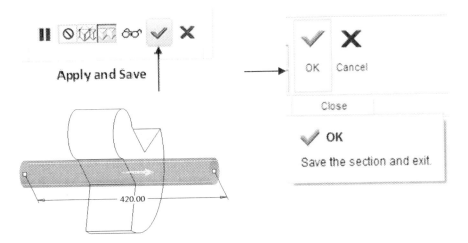

Step 4: Create the third feature.

Select the icon of **Extrude.** Select the icon of **Cut**. Select the icon of **Symmetry**, and set the distance value to *40*.

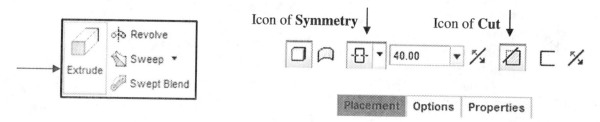

In the model tree, click **RIGHT** (sketching plane). Click the icon of **Sketch View** to orient the sketching plane parallel to the screen.

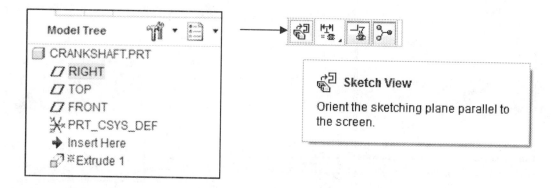

Before sketching, click the icon of **References** from the **Sketch** tab. Pick the circle as a new reference to define the center for the circle to be sketched. After defining this new reference, click **Close**.

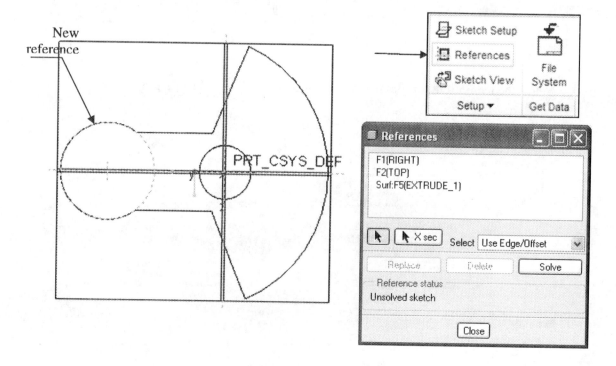

Click the icon of **Circle** and sketch a circle, as shown below. The diameter value is 50.

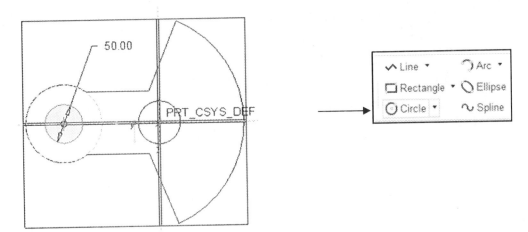

Select the icon of **OK** to complete the 2D sketch. Make sure that the cutting direction is towards the outside of the sketched circle, as shown.

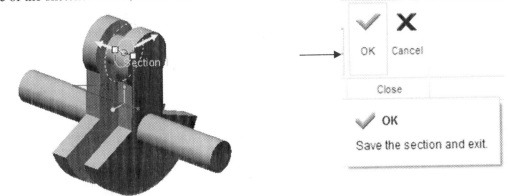

Click the icon of **Apply and Save**, thus completing the creation of the cut feature.

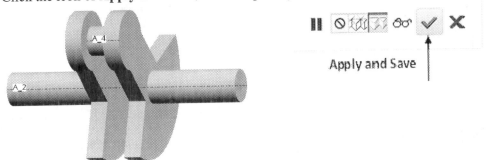

Step 5: Create the fourth feature.
Select the icon of **Extrude.** Select the icon of **Cut**. Select the icon of **Symmetry**, and set the distance value to *30*.

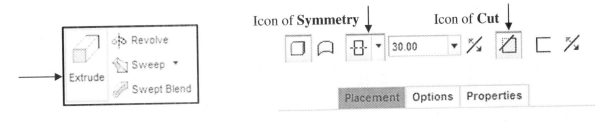

In the model tree, click **RIGHT** (sketching plane). Click the icon of **Sketch View** to orient the sketching plane parallel to the screen.

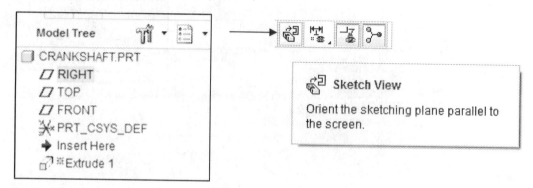

Before sketching, click the icon of **References** from the **Sketch** tab. Pick the circle as a new reference to define the center for the circle to be sketched. After defining this new reference, click **Close**.

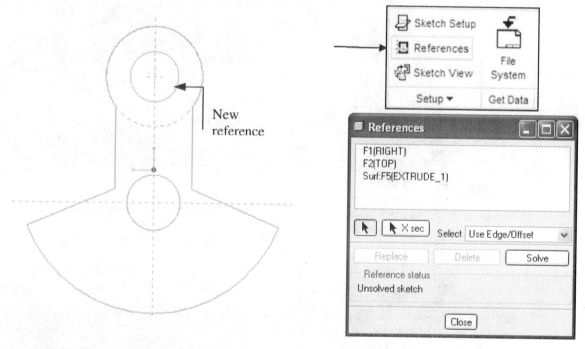

Click the icon of **Circle** and sketch a circle, as shown below. The diameter value is 40.

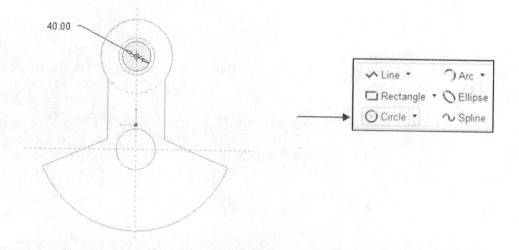

Select the icon of **OK** to complete the 2D sketch. Make sure that the cutting direction is towards the outside of the sketched circle, as shown.

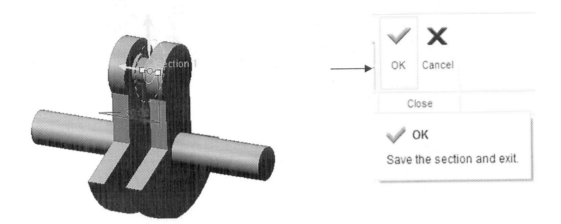

Click the icon of **Apply and Save**, thus completing the creation of the cut feature.

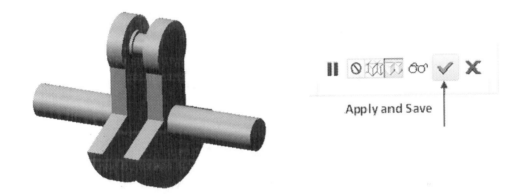

To increase the beauty of this 3D solid model for the crankshaft component, from the Render tab, click **View** from the top menu > **Render Window.**

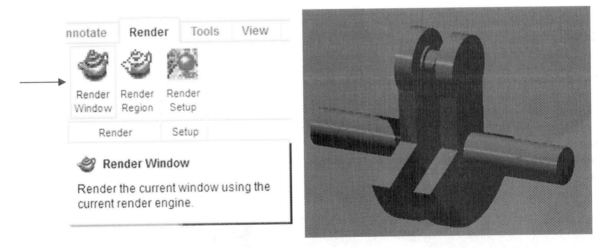

Click Saved Orientation and click Standard Orientation to go back to the display of standard orientation.

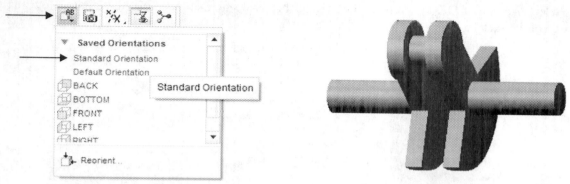

At this time the user has successfully completed the design of crankshaft, he or she should save all the work with the 3D solid model. Select **Save** from the main toolbar > **OK**.

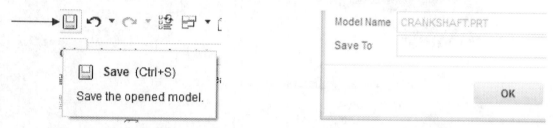

To prepare an engineering drawing of this object, follow the procedure described in Example 5-1 and Example 2 in Chapter 4.

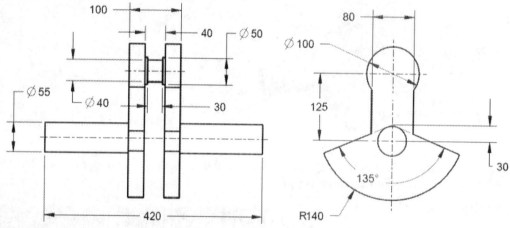

5.3   Example 5-3: Add Color to an Object

The use of color in engineering drawings is really a new subject. It is the introduction of computer graphics to the engineering design that provides a unique opportunity to use the parameter Color to help identify the different components in an assembly or to produce a more realistic view when using a screen-capture option to create a graphics file. Adding color to engineering drawings represents an integration of art and engineering design. Color also facilitates the communication of the function of a design to others.

The above figure presents two 3D solid models with 2 different color settings. The color of the 3D solid model on the left side is the color of default shading. The color of the 3D solid model on the right side is a user-defined color. The procedure to have a user-defined color is listed below. It starts from selecting the icon of **Appearance Gallery** listed in the Render tab or in the View tab. In My Appearances, a user may select a color type. For example, the color type of red is selected. From the model tree, the user may just click LEGO_PART1.PRT > **OK**.

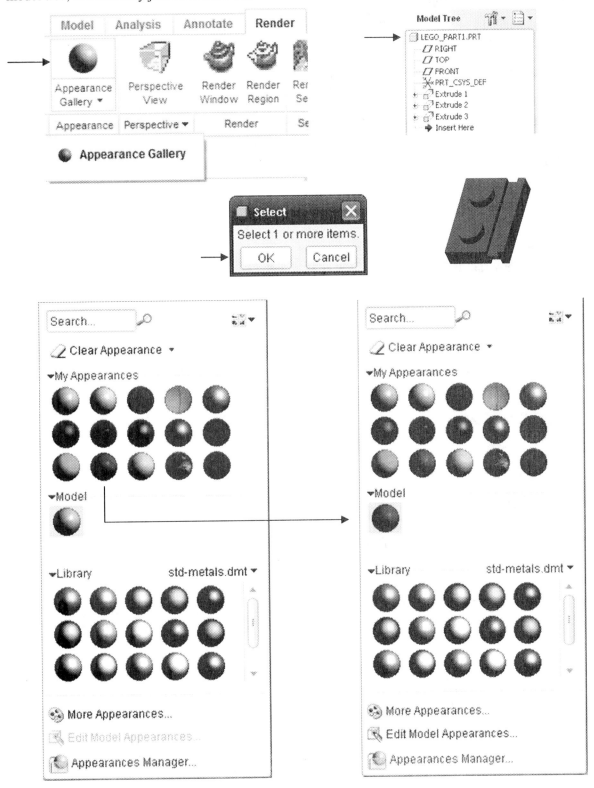

If a user would like to add a new type of color on his/her own, instead of picking a type of color, click the box of **Edit Model Appearance**. In the pop up window called **Model Appearance Editor**, click the colored rectangular area to open the **Color Editor** > the **Color Wheel** appears. > select the desired color, then click the box of **Close** to close the **Color Editor** window, and return to the **Appearance Editor** window. At this moment, users should be able to observe that the color has the new color type > **Close** to complete the process of adding a new type of color to the 3D solid model.

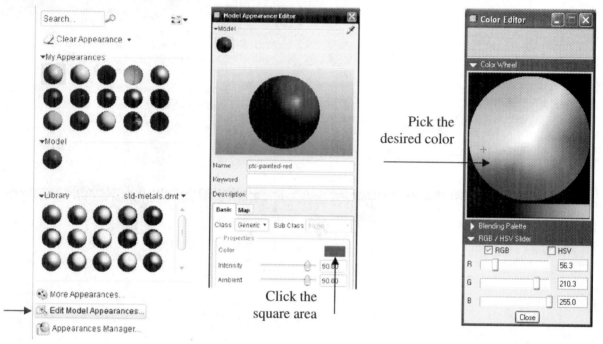

In the **Model Appearance Editor** window, adjust the Transparency control bar to control the degree of transparency.

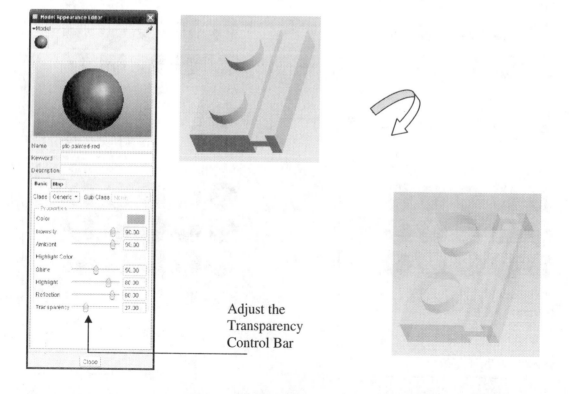

Adjust the Transparency Control Bar

5.4 References

1.   F. L. Amirouche, <u>Computer-aided Design and Manufacturing</u>, Prentice Hall, Englewood Cliffs, New Jersey, 1993.

2.   B. L. Davids, A. J. Robotham and Yardwood A., <u>Computer-aided Drawing and Design</u>, London, 1991.

3.   J. H. Earle, <u>Graphics for Engineers, AutoCAD Release 13</u>, Addison-Wesley, Reading, Massachusetts, 1996.

4.   G. Farin, <u>Curves and Surfaces for Computer-aided Geometric Design</u>, New York, 1988.

5.5 Exercises

1.   A designed part is shown below. List the manufacturing processes so that the designed part can be manufactured. How many features are there? How many manufacturing processes are needed? Is there any relation between the number of features and the number of the manufacturing processes required? Use a drilling process and a milling process to demonstrate the relationship between the feature-based design and the manufacturing planning.

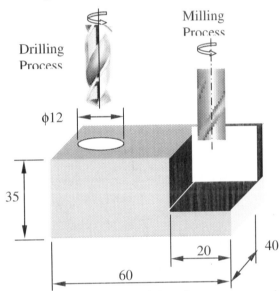

2.   Use Creo Parametric to construct a 3D solid model, and prepare an engineering drawing.
    (1)   Use roundness to round all corners. Select radii as you see fit.
    (2)   Use Shading to display the model on screen.

Through Hole Diameter = 32

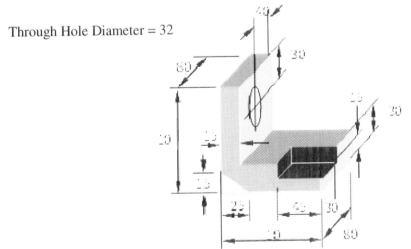

3. Construct a 3D solid model and prepare an engineering drawing.

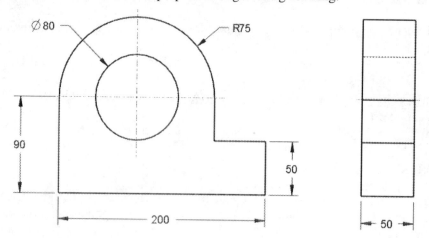

4. Construct a 3D solid model and prepare an engineering drawing.

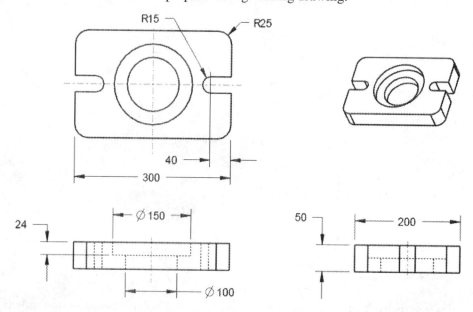

5. How to add color to some of the surfaces? Pick Surface from the box shown below.

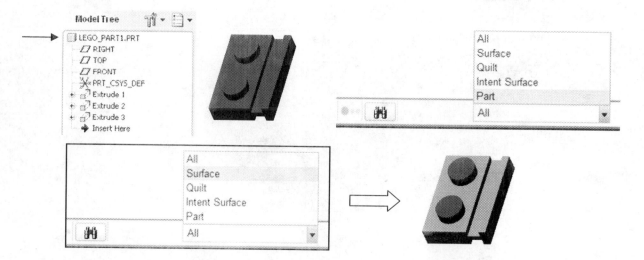

CHAPTER 6

PREPARATION OF ENGINEERING DRAWINGS

6.1   Units of Engineering Drawings and Full Section View

As discussed in Chapter 3, there are two unit systems currently used in the United States of America. These two unit systems are the inch-unit system adopted by ANSI and the mm-unit system adopted by ISO. The default unit system used by the Creo Parametric design system is the inch-unit system. However, users can set the mm-unit system with ease. In the following example, we will use the mm-unit system to create a 3D solid model and prepare an engineering drawing of the 3D solid model.

Example 6-1:   Use the mm-unit System to create a 3D solid model and prepare an engineering drawing with a full section view.

A 3D view of the object and an engineering drawing are shown below. As indicated in the engineering drawing, the front view is a full section view, which is marked as SECTION A-A. In the full section view, the dashed lines representing the hole at the central location are replaced by solid lines because the hidden geometry of the hole becomes visible when part of the 3D solid model is removed in the sectioning process.

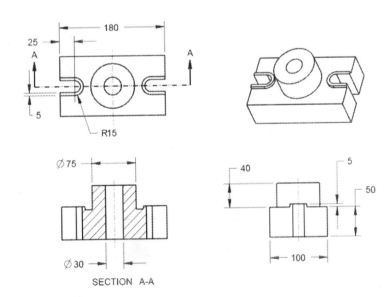

SECTION A-A

Based on the feature-based modeling approach, we will create the following 4 features:

Feature 1: block with size: 180 x 100 x 50 mm.

Feature 2: cylinder with size: ϕ75 x40 mm.

Feature 3: Create a through hole at the central location with size: ϕ30 mm.

Feature 4: Create a set of 2 built-slot features.

From the **File** menu click **New > Part.** Type *ex6_1* as the file name and clear the icon of **Use default template**.

Select **mmns_part_solid** (units: Millimeter, Newton, Second) and type *block_component* in **DESCRIPTION**, and *student* in **MODELED_BY**, then **OK**.

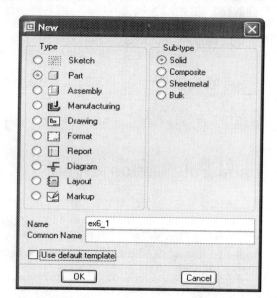 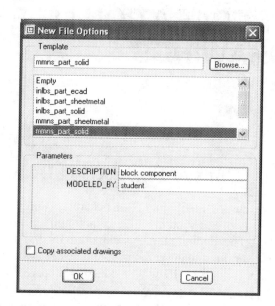

Select the icon of **Extrude** from the **Model** tab. Specify *50* as the extrusion distance.

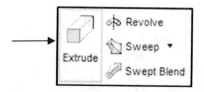 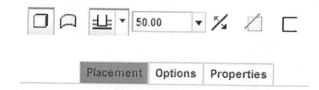

In the model tree, click **TOP** (sketching plane). Click the icon of **Sketch View** to orient the sketching plane parallel to the screen.

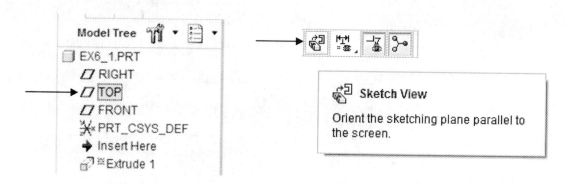

Select the icon of **Rectangle** from the Sketch group. Select Center Rectangle and sketch a rectangle centered at the origin. Modify the two dimensions to 180 and 100, respectively.

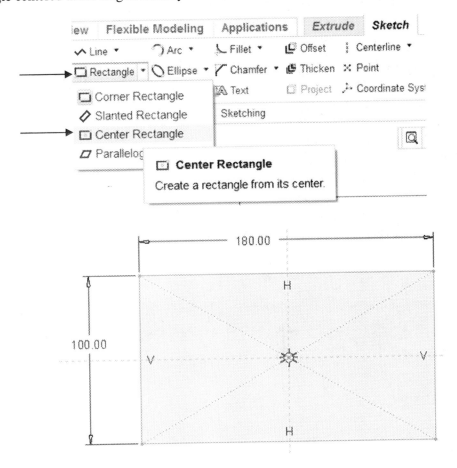

Click the icon of **OK,** and click the icon of **Apply and Save**.

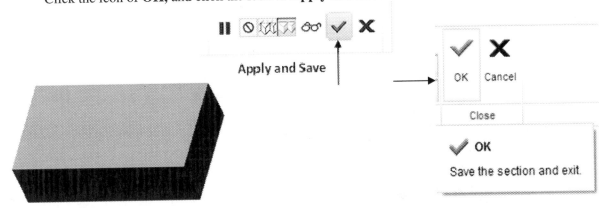

Now let us create the second feature, a cylinder: φ75 x 40 mm. Click the icon of **Extrude.** Specify 40 as the extrusion distance.

Click the top surface of the block (sketching plane). Click the icon of **Sketch View** to orient the sketching plane parallel to the screen.

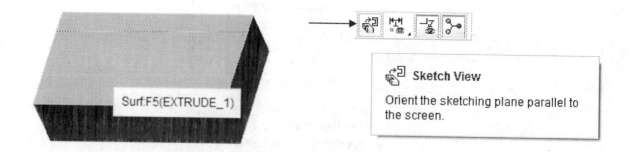

Select the icon of **Circle** to draw a circle with diameter equal to 75.

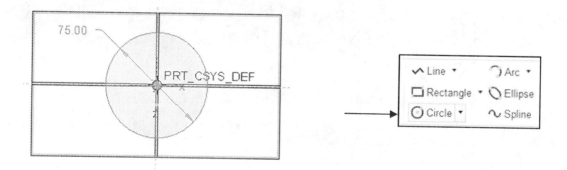

Click the icon of **OK,** and click the icon **of Apply and Save.**

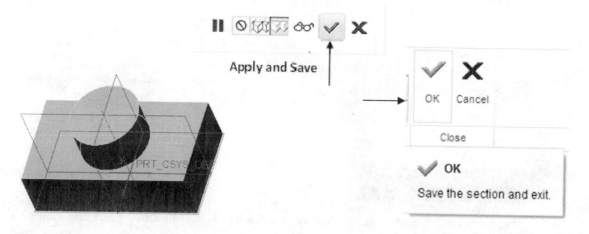

After creating the cylindrical feature, we create the third feature, a through hole with diameter equal to φ30. click the icon of **Hole** from the Model tab. On the dashboard, type *30* as the diameter value and select **Through All** as the depth choice (click the black arrow on the Depth Options Flyout).

Click the **Placement** box, and select the axis displayed on screen and the top surface of the cylinder as the 2 placement settings while holding down the Ctrl key. Click the icon of **Apply and Save** to complete the creation of the hole feature.

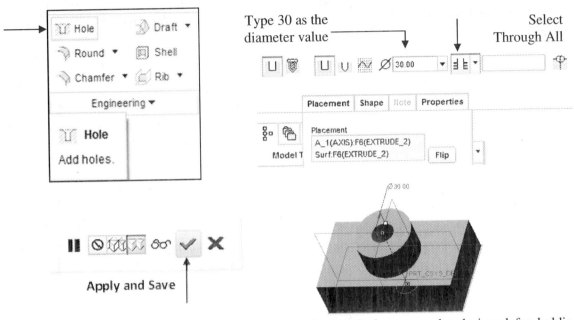

Type 30 as the diameter value

Select Through All

Apply and Save

After creating the hole feature, we create the fourth feature, a slot designed for holding this component. Click **Extrude** from the Model tab. Specify *5* as the height value.

Click the top surface of the block (sketching plane). Click the icon of **Sketch View** to orient the sketching plane parallel to the screen.

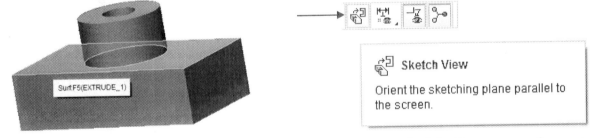

Sketch View

Orient the sketching plane parallel to the screen.

Click **References** from the Sketch tab. Pick the vertical edge on the left side as a new reference > **Close** the reference window.

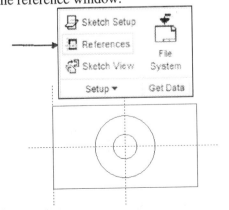

15. Click the icon of Centerline from the Sketch tab. Sketch a vertical centerline with a dimension of

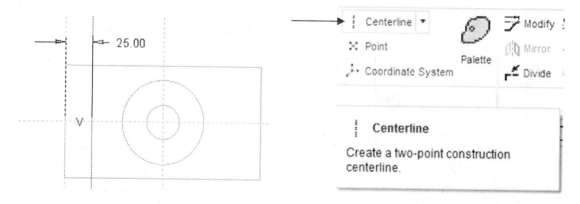

Click the icon of **Circle** and sketch a circle, as shown.

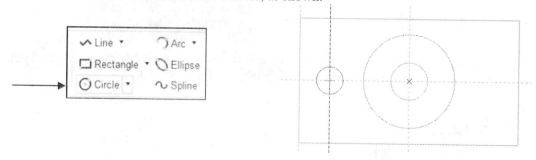

Click the icon of Delete and delete half of the sketched circle. Specify 15 as the radius value.

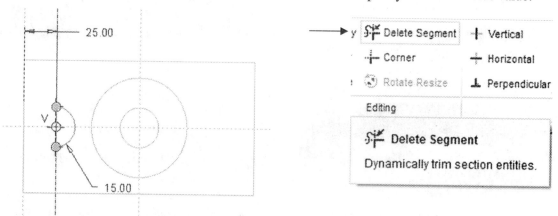

Click the icon of **Line** and sketch 3 lines, forming a closed sketch.

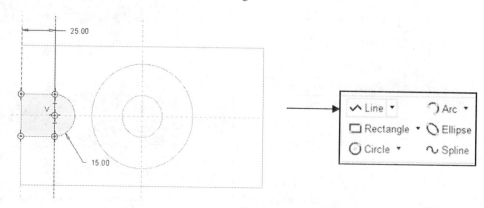

Upon completing the sketch, click the icon of **OK.** Click the icon of **Apply and Save**.

To cut a slot, click the icon of **Extrude**. Select the icon of **Cut** and select **Through All** as the depth choice.

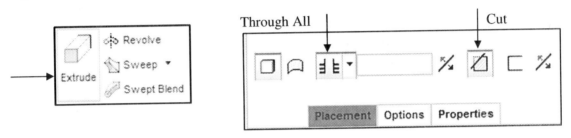

Click the top surface of the built step as the sketching plane. Click the icon of **Sketch View** to orient the sketching plane parallel to the screen.

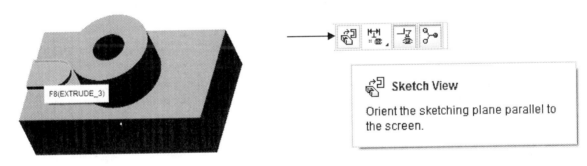

Click **References** from the Sketch tab. Pick the vertical edge on the left side as a new reference > **Close** the reference window.

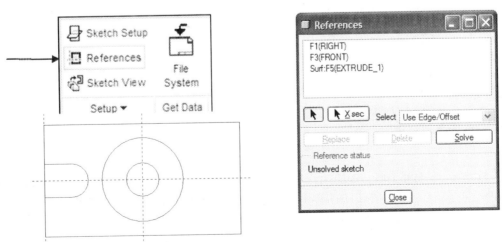

Click the icon of **Use Edge with Offset**. Click the half circle. Specify *-5* as the offset value. The negative sign indicates the offset is in the opposite direction of the arrow, and press the **Enter** key.

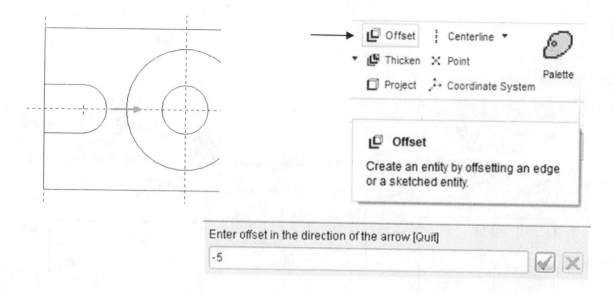

Click the icon of **Line** to sketch 3 lines, forming a closed sketch, as shown.

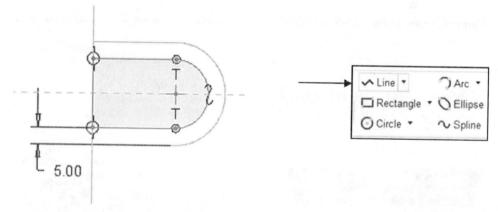

Upon completing the sketch, click the icon of **OK**. Click the icon of **Apply and Save**.

At this moment, let us use **Mirror** to create another set of the built-cut feature on the right side of the block. In the model tree, pick these 2 features while holding down the **Ctrl** key, click the icon of Mirror Tool > click the **RIGHT** datum plane for the mirroring operation > click the icon of **Apply and Save**.

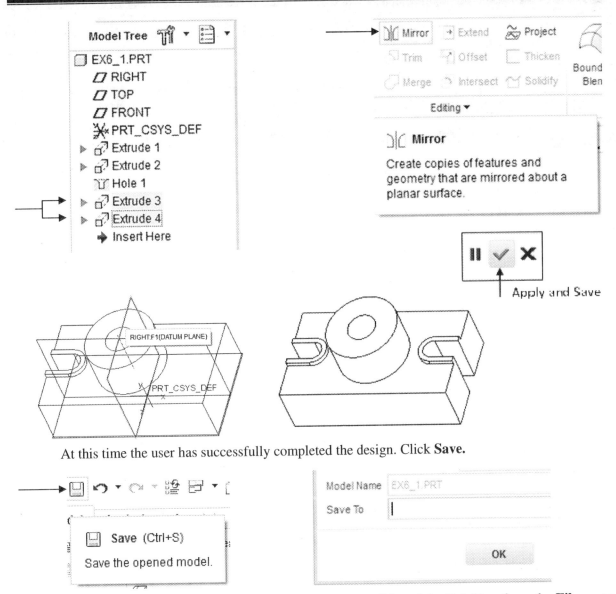

At this time the user has successfully completed the design. Click **Save.**

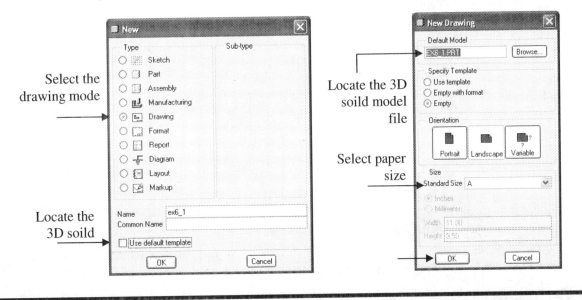

To prepare an engineering drawing based on the 3D solid model, click **New** from the **File** menu and click **Drawing**. Type *ex6_1* as the file name. Clear the box of **Use default template**, and click **OK**.

Select the drawing mode

Locate the 3D soild

Locate the 3D soild model file

Select paper size

This brings up the drawing screen. Click the **Layout** tab. Click the icon of **General.** In the **Select Combined State** window, click **OK** to accept **No Combined State**.

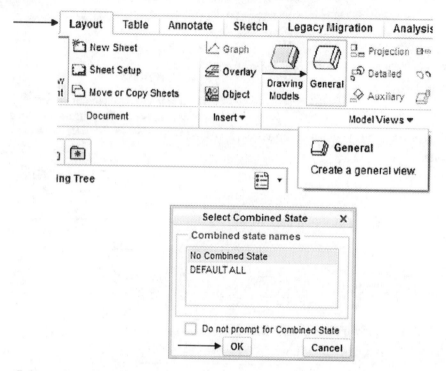

Select a location on the drawing screen as the center point for the **General View**. A general view appears on the screen.

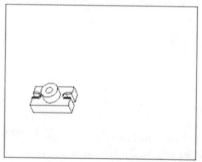

In the pop-up **Drawing View** window, select **FRONT > Apply > Close**, the construction of the front view is completed.

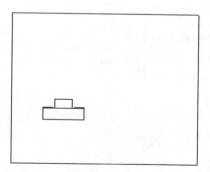
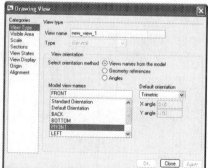

To insert the right side view, pick the **FRONT** View just created so that the Front View is activated, click the icon of **Projection** and make a left click at the right side of the Front View.

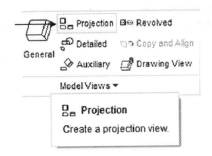

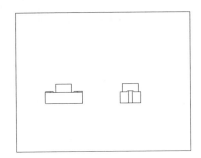

Follow the same procedure to create the top view, as shown below.

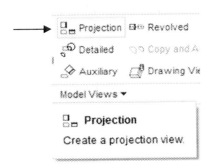

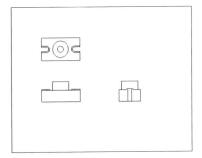

Click the icon of **General.** In the **Select Combined State** window, click OK to accept **No Combined State**. Select a location on the drawing screen as the center point for the 3D View (click the left button of mouse). A general view appears on the screen. In the pop-up Drawing View window, select **Standard Orientation > Apply > Close**, the construction of the 3D View is completed.

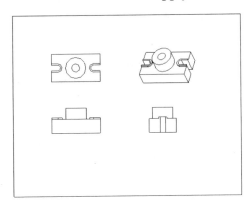

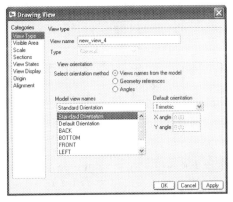

Note that the hole feature and part of the slot features are invisible in the FRONT view. In order to have a visible version of the hole feature and the slot feature located in the center of the block, we use a section view. To do so, let us modify the FRONT view to a full section view.

First, let us enable the display of datum planes. Click the icon of **Plane Display**.

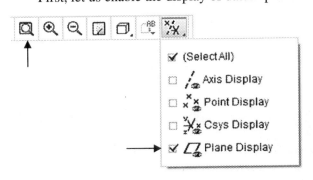

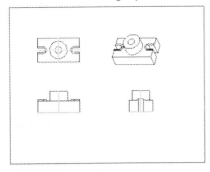

Now click the **FRONT** view through a left click of mouse. Afterwards, right click and hold, select **Properties.**

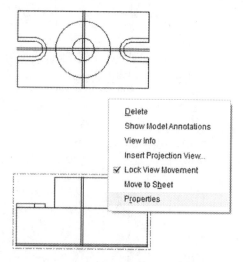

In the Drawing View window, select **Sections** and **2D cross-section.** Click the icon of **Add** (plus sign) to add cross-section. In the pop up window, accept **Planar** and **Single > Done.**

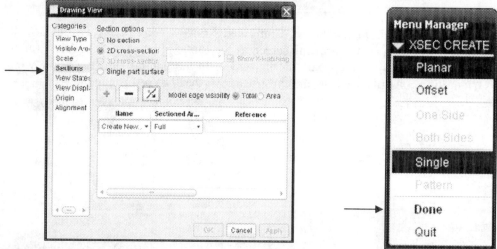

The software system is asking the user to enter a name for cross-section. Type *A* as the name for cross-section and press the **Enter** key.

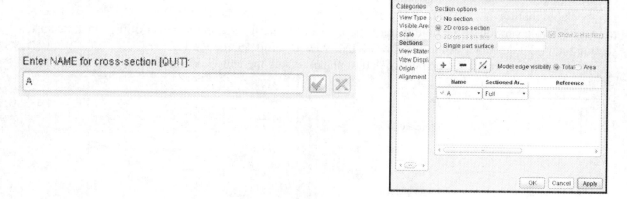

On the screen display, select the **FRONT** datum plane from the Top View > click the box of **Apply**, a cross-section is added to the Front view.

Pick FRONT DATUM PLANE

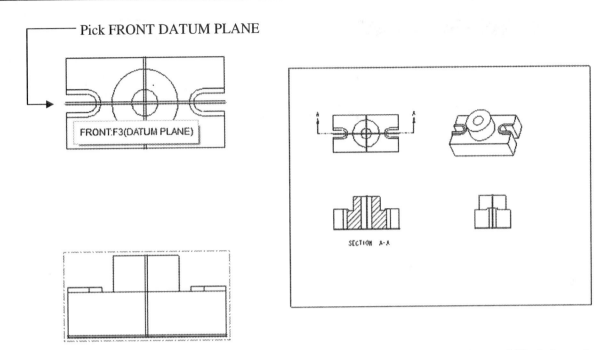

If the user has difficulty in picking the **FRONT** datum plane, click the icon of **Find** from the menu bar located at the left-lower corner.   In the **Search Tool** window, select Datum Plane under Look for. Select **FRONT** as the Value in the box of Criteria. Click **Find Now**. When identifying the **FRONT** datum plane, click the arrow button in the middle so that the search result goes into effect > **Close**.

To add an arrow indicating the direction of the cross-section view, activate **Arrow Display** from the **Drawing View** window > click the Top view > **Apply** and two arrows marked as A appear together with SECTION A-A > **Close**.

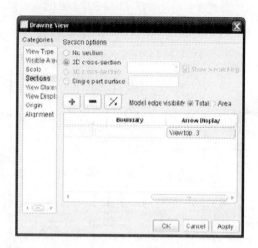
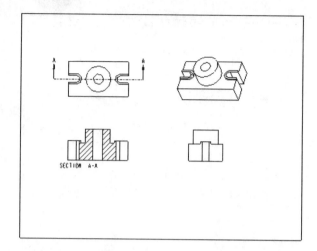

Upon completing the drawing layout, users should add dimensions and centerlines, following the instructions described in the previous examples.

At this time the user has successfully completed the engineering drawing, he or she should save all the work with the drawing. Select **Save** from the main toolbar > **OK**.

6.2   Diameter Dimensions for 3D Models Created Using Revolve

A significant amount of parts are made on lathe where the workpiece rotates and a cutting tool removes material from the rotating workpiece. Example 6-2 is to create a shaft component using the function called **Revolve** under the Creo Parametric design environment.

Example 6-2:   Create a shaft component, which is shown below with an engineering drawing.

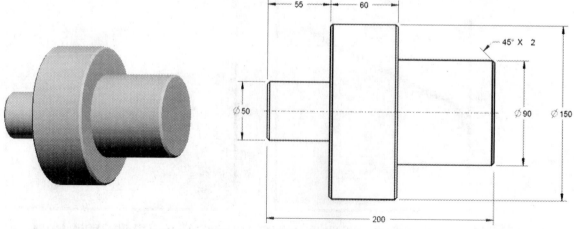

Based on the feature-based modeling approach, we will create the following 2 features:
Feature 1: revolving feature for the shaft
Feature 2: chamfers at the sharp edges

Click **New** from the File menu. Select **Part** > type *ex6_2* as the file name and clear the icon of **Use default template** to set the mm-unit system > **OK**. In the New File Option window, type Shaft as description and type student as modeled_by. Click> **OK**.

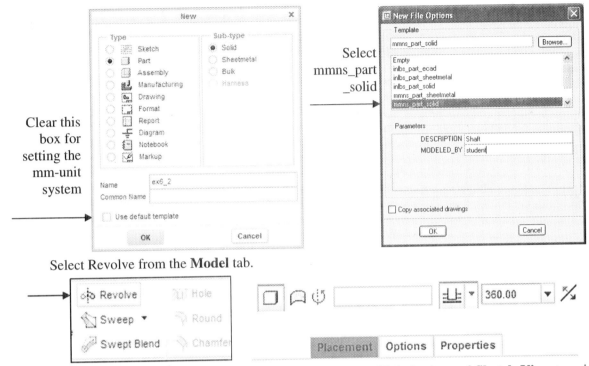

Select Revolve from the **Model** tab.

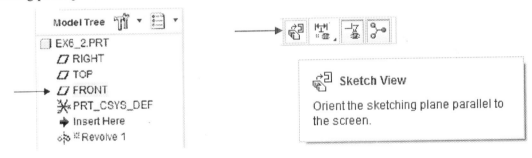

From the model tree, click FRONT (sketching planer). Click the icon of **Sketch View** to orient the sketching plane parallel to the screen.

Right-click and hold, select Axis of Revolution. Afterwards, sketch a horizontal centerline.

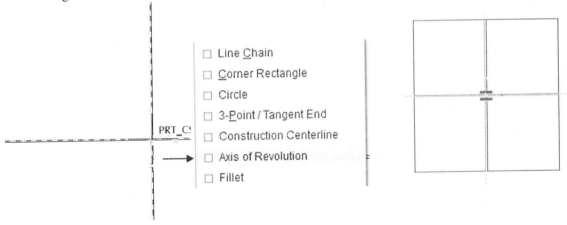

Select the icon of **Line** from the Sketch tab. Sketch 2 lines. Modify the 2 dimensions to 50 and 55, respectively.

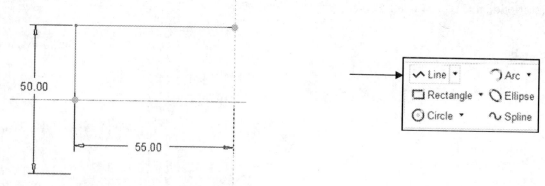

Select the icon of **Line** from the Sketch tab. Sketch 2 lines. Modify the 2 dimensions to 150 and 60, respectively.

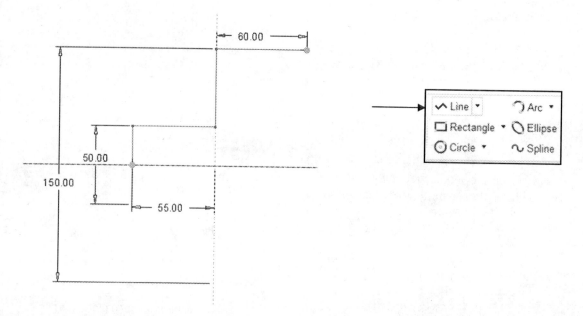

Select the icon of **Line** from the Sketch tab. Sketch 4 lines to form a closed sketch. Modify the 2 dimensions to 90 and 200, respectively.

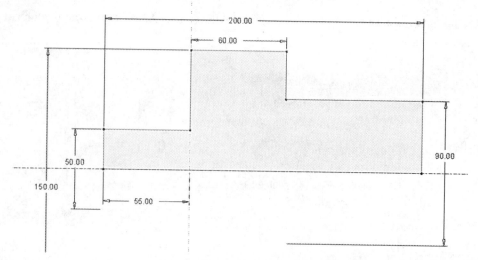

Users may need to click the icon of **Normal** to define the dimension of 200. Users need to make 2 left clicks and one click on the middle button of mouse.

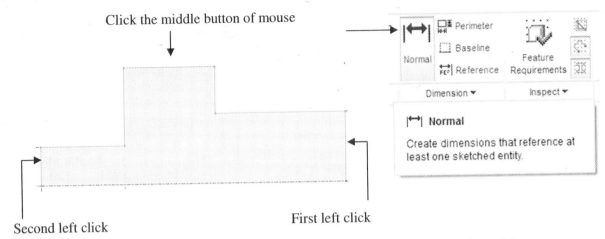

Click the middle button of mouse

Second left click

First left click

Upon completing this sketch, click the icon of **OK.** Click the icon of **Apply and Save**.

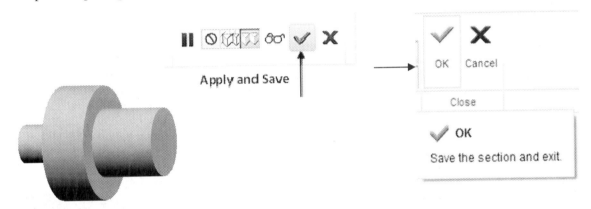

Apply and Save

After creating the revolved feature, we create the second feature: chamfers at the sharp edges. Click the icon of **Edge Chamfer** from the toolbar of feature creation. On the dashboard, specify 45xD and 2 as the size of the chamfer. While holding down the **Ctrl** key, pick the 4 edges. Click the icon of **Apply and Save**.

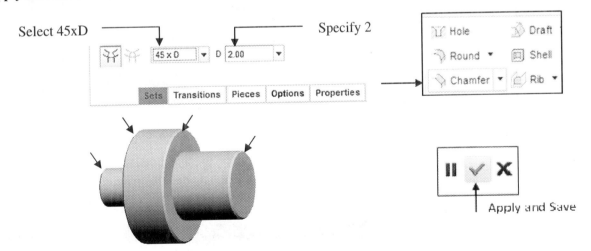

Select 45xD

Specify 2

Apply and Save

At this time the user has successfully completed the design of shaft component, he or she should save all the work with the 3D solid model. Select **Save** from the main toolbar > **OK**.

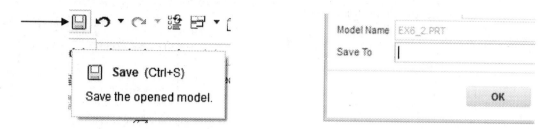

To prepare an engineering drawing based on the 3D solid model, click **New** from the **File** menu and click **Drawing**. Type *ex6_2* as the file name. Clear the box of **Use default template**, and click **OK**.

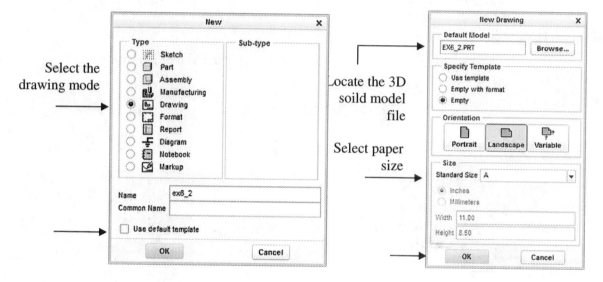

Select the drawing mode

Locate the 3D soild model file

Select paper size

This brings up the drawing screen. Click the **Layout** tab. Click the icon of **General**. In the **Select Combined State** window, click **OK** to accept **No Combined State**.

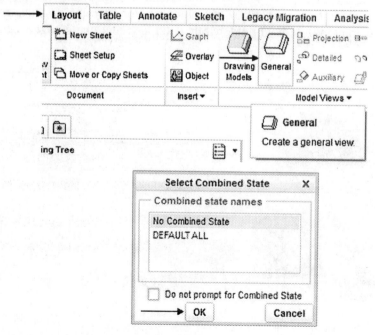

Note that one view is sufficient to meet the criterion for clarification. Locate a position as the CENTER POINT of the front view. From the Drawing View Window, select **FRONT > Apply > Scale > Custom scale > 0.50 > Apply > Close.** The construction of the front view is completed.

 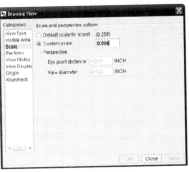 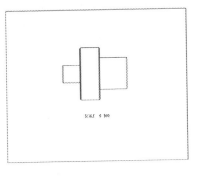

Upon completing the layout, add dimensions and a centerline to the drawing.

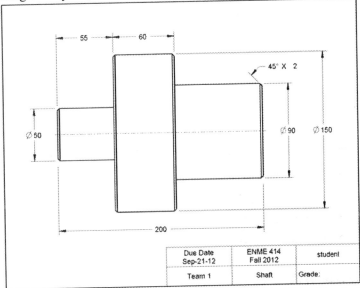

At this time the user has successfully completed the engineering drawing of the designed shaft component, he or she should save all the work with the drawing. Select **Save** from the main toolbar > **OK**.

Note that there is a title box placed in the engineering drawing. The title box contains the information on the part name, the designer's name, the date of design completion. In industry, the title box may list the company name, part name, part material, designer's name, signature of the person in charge of making approval. We will discuss the format issue in the following example, or Example 6-3.

6.3 Creation of a Format Used in Engineering Drawing

In this section, we present the procedure to create a format file. The procedure consists of two steps: creating a frame and creating a table.

Example 6-3: Create a format for paper size A (11 x 8.5 inch)

As illustrated, the frame is formed by 4 lines. Each line is so positioned to meet the margin requirements. The margin on the left side is 0.50 inch. The margins on the other 3 sides are 0.25 inch. Assuming the left-lower corner is the origin, the coordinates of the four corners of the frame are shown in the following figure.

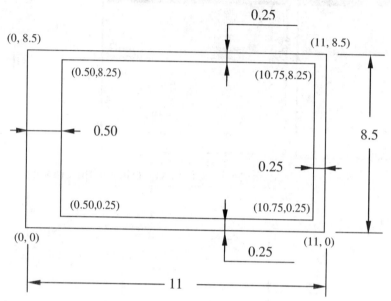

A title box is a table. As shown, the table has 3 columns and 2 rows. The table is located at the right-lower corner.

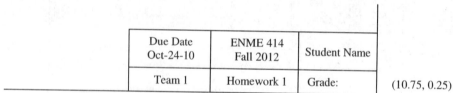

Due Date Oct-24-10	ENME 414 Fall 2012	Student Name
Team 1	Homework 1	Grade:

(10.75, 0.25)

From the **File** menu, click **New > Format**. Type *exercise_format* as the file name > **OK.** A window of **New Format** appears. Select **Empty**, **Landscape** and **Standard size A > OK.**

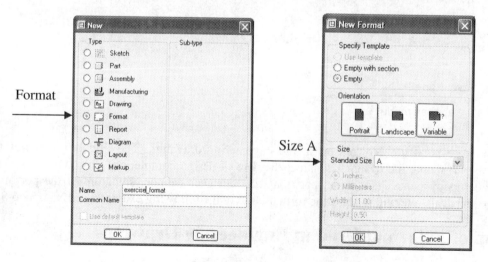

From the **Sketch** tab, click the icon of **Line.** On the screen, right-click and hold, and a pop up window appears. Select **Absolute Coordinates.** Type 0.50 for X and 0.25 for Y, press the **Enter** key.

Repeat this procedure: right-click and hold, and select **Absolute Coordinates** in the pop up window. Type 10.75 for X and 0.25 for Y, thus completing the creation of the first line, which is a horizontal line at the lower position.

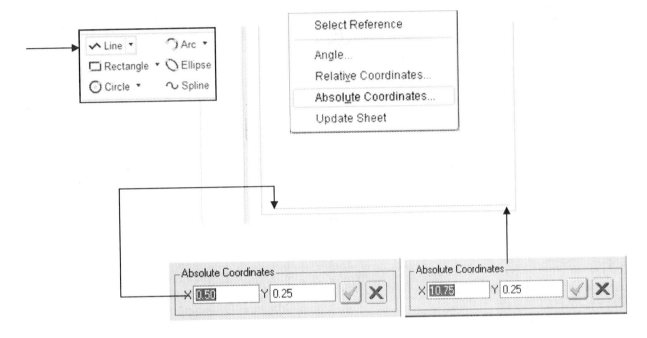

Repeat the previous procedure to create another horizontal line. The coordinates of the left end are *0.50* for x coordinate and *8.25* for y coordinate. The coordinates of the right end are *10.75* for x coordinate and *8.25* for y coordinate.

Repeat the previous procedure to create a vertical line on the left side. The coordinates of the upper end are *0.50* for x coordinate and *8.25* for y coordinate. The coordinates of the lower end are *0.50* for x coordinate and *0.25* for y coordinate.

Repeat the previous procedure to create a vertical line on the right side. The coordinates of the upper end are *10.75* for x coordinate and *8.25* for y coordinate. The coordinates of the lower end are *10.75* for x coordinate and *0.25* for y coordinate.

Upon completing this frame, close the window of Snapping References.

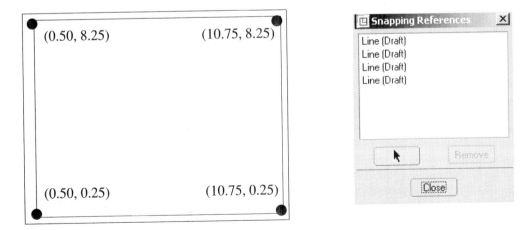

To create the title box with three columns and two rows, click the **Table** tab and > click the icon of **Table > Insert Table.**

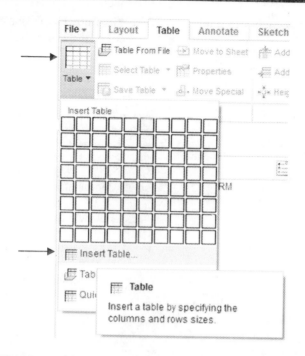

In the Insert Table window, select the icon of leftward and ascending. Specify 2 rows and 3 columns. Clear the box of Automatic Height Adjustment. Set 3 as the height of row and 14 as the width of column. Click **OK**. In the Select Point window, pick Absolute Coordinates and specify 10.75 for X and 0.25 for Y. Click **OK**, completing the creation of a table.

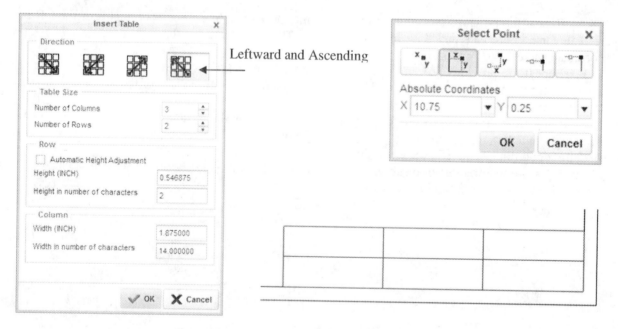

To enter text at a given cell, for example, to enter Team 1 at the left-upper cell, double click the cell and a window of **Note Properties** appears. Type *&todays_date*. To justify its position within the cell, click the box of **Text Style**. In the pop up window, select **Center** for the horizontal and **Middle** for the vertical. Click **OK** to complete the process of entering the text. Note the use of symbol **&,** which tracks the name of the parameter used in the design process. As a result, when the format file is being used, the actual date will appear in the title box.

Double click the middle cell on the top row, type in *ENME 414 <enter> Fall 2012* and justify the text to the center horizontally and the middle vertically.

Double click the right cell on the top row, type in *&modeled_by* (your name will appear if you specify your name in *modeled_by* when creating a new file in the part mode) and justify the text to the center horizontally and the middle vertically.

Double click the left cell on the bottom row, type in *Team 1* and justify the text to the center horizontally and the middle vertically.

Double click the middle cell on the bottom row, type in *&description* and justify the text to the center horizontally and the middle vertically.

Double click the right cell on the bottom row, type in *Grade:* and justify the text to the left horizontally and the middle vertically.

&todays_date	ENME414 Fall 2012	&modeled_by
Team 1	&description	Grade:

At this stage, we have completed the creation of a format, which is shown below. At this time, save the format file. Click the icon of **Save > OK**.

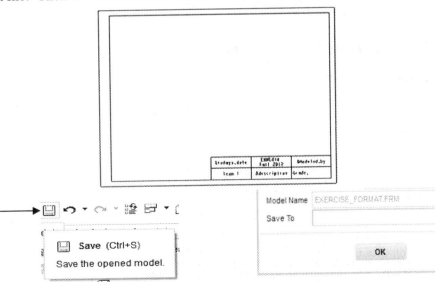

How to insert such a format into a drawing? In the following, we demonstrate the procedure to insert this format to the shaft drawing of Example 6-2.

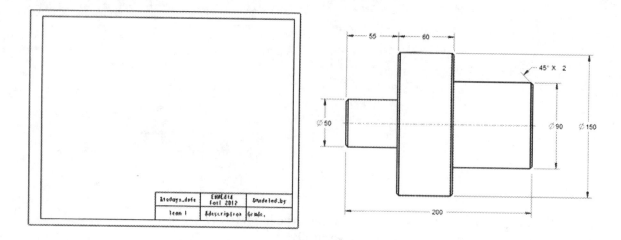

Click the Layout tab. Click **Sheet Setup** > Using **Browse** to locate the format file, which is *exercise_format* > **Open** > select **Show format** > **OK.**

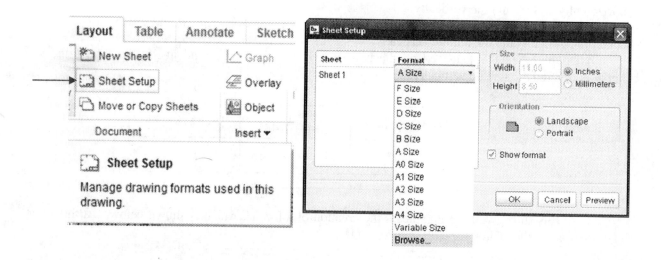

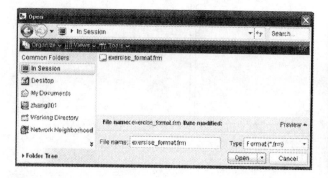
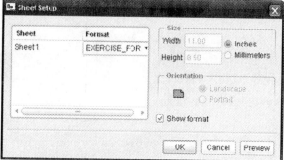

Note that we used student as the name under modeled_by, and Shaft under description when creating the part model in Example 6-2. As a result, student and Shaft have appeared in the title box.

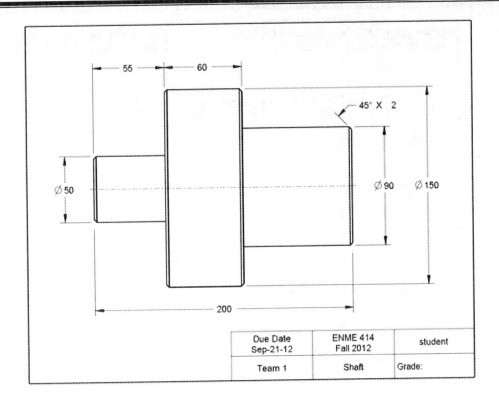

Due Date Sep-21-12	ENME 414 Fall 2012	student
Team 1	Shaft	Grade:

Example Rocket Model: Create a rocket model, which is shown below with an engineering drawing.

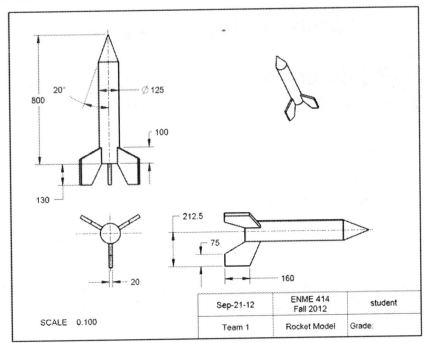

Sep-21-12	ENME 414 Fall 2012	student
Team 1	Rocket Model	Grade:

Based on the feature-based modeling approach, we will create the following 3 features:

Body: revolving feature

Support: extrusion feature

Pattern the support to create 2 more supports

From the File menu, Click **New > Part**. Type *rocket_model* as the file name and clear the icon of **Use default template** to set the mm-unit system > **OK.**

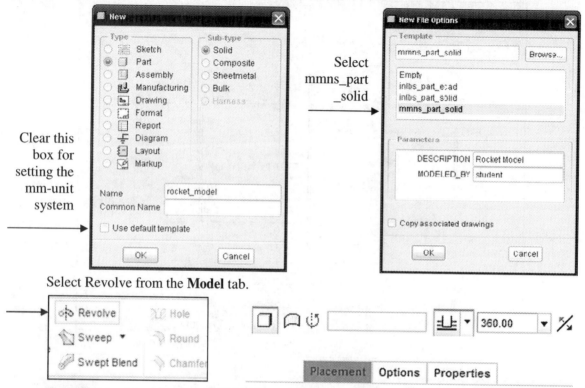

Clear this box for setting the mm-unit system

Select mmns_part _solid

Select Revolve from the **Model** tab.

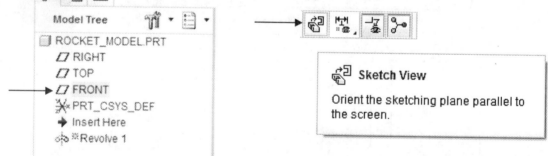

From the model tree, click **FRONT** (sketching planer). Click the icon of **Sketch View** to orient the sketching plane parallel to the screen.

Sketch View

Orient the sketching plane parallel to the screen.

Right-click and hold, select Axis of Revolution. Sketch a vertical centerline. This centerline will serve as the axis for the revolving operation.

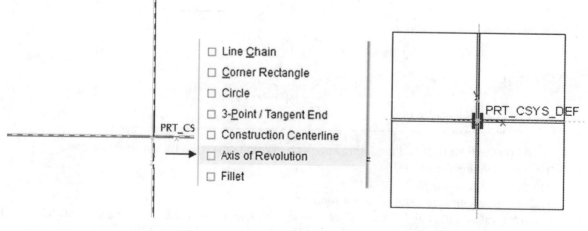

Select the icon of **Line** from the Sketch tab. Sketch a vertical line. Modify the dimensions to 800.

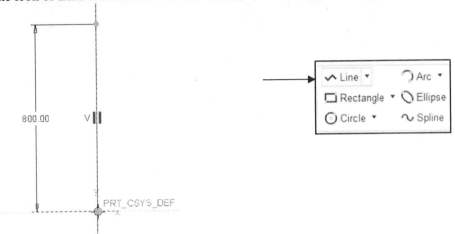

Select the icon of **Line** from the Sketch tab. Sketch 3 lines to form a closed sketch. Modify the 2 dimensions to 40 and 125.

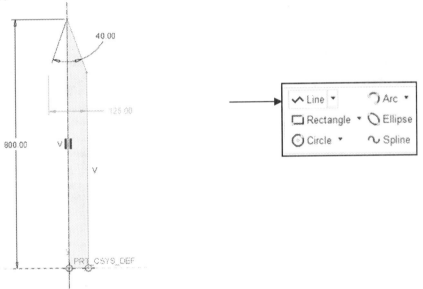

Upon completing this sketch, click the icon of **OK.** Click the icon of **Apply and Save**.

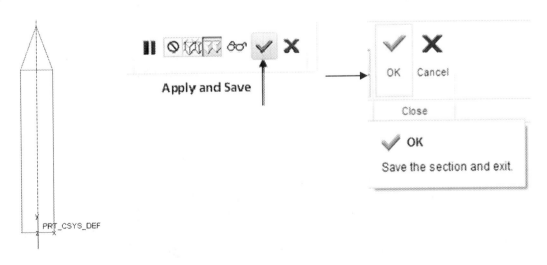

To create the support feature, click the icon of Extrude. Select the icon of Symmetry; and specify *20* as the depth of extrusion.

In the model tree, click **FRONT** (sketching plane). Click the icon of **Sketch View** to orient the sketching plane parallel to the screen.

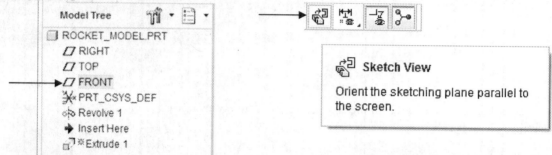

Before sketching, click the icon of **References** from the **Sketch** tab. Pick the edge representing the cylindrical surface as a new reference. After defining this new reference, click **Close**.

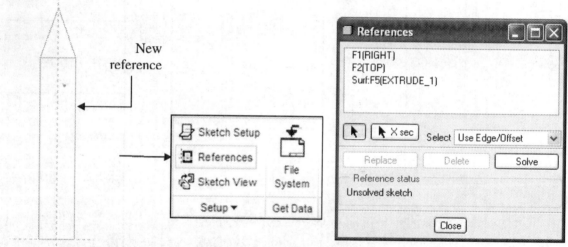

Select the icon of **Line** from the Sketch tab. Sketch 5 lines and modify the dimensions, as shown below.

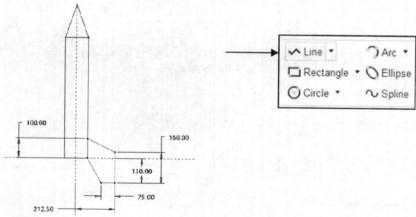

Click the icon of **OK**, and click the icon of **Apply and Save**.

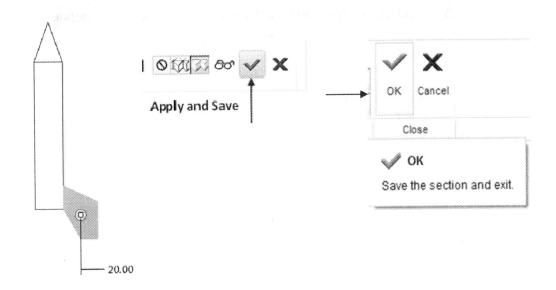

From the model tree, highlight Extrude 1, right-click to select **Pattern**. In the **Pattern** window, select **Axis** and pick the axis from the created model. Specify 3 as the total number of copies and type 120 so that the 3 copies are uniformly distributed.

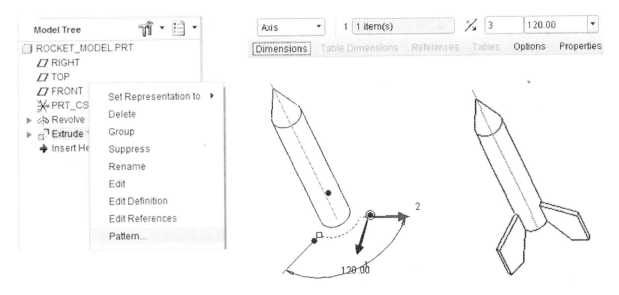

At this time the user has successfully completed the design of rocket model, he or she should save all the work with the 3D solid model. Select **Save** from the File menu > **OK**.

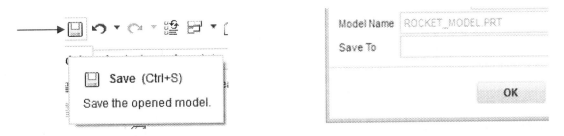

Users are asked to prepare an engineering drawing based on the 3D revolved solid model.

Example 6-4:   Construct a belt wheel with a half section view and an offset section view.

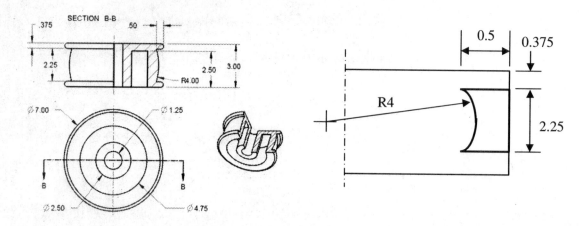

Step 1:   Create a file for the 3D solid model.
From the **File** menu, click **New > Part**. Type *ex6_4* as the file name and clear the icon of **Use default template**.
Select **inlbs_part_solid** (units: Inch, Pound, Second) and type *belt wheel* in **DESCRIPTION**, and *student* in **MODELED_BY**, then **OK**.

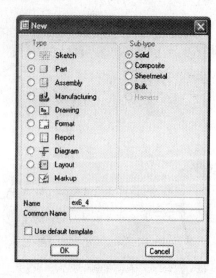 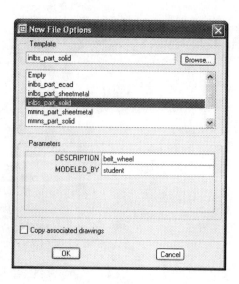

Step 2:   Create a 3D solid model.
Feature 1: a cylinder with size: ⌀7 x 3 inch.
From the Model tab, click the icon of **Extrude.** Specify *3* as the depth of extrusion.

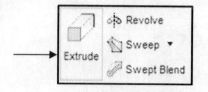 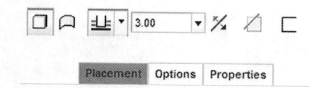

From the model tree, click **FRONT** (sketching planer). Click the icon of **Sketch View** to orient the sketching plane parallel to the screen.

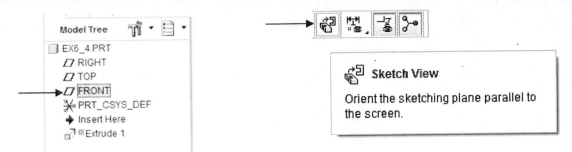

Select the icon of **Circle** from the Sketch tab. Sketch a circle and modify the diameter dimension to 7.

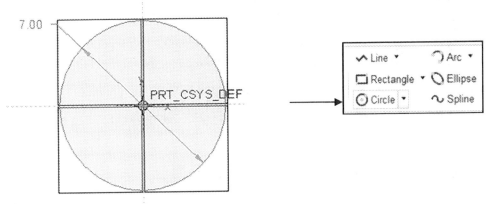

Click the icon of **OK.** Click the icon of **Apply and Save.**

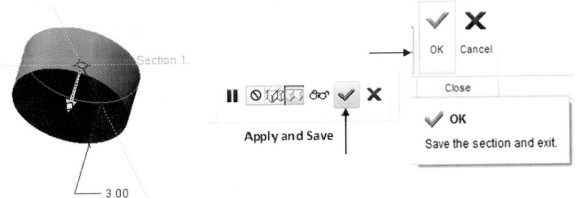

Feature 2: place a through hole in the central location. Its size: ϕ1.25 x 3.

Click the icon of **Hole** from the **Model** tab. Type 1.25 as the diameter value and set the depth choice to **Thru All**. Select the axis of the cylinder as the Primary Reference. While holding down the **Ctrl** key, pick the front surface of the cylinder as the secondary reference. Select the icon of **Apply and Save**, completing the placement of the hole feature.

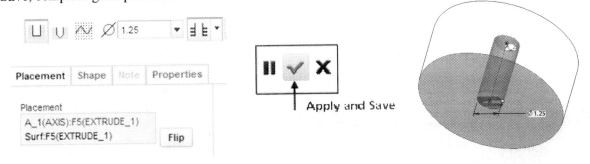

Feature 3: use **Revolve** to cut a ring-shape. Its size: $\phi4.75 \times \phi2.5 \times 2.5$.
Click the icon of **Revolve.** Select the icon of **Cut**.

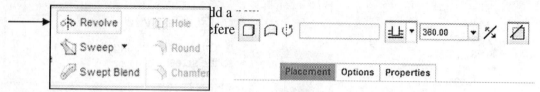

From the model tree, click **TOP** (sketching planer). Click the icon of **Sketch View** to orient the sketching plane parallel to the screen.

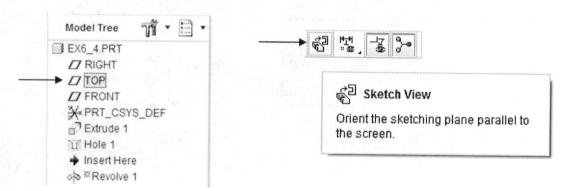

Before sketching, click the icon of **References** from the **Sketch** tab. Pick the edge representing the front surface of the disk as a new reference. After defining this new reference, click **Close**.

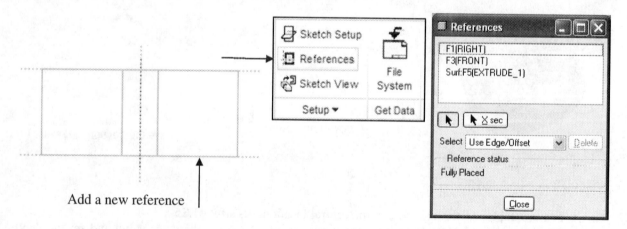

Add a new reference

Right-click and pick the icon of Axis of Revolution. Sketch a vertical centerline along the z-axis.

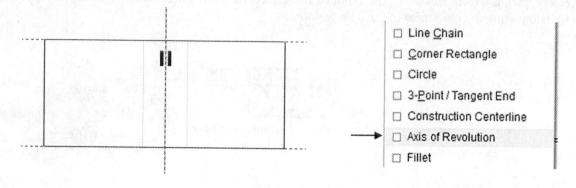

Select the icon of **Rectangle** to sketch a rectangle with the dimensions shown below. The diameter dimensions are 2.50 and 4.75, respectively. The height dimension is 2.5.

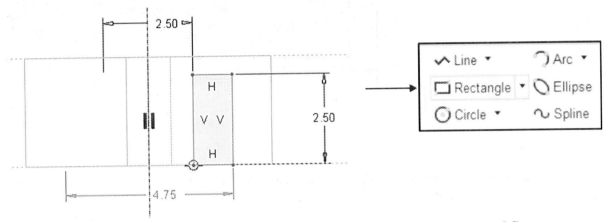

Upon completing this sketch, pick the icon of **OK**. Click the icon of **Apply and Save**.

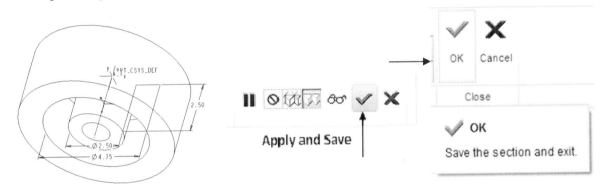

Feature 4: use **Revolve** to cut another ring-shape. Its size is shown below:

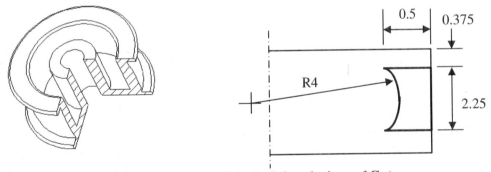

Click the icon of **Revolve** from the Model tab. Select the icon of **Cut**.

From the top menu, click **Sketch > References**. Pick the edge representing the cylindrical surface as a new reference to facilitate sketching.

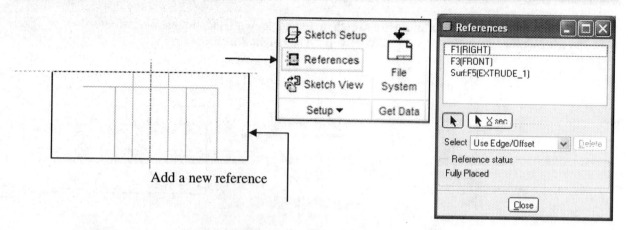

Add a new reference

Click the icon of **Centerline** to draw a vertical centerline along the z-axis. Pick this centerline and right-click to select **Axis of Revolution**.

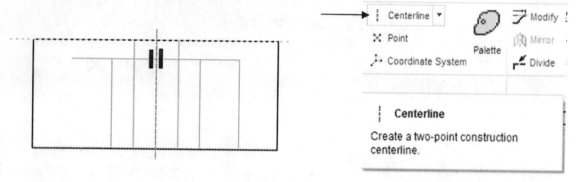

Click the icon of **Line** and make a U-shaped sketch. Modify the dimensions, as shown.

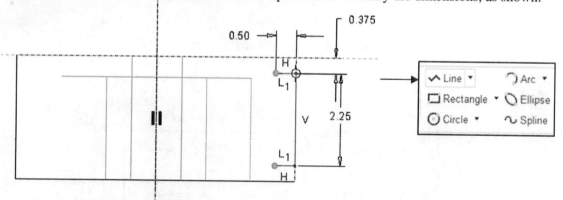

Click the icon of **Arc** to sketch an arc with the radius value equal to 4, as shown below.

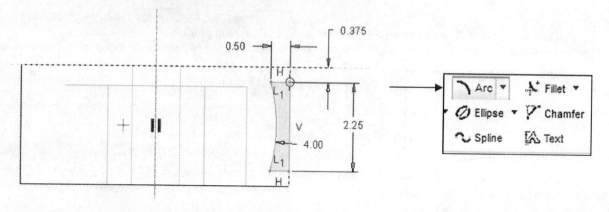

Upon completing this sketch, pick the icon of **OK.** Click the icon of **Apply and Save**.

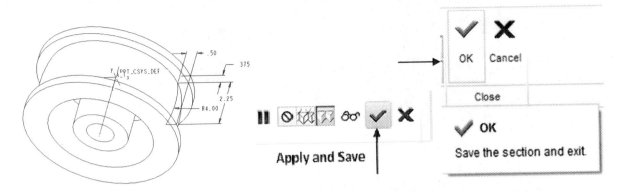

Feature 5: add roundness to the two edges (full round)
Click the icon of **Round** from the Model tab. While holding down the **Ctrl** key, pick 2 edges to form a pair. Click the icon of **Set > Full round.** Click the icon of **Apply and Save**.

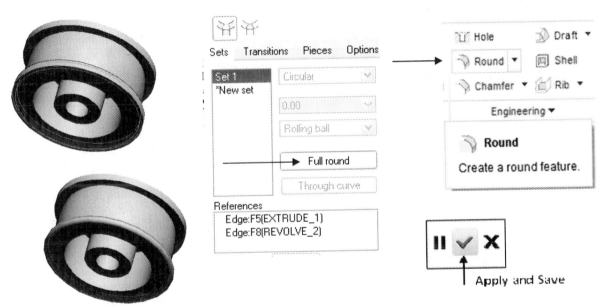

Repeat this process to create the second full round feature using the other 2 edges.
At this time the user has successfully completed the design of the belt wheel component, he or she should save all the work with the 3D solid model. Select **Save** from the **File** menu > **OK**.

Step 3: Create an engineering drawing with a half section view and an offset section view.
(1)   To prepare an engineering drawing based on the 3D solid model, we open a new file under the module of **Drawing**. First, we select the icon of **Create a new object** from the tool bar. Type *ex6_4* as the name of the file, as shown. Clear the box of **Use default template** and click the box of **OK**.

In the window of New Drawing, make sure that the file of the 3D solid model called *ex6_4* is shown. Otherwise, use "**Browse**" to locate it. Select **Empty** under Specify Template, and select the paper size to be **A**. Afterwards, click the button of **OK**.

This brings up the drawing screen. Click the **Layout** tab. Click the icon of **General.** In the **Select Combined State** window, click **OK** to accept **No Combined State**.

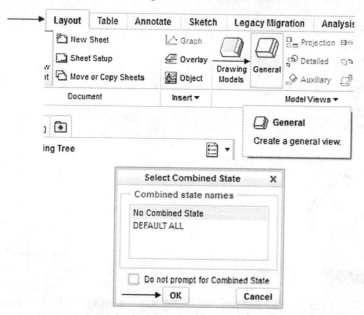

We first insert the front view. Just locate a position as the CENTER POINT of the front view. From the Drawing View Window, select **FRONT > Apply > Scale > Custom scale > 0.40 > Apply > Close.** The construction of the front view is completed.

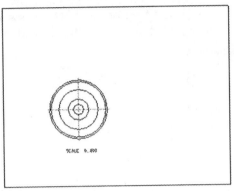

To insert the top view through projection, click the icon of **Projection**. Move the cursor to a location above the front view and click the left button of mouse, and the construction of the top view is completed.

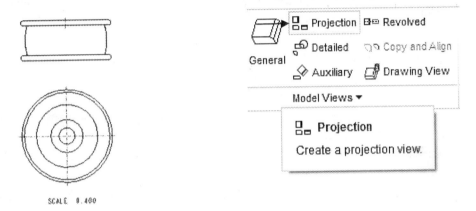

Now let us modify the top view to a half section view. Before sectioning, make sure the display of datum planes is enabled.

Now click the **TOP** view through a left click of mouse. Afterwards, right click and hold, select **Properties.**

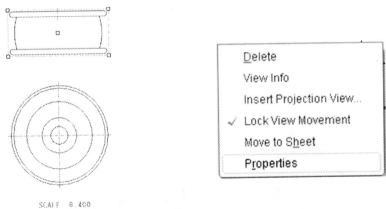

In the **Drawing View** window, select **Sections** and **2D cross-section.** Click the icon of **Add** (plus sign) to add cross-section. In the pop up window, accept **Planar** and **Single > Done**.

The software system is asking the user to enter a name for cross-section. Type *A* as the name for cross-section and press the **Enter** key. On the screen display, select the **TOP** datum plane from the Front View, as shown.

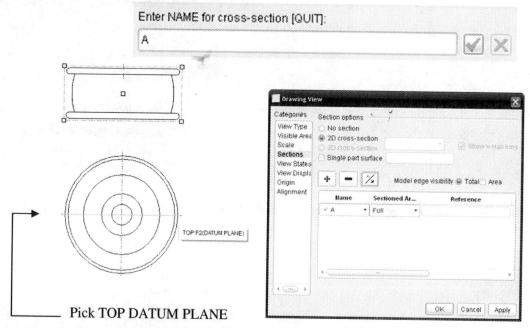

Pick TOP DATUM PLANE

In the drawing window, change **Full** to **Half**, as shown. Select RIGHT as the reference plane for the half section view > **Apply** > **Close**.

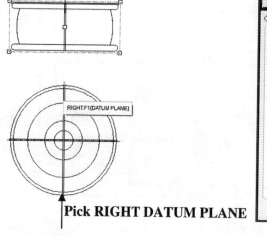

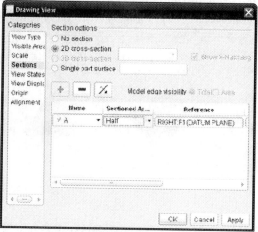

Pick RIGHT DATUM PLANE

To add an arrow indicating the direction of the cross-section view, activate **Arrow Display** from the **Drawing View** window > click the Front View > **Apply** and two arrows marked as A appear together with SECTION A-A > **Close**.

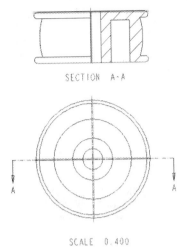

Select the icon of **General** to create a 3D view. Select a position at the middle and right portion as the CENTER POINT of the 3D view > left click of mouse > from the **Drawing View** window, select **Standard Orientation > Apply.** Click **Scale > Custom scale > 0.40 > Apply > Close**, the construction of the 3D view is completed.

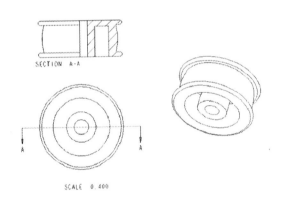

Now let us modify the 3D view with an offset section view.

First we need to create a set of cutting planes so that the offset section view can be created. This creation of a set of cutting planes must be done in the part mode. Therefore, let us go back to the part mode. From the top menu, click **Window** > select EX6_4.PRT.

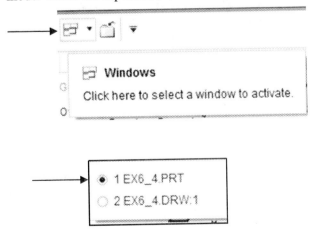

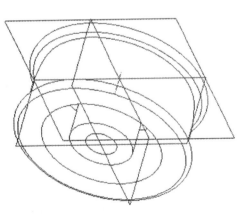

From the top menu, select **View > View Manager**. In the pop up View Manager window, **Xsec > New** > type *B* and press the **Enter** key > **Offset > Both Sides > Single > Done**.

In the **View Manager** window, click **Xsec** > New > type *B* and press **Enter** key. Select Offset > Both Sides > Single > Done.

Setup New > Plane > Pick the **FRONT** datum plane as the sketch plane > **Okay** to accept the feature creation direction > **Default** to accept the orientation of the sketch plane. Click Sketch View to orient the sketching plane parallel to the screen

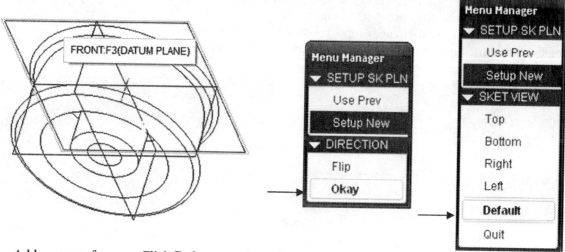

Add a new reference. Click **References** from the Sketch tab. Pick the outside circle as the new reference. Upon completion, click **Close**.

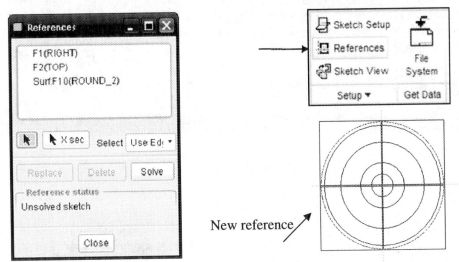

Click the icon of **Line** and drawing 2 lines, as shown. Upon completion, select the icon of **OK.** The created offset section planes are on display. Click **Close** to complete the creation of the 2 offset section planes.

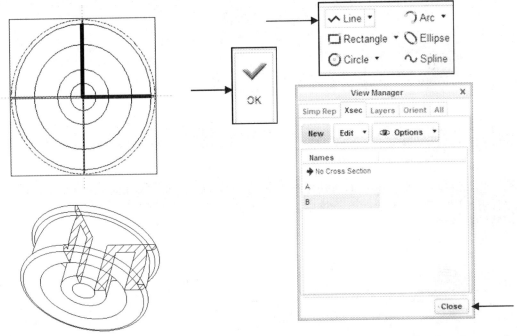

To create an offset section view in the engineering drawing, let us go back to the drawing mode. From the top menu, click **Window** > select EX6_4.DRW.

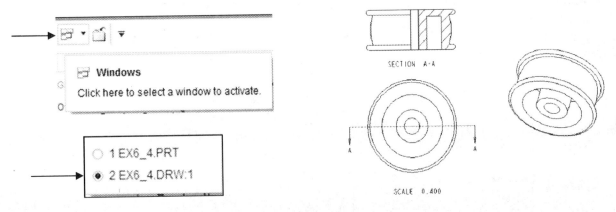

Now make a left-click to activate the 3D view. Right-click and hold to pick **Properties**. In the Drawing View window, click **Sections** > **2D cross-section** > click the plus sign or **Add** and pick *B* as the cutting planes > **Apply** > **Close**.

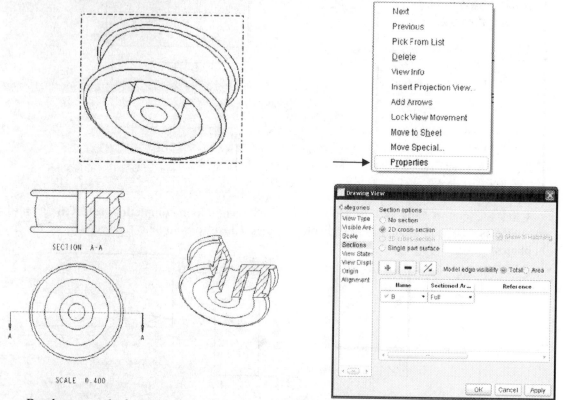

Readers are asked to add dimensions and centerlines to this engineering drawing, as shown at the beginning of this example.

At this time the user has successfully completed the engineering drawing of the designed belt wheel component, he or she should save all the work with the drawing. Select **Save** from the main toolbar > **OK**.

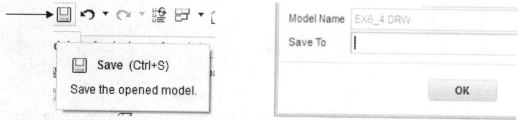

Example 6-5: Use Blend to construct a bridge base with straight edges.

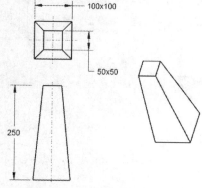

Step 1: Create a file for the 3D solid model.

From the **File** menu, click **New > Part.** Type *ex6_5* as the file name and clear the icon of **Use default template.** Select **mmns_part_solid** (units: Millimeter, Newton, Second) and type *student* in **MODELED_BY**, and *bridge base* in **DESCRIPTION**, then **OK.**

Note that there are 2 sections. Each of the 2 sections is a square. The dimensions of the 2 squares are 100x100, and 50x50, respectively. These 2 squares are separated by a distance. The value of this distance is 250 mm. To create a 3D solid model, we start with sketching the first square of 100x100, and the second square of 50x50, afterwards.

Step 2: From the Model tab, expand **Shapes** > click **Blend**. Click **Sections**

Section 1 is shown. Click **Define** to sketch the geometry.

From the display, pick **TOP** as the sketching plane. In the Sketch window, click **Sketch**.

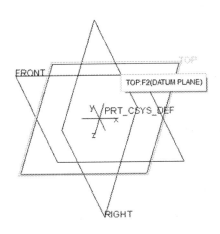
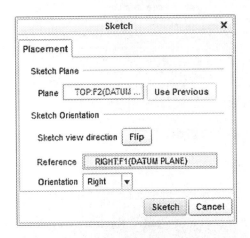

To orient the sketching plane parallel to the screen, click the icon of **Sketch View**.

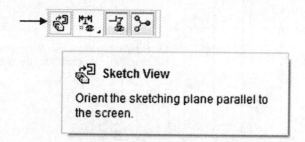

Sketch View

Orient the sketching plane parallel to the screen.

Select the icon of **Center Rectangle** to sketch a center rectangle, which starts at the origin of the default coordinate system. Modify the 2 dimensions to 100 and 100. Pay attention to the location of the arrow, which indicates the starting point. Click **OK** to complete the creation of Section 1.

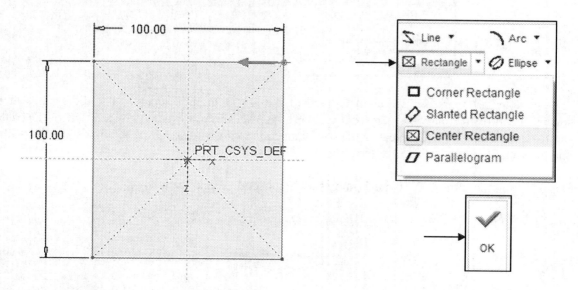

Click **Sections**. Section 2 is shown. Specify *250* as the offset value from Section 1. Click **Sketch** to define the geometry of Section 2.

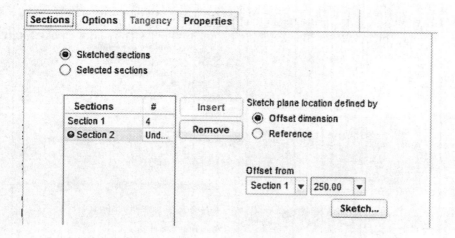

Select the icon of **Center Rectangle** to sketch a center rectangle, which starts at the origin of the default coordinate system. Modify the 2 dimensions to 50 and 50. Pay attention to the location of the arrow, which indicates the starting point of Section 2. This location should be the same as the location of the starting point of Section 1. Click **OK** to complete the creation of Section 2.

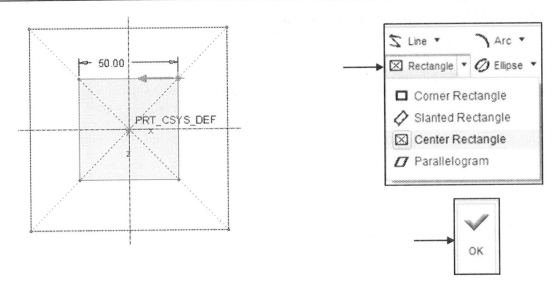

Upon completion of the 2 section sketches, click the icon of **OK**. Click the icon of **Apply and Save**.

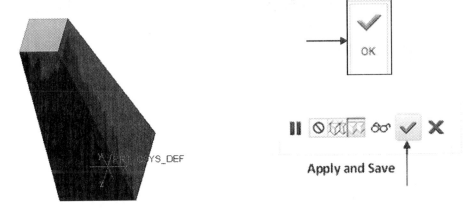

Step 3: Create a vertical axis for preparing the engineering drawing.

Pick the icon of **Datum Axis** from the Model tab. While holding down the **Ctrl** key, pick both the **FRONT** and **RIGHT** datum planes. An axis is created, and click **OK**.

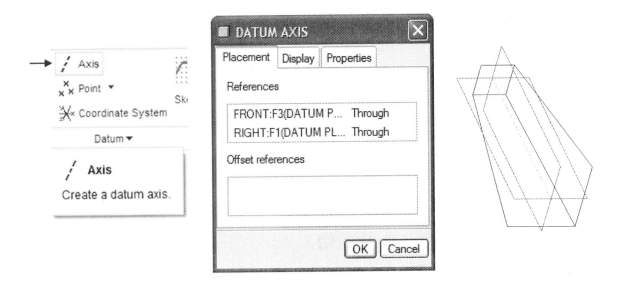

At this time the user has successfully completed the solid model of the designed component, he or she should save the solid model. Select **Save > OK**.

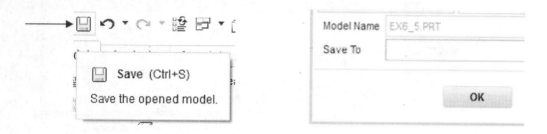

Step 4: Create an engineering drawing for the 3D model together with the drawing format.
From the **File** menu, click **New > Drawing.** Type *ex6_5*, clear the box of **Use default template**, and **OK**
Identify the file called ex6_5.*prt* in the **Default Model**, use **Empty**, select the **A** size and **OK**.

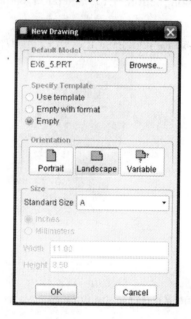

This brings up the drawing screen. Click the **Layout** tab. Click the icon of **General.** In the **Select Combined State** window, click **OK** to accept **No Combined State**.

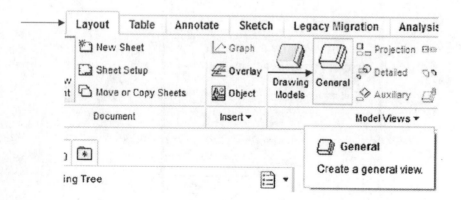

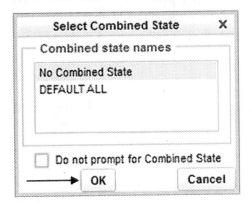

Select a location on the drawing screen as the center point for the **General View**. A general view appears on the screen.

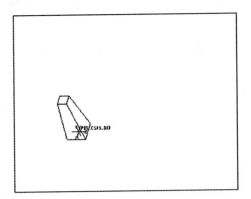

We first create the FRONT view. From the Drawing View Window, select **TOP > Apply > Close.** The construction of the front view is completed.

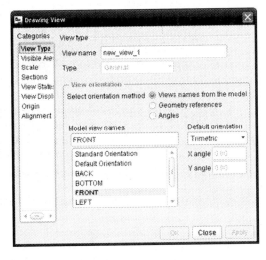

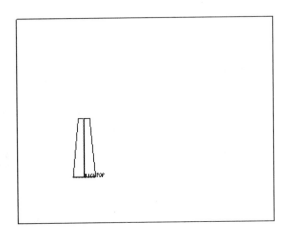

To insert the top view through projection, click the icon of **Projection**. Move the cursor to a location above the front view and click the left button of mouse, and the construction of the top view is completed.

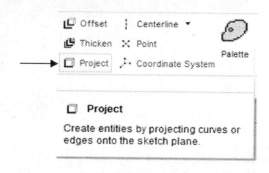

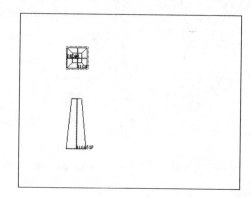

Click the icon of **General.** In the **Select Combined State** window, click **OK** to accept **No Combined State.** Select a position at the middle and right portion as the CENTER POINT of the 3D view > left click of mouse > from the **Drawing View** window, select **Standard Orientation > Apply > Close,** the construction of the 3D view is completed.

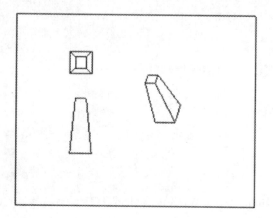

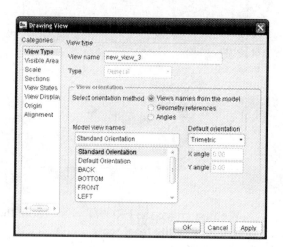

Upon completing the layout, we start adding dimensions. Click the **Annotate** tab.Click Show Model Annotation.

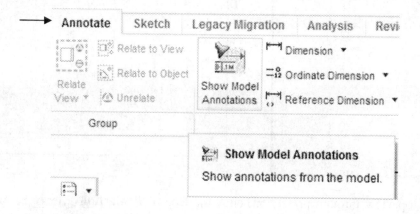

Select the icon of **Dimensions.** From the model tree, click Protrusion id 40. Three dimensions of 50, 100 and 250 associated with the protrusion feature are shown. Click the box of **Accept All > Apply.**

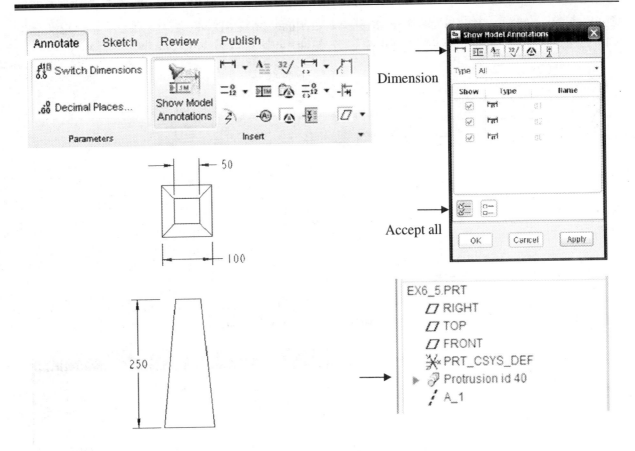

To add centerlines, select the box of centerlines. Click A-1 listed in the model tree. A set of centerlines are on display > click the box of **Accept All > OK.**

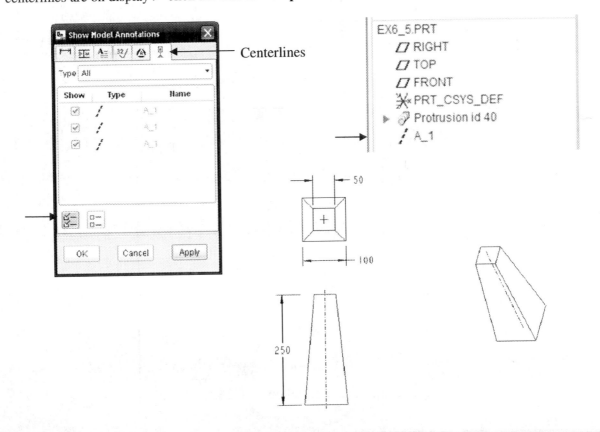

In general, there is no need to display centerlines on a 3D view. To delete the displayed centerline on the 3D view, click the centerline first. Afterwards, click **Delete** from the Annotation menu.

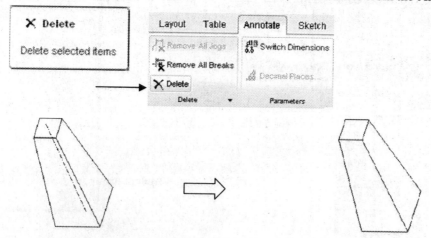

To insert the drawing format, from the Layout tab, click **Sheet Setup >** Using **Browse** to locate the format file, which is *exercise_format* > **Open** > select **Show format** > **OK.**

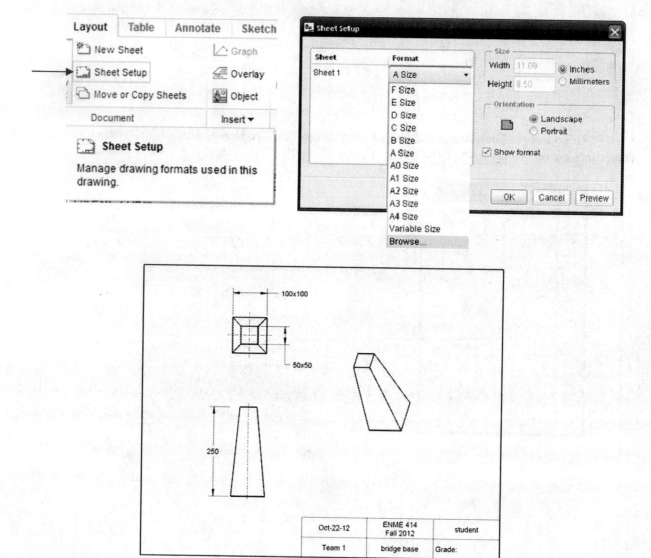

At this time the user has successfully completed the engineering drawing of the designed component, he or she should save the drawing. Select **Save** from the **File** menu > **OK**.

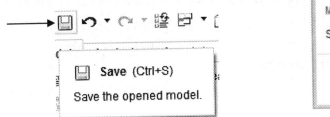 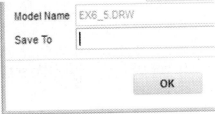

Example 6-6: **Use Blend to construct a bridge base with curved edges and add 2 revolved section views**

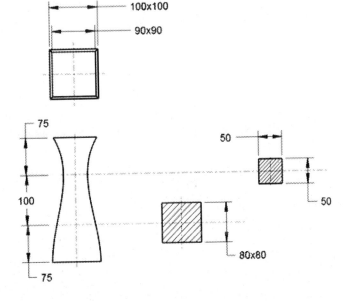

Step 1: Create a file for the 3D solid model.

From the **File** menu, click **New > Part**. Type *ex6_6* as the file name and clear the icon of **Use default template.** Select **mmns_part_solid** (units: Millimeter, Newton, Second) and type *Student* in **MODELED_BY**, and *curved base* in **DESCRIPTION**, then **OK.**

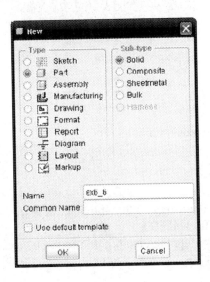 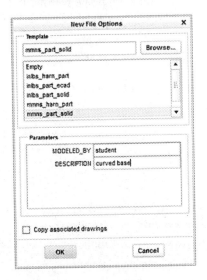

Note that there are 4 sections. Each of the 4 sections is a square. The dimensions of the 4 squares are 100x100, 80x80, 50x50 and 90x90, respectively. These 4 squares are separated by 3 distances. These 3 distances are 70 mm, 100 mm and 75 mm, respectively. To create a 3D solid model, we start with sketching the first square of 100x100, the second square of 80x80, the third square of 50x50, and the fourth square of 90x90.

Step 2: From the **Model** tab, expand **Shapes** > click **Blend**. Click **Sections**.

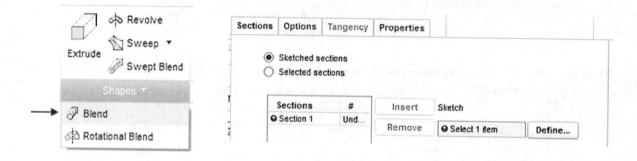

Section 1 is shown. Click **Define** to sketch the geometry.
From the display, pick **TOP** as the sketching plane. In the Sketch window, click **Sketch**.

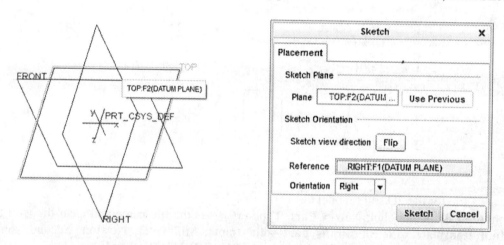

To orient the sketching plane parallel to the screen, click the icon of **Sketch View**.

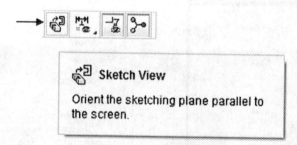

Select the icon of **Center Rectangle** to sketch a center rectangle, which starts at the origin of the default coordinate system. Modify the 2 dimensions to 100 and 100. Pay attention to the location of the arrow, which indicates the starting point. Click **OK** to complete the creation of Section 1.

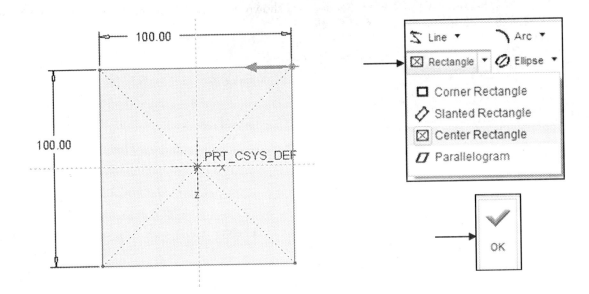

Click **Sections**. Section 2 is shown. Specify *75* as the offset value from Section 1. Click **Sketch** to define the geometry of Section 2.

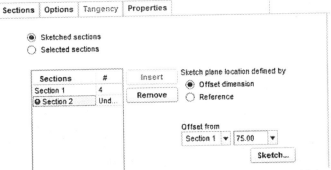

Select the icon of **Center Rectangle** to sketch a center rectangle, which starts at the origin of the default coordinate system. Modify the 2 dimensions to 80 and 80. Pay attention to the location of the arrow, which indicates the starting point of Section 2. This location should be the same as the location of the starting point of Section 1. Click **OK** to complete the creation of Section 2.

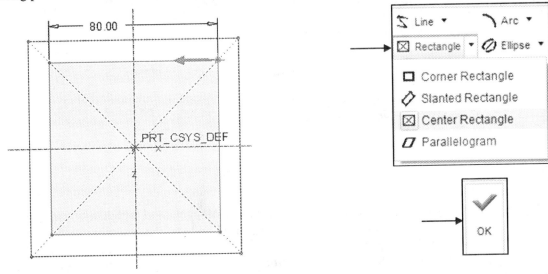

Click **Sections**. Click **Insert**. Section 3 is shown. Specify *100* as the offset value from Section 2. Click **Sketch** to define the geometry of Section 3.

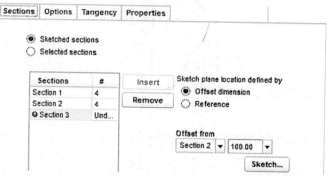

Select the icon of **Center Rectangle** to sketch a center rectangle, which starts at the origin of the default coordinate system. Modify the 2 dimensions to 50 and 50. Pay attention to the location of the arrow, which indicates the starting point of Section 3. This location should be the same as the location of the starting point of Section 1 and Section 2. Click **OK** to complete the creation of Section 3.

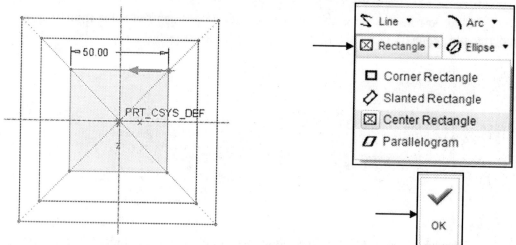

Click **Sections**. Click **Insert**. Section 4 is shown. Specify *75* as the offset value from Section 3. Click **Sketch** to define the geometry of Section 4.

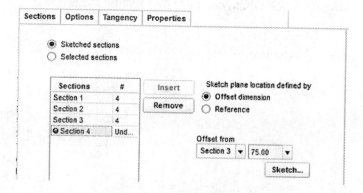

Select the icon of **Center Rectangle** to sketch a center rectangle, which starts at the origin of the default coordinate system. Modify the 2 dimensions to 90 and 90. Pay attention to the location of the arrow, which indicates the starting point of Section 4. This location should be the same as the location of the starting point of Section 1, Section 2 and Section 3. Click **OK** to complete the creation of Section 4.

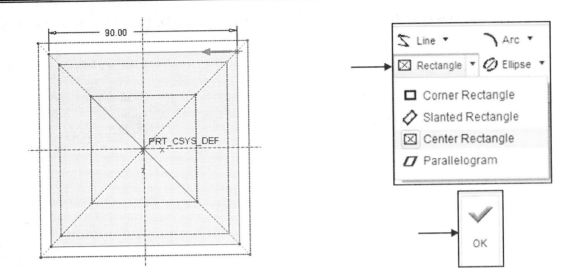

Upon completion of the 3 section sketches, click the icon of **OK**. Click the icon of **Apply and Save**.

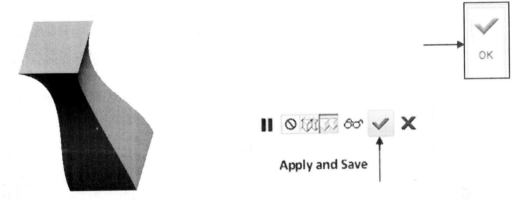

Apply and Save

Step 3: Create a vertical axis and two (2) datum planes for preparing the engineering drawing.
Pick the icon of **Datum Axis** from the Model tab. While holding down the **Ctrl** key, pick both the **FRONT** and **RIGHT** datum planes. An axis is created, and click **OK**.

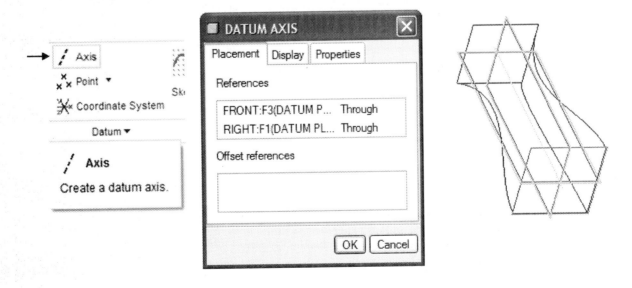

Pick the icon of **Datum Plane** from the **Model** tab. Click **TOP** from the model tree and specify 75 as the offset value. Click **OK**. **DTM** 1 is created.

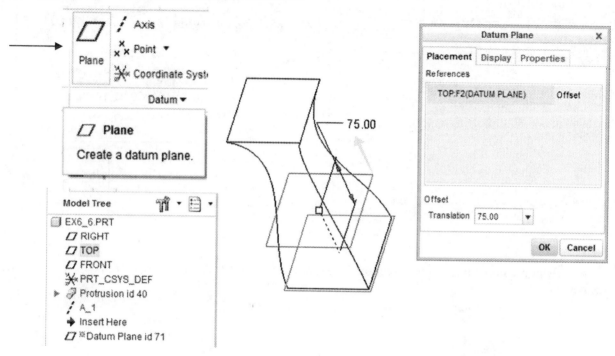

Pick the icon of **Datum Plane** from the **Model** tab. Click **TOP** from the model tree and specify 175 as the offset value. Click **OK**. **DTM2** is created.

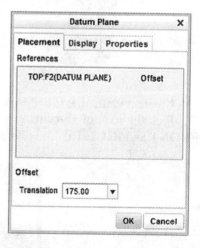

At this time the user has successfully completed the solid model of the designed component, he or she should save the solid model. Select **Save** from the main toolbar > **OK**.

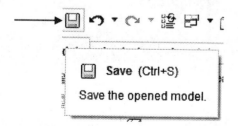
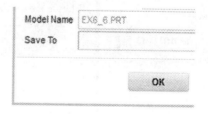

Step 4: Create an engineering drawing for the 3D model together with the drawing format.
From the **File** menu, click **New >Drawing.** Type *ex6_6*, clear the box of **Use default template**, and **OK**
Identify the file called ex6_6.*prt* in the **Default Model**, use **Empty**, select the **A** size and **OK**.

This brings up the drawing screen. Click the **Layout** tab. Click the icon of **General.** In the **Select Combined State** window, click **OK** to accept **No Combined State**.

Select a location on the drawing screen as the center point for the **General View**. A general view appears on the screen.

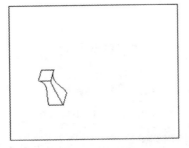

Select CENTER POINT for drawing view.

We first create the **FRONT** view. From the Drawing View Window, select **TOP > Apply > Close.** The construction of the front view is completed.

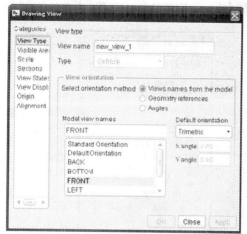
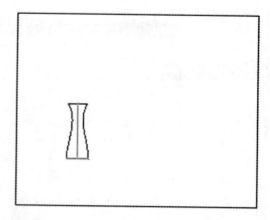

To insert the top view through projection, click the icon of **Projection.** Move the cursor to a location above the front view and click the left button of mouse, and the construction of the top view is completed.

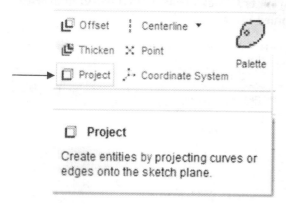
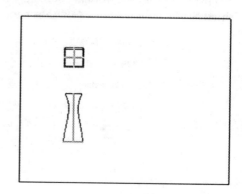

To insert a revolved section view for the lower section (80x80), click **Revolved** from the **Layout** tab.

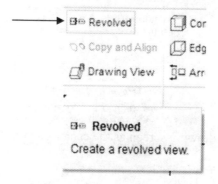

Click the **FRONT** view as the parent view for the revolved view to be created.
Locate a position for the revolved view.
Planar > Single > Done.
Type *A* as the name as the cross-section, and press **Enter.**
Select **DTM1** as the cross section plane > select the **FRONT** datum plane as the symmetry axis > **Apply > Close.**

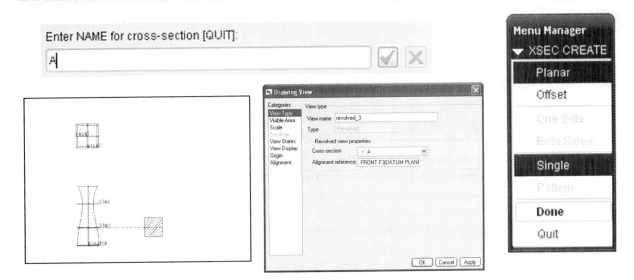

Follow the same procedure to insert another revolved section view for the upper section (50x50). In the Drawing View window, select **Create New**, instead of A, in Cross-section.

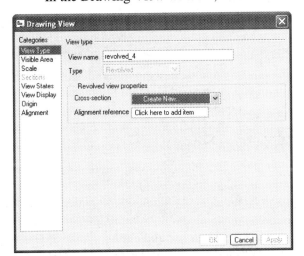
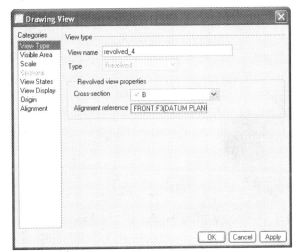

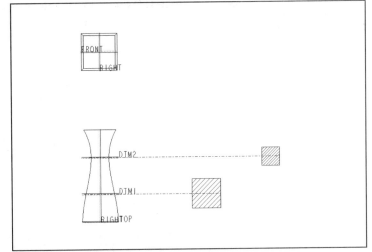

Users may add a 3D view and add the required dimensions and centerlines.

At this time the user has successfully completed the engineering drawing of the designed component, he or she should save the drawing. Select **Save** from the main toolbar > **OK**.

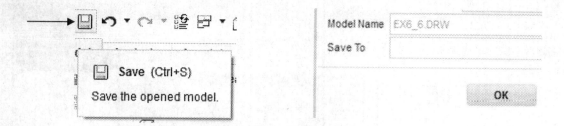

Save (Ctrl+S)
Save the opened model.

Model Name EX6_6.DRW

Save To

OK

Example 6-7:   Use Blend to create a 3D solid model for a diamond.

We assume that a diamond component consists of 3 parallel planes with 3 hexagons. As shown in the above drawing, the dimensions of the 3 hexagons are 1.5, 10 and 2.5 mm, respectively.   The 2 distances between the 2 neighboring planes are 10 and 5 mm, respectively. The sharp edges and corners on the middle plane are removed to demonstrate the beauty of the diamond component.

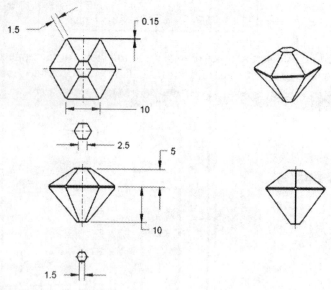

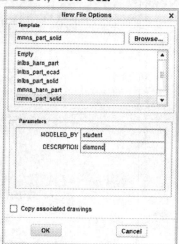

Step 1: Create a file for the 3D solid model.

From the **File** menu, click **New > Part.** Type *ex6_7* as the file name and clear the icon of **Use default template.** Select **mmns_part_solid** (units: Millimeter, Newton, Second) and type *Student* in **MODELED_BY**, and *Diamond* in **DESCRIPTION**, then **OK.**

Note that there are 3 sections. In section 1, we sketch a hexagon and the side dimension equal to 1.5 mm. In section 2, we sketch a hexagon and the side dimension equal to 10 mm. In section 3, we sketch a hexagon and the side dimension equal to 2.5 mm. These 3 sections are parallel to each other.

The distance between the first and second sections is 10 mm and the distance between the second and third sections is 5 mm.

Step 2: From the Model tab, expand **Shapes** > **Blend.** Click **Sections**.

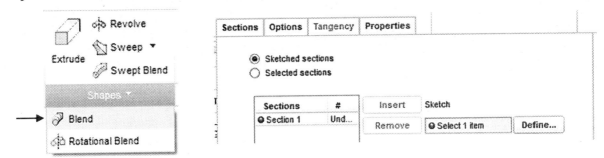

Section 1 is shown. Click **Define** to sketch the geometry.

From the display, pick **TOP** as the sketching plane. In the Sketch window, click **Sketch**.

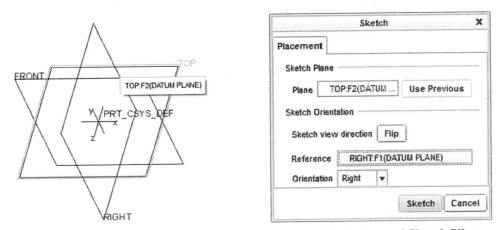

To orient the sketching plane parallel to the screen, click the icon of **Sketch View**.

Click the icon of **Palette** > **Polygons** > double-click **Hexagon**. Move the cursor to the intersection point of the 2 axes or the origin of the default coordinate system and make a left click to place a hexagon, as shown.

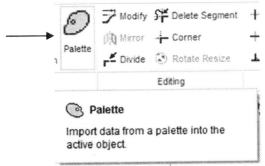

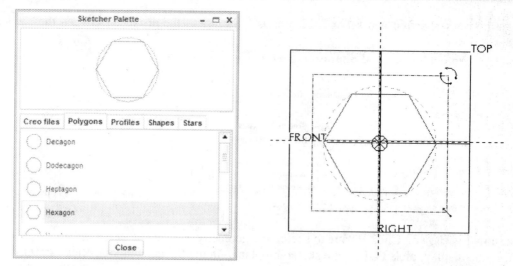

Change the value of the scaling factor to 1.5 or modify the dimension to 1.5. Click **OK**.

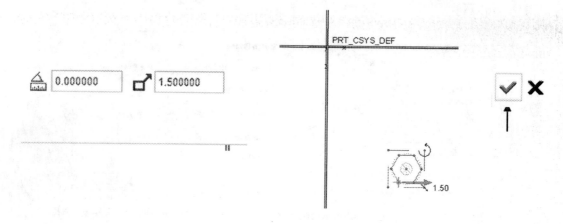

It is always the case that the center of the imported hexagon is not located at the intersection point or the origin of the default coordinate system. We need to add 2 Coincident constraints to reposition the center of the hexagon to the intersection point. Click the icon of **Coincident.** Click the center of the hexagon and the vertical axis for the alignment. Click the center of the hexagon and the horizontal axis for the alignment. It is important to note the starting point with an arrow mark. Click **OK** to complete the creation of Section 1.

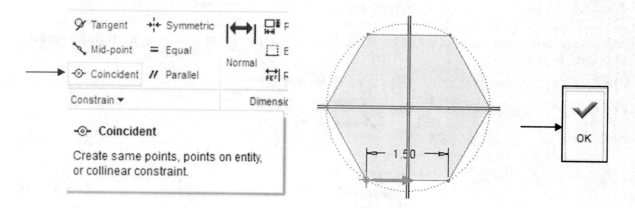

Click **Sections**. Section 2 is shown. Specify 10 as the offset value from Section 1. Click **Sketch** to define the geometry of Section 2.

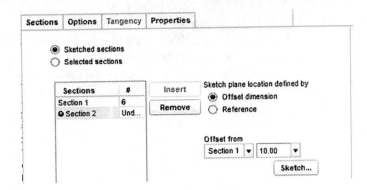

Click the icon of **Palette > Polygons >** double-click **Hexagon**. Move the cursor to the intersection point of the 2 axes or the origin of the default coordinate system and make a left click to place a hexagon, as shown.

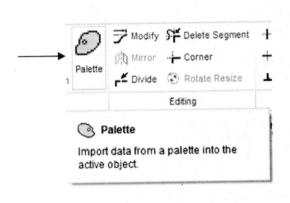

In the **Scale Rotate** window, change the scale to 10 > click the check mark or **OK** and close the **Sketcher Palette** window.

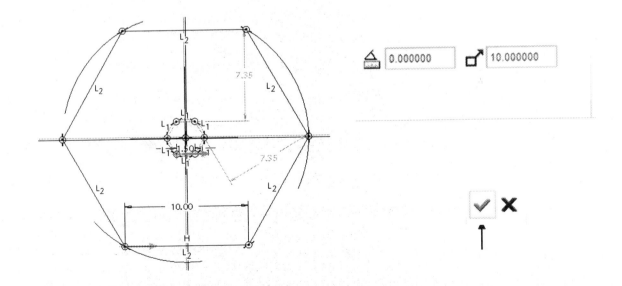

We still need to add 2 Coincident constraints to reposition the center of the hexagon to the intersection point. Click the icon of **Coincident**. Click the center of the hexagon and the vertical axis for the alignment. Click the center of the hexagon and the horizontal axis for the alignment. It is important to note the starting point with an arrow mark. Click **OK** to complete the creation of Section 2.

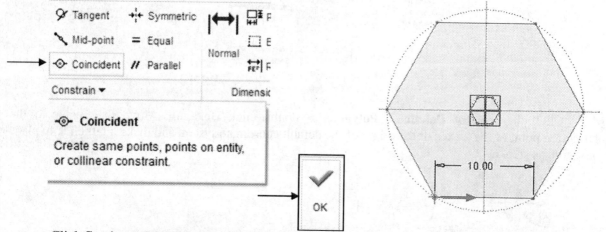

Click **Sections**. Click **Insert** and Section 2 is shown. Specify 5 as the offset value from Section 2. Click **Sketch** to define the geometry of Section 3.

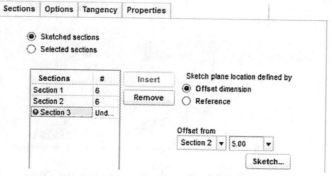

Click the icon of **Palette > Polygons >** double-click **Hexagon**. Move the cursor to the intersection point of the 2 axes or the origin of the default coordinate system and make a left click to place a hexagon, as shown.

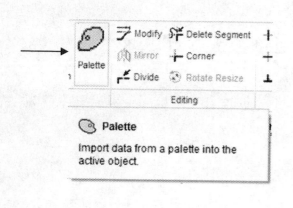

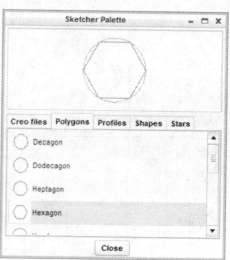

In the **Scale Rotate** window, change the scale to 2.5 > click the check mark or **OK** and close the **Sketcher Palette** window.

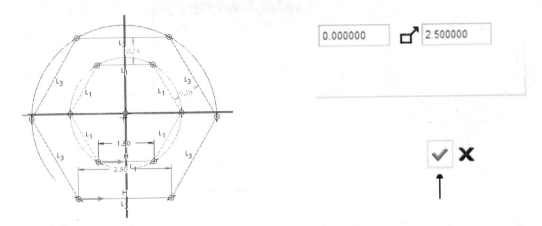

We still need to add 2 Coincident constraints to reposition the center of the hexagon to the intersection point. Click the icon of **Coincident**. Click the center of the hexagon and the vertical axis for the alignment. Click the center of the hexagon and the horizontal axis for the alignment. It is important to note the starting point with an arrow mark. Click **OK** to complete the creation of Section 3.

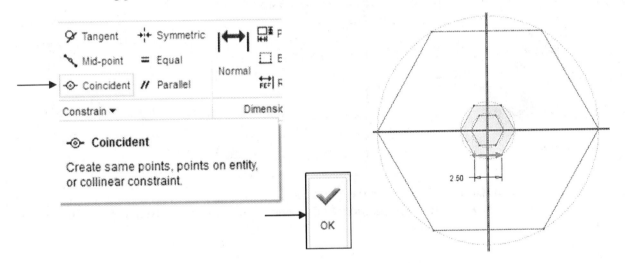

Upon completing the 3 section sketches, select the icon of **OK.** Click the icon of **Apply** and **Save**.

Step 3: Create a datum axis and a datum plane
        Pick the icon of **Datum Axis**. While holding down the **Ctrl** key, pick the Right datum plane and the Front datum plane > **OK**.

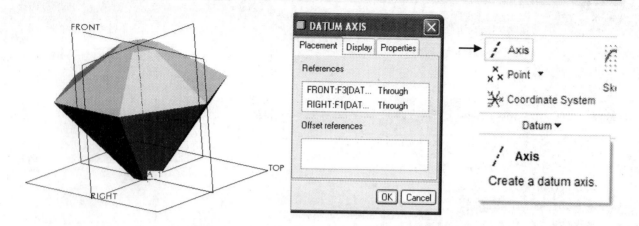

Pick the icon of **Datum Plane** from the Model tab. Select the **TOP** datum plane, change to Parallel. While holding down the **Ctrl** key, pick the vertex, as shown > **OK**.

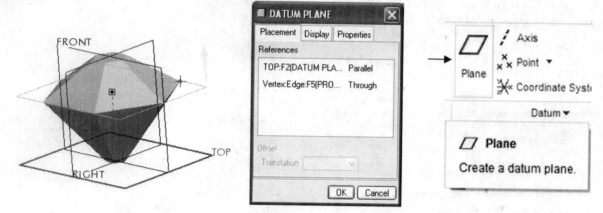

Step 4: Create a small flat surface at each of the 6 vertices.

Pick the icon of **Extrude** from the Model tab. Select **Cut** and choose **Symmetry** as the depth choice > specify 2 as the depth value.

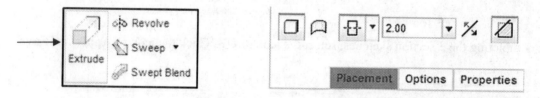

From the model tree, click **DTM1** (sketching plane). Click the icon of **Sketch View** to orient the sketching plane parallel to the screen.

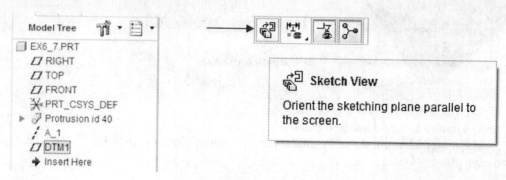

Click the icon of **References** from the Sketch tab. Pick 2 edges as 2 new references > **Close**.

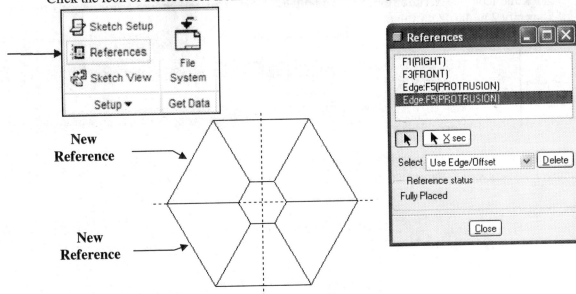

Pick the icon of **Line** and sketch a triangle along the 2 newly added references. Only one dimension is needed and set its value to 1.5. Click the icon of **OK**, and click the icon of **Apply and Save**.

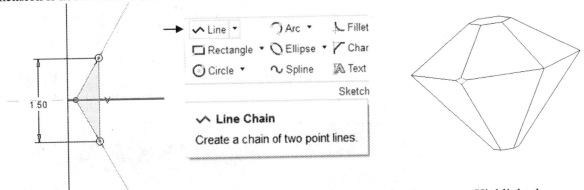

Now let us apply **"Pattern"** to obtain the other 5 flats at the other 5 corners. Highlight the group feature just created in the model tree > right-click, hold and select **Pattern**.

Select **Axis** as the pattern operation > pick A-1 as the axis to be used for the pattern operation > set the number value to 6 and the incremental angle to 60 (degrees) > click the icon of **Apply and Save**.

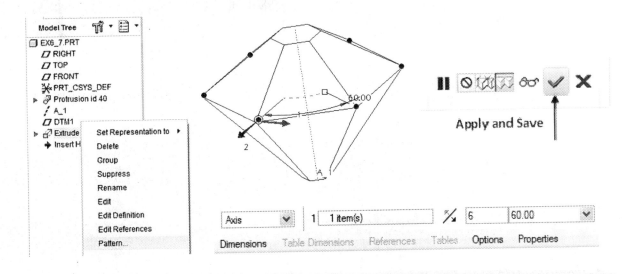

Step 5: Create a small flat surface along each of the 6 edges.

Pick the icon of **Extrude** from the **Model** tab. Select **Cut** and choose **Symmetry** as the depth choice > specify 2 as the depth value.

From the model tree, click **DTM1** (sketching plane). Click the icon of **Sketch View** to orient the sketching plane parallel to the screen.

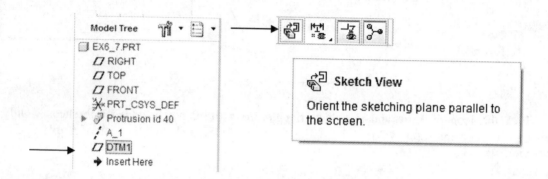

Before making a sketch, click the icon of **References** from the Sketch tab. Pick 2 edges as 2 new references > **Close**.

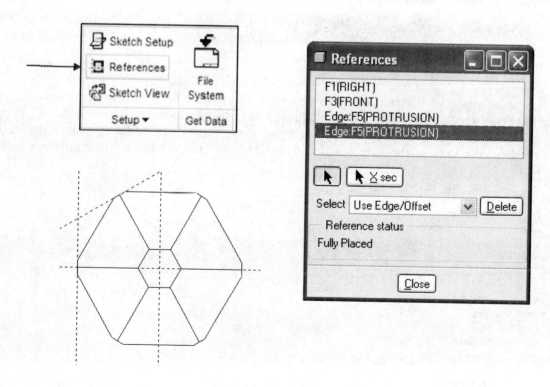

Pick the icon of **Projection** to define one line and pick the icon of **Line** to sketch a parallel line. The distance is 0.15. Add 2 small lines to close the sketch.

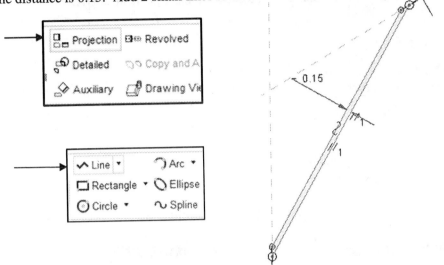

Upon completing the sketch, click **OK.** Click the icon of **Apply and Save.**

Now let us apply **"Pattern"** to obtain the other 5 flats along the other 5 edges. Highlight the cut feature just created in the model tree > right-click, hold and select **Pattern**.

Select **Axis** as the pattern operation > pick A-1 as the axis to be used for the pattern operation > set the number value to 6 and the incremental angle to 60 (degrees) > click the icon of **Done.**

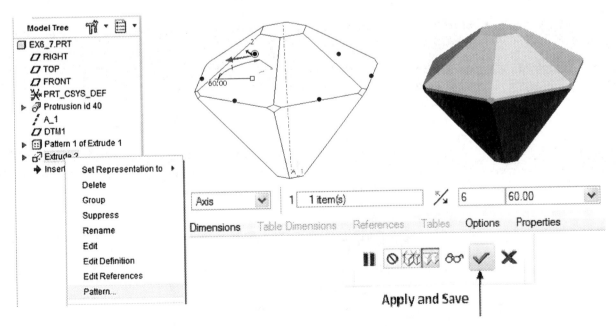

At this time the user has successfully completed the solid model of the designed diamond component, he or she should save the solid model. Select **Save** from the **File** menu > **OK**.

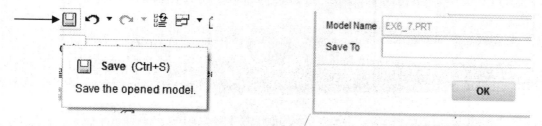

Step 6: Prepare an engineering drawing for the diamond.
From the **File** menu, click **New** > **Drawing.** Type *ex6_7*, clear the box of **Use default template**, and **OK**
Identify the file called ex6_7.*prt* in the **Default Model**, use **Empty**, select the **A** size and **OK**.

Click the **Layout** tab. Click the icon of **General.** In the **Select Combined State** window, click **OK** to accept **No Combined State**.

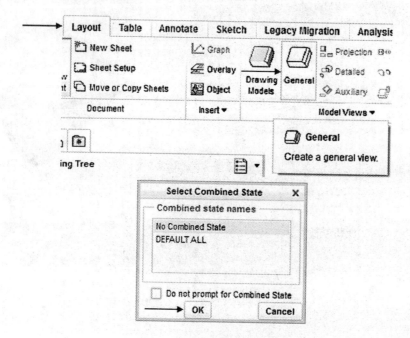

Select a location on the drawing screen as the center point for the **General View**. A general view appears on the screen. From the Drawing View Window, select **TOP > Apply > Close.** The construction of the front view is completed.

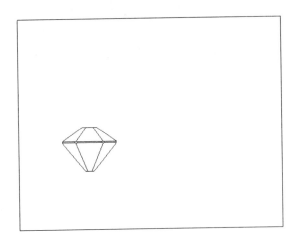

To insert the top view through projection, click the icon of **Projection**. Move the cursor to a location above the front view and click the left button of mouse, and the construction of the top view is completed.

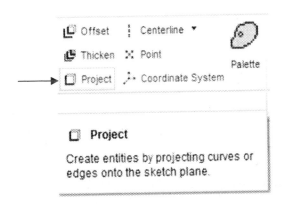

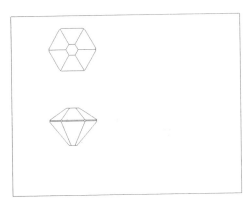

To insert an auxiliary view, from the **Layout,** select **Auxiliary**. Pick the bottom surface and move the cursor downward to obtain a projection, as shown.

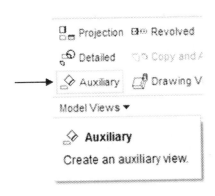

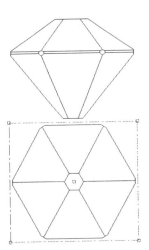

Right-click and hold > **Properties**. In the window of **Drawing View**, click **Visible Area**.

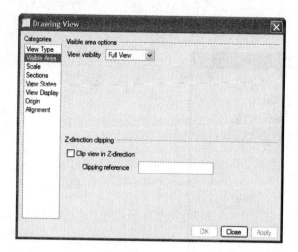

In the lower part marked as Z-direction clipping, click the box to activate this function. On the projection, click the middle location of the smallest hexagon.   A message is on display, indicating that the geometry behind the selection point will be hidden. Click **OK**.

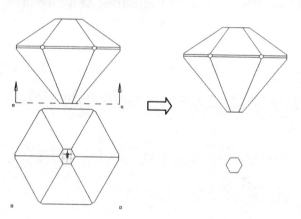

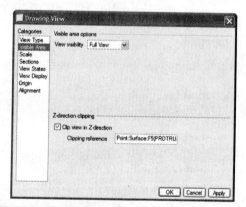

⚠ Geometry behind the selected point will be hidden.

Repeat the above procedure to create another auxiliary view to show the hexagon on the top surface.

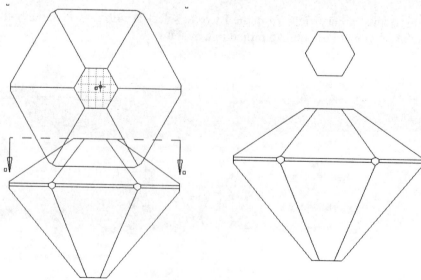

Add dimensions, centerlines and the required format to the drawing.

At this time the user has successfully completed the engineering drawing of the designed component, he or she should save the drawing. Select **Save** from the main toolbar > **OK**.

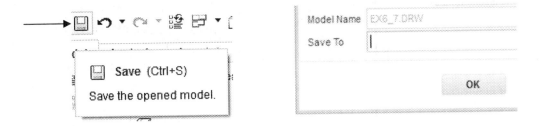

6.4 Creation of Spring and Thread Component Using Sweep

Mechanical components, such as the spring component shown below, are manufactured by the use of steel bars with small diameters or steel wires in general. Those components share a common characteristic, namely, their cross section areas are identical. Under the Creo Parametric design environment, a built-in function called **SWEEP** is used to create features that have identical cross sections.

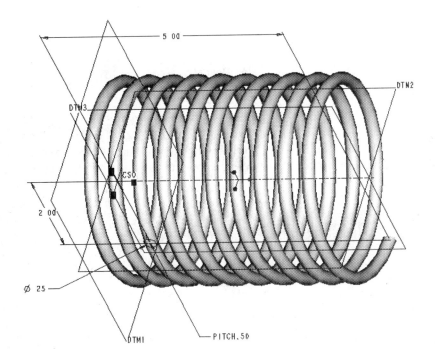

Example 6-11: Use the Inch System to create a cylindrical spring using Helical Sweep.

We first create a helical trajectory with pitch 0.5 inch, and then create a circular cross section with diameter equal to 0.25 inch.

Step 1: We establish a file: *cylindrical_spring.prt, and define the sketch plane*

From the **File** menu, click **New > Part**. Type *cylindrical_spring* as the file name and clear the box of **Use default template**. Select **inlbs_part_solid** (units: inch, lb, second) and type Cylindrical Spring in **DESCRIPTION**, and student in **MODELED_BY**, then **OK**.

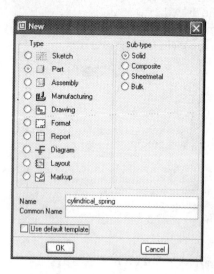
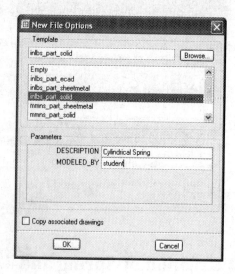

From the Model tab, select **Helical Sweep**.

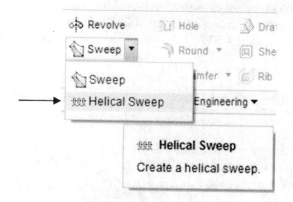

Click **References** > **Define**. Click **FRONT** (sketching plane) > **Sketch** to accept the default setting for orientation. Click the icon of Sketch View to orient the sketching plane parallel to the screen.

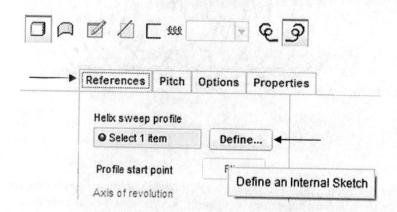

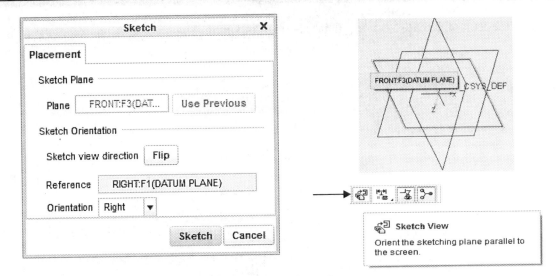

Step 2: Create a centerline for the helical sweep
   Right click and pick Axis of Revolution. Sketch a horizontal centerline along the X-axis.

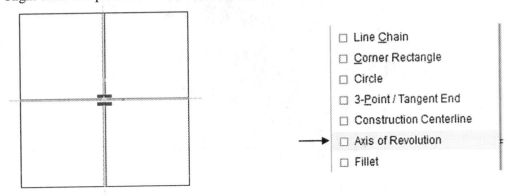

Step 3: Sketch the trajectory and the cross section
   Click the icon of **Line** and sketch a line with the dimensions shown below:

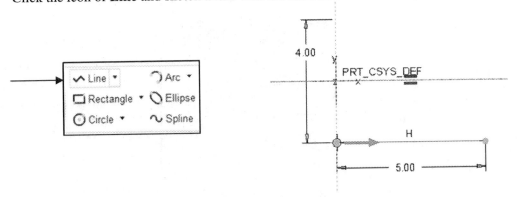

Upon completion, select the icon of **OK**. Specify the pitch value: 0.5, and select Right Hand.

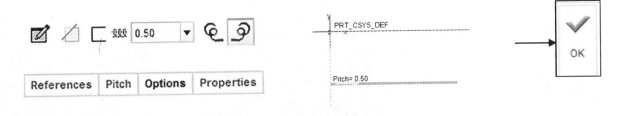

Click the icon of **Create Section**. Click the icon of Circle. Upon completion, select the icon of **OK**.

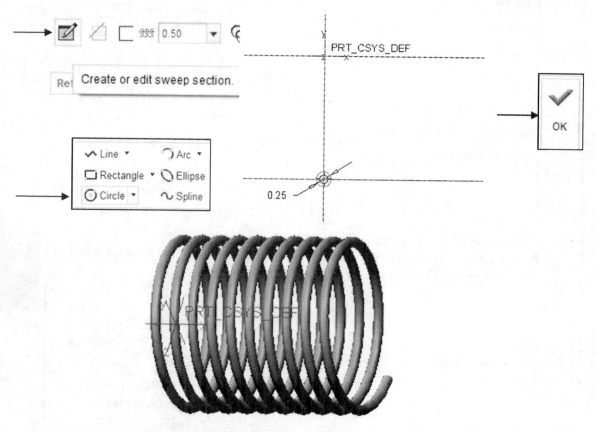

Step 4: Create a datum axis for preparing an engineering drawing.

Pick the icon of Datum axis > while holding down the **Ctrl** key, pick the **FRONT** and **TOP** datum planes and a datum axis is created > **OK**.

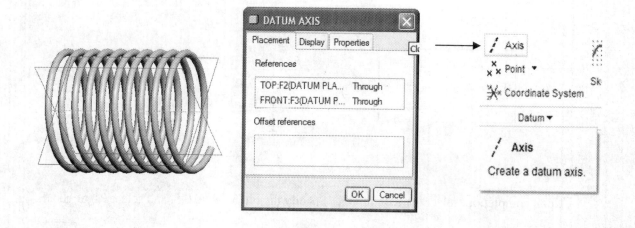

Step 5: Create an engineering drawing with the required drawing format.

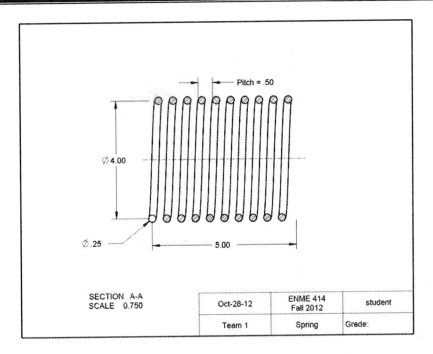

Example 6-8: Use the mm-unit System to create a 3D solid model of a thread component shown in Figure 6-4 and prepare an engineering drawing with a detailed view.

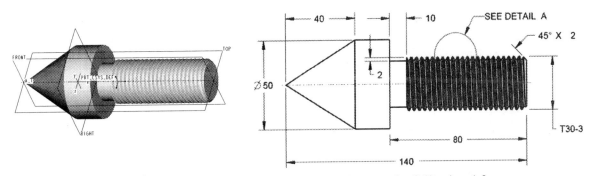

Based on the feature-based modeling approach, we will create the following 4 features:
Feature 1: the cylindrical stepped bar (revolve).

Feature 2: Add a chamfer at the right end. The dimension is 45°x2.

Feature 3: Add a slot for the cutting tool retreat, The two dimensions of the slot: 10 and 2 mm.

*Feature 4: create the thread part. Use **Helical Sweep** and the pitch value is 3 mm.*

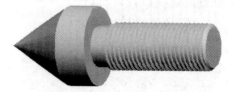

Create a file for the 3D solid model and set up the mm-unit system.

From the **File** menu, click **New > Part**. Type *ex6_8* as the file name and clear the icon of **Use default template** because of setting the mm-unit system > **OK.** In the window of **New File Options**, Select **mmns_part_solid** (units: Millimeter, Newton, Second) and type in *EX 6_8* in **DESCRIPTION**, and *student* in **MODELED_BY**, then **OK**

Create a 3D solid model and start with Feature 1, using **Revolve**

Select **Revolve** from the Model tab. In the model tree, highlight **FRONT** (sketching plane). Click the icon of Sketch View to orient the sketching plane parallel to the screen.

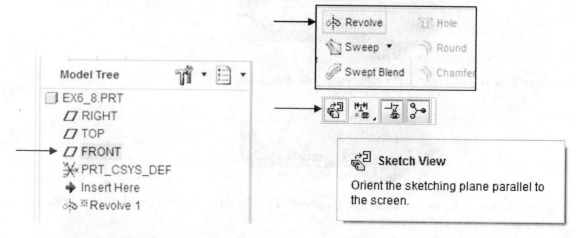

Right click and pick **Axis of Revolution**. Sketch a horizontal centerline.

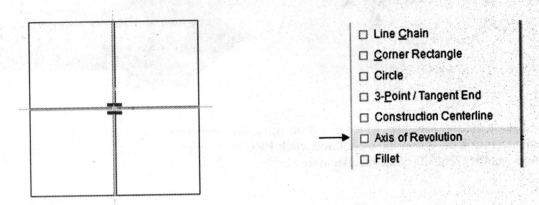

Select the icon of **Line** to make a 2D sketch as shown below. Make sure that the sketch is a closed one. This means that the starting point meets the ending points at the end of the sketch process.

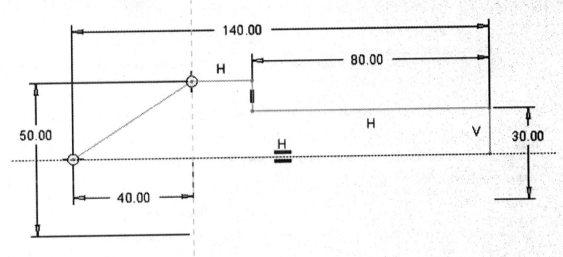

Upon completing this sketch, click the icon of **OK**. Click the icon of Apply and Save.

Create the second feature: chamfers at the sharp edges. Click the icon of **Edge Chamfers**, specify 45xD and 2 as the size of the chamfer. Click the icon of **Apply and Save**.

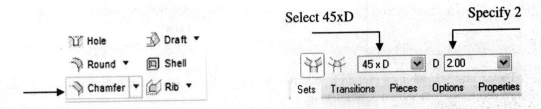

Apply and Save

Create the third feature, which is a slot, using **Revolve** with **Cut**. Click the icon of **Revolve**. Select the icon of **Cut**. From the model tree, click **FRONT** (sketching plane). Click the icon of Sketch View to orient the sketching plane parallel to the screen.

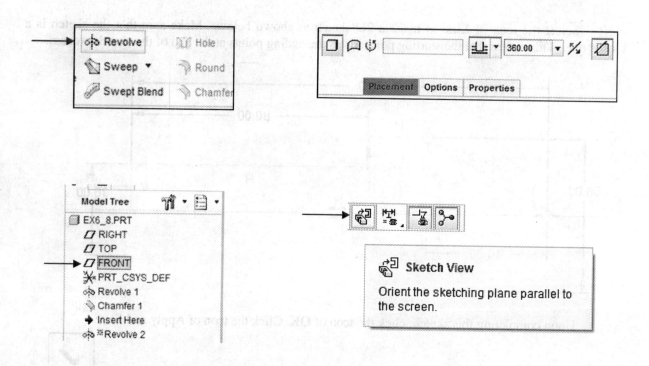

Sketch View

Orient the sketching plane parallel to the screen.

Right click and pick Axis of Revolution. Sketch a horizontal centerline along the X-axis.

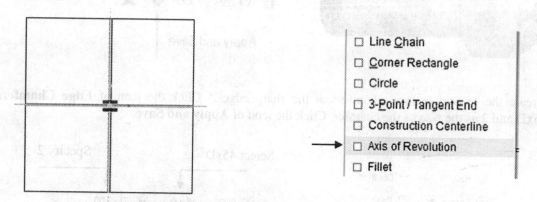

☐ Line Chain
☐ Corner Rectangle
☐ Circle
☐ 3-Point / Tangent End
☐ Construction Centerline
☐ Axis of Revolution
☐ Fillet

To facilitate sketching a rectangle, add two new references. Click **References** from the Sketch tab. Pick 2 new references, as shown. Click **Close**.

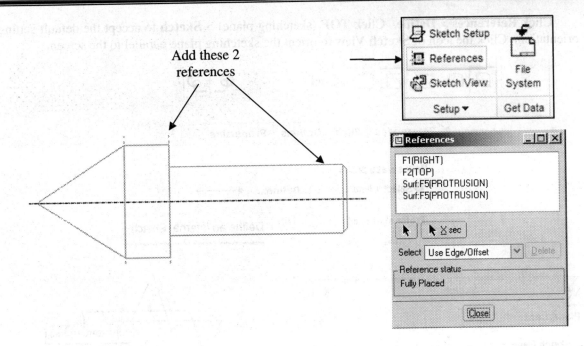

Click the icon of Rectangle, and sketch a rectangle with the 2 dimensions equal to 2 and 10, respectively.

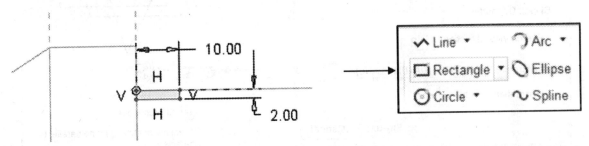

Click the icon of **OK.** Click the icon of **Apply and Save** to complete the creation of the cylindrical feature, as shown below:

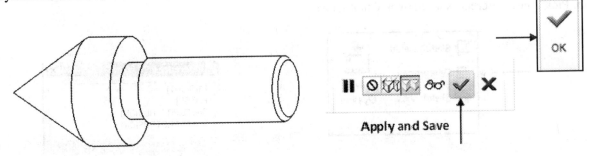

Create the thread feature using Helical Sweep. Click the icon of **Helical Sweep** from the **Model tab > Cut.**

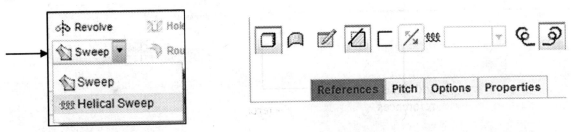

Click **References > Define**. Click **TOP** (sketching plane) **> Sketch** to accept the default setting for orientation. Click the icon of **Sketch View** to orient the sketching plane parallel to the screen.

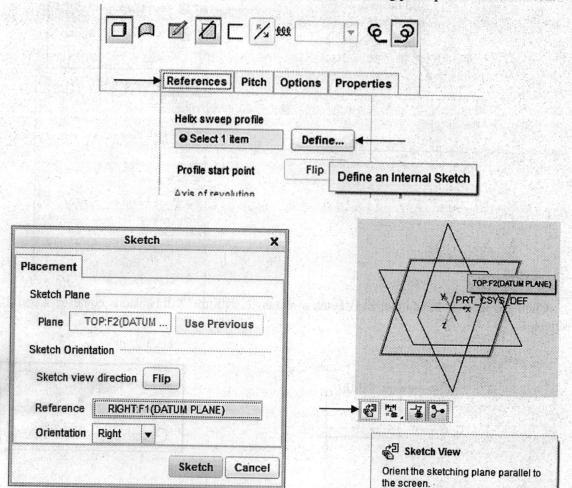

To facilitate sketching a rectangle, add two new references. Click **References** from the **Sketch** tab. Pick 2 new references, as shown. Click **Close**.

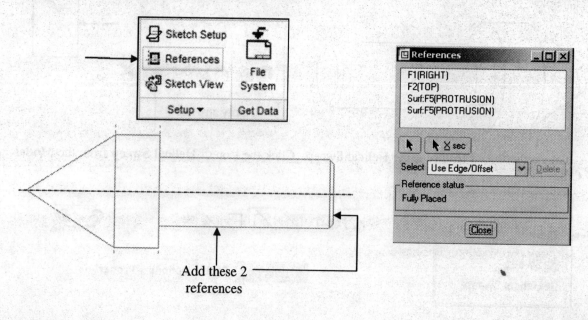

Add these 2
references

Click the icon of **Line** and sketch a line with the dimensions shown below:

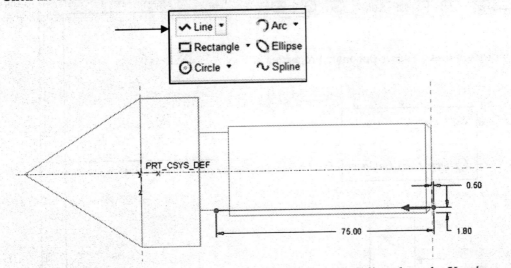

From the **Sketch** tab, click the icon of **centerline**; draw a centerline along the X-axis.

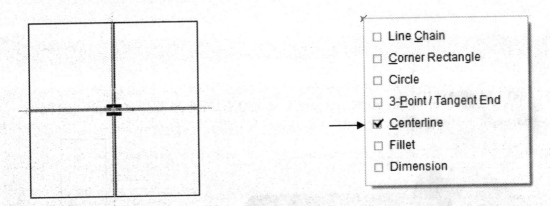

Pick the sketched centerline and right-click to pick **Axis of Revolution**.
Upon completion, select the icon of **OK**. Specify the pitch value: 3.0, and select **Right Hand**.

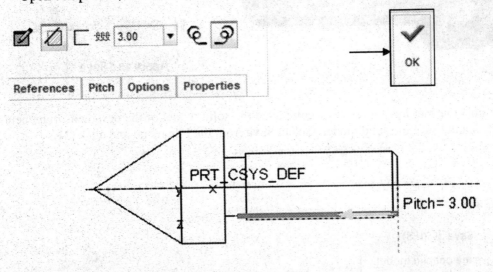

Click the icon of **Create Section**. Click the icon of Circle. Upon completion, select the icon of

OK.

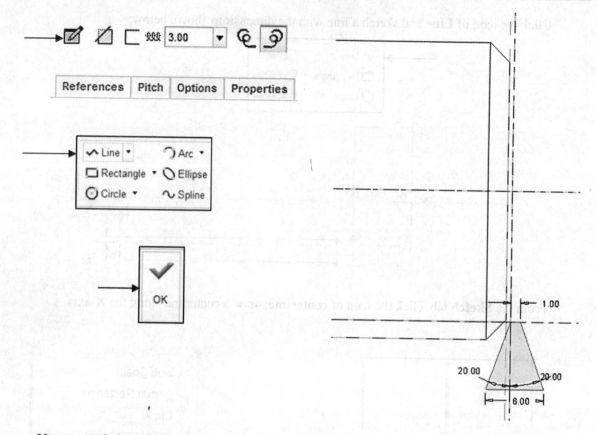

Upon completion of this sketch, pick the icon of **OK.** Click the icon of **Apply and Save**.

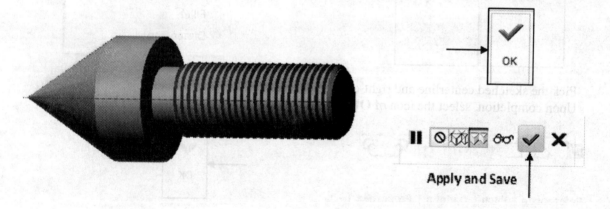

Apply and Save

At this time the user has successfully completed the solid model of the designed component with thread, he or she should save the solid model. Select **Save** from the File menu and click **OK**.

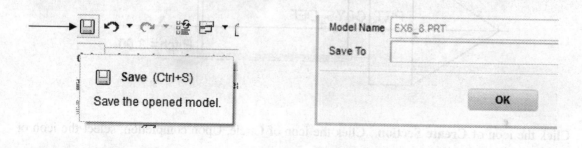

Model Name	EX6_8.PRT
Save To	

To prepare an engineering drawing based on the 3D thread model, we open a new file under the Mode of **Drawing**. First, we select the icon of **Create a new object** from the tool bar. Type ex6_8 as the name of the file. Clear the box of **Use default template** and click the box of **OK**.

In the window of New Drawing, make sure that the file of the 3D solid model called *ex6_8* is shown. Otherwise, use "**Browse**" to locate it. Select **Empty** under Specify Template, and select the paper size to be **A**. Afterwards, click the box of **OK**.

Click the **Layout** tab. Click the icon of **General.** In the **Select Combined State** window, click **OK** to accept **No Combined State**.

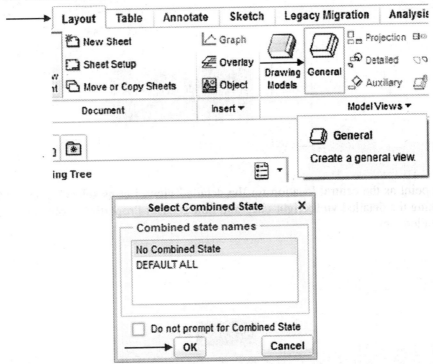

Select a location on the drawing screen as the center point for the **General View**. A general view appears on the screen. From the Drawing View Window, select **FRONT > Apply > Scale > Custom scale > 1.0 > Apply > Close.** The construction of the front view is completed.

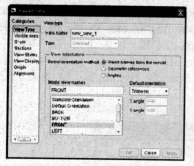
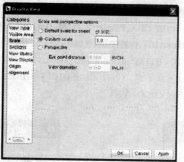
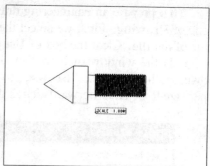

In order to provide some detailed information on the thread feature, we add a detailed view. Click **Detailed** from the **Layout** tab.

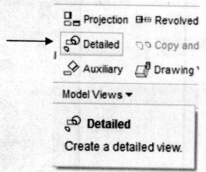

Select a location from the projection where the detailed view is needed. This location will serve as the center point for sketching a spline around it. Let us select a point around the middle of the top of the thread portion.

Sketch a spline around the selected location. Press the middle button of mouse to complete it.

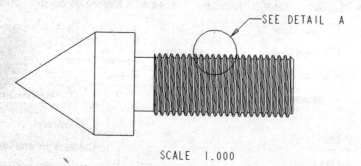

SEE DETAIL A

SCALE 1.000

Select a point as the central location for the detailed view. Let us select a point at the left lower portion. By picking the detailed view (right-click and hold), select Properties to obtained the information related to the detailed view.

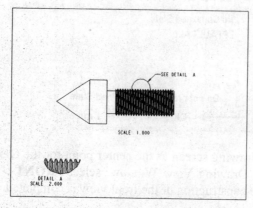

SEE DETAIL A

SCALE 1.000

DETAIL A
SCALE 2.000

To add dimensions, click **Annotate > Show Model Annotations** > select the icon of **Dimensions**. To add centerlines, select the icon of **Centerlines**.

From the model tree, click Revolve. A set of dimensions are shown. Click the box of **Accept All > Apply**.

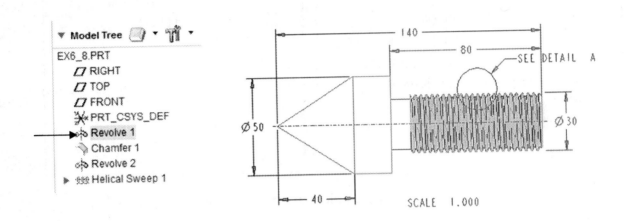

To modify φ30 to T30-3, pick φ30 and right-click and hold from the pop up window, pick **Properties > Display** > delete φ, and add T in the Prefix box, and add -3 in the Postfix box, as shown.

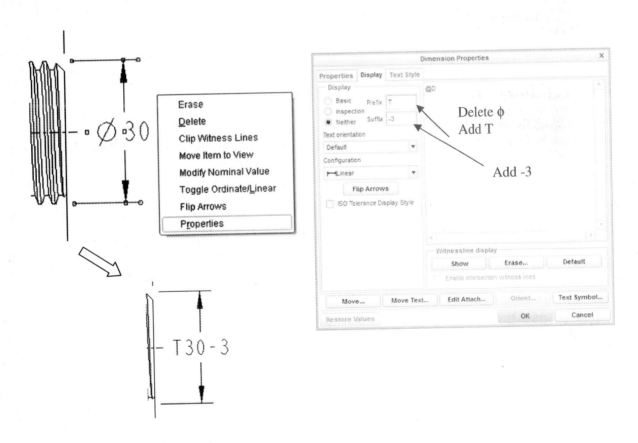

In order to add "Pitch" in front of the value of 3, pick the dimension of 3. Right-click and hold > from the pop up window, pick **Properties > Display**. In the Prefix box, type *Pitch=* > **OK**.

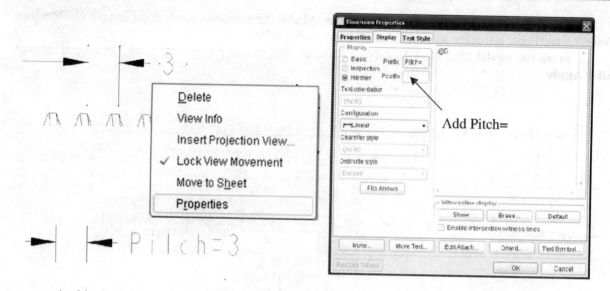

At this time, let us save the drawing file. Click **Save** from the **File** menu and click **OK**.

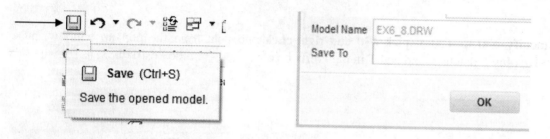

6.5 Creation of a Beam Structure Using Sweep

The following figure illustrates a beam or truss structure. Because the loading condition on each beam varies, each beam has its own section area. To create such a truss structure, we use SWEEP. In general, datum curves and/or sketched curves are needed for sweeping operations.

Example 6-9: Use the mm-unit System to create a 3D solid model of a truss structure shown below.

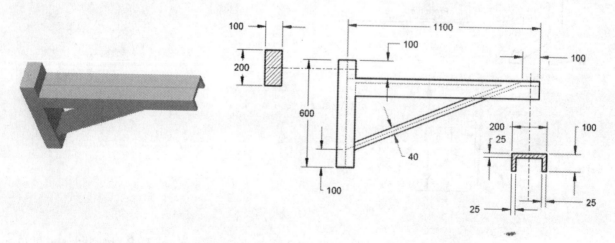

Based on the feature-based modeling approach, we view each beam as a feature. There are three beams, and we will create the 3 beam features.

From the **File** menu, click **New > Part**. Type *ex6_9* as the file name and clear the icon of **Use default template** because of setting the mm-unit system > **OK**.

In the window of **New File Options**, Select **mmns_part_solid** (units: Millimeter, Newton, Second) and type *ex6-9* in **DESCRIPTION**, and *student* in **MODELED_BY**, then **OK**

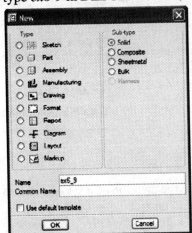 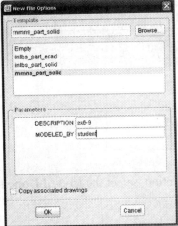

Before creating the first feature, let us create a set of datum curves representing the frame of the truss structure. Click the icon of Sketch from the **Model** tab. Select the **FRONT** datum plane displayed on screen, and click the box of **Sketch** to accept the **RIGHT** datum plane as the default reference to orient the sketch plane, as illustrated below.

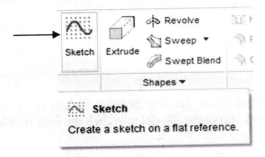

Select the **FRONT** datum plane displayed on screen, and click the box of **Sketch** to accept the **RIGHT** datum plane as the default reference to orient the sketch plane. Click the icon of **Sketch View** to orient the sketching plane parallel to the screen.

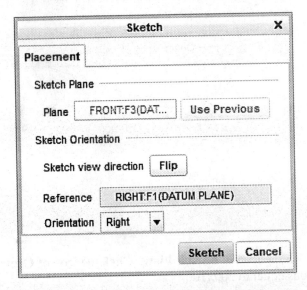 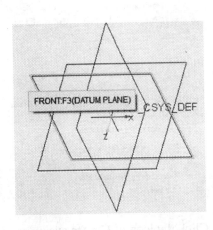

Select the icon of **Line** from the toolbar of sketcher to make the following sketch.

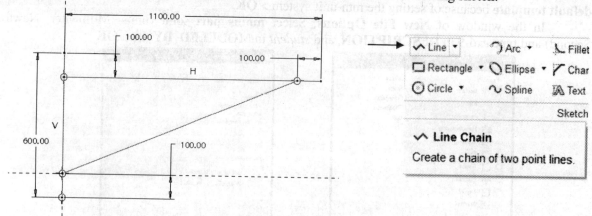

Upon completion, select the icon of **Done** to complete the creation of a set of 3 datum curves.

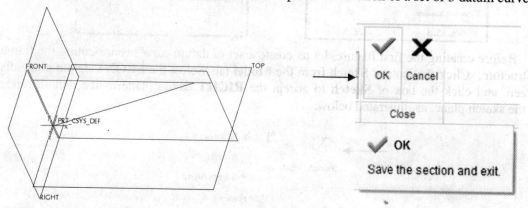

Now let us use **SWEEP** to create the first beam, which is the vertical beam with a rectangle section. The size is 200 x 100 mm. From the **Model** tab, click the icon of **Sweep**. Click **References** and pick the vertical datum curve.

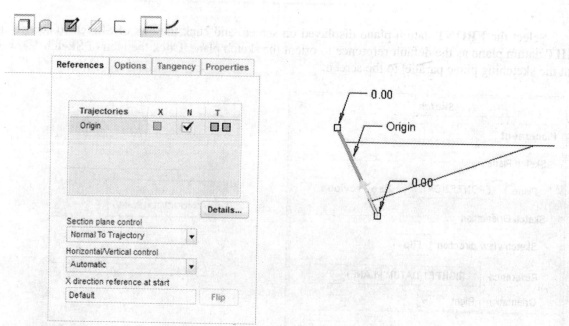

Click the icon of **Create sweep section**. Click the icon of **Sketch View**. Click the icon of **Center Rectangle** to sketch a rectangle with the 2 dimensions equal to 200x100.

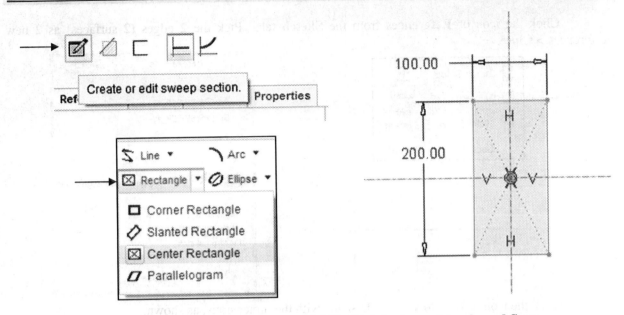

Upon completing the sketch, pick the icon of **OK.** Click the icon of **Apply and Save**.

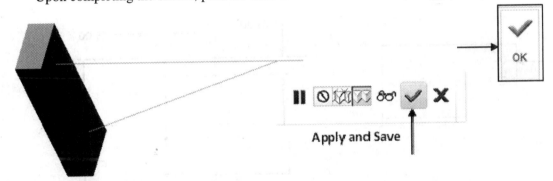

Now let us use **SWEEP** to create the second beam, which is the horizontal beam with a U-shaped section. From the **Model** tab, click the icon of **Sweep**. Click **References** and pick the horizontal datum curve.

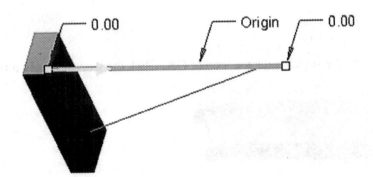

Click the icon of **Create sweep section**. Click the icon of **Sketch View**.

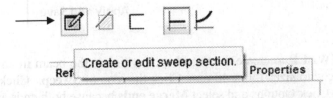

Click the icon of **References** from the **Sketch** tab. Pick the 2 edges (2 surfaces) as 2 new references > **Close**.

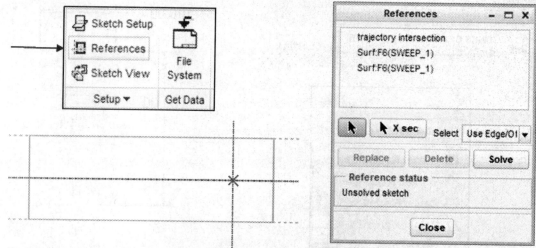

Click the icon of **Line** to sketch a U-shape with the dimensions, as shown.

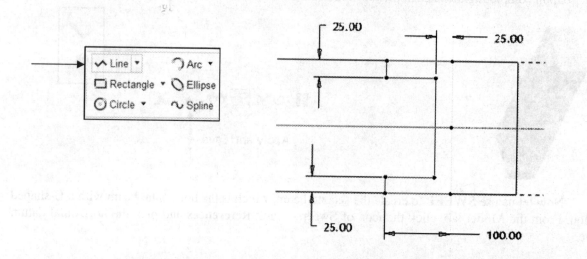

Upon completing the sketch, pick the icon of **OK.** Click the icon of **Apply and Save**.

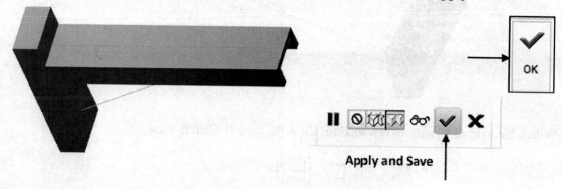

Now let us use **SWEEP** to create the third beam, which is the beam in an inclined position. Its section area is a rectangle with size: 150 x 40 mm. Click the icon of **Sweep**. Click **References** and pick the inclined datum curve. Click Options and select **Merge ends** because both ends are not free.

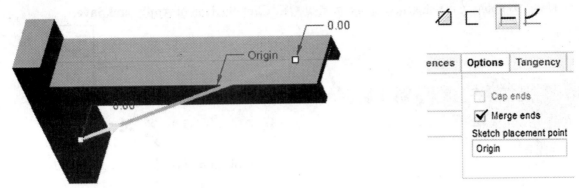

Click the icon of **Create sweep section**. Click the icon of **Sketch View**.

Click the icon of **References** from the **Sketch** tab. Pick the 2 edges (2 surfaces) as 2 new references > **Close**.

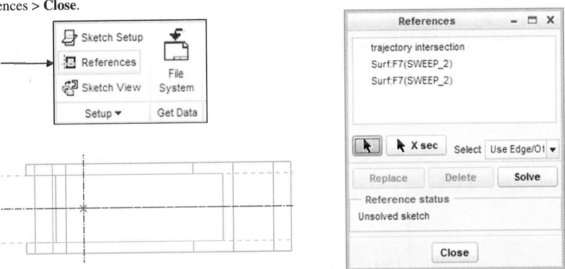

Click the icon of **Center Rectangle** to sketch a rectangle with the 2 dimensions equal to 150x40 as shown.

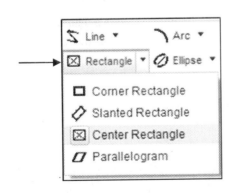

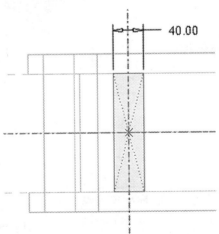

Upon completing the sketch, pick the icon of **OK.** Click the icon of **Apply and Save**.

Apply and Save

We need to create two datum planes, which will be used for creating 2 revolved section views.
Pick the icon of **Datum Plane** from the **Model** tab. Select the top surface from the U-shaped beam as the reference, type 50 as the offset value. Click **OK** and **DTM1** is created.

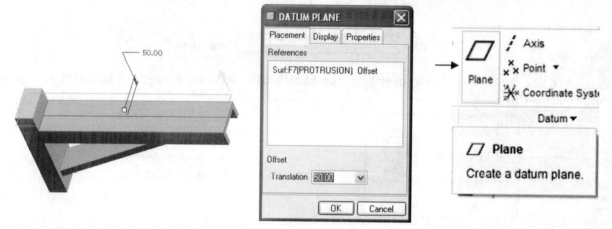

Pick the icon of **Datum Plane** from the **Model** tab. Select the surface at the right free-end of the U-shaped beam as the reference, type *50* (you may type -50), and click **OK**. **DTM2** is created.

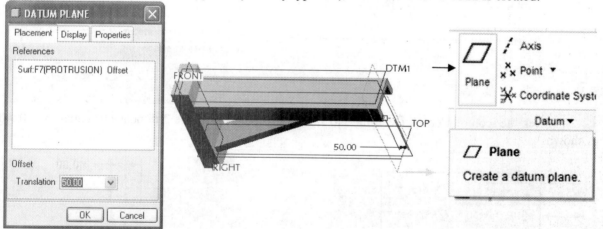

At this time the user has successfully completed the solid model of the designed truss structure, he or she should save the solid model. Select **Save** from the **File** menu > **OK**.

We open a new drawing file. First, we select the icon of **Create a new object** from the main toolbar. Type *ex6_9,* as the name of the file. Clear the box of **Use default template** and click the box of **OK**.

In the window of New Drawing, make sure that the file of the 3D solid model called *ex6_9* is shown. Otherwise, use "**Browse**" to locate it. Select **Empty** under Specify Template, and select the paper size to be **A**. Afterwards, click the box of **OK**.

Click the **Layout** tab. Click the icon of **General.** In the **Select Combined State** window, click **OK** to accept **No Combined State**.

Select a location on the drawing screen as the center point for the **General View**. A general view appears on the screen. From the Drawing View Window, select **FRONT > Apply > Scale > Custom scale > 0.1 > Apply > Close.** The construction of the front view is completed.

  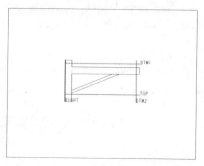

To insert a revolved section view for the vertical rectangle beam, click **Revolved** from the **Layout** tab.

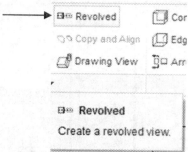

Click the **FRONT** view as the parent view for the revolved view to be created.

Locate a position for the revolved view.

Planar > Single > Done.

Type *A* as the name as the cross-section, and press **Enter**.

Select **DTM1** as the cross section plane > select the **FRONT** datum plane as the symmetry axis > **Apply > Close**.

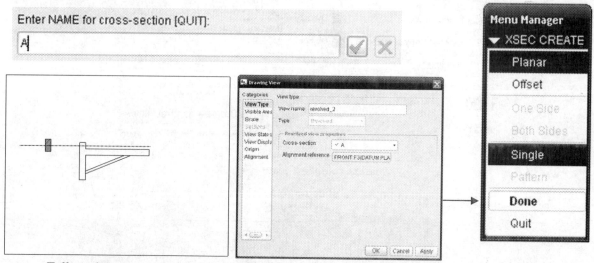

Follow the same procedure to insert another revolved section view for the horizontal U-shaped beam. In the Drawing View window, select **Create New**, instead of A, in Cross-section.

Click **Layout** > expand Model View to locate **Revolved**.

Click the **FRONT** view as the parent view for the revolved view to be created.

On the drawing, select a location as the center point for the second revolved section view.

Planar > Single > Done

Type *B* as the name as the cross-section, and press **Enter**.

Select **DTM2** as the cross section plane > select the **FRONT** datum plane as the symmetry axis > **Apply > Close**.

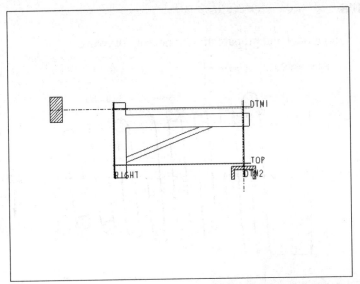

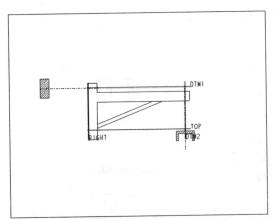

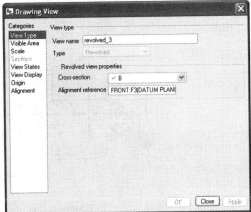

Users may add dimensions and centerlines to the drawing and insert the format file as well.

At this time the user has successfully completed the engineering drawing of the designed component, he or she should save the drawing. Select **Save** from the **File** menu > **OK**.

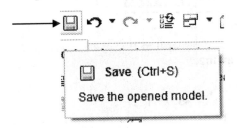

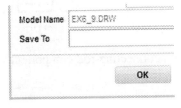

6.6 References

1. F. L. Amirouche, <u>Computer-aided Design and Manufacturing</u>, Prentice Hall, Englewood Cliffs, New Jersey, 1993.
2. R. E. Barnhill, <u>IEEE Computer-Graphics and Applications</u>, 3(7), 9-16, 1983.
3. H. R. Buhl, <u>Creative Engineering Design</u>, Iowa State University Press, Ames, Iowa, 1960.
4. B. L. Davids, A. J. Robotham and Yardwood A., <u>Computer-aided Drawing and Design</u>, London, 1991.
5. C.S. Krishnamoorthy, <u>Finite Element Analysis, Theory and Programming</u>, 2nd Ed., 1995.
6. D. Hearn, M. P. Baker, Computer Graphics, Englewood Cliffs, NJ, 1986

6.7   Exercises

1.   Create a 3D solid model and prepare an engineering drawing..

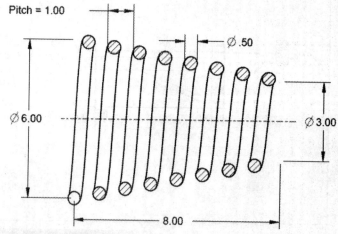

2.   Create a 3D model first and prepare an engineering drawing .

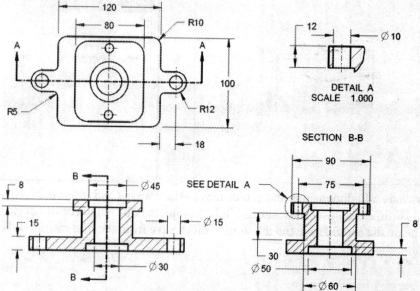

3.   Create a connecting-rod component with an engineering drawing.

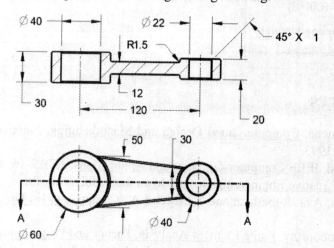

3.   Creation of a thin wall structure using Revolving with an engineering drawing. Add a format.

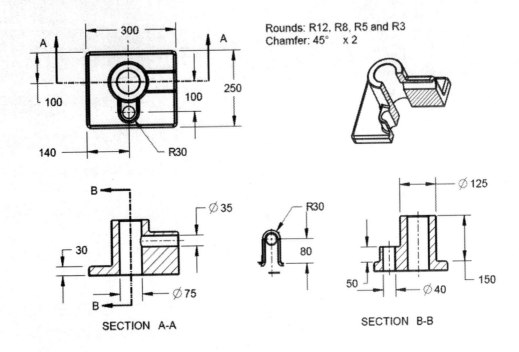

4.   Creation of a 3D solid model and preparation of an engineering drawing of it.

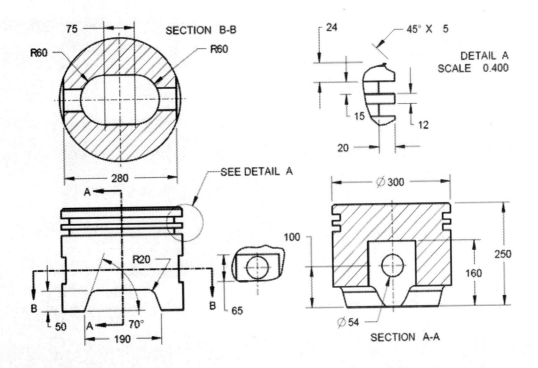

CHAPTER 7

ASSEMBLY OF COMPONENTS

7.1   Introduction

Almost every product on the market is assembled from components. A pencil used to take notes may consist of three or four components. The cars we drive are assembled from thousands of components. Assembly involves the joining together of two or more separate components to form a new entity, called a subassembly or an assembly. The method to accomplish the assembly of these components may be mechanical fastening, welding, adhesive bonding, etc. Assembly of components is one of the critical tasks in product development. In fact, the Creo Parametric design system provides a virtual environment to simulate the physical assembly process carried out on the shop floor.

Example of constraints used in the process of assembling two blocks.

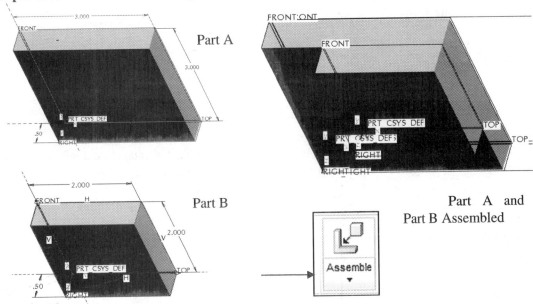

Let us first create a 3D solid model for Part A.

From the **File** menu, click **New > Part**. Type *Part_A* as the file name and clear the box of **Use default template** for setting the inch-unit system > **OK.** In the window of **New File Options,** Select **inlbs_part_solid** (units: inch, lbf, second) and type *Part A* in **DESCRIPTION**, and *student* in **MODELED_BY**, then **OK.**

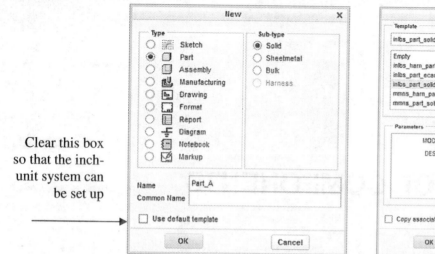
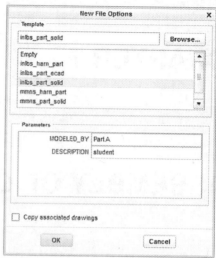

Clear this box
so that the inch-
unit system can
be set up

Select the icon of **Extrude** from the **Model** tab. Specify 0.50 as the extrusion distance.

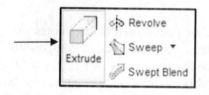
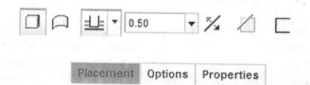

In the model tree, click **FRONT** (sketching plane). Click the icon of **Sketch View** to orient the sketching plane parallel to the screen.

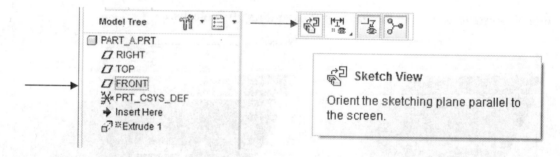

Select the icon of **Rectangle** from the **Sketch** group. Select Center Rectangle and sketch a rectangle centered at the origin. Modify the two dimensions to 180 and 100, respectively.

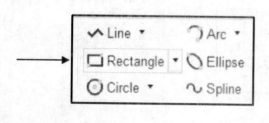
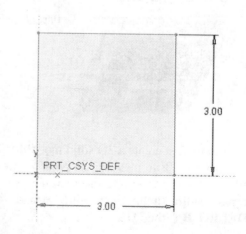

Click the icon of **OK,** and click the icon of **Apply and Save**.

To create a 3D solid model for Part B, from the **File** menu, click **New > Part**. Type *Part_B* as the file name and clear the box of **Use default template** for setting the inch-unit system > **OK.** In the window of **New File Options**, Select **inlbs_part_solid** (units: inch, lbf, second) and type *Part B* in **DESCRIPTION**, and *student* in **MODELED_BY**, then **OK.**

Clear this box so that the inch-unit system can be set up

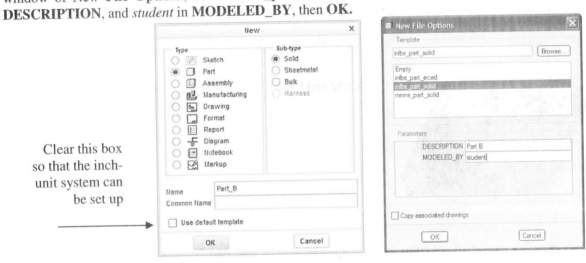

Select the icon of **Extrude** from the **Model** tab. Specify *0.50* as the extrusion distance.

In the model tree, click **FRONT** (sketching plane). Click the icon of **Sketch View** to orient the sketching plane parallel to the screen.

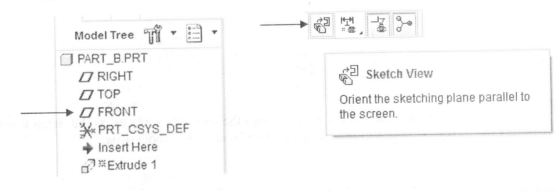

Select the icon of **Rectangle** from the Sketch group. Select **Rectangle** and sketch a rectangle. Modify the two dimensions to 2 and 2, respectively.

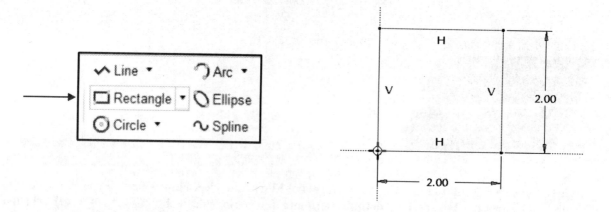

Click the icon of **OK,** and click the icon of **Apply and Save**.

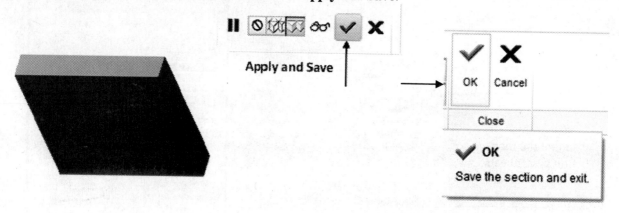

Now we have two (2) solid models, namely, Part A and Part B. A physical entity in a 3D space possesses 6 degrees of freedom: 3 degrees of freedom are translational, and the other 3 degrees of freedom are in rotation. To uniquely define the position and the orientation of a physical entity, the 6 degrees of freedom have to be constrained. We use the example of assembling the 2 blocks to demonstrate the basic steps involved in the assembly on the shop floor. In the meantime, we demonstrate the procedure of assembling these two blocks under the Creo Parametric design environment.

It is extremely important that we assemble the first component or Part A to the ground so that the position of Part A in space is uniquely defined. Afterwards, we assemble Part A and Part B under the assembly environment. For example, we let the top surface of Part A to be in contact with the bottom surface of Part B. This process is called **Mate** in Creo Parametric because we are adding a specific constraint to both parts.

Constraint Type: **Mate**

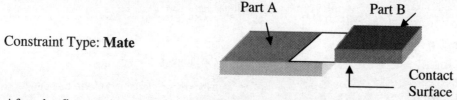

After the first mating constraint is defined, we align the two right surfaces, as illustrated below. This process is called **Align** because we are adding the second constraint to both parts.

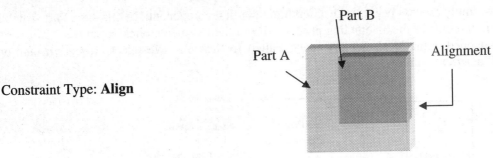

Constraint Type: **Align**

To uniquely define the relative position between Part A and Part B, we need one more constraint. We use "**Align**" again to add the third constraint to align the top surfaces of both parts. After adding the third constraint, we have completed the assembly process because the two parts are fully constrained, or the relative position of the two parts with respect to each other has been uniquely defined.

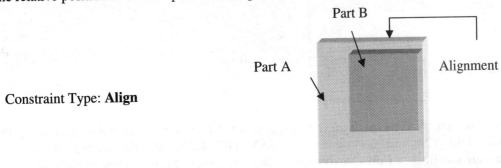

Constraint Type: **Align**

To summarize the assembly process under the Creo Parametric design system, there are 2 steps. The first step is to assemble the first component to the assembly system by positioning the default coordinate system of the first component to the location of the default coordinate system of the assembly system with the aligned orientations. The second step is to assemble the coming component by defining 3 constraints to uniquely define the relative positions of the coming component with respect to the assembled component(s), such as the mating constraint and the 2 alignment constraints.

7.2   Assembling Two Components

Now let us demonstrate the procedure of assembling these two parts under the Creo Parametric.
Example 7-1:   Assemble two blocks.
We have 2 components: Part A and Part B. Part A is a block of 3 x 3 x 0.5 inch. Part B is also a block of 2 x 2 x 0.5 inch. The names of these two files are Part_A.prt and Part_B.prt, respectively.
To assemble these 2 blocks together, create a file for the assembly.
File > New > Assembly > type *ex7-1* as the file name **> OK.** The default unit system is inch.

Select Assembly Mode

Type *ex7_1*

Click **OK**

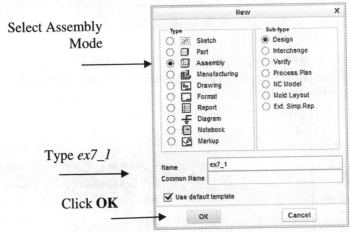

The assembly process begins with assembling the first component. In this case, Part A will be the first component to come to the assembling process. From the top menu, click **Assemble**. This brings us with the files opened in the local memory space, called **In Session**. We select *Part_A.prt*, and open it. Activate the **Placement** window.

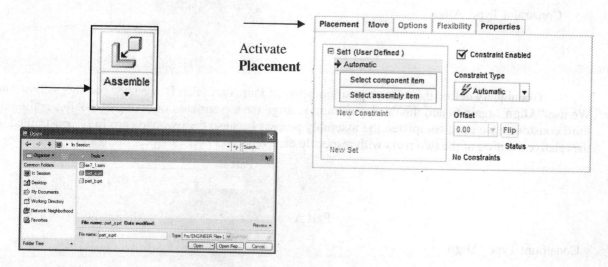

Activate
Placement

Under the **Constraint Type**, pick the icon of **Default**, which means automatically placing the origin of the PART_DEF_CSYS to the origin of the ASM_DEF_CSYS and the orientations of the 2 coordinate systems are identical > **Full Constrained** is indicated under **Status**> click the icon of **Apply and Save**.

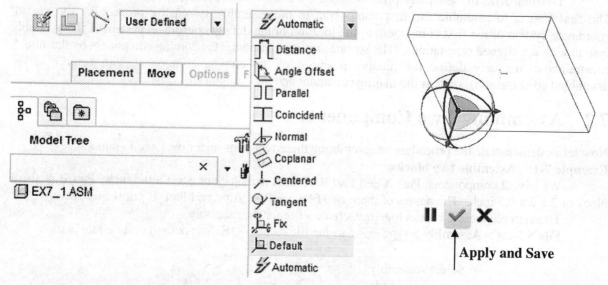

Apply and Save

It is extremely important that users apply the function of **Default** when assembling the first component. Generally speaking, we do not use any other functions when assembling the first component.

Now we assemble Part B to the assembly. Following the same procedure, click the icon of **Assemble**, and open the file called Part_B from **In Session**.

Activate the **Placement**. pick the front surface of Part A and the back surface of Part B. A constraint called Coincident is created. Click New Constraint because of the partial constrained condition is displayed.

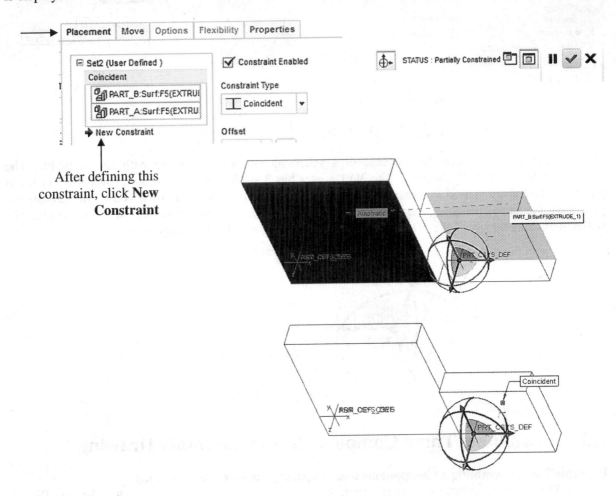

After defining this constraint, click **New Constraint**

To define the second constraint, click the surface on the right side of Part A and the surface on the right side of Part B. Select Coincident. Click the icon of New Constraint to continue.

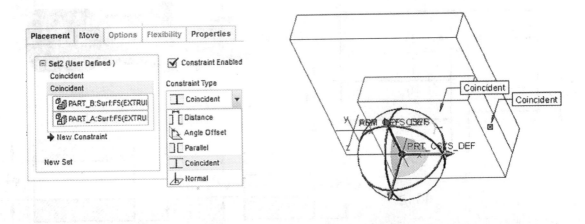

To define the third constraint, click the surface on the top of Part A and the surface on the top of Part B. Select **Coincident**. The assembly process is completed. Click the icon of **Apply and Save.**

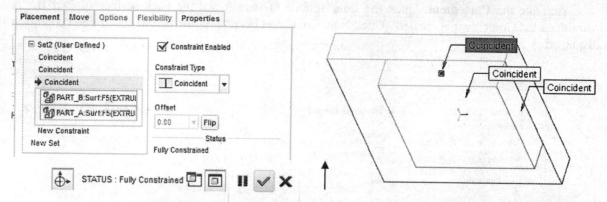

Readers may notice the presence of a spherical ball when working with an assembly. The spherical ball is called 3D Dragger. The 3D Dragger has 3 shaded arcs, 3 shaded arrows and a centroid point. A shaded arc is used to rotate the part about a given axis. A shaded arrow is used to translate the part along the axial direction. The centroid point allows the user to move the part in the 3D space. We will demonstrate the use of the 3D Dragger when assembling a belt-roller-support system.

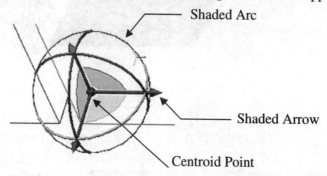

7.3   Assembling Three Components and Assembly Drawing

Example 7-2: Assembling 3 Components and Preparing an Assembly Drawing

The following figure presents an assembly, which consists of three components. They are Ring 1, Ring 2 and Shaft, as shown below. We first create these three components with file names: ring1.prt, ring2.prt, and shaft.prt, respectively. We save these 3 files to a directory called ex7_2.

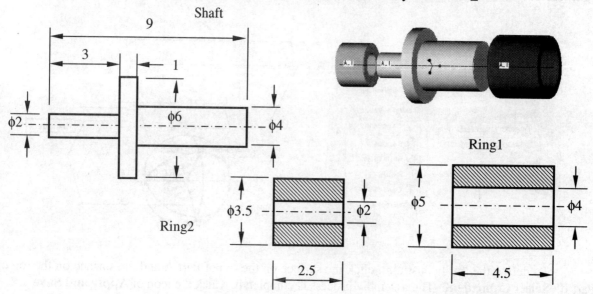

Let us create a 3D solid model for Ring 1.

Click **New** from the File menu. Select **Part** > type *ring1* as the file name and clear the icon of **Use default template** to set the inch-unit system > **OK.** In the New File Option window, type *Ring 1* as description and type *student* as modeled_by. Click> **OK**.

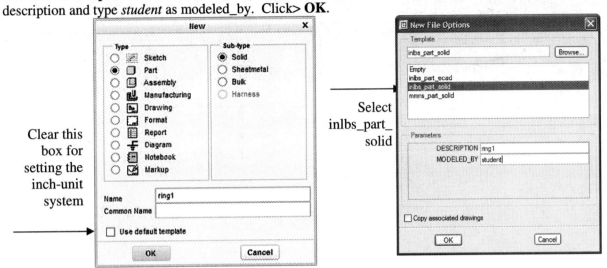

Select **Revolve** from the **Model** tab.

From the model tree, click **FRONT** (sketching planer). Click the icon of **Sketch View** to orient the sketching plane parallel to the screen.

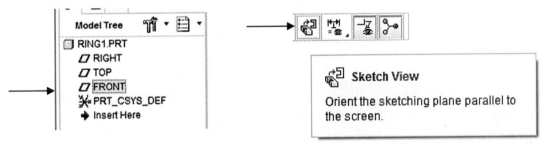

Right-click and hold, pick Axis of Revolution. Sketch a horizontal centerline. This centerline will serve as the axis for the revolving operation.

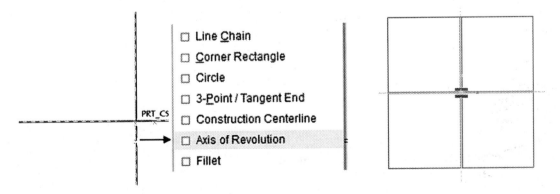

Select the icon of **Rectangle** from the Sketch tab. Sketch a rectangle. Modify the 3 dimensions to 5, 4.5 and 4, respectively.

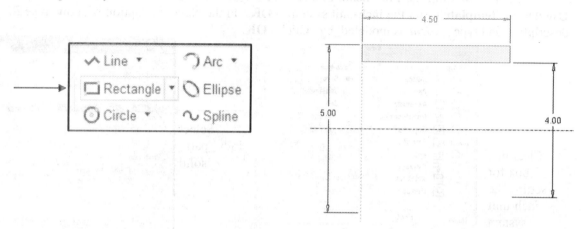

Upon completing this sketch, click the icon of **OK.** Click the icon of **Apply and Save**.

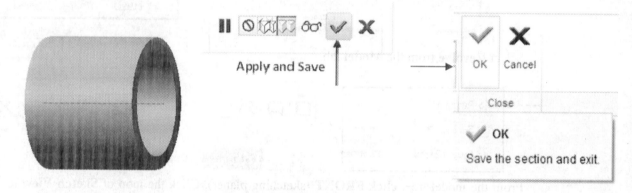

Click the icon of **Save**. Click **OK** to save the work.to the file called Ring1.prt.

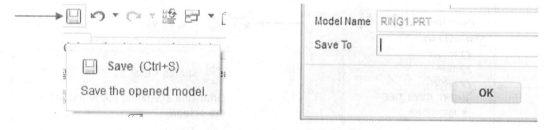

Because of the similarity between Ring 1 and Ring 2, we use **Save a Copy** to create the file of ring2.prt. From the top menu, click **File** > Save As > **Save a Copy**. Type *ring2* as the file name > **OK**.

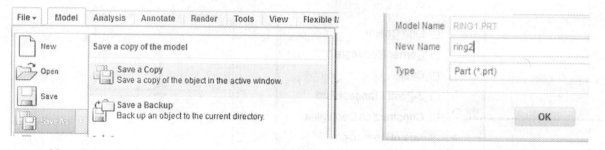

Now let us open the ring2 file. From the top menu, click **File** > **Open** > highlight the file called ring2.prt > **Open**.

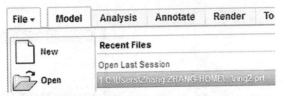

To modify the 3 dimensions, highlight Revolve 1 listed in the model tree > right-click and pick **Edit Definition**. Click Placement > Edit. Modify the 3 dimensions to 3.5, 2.5 and 2, respectively. Click OK. Click the icon of **Apply and Save**.

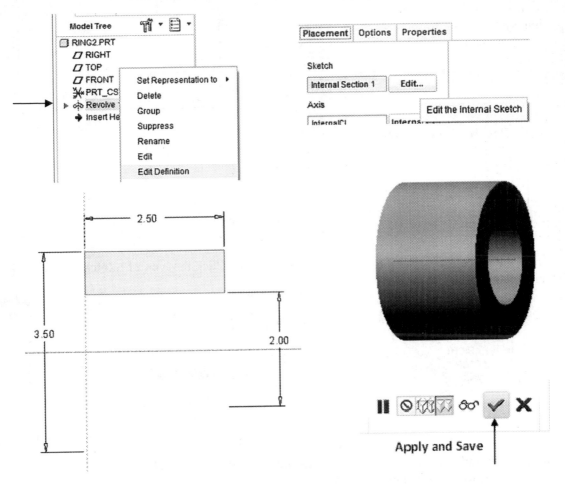

Apply and Save

Click the icon of **Save**. Click **OK** to save the work.to the file called Ring2.prt.

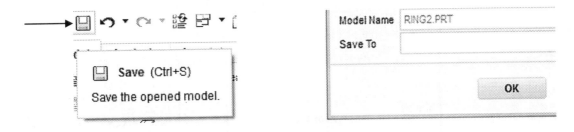

Let us create a 3D solid model for the Shaft component.

File > New > Part > type *shaft* as the file name and clear the box of **Use default template** for setting the inch-unit system > **OK.** In the window of **New File Options**, Select **inlbs_part_solid** (units: inch, lbf, second) and type *shaft* in **DESCRIPTION**, and *student* in **MODELED_BY**, then **OK.**

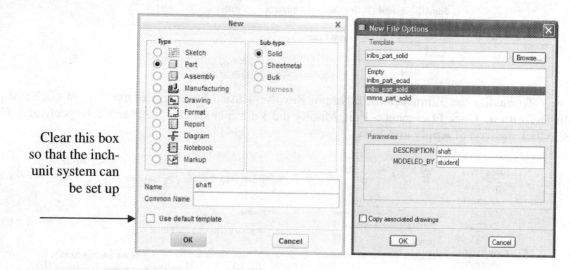

Clear this box so that the inch-unit system can be set up

Select **Revolve** from the **Model** tab.

From the model tree, click **FRONT** (sketching planer). Click the icon of **Sketch View** to orient the sketching plane parallel to the screen.

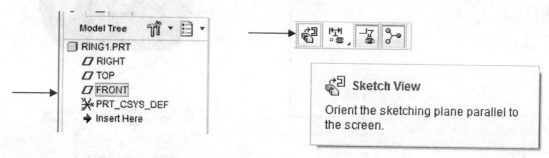

Right-click and hold, **pick** Axis **of Revolution**. Sketch a horizontal centerline. This centerline will serve as the axis for the revolving operation.

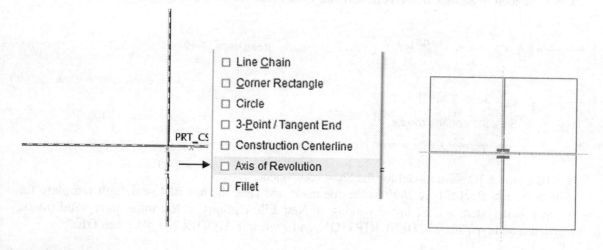

Select the icon of **Rectangle** from the Sketch tab. Sketch a rectangle. Modify the 3 dimensions to 5, 4.5 and 4, respectively.

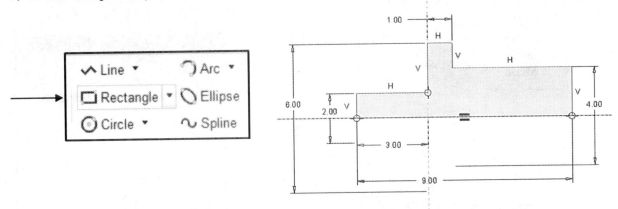

Upon completing this sketch, click the icon of **OK.** Click the icon of **Apply and Save**.

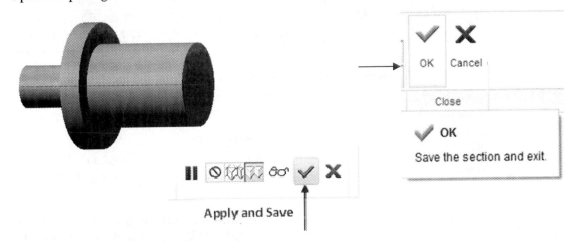

Apply and Save

Click the icon of **Save**. Click **OK** to save the work.to the file called Shaft.prt.

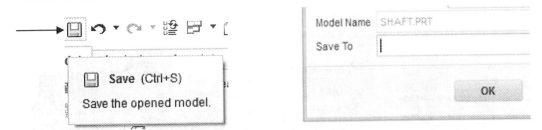

Now we have the 3 parts. The 3 file names are *ring1.prt, ring2.prt, and shaft.prt*, respectively. These 3 files are saved in the folder called **EX7_2**. The uniqueness of this assembly process is that the centerlines of the two rings are aligned with the centerline of the shaft component.

In the assembly process, we assume that the Shaft component is the first component to be assembled for establishing the assembly system. Afterwards, we assemble Ring 1. Finally, we assemble Ring 2. We outline the major steps as follows:

- When assembling the Shaft component, we use **Default** so that the PART_DEF_CSYS of the Shaft component is placed to the location of ASM_DEF_CSYS, and the orientations of the 2 coordinate systems are fully aligned, thus establishing the Assembly Reference.
- When assembling the component of Ring 1, we use the three-click process and make sure the status of Fully Constrained is reached.
- Finally, assemble the component of Ring 2, using the three-click process until the status of Fully Constrained is reached.

Now let us create an assembly file. **File > New > Assembly** > type *ex7-2* as the file name > clear the box > **OK**. Select the inlbs_asm_design system. Type *7-2 Assembly* in the Description box and type *student* in the Modeled_by box > **OK**.

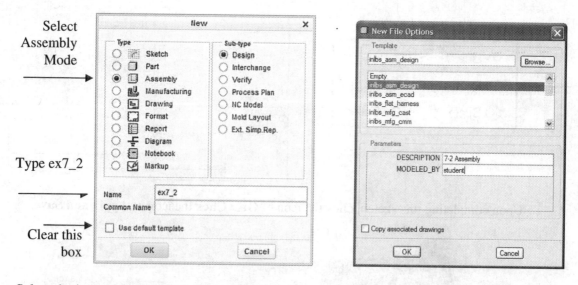

Select the icon of **Assemble** from the assembly icon list. From the local memory, or **In Session**, select *shaft.prt*, and open it.

Under the **Constraint Type**, pick the icon of **Default**, which means automatically placing the origin of the PART_DEF_CSYS to the origin of the ASM_DEF_CSYS and the orientations of the 2 coordinate systems are identical > **Full Constrained** is indicated under **Status**> click the icon of **Apply and Save**.

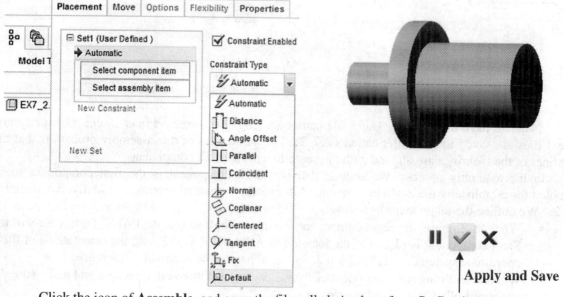

Click the icon of **Assemble**, and open the file called *ring1.prt* from **In Session**.

Activate the **Placement** window. We start the three-click process. The first click is to pick the axis from the shaft component and the second click is to pick the axis from the ring1 component. A coincident constraint is defined. The third click is to click **New Constraint** to continue the assembly process between the shaft component and the ring 1 component.

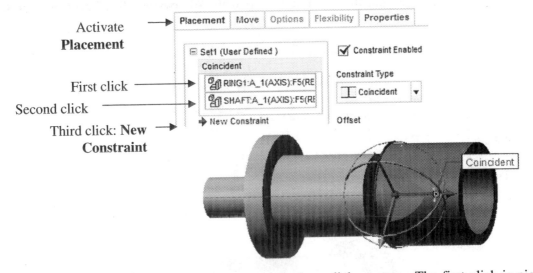

After clicking **New Constraint,** we start a new three-click process. The first click is pick the surface from the shaft component and the second click is to pick the surface from the ring1 component, as shown. A second coincident constraint is defined. Because **Full Constrained** is indicated under **Status**, click the icon of **Apply and Save** to complete the process of assembling the Ring1 component.

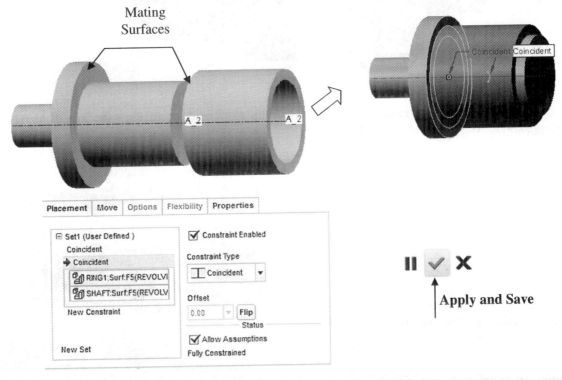

Follow the same procedure to assemble Ring 2. Click the icon of **Assemble**, and open the file called *ring2.prt* from **In Session**.

Activate the **Placement** window. The first click is to pick the axis from the shaft component and the second click is to pick the axis from the ring2 component. Afterwards, click **New Constraint**.

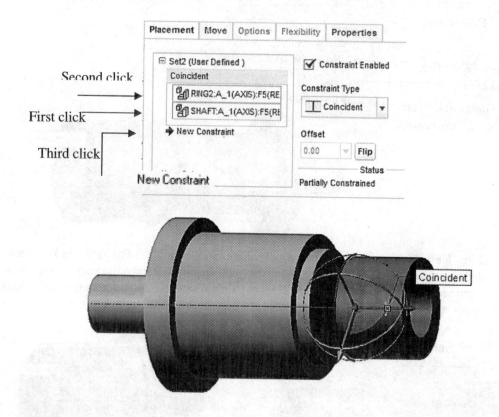

To move the Ring2 component to the left side of the shaft component, click the icon of **Move** and pick Ring2 and move it to the left side of Shaft.

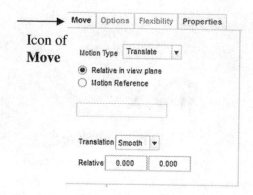

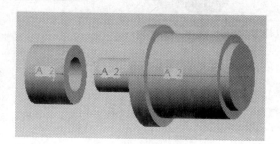

Now let us start the three-click process to define the second constraint. The first click is to pick the surface from the ring2 component and the second click is to pick the surface from the shaft component, as shown. Because **Full Constrained** is indicated under **Status**, click the icon of **Apply and Save** to complete the process of assembling the Ring2 component.

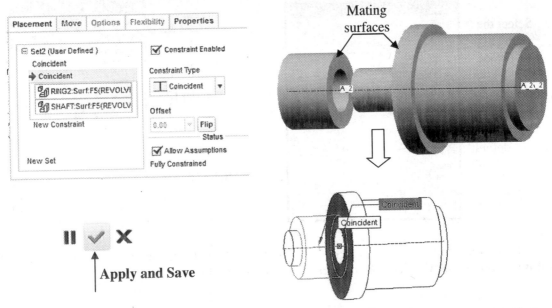

Mating surfaces

Apply and Save

At this time the user has successfully completed the assembly of the 3 components, he or she should save all the work with the 3D solid model of assembly. Select **Save** from the main toolbar > **OK**.

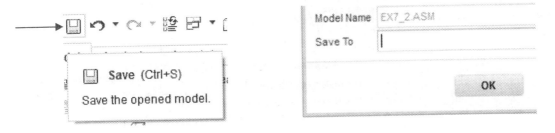

Now let us prepare an assembly drawing for this assembly. There exist several significant differences between an assembly drawing and the engineering drawing of a component. First, these two types of drawings serve two different purposes in design:

- Component drawing: Detailed information on geometry, dimensions and tolerances.
- Assembly drawing: Relationship among all components, especially how to assemble them together.

The basic requirements of an assembly drawing are

- Projections of the assembly.
- Maximum dimensions and key dimensions indicating the connections.
- Bill of Material listing the number of components, quantity for each component, the material type used for an individual component, standard parts, etc.
- BOM Balloons clearly specifying the correspondence between the components and the items listed in BOM.

To prepare an engineering drawing based on the assembled model, we open a new file under the Mode of **Drawing**. First, we select the icon of **Create** a new object from the main toolbar. Type *ex7_2* as the file name. Clear the box of Use default template and click the box of **OK**.

In the window of **New Drawing**, make sure that the file of the assembled model called *ex7-2* is shown. Otherwise, use "**Browse**" to locate it. Select **Empty** under Specify Template, and select the paper size to be **A**. Afterwards, click the box of **OK**.

Select the drawing mode

Clear the default box

Locate the 3D solid model file

Select paper size

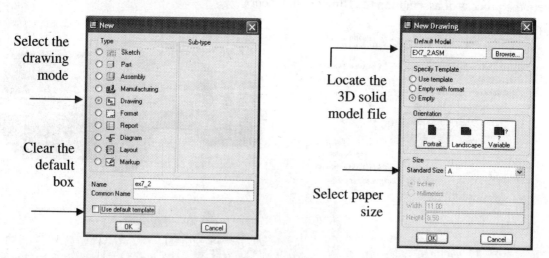

This brings up the drawing screen. Click the **Layout** tab. Click the icon of **General.** In the **Select Combined State** window, click **OK** to accept **No Combined State**.

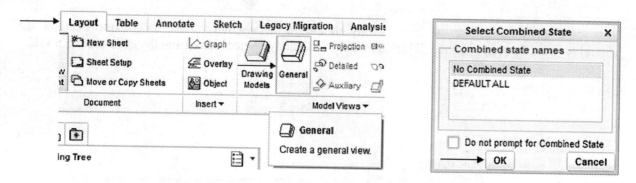

In the pop-up **Drawing View** window, select **FRONT > Apply**, the construction of the front view is completed.

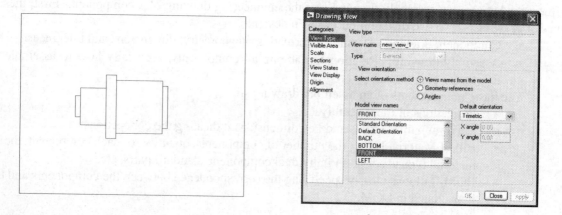

To control the scale of the FRONT view, select **Scale > Custom scale >** type 0.5 **> Apply** to make sure the selected scale fits the need **> OK**.

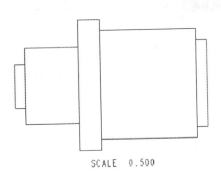 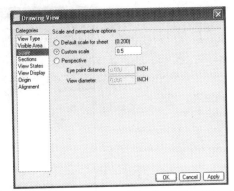

In order to show detailed information on the assembly process, we modify the FRONT view to a full section view. Let us turn on the display of datum planes in the model tree. Click the icon of **Settings** from the model tree. Click **Tree Fillers**. In the Model Tree window, activate **Features > OK**. ASM_FRONT is displayed in the model tree.

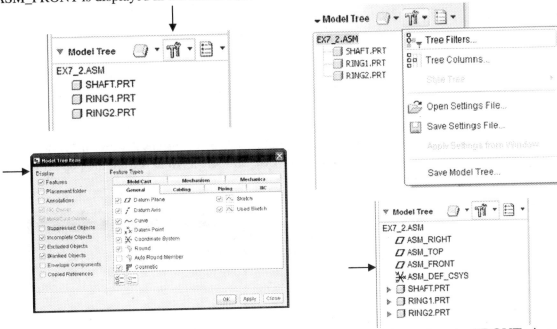

To modify the FRONT view to a full section view, left-click to select the **FRONT** view > right-click and hold, select **Properties.** In the

Sections and **2D cross-section** > Click the icon of **Add** (plus sign) to add cross-section > **Planar > Single > Done**. Type *A* as the name for cross-section.

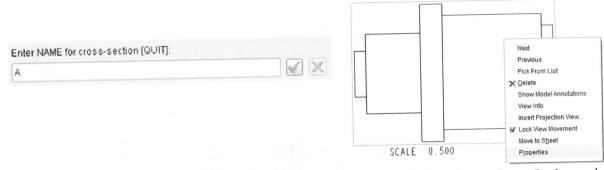

On the screen display, the user is being asked to select an assembly datum plane. In the model tree, select **ASM_FRONT** > click **APPLY > Close**.

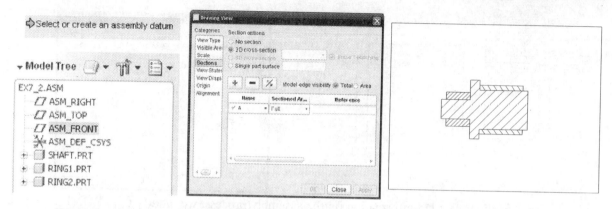

From the front view, pick **Xhatch,** using a left-click. Afterwards, right-click and hold, and select **Properties.**

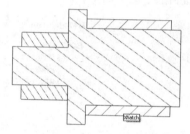

If the user has difficulty to directly pick **Xhatch**, select the FRONT view, using left–click. Afterwards, right-click and hold, and select **Pick from List**, and select **Xhatch** from the pop up window > OK.

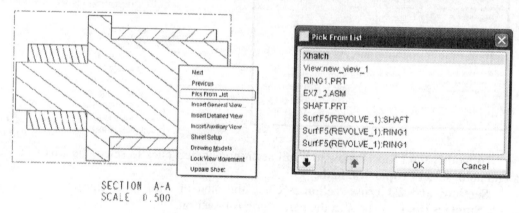

Right-click and hold > **Properties**.

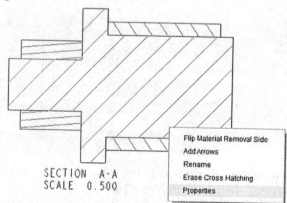

Use X-Component > **Next** to identify the shaft component as shown. Pick **Exclude > Done** to eliminate the hatched lines associated with the shaft component. No hatched line for shaft components is a general rule adopted by both ANSI and ISO standards. For Ring 1 and Ring 2, users may click the icon of **Angle** to select 45 degrees or 135 degrees for the hatched lines, as shown.

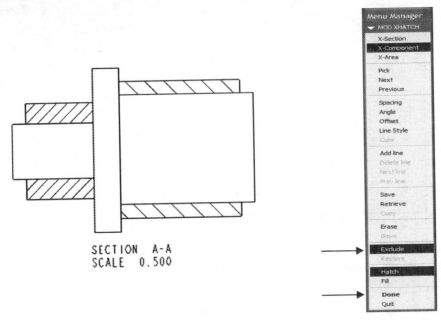

Upon completing the layout, we add dimensions. Select the icon of **Annotation > Show Model Annotation.** In the model tree, click the Revolve feature from SHAFT.PRT. Select 2 dimensions: 6 and 9. Click Apply, thus adding the 2 maximum dimensions.

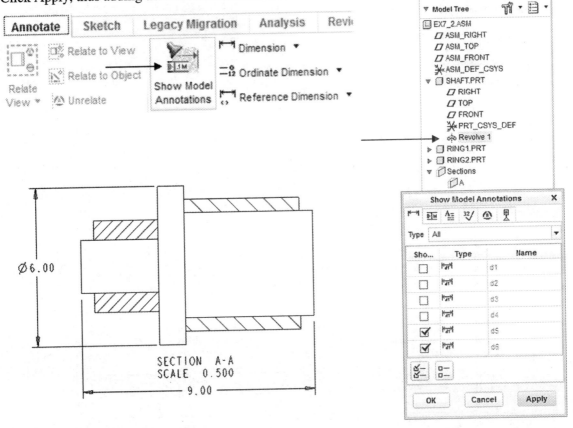

To add a centerline to the drawing, click the icon of **Show Model Datum**, click the projection on display. A centerline is on display. Click **Apply > Cancel**.

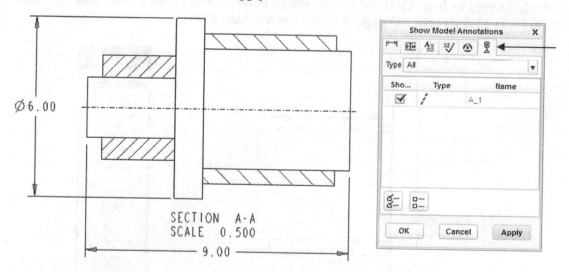

To insert the format, click Layout > Sheet Setup. Use **Browse** to locate the format file, which is *exercise_format* > **Open** > select **Show format** > **OK.**

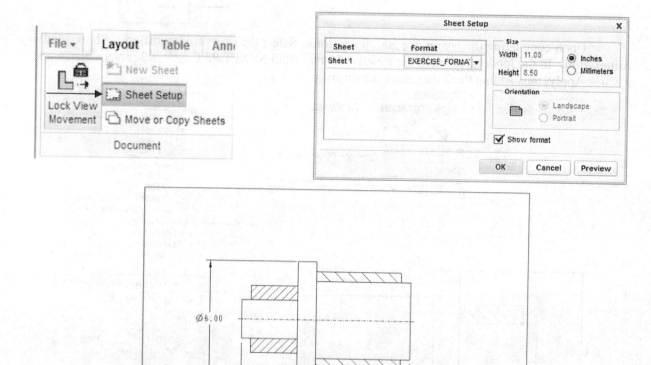

7.4   Special Notes on Assembling Components

In presenting Example 7-1 and Example 7-2, we emphasized two important concepts. The first concept was, when assembling the first component, we use **Default** Location. This means that we assemble the default coordinate system of the first component with the default coordinate system of the assembly system through **OVERLAPPING**. The original of the default coordinate system of the first component is located at the origin of the default coordinate system of the assembly system. The orientations of the x-axis, y-axis and z-axis of the default coordinate system of the first component are identical to the orientations of the x-axis, y-axis and z-axis of the default coordinate system of the assembly system.

The second concept is Creo Parametric design system has the built-in artificial intelligence to detect the nature of a constraint type, such as **Distance, Coincident,** etc. Users should have noticed the constraint type called **Automatic** is always picked by the system first during the assembling process. Because of this characteristic, users do not need to select Distance or Coincident before picking the surfaces or datum planes from the parts. By leaving **Automatic** untouched or in effect, users can directly pick the surfaces or axes or datum planes from the parts. When the picking is completed, the system will show the type of constraint, such as **Coincident**. This will speed up the assembling process.

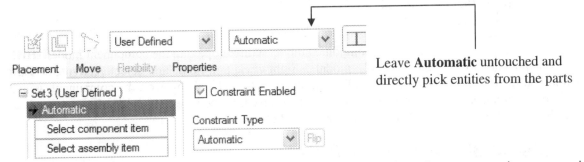

Leave **Automatic** untouched and directly pick entities from the parts

As illustrated in ex7_2, moving the position and/or orientation of a component is necessary in the assembly process. In addition to the method of using **Move**, the following 2 combinations, as shown in following figure, will also allow the users to move and rotate the component during assembling.

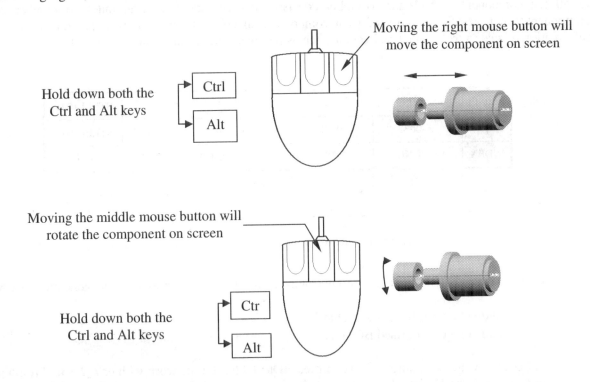

Moving the right mouse button will move the component on screen

Hold down both the Ctrl and Alt keys

Moving the middle mouse button will rotate the component on screen

Hold down both the Ctrl and Alt keys

There are 2 additional notes about the unique characteristic of the Creo Parametric design system. The first characteristic is called Associativity. When a change is made, at the part modeling level, to one of the components that have been assembled, there is no need to make the corresponding changes in the assembly. The only thing the designer needs to do is to regenerate the assembly model so that the change made at the part modeling level will be reflected in the assembly. By selecting Edit from the system tool bar > Regenerate, an automatic generation will be made to reflect the change at the assembly level. Users may directly pick the icon of **Regenerate** displayed on the system icon list of the tool bar.

The second characteristic is the communication between the part model and the assembly model. The model tree of the assembly lists all the components that have been assembled. Highlight the name of the component listed in the model tree. Right-click and hold, and select **Open**. This procedure opens the component model without going back to **Open** from **File** listed on the main toolbar.

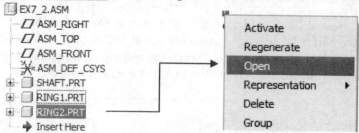

Users can also make changes to a component model without opening the component model. High light the component listed in the assembly model > right-click and hold, and select **Activate** > **Edit Definition** and the dashboard appears, thus allowing the user to make changes on the component, which has been activated under the assembly environment. To go back to the assembly mode, the user needs to highlight **EX7_2.ASM** > right-click and hold, and select **Activate**.

7.5   Table of Bill Of Material (BOM)

There is a table associated with an assembly drawing. The table is called Bill of Materials, or BOM table. The following figure presents a typical user-defined BOM table. As illustrated, the table lists the names of all the components, which the assembly consists of. The table uses an index to number the components, indicates the quantity of each component, specifies the type of raw material used, and information related to the product realization, such as purchased items and standard parts (bolts, washers, etc.).

INDEX	PART NO	PT NAME	PRICE	QTY	MATS
2	A-006	BOLT	2	4	STEEL1040
1	A-007	BASE_PART	50	1	STEEL1020

Ascending ↑ 3

Width below columns: 5, 10, 12, 7, 5, 6

[5, 10, 12 7 5 6] Width of Each Column = number of characters

Under the Pro/ENGINEER design environment, there are two approaches to generate a BOM table.

- Creation of a simplified BOM table.
- Creation of a user-defined BOM table.

Let us start with the creation of a simplified BOM table. Let us work with ex7_2.asm. From the system tool bar, click the Model tab. Under the Investigate group, click the icon of **Bill of Materials**. A new window called BOM appears. Select **Top Level** and **OK.**

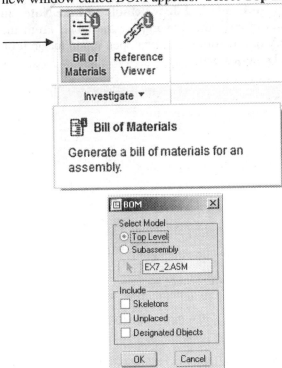

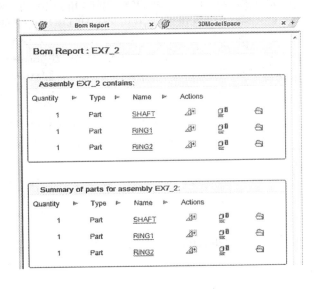

A bill of materials document is on display immediately. Close the file after reviewing it. Note that this document file is automatically saved into your working directory. You may save the file on your disk so that it can be easily identified. The file name is *ex7_2*.bom.

current_session.pro	6/23/2012 10:38 PM	PRO File	1 KB
ex7_2.asm	6/23/2012 9:41 PM	Creo Versioned File	58 KB
ex7_2.asm	6/23/2012 9:41 PM	Creo Versioned File	58 KB
ex7_2.bom	6/23/2012 10:58 PM	Creo Versioned File	1 KB
ring1.prt	6/23/2012 4:26 PM	Creo Versioned File	74 KB
ring2.prt	6/23/2012 4:32 PM	Creo Versioned File	75 KB
ring2.prt	6/23/2012 4:45 PM	Creo Versioned File	75 KB
shaft.prt	6/23/2012 5:27 PM	Creo Versioned File	83 KB

In order to place such a bill of materials on a new sheet in the drawing, we need to work with EX7_2.DRW. We first add a new sheet to the current sheet so that we have a new sheet for the simplified **BOM** table. The procedure to add a new sheet, or sheet number 2, is as follows. From the menu bar, click **Layout > New Sheet**.

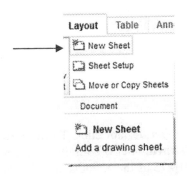

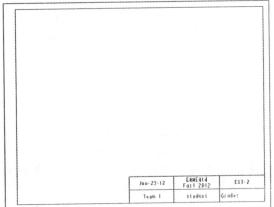

The procedure to add the simplified BOM table is as follows:

Annotation > Note. In the pop up window, select **No Leader > File > Default > Make Note.** In the Select Point window, select **Free Point**. Locate a position in the drawing for the table. From the working directory or your disk containing the file, identify the file of *ex7_2.bom*, open it and locate it on the new sheet (you may need to use All Files to locate) > **Done/Return.**

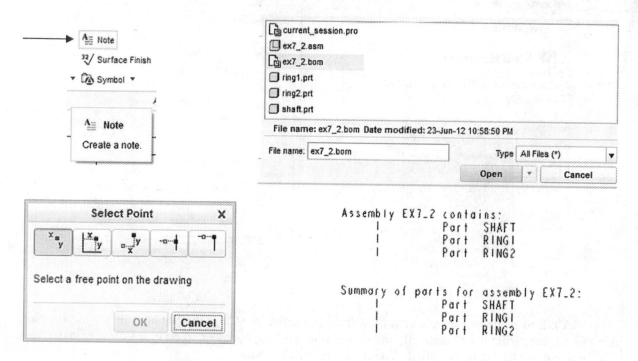

The simplified BOM table lists the information related to quantity, the nature of the model file and the names of the components. For example, there are three components, and the quantities and their names are displayed. As illustrated, the quantity of each component is one in the current case. The nature of each component is Part, not Assembly.

To create a user-defined BOM table, let us copy the sheet with the assembly drawing. To do so, highlight Sheet 1 listed at the bottom of the screen. Click **Move or Copy**. In the pop up window, check the box to create a copy after Sheet 2 > **OK**. Users may add the critical dimensions to it if those dimensions are not shown in Sheet 3.

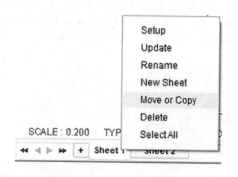
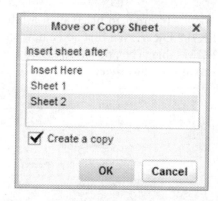

To create a user-defined BOM, From the menu bar, from the **Table** tab, click **Table > Insert Table.** . In the pop up window, click the arrow of **Ascending & leftward.** Set 6 columns and 2 rows. Specify the row height to 1 and the column with to 4 > OK. . Specify 10.75 as the X value and 1.34 as the Y value to define the anchor point for locating the BOM table > OK. A 6x2 table is created.

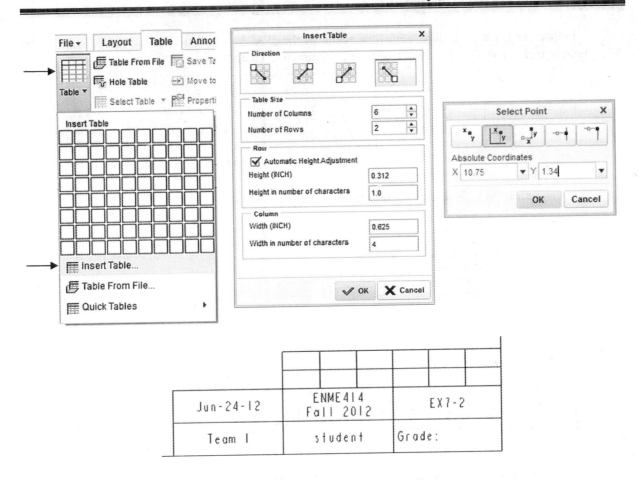

Now let us adjust the widths of columns. From the filter listed on the bottom of the display screen, set to **Column Width**. Pick the second column and right-click to set the width to 9 characters.

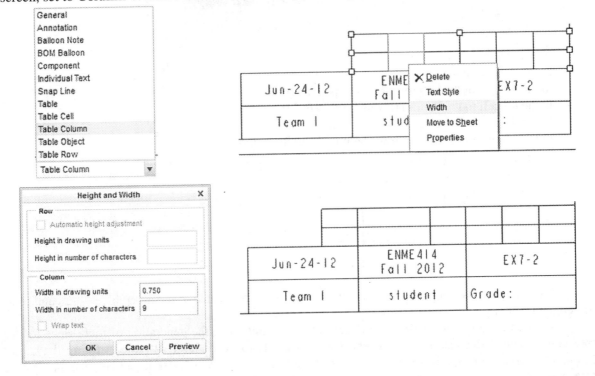

Follow the same procedure, adjust the width of the 3rd column to 11 characters, the width of the 4th column to 6 characters, and the width of the 6th column to 5 characters.

Jun-24-12	ENME414 Fall 2012		EX7-2		
Team 1	student		Grade:		

Let us return the filter setting from Column Width to General.

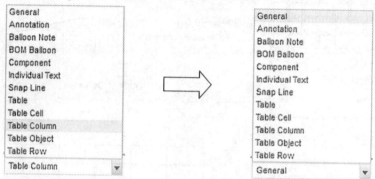

To fill in the contents of the bottom row, do the following:

Double click the first cell (on the left side), type INDEX, click Text Style, and set to Center in Horizontal and Middle in Vertical.

Repeat the process for the 5 other cells.
In the 2nd cell in the bottom row and type PART NO
In the 3rd cell in the bottom row and type PT NAME
In the 4th cell in the bottom row and type PRICE
In the 5th cell in the bottom row and type QTY
In the 6th cell in the bottom row and type MATS (materials)

INDEX	PART NO	PT NAME	PRICE	QTY	MATS
Jun-24-12		ENME414 Fall 2012		EX7-2	
Team 1		student		Grade:	

Step 2: Defining a repeat region to enter the information related to the assembly system and user-defined parameters.

We will use the information on the second row to automate the generation of more rows for the three components. Because of this, a repeat region needs to be defined. Before defining the repeat region, a few things need to be explained. First, the numerical value of **INDEX** can be generated by the software system itself. The PT NAMEs, such as SHAFT, RING1 and RING2, are the names of the three computer files, such as *shaft.prt, ring1.prt* and *ring2.prt*. Therefore, the software system is able to insert these file names into the **BOM** table. The numerical value of **QTY** can be obtained by the software system through counting the number of identical parts used in the assembly.

On the other hand, information on PART NO, PRICE and MATS has to be made available in the process of constructing the **BOM** table. For each of these 3 components, we need to add these 3 parameters. Let us first open the file of shaft.prt. From the model tree, highlight SHAFT.PRT. Right click and hold, select **Open**.

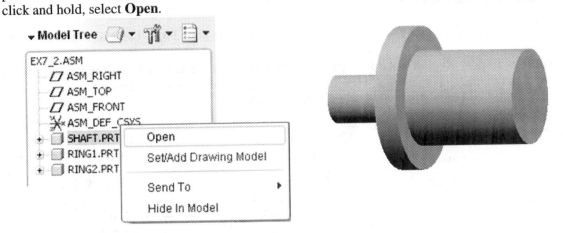

Click **Tools** from the main toolbar > **Parameters** > **Add Parameter** or click the Plus sign.
Type *PART_NO*, select String, and type *A-001*
Add Parameter (or click the plus sign)
Type *PRICE*, select Real Number, and type *50*
Add Parameter (or click the plus sign)
Type *MATS*, select String, and type *1020*
Upon completion, click **OK**.

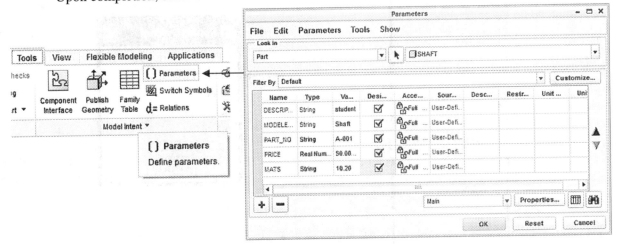

Open the file of *ring_1.prt,* and select **Tools** from the main toolbar,
Parameters > **Add Parameter** or click the Plus sign.
Type *PART_NO*, select String, and type *A-002*
Add Parameter or click the Plus sign
Type *PRICE*, select Real Number, and type *20*
Add Parameter or click the Plus sign
Type *MATS*, select String, and type *1040*
Upon completion, click **OK**.

Open the file of *ring_2.prt,* and select **Tools** from the main toolbar,

Parameters > Add Parameter or click the Plus sign.
Type *PART_NO*, select String, and type *A-003*
Add Parameter or click the Plus sign
Type *PRICE*, select Real Number, and type *30*
Add Parameter or click the Plus sign
Type *MATS*, select String, and type *COPPER*
Upon completion, click **OK**.

Upon completing this process, let us define the repeat region. From the main toolbar of the assembly window,
Table > Repeat Region > Add > Simple. Click or select the first cell and the last cell of the second row to define the repeat region.> **Attributes >** select the repeat region just defined.
No Duplicate > Flat > Bln by Part > Done/Return > Done.

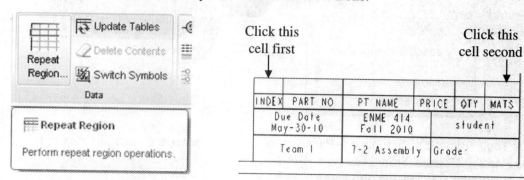

Double click the first cell (the very left cell) of the second row. A window of Report System appears. Select rpt... > index.

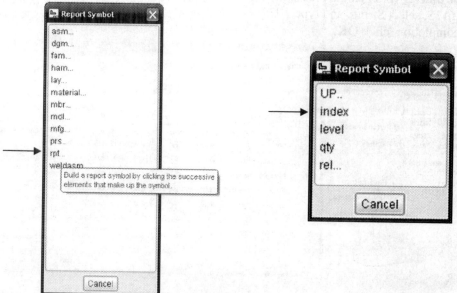

Double click the second cell, select **asm... > mbr > user defined** > type PART_NO and press the **Enter** key.
Double click the third cell, select **asm... > mbr... > name**.
Double click the fourth cell, select **asm... > mbr... > user defined** > type PRICE and press the **Enter** key.
Double click the fifth cell, select **rpt... > qty**.
Double click the sixth cell, select **asm... > mbr... > user defined** > type MATS and press the **Enter** key.
Table > Repeat Region > Update Tables. The table should be displayed, as shown below. The

user may need to center the text contents. To do so, left-click the cell > right-click and hold > select **Properties** > **Text Style** > **Center** in **Horizontal** and **Middle** in **Vertical**.

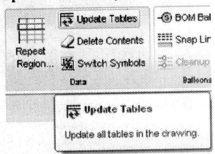

3	A-001	SHAFT	50.000	1	10.20
2	A-003	RING2	30.000	1	COPPER
1	A-002	RING1	20.000	1	1040
INDEX	PART NO	PT NAME	PRICE	QTY	MATS
Jun-24-12		ENME414 Fall 2012		EX7-2	
Team 1		student		Grade:	

The user may need to center the text contents. To do so, left-click the cell > right-click and hold > select **Properties** > **Text Style** > **Center** and **Middle** > **OK**.

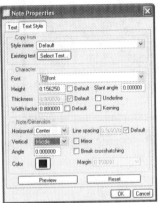

To adjust the decimal number from 3 to 2 (changing 50.000 to 50.00), left-click to select the cell of 50.000 > right-click and hold > Properties > type in [.2] immediately after PRICE > **OK**. From the main toolbar, select **Table** > **Repeat Region** > **Update Table**.

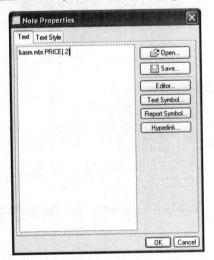

3	A-001	SHAFT	50.00	1	10.20
2	A-003	RING2	30.00	1	COPPER
1	A-002	RING1	20.00	1	1040
INDEX	PART NO	PT NAME	PRICE	QTY	MATS
Jun-24-12		ENME414 Fall 2012		EX7-2	
Team 1		student		Grade:	

If you find that the engineering drawing is on sheet 1, and the formal BOM table is on sheet 3. You are still able to move the engineering drawing from sheet 1 to sheet 3 (or move the BOM table from sheet 3 to sheet 1). Turn the sheet number shown on the bottom of the screen to Sheet 1.

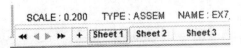

Pick the FRONT view. Right click and hold, select **Move Item to Sheet**. In the Move or Coly Sheet window, select Sheet 3 > OK.

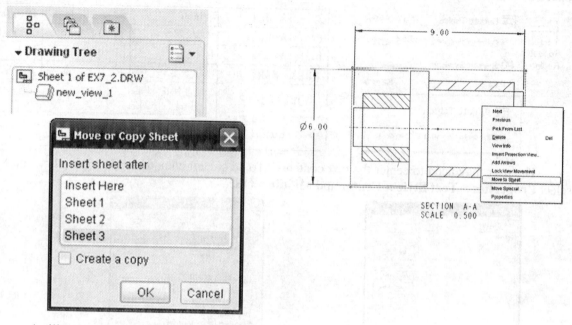

As illustrated, the engineering drawing and the formal BOM table are on the same sheet.

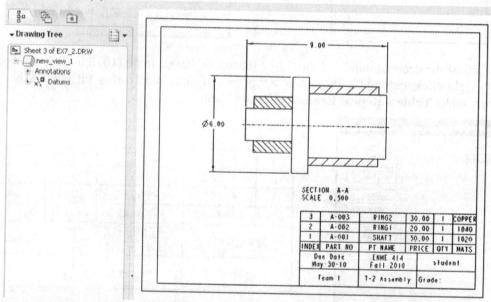

At this time the user has successfully completed the assembly drawing, he or she should save all the work with the drawing. Select **Save** from the main toolbar > **OK.**

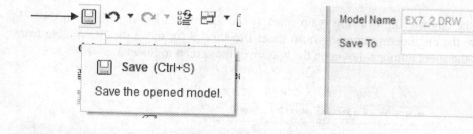

7.6   Creation of an Exploded View and Addition of Colors

Exploded views of assemblies have been widely used in industry. When we buy a product, such as a table or a chair, we need to put pieces together. An exploded view would be one of the best documents to guide the assembly process. It is very important to note that the creation of an exploded view has to be carried on in the assembly environment.

Under the Creo Parametric design environment, there are two approaches to create an exploded view.
- Creation of the default exploded view.
- Creation of a user-defined exploded view.

Let us start with the construction of the default exploded view. Open the file called ex7_2.asm. From the View or Model tab, select **Exploded > Explode View.** To go back to an unexploded view, just click the exploded view icon, again.

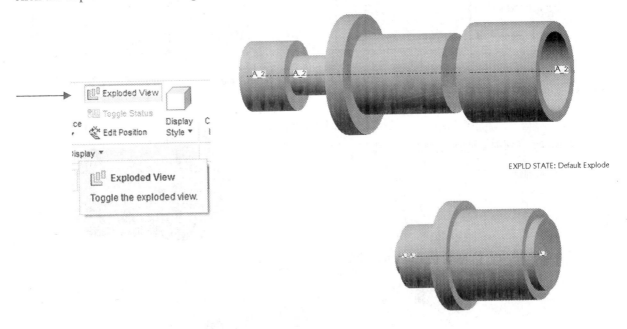

EXPLD STATE: Default Explode

To create a user-defined exploded view, from **View** tab, click **Manage Views > View Manager.** In the **View Manager** window, click **Explode > New**.

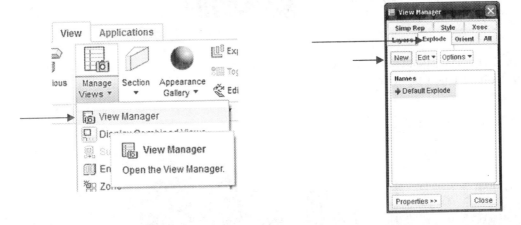

Type *Exploded_1* as the name for the exploded view in this case study > press **Enter** > Click **Properties** > click the icon of **Position.**

Specify the name for the exploded view and press **Enter**

Click **Properties**

Click **Position**

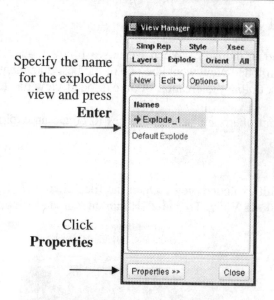
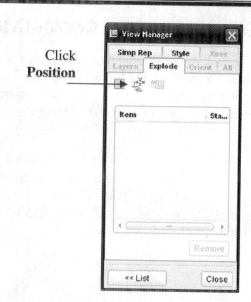

Pick Ring2 and a coordinate system is on display. Select the X- axis, drag Ring2 to the left side and left click to finalize its new position.

Pick Ring2

Drag Ring2 to a new location

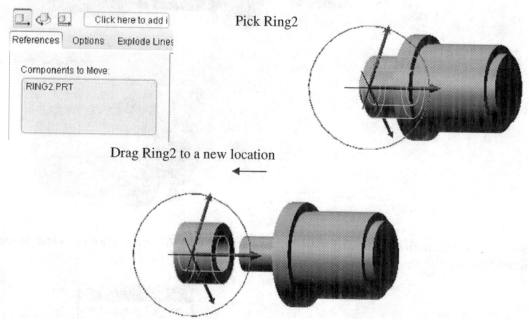

Pick Ring1 and a coordinate system is on display. Select the X- axis, drag Ring1 to the right side and left click to finalize its new position.

Pick Ring1

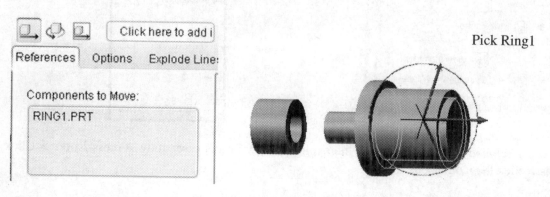

Drag Ring1 to a new location

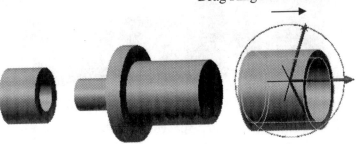

Click the icon of **Apply and Save**. In the View Manager window, click the icon of **List** > click the icon of **Edit** > **Save.**

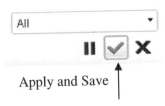

Apply and Save

In the Save Display Elements window, click OK > Close.

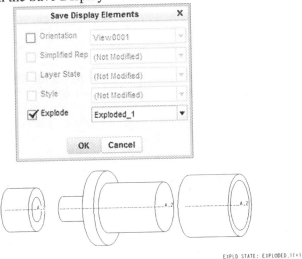

When an assembly consists of a significant amount of components, such as the transmission of a car, using color as a means to enhance the graphical representation is very helpful and effective. In Chapter 5, we discussed how to add a desired color to a component. In this chapter, we present the procedure to add a set of colors to individual components. Let us add a set of three different colors to the three components, as show below.

EXPLD STATE: EXPLODED_I(+)

From the View tab, click the icon of **Appearance Gallery.** The Appearance Gallery window appears. Pick the color, say yellow. Set the filter to component, and use the brush to pick a component (Ring 1). Click **OK**. The yellow color is assigned to Ring1 component.

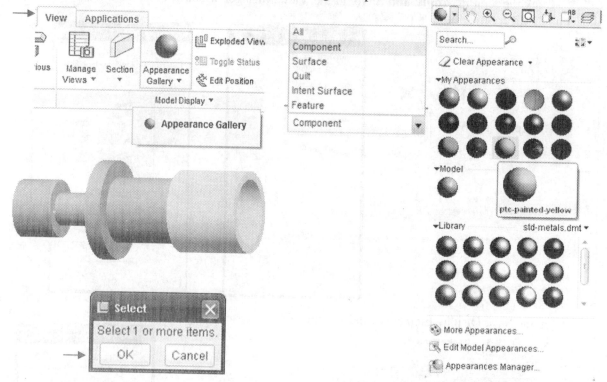

To add color of blue to the Shaft component, pick the blue color from the color map > use the brush to pick the shaft component > **OK**. The blue color is added to Shaft component.

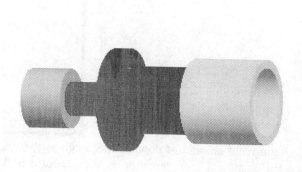

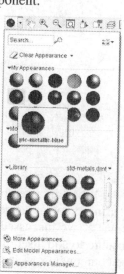

To add color of green to the Ring2 component, pick the green color from the color map > use the brush to pick Ring2 component > **OK**. The green color has been added to Ring2 component.

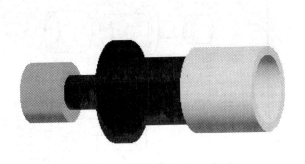

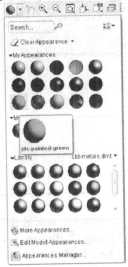

Finally, let us prepare an engineering drawing with the exploded view and add the BOM balloons to the exploded view. First let us return to the drawing mode, or let us activate *ex7-2.drw*, and copy the sheet with the assembly drawing and the user-defined BOM table, or Sheet 3. To do so, highlight Sheet 3 listed at the bottom of the screen. Click **Move or Copy**. In the pop up window, check the box to create a copy after Sheet 3 > **OK**.

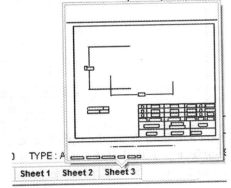

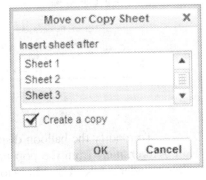

Now let us delete the projection view and add the 3D view in the standard orientation.

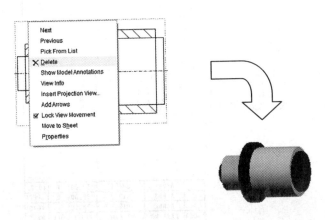

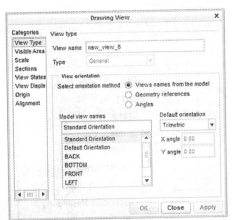

In the Drawing View window, click **View States**. Pick Exploded components in view, and select **Exploded_1** > **Apply** and **Close**.

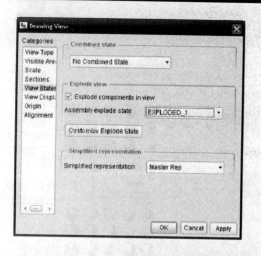

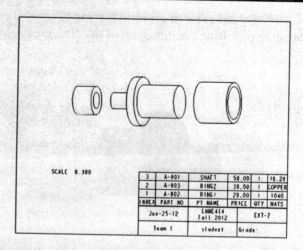

Now let us add BOM balloons to the exploded view. From the main toolbar, Click the Table tab, click **Create Balloons** > Create Balloons – All. Select the repeat region (lift-click the BOM table) > **OK**. The 3 balloons appear on the screen.

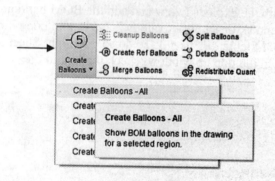

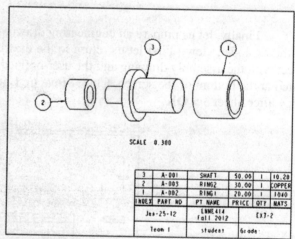

To modify the balloon display, pick a balloon and hold down the right button of mouse and pick **Edit Attachment** from the pop up menu > **On Surface** > **Filled Dot** > select a new location for the balloon leader > OK. Use **Move** to reposition balloons as necessary. Repeat this procedure to modify the leaders of the other 2 balloons.

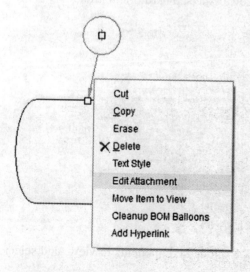

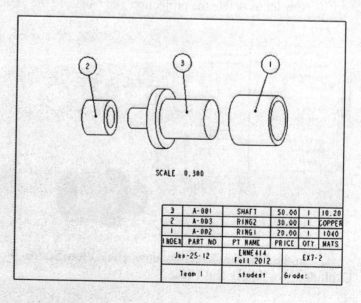

7.7   Creation of an Assembly of a Belt-Roller-Support System

A belt-roller-support system is shown below. As illustrated, the assembly system consists of 7 components. Those components are Shaft, Wheel, Sleeve, Support, Base, Washer and Bolt. An exploded view of the assembly depicts the relative positions of those components during the assembly process.

In this exercise, we first create the 3D solid model for each of the 7 components. Afterwards, we assemble them together. Finally, we reassemble them through the use of Mechanism and add a servo motor to drive the roller in motion.

Part Name	QTY
Shaft	1
Wheel	1
Sleeve	2
Support	2
Base	1
Washer	4
Bolt	4

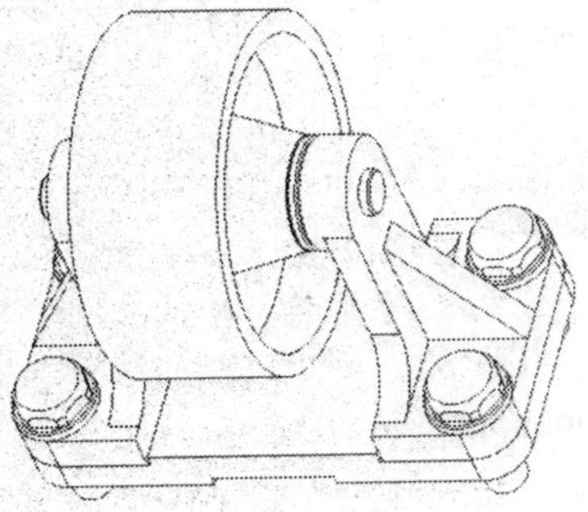

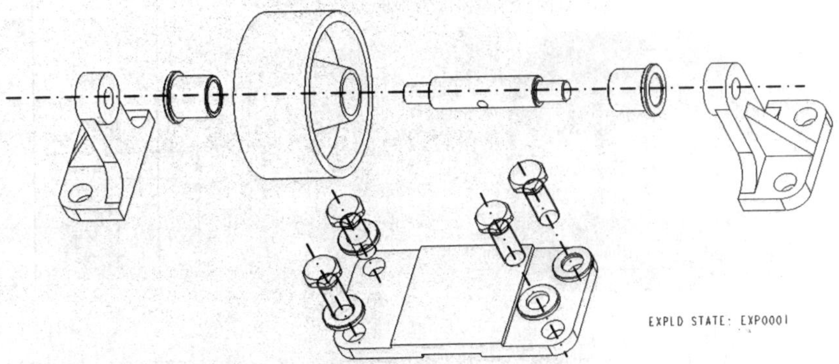

EXPLD STATE: EXP0001

7.7.1 Creation of the 7 Components

Before creating the 7 components, we ask readers a question: "What is the criterion or criteria for selecting a datum plane to be the sketching plane when we are working on the creation of the first feature?" Up to this moment, readers have created quite a few 3D solid models. In the previous chapters, we asked readers to follow the instruction to select the Front datum plane or the Top datum plane. We did not make any explanation(s) to "Why should the sketching plane be the Front datum plane?" In this section, we will answer this question to our readers.

When examining the exploded view shown above, each component has its own unique orientation in the assembly of the product. It is those unique orientations of those components in the assembly, which provide the reason(s) for selecting a specific datum plane to be the sketching plane when creating the first feature. For example, assume **Revolve** will be used to create the wheel component. We should use the Front datum plane as the sketching plane because the rotation axis of the revolving feature will be in the same orientation as the orientation of the axis of the assembled product. Take the base component as another example. Assume **Extrude** will be used to create the plate feature, we should select the Top datum plane as the sketching plane so that the 2 support components can be placed on the base component in the orientation, as illustrated in the above exploded view.

In the following, the geometry and dimensions of the 7 components are shown with their orientations illustrated in the exploded view.

Shaft component

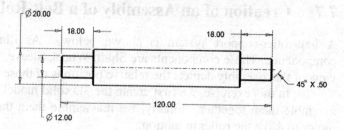

Sleeve component

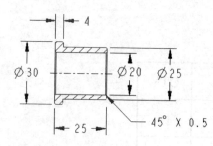

Wheel component

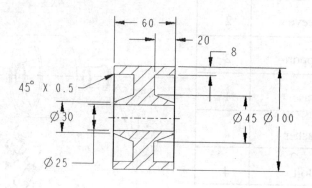

Support component

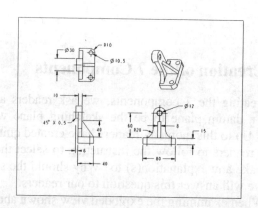

Base component

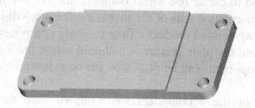
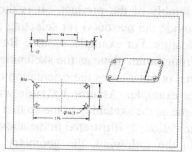

Washer component

Bolt component

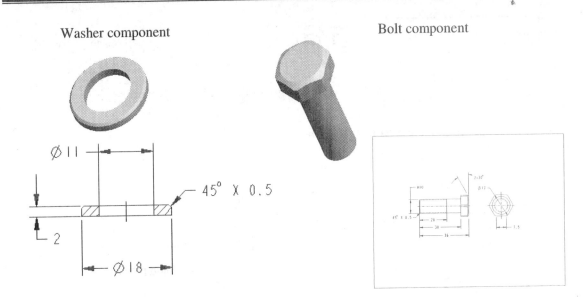

Before creating 3D solid models for the 7 components, let us set the working directory to roller_system. From the top menu, click **Home > Set Working Directory** > locate directory called roller_system > **OK**.

Let us first create the shaft component.

Step 1: Create a file for the 3D solid model. **File > New > Part** > type *shaft* as the file name and clear the box of **Use default template > OK.**

Select **mmns_part_solid** (units: Millimeter, Newton, Second) and type *Shaft* in **DESCRIPTION**, and *student* in **MODELED_BY**, then **OK.**

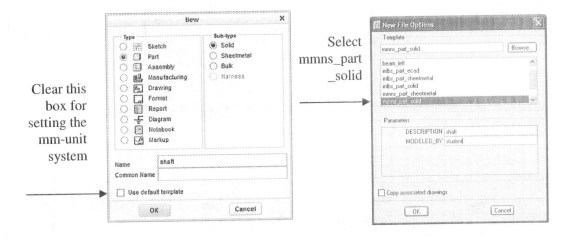

Clear this box for setting the mm-unit system

Select mmns_part _solid

To create a revolved feature, in the Model tab, select **Revolve.**

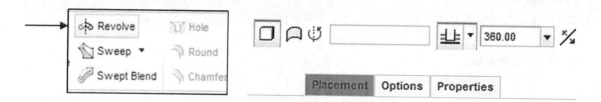

From the model tree, click **FRONT** (sketching planer). Click the icon of **Sketch View** to orient the sketching plane parallel to the screen.

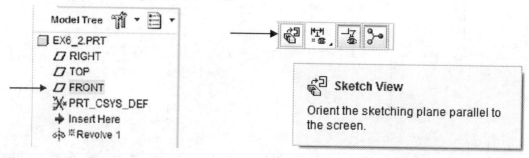

Right-click and hold, select **Axis of Revolution**, and sketch a horizontal centerline.

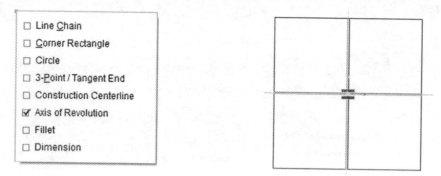

Select the icon of **Line** from the Sketch tab. Sketch 3 lines. Modify the 3 dimensions to 12, 20 and 18, respectively.

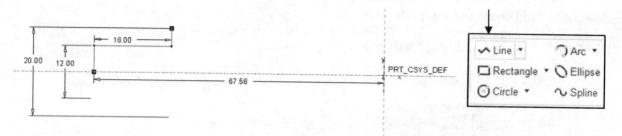

Click the icon of **Centerline** from the Sketch tab. Sketch a vertical centerline.

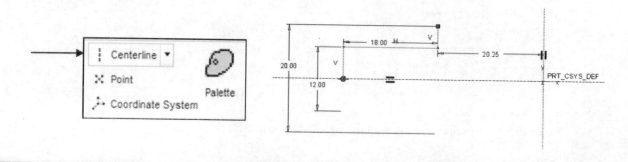

While holding down the **Ctrl** key, pick the 3 sketched lines. Select the icon of **Mirror** to obtain a set of 3 lines on the other side of the default coordinate system.

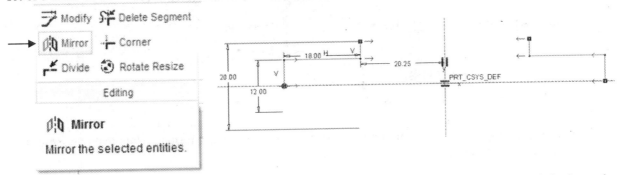

Select the icon of **Line** from the Sketch tab. Sketch 2 lines so that a closed sketch is formed. Click the icon of Normal to define the horizontal dimensions to 120.

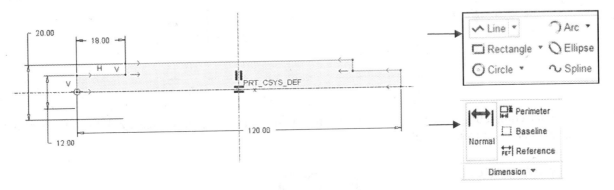

Upon completing this sketch, click the icon of **OK.** Click the icon of **Apply and Save**.

After creating the revolved feature, we create the second feature: chamfers at the sharp edges. Click the icon of **Edge Chamfer** from the toolbar of feature creation. On the dashboard, specify 45xD and 0.5 as the size of the chamfer. While holding down the **Ctrl** key, pick the 4 edges. Click the icon of **Apply and Save**.

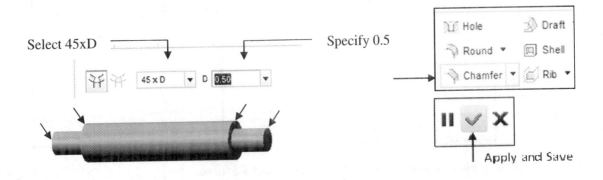

At this time the user has successfully completed the design of shaft component, he or she should save all the work with the 3D solid model. Select **Save** from the main toolbar > **OK**.

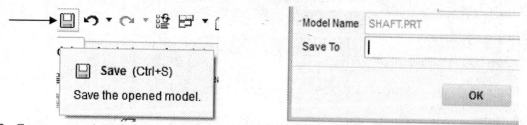

Step 3: Create an engineering drawing for the shaft and add the drawing format. Note that one view is sufficient to meet the criterion for clarification.

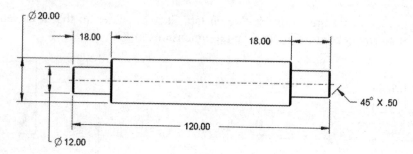

After completing the 3D solid model for the shaft component, let us create a 3D solid model for the sleeve component using **Revolve**.

Step 1: Create a file for the 3D solid model.
   File > New > Part > type *sleeve* as the file name and clear the box of **Use default template**
   Select **mmns_part_solid** (units: Millimeter, Newton, Second) and type *sleeve* in **DESCRIPTION**, and *student* in **MODELED_BY**, then **OK**.

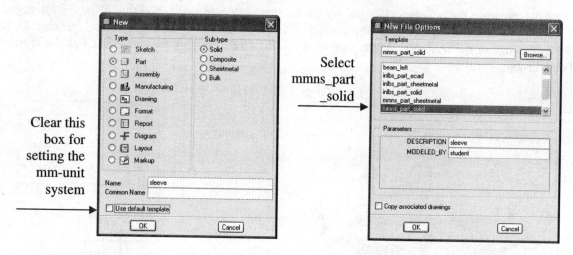

To create a revolved feature, in the Model tab, select **Revolve.**

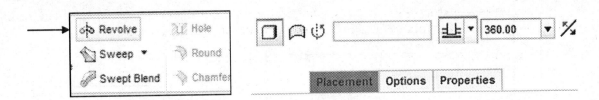

From the model tree, click **FRONT** (sketching planer). Click the icon of **Sketch View** to orient the sketching plane parallel to the screen.

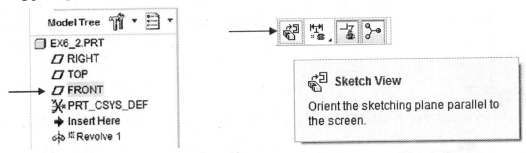

Right-click and hold, select **Axis of Revolution**, and sketch a horizontal centerline.

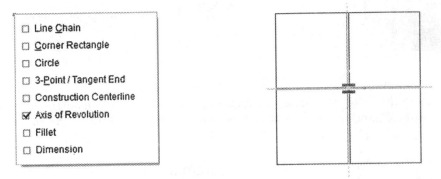

Select the icon of **Line** from the Sketch tab. Sketch 3 lines. Modify the 4 dimensions to 20, 30, 25 and 4, respectively.

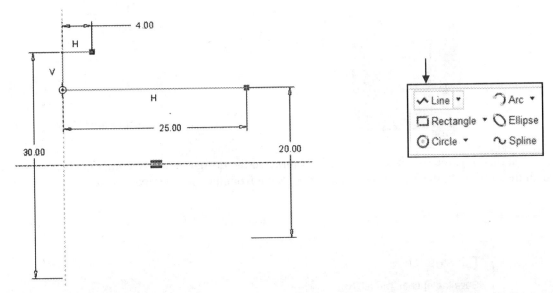

Select the icon of **Line** from the Sketch tab. Sketch 2 lines so that a closed sketch is formed. Modify the dimension to 25, as shown.

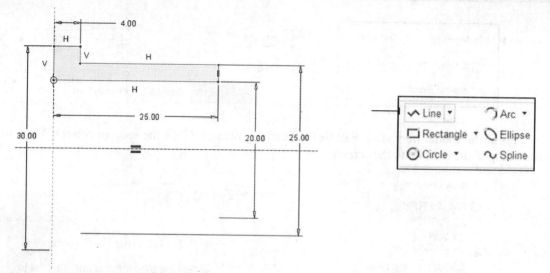

Upon completing this sketch, click the icon of **OK.** Click the icon of **Apply and Save**.

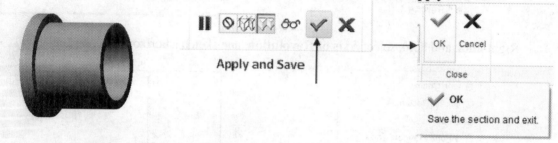

After creating the revolved feature, we create the second feature: chamfers at the sharp edges. Click the icon of **Edge Chamfer** from the Model tab. Specify 45xD and 0.5 as the size of the chamfer. While holding down the **Ctrl** key, pick the 5 edges. Click the icon of **Apply and Save**.

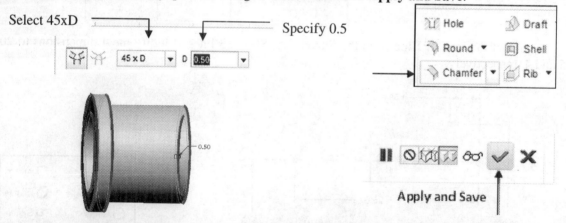

At this time the user has successfully completed the design of sleeve component, he or she should save all the work with the 3D solid model. Select **Save** from the main toolbar > **OK**.

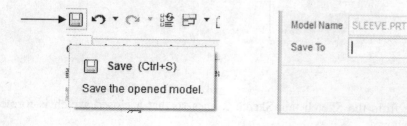

Step 3: Create an engineering drawing for the sleeve and add the drawing format. Note that one view is sufficient to meet the criterion for clarification.

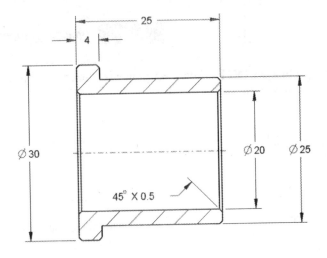

Creation of a 3D solid model for the wheel component using **Revolve**.

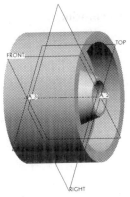

Step 1: Create a file for the 3D solid model.
    File > New > Part > type in *wheel* as the file name and clear the box of **Use default template**
    Select **mmns_part_solid** (units: Millimeter, Newton, Second) and type *wheel* in
    DESCRIPTION, and *student* in **MODELED_BY**, then **OK.**

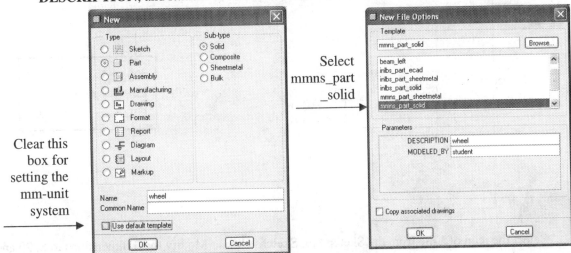

To create a revolved feature, in the Model tab, select **Revolve.**

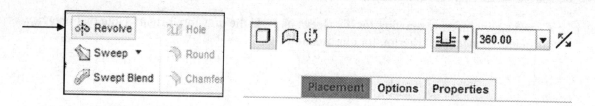

From the model tree, click **FRONT** (sketching planer). Click the icon of **Sketch View** to orient the sketching plane parallel to the screen.

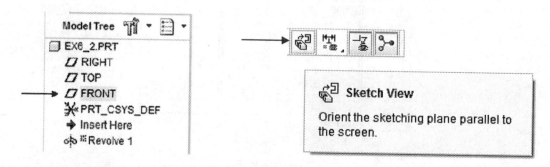

Right-click and hold, select **Axis of Revolution**, and sketch a horizontal centerline.

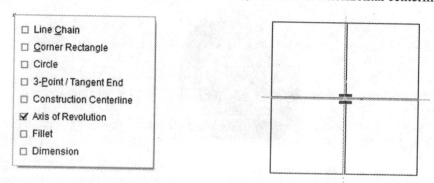

Select the icon of **Line** from the Sketch tab. Sketch 3 lines. Modify the 3 dimensions to 25, 30, and 100, respectively.

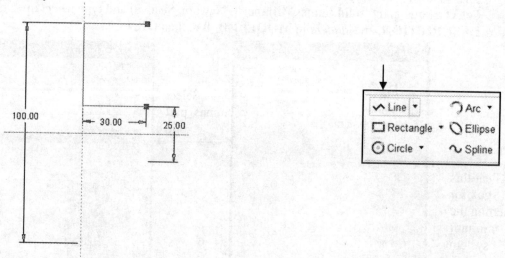

Select the icon of **Line** from the Sketch tab. Sketch 3 lines. Modify the 3 dimensions to 8, 20 and 45, respectively.

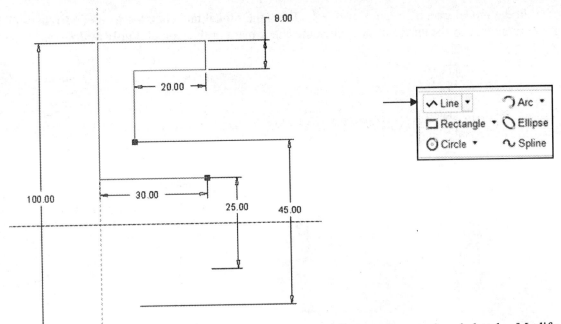

Select the icon of **Line** from the Sketch tab. Sketch 3 lines to form a closed sketch. Modify the dimension to 30, as shown.

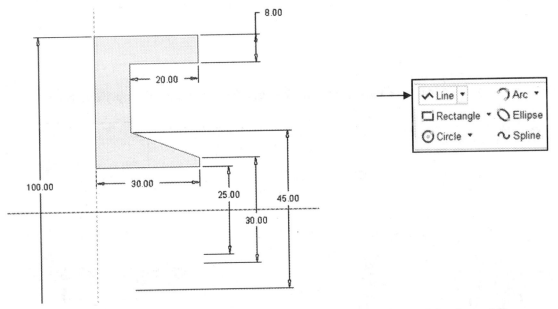

Upon completing this sketch, click the icon of **OK.** Click the icon of **Apply and Save**.

Step 2: Create the other half of the 3D solid model through **Mirror** operation.

In the model tree, highlight Revolve 1. From the Model tab, click the icon of **Mirror** > pick the **Right** datum plane as the mirror plane > click the check mark or the icon of **Apply and Save**.

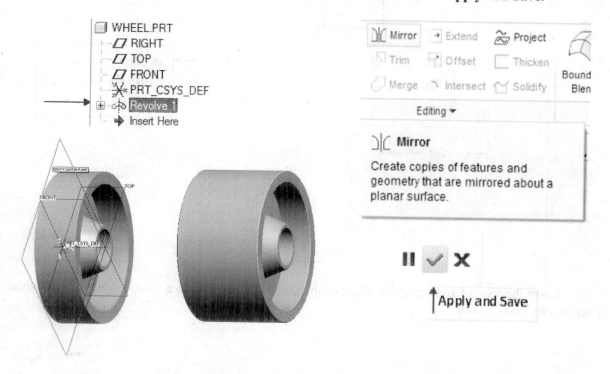

Step 3: Create chamfers on the sharp edges.

Click the icon of **Edge Chamfer** from the Model tab. Specify 45xD and 0.5 as the size of the chamfer. While holding down the **Ctrl** key, pick the 8 edges. Click the icon of **Apply and Save**.

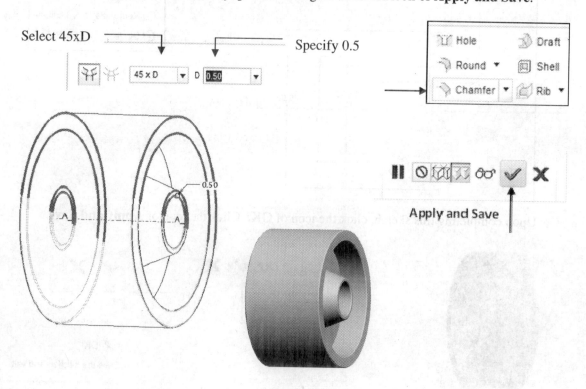

To save this file, click the icon of Save, and click **OK**.

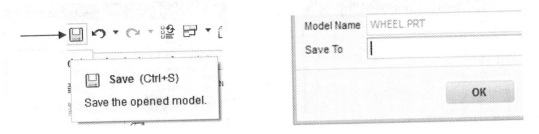

Step 4: Create an engineering drawing for the wheel and add the drawing format. Note that one view is sufficient to meet the criterion for clarification.

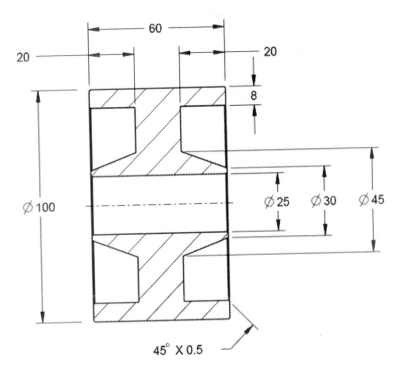

Creation of a 3D solid model for the support component using **Revolve** for the first feature.

Step 1: Create a file for the 3D solid model.

From the main toolbar, **File > New > Part** > type *support* as the file name and clear the box of **Use default template**

Select **mmns_part_solid** (units: Millimeter, Newton, Second) and type support in **DESCRIPTION** and type student in **MODELED_BY > OK**.

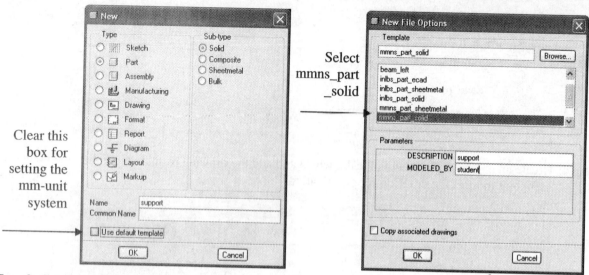

Clear this box for setting the mm-unit system

Select mmns_part_solid

Step 2: Create a 3D Solid Model.

To create a revolved feature, in the Model tab, select **Revolve**.

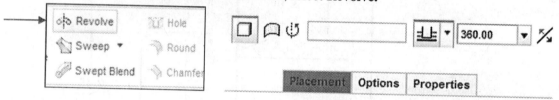

From the model tree, click **FRONT** (sketching planer). Click the icon of **Sketch View** to orient the sketching plane parallel to the screen.

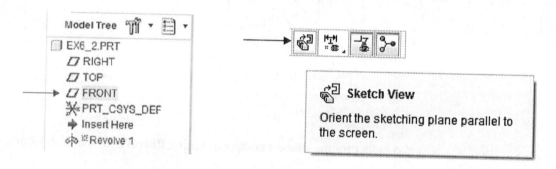

Right-click and hold, select **Axis of Revolution**, and sketch a horizontal centerline.

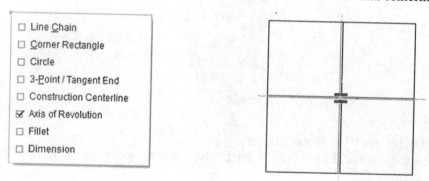

Select the icon of **Rectangle** from the Sketch tab. Sketch a corner rectangle. Modify the 3 dimensions to 12, 30, and 10, respectively.

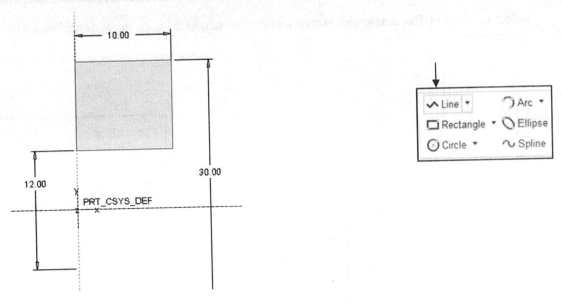

Upon completing this sketch, click the icon of **OK.** Click the icon of **Apply and Save**.

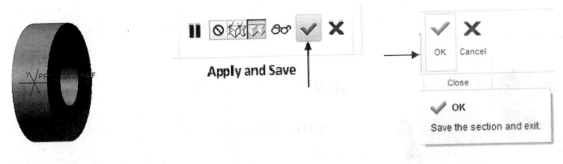

To create the plate portion, from the Model tab, select **Extrude.** Select Symmetry and set the depth value to 80.

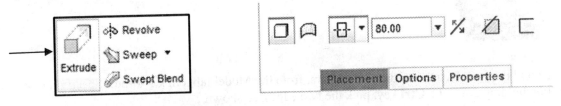

In the model tree, click **FRONT** (sketching plane). Click the icon of **Sketch View** to orient the sketching plane parallel to the screen.

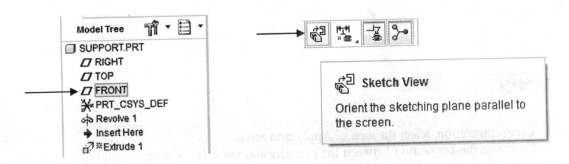

Select the icon of **Rectangle** and sketch a corner rectangle. Modify the 3 dimensions to 40, 10 and 60, respectively.

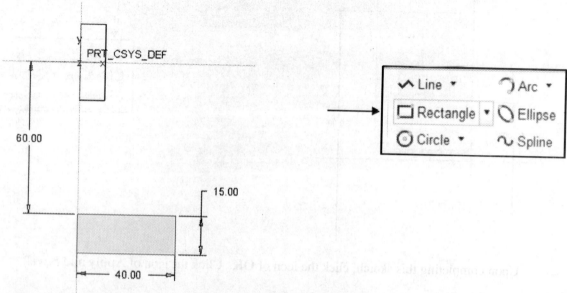

Pick the icon of **Done**, and click the icon **Apply and Save** to complete the creation of the block feature, as shown below:

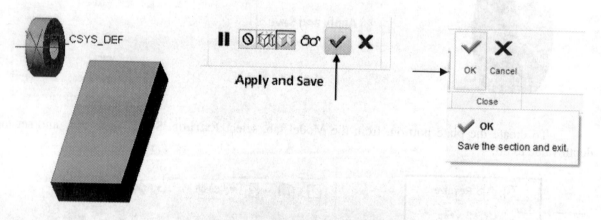

To add the round feature to the two corners, from the Model tab, click **Round.** Specify the radius to 10. While holding down the **Ctrl** key, pick the two edges, as shown.

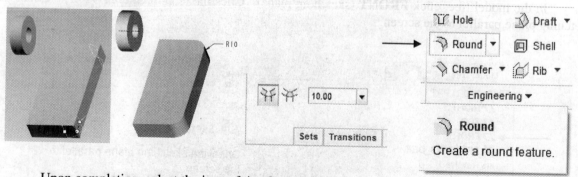

Upon completion, select the icon of **Apply and Save.**

To create the connection between the cylinder and the plate portions, from the Model tab, click **Extrude.** Specify 10 as the depth of extrusion.

Pick the surface on the left side as the sketching plane, and click the icon of **Sketch View** to orient the sketching plane parallel to the screen.

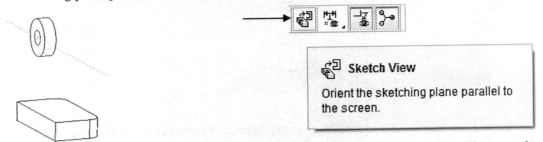

From the Sketch tab, click the icon of **References** > Add 2 new references. They are the top surface of the plate and the outer surface of the cylinder, as shown > **Close**.

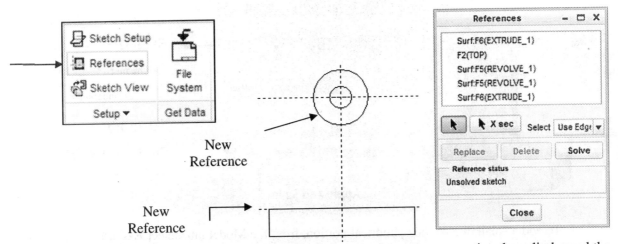

Click the icon of **Line** and the icon of **Arc** to sketch the geometry connecting the cylinder and the plate, as shown. No dimension is needed for the sketch.

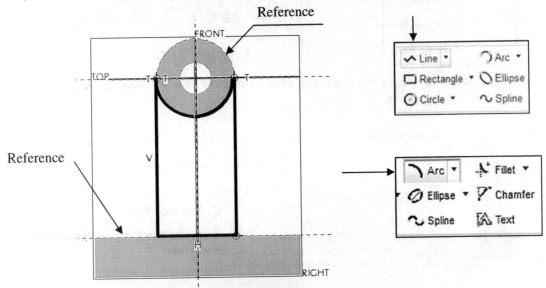

Pick the icon of **Done**, and click the icon **Apply and Save** to complete the creation of the connecting feature, as shown below:

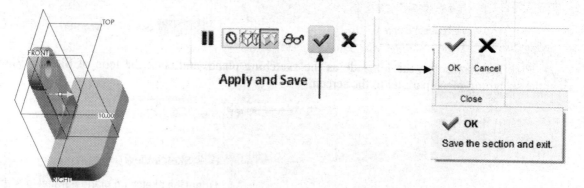

To add the round feature to the two edges, from the Model tab, click **Round.** Specify the radius to 20. While holding down the **Ctrl** key, pick the two edges, as shown. Upon completion, select the icon of **Apply and Save.**

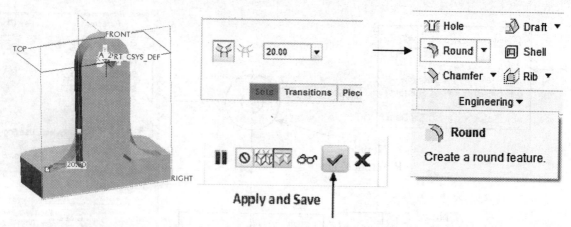

To add a small disk to the cylindrical portion, from the Model tab, select **Extrude.** Specify 6 as the extrusion depth.

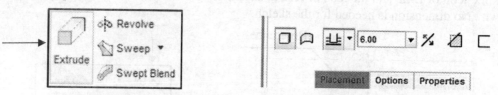

Select the circular surface as the sketching plane. Click the icon of **Sketch View** to orient the sketching plane parallel to the screen.

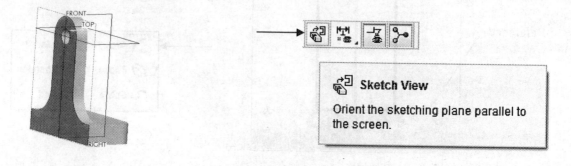

Add two references: the two created circles. Click the icon of Circle to create the following sketch and no dimension is needed. Upon completion, click **Done** and the icon of **Apply and Save** from the feature control panel.

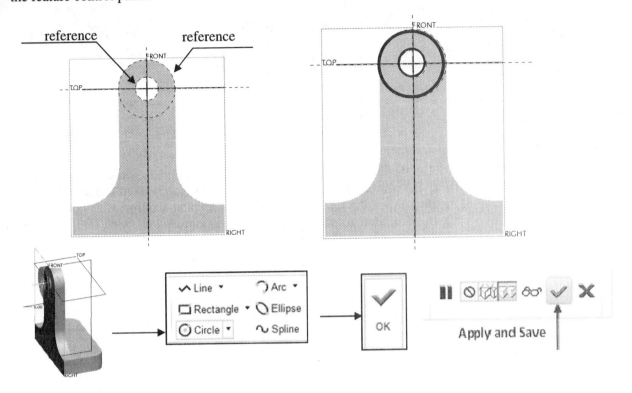

Click the icon of **Edge Chamfer** from the Model tab. Specify 45xD and 0.5 as the size of the chamfer. While holding down the **Ctrl** key, pick the 3 edges. Click the icon of **Apply and Save**.

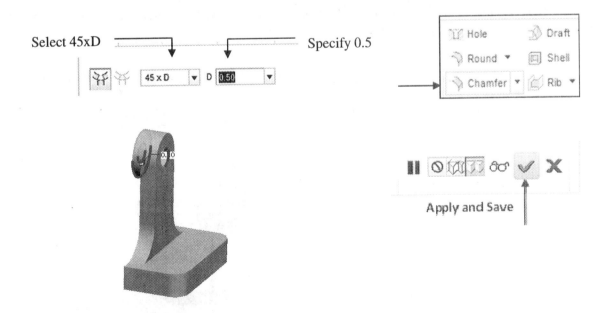

To have the two holes on the plate portion, we create a centerline at one corner using the round feature. From the Model tab, select the icon of **datum axis**, pick the corner surface, as shown > **OK**, and a centerline is created.

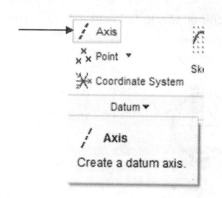
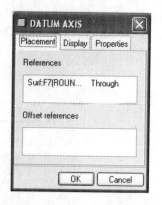

From the Model tab, select the icon of **Hole**.> set the diameter value to 10.5 and the depth choice to **Thru All**. Select the axis as the primary reference (**Coaxial**) and the top surface of the plate as the secondary reference while holding down the Ctrl key > select the icon of **Complete** to complete the placement of the hole. Repeat this procedure to place the other hole, as shown.

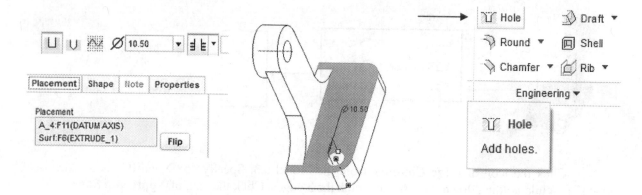

To create the second hole, let us use **Mirror**. From the Model tab, click Mirror, pick the FRONT datum plane as the mirror plane and click the icon of **Done**.

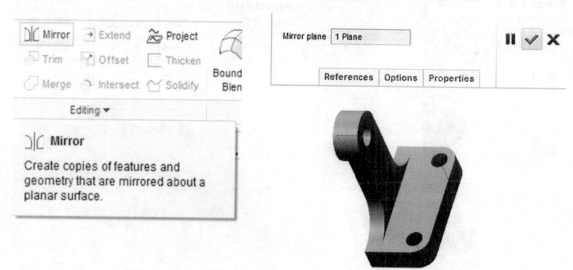

To create a rib to strengthen the rigidity of the support component, from the Model tab , click Rib > Profile Rib. From the model tree, select **FRONT** as the sketching plane, and click Sketch View to orient the sketching plane parallel to the screen. Click the icon of References, add three new references.

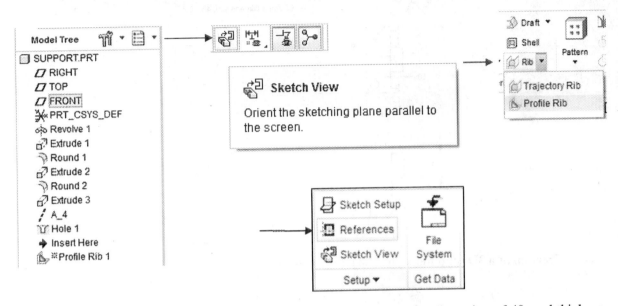

Click the icon of **Line** to sketch a line, as shown and specify the dimension of 40, and thickness of the rib is set to 8. Upon completion, click the icon of **Apply and Save**.

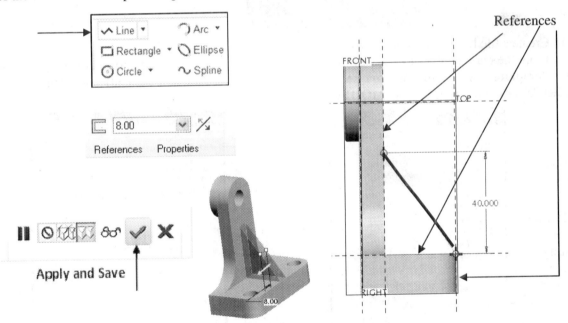

To save this file, click the icon of Save, and click **OK**.

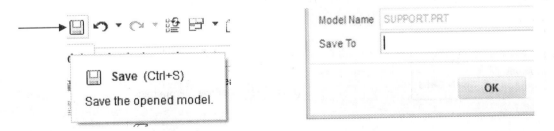

Step 3: Create an engineering drawing for the support and add the drawing format.

Chamfer Dimensison: 45° x0.5

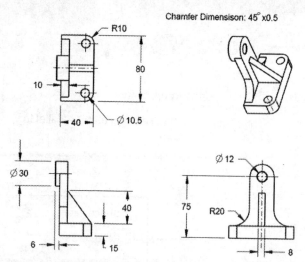

Creation of a 3D solid model for the base component.

Step 1: Create a file for the 3D solid model.

From the main toolbar, **File > New > Part >** type *base* as the file name and clear the box of **Use default template.** Select **mmns_part_solid** (units: Millimeter, Newton, Second) and type *base* in **DESCRIPTION** and type *student* in **MODELED_BY > OK.**

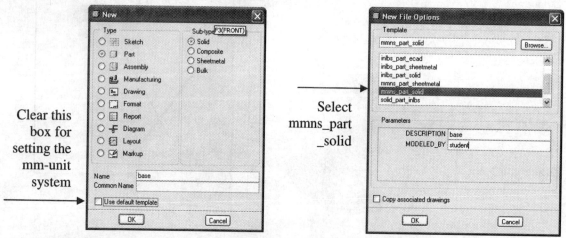

Clear this box for setting the mm-unit system

Select mmns_part _solid

From the Model tab, click the icon of **Extrude.** Set the depth value of extrusion to 12.

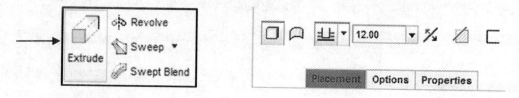

Select the **TOP** datum plane as the sketching plane, and click the box of **Sketch View** to orient the sketching plane parallel to the screen.

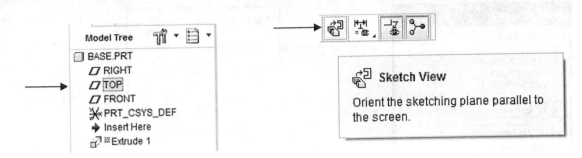

Click the icon of Rectangle and sketch a center rectangle. Modify the 2 dimensions to 176 and 80, respectively. Select the icon of **Done**. Select the icon of **Apply and Save.**

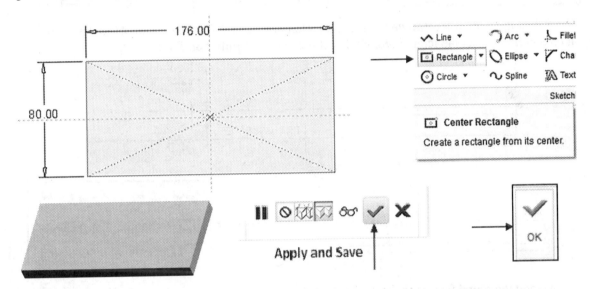

To cut the 2 slots, from the main toolbar, from the Model tab, click the icon of **Extrude.** Select Cut, and set the depth choice to **Thru All**.

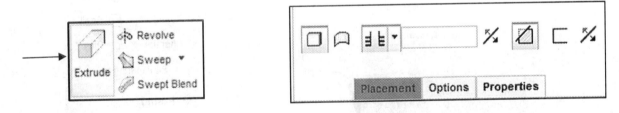

Select the front surface of the plate as the sketching plane, and click the icon of **Sketch** View to orient the sketching plane parallel to the screen.

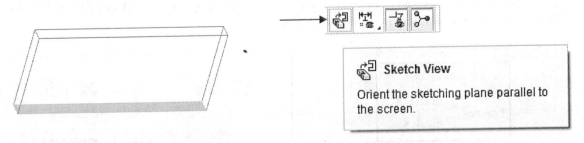

Add three new references: the top surface of the base, the left and right sides.

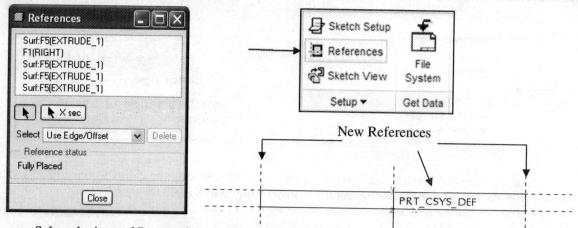

New References

Select the icon of **Rectangle** to sketch 2 rectangles. The 2 dimensions are 41 and 3, respectively. Upon completion, select the icon of **Done**. Select the icon of **Apply and Save.**

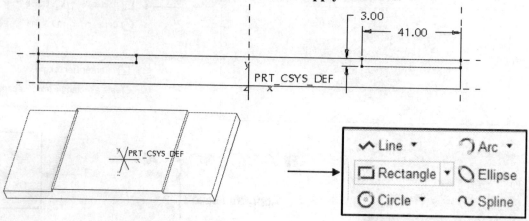

To add the round feature to the 4 corners, from the Model tab, click **Round.** Specify the radius to 10. While holding down the **Ctrl** key, pick the 4 edges, as shown.

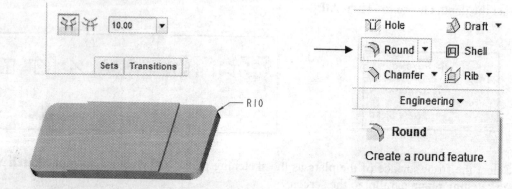

To add 4 holes to the bottom plate through a cut operation, from the Model tab, click of **Extrude**. Select the icon of **Cut** and set the depth choice to **Thru All**.

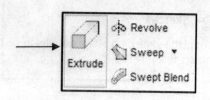

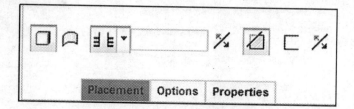

Select the top surface of the cut step as the sketching plane, and click the icon of **Sketch View** to orient the sketching plane parallel to the screen.

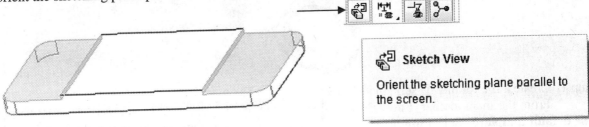

In the Extrude group, click **References** and add 4 additional references, i.e., the arc at each of the 4 corners so that the locations of the 4 centers can be identified. Select the icon of **Circle** to sketch 4 circles. The diameter is 10.5. Upon completion, select the icon of **Done**, and select the icon of **Apply and Save**.

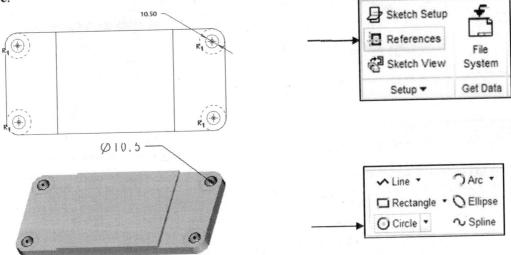

To save this file, click the icon of **Save**, and click **OK**.

Step 3: Create an engineering drawing for the base and add the drawing format.

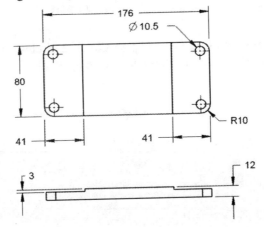

Creation of a 3D solid model for the washer component.

Step 1: Create a file for the 3D solid model of washer.

From the main toolbar, **File > New > Part** > type *washer* as the file name and clear the box of **Use default template.** Select **mmns_part_solid** (units: Millimeter, Newton, Second) and type *washer* in **DESCRIPTION** and type *student* in **MODELED_BY > OK**.

Clear this box for setting the mm-unit system

Select mmns_part_solid

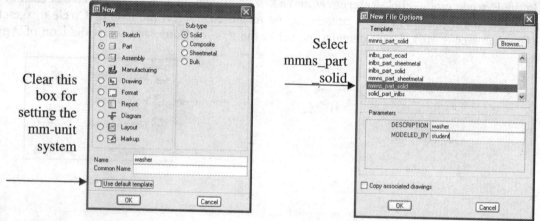

From the Model tab, click the icon of **Extrude.** Specify 2 as the height value.

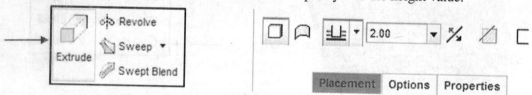

From the model tree, select the **TOP** datum plane as the sketching plane, and click the icon of **Sketch View** to orient the sketching plane parallel to the screen.

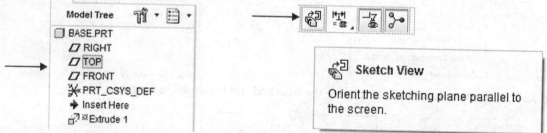

Click the icon of **circle** from the Extrude group to sketch 2 circles. Their diameters are 11 and 18, respectively. Select the icon of **Done**, and click the icon of **Apply and Save.**

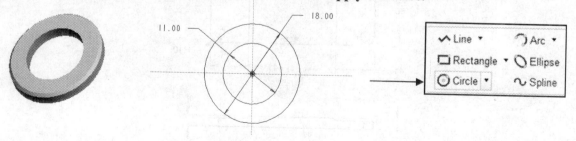

Click the icon of **Edge Chamfer** from the Model tab. Specify 45xD and 0.5 as the size of the chamfer, and pick the edge. Click the icon of **Apply and Save**.

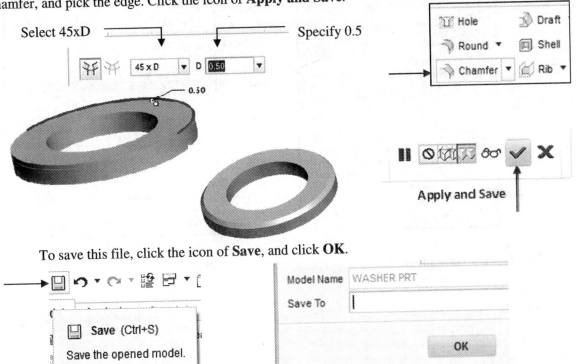

Select 45xD — Specify 0.5

Apply and Save

To save this file, click the icon of **Save**, and click **OK**.

Save (Ctrl+S)
Save the opened model.

Model Name WASHER PRT
Save To
OK

Step 3: Create an engineering drawing for the washer component and add the drawing format. Note that one view is sufficient to meet the criterion for clarification.

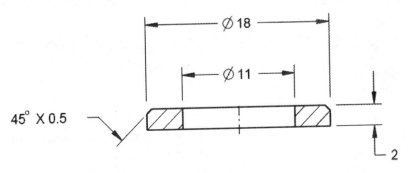

Ø 18

Ø 11

45° X 0.5

2

Creation of a 3D solid model for the bolt component.

Step 1: Create a file for the 3D solid model of bolt.

From the main toolbar, **File > New > Part >** type *bolt* as the file name and clear the box of **Use default template.** Select **mmns_part_solid** (units: Millimeter, Newton, Second) and type *bolt* in **DESCRIPTION** and type *student* in **MODELED_BY > OK**.

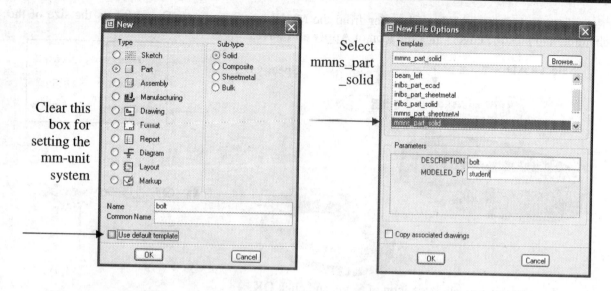

Clear this box for setting the mm-unit system

Select mmns_part _solid

To create a revolved feature, in the Model tab, select **Revolve.**

From the model tree, click **FRONT** (sketching planer). Click the icon of **Sketch View** to orient the sketching plane parallel to the screen.

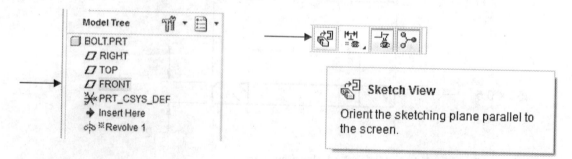

Right-click and hold, select **Axis of Revolution**, and sketch a vertical centerline.

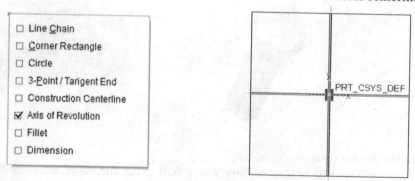

Select the icon of **Line** from the Sketch tab. Create the following sketch with the specified dimensions. Upon completing this sketch, click the icon of **OK.** Click the icon of **Apply and Save.**

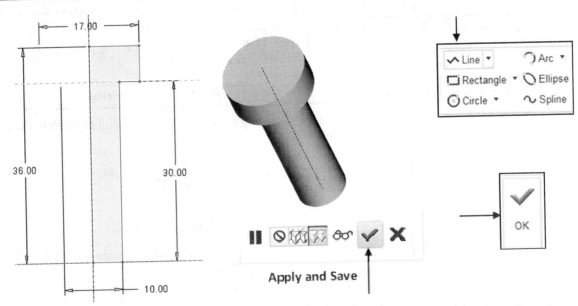

To create a 30 degree chamfer on the bolt head, directly pick the icon of **Chamfers** from the Model tab. Select **AnglexD** and specify *30* and *2* as the chamfer dimensions. Pick the edge on the top surface. Upon completion, select the icon of **Apply and Save** from the feature control panel.

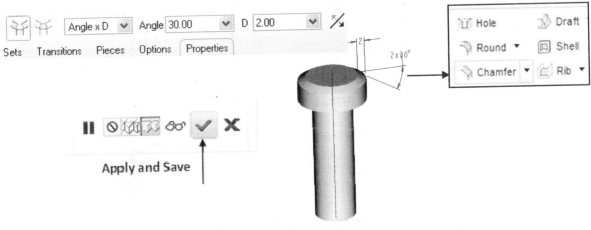

To create a 45 degree chamfer on the bolt head, from the Model tab, pick the icon of **Chamfer.** Select **45xD** and specify *0.5* as the chamfer dimensions. Pick the edge on the bottom corner. Upon completion, select the icon of **Apply and Save.**

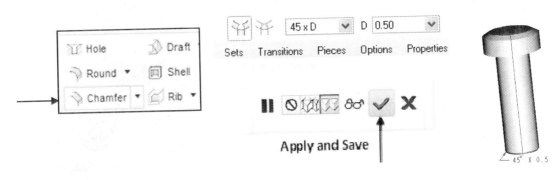

To create the hex shaped head, from the Model tab, select **Extrude.** Click the icon of **Cut** and set the depth choice to **Thru All**.

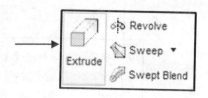

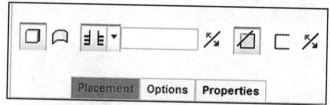

Select the bottom surface of the head as the sketching plane, and click the icon of **Sketch View** to orient the sketching plane parallel to the screen.

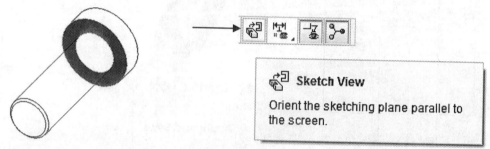

Add a reference, i.e., the outside circular surface. Sketch a line, as shown below with a dimension of 7.5. Select the icon of **Done**, and click the icon of **Apply and Save.**

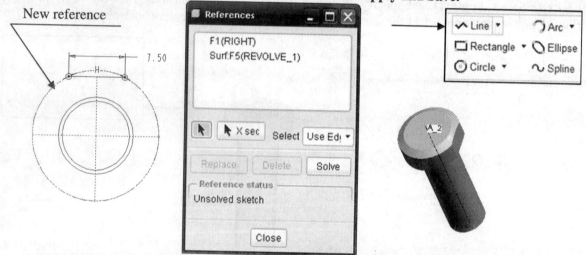

Use the function of **Pattern** to create the other 5 cuts. From the model tree, highlight the cut feature, right-click and hold > **Pattern**. Change **Dimension** to **Axis** > Pick the axis of the bolt.

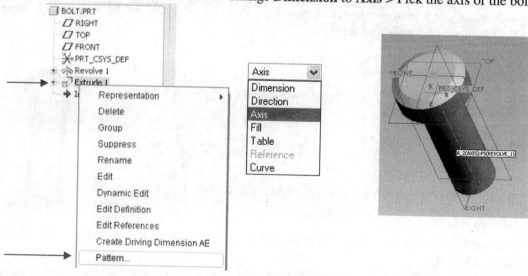

Set the total copies of the cut to 6, which includes the current cut, and set the incremental angle to 60 degrees > click **Apply and Save** from the feature control panel.

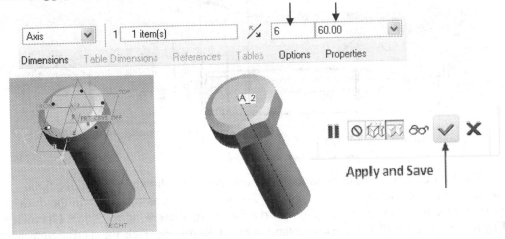

To define the thread feature, from the Model tab, click **Engineering** > **Cosmetic Thread**. Select the cylindrical surface as the thread surface. Select the bottom surface as the starting surface for creating the thread. Specify 25 as the thread length and set the pitch value to 0.5. Click the icon of **Apply and Save**.

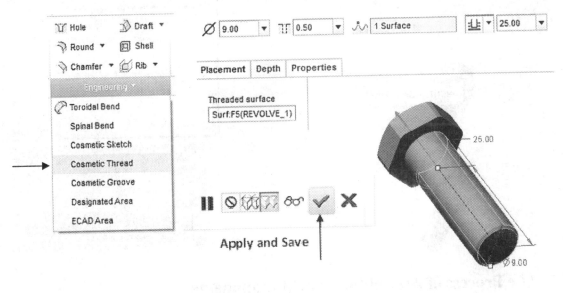

To save this file, click the icon of **Save**, and click **OK**.

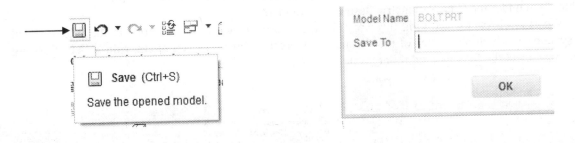

Step 3: Create an engineering drawing for the shaft and add the drawing format.

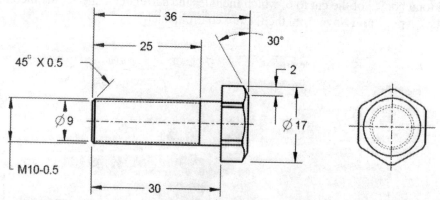

The Front View may not be in the same orientation as shown in the above figure. How to set the orientation of the bolt on the drawing screen? The procedure is as follows. In the drawing mode, click **General** to have the 3D view on display. In the **Drawing View** window, select **Geometry References**. Set **Front** and pick the FRONT datum plane, and set **Right** and pick the TOP datum plane. The new orientation is set and click **OK**.

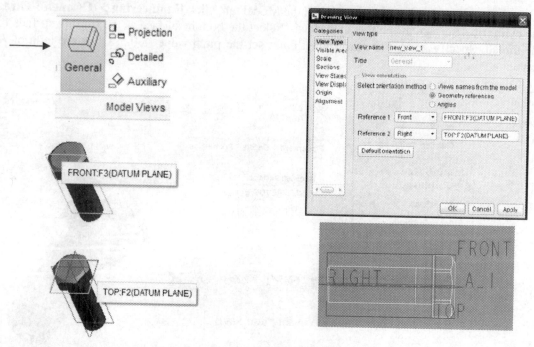

7.7.2 The Process of Assembling the 7 Components

In the previous section, we have created the solid models for the 7 components. In this section, we will assemble them under the Creo Parametric design environment.

We first check the working directory to make sure the working directory is the folder called roller_system, in which the 7 files of the 7 components reside. From the top menu, **File > Set Working Directory** > select the folder called roller_system > **OK**.

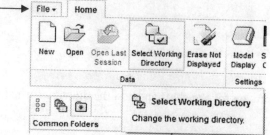

Step 1: Create a file for assembling the 3D solid models under the directory of roller_system.

      File > New > Assembly > type *belt_roller_support* as the file name and clear the box of **Use default template > OK**. Select **mmns_asm_design** (units: Millimeter, Newton, Second) and type *assembly* in **DESCRIPTION** and type *student* in **MODELED_BY > OK**.

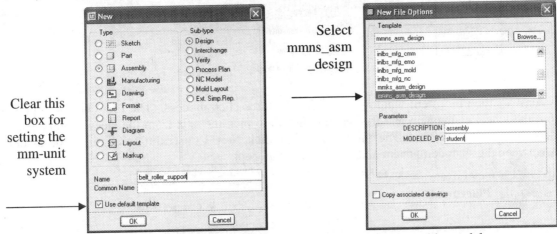

Step 2: Assemble the wheel with the default coordinate system of the assembly model.

      The first step in assembling components is to assemble the default coordinate system of the first component with the ASM_DEF_CSYS. In this case, the wheel component, or *wheel.prt,* will be the first component to be assembled to the assembly.

      Select the icon of **Assemble** from the assembly icon list. From the local memory, or **In Session**, select *wheel.prt*, and open it.

      Under the **Constraint Type**, pick the icon of **Default**, which means automatically placing the origin of the PART_DEF_CSYS to the origin of the ASM_DEF_CSYS and the orientations of the 2 coordinate systems are identical > **Full Constrained** is indicated under **Status**> click the icon of **Apply and Save**.

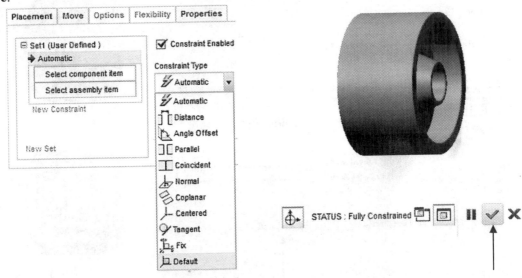

Click the icon of **Assemble**, and open the file called *sleeve.prt* from **In Session**.

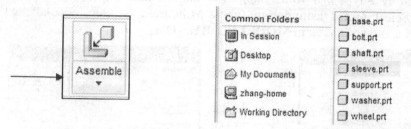

Activate the **Placement** window. We start the three-click process. The first click is to pick the axis from the wheel component and the second click is to pick the axis from the sleeve component. A coincident constraint is defined. The third click is to click **New Constraint** to continue the assembly process between the shaft component and the ring 1 component.

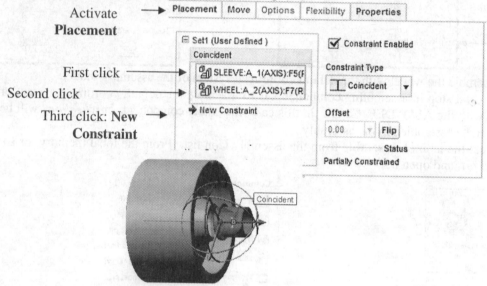

To define the second constraint, the first click is to pick the flat surface from the wheel component, and the second click to pick the flat surface from the sleeve. A coincident constraint is defined. To flip the orientation, click Flip. Click the icon of Apply and Save/

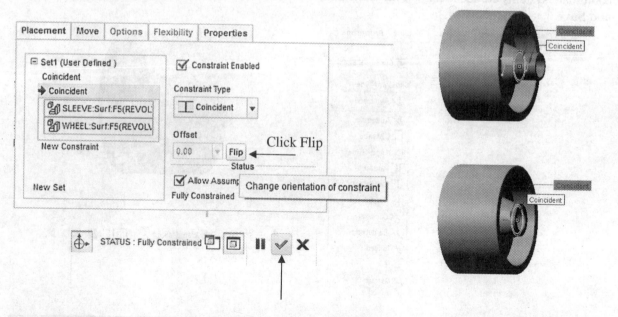

To assemble the second component of sleeve on the left side of the wheel component, click the icon of **Assemble**. Let us work with the displayed **3D Dragger**. Pick the shaded arrow in the X direction and drag it to translate the position of the sleeve component to the left side of the wheel component.

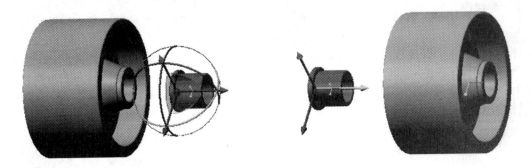

Now let us repeat the procedure to assemble the first sleeve component with 2 coincident constraints.

Step 4: Assemble the shaft component with the assembly, which contains the wheel component and 2 sleeve components.

Click the icon of **Assemble**, and open the file called *shaft.prt* from **In Session**.

Under the **Constraint Type**, pick the icon of **Default**, which means automatically placing the origin of the PART_DEF_CSYS to the origin of the ASM_DEF_CSYS and the orientations of the 2 coordinate systems are identical > **Full Constrained** is indicated under **Status**> click the icon of **Apply and Save**.

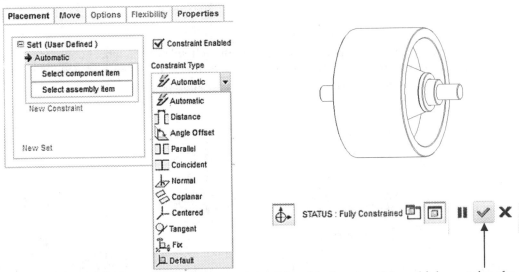

Step 5: Assemble the support component on the right side with the assembly, which contains the wheel component, 2 sleeve components and a shaft component.

Select the icon of **Assemble** > select *support.prt*, and open it.

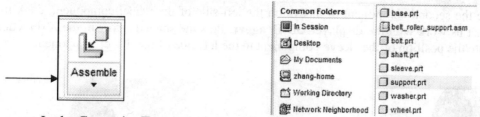

In the Constraint Type, use **Automatic** > pick the two centerlines > **Coincident** is automatically set. Click **New Constraint** > Automatic, pick the 2 surfaces, as shown. In the Placement Status window, a message Full Constrained appears > **OK**. Click the icon of **Apply and Save** to complete the process of assembling the first support component.

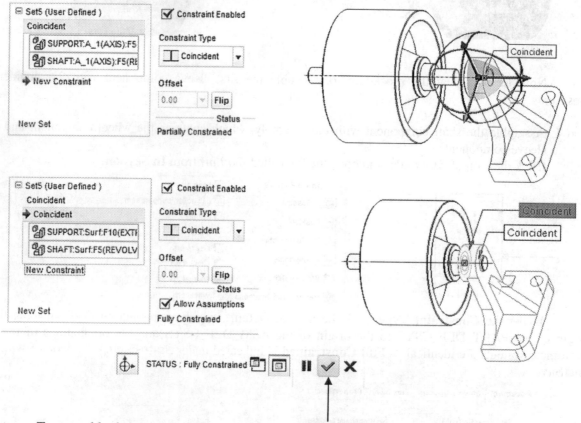

To assemble the second support component on the left side of the wheel component, let us work with the displayed **3D Dragger**. Pick the shaded arrow in the X direction and drag it to translate the position of the support component to the left side of the wheel component.

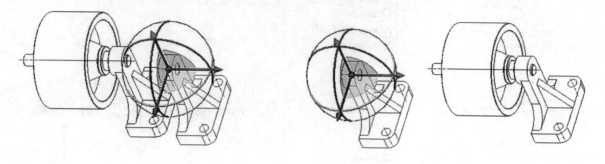

Now pick the shaded arc to rotate 180 degrees about the Y axis, as shown.

Now let us repeat the procedure to assemble the first support component with 2 coincident constraints.

Sometimes, users may have an assembly where the second support is in an opposite position after exiting from the assembly process, as shown. Under such a circumstance, in the model tree, highlight this support component, right-click and hold and select **Edit Definition > New Constraint**. At this moment, we add one more constraint.

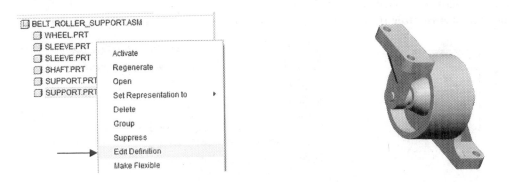

Let us work with the displayed **3D Dragger**. Pick the shaded arc and rotate 90 degrees, as shown.

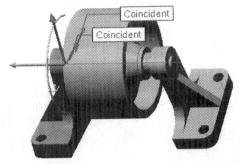

Pick two datum planes to define a new coincident constraint. These 2 datum planes are ASM_TOP and the TOP datum plane from the support component Click the icon of **Apply and Save.**

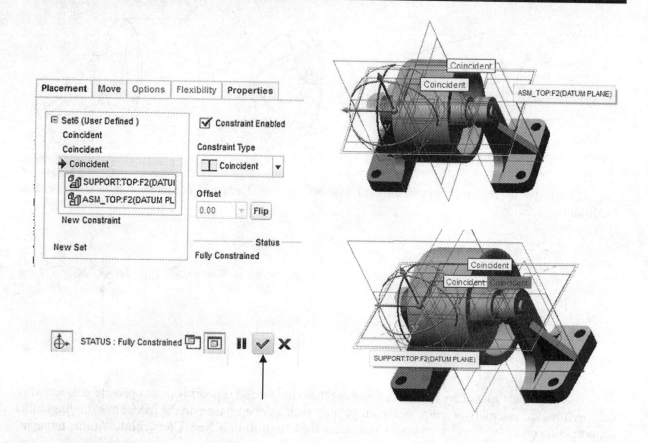

Step 6: Assemble the base part with the assembly, which contains the wheel component, 2 sleeve components, a shaft component and a support component.

Select the icon of **Assemble** from the toolbar of assembly creation > select *base.prt*, and open it.

In the Constraint Type, use **Automatic** > pick the bottom surface from the support component and pick the top surface from the base component, as shown > **Coincident** is automatically set.

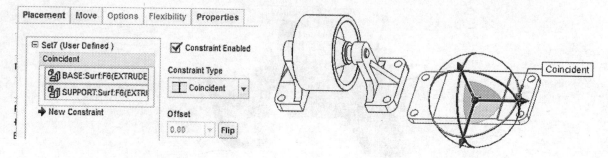

Click **New Constraint** > Automatic, pick the front side surface from the support component and the front side surfaces from the base component, as shown > **Coincident** is automatically set.

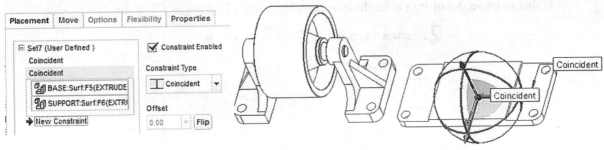

Click **New Constraint** > Automatic, pick the right side surface from the support component and the right side surface from the base component, as shown. Pick **Coincident** as the constraint type. In the Placement Status window, a message **Full Constrained** appears > **OK**.Click the **Apply and Save** icon.

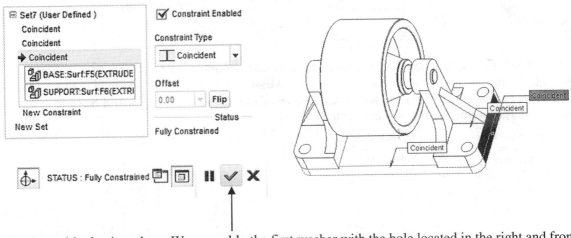

Step 7: Assemble the 4 washers. We assemble the first washer with the hole located in the right and front. Select the icon of **Add** from the toolbar of assembly creation > select *washer.prt*, and open it.

In the Constraint Type, use **Automatic** > pick the bottom surface from the washer component and pick the top surface from the support component. Select **Coincident.**

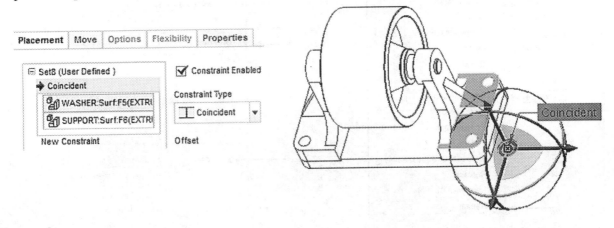

At this moment, let us turn off or hide the display of the 3D dragger. Click the icon of Hide

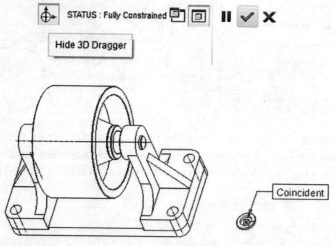

Click **New Constraint > Automatic**, pick the axis from the washer component and the axis from the hole of the support component, as shown > **Align** is automatically set. In the Placement Status window, a message **Full Constrained** appears > **OK**. Click the icon of **Apply and Save** to complete the process of assembling the first washer component.

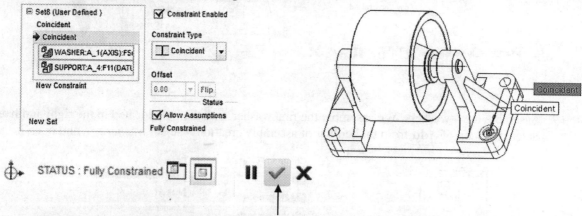

To assemble the other 3 washers, use **Repeat**. In the model tree, highlight WASHER.PRT. Right click and pick **Repeat**. In the **Repeat Component** window, highlight the 2 **Coincidents > Add**.

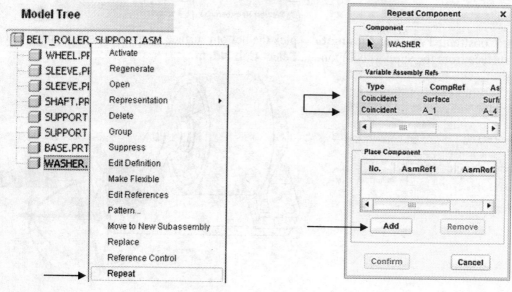

On the display, click the top surface of the support component and the axis of a hole. Repeat this procedure 2 more times > **Confirm**. Three more washer components have been assembled.

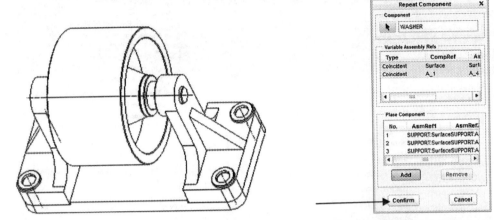

Step 8: Assemble the 4 bolts. We assemble the first bolt with the washer first assembled.
Select the icon of **Add** from the toolbar of assembly creation > select *bolt.prt*, and open it.

In the Constraint Type, use **Automatic** > pick the bottom surface of the bolt head and the top surface of the washer component, as shown > **Coincident** is automatically set.

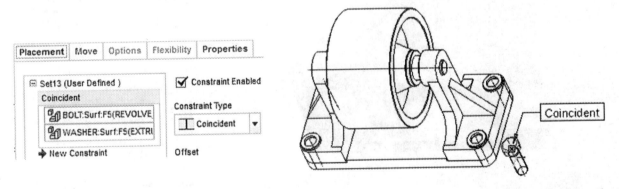

New Constraint > Automatic > pick the axis from the bolt component and the axis from the washer component, as shown > **Coincident** is automatically set. Click the icon of **Apply and Save**.

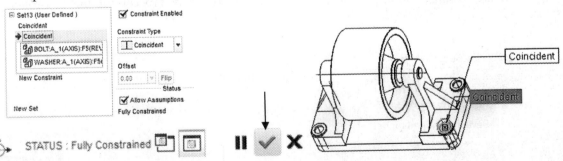

To assemble the other 3 bolts, use **Repeat**. In the model tree, highlight BOLT.PRT. Right click and pick **Repeat.** In the Repeat Component window, highlight the 2 **Coincidents > Add**.

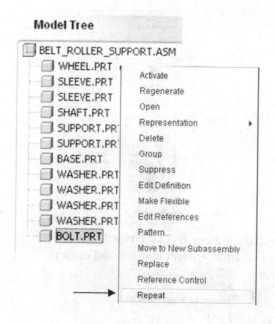

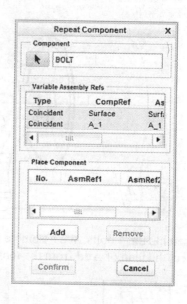

On the display, click the top surface of the washer component and the axis of the washer component. Repeat this procedure 2 more times > **Confirm**. Three bolt components have been assembled.

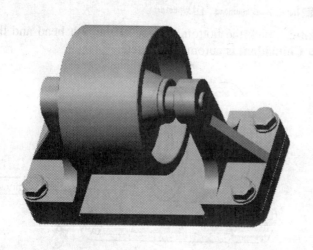

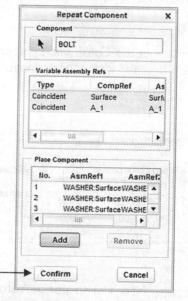

At this moment, we have completed the entire assembly process for the belt-roller-support system. To save this assembly file, click the icon of **Save**, and click **OK**.

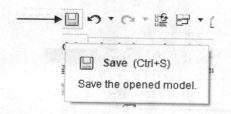

To prepare an engineering drawing based on the assembled model, we open a new file under the Mode of **Drawing**. First, we select the icon of **Create** a new object from the main toolbar. Type *assembly_drawing* as the file name. Clear the box of Use default template and click the box of **OK**.

In the window of **New Drawing**, make sure that the file of the assembled model called *belt_roller_support* is shown. Otherwise, use "**Browse**" to locate it. Select **Empty** under Specify Template, and select the paper size to be **A**. Afterwards, click the box of **OK**.

Select the drawing mode

Clear the default box

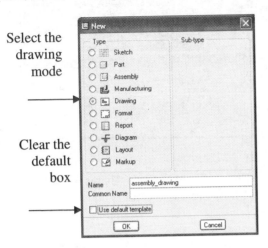

Locate the 3D solid model file

Select paper size

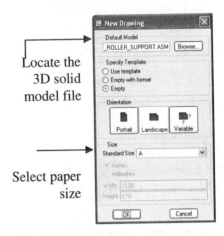

A window called **Select Presentation** appears. Keep the default choice of **No Presentation** and click the box called **Do not prompt for Presentation > OK**.

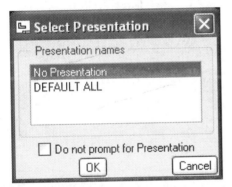

This brings up the drawing screen. Click the **Layout** tab. Click the icon of **General.** In the **Select Combined State** window, click **OK** to accept **No Combined State**.

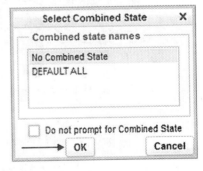

Click the icon of **Layout**. Select the icon of **General** which is displayed on the tool bar. Select a location on the drawing screen as the center point for the **General View** in its standard orientation appears on the screen.

From the Drawing View Window, select **Standard Orientation > Apply > Close**, the construction of the 3D view is completed (user may need to change the scale to 0.75, as shown).

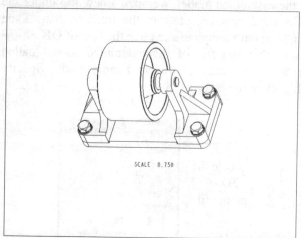 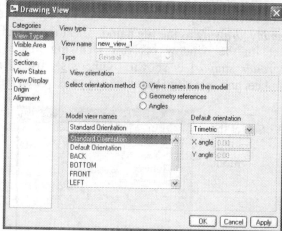

To insert the format, select **File** from the main toolbar > **Sheet Setup** > Using **Browse** to locate the format file, which is *exercise_format* > **Open** > select **Show format** > **OK.**

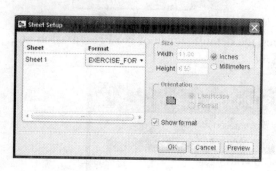 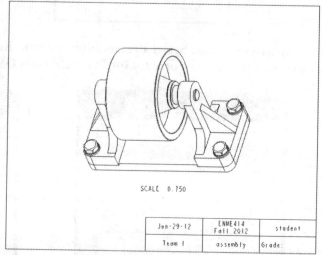

To modify the created 3D view with an offset view, we need to go back to the assembly mode. From the **View** tab. click **View Manager** > **Sections** . Click **New** > type *A* and press **Enter.**

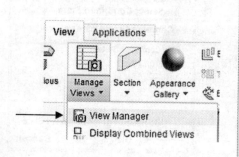 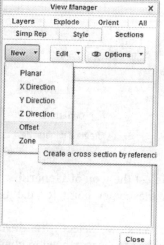 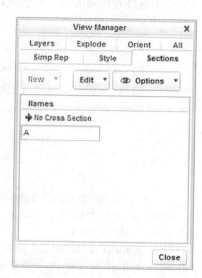

From the model tree, pick **ASM_RIGHT** (this means that you have chosen the **ASM_RIGHT** as your sketching plane). Click the icon of Sketch View to orient the sketching plane parallel to the screen.

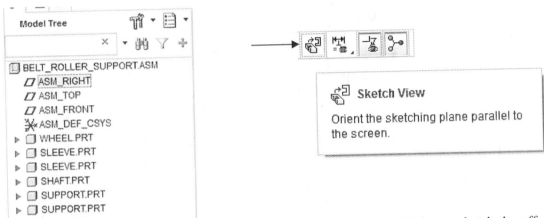

Select the outer diameter as a new reference. Select the icon of **Line** to sketch the offset plane along the y and z positive directions > select the icon of **Done.** Click the Preview without clipping. Click the check mark to **Close.**

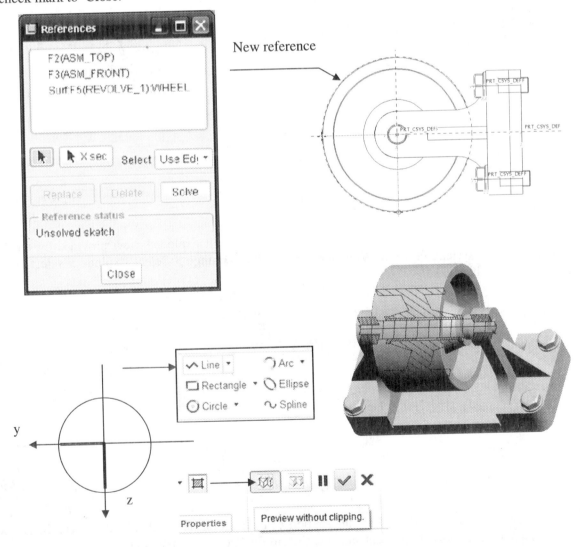

Now let us go back to the drawing mode. Click **Layout**. Left-click to select the 3D view > right-click and hold and select **Properties**.

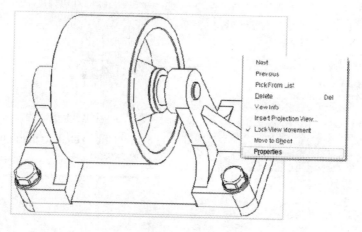

From the Drawing View window, select **Section** > **2D cross-section** > select *A* > **Apply** > **Close**.

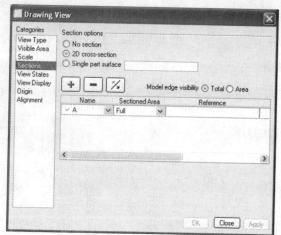

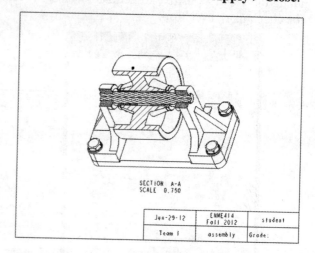

To obtain an exploded view, we first utilize the default exploded view provided by the Creo Parametric design system. From the **View** tab, click **View Manage** > Select **Explode** > select **Default Explode**, and double click it.

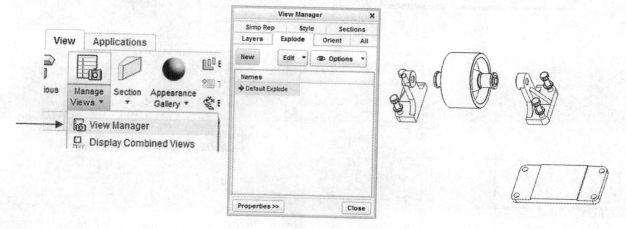

Click the icon of **Position.** Pick the support component on the right side and select the X- axis, drag the support component to the right, and left click to finalize its new position.

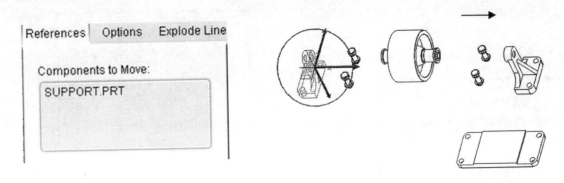

Follow this procedure to relocate the components. Click the icon of **Apply and Save**.

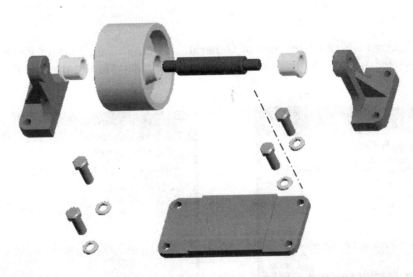

To save your work, click the icon of **List > Edit > Save > OK** to complete the modification to the default exploded view.

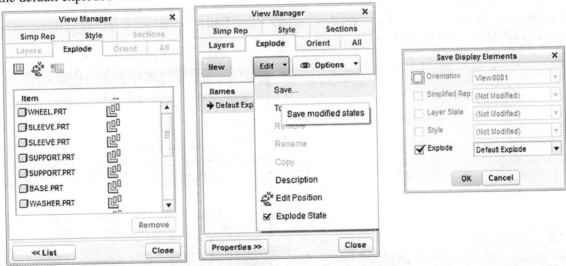

To go back to an unexploded view, just click the icon of Exploded View. Now let us insert this modified exploded view to the engineering drawing. We first add a new sheet to the current drawing. Click **Layout > New Sheet**. A new sheet (number 2) appears on the screen

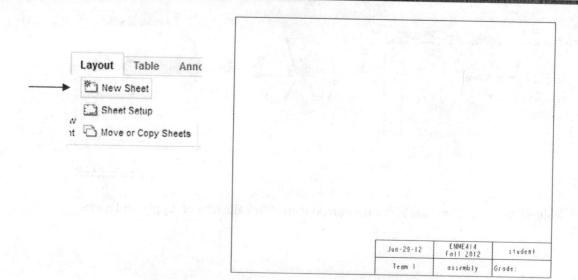

From the **Layout** tab, select the icon of **General**. A window called **Select Presentation** appears. Keep the default choice of **No Presentation** and click the box called **Do not prompt for Presentation > OK**.

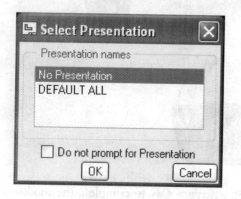
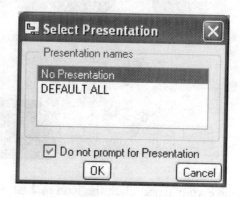

Select a location on the drawing screen as the center point for the **Front View** (click the left button of mouse). In the Drawing View window, select **View States** > choose **Explode** component in view > select **Default** > **Apply** > **Close**.

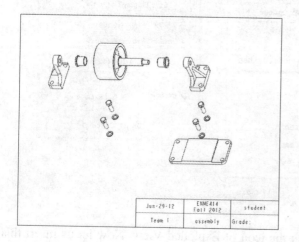
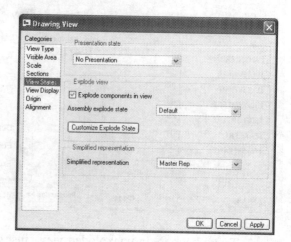

To save this file, click the icon of **Save**, and click **OK**.

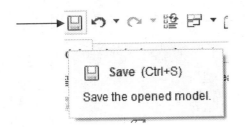

7.7.3 Preparation of an Engineering Drawing

Step 1: Establish a file for the drawing.

File > New > type *roller_system* as the file name, clear the box of **Use default template**, and **OK.** Identify the assembly file, use **Empty**, select the **A** size and **OK.**

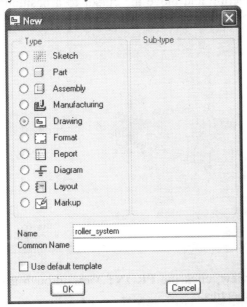

Step 2: Create the Front and Right-Sided views.

From the **Layout**, click the icon of **General**. A window called **Select Presentation** appears. Keep the default choice of **No Presentation** and click the box called **Do not prompt for Presentation > OK.**

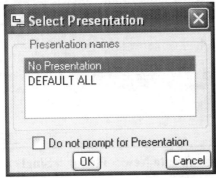

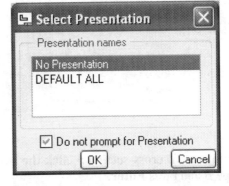

We first insert the front view. Just pick the central location of screen as the CENTER POINT for the standard orientation view. From the Drawing View window, select **Front > Apply > Close**, the construction of the 3D view is completed.

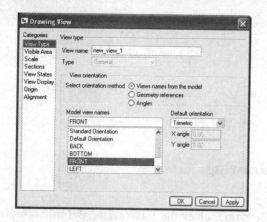

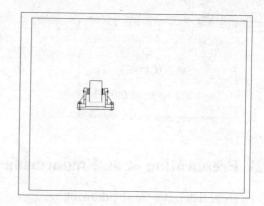

To create the right-sided view, click **Projection** and move the cursor to a position right to the front projection and left click to insert the right-sided view.

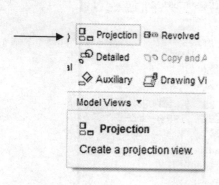

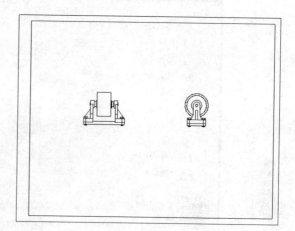

To modify the front view with a section view, click the **PRONT** view through a left click of mouse. Afterwards, right click and hold, select **Properties.**

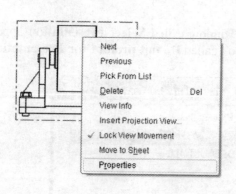

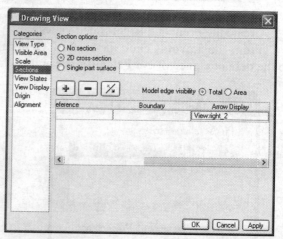

Sections > 2D cross-section > click the icon of Add > Create New > Planar > Single > Done.
Type *B* and press **Enter.**
From the display, select **ASM_FRONT > OK.**
To add the arrows to the Right-Sided view, locate **Arrow Display** within the **Drawing View** window and click the empty space below > for selecting item, pick the Right-Sided view > **Apply > Close.**

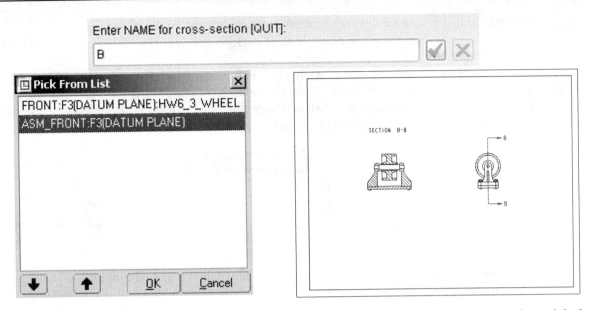

Enter NAME for cross-section [QUIT]:

B

Pick From List

FRONT:F3(DATUM PLANE):HW6_3_WHEEL
ASM_FRONT:F3(DATUM PLANE)

OK   Cancel

SECTION B-B

To modify the hatched lines in terms of its presence, spacing, and angle of orientation, pick the Front View from the display, right-click and hold and choose **Pick from List**. Make sure that you select **Xhatch > OK**. Afterwards, right-click and hold and select **Properties** to carry out the modifications of hatched lines for each of the components. Note that there are no hatched lines for the shaft component.

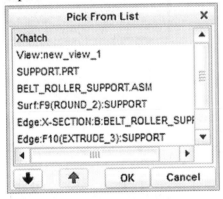

Pick From List

Xhatch
View:new_view_1
SUPPORT.PRT
BELT_ROLLER_SUPPORT.ASM
Surf:F9(ROUND_2):SUPPORT
Edge:X-SECTION:B:BELT_ROLLER_SUPF
Edge:F10(EXTRUDE_3):SUPPORT

OK   Cancel

Step 4: Add critical dimensions to the assembly drawing.
To add centerlines, from the **Annotation,** click **Dimension**.

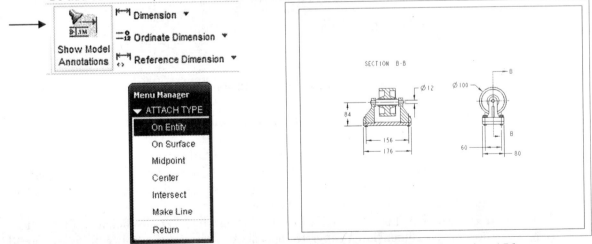

Show Model Annotations

Dimension
Ordinate Dimension
Reference Dimension

Menu Manager
ATTACH TYPE
On Entity
On Surface
Midpoint
Center
Intersect
Make Line
Return

SECTION B-B

⇨ Pick the two vertical centerlines in the front view to create the dimension 156.
⇨ Pick the two horizontal centerlines in the right side view for the dimension 60.

⇨ Pick the two horizontal lines of the shaft in the front view for the dimension 12.

⇨ Pick the outer diameter of the circle (double click) in the right side view for the dimension φ100.

To add centerlines, from the **Annotation** tab, click **Show Model Annotations.** In the Show Model Annotation window, click Centerlines. From the model tree, click SHAFT.PRT. Click the box of Accept. The centerlines associated with the shaft component are on display. Follow the same procedure, the user may add the centerlines associated with the bolt components.

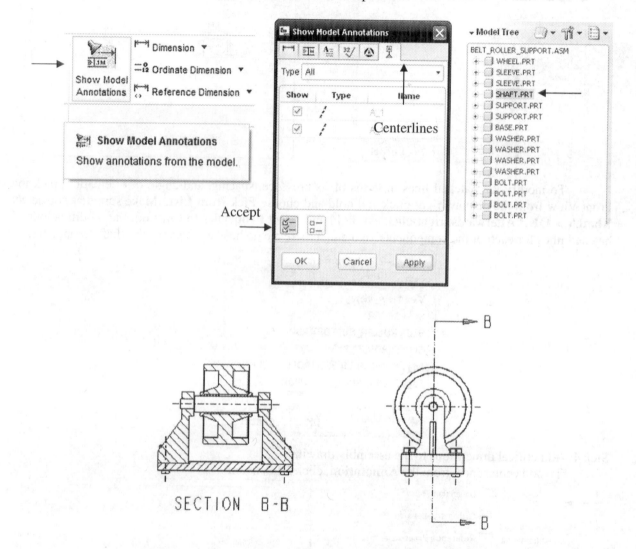

SECTION B-B

Dimensions 156 and dimension 60 indicate the dimensions of the locations of the 4 holes for placing this assembly on the ground.

Dimension φ12 indicates that the diameter of the shaft, which is supposed to be connected with another component to drive the bell_roller_support system.

Dimension 84 indicates the distance of the centerline of the shaft with respect to the ground.

Dimension φ100 indicates one of the maximum dimensions of the assembly. This dimension also indicates the height of the assembly when adding the dimension of 84. The dimensions of 176 and 80 also indicate the maximum dimensions of the assembly on the ground.

To add a symbol, φ, to the dimension of 12, pick the dimension and **right-click** and **Properties.**

A new window called **Dimension Properties** appears on the screen. You will be able to add symbols as prefix or postfix. There is a build-in table called **Symbol Palette** available for you to select the symbol or symbols.

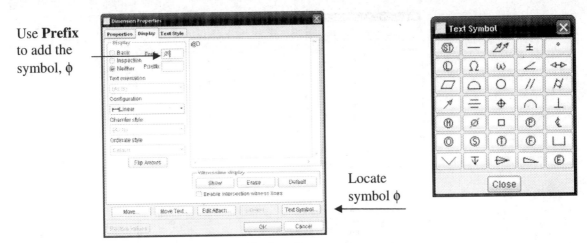

Use **Prefix** to add the symbol, φ

Locate symbol φ

Step 5: Add a drawing format to the assembly drawing.
File > Sheet Setup > Browse > identify the format file and open it.

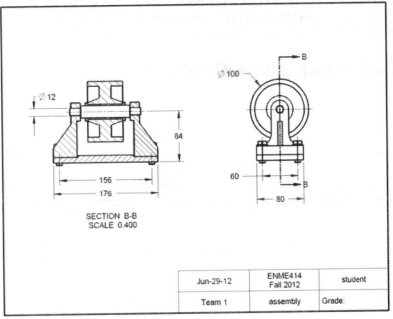

| Jun-29-12 | ENME414 Fall 2012 | student |
| Team 1 | assembly | Grade: |

SECTION B-B
SCALE 0.400

Task 5: Generation of a simplified BOM table
Open the assembly file: *belt_roller_support.asm.*
On the main menu, select **Info > Bill of Materials**. A new window called **BOM Report** appears.
Select **Top Level** and **OK.**

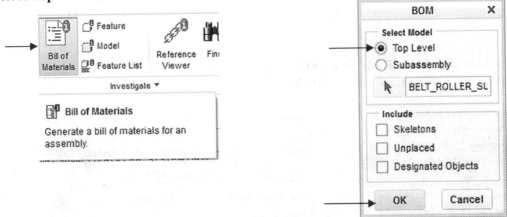

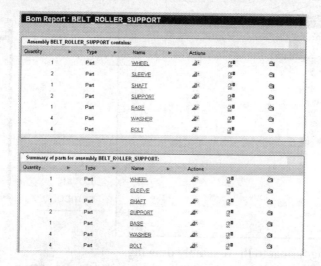

A bill of materials document is on display immediately. Close the file after reviewing it. Note that this document file is automatically saved into your working directory. It is very important that you modify the file name from *.bom to *.csv. You may open Microsoft EXCEL to do so.

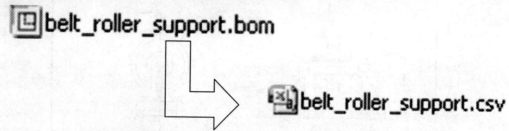

In order to place such a bill of materials in the drawing, we first add a new sheet to the current drawing. Click **Layout > New Sheet**. A new sheet (number 2) appears on the screen

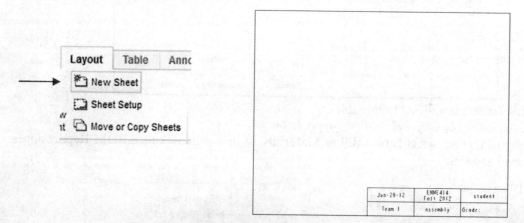

Click the icon of **Table > Table From File**. Select the belt.roller_support.csv file and pick select a free point on the drawing to position the BOM table.

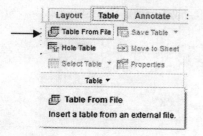

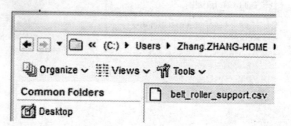

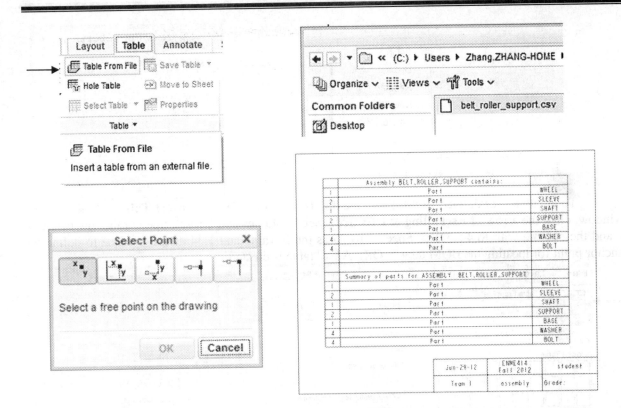

In the simplified BOM table, the information related to quantity, the nature of the model file and the names of the components are listed. For example, there are 4 pieces of the component *BOLT*. The nature of this component is *Part*, not Assembly.

In order to creation of a formal or a user-defined BOM table, there are two steps.

- Creating a table.
- Defining a repeat region and specifying the information for the repeating process.

Step 1: Create a table with the format shown below.

This table has 2 rows and 6 columns. The column width varies for each of the 7 columns.

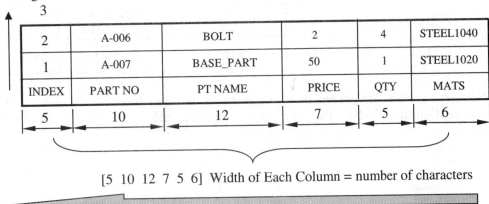

2	A-006	BOLT	2	4	STEEL1040
1	A-007	BASE_PART	50	1	STEEL1020
INDEX	PART NO	PT NAME	PRICE	QTY	MATS

[5 10 12 7 5 6] Width of Each Column = number of characters

Leftward

To create a user-defined BOM table, let us copy the sheet with the assembly drawing. To do so, highlight Sheet 1 listed at the bottom of the screen. Click **Move or Copy**. In the pop up window, check the box to create a copy after Sheet 2 > **OK**. Users may add the critical dimensions to it if those dimensions are not shown in Sheet 3.

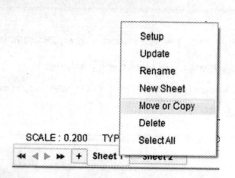

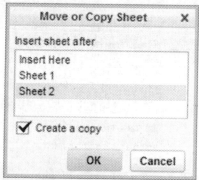

To create a user-defined BOM, From the **Table** tab, click **Table > Insert Table**. . In the pop up window, click the arrow of **Ascending & leftward.** Set 6 columns and 2 rows. Specify the row height to 1 and the column with to 4 > OK. . Specify 10.75 as the X value and 1.34 as the Y value to define the anchor point for locating the BOM table > OK. A 6x2 table is created.

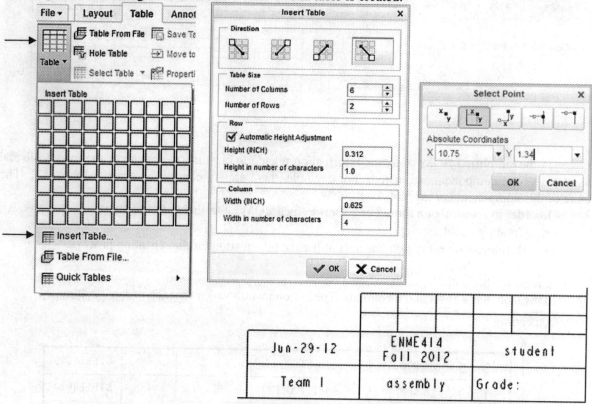

Now let us adjust the widths of columns. From the filter listed on the bottom of the display screen, set to **Column Width**. Pick the second column and right-click to set the width to 9 characters.

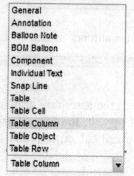

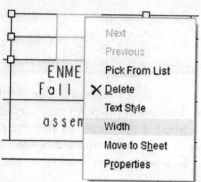

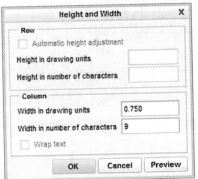

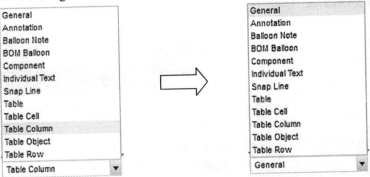

Follow the same procedure; adjust the width of the 3rd column to 11 characters, the width of the 4th column to 6 characters, and the width of the 6th column to 5 characters.

Let us return the filter setting from Column Width to General.

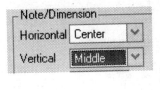

To fill in the contents of the bottom row, do the following:

Double click the first cell (on the left side), type INDEX, click Text Style, and set to Center in Horizontal and Middle in Vertical.

Repeat the process for the 5 other cells.

In the 2nd cell in the bottom row and type PART NO

In the 3rd cell in the bottom row and type PT NAME

In the 4th cell in the bottom row and type PRICE

In the 5th cell in the bottom row and type QTY

In the 6th cell in the bottom row and type MATS (materials)

INDEX	PART NO	PT NAME	PRICE	QTY	MATS
	Jun-29-12	ENME414 Fall 2012		student	
	Team 1	assembly	Grade:		

Step 2: Defining a repeat region to enter the information related to the assembly system and user-defined parameters.

We will use the information on the second row to automate the generation of more rows for the three components. Because of this, a repeat region needs to be defined. Before defining the repeat region, a few things need to be explained. First, the numerical value of **INDEX** can be generated by the software system itself. The PT NAMEs, such as WHEEL, SHAFT… are the names of the 7 computer files, such as *shaft.prt, wheel.prt*, …and *bolt.prt*. Therefore, the software system is able to insert these file names into the **BOM** table. The numerical value of **QTY** can be obtained by the software system through counting the number of identical parts used in the assembly.

On the other hand, information on PART NO, PRICE and MATS has to be made available in the process of constructing the **BOM** table. For each of these 7 components, we need to add these 3 parameters. Let us define the value for each of the three user-defined parameters for each component.

Let us first open the file of shaft.prt. From the model tree, highlight SHAFT.PRT. Right click and hold, select **Open**.

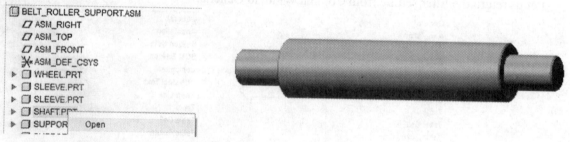

From the **Tools** tab, select **Parameter** > click the plus sign or click the box of **Parameter** on the pop up window > **Add Parameter,** and type the following information to the boxes, as shown.

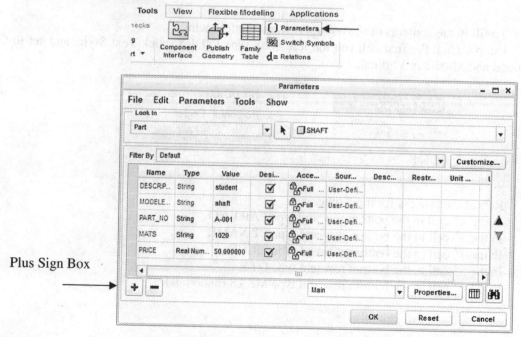

PART_NO > **String** > *A-001*
MATS > **String** > *1020*
PRICE > **Real Number** > *50.00*

Open the file of *bolt.prt*.   From the main menu, select **Tools > Parameter >** click the plus sign or click the box of **Parameter** on the pop up window > **Add Parameter** or click the Plus Sign box, and type the following information to the boxes, as shown.

PART_NO > **String** > *A-007*
MATS > **String** > *1020*
PRICE > **Real Number** > *2.00*

Repeat the above procedure for the 5 remaining components based on the information shown in the BOM table (page 369). Upon completing this process, from the Table tab, click the icon of **Repeat Region > Add > Simple.**

Click or select the first cell and the last cell of the second row to define the repeat region.> **Attributes >** select the repeat region just defined.

No Duplicate > Flat > Bln by Part > Done/Return > Done.

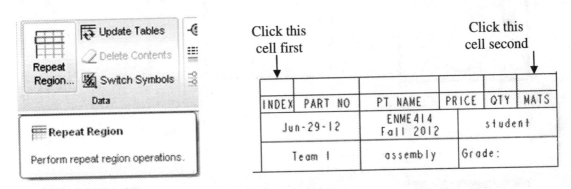

To fill in the contents of the second row, or the repeat region, do the following:
Double click the first cell (on the right side) of the second row
⇨ **rpt... > index**.

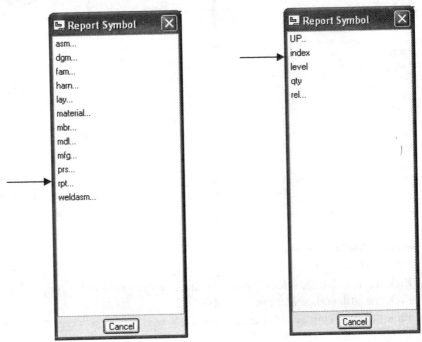

⇨ Pick the second cell, select **asm... > mbr > user defined** > type *PART_NO*.

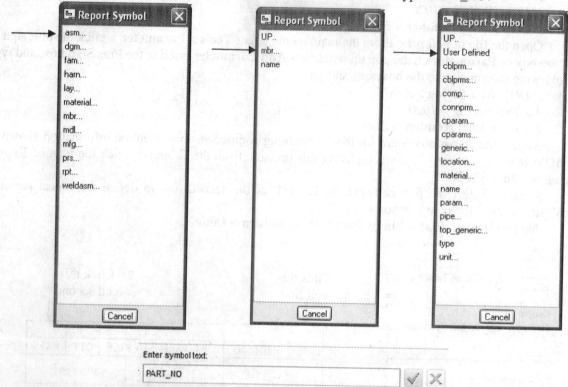

Enter symbol text:

PART_NO

⇨ Pick the third cell, select **asm... > mbr... > name**.

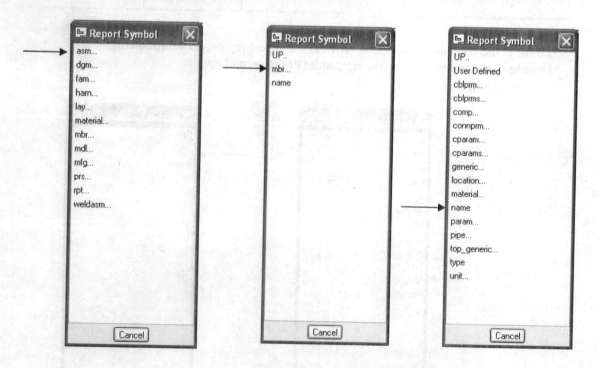

⇨ Pick the fourth cell, select **asm... > mbr... > user defined** > type *PRICE*.
⇨ Pick the fifth cell, select **rpt... > qty**.
⇨ Pick the sixth cell, select **asm... > mbr... > user defined** > type *MATS*.

Repeat Region > Update Tables. The table should display the BOM information shown below:

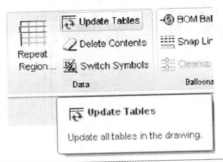

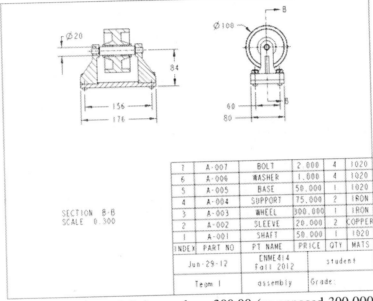

In order to control the number of digits, such as 300.00 (as opposed 300.000 shown), select the leading cell for the parameter of PRICE. The cell to be selected should be the cell just above the cell of PRICE. Right click of mouse, **Properties**, add [.2] just following the word PRICE and **OK**.

From the main bar, select **Table > Repeat Region > Update** the repeat region.

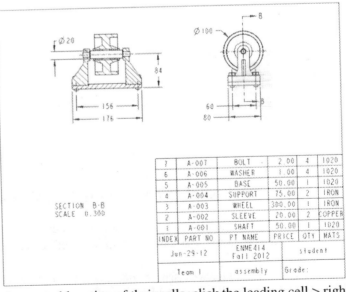

To adjust the displayed numbers to the central location of their cells, click the leading cell > right-click and hold > **Properties**.

In the Note Properties window > **Text Style > Center** in the **Horizontal** Note > **Middle** in the **Vertical** Note.

From the **Table** tab, click **Repeat Region > Update Table**.

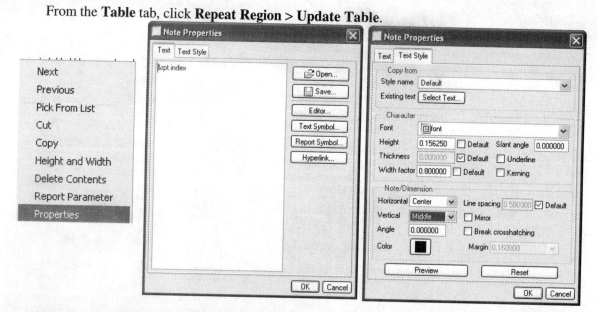

Now let us add BOM balloons. From the **Table** tab, click **Create Balloons** > Create Balloons – All. The 7 balloons appear on the screen. To modify the balloon display, pick a balloon and hold down the right button of mouse and pick **Edit Attachment** from the pop up menu > **On Surface** > **Filled Dot** > select a new location for the balloon leader > OK. Use **Move** to reposition balloons as necessary. Repeat this procedure to modify the leaders of the other 6 balloons.

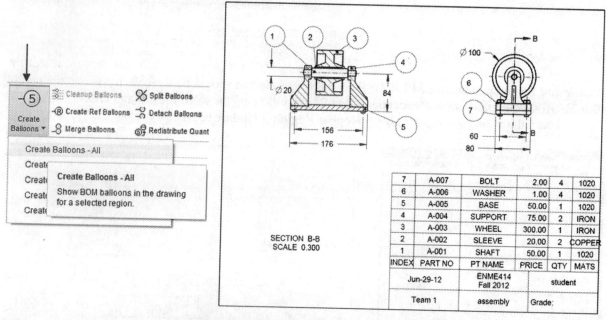

INDEX	PART NO	PT NAME	PRICE	QTY	MATS
7	A-007	BOLT	2.00	4	1020
6	A-006	WASHER	1.00	4	1020
5	A-005	BASE	50.00	1	1020
4	A-004	SUPPORT	75.00	2	IRON
3	A-003	WHEEL	300.00	1	IRON
2	A-002	SLEEVE	20.00	2	COPPER
1	A-001	SHAFT	50.00	1	1020

Jun-29-12	ENME414 Fall 2012	student	
Team 1	assembly	Grade:	

SECTION B-B
SCALE 0.300

7.8   Visualization of Product Function through Mechanism

To visualize the function of a designed product, such as the assembly of the belt_roller_support system, adding mechanism to the assembly system is an effective way to incorporate motion into the assembly system.

In this example, we assume that a servo motor is connected to the shaft component. The two sleeve components will be assembled with the shaft through an interference fit so that they rotate as the shaft is driven by the servo motor. We also assume that the wheel component is assembled to the two sleeve components so that the wheel rotates as the two sleeve components rotate.

We assume that all other components in this assembly do not move, or those components are in a stationary status. Our objective is to visualize the motion of this assembly when the servo motor drives the shaft component through a specific mode called **Mechanism**. Readers can find this module by selecting **Applications** from the main toolbar > **Mechanism**.

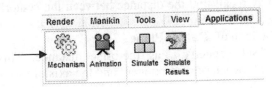

7.8.1 Guidelines of Incorporating Mechanism in the Assembly

There are several guidelines to incorporating mechanism in the assembly. The first guideline is to determine which components will be in motion and which components will be stationary when a servo motor is added into the system and drive the system in motion. More important is the fact that during the assembly process, the components in motion cannot be "touched" by those so-called stationary components. In this example, we assume the components in motion are Shaft, Sleeve and Wheel. The stationary components are Support, Base, Washers and Bolts. The second guideline is, when connecting an axis to a servo motor, a function called **Connection** should be used. The **Connection** function includes Pins, Slides, Ball Joints, and many others. The third guideline is that the assembly default coordinate system serves as the fixed coordinate system, or the ground. Consequently, the three default datum planes, namely, ASM_FRONT, ASM_TOP and ASM_RIGHT are also reviewed as the ground.

The fourth guideline, which is the most important guideline among all, is the "two-body principle". This principle emphasizes entities selected in the process of defining a set of constraint conditions have to be from 2 bodies so that an explicit motion transmission from one component to another can be realized.

7.8.2 Demonstration Example

To demonstrate the implementation of those guidelines in the process of incorporating mechanism in the assembly, we use the belt-roller-support system. To distinguish the file name used previously, we now use a new name for the assembly file. The new name is *motor_roller_support*.

Let us set the working directory to roller system. In the folder of roller system, the 7 files of the 7 components reside. Under this working directory, we create a file for the assembly.

File > New > Assembly > type *motor_roller_support* as the file name > clear the box of **Use default template > OK**. Select **mmns_asm_design** (units: Millimeter, Newton, Second) and type *mechanism* in **DESCRIPTION** and type *student* in **MODELED_BY > OK**.

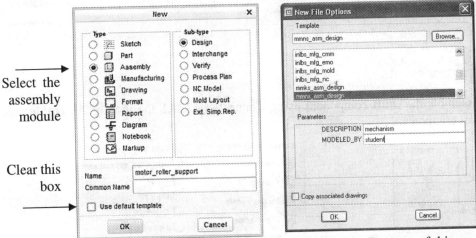

In order to drive the shaft in motion, we will use a servo motor. Because of this reason, the shaft has to be assembled through the use of **Connections** so that a pin connection can be defined. In order to define a pin connection, an axis associated with the assembly coordinate system (the ground) is needed. Because of this reason, we first create a datum plane called ADTM1, which is parallel to the ASM_TOP and the offset distance is 75. We may recall that the distance between the centerline of the hole and the bottom surface of the base component is 75 mm.

From the Model tab, click the icon of **Datum Plane.**

Pick **ASM_TOP** and use **Offset** > specify 75 as the offset distance. This distance is the height distance between the bottom surface of the support component and the axis of the shaft component.

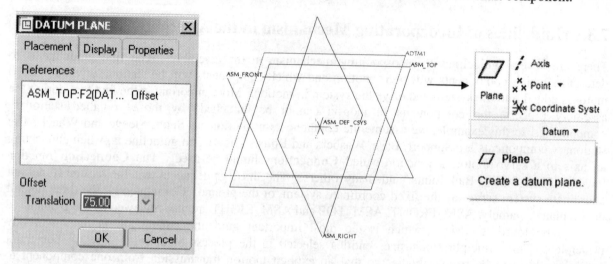

To create an axis, click the icon of datum axis. The required axis is the intersection of 2 planes. While holding down the **Ctrl** key, pick ASM_FRONT and ADTM1. The axis is named as AA_1 listed in the model tree.

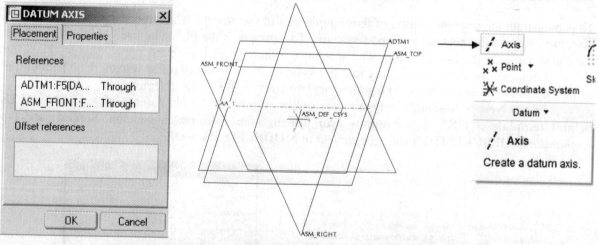

To assemble the **shaft** component using Connections, click the icon of **Assemble,** and open the file of the shaft component.

From User Defined, select Pin.

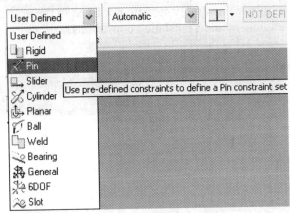

To define a pin connection, two (2) constraints are needed. The first constraint is Axis alignment. The second constraint is Translation Restriction. For the axis alignment constraint, we select AA_1 from the assembly system and the axis of the shaft component (A_1).

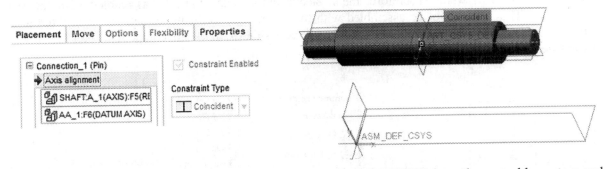

For the translation restriction constraint, we select **ASM_RIGHT** from the assembly system and the **RIGHT** datum plane from the shaft component. A message "Connection Definition Complete" appears > Click the icon of **Apply and Save**.

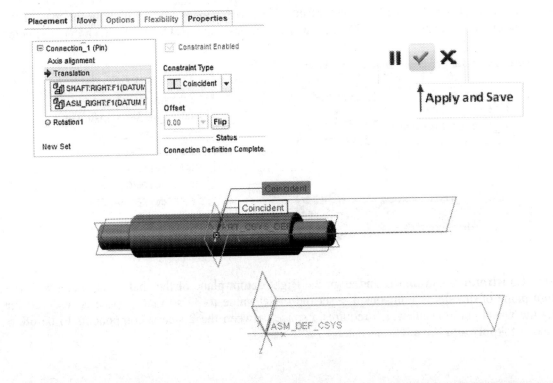

When examining the model tree, there is a small square attached to SHAFT.PRT, indicating the shaft component is movable within the assembly system, not fixed to the assembly system. Connection_1 is also listed, including Axis alignment and Translation constraints.

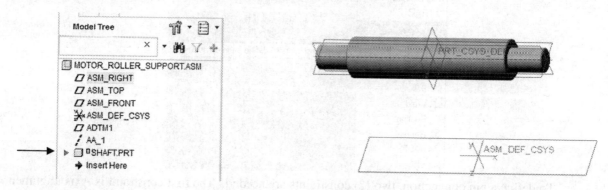

There are 2 sleeve components attached to the shaft component. As the shaft rotates, the 2 sleeve components rotate as well. Therefore, the 2 sleeve components must be assembled with the shaft component. They should not be assembled with the assembly coordinate system which is fixed to the ground. To assemble the sleeve component to the left side of the shaft component, pick the icon of **Assemble**, and open the file of the sleeve component.

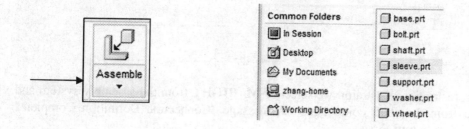

Align the axis of the shaft with the axis of the sleeve component. When picking the axis of the shaft, right-click on the axis and hold, use **Pick from List** to make sure **SHAFT: A_1(AXIS)** is selected >**OK**.

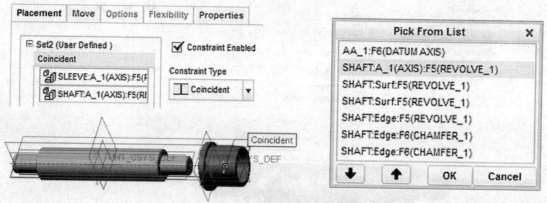

New Constraint > Automatic and align the Right datum plane of the shaft component with the Right datum plane of the sleeve component > set the offset value to 34 so that a space is reserved for assembling the wheel component, which requires a space between the 2 sleeve components to be 68. > Click the icon of **Apply and Save**.

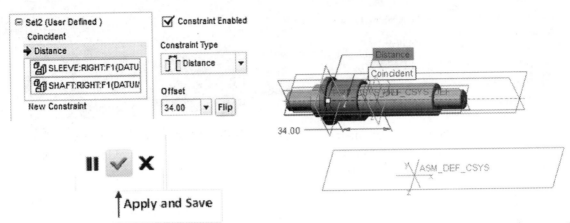

If examining the model tree, there is a small square attached to the sleeve component because the sleeve component will rotate as the shaft rotates. The placement folder indicates there is a Coincident constraint and a distance constraint defined.

Let us assemble the second sleeve component. Click the icon of **Assemble**, and open the file of the sleeve component.

Let us work with the displayed **3D Dragger**. Pick the shaded arc and rotate the sleeve component for 180 degrees.

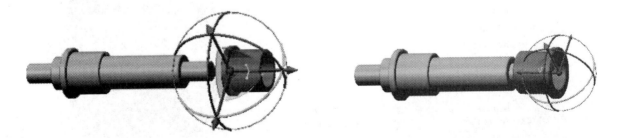

Following the same procedure, we assemble the sleeve component to the right side of the shaft component. Note the offset distance equal to 34.

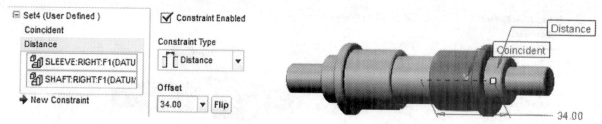

If examining the model tree, there is a small square attached to this sleeve component as well because this sleeve component will rotate as the shaft rotates. The placement folder indicates there are a Coincident constraint and a distance constraint.

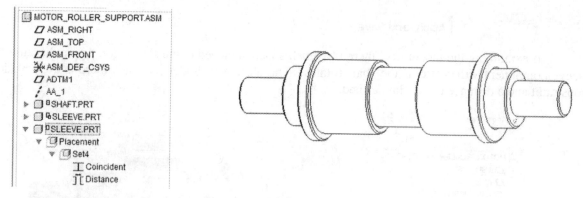

Now let us assemble the wheel component.

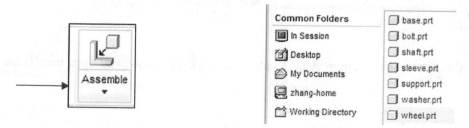

Based on the two body principle, in the assembly process, we assemble the wheel component to the sleeve component on the left side of the shaft component.

Align the axis of the wheel with the axis of the sleeve component. When picking the axis of the sleeve, right-click on the axis and hold, use **Pick from List** to make sure **SLEEVE:A_1(AXIS)** is selected >**OK**.

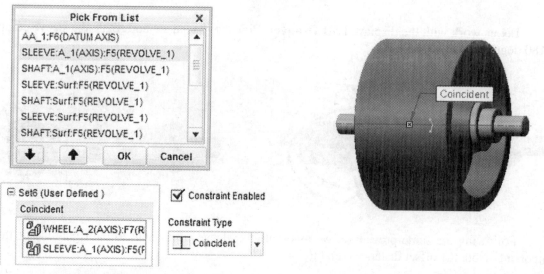

New Constraint > Automatic. Pick one surface from the sleeve and one surface from the wheel. Select Coincident and **Mate** is automatically set. The message of Full Constrained appears. Click the icon of **Apply and Save**.

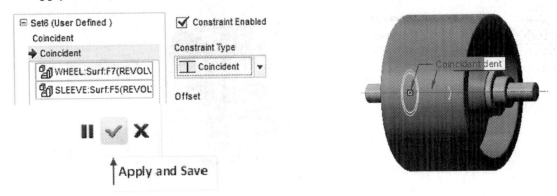

Up to this point, all the components in motion have been assembled. Now let us assemble the stationary components. Let us start with the base component.

Because the base component does not move in operation, it should be assembled to the ground. Therefore, the surface of the base component, which is in contact with the support component, is aligned with **ASM_TOP**. **ASM_FRONT** is aligned with the **FRONT** datum plane of the base component. **ASM_RIGHT** is aligned with the **RIGHT** datum plane of the base component. Note that there is no small square attached to BASE.PRT when examining the model tree of the assembly system, indicating that the base component is in the stationary status.

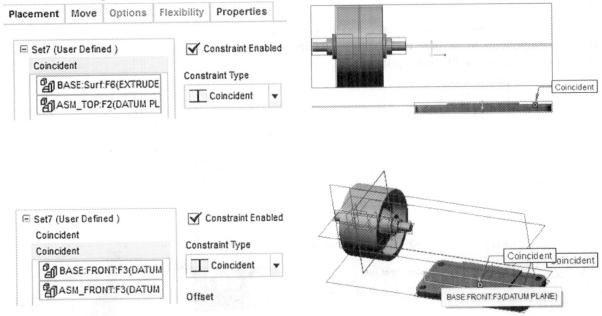

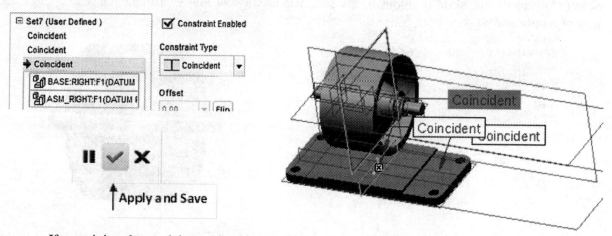

If examining the model tree, there is no small square attached to the base component because the base component will not rotate as the shaft rotates. The placement folder indicates there are 3 alignment constraints and the base component is in stationary status.

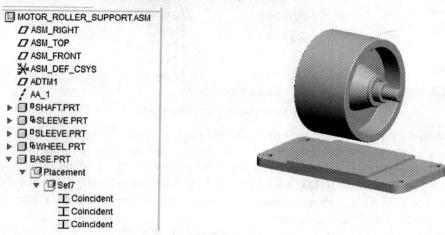

There are 2 support components, and they are in stationary status. As a result, we assemble the 2 support components to the base component. We first assemble the support to the right side of the plate component based on the two-body principle.

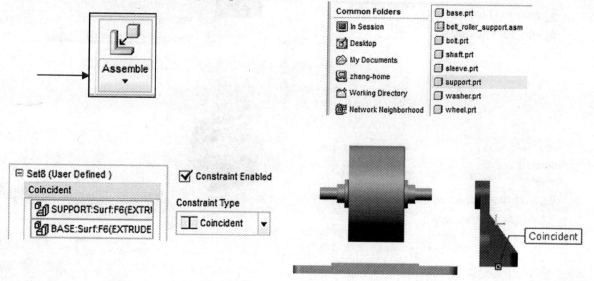

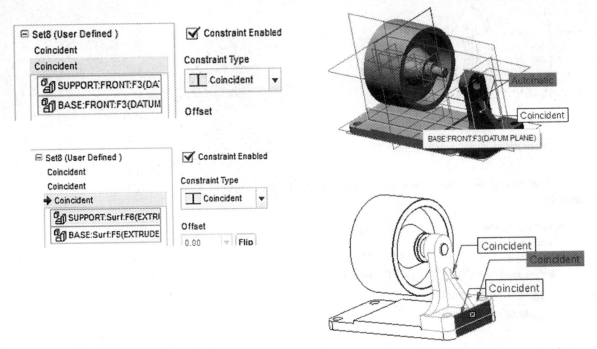

If examining the model tree, there is no small square attached to the support component because the support component will not rotate as the shaft rotates. The placement folder indicates there are 3 Coincident constraints.

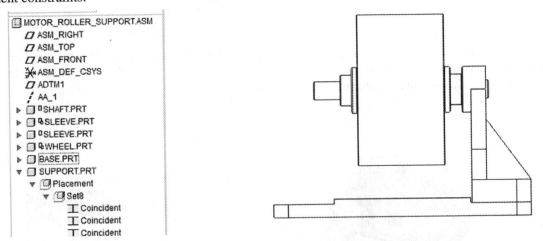

Let us assemble the second support component. Click the icon of **Assemble**, and open the file of the support component.

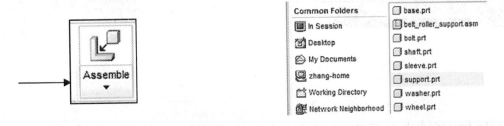

Let us work with the displayed **3D Dragger**. Pick the shaded arc and rotate the support component for 180 degrees. Pick the shaded arrow to move the support to the left side.

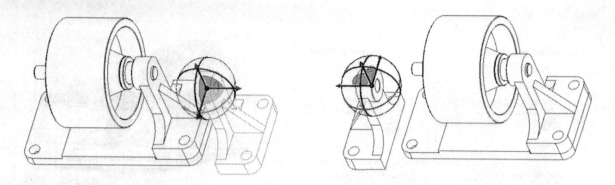

Following the same procedure, we assemble the support component to the left side of the assembly.

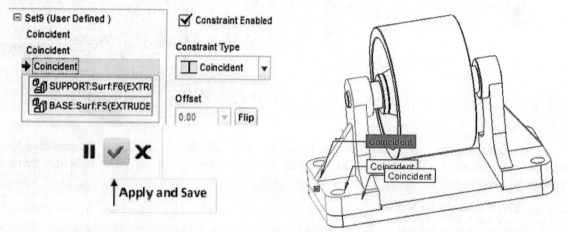

Assemble the four (4) washer components to the Support components. Reader should refer to the material presented in the previous section or Section 7.7.2. We assemble the first washer. After afterwards, use **Repeat** to assemble the other 3 washers.

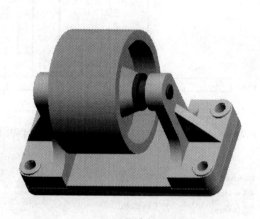

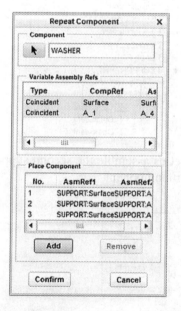

Assemble the four (4) bolt components to the 4 washer components. Reader should refer to the material presented in the previous section or Section 7.7.2. We assemble the first bolt to the washer. After afterwards, use **Repeat** to assemble the other 3 bolts.

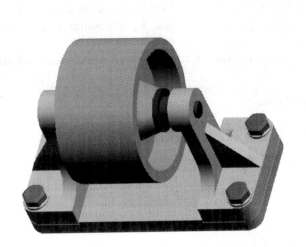

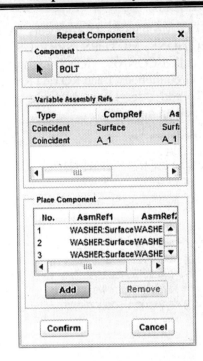

When examining the model tree of this assembly, there are 4 components with the movable status. They are SHAFT.PRT, SLEEVE.PRT, SLEEVE.PRT and WHEEL.PRT. A small square is attached to each of the 4 components.

There are 10 components with the stationary status. They are PLATE.PRT, 2 SUPPORT.PRTs, 4 WASHER.PRTs and 4 BOLT.PRTs.

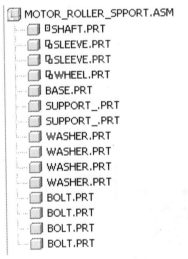

7.8.3 Incorporation of Mechanism

Form the **Applications** tab, click **Mechanism**.

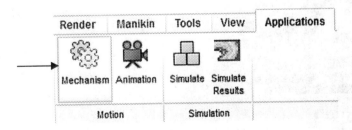

The Mechanism Tree appears. A set of functions are listed in the Mechanism Tree, such as CONNECTIONS, MOTORS, SPRINGS, ... ANALYSES, and PLAYBACKS. Let us now expand the function called CONNECTIONS, expand JOINTS, and expand Connection_1. . Three items are listed. They are Ground, body 1 and ROTATIONAXIS.

To add a servo motor, highlight ROTATIONAXIS. Make a right-click to select Servo Motor from the pop up menu.

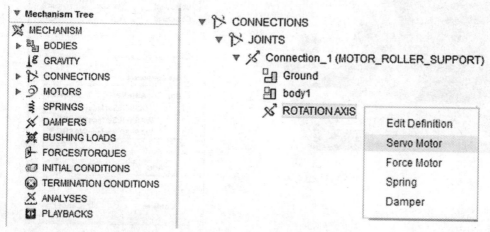

In the Servo Motor Definition window, the design system automatically selects the pin axis as the rotation axis because there is only one joint defined. Click **Profile**, select Velocity > Constraint, and specify 360 as the magnitude, or one revolution per second as the rotation speed. Click **OK**.

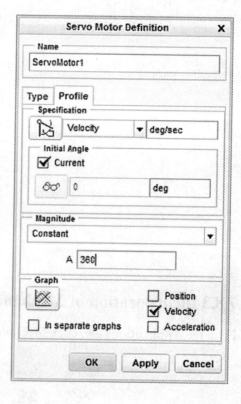

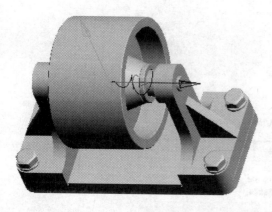

In the Mechanism tab, click the icon of Mechanism Analysis. In the Analyses window, click Run. The wheel component starts to rotate at a speed 360 degrees per second. Click **OK** to complete the analysis. To make a movie file, click the icon of Playback. In the Playback window, click the box of play current result set.

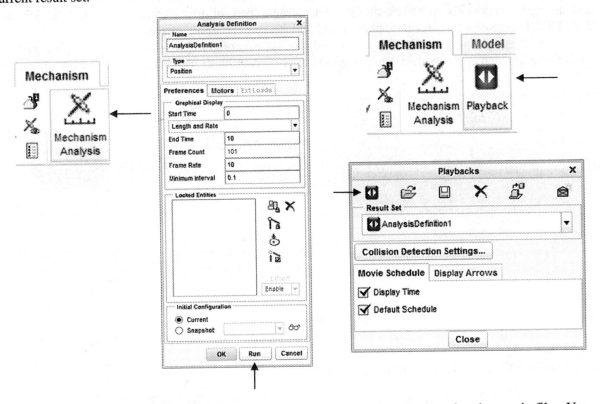

On the pop up window called Animate, users may adjust the speed to play the movie file. Upon obtaining an appropriate setting for speed, click Capture to generate a MPEG file for showing the motion driven by the servo motor and the defined connections.

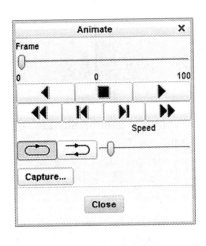

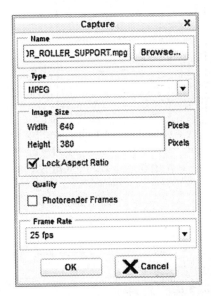

It is important to note that the MPEG file is automatically saved in the working directory with the file name : motor_roller_support.mpeg for later use.

7.9 Creation of a PCB Assembly with Electronic Components

In this section, we use conceptual parts to represent resistors, IC chips and capacitors. We assemble them through the use of a special function called **Package**. This function allows designers to quickly visualize and arrange components in an assembly. The second part of this exercise is to use **COPY** and **PATTERN** to create holes on a base plate, which holds those electronic components.

As illustrated in the following figure, the product we are going to work with is a typical printing circuit board, which contains electronic components, such as resistors, capacitors and IC chips.

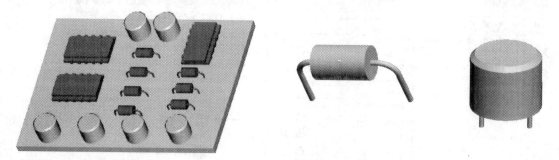

Let us assume that a directory called PCB_assembly is created. Let us now set the working directory to PCB_assembly. From the top menu, click **File > Set Working Directory** > locate directory called PCB_assembly > **OK**.

Step 1: Create a file for the 3D solid model of a resistor.

From **File,** click **New > Part** > type *resistor* as the file name and clear the box of **Use default template > OK.** Select **mmns_part_solid** (units: Millimeter, Newton, Second) and type *Resistor* in **DESCRIPTION**, and *student* in **MODELED_BY**, then **OK**.

Feature 1: create a datum curve to be used for sweeping

From the model tree, pick **FRONT**. From the Model tab, click the icon of **Sketch**. Click the icon of **Sketch View** to orient the sketching plane parallel to the screen.

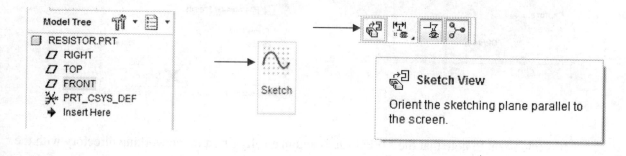

Create a centerline along the vertical axis. Click the icon of **Line** to sketch 3 lines, as shown.

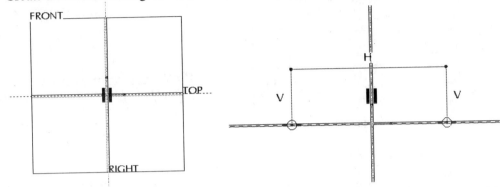

Click the icon of **Circular Fillet** to create 2 rounds at the 2 corners, as shown. Note that the tangency at each of the connecting points is guaranteed.

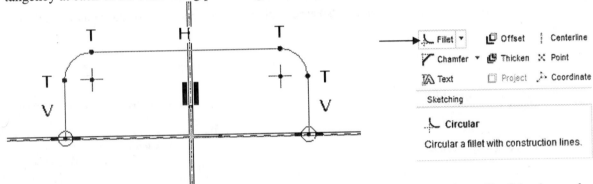

Click the icon of **Equal Radii** from the Constraint group to enforce the radii of the 2 rounds are equal to each other.

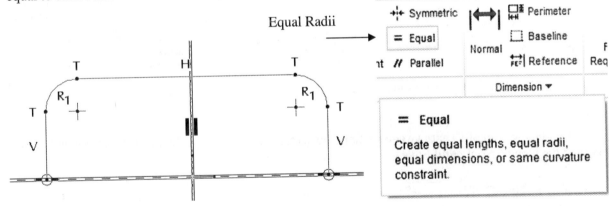

Click the icon of **Symmetry** from the Constraint group. Click the vertical centerline first and 2 points afterwards to add a symmetric constraint.

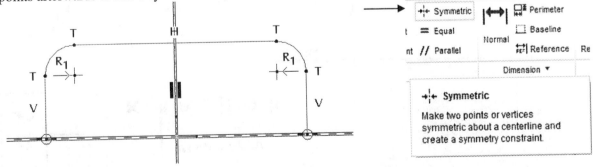

Specify the dimensions, as shown.

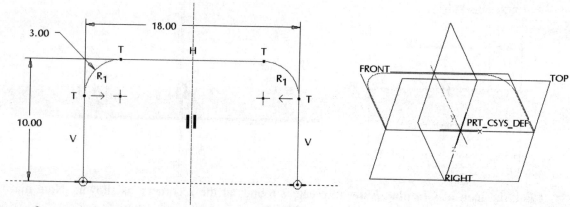

Feature 2: creation of a connecting wire. The diameter of the wire is φ1 mm.

From the Model tab, click the icon of **Sweep.** Select the sketched datum curve as the selected trajectory.

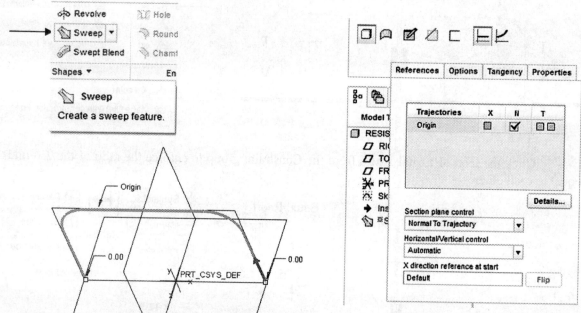

Click the icon of **Create sweep section** and sketch a circle and the diameter dimension is 1. Click **OK** and the icon of **Apply and Save.**

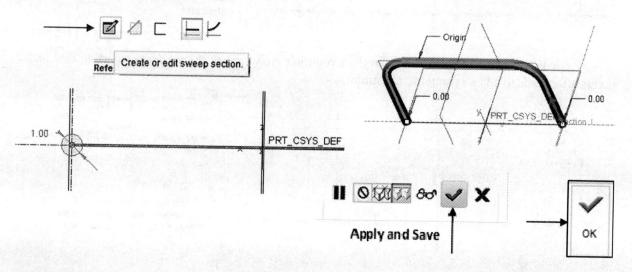

Feature 3: create a cylinder with size: φ6 x 10 mm.

From the **Model** tab, click the icon of **Extrude.** Select Symmetry and specify 10 as the extrusion distance.

From the model tree, click **RIGHT**, and click the icon of **Sketch View** to orient the sketching plane parallel to the screen.

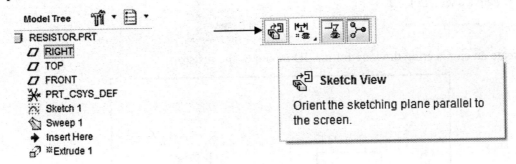

Click the icon of References. Pick the circle as the new reference > **Close**.

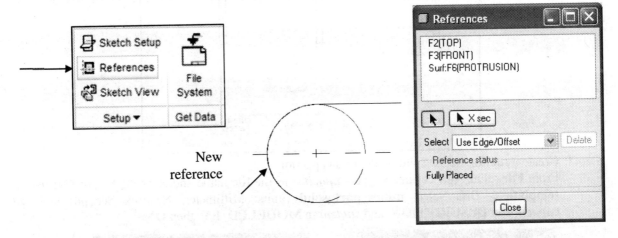

Click the icon of **Circle** to sketch a circle. The diameter is 6. Upon completion, select the icon of **OK**, and the icon of **Apply and Save** from the feature control panel.

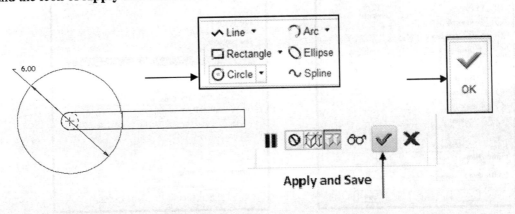

Now let us create an axis, which will be used in the assembly process. Click the icon of Axis and pick 2 datum planes: FRONT and RIGHT. Click OK/

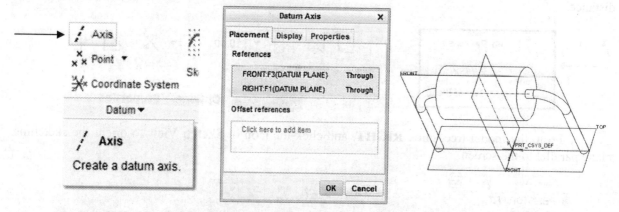

Create an engineering drawing for the 3D model of the resistor.

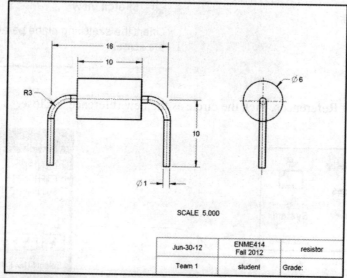

Step 2: Create a file for the 3D solid model of a capacitor.

From **File**, click **New > Part >** type *capacitor* as the file name and clear the box of **Use default template > OK.** Select **mmns_part_solid** (units: Millimeter, Newton, Second) and type *capacitor* in **DESCRIPTION**, and *student* in **MODELED_BY**, then **OK.**

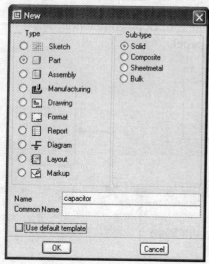

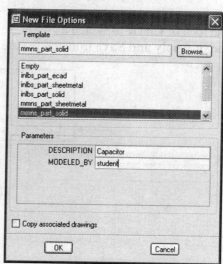

Feature 1: cylinder with size: φ15 x 12 mm.
    From the **Model** tab, click the icon of **Extrude.** Specify 12 as the extrusion height.

    From the model tree, click **TOP**, and click the icon of **Sketch View** to orient the sketching plane parallel to the screen.

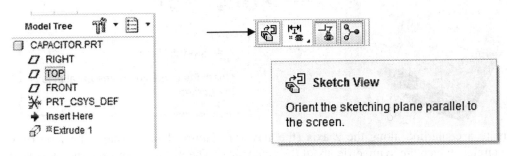

    Select the icon of **Circle** to sketch a circle. The diameter is 15. Upon completion, select the icon of **Done.** From the dashboard, set the depth value to 12, and select the icon of **Apply and Save** from the feature control panel.

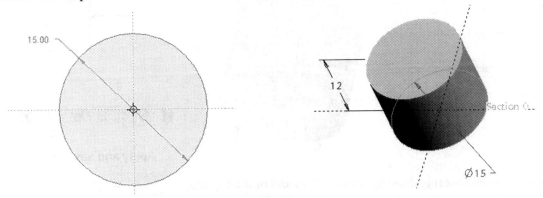

Feature 2: a chamfer on the circumference on the top surface.
    From the Model tab, click the icon of **Edge Chamfers.** Select **45xD** and specify *1.0* as the chamfer dimension. From the display, pick the edge on the top surface. Click the icon of **Apply and Save.**

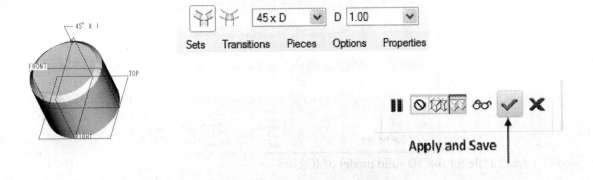

Feature 3: 2 cylinders as the connecting wires. The size is φ1 x 5 mm.
Click the icon of **Extrude**. Specify 5 as the extrusion distance.

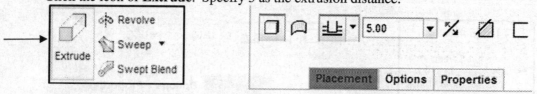

Pick the bottom surface from the cylinder as the sketching plane, and click the icon of **Sketch View** to orient the sketching plane parallel to the screen.

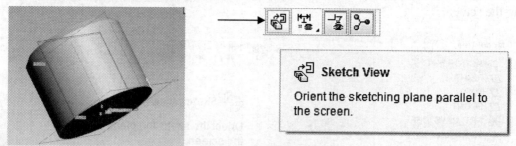

Create a centerline along the z axis (the **RIGHT** datum plane). Select the icon of **Circle** to sketch two circles, which are symmetric about the centerline. The distance between the two centers of the two circles is 10 mm. Both diameters of the two circles are 1 mm. Upon completion, select the icon of **OK**, and the icon of **Apply and Save**.

Create an engineering drawing for the 3D model of the capacitor.

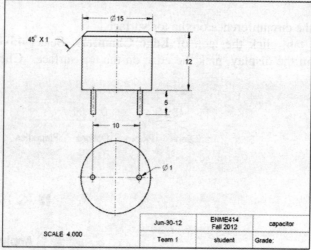

Step 3: Create a file for the 3D solid model of IC chip.

File > New > Part > type *ic_chip* as the file name and clear the box of **Use default template >** **OK.** Select **mmns_part_solid** (units: Millimeter, Newton, Second) and type *IC chip* in **DESCRIPTION**, and *student* in **MODELED_BY**, then **OK.**

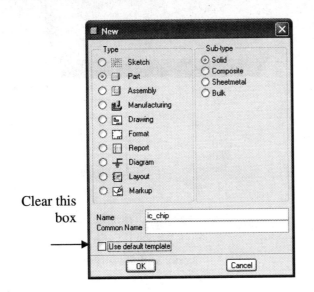
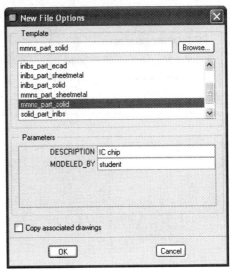

Feature 1: Create a block: 30 x 15 x 4 mm
Click the icon of **Extrude.** Specify 4 as the thickness of the plate.

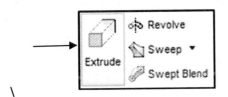
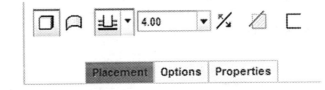

From the model tree, click **TOP**, and click the icon of **Sketch View** to orient the sketching plane parallel to the screen.

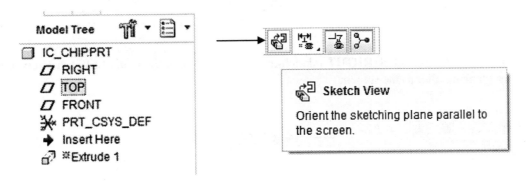

Click the icon of **Rectangle** and select **Centered Rectangle** to sketch a rectangle, which is symmetric about the x axis and the z axis. The 2 dimensions are 30 and 15, respectively. Upon completion, select the icon of **OK**, and click the icon of **Apply and Save.**

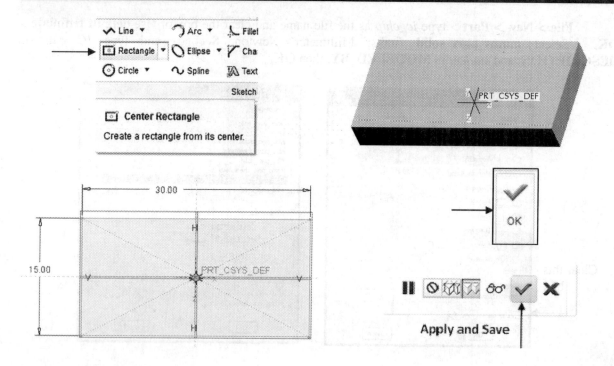

Feature 2: Add 2 steps to the block: 30 x 2 x 2.25 mm

Directly select the icon of **Extrude** from the toolbar of feature creation. From the dashboard, select the icon of **Symmetry**, and set the depth (both sides) equal to 30. Click **Placement > Define**. From the screen display, select the **Right** datum plane as the sketch plane and use the **Top** datum plane to orient the sketch plane.

From the model tree, click **RIGHT** (sketching plane), and click the icon of **Sketch View** to orient the sketching plane parallel to the screen.

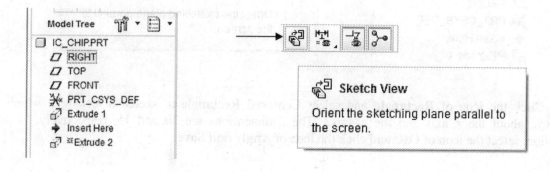

Click the icon of **References**. Pick the 2 surfaces, as shown > **Close**.

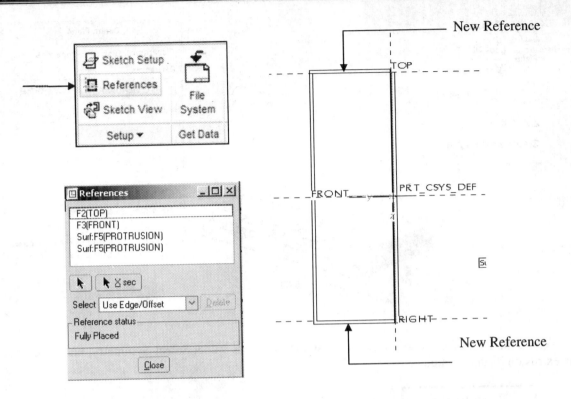

Click the icon of **Rectangle**, and sketch the two rectangles, as shown. The 2 dimensions are 2 x 2.25 mm. Upon completion, select the icon of **OK**, and click the icon of **Apply and Save**.

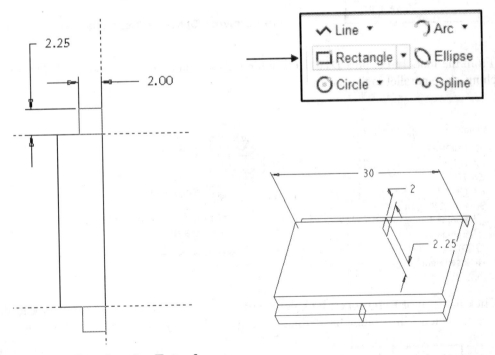

Feature 3: Create the first pin using **Extrude**

The first pin is located in a plane parallel to the left side of the chip at a distance equal to 5. As we notice that there is no datum plane at this location. In order to create a sketch at that location, we need to create a datum plane at that location.

Click the icon of **Datum Plane**. Pick the surface on the left side, as shown. Specify 5 as the offset distance > **OK**.

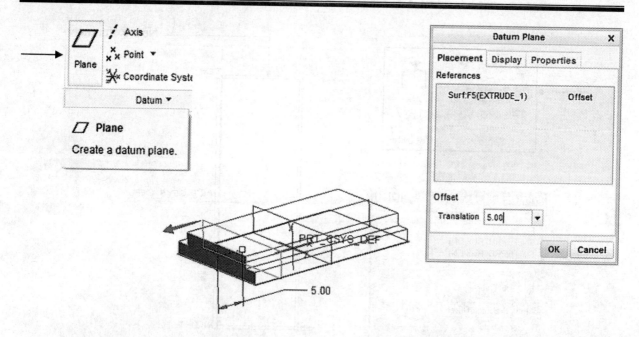

Click the icon of Extrude. Specify 0.5 as the thickness value. Select Symmetry, and specify 1.8 as the extrusion distance value.

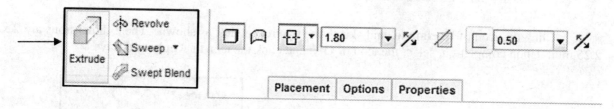

From the model tree, pick DTM1 (sketching plane), and click the icon of **Sketch View** to orient the sketching plane parallel to the screen.

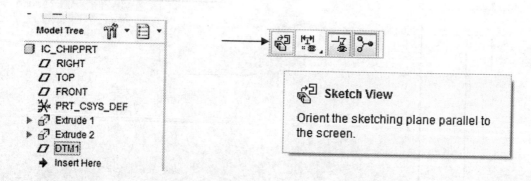

Click the icon of **References**. Pick the 3 surfaces as new references, as shown > **Close**. Click the icon of Line to sketch 2 lines along the defined references. Specify 7 as the length of the line, as shown.

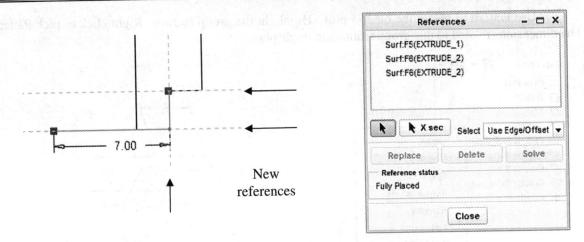

New references

Click the icon of **OK**, and click the icon of **Apply and Save**.

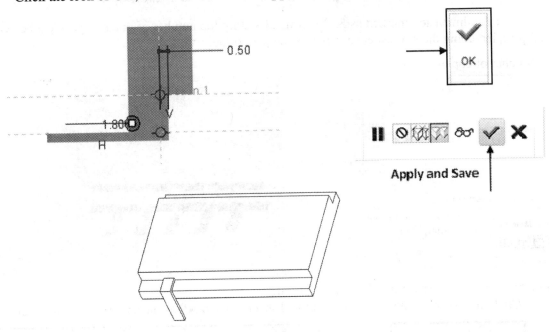

OK

Apply and Save

When the extrusion feature is completed, we need to group it with the datum plane feature. In the model tree, select both DTM1 and Extrude 3 while holding down the Ctrl key. Right-click and hold to pick **Group**.

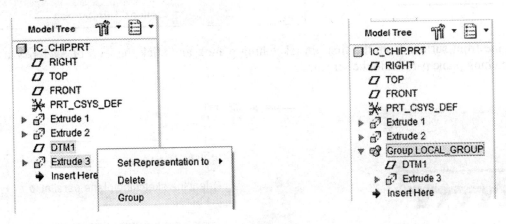

Use Pattern to obtain the other 4 pins. Highlight the group feature. Right click to pick Patterns. The dimensions related to this group feature are on display.

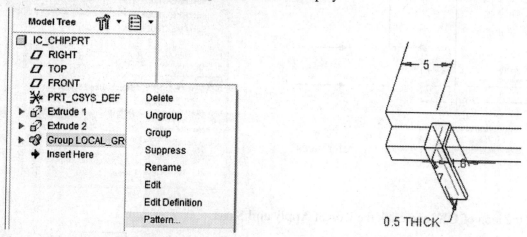

Pick the dimension marked as 5. In terms of setting the number of copies, specify 5 because we need 5 pins, including the pin just created before the pattern operation.

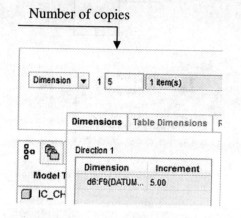

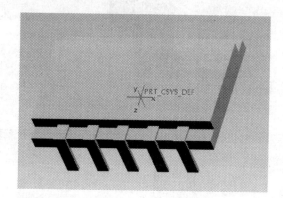

Feature 5: Use Cut to reshape the end of the first pin.

Click the icon of **Extrude**. Select **Cut** and specify **Thru All** as the choice of depth of cut.

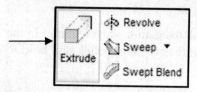

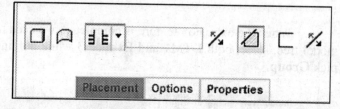

Pick the front surface from the first pin (sketching plane), and click the icon of Sketch View to orient the sketching plane parallel to the screen.

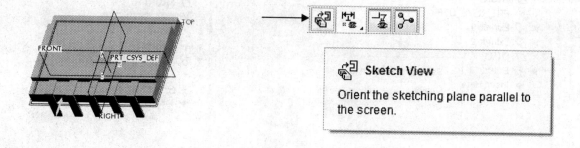

Click the icon of References. Add 2 new references, as shown. Click **Close**.

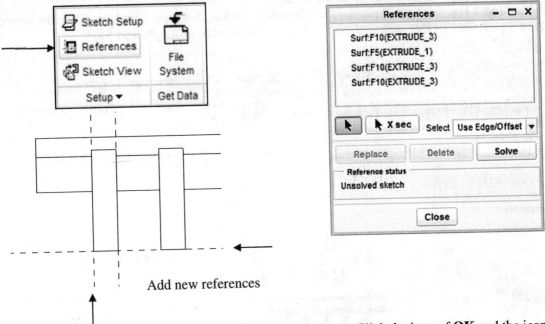

Add new references

Click the icon of Line to sketch 2 triangles, as shown. Click the icon of **OK** and the icon of **Apply and Save**.

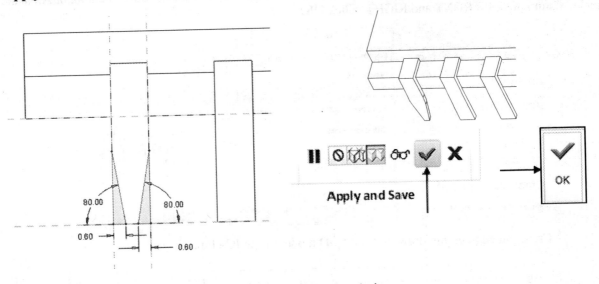

Feature 6: Use Reference Pattern to map the cut to the other 4 pins.

From the model tree, highlight the cut feature (Extrude 8), right click to pick **Pattern**. Note that **Reference** is shown. Just click the icon of **Apply and Save**.

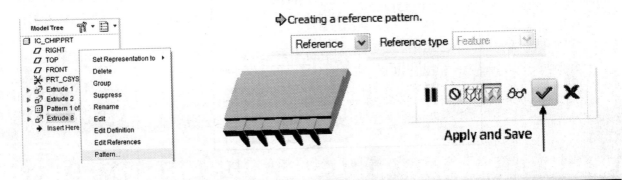

Now let us the **Mirror Tool** to create the other five pins with the cuts on the other side of the IC chip. The symmetric plane is the **FRONT** datum plane.

In the Model Tree, pick the 2 pattern features while holding down the **Ctrl** key. Click the icon of **Mirror Tool** > pick the **FRONT** datum plane > click the check mark or **Apply and Save**.

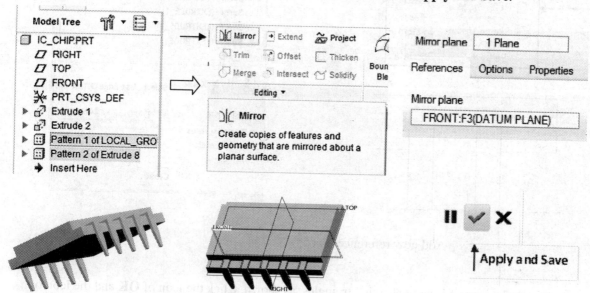

Now let us create an axis, which will be used in the assembly process. Click the icon of **Axis** and pick 2 datum planes: FRONT and RIGHT. Click OK/

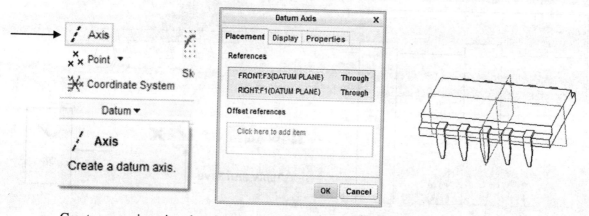

Create an engineering drawing for the 3D model of the IC-chip.

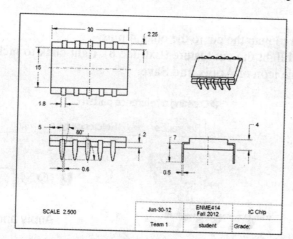

Step 4: Create a file for the 3D solid model of the base plate.
File > New > Part > type *plate* as the file name and clear the box of **Use default template > OK.**
Select **mmns_part_solid** (units: Millimeter, Newton, Second) and type *Plate* in **DESCRIPTION,**
and *student* in **MODELED_BY**, then **OK.**

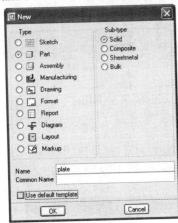 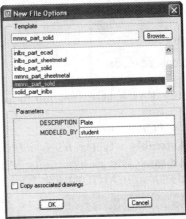

Feature 1: Create a block: 135 x 100 x 5 mm
Click the icon of **Extrude.** Specify 5 as the height of the extrusion distance.

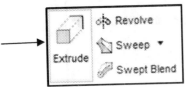 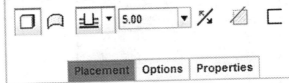

From the model tree, click **TOP**, and click the icon of **Sketch View** to orient the sketching plane parallel to the screen.

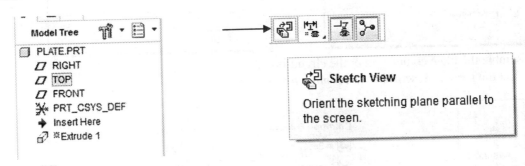

Click the icon of **Rectangle** and select **Centered Rectangle** to sketch a rectangle, which is symmetric about the x axis and the z axis. The 2 dimensions are 135 and 100, respectively. Upon completion, select the icon of **OK**, and click the icon of **Apply and Save**.

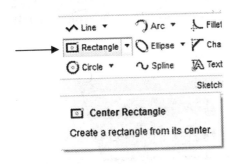 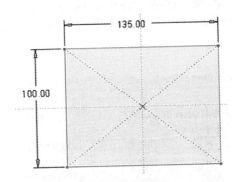

At this time the user has successfully completed the design of plate feature. Let us save it first. We will work on the plate component when getting on the assembly. Select **Save** from the main toolbar > **OK**.

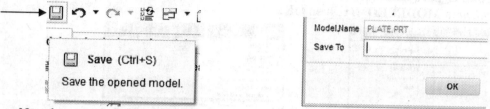

Now let us use the **PACKAGE** function to assemble 3 IC chips, 7 resistors and 6 capacitors on the base plate.

Step 1: create a file for the PCB assembly.

File > New > Assembly > type *pcb_assembly* as the file name and clear the box of **Use default template > OK**. Select **mmns_asm_design** (units: Millimeter, Newton, Second) and type *PCB assembly* in **DESCRIPTION**, and *student* in **MODELED_BY**, then **OK**.

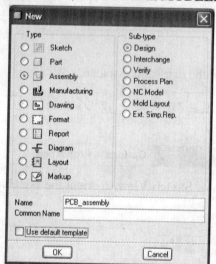
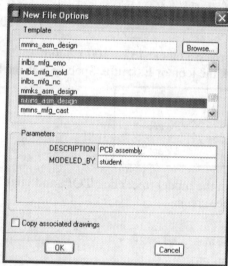

Step 2: assemble the plate component or the circuit board.

Select the icon of **Assemble**. select *plate.prt*, and open it.

Under the **Constraint Type**, pick the icon of **Default**, which means automatically placing the origin of the PART_DEF_CSYS to the origin of the ASM_DEF_CSYS and the orientations of the 2 coordinate systems are identical > **Full Constrained** is indicated under **Status**> click the icon of **Apply and Save**.

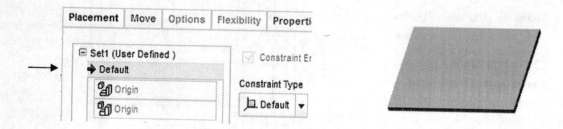

Step 3:   Add a column to the Model Tree to display the model status and monitor the progress of packaging.
Activate **Settings** > **Tree Columns** > highlight **Status** under **Not Displayed** > click the button located in the middle to shift **Status** column from **Not Displayed** box to the **Displayed box** > **OK.**
Note that the phrase **Regenerated** appears in the column of **Status**, indicating that the plate component is fully constrained.

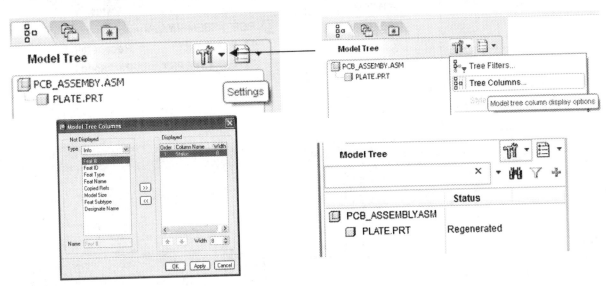

Step 4: Place 3 IC chips on the circuit board.
In the Assembly group, click Package. In the pop up window, click **Add** > **Open** > open the file: ic_chip.prt.

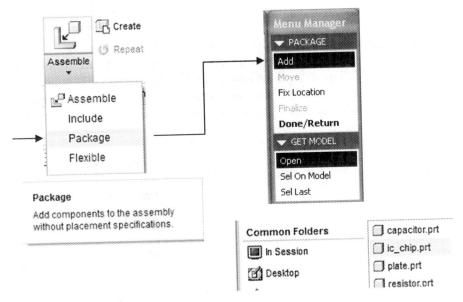

A new window called **Move** appears.   Select **Translate** from **Motion Type** > from the orientation setting, select **TOP** and move the IC chip to a new or a desired location, as shown. How to move the IC chip? Use the left button of mouse to pick the IC chip, and just move it (do not hold down the left button when moving the IC chip), and OK after positioning the IC chip in a location for the moment, or as an initial assembly consideration). When examining the Model Tree, IC_CHIP.PRT has been added. Notice the word **Packaged** appears along the line of IC_CHIP. It indicates that the IC component has been packaged, but not fully constrained.

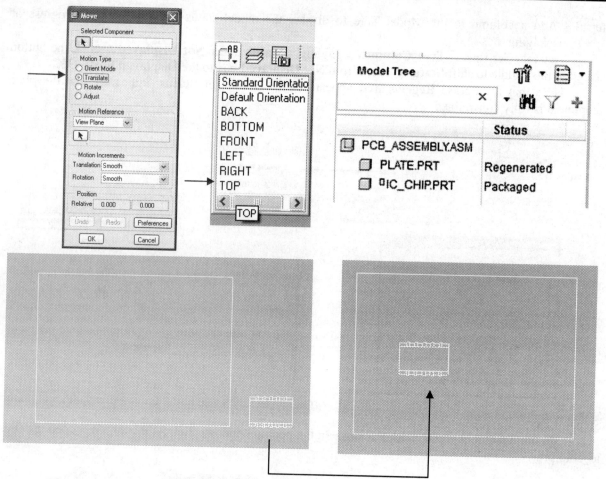

To package the second IC chip,

Add > Sel On Model > select IC_CHIP from the list of the model tree. Users may also use **Sel Last** instead of using **Sel on Model**. Make sure that you select **Translate** from **Motion Type** before moving the newly entered IC chip. Notice the change in the Model Tree. There are 2 IC_CHIP.PRTs on the list. Both are marked with **Packaged**, not **Regenerated**. Also notice an additional little square next to each of the 2 IC_CHIPs, indicating that they are not fully constrained, and they are only packaged.

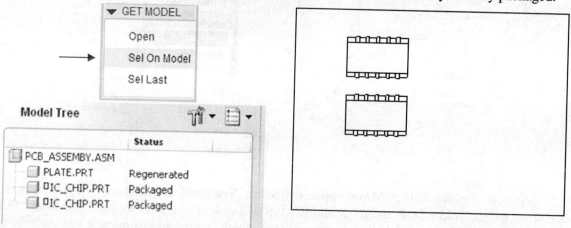

To package the third IC chip,

Add > Sel Last, and another IC chip appears on screen immediately. Make sure that you select **Translate** from **Motion Type**. Use a left click (do not hold the left button) to position the IC chip on the circuit board, and **OK** to close the dialog box. Notice the change in the Model Tree. There are 3 IC

PRTs on the list. All are marked with **Packaged**, not **Regenerated**. Also notice a small square next to each of the 3 IC CHIPs.

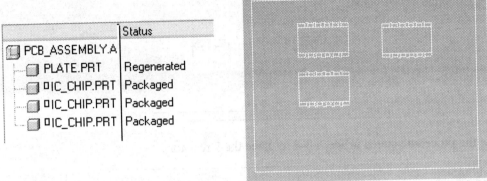

To rotate the 3rd IC chip for a new orientation, from the **Move** window, select **Rotate** and type 90 as **Motion Increment**. Use a lift click and rotate the IC chip so that a rotation of 90° is made.

Change to
Rotate

Select 90 or
type 90

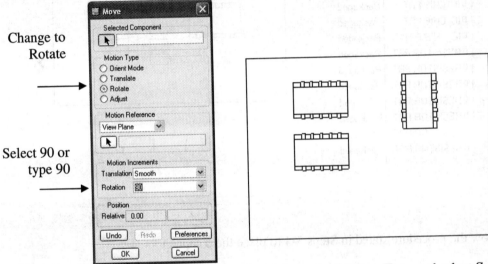

Afterwards, on the Move window, select **Translate** under **Motion Type** and select **Smooth** under **Motion Increments**.

Return to
Translate

Return to
Smooth

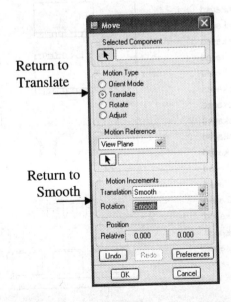

Now let us select **FRONT** from the **Saved Views** listed on the main menu. We may notice the positions of 3 IC chips in the direction are at different levels. Let us move them to a level with, approximately, the same height value.

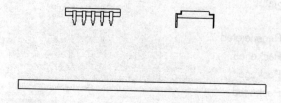

Step 5: Follow the procedure stated in Steps 3-4 to place the 7 resistors.

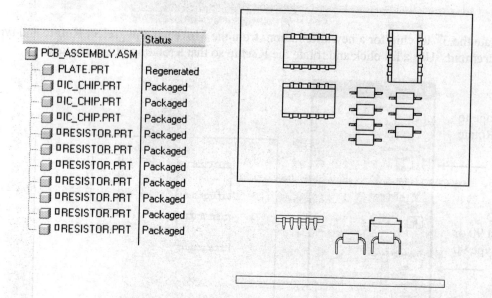

Step 6: Follow the procedure stated in Steps 3-4 to place the 6 capacitors.

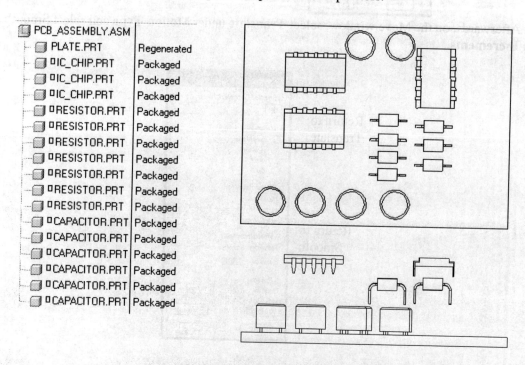

Step 7: Finalize the design of layout.

Let us assume that the 3 IC chips should be in the following configuration.

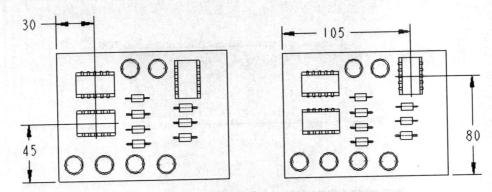

Let us assume that the 7 resistors should be in the following configuration.

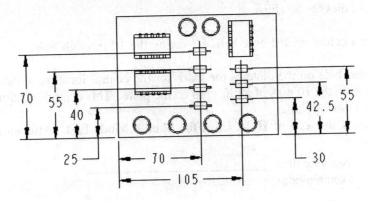

Let us assume that the 6 capacitors should be in the following configuration.

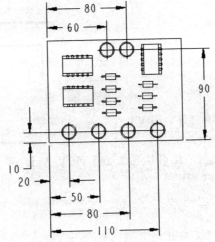

Let us save this assembly file. Select **Save** from the main toolbar > **OK**.

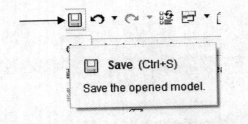

Model Name   PCB_ASSEMBLY.ASM

Save To

OK

Now let us go back to plate.prt to create holes in the plate component so that those electronic components can be positioned at their required locations. When those holes are available, we assemble them to the plate.

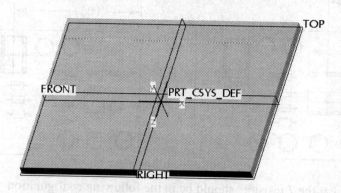

Task 1: Creation of 3 sets of holes for IC chips.

Step 1: Use **Hole** to create a center drilled hole before creating the 10 through holes as a single feature for the IC chip.

Create a center-drilled hole on the plate as the mark for the central location of the 10 distributed holes, which are used to position the 10 pins of an IC chip on the plate. This central location serves as the reference to determine the 10 through holes.

In the **Model** tab, click the icon of **Hole**. Click the **Sketch Mode** first. Afterwards, activate or click **Sketcher**, as shown below.

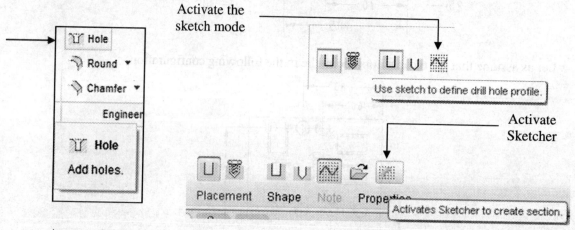

A new sketch window appears. Right-click and click **Axis of Revolution** from the pop up window. Afterward sketch a vertical centerline.

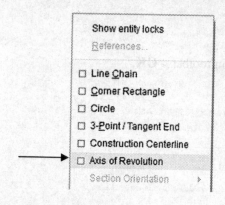

Select the icon of **Line** to sketch a triangle. The two dimensions are 1 and 60°, respectively. Click the icon of **OK** to return to the hole-making page.

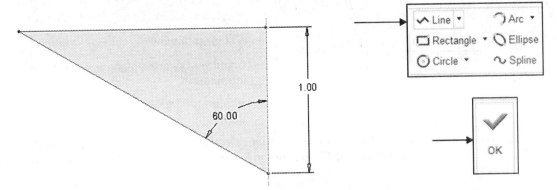

On Hole Placement, pick the top surface of the plate. For the offset references, pick the two surfaces, parallel to the **FRONT** and RIGHT datum planes of the plate, respectively (holding down the **Ctrl** key). The two distances with respect to the 2 surfaces are 45 and 30, respectively.

From the feature control panel, select the icon of **Apply and Save** to complete the creation of the center drill hole.

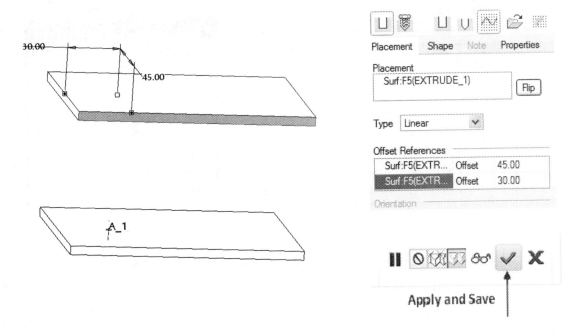

To create the 10 holes, click the icon of **Extrude**. Select **Cut** and set the depth option to **Through All**.

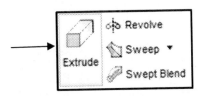
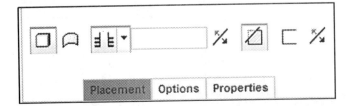

Select the top surface of the plate component as the sketching plane. Click the icon of **Sketch View** to orient the sketching plane parallel to the screen.

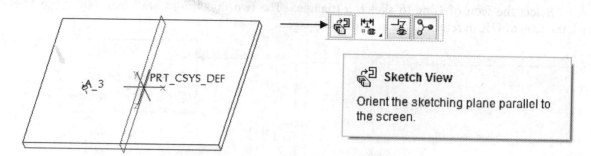

Click the icon of **References**. Add a new reference by selecting the axis of the center drilled hole as the new reference > **Close**. Click the icon of Centerline and sketch 2 centerlines through the center of the drill hole.

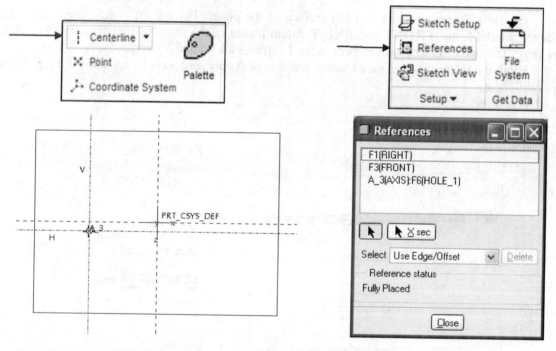

Sketch another horizontal centerline with an offset value equal to 10, as shown.

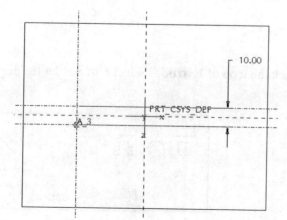

Sketch 3 circles, as shown. The first circle is on the intersection of the vertical and the second horizontal centerlines. The other 2 circles are offset from the first circle with the offset values equal to 5 and 10, respectively. The diameter of the 3 circles is 2.

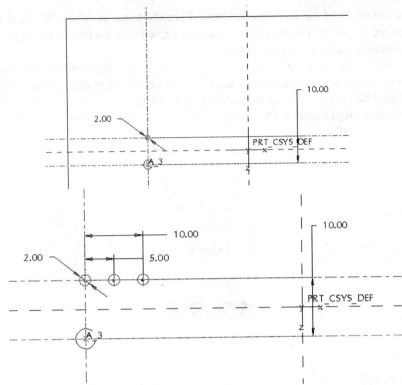

While holding down the **Ctrl** key, pick the second and the third circles. Select the icon of **Mirror**, and select the vertical axis to obtain the 4th and 5th circles located on the other side of the vertical centerline.

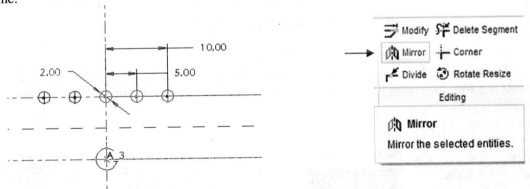

While holding down the **Ctrl** key, pick all 5 circles. Select the icon of **Mirror**, and select the horizontal axis to obtain the 6th, 7th, 8th, 9th and 10th circles located on the other side of the horizontal centerline. Upon completion, select the icon of **OK**, and the icon of **Apply and Save.**

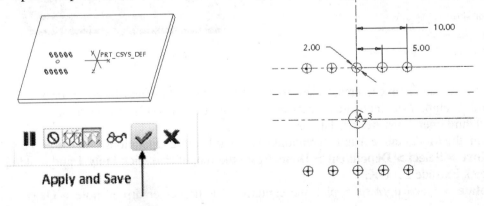

Note that the diameter of the 10 holes is 2 mm. Five (5) holes are above the horizontal centerline, and the other 5 holes are below. The horizontal centerline serves as the axis of symmetry. The 5 holes in each side are 5 mm distance away from each other.

Step 2: Use **COPY** and **Move** to create a new set of the center drilled hole and the 10 through holes for the 2nd IC chip, which has the same orientation as the first IC chip during assembling.

From the Model tab, expand Operations and click Feature Operations. In the pop up menu, click **Copy > Move > Select > Dependent > Done.** From the model tree, pick **Hole 1** and, holding down the **Ctrl** key, pick Extrude 2 > **OK.**

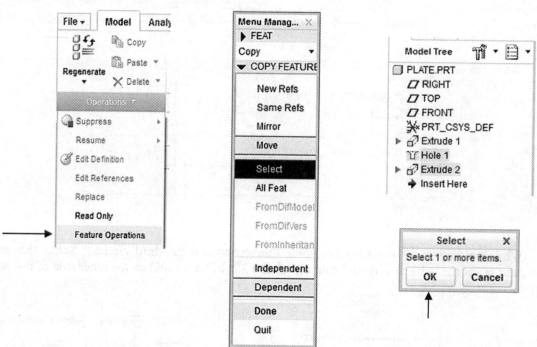

Translate > Plane > pick **FRONT** > accept the arrow direction if it directs to the 2nd IC chip, otherwise use **Flip** to reverse the direction > **Okay** > type in *30* > **Done Move > Done** to accept all the dimensions > **OK.**

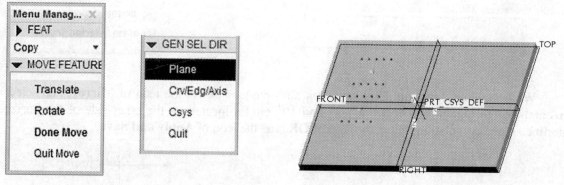

Step 3: Use **Copy** and **Move** to create a second set of center drill hole and 10 holes for positioning the third IC chip. Note there are 3 operations. The first operation is a 90° rotation and the second and third operations are translations.

From the Model tab, expand Operations and click Feature Operations. In the pop up menu, click **Copy > Move > Select > Dependent > Done.** From the model tree, pick **Hole 1** and, holding down the **Ctrl** key, pick Extrude 2 > **OK.**

Rotate > Crv/Edg/Axis > pick the centerline of the center drilled hole > Okay to accept the arrow direction if it follows the direction of y axis > type *90.*

      Translate > **Plane** > pick **FRONT** > accept the arrow direction if it directs to the 3rd IC chip, otherwise use **Flip** to reverse the direction > **Okay** > type *35.*

      Translate > **Plane** > pick **RIGHT** > accept the arrow direction if it directs to the 3rd IC chip, otherwise use **Flip** to reverse the direction, > type *75* > **Done Move** > **Done** to accept all the dimensions > **OK.**

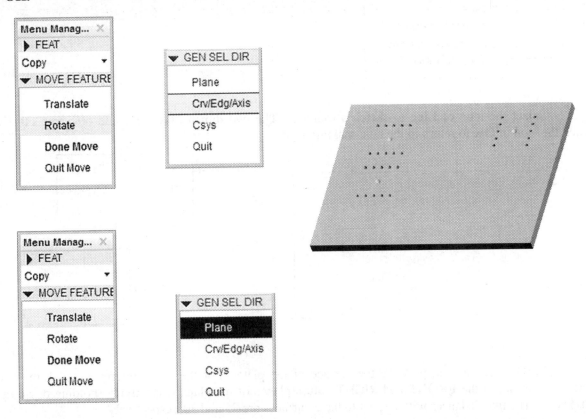

Task 2: Creation of a pattern table for the 7 resistors.

      In this example, we have 11 resistors. We use Pattern Table to create the holes for those resistors.

Step 1: Use **Hole** to create a center drill hole as the mark for a resistor placed on the plate.

      In the **Model** tab, click the icon of **Hole**. Click the **Sketch Mode** first. Afterwards, activate or click **Sketcher**, as shown below.

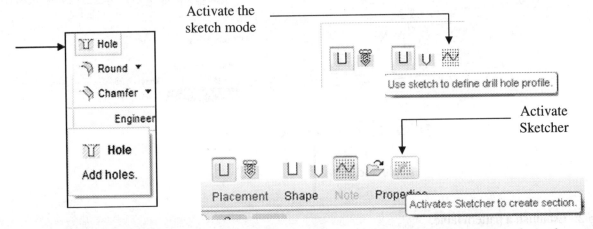

      A new sketch window appears. Right-click and click **Axis of Revolution** from the pop up window. Afterward sketch a vertical centerline.

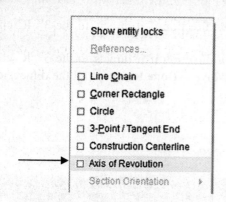

Select the icon of **Line** to sketch a triangle. The two dimensions are 1 and 60°, respectively. Click the icon of **OK** to return to the hole-making page.

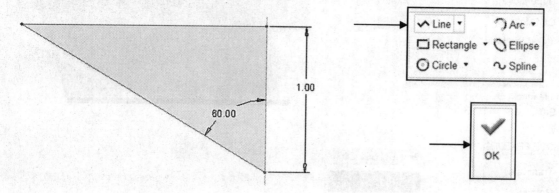

On Hole Placement, pick the top surface of the plate. For the offset references, pick the two surfaces, parallel to the **FRONT** and RIGHT datum planes of the plate, respectively (holding down the **Ctrl** key). The two distances with respect to the 2 surfaces are 25 and 70, respectively.

From the feature control panel, select the icon of **Apply and Save** to complete the creation of the center drill hole.

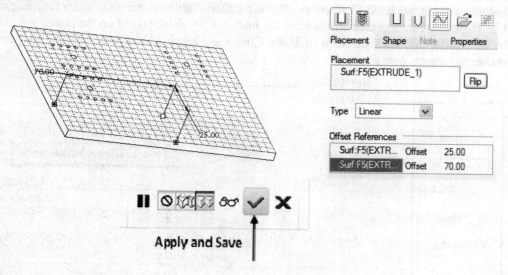

Step 2: Establish a pattern table.

The location of a resistor requires two coordinates, namely, its x coordinate and the z coordinate because we are working on a plane which is parallel to the **TOP** datum plane. As a result, the pattern table to be created requires 2 columns; one column is for x_position and the other for z_position. Assign names to the two columns by using 2 symbols to represent the two dimensions, 70 and 25.

From the model tree, highlight Hole 2 and right-click and hold, Pick **Edit** and the 4 dimensions associated with **Hole 2** are on display. Select 70 and right click to pick **Properties**. In the Dimension Properties window, change d51 to x_position.

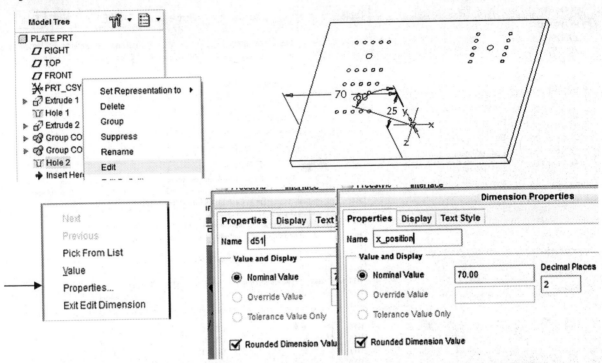

Select 25, and right click to pick Properties. In the **Dimension Properties** window, change d50 to z_position. In the Component Interface tab, expand Model Intent and pick Switch Symbols. The symbolic names of the dimensions 70 and 25 are on display.

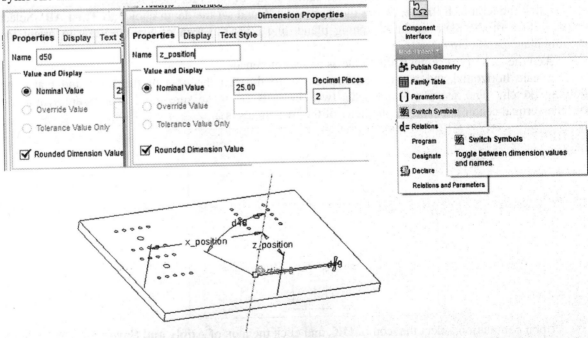

From the model tree, highlight the Hole feature, right click and hold, and select **Pattern**. From the dashboard, select **Table** and activate **Table Dimensions**. Pick x_position and z_position from the display while holding down the Ctrl key. Click **Edit** and a **Pattern Table** appears. In this table each row stands for a new instance in the pattern and is assigned to an index name, or idx, together with its x and z positions. Type the following information for the 6 new instances to the table.

Note that an asterisk, "*", is used for those x coordinates sharing the same value (namely, 70) with the driving dimension in the x direction > **Exit** from the table. Click the icon of **Apply and Save**.

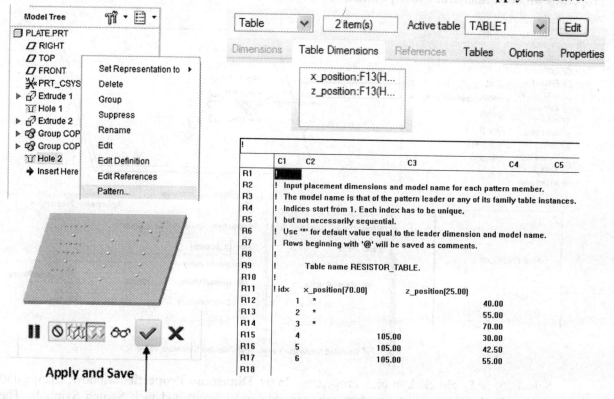

Apply and Save

	C1	C2	C3	C4	C5
R1					
R2	! Input placement dimensions and model name for each pattern member.				
R3	! The model name is that of the pattern leader or any of its family table instances.				
R4	! Indices start from 1. Each index has to be unique,				
R5	! but not necessarily sequential.				
R6	! Use '*' for default value equal to the leader dimension and model name.				
R7	! Rows beginning with '@' will be saved as comments.				
R8	!				
R9	! Table name RESISTOR_TABLE.				
R10	!				
R11	! idx	x_position[70.00]	z_position[25.00]		
R12	1	*	40.00		
R13	2	*	55.00		
R14	3	*	70.00		
R15	4	105.00	30.00		
R16	5	105.00	42.50		
R17	6	105.00	55.00		
R18					

Step 3: Use Reference Pattern to complete the creation of the 14 holes for the 7 resistors.

Click the icon of **Extrude.** Select the icon of **CUT** and set the depth choice to **Thru All**. Select the top surface of the plate as the sketching plane, and click the icon of Sketch View to orient the sketching plane parallel to the screen.

Add the axis of the center drilled hole as a new reference.

Create horizontal and vertical centerlines to go through the axis of the hole, and make the following sketch: The distance between the two circles is 18, make sure the 2 centers are symmetric about the vertical center line, and the diameter of the two circles is 2.

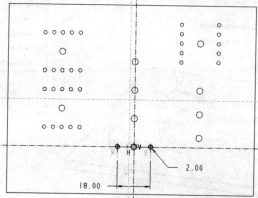

Upon completion, select the icon of **OK,** and click the icon of **Apply and Save.**

From the Model Tree, highlight the cut feature, right click and hold, and select **Pattern**. On the dashboard, the **Reference** choice is selected by default. Simply click the icon of **Apply and Save.**

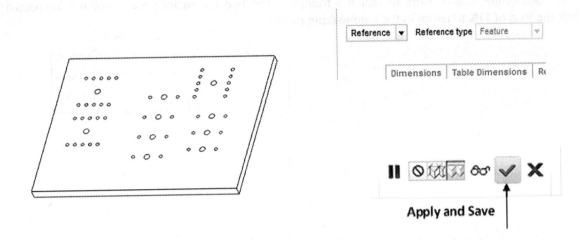

Apply and Save

Task 3: Creation of a pattern table for the 6 capacitors.

We use the pattern table method to create the holes for the 6 capacitors.

Step 1: Use **Hole** to create a center drilled hole as a mark for the location of a capacitor on the plate.

In the **Model** tab, click the icon of **Hole**. Click the **Sketch Mode** first. Afterwards, activate or click **Sketcher**, as shown below.

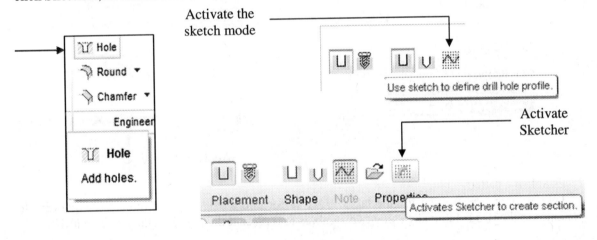

A new sketch window appears. Right-click and click **Axis of Revolution** from the pop up window. Afterward sketch a vertical centerline.

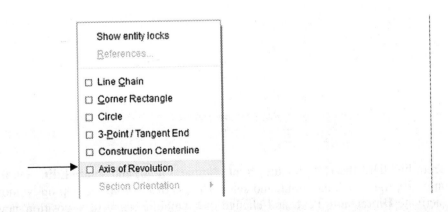

Select the icon of **Line** to sketch a triangle. The two dimensions are 1 and 60°, respectively. Click the icon of **OK** to return to the hole-making page.

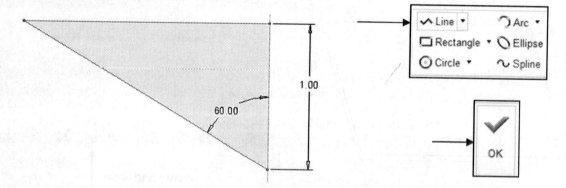

On Hole Placement, pick the top surface of the plate. For the offset references, pick the two surfaces, parallel to the **FRONT** and RIGHT datum planes of the plate, respectively (holding down the **Ctrl** key). The two distances with respect to the 2 surfaces are 10 and 20, respectively.

From the feature control panel, select the icon of **Apply and Save** to complete the creation of the center drill hole.

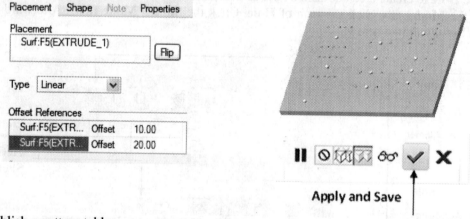

Apply and Save

Step 2: Establish a pattern table.

Two columns are needed for the table. One is for coordinate and the other for z_coordiante. Assign names to the two columns by using two symbols to represent the two dimensions, 20 and 10.

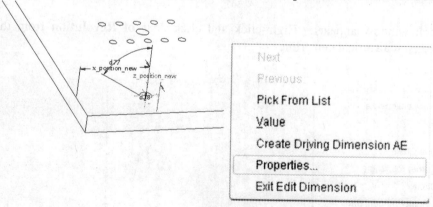

From the Model Tree, highlight the Hole feature, right click and hold, and select **Edit**. On the display, pick the dimension of 20, right click and hold, and select **Properties**. From the pop up window of Dimension Properties, activate **Dimension Text**, and change the symbolic name to x_position_new.

Following the same procedure, change the symbolic name of dimension equal to 10 to z_position_new.

From the Model Tree, highlight the Hole feature, right click and hold, and select **Pattern**. From the dashboard, select Table and activate Table Dimensions. Pick x_position_new and z_position_new from the display.

Activate **Edit**, and a Pattern Table appears on screen. In this table each row stands for a new instance in the pattern and is assigned to an index name, or idx, together with its x and z positions. Type the following information for the 5 new instances to the table.

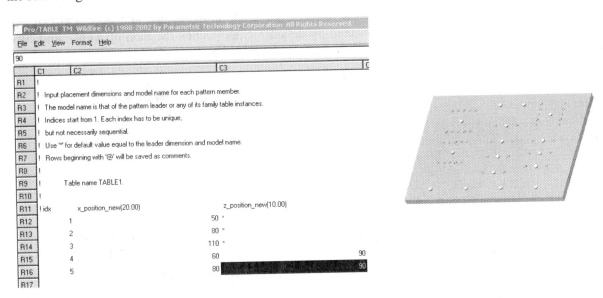

Step 3: Use Reference Pattern to complete the creation of the 12 holes for the 6 capacitors.

To create the 12 holes, directly select the icon of **Extrude** from the feature toolbars. From the dashboard, select the icon of **CUT** and set the depth choice to **Thru All**. Click **Placement > Define**.

Select the top surface of the plate as the sketch plane, and use the **RIGHT** datum plane to orient the sketch plane.

Add the axis of the center drilled hole as a new reference.

Create horizontal and vertical centerlines to go through the axis of the hole, and make the following sketch: The distance between the two circles is 10, make sure that the 2 centers are symmetric about the vertical center line, and the diameter of the two circles is 2.

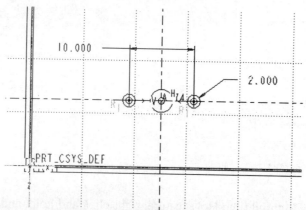

Upon completion, select the icon of **Done**. From the dashboard, select the icon of **Complete** from the feature control panel.

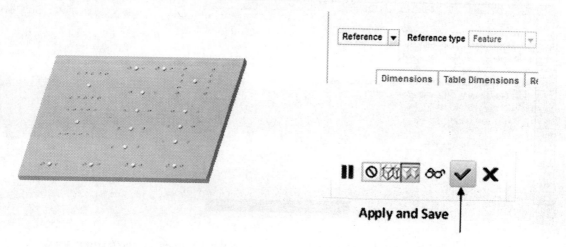

From the model tree, highlight the cut feature, right click on the mouse, and select **Pattern**. On the dashboard, the Reference choice is selected by default. Simple click the icon of **Apply and Save** from the feature control panel to complete the creation of the 12 holes.

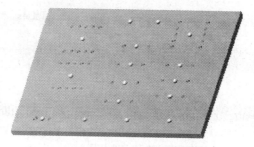

Create the engineering drawings for the IC chip layout.

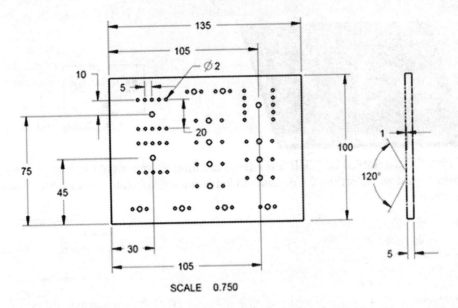

SCALE   0.750

Layout of the 3 IC Chips

At this moment, we have all the holes with the plate component. We are able to easily finalize the PCB assembly. Let us open the file called PCB_ASSEMBLY. We start with assembling the 3 IC chips.

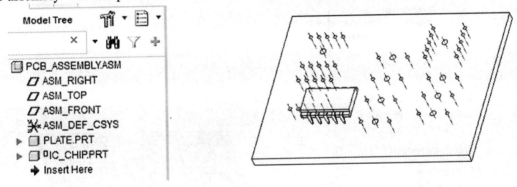

Highlight IC_CHIP.PRT, and right-click to pick **Edit Definition**. Turn off or hide the 3D Dragger. Click the axis from IC_Chip and the axis from the central hole for the IC chip component to define the first Coincident constraint. Click the top surface of plate and the bottom surface from the chip body to define the second Coincident constraint. Click the icon of **Apply and Save**.

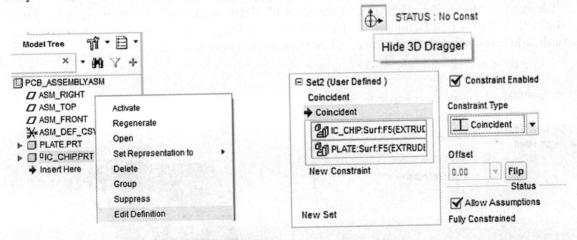

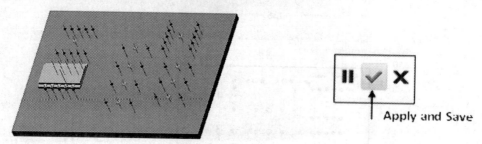

Apply and Save

Let us pick this assembled IC_CHIP.PRT from the Model Tree, right-click to pick **Repeat.** In the Repeat Component window, select the 2 Coincident Constraints. Click Add to assemble 2 more IC_CHIP components, as shown.

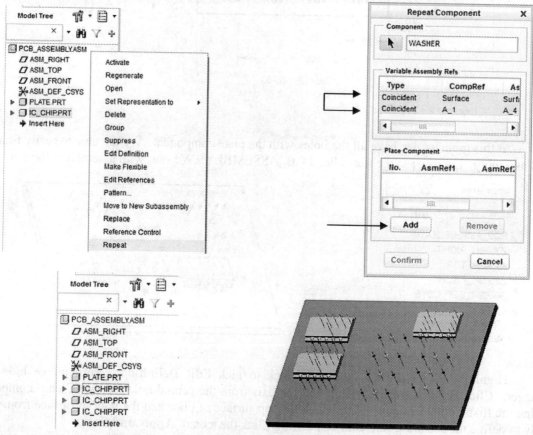

We need to modify the orientation of the third IC_CHIP assembled. Highlight it in the Model Tree. Right-click to pick Edit Definition. Turn on or show 3D Dragger and rotate the IC chip 90 degrees. Afterwards, add a new coincident constraint. Click the icon of **Apply and Save.**

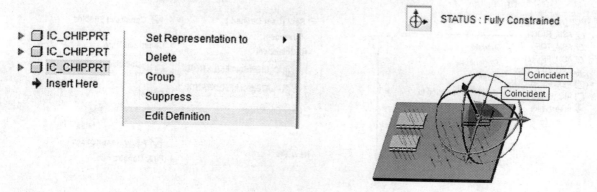

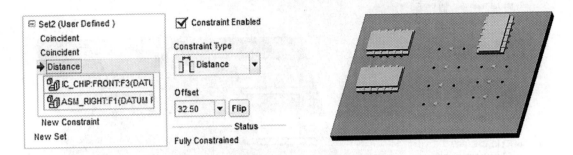

Highlight CAPACITOR.PRT, and right-click to pick **Edit Definition**. Turn off or hide the 3D Dragger. Click the axis from CAPACITOR and the axis from the central hole for the CAPACITOR component to define the first Coincident constraint. Click the top surface of plate and the bottom surface from the CAPACITOR to define the second Coincident constraint. Click the icon of **Apply and Save**.

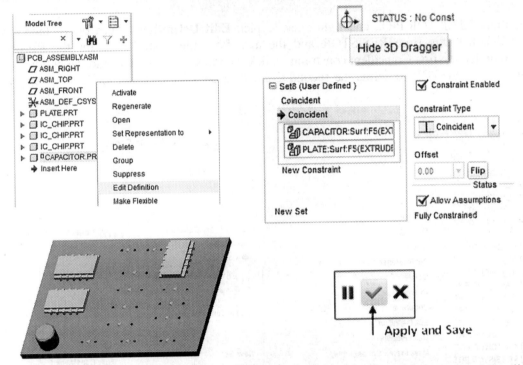

Apply and Save

Let us pick this assembled IC_CAPACITOR.PRT from the Model Tree, right-click to pick **Repeat.** In the Repeat Component window, select the 2 Coincident Constraints. Click Add to assemble 5 more CAPACITOR components, as shown.

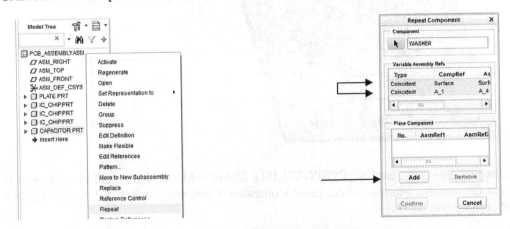

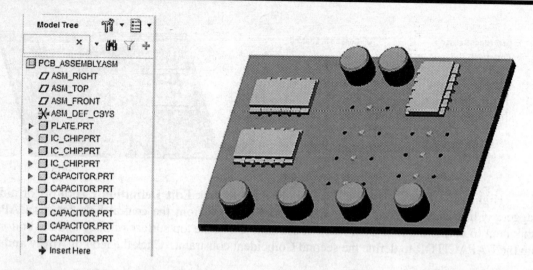

Highlight RESISTOR.PRT, and right-click to pick **Edit Definition**. Turn off or hide the 3D Dragger. Click the axis from RESISTOR and the axis from the central hole for the RESISTOR component to define the first Coincident constraint. Click the top surface of plate and the bottom surface from the wire of RESISTOR to define the second Coincident constraint. Click the icon of **Apply and Save**.

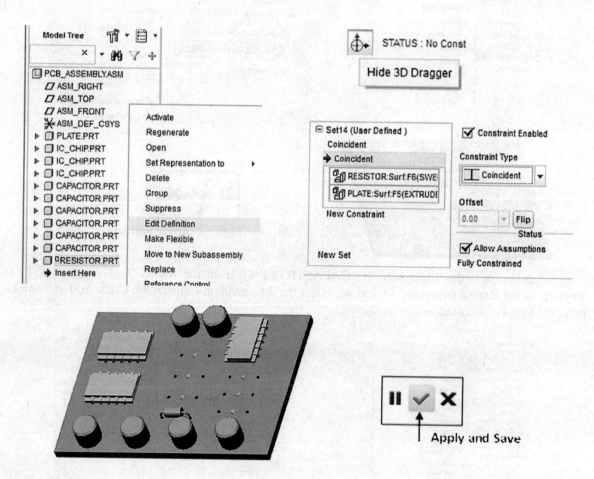

Let us pick this assembled IC_RESISTOR.PRT from the Model Tree, right-click to pick **Repeat.** In the Repeat Component window, select the 2 Coincident Constraints. Click Add to assemble 6 more RESISTOR components, as shown.

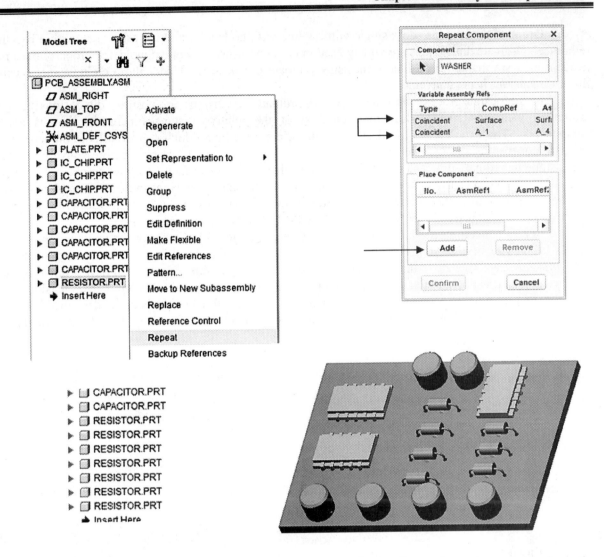

Create an assembly drawing for the printed circuit board using linear dimensions. Let us have the name of the drawing file as *pcb_linear.drw*.

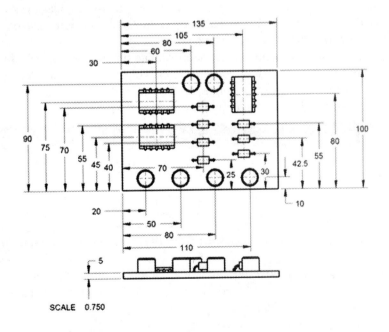

Ordinate dimensions use a single witness line with no leader, and are associated with a baseline reference. Ordinate dimensions are widely used in civil engineering. For example, the property lines in a resident area are marked on a blue print using ordinate dimensions. Under those circumstances, using linear dimensions is not convenient.

In the design process, designer also use ordinate dimensions for position dimensions because ordinate dimensions give a clear representation of the relative distances between features and/or components. The Creo Parametric design system offers a method, which converts linear dimensions to ordinate dimensions and vice versa. However, special attention has to be paid before converting linear dimensions to ordinate dimensions. It is important that all linear dimensions have to share a common reference, which can be used to define as the base for the ordinate dimensions in the process of converting the linear dimensions to their corresponding ordinate dimensions. Note that in this exercise, the right and lower corner is assumed to be the origin, or x=0 and z=0, for the conversion.

Before converting the linear dimensions to the ordinate dimensions for the engineering drawing of this PCB assembly, let us use "Save As" to save the above drawing to a file with another name, say *pcb_ordinate.drw*. Then open the file called *pcb_ordinate.drw*. In this way, we will have 2 drawing files. One is associated with the linear dimensions and the other is associated with the ordinate dimensions.

The procedure to convert the linear dimensions to their ordinate dimensions is described below:
Pick the linear dimension on display, right click and hold, and select **Toggle ordinate/linear**.

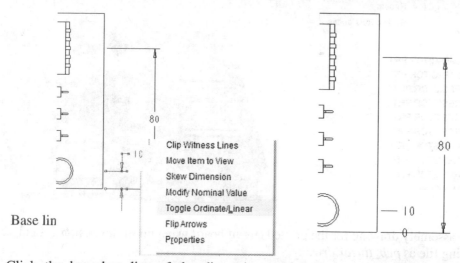

Click the boundary line of the dimension, which serves as the base line for the ordinate dimension. To convert the ordinate dimension back to its linear dimension, just do the same as the procedure to convert the linear dimension to the ordinate dimension.

For converting a set of linear dimensions to their ordinate dimensions, which share the same base line, special attention should be paid to "How many "0"s do you need?" Generally speaking, we only need a single "0" for the x-direction, and/or a single "0" for the y-direction. In such cases, make sure click "**Yes**" when such a question appears on screen to avoid having many zeros.

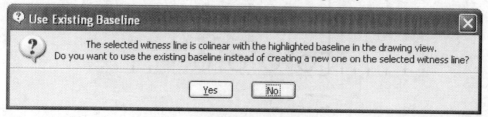

Another way for the conversion is select **Edit** from the main menu > **Toggle ordinate/linear** > pick a linear dimension from the display.

Sometimes, jogs are needed to move the numerical values to other locations for clarity purpose. Just pick the dimension line where a jog is needed, right click on the mouse and select **Insert Jog** > on the display, pick the location where a jog starts.

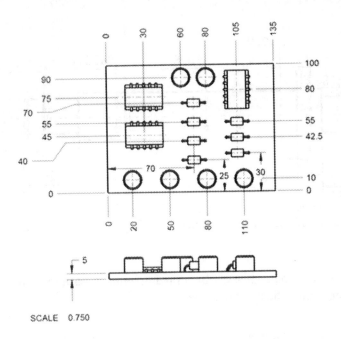

SCALE 0.750

7.10 References

1. F. L. Amirouche, <u>Computer-aided Design and Manufacturing</u>, Prentice Hall, Englewood Cliffs, New Jersey, 1993.
2. R. E. Barnhill, <u>IEEE Computer-Graphics and Applications</u>, 3(7), 9-16, 1983.
3. D. D. Bedworth, M. R. Henderson, and P. M. Wolfe, <u>Computer-Integrated Design and Manufacturing</u>, McGraw-Hill, New York, NY, 1991.
4. D. Hearn, M. P. Baker, Computer Graphics, Englewood Cliffs, NJ, 1986
5. P. Ingham P. <u>CAD System in Mechanical and Production Engineering</u>, London, 1989.
6. M. Mantyla, <u>An introduction to Solid Modeling</u>, Rockville IN:Computer Science Press., 1988

7.11 Exercises

1. Use Creo Parametric to prepare the following assembly drawing.
    Components: 2 Medium 305W Radial Bearings
                  A gear component (You specify the required tolerances)
                  A special nut for fastening the gear component (You design the detail)
                  A shaft (You specify the required tolerances)

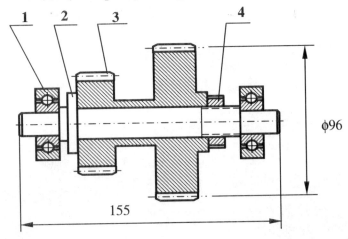

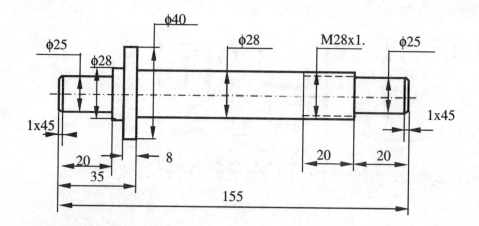

2.   Use Creo Parametric to prepare an assembly drawing with, at least, two projections, a BOM table, three BOM balloons, and critical dimensions.

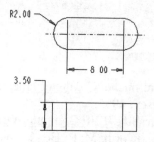

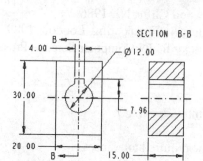

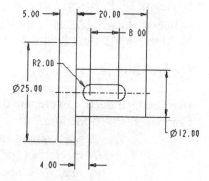

CHAPTER 8

DETAILING WITH TOLERANCES

8.1 Engineering Drawings with Dimensional Tolerances

The engineering drawings shown in the examples presented in Chapters 5, 6 and 7 had dimensions with them. However, no information on tolerances was presented. In the process of product development, tolerances are used to control the deviations allowable for the purpose of maintaining quality assurance and product exchangeability, as discussed in Chapter 3. The following figure presents an engineering drawing, which has the tolerance information associated with some of the dimensions specified in the drawing.

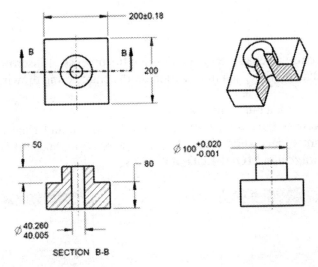

SECTION B-B

For example, the maximum and minimum dimensions of the hole allowable are 40.260 and 40.005, respectively. The deviations allowable for the width dimension of 200 are ±0.18, as shown, and the dimension of 200 is the nominal value, about which the deviations are measured. Under the Pro/ENGINEER design environment, tolerances can be specified in the following formats, or tolerance modes:

- Nominal without tolerances
- Symmetric, 200±0.18
- Limits, $\phi_{40.005}^{40.260}$
- Plus-Minus, $\phi 100_{-0.001}^{+0.020}$

Example 8-1: Create a 3D solid model based on the information presented in Figure 8-1, prepare an engineering drawing (a full section view and an offset section view) and add tolerance information to the engineering drawing.

Let us launch Creo Parametric. Click **File > Options.** In the Creo Parametric Options window, click Configuration Editor. The default setting for tolerance is ANSI. Click OK to close this window.

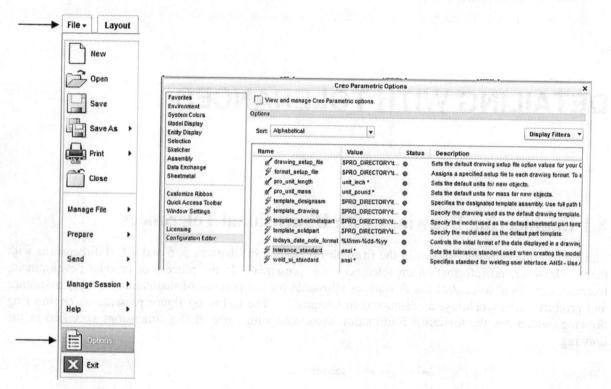

In the following, we use an example to demonstrate the process of inserting tolerance information into the 3D solid model and displaying such information on the engineering drawing.

Step 1: Create a solid model for tolerance specifications.

From **File,** click **New > Part** > type *ex8_1* as the file name and clear the box of **Use default template > OK.** Select **mmns_part_solid** (units: Millimeter, Newton, Second) and type *Example 8-1* in **DESCRIPTION** and type *student* in **MODELED_BY > OK.**

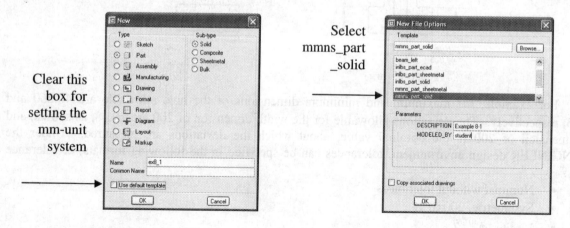

Let us create the first feature: a block with size: 200 x 200 x 80 mm.
From the Model tab, click **Extrude.** Specify 80 as the value of extrusion distance.

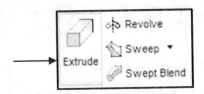
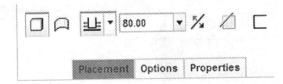

Select the **TOP** datum plane as the sketching plane, and click the icon of **Sketch View** to orient the sketching plane parallel to the screen.

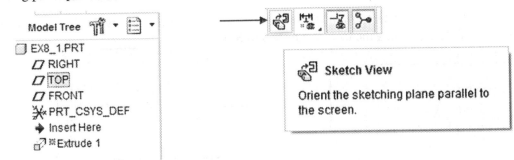

Select the icon of **Center Rectangle** from the Model tab, and sketch a rectangle. The two dimensions are 200 and 200. Click **OK** and click the icon of **Apply and Save.**

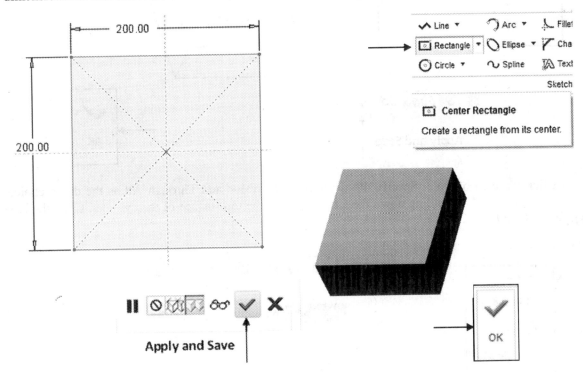

Click the icon of Extrude. Specify 50 as the value of the extrusion distance.

Select the top surface of the block as the sketching plane. Click the icon of Sketch View to orient the sketching plane parallel to the screen.

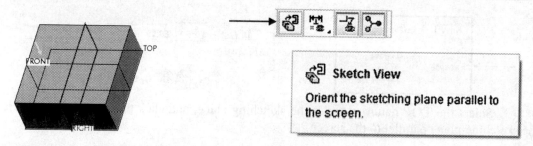

Sketch View

Orient the sketching plane parallel to the screen.

Select the icon of **Circle** from the Model tab, and sketch a circle with diameter equal to 100. Click the icon of **OK**, and click the icon of **Apply and Save**.

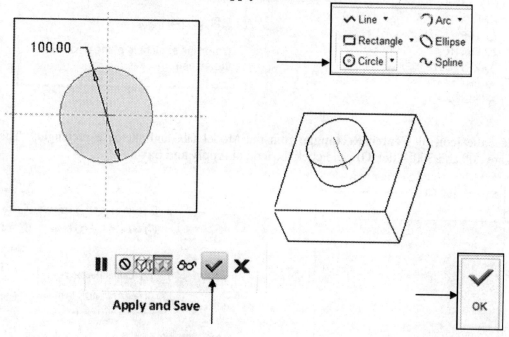

✓ Line ▾   ↱ Arc ▾
◻ Rectangle ▾   ◯ Ellipse
◯ Circle ▾   ∿ Spline

100.00

Apply and Save

OK

Click the icon of Hole. Specify 40 as the diameter value and Through All as the depth choice. Pick the Axis first. While holding down the **Ctrl** key, pick the top surface of the cylinder. Click the icon of **Apply and Save**.

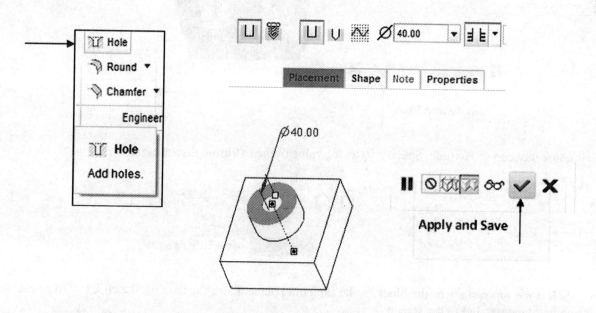

⊔ Hole
⤾ Round ▾
⤾ Chamfer ▾
Engineer
⊔ Hole
Add holes.

⌀ 40.00

Placement   Shape   Note   Properties

⌀40.00

Apply and Save

To prepare an offset section view to depict the geometrical characteristics of the inner side, we need to create an offset section, which consists of 2 planes, as shown.

From the top menu, select **View > View Manager.**

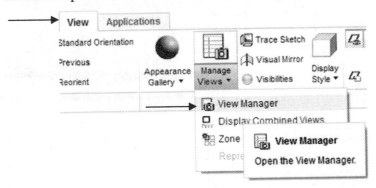

In the **View Manager** window, click **Section > New > Offset.**

type *B* and press **Enter** key.

Select **Offset > Both Sides > Single > Done.**

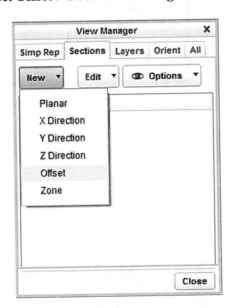

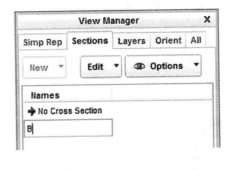

Setup New > Plane > Pick the **FRONT** datum plane as the sketch plane > **Okay** to accept the feature creation direction > **Default** to accept the orientation of the sketch plane. Click Sketch View to orient the sketching plane parallel to the screen

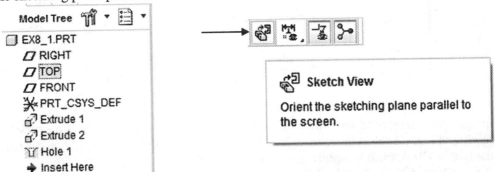

Add 2 new references. Click the icon of **References**. Pick the surface on the right side (positive x direction) and the surface at the bottom side (positive z direction) as the 2 new references > **Close**

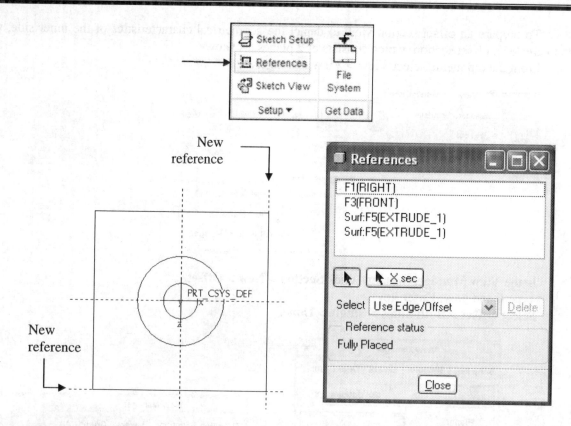

New reference

New reference

Click the icon of **Line** and drawing 2 lines, as shown. Upon completion, select the icon of **OK**. The created offset section planes are on display. Click **Close** to complete the creation of the 2 offset section planes.

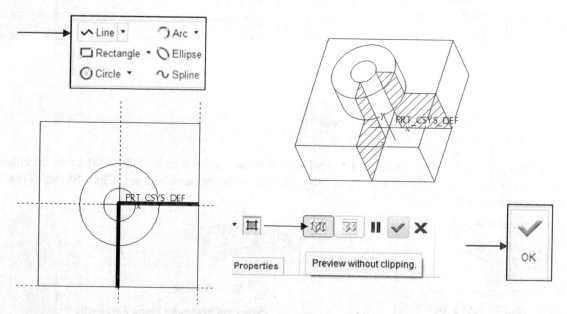

To prepare an engineering drawing based on the 3D solid model, we open a new file under the Mode of **Drawing**. First, we select the icon of **New** from the main toolbar. Type *ex8_1* as the name of the file. Clear the box of **Use default template** and click the box of **OK**.

In the window of **New Drawing**, make sure that the file of the 3D solid model called *ex8-1* is shown. Otherwise, use "**Browse**" to locate it. Select **Empty** under Specify Template, and select the paper size of **A**. Afterwards, click the box of **OK**.

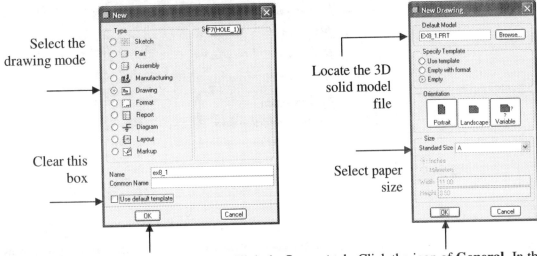

Select the drawing mode

Clear this box

Locate the 3D solid model file

Select paper size

This brings up the drawing screen. Click the **Layout** tab. Click the icon of **General.** In the **Select Combined State** window, click **OK** to accept **No Combined State**.

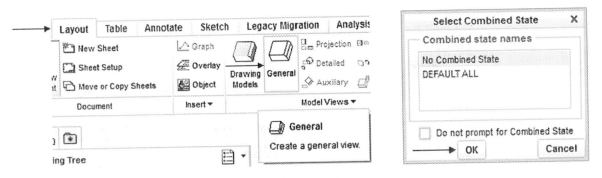

In the pop-up **Drawing View** window, select **FRONT > Apply > Close**, the construction of the front view is completed.

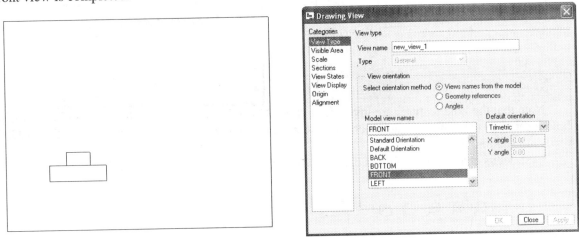

To insert the right-sided view through projection, click the icon of **Projection**. Move the cursor to a location right to the front view and click the left button of mouse, the construction of the right-sided view is completed. Repeat this procedure for creating the top view. Click the icon of **Projection** and move the cursor to a location above the front view and click the left button of mouse, the construction of the top view is completed.

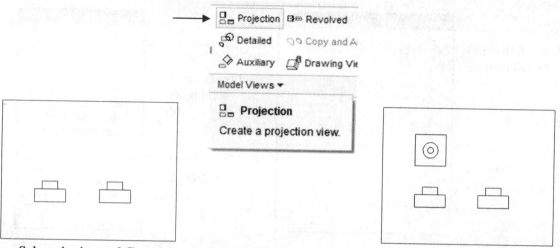

Select the icon of **General** to create a 3D view. Select a location on the drawing screen as the center point for the 3D view (click the left button of mouse). A general view appears on the screen. select **Standard Orientation > Apply > Close**, the construction of the 3D view is completed.

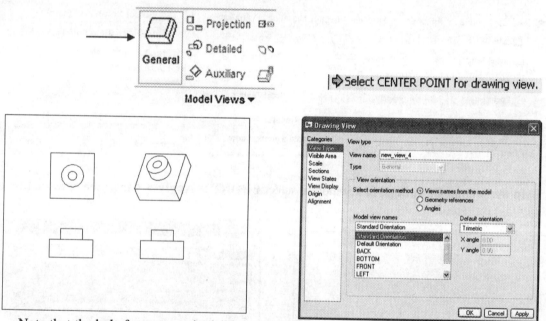

Note that the hole features are invisible in the FRONT view. In order to have a visible version of the hole located in the center of the block, we use a section view. To do so, let us modify the FRONT view to a full section view.

First, let us enable the display of datum planes. Click the icon of **Plane Display**.

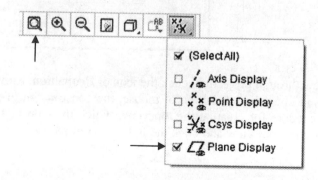

Select the FRONT view by a left click of mouse. Afterwards, right click and hold, select **Properties** > select **Sections** and **2D cross-section** > Click the icon of **Add** (plus sign) to add cross-section > **Create New** > **Planar** > **Single** > **Done**.

Type *A* as the name for cross-section and press **Enter** > select the FRONT datum plane from the Top View > **Apply**, a cross-section is added to the Front view.

To add an arrow indicating the position and direction of the cross-section view, activate **Arrow Display** from the **Drawing View** window > click the Top view > **Apply** and two arrows marked as A appear together with SECTION A-A > **Close**.

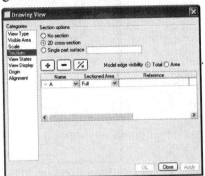 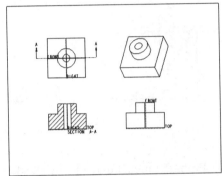

To modify the 3D view to an offset section view, select the 3D view by a left click of mouse. Afterwards, right click and hold, select **Properties** > select **Sections** and **2D cross-section** > Click the icon of **Add** (plus sign) to add cross-section > pick **B** > **Apply** > **Close**.

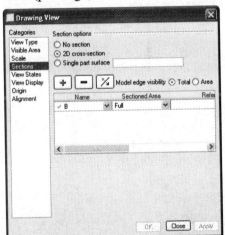 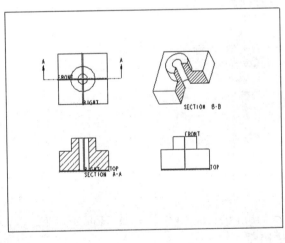

Upon completing the layout, we start adding dimensions. Click the **Annotate** tab > **Show Model Annotation**.

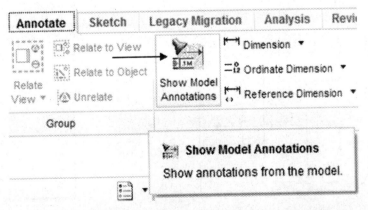

Select the icon of **Dimensions**. From the model tree, click Extrude 1. Three dimensions of 80, 200 and 200 associated with Extrude 1 are shown. Click the box of **Accept All > Apply**.

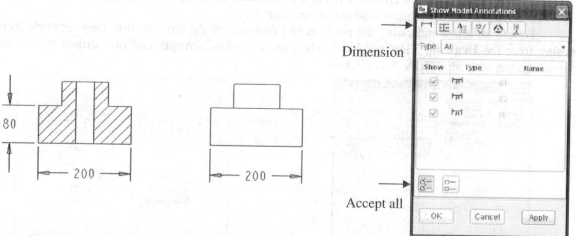

From the model tree, click Extrude 2. Two dimensions of Ø100 and 50 are shown. Click the box of **Accept All > Apply**.

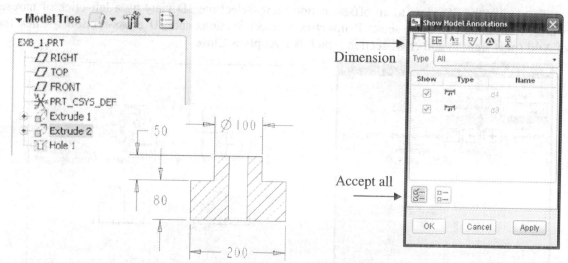

From the model tree, click Hole 1. The dimension of Ø40 is shown. Click the box of **Accept All > Apply**.

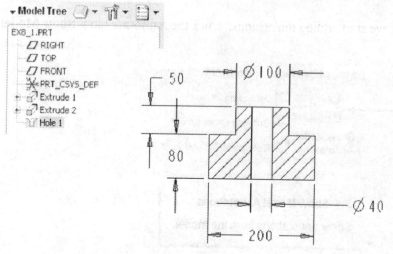

In the **Show Model Annotation** window, click Centerline. From the model tree, click Hole 1. pop-up window, select the icon of dimension and the icon of axis > **Show All** > **Yes** > **Accept** > **Close.**

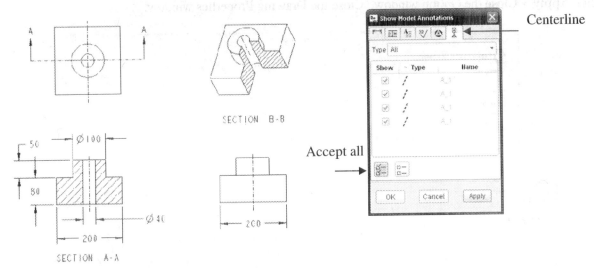

You may use the icon of **Pick** to move the dimensions to appropriate locations.

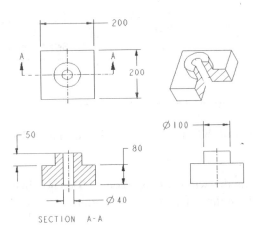

To add dimensional tolerances to the engineering drawing, the function of **Tolerance** should be activated. Let us add the symmetric form of tolerance labeled as ±0.18 to the width dimension of 200. From the top menu, click **File** > Prepare > **Drawing Properties.**

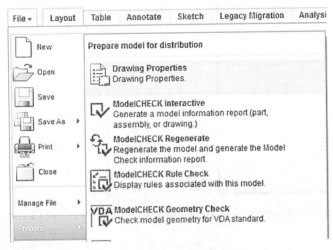

In the Drawing Properties window, Click **change**. In the Options window, type *tol_display* in the box called **Option**, press the **Enter** key, and replace the choice of **no** with **yes** > click **Add/Change** > click **Apply** > **Close** the Option window. Close the Drawing Properties window.

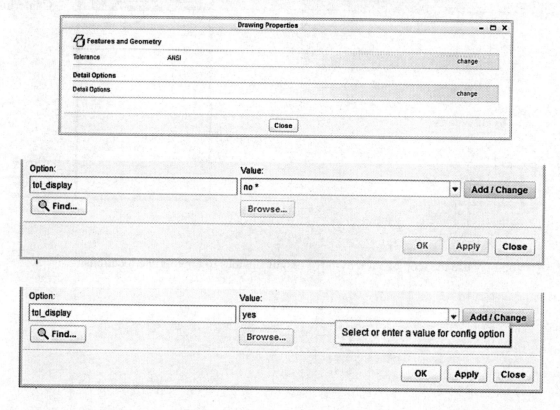

Select the width dimension of 200, right-click and hold, and select **Properties** from the pop up window.

Tolerance Mode: **Symmetric** for the width of the block. The nominal value is 200. The deviation about 200 is 0.18 mm. The deviation requires 2 decimal places.

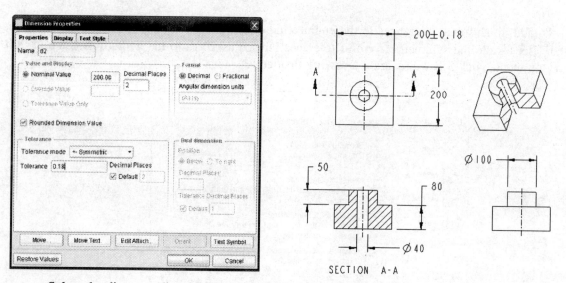

Select the diameter dimension of 100, right-click and hold, and select **Properties** from the pop up window.

Tolerance Mode: **Plus-Minus** for the diameter of the cylinder. The nominal value is 100. The plus deviation about 100 is 0.020 mm, and the minus deviation about 100 is –0.001. Both deviations require 3 decimal places.

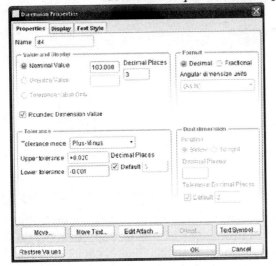
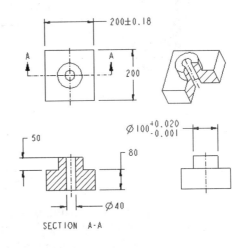

Select the diameter dimension of 40, right-click and hold, and select **Properties** from the pop up window.

Tolerance Mode: **Limits** for the diameter of the hole. The maximum dimension is 40.260 mm, and the minimum dimension is 40.005 mm. Both dimensions require 3 decimal places.

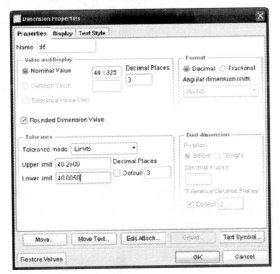
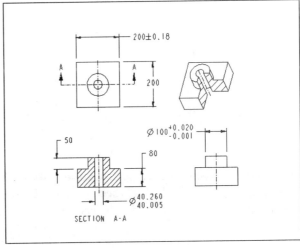

The tolerance modes for the other width of the block, the thickness of the block and the height of the cylinder are set to **Nominal** to show no limits. Finally, insert the format to the drawing.

8.2 Engineering Drawings with Surface Finish Requirements

For quality assurance of the functional requirements of products, sustaining certain surface conditions, such as smoothness and flatness are important. The following figure presents an engineering drawing showing the requirements on surface finish, which is usually measured by a surface profilometer in the unit of micro inches, or μinch. For machined surfaces, both ANSI and ISO have their standards on surface finish. In the following figure, the symbols used for specifying surface finish are commonly used for machined surfaces.

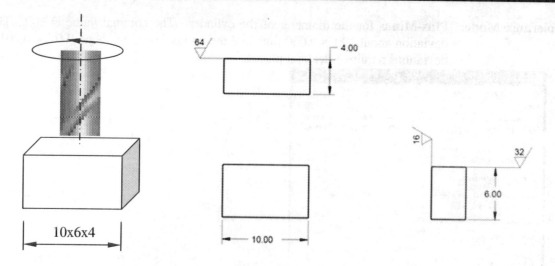

10x6x4

Example 8-2:   The engineering drawing of a block component is shown below. The requirements for surface finish are specified. They are 16 μinch, 32 μinch, and 64 μinch, respectively. Add the three surface finish requirements to the engineering drawing, as shown.

In this example, we assume that an engineering drawing with dimensions, as shown below, has been prepared. Now we are to add the surface finish requirement on the engineering drawing.

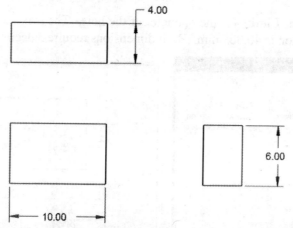

From the main toolbar, select **Annotation > Surface Finish > Retrieve** the files for surface finish > open the fold called **Machined** > select **standard1.sym** > **Normal** > pick the surface where the surface finish requirement is needed > type in the value (the unit is μinch by default), say 64 for the top surface.

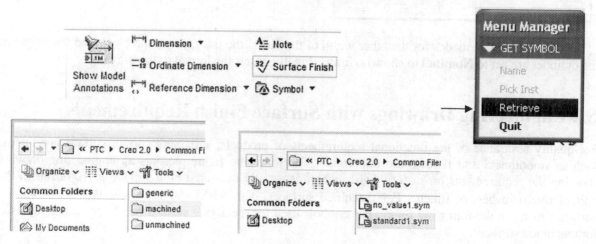

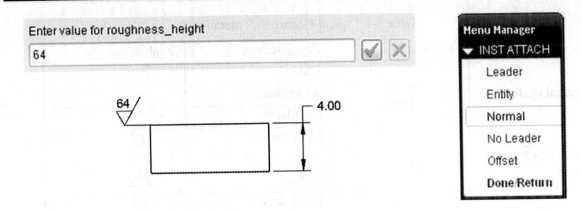

Readers may repeat the above procedure to add more symbols and move the surface finish symbols to their appropriate positions, as shown.

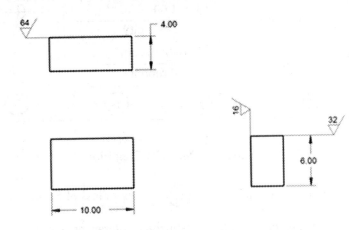

8.3 Engineering Drawings with Geometrical Tolerances

In section 8.2, we discussed the dimensional tolerances. A dimensional tolerance is the permissible variation on the dimension it relates to. The values of a tolerance may determine the performance of the component, and a product. On the other hand, the permissible variation is related to the manufacturing process or processes, from which a component is fabricated. As a result, design engineers have the responsibility of assigning appropriate values to the permissible variation on each dimension of a component. Besides the dimensional tolerances, there is another type of tolerances, called as geometric tolerances. Those tolerances are related to the specifications of the maximum variation that can be allowed in form or position from true geometry. The characteristic symbols listed in Table 8-1are those that have adopted for use in lieu of notes to express positional and form tolerances.

Expressions of geometrical tolerances are significantly different from the ways, by which the dimensional tolerances are presented. As illustrated in the following figure, the feature control frame consists of three parts: the box of Feature Control Symbol, the box of Tolerance, and the box of Datum Reference.

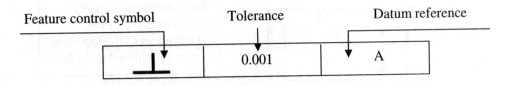

Table 8-1 Typical Geometric Tolerances

	Tolerance	Characteristic	Symbol
Individual Feature	Form	Flatness	⬮
		Straightness	—
		Circularity	○
		Cylindricity	⌭
Individual or Related Features	Profile	Line	⌒
		Surface	⌓
Related Features	Orientation	Parallelism	//
		Perpendicularity	⊥
		Angularity	∠
	Location	Position	⊕
		Concentricity	◎
	Runout	Circular runout	↗
		Total runout	⍁
Supplementary Symbols	Ø	Ⓜ	Ⓛ	Ⓢ

Ø Diameter   Ⓜ   At Maximum Material Condition

Ⓛ   At Least Material Condition   Ⓢ   Regardless of Feature Size

Are there any relationships between the dimensional tolerances and the geometrical tolerances? The answer is YES. The following example illustrates the relationship between tolerances of dimension and tolerances of geometry. Regarding the dimension of 6 inches, its maximum and minimum dimensions allowed to vary are 6.025 and 5.975, respectively.

Case 1: When only a size tolerance is specified, the limits of the dimension control both size and geometric forms. For example, the flatness of the top surface is assumed to be better than 0.05 inch.

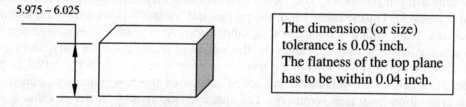

5.975 – 6.025

The dimension (or size) tolerance is 0.05 inch.
The flatness of the top plane has to be within 0.04 inch.

Case 2: When both a size tolerance and a geometric tolerance are specified, the limits of the dimension control the size and the geometric tolerance controls the form, such as the flatness within 0.01 inch, as shown below.

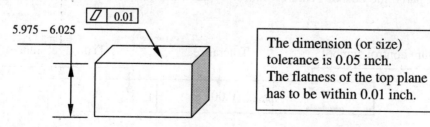

5.975 – 6.025

⬮ | 0.01

The dimension (or size) tolerance is 0.05 inch.
The flatness of the top plane has to be within 0.01 inch.

Example 8-3   Implementation of four types of geometrical tolerances, which do not require a datum for specification.

Straightness	Flatness	Circularity	Cylindricity
——	▱	◯	⌭
line	plane	circle	cylinders

Case Study 1:   Display the flatness of 0.01 inch in the engineering drawing of the block. We use the 3D model of the block used in Example 8-2 for surface finish study.

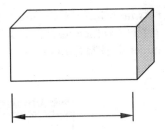

From the main toolbar, select **Annotation > Geometric Tolerance** > select the flatness from the window of geometric tolerance > select **Surface** under the **Reference > Select Entity** and pick the top surface on the top view > **Dimension** under the **Placement** and pick the dimension of 4. For changing the tolerance value, click the button of **TolValue,** and type the desired value > **OK.**

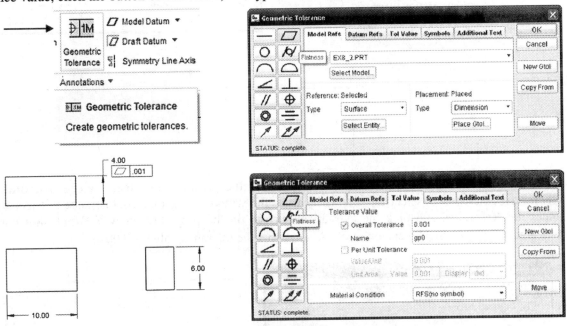

Case Study 2:   Display the straightness and circularity on the engineering drawing of a cylinder.

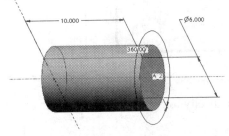

Assume that the engineering drawing with the 2 dimensions and a dimensional tolerance has been prepared, as shown.

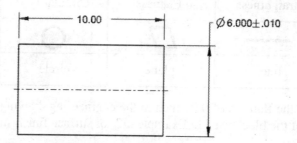

From the main toolbar, select **Annotation** > **GeometricTolerance** > select the straightness from the window of geometric tolerance > select **Surface** under the **Reference** and pick the cylindrical surface on the projection view > **Dimension** under the **Placement** and pick the dimension of 10. Assume that the tolerance value is 0.001.

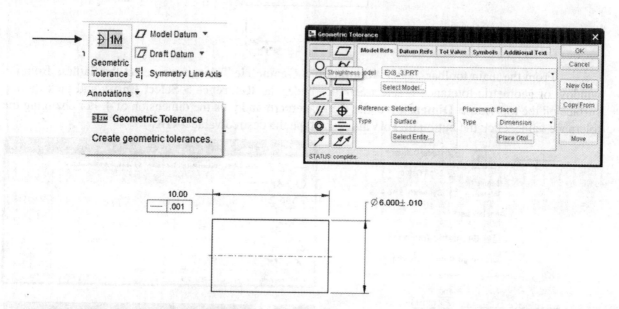

To add the circularity tolerance, from the main tool bar, select **Annotation** > **GeometricTolerance** > select the circularity from the window of geometric tolerance > select **Surface** under the **Reference** and pick the cylindrical surface on the projection view > **Dimension** under the **Placement** and pick the dimension of φ6. Assume that the tolerance value is 0.001.

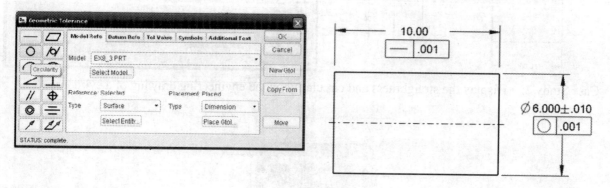

Case Study 3: Display the concentricity tolerance of 0.003 on the engineering drawing of a cylinder.

Under circumstances, the requirement of concentricity tolerance needs to be specified, instead of showing the circularity. Let us delete the circularity first.

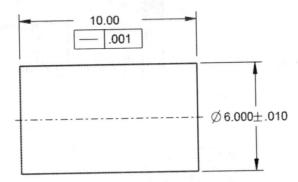

To add the concentricity tolerance, select **GeometricTolerance** > select the concentricity from the window of geometric tolerance > select **Surface** under the **Reference** and pick the cylindrical surface on the projection view > **Dimension** under the **Placement** and pick the dimension of φ6. To change the tolerance value, say from 0.001 (default value) to 0.002, click the button of **TolValue** > type 0.002 > **OK.**

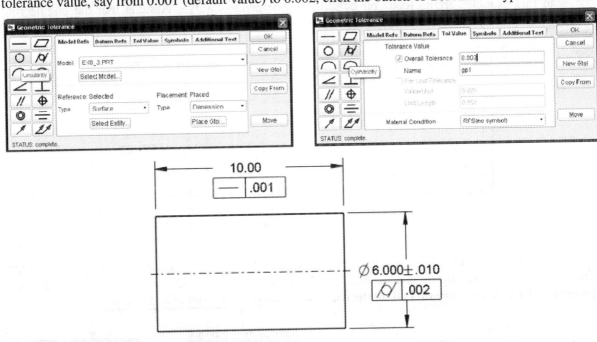

Example 8-4 Implementation of Perpendicularity

Perpendicularity, angularity and parallelism are orientation tolerances and they are datum related, as shown below:

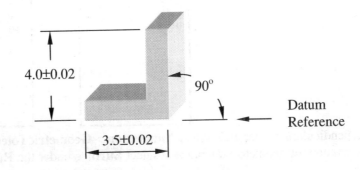

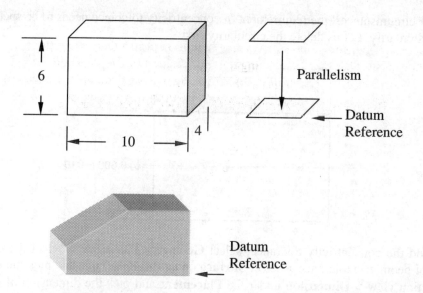

In this example, let us focus on defining the perpendicularity. Assume that the engineering drawing of the V-shape object is available, as shown.

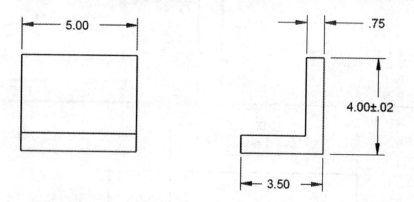

First, we need to define the datum reference before specifying the perpendicularity tolerance. Turn on the display of datum planes, pick the **TOP** datum plane, right-click and hold, and select **Properties**. Change the name of **TOP** to the name of A, activate the symbol sign > **Set** > **OK**.

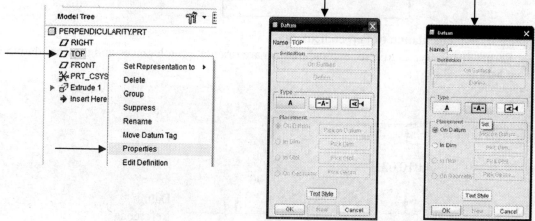

To specify the perpendiculariity tolerance, select **Annotation** > **GeometricTolerance** > select the perpendicularity from the window of geometric tolerance > select **Surface** under the **Reference** and pick the vertical surface on the right side projection view > **Dimension** under the **Placement** and pick the dimension of 4.

To add the reference symbol of A to the feature control frame, click the box of **Datum Refs** > under **Basic**, choose A > **OK**, thus completing the specification of the perpendicularity.

Move these references to appropriate positions by picking them up and relocating them.

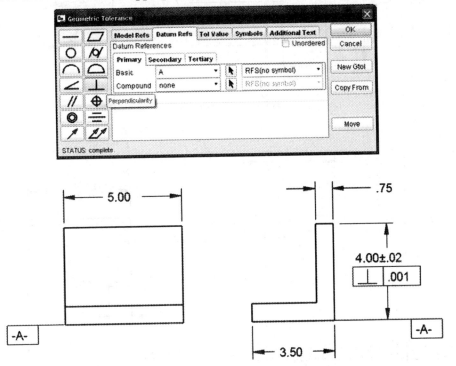

8.4   Dimensional Tolerances with an Assembly

An assembly consists of components. The tolerances assigned to components will be certainly reflected on the tolerances of the assembly. In Section 3.61, an example was presented to illustrate the relation between the tolerances of components to the tolerance of its assembly, as shown below:

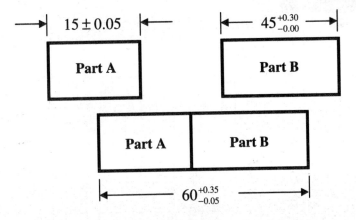

For the purpose of demonstrating such a concept, the following 2 engineering drawings represent Part A and Part B, respectively. The dimension, marked as 15±0.05, is shown in Part A. The dimension, marked as 45+0.3, is shown in Part B.

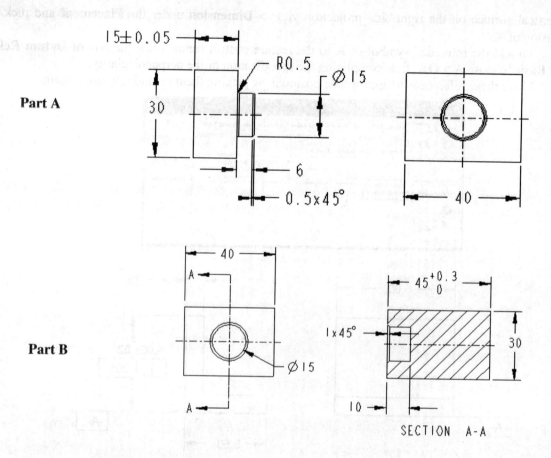

Part A

Part B

When we assemble Part A and Part B, a 3D solid model of this assembly and an engineering drawing are shown below.

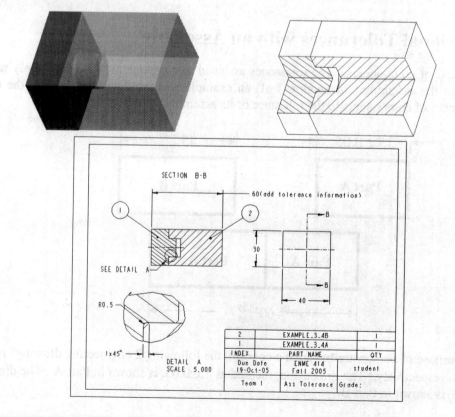

In the above engineering drawing, we are asking the readers to provide the solution to the dimension representing the length after being assembled. Certainly, the solution is $60^{+0.35}_{-0.05}$.

Pay attention to the information presented in the detailed view, marked as Detail A. The dimension of the round on Part A is 0.5 mm. The dimension of the chamfer on Part B is 1x45°, or the width of the chamfer is 1.0 mm, which is greater than the value of the round, ensuring no clearance on the interface between Part A and Part B after assembling them together.

8.5 Creation of Annotation Features and Layer Structures

As we recall, the dimensions presented by an engineering drawings are associated with projection views, or are associated with 2D representations. It is natural to ask a question: Can we present dimensions in a 3D space? The following figure presents 2 dimensions specified in a 3D space. These dimensions are called Annotation features.

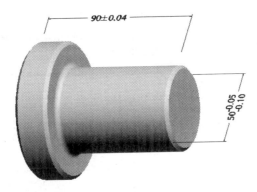

Annotation features are data features. Users are able to use annotation features to manage the model annotation and propagate model information to other models. Remember that annotation features do not create any geometry. Because of this reason, the created annotation features are only displayed in the Model Tree. Users are not able to select an annotation feature directly from the screen.

In this section, we present the procedure to create 2 types of annotations. The first annotation feature is **Driven Dimension**. The second annotation feature is **Surface Finish**. We use a 3D model of a block to begin with. Let us first create a 3D solid model for the block, assuming that the three dimensions are 100, 60 and 40 mm, respectively.

Step 1: Create a 3D solid model for the block object.

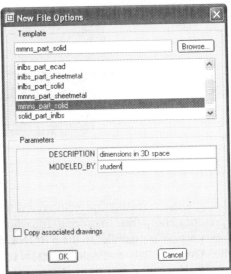

Let us use **Extrude** to create the block object. select the icon of **Extrude**. Set the depth equal to 40 and pick the **FRONT** datum plane as the sketching plane and click the icon of Sketch View to orient the sketching plane parallel to the screen.

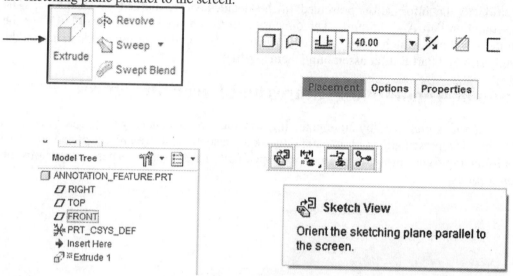

Pick the icon of **Rectangle** and sketch a rectangle along the x-axis and y-axis. The 2 dimensions are 100 and 60.

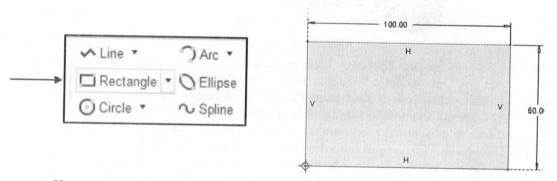

Upon completing the sketch, select the icon of **OK** and select the icon of **Apply and Save.**

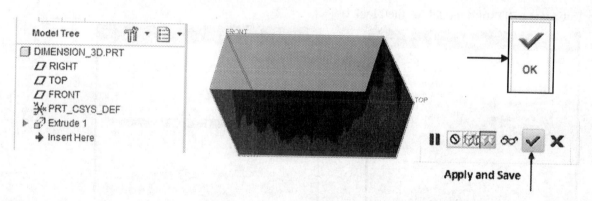

Step 2: Create an annotation feature for the driven dimension equal to 100.

It is important to note that, in order to measure this dimension, we have to use the FRONT datum plane, or any planes which are parallel to the **FRONT** datum plane.

Click the **Annotate** tab, and select **FRONT**. Click the icon of Annotation feature. A window called **Annotation Feature** appears. From the window, select the icon of **Create a driven dimension**.

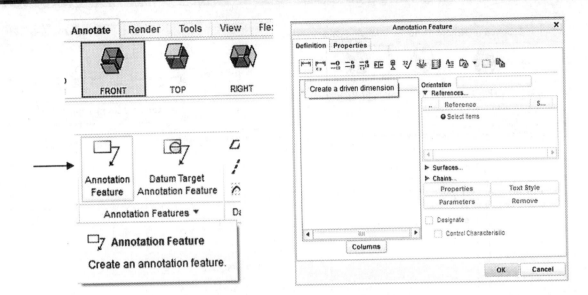

In the ATTACH TYPE window, the command of **On Entity** is highlighted. The software system is asking the user to select an entity so that the measurement of 100 can be taken. Let us pick the horizontal edge on the top surface of the block, and locate a position for the dimension and press the middle button of mouse. The annotation feature is created, as shown below.

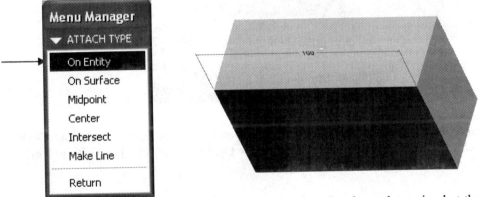

It is very important to note that a reference plane has been determined at the time the horizontal edge is picked. The Reference Description indicates the **FRONT** datum is used. Click **OK** to complete the creation of the first annotation feature.

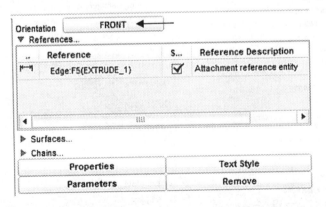

Let us create the second annotation feature. Click the **Annotate** tab, and select **RIGHT** (the reference datum plane). Click the icon of **Annotation feature**, and select **Create a driven dimension**. Click the edge, as shown, to display the dimension of 40. Click **OK** to complete the creation.

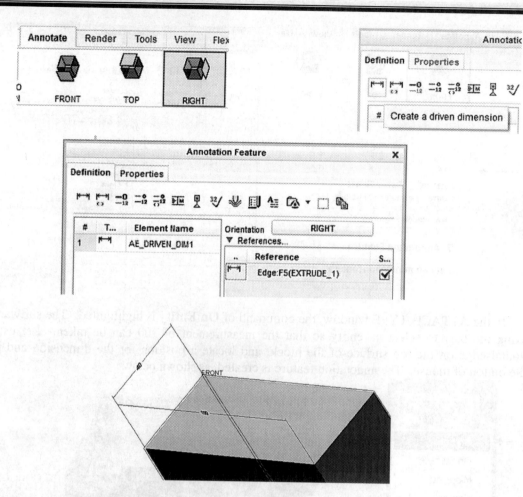

To add tolerance information, say 100±0.15, Click **File** and click Configuration Editor. Click Add and type *tol_display*. Click Find. In the **Creo Parametric Options** window, change **No** to **Yes**. Click **OK**.

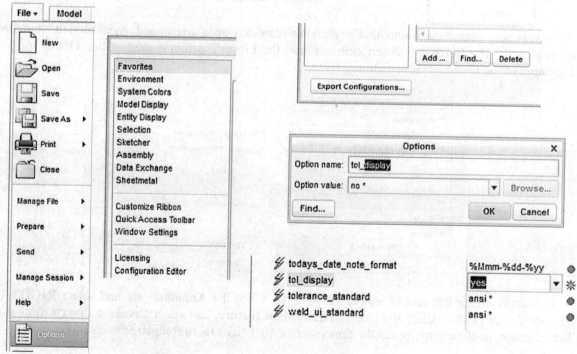

Afterwards, from the model tree, highlight **Annotation 1** and right-click and hold > **Edit Definition**. In the Annotation Feature window, select the defined feature and right-click to select Properties.

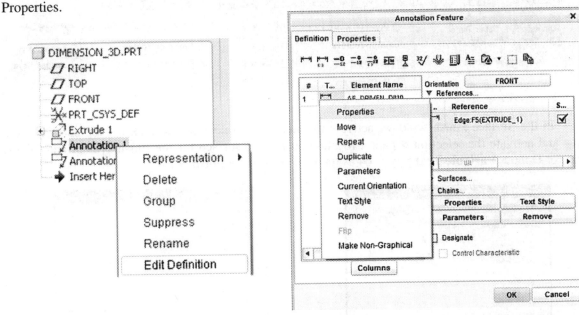

In the **Dimension Properties** window, select +- Symmetric and specify 0.01 as the tolerance value. Click OK to add the tolerance information to the defined annotation feature.

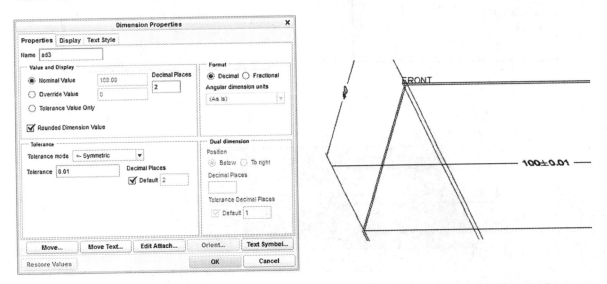

Step 3: Create an annotation feature for the surface requirement on the top surface of the block.
Click the Annotate tab. and select TOP (reference plane). Click the icon of Annotation Feature. Select the icon of Create a surface finish.
To create the surface finish symbol, click machined and click standard1_sys.

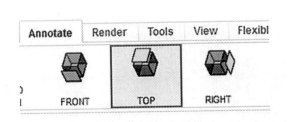

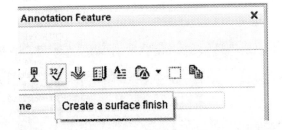

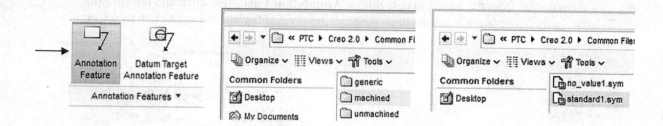

In the Surface Finish window, activate the **Reference** selection and pick the top surface > **On Entity** and activate the selection > pick a location on the top surface for the finish symbol and middle button for Done > **Variable Text** > type 64 as the value of surface finish >**OK**.

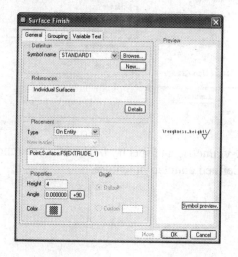 

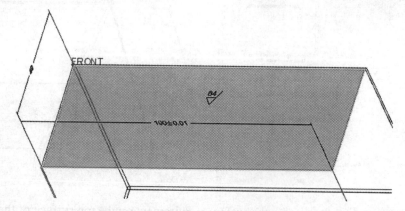

When examining the model tree, there are 3 annotation features listed.

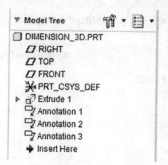

Step 4: Organize the 3 annotation features into a layer structure to facilitate the display or hiding.

From the Model Tree, select **Show > Layer Tree**, and the layers associated with this 3D solid models appear.

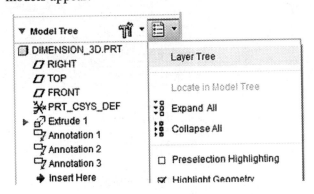
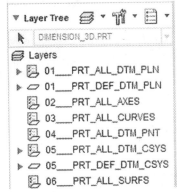

To create a new layer for organizing the annotation features, click **Layer > New Layer** > type *annotation_features* as the layer name.

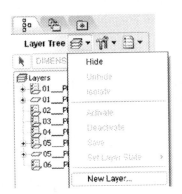

Pick the 3 annotation features > **OK**.

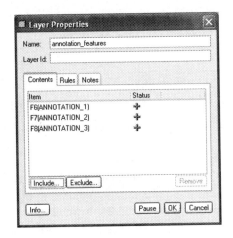
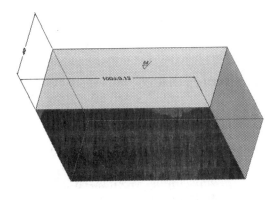

We may notice that the layer called annotation_features has already been displayed in the Model Tree.

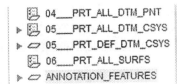

If we do not want to show those annotation features, we may hide this layer called annotation_features. Just pick this layer from the model tree > right-click and select Hide, and the created annotation features are not on display.

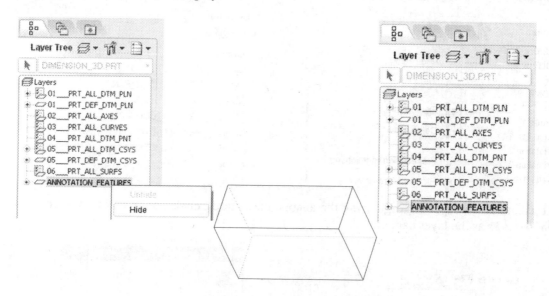

From this example, we have learned the procedure to create a layer structure, which can be effectively used to organize the data information, such as on display or hiding. It is not uncommon that a designer opens a file of 3D solid model and he/she does not observe all features on display. Under such a circumstance, check the layer structures because some of the layers may be in a status called Hide.

8.6 References

1. F. L. Amirouche, <u>Computer-aided Design and Manufacturing</u>, Prentice Hall, Englewood Cliffs, New Jersey, 1993.
2. R. E. Barnhill, <u>IEEE Computer-Graphics and Applications</u>, 3(7), 9-16, 1983.
3. D. D. Bedworth, M. R. Henderson, and P. M. Wolfe, <u>Computer-Integrated Design and Manufacturing</u>, McGraw-Hill, New York, NY, 1991.
4. H. R. Buhl, <u>Creative Engineering Design</u>, Iowa State University Press, Ames, Iowa, 1960.
5. B. L. Davids, A. J. Robotham and Yardwood A., <u>Computer-aided Drawing and Design</u>, London, 1991.
6. M. P. Groover and E. W. Zimmers, <u>Computer-aided Design and Manufacturing</u>, Englewood Cliffs, NJ, 1984.
7. C.S. Krishnamoorthy, <u>Finite Element Analysis, Theory and Programming</u>, 2nd Ed., 1995.
8. D. Hearn, M. P. Baker, Computer Graphics, Englewood Cliffs, NJ, 1986
9. P. Ingham P. <u>CAD System in Mechanical and Production Engineering</u>, London, 1989.
10. M. Mantyla, <u>An introduction to Solid Modeling</u>, Rockville IN:Computer Science Press., 1988

8.7 Exercises

8-1.   Construct a 3D solid model of the object shown below. Prepare an engineering drawing of it. Specify the tolerances as indicated.

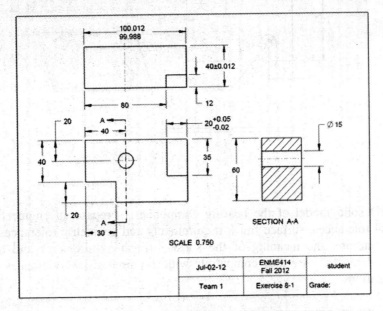

8-2.   Construct a 3D solid model of the object shown below. Prepare an engineering drawing of it. Specify the tolerances as indicated.

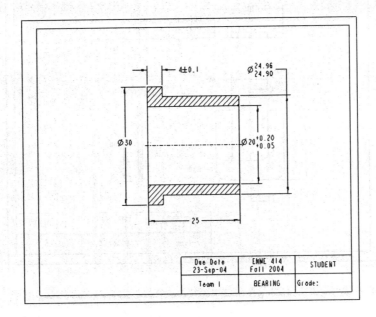

8-3.   Create a 3D solid model of the bearing component. Prepare an engineering drawing. Add dimensional tolerances to the engineering drawing.

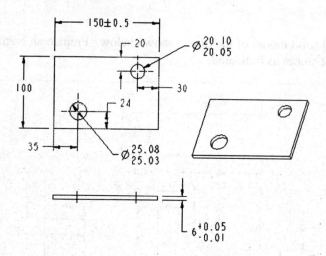

8-4. Create a 3D solid model of the bearing component. Prepare an engineering drawing. Add dimensional tolerances, surface finish requirements and geometric tolerances to the engineering drawing. Interpret the meaning of the surface finish requirements and the meaning of the geometric tolerances. Are they compatible with the dimensional tolerances specified? Provide your explanations.

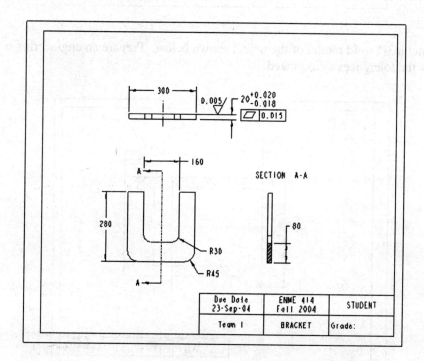

CHAPTER 9

SPECIAL FUNCTIONS IN Creo Parametric

9.1 Creation of 3D Solids Using Shell and Draft

In the process of creating 3D solid models with thin wall structures, the function called **Shell** is often used as demonstrated in Example 9-1. We use **Shell** to create a bath tub. In the manufacturing processes, such as casting and forging, the function of draft is often used to ensure the manufacturability. In this example, we also demonstrate the use of **Draft** in the 3D solid modeling.

Example 9-1: Creation of a 3D solid model of bath tub using Shell and Draft

The following figure presents a bath tub we use in our daily life. Products of bath tub are manufactured through ejection molding. The geometric characteristics and dimensions are shown below.

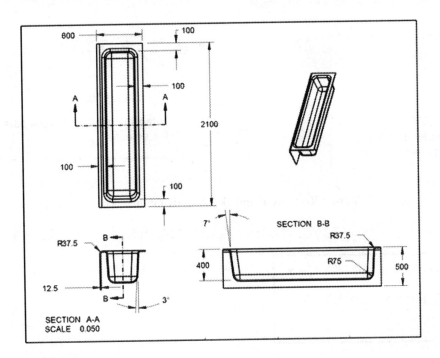

Step 1: Create a 3D solid model
Create a file for the 3D solid model.
File > New > Part > type *bath_tub* as the file name and clear the icon of **Use default template**.

Select mmns_part_solid (units: Millimeter, Newton, Second) and type *Bath Tub Structure* in **DESCRIPTION**, and *Student* in **MODELED_BY**, then **OK**.

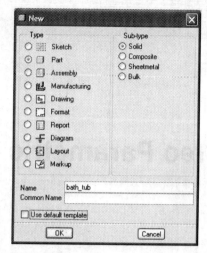
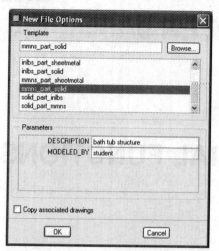

The first feature is a block. The three dimensions are 500 x 600 x 2100 mm. Click the icon of **Extrude.** Set the depth value to 2100.

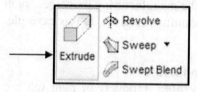
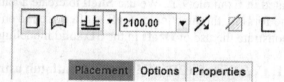

Select the **FRONT** datum plane as the sketching plane, and click the icon of **Sketch** View to orient the sketching plane parallel to the screen.

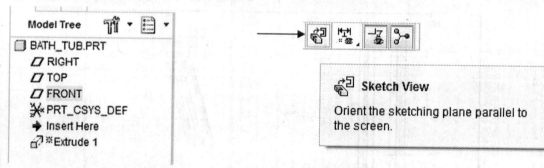

Select the icon of **Corner Rectangle** and sketch a rectangle. The 2 dimensions are 600 and 500, as shown.

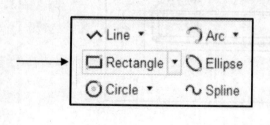
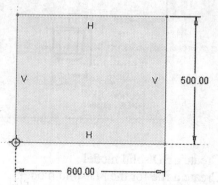

Upon completion, pick the icon of **OK,** and click the icon of **Apply** and **Save**.

Step 2: Create a cut feature, which is a rectangular block, leaving the thickness value equal to 10 mm, and the depth of cut is 400.

Select the top surface of the block as the sketching plane, and click the icon of Sketch View to orient the sketching plane parallel to the screen.

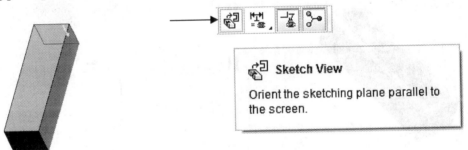

Add 2 new references before sketching. Click the icon of **References**. Pick the 2 surfaces, as shown. Click **Close**.

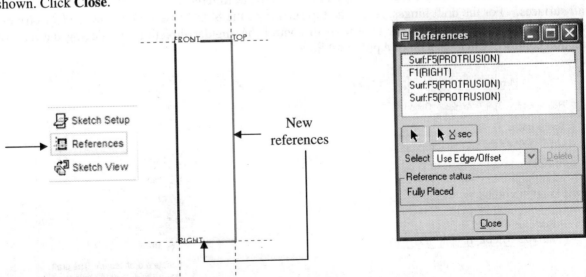

Pick the icon of **Rectangle** and sketch a rectangle so that the thickness value at each side is 100 mm, as shown.

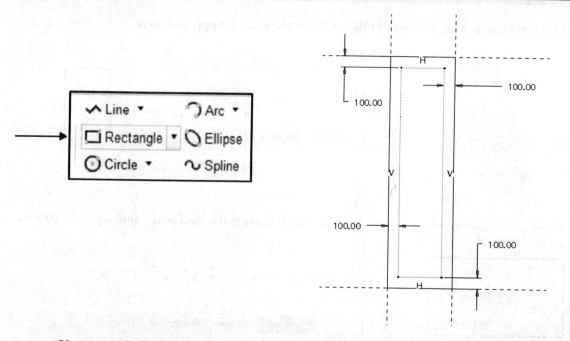

Upon completing the sketch, select the icon of **OK,** and click the icon of **Apply and Save**.

Apply and Save

OK

Step 3: Create draft on three surfaces so that water can flow downward.

Click the icon of **Draft** from the Model tab. Activate References > select the 3 surfaces as the draft surfaces. For the draft hinges, select the top surface of the block, as shown below, and specify the draft angle equal to 3 degrees (user may need to control the angular direction by clicking the icon of direction control). Click the icon of **Apply and Save**.

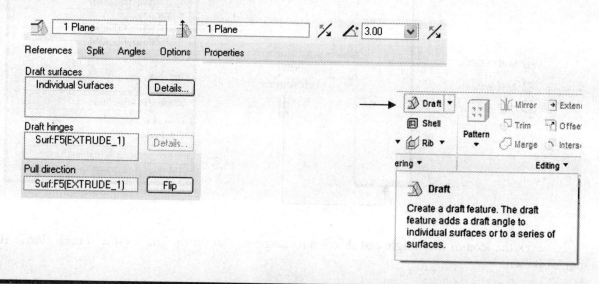

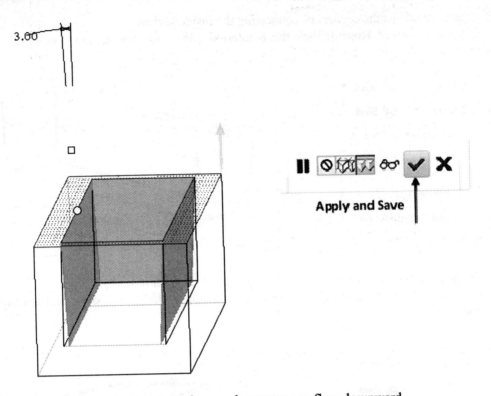

Step 4: Create draft on the fourth surface so that water can flow downward.

Activate **References** > select the surface as the draft surface. For the draft hinges, select the top surface of the block, as shown below, and specify the draft angle equal to 7 degrees. Click the icon of **Apply and Save**.

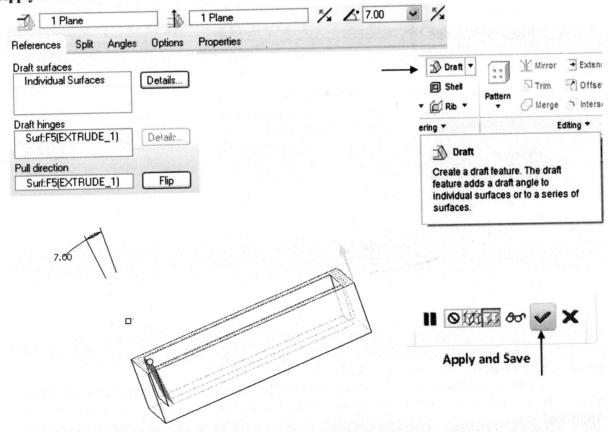

Step 5: Create rounds on the corners of connecting the inside surfaces.

Click the icon of **Round**. Pick the 8 internal edges, as shown, and specify 75 as the radius dimension.

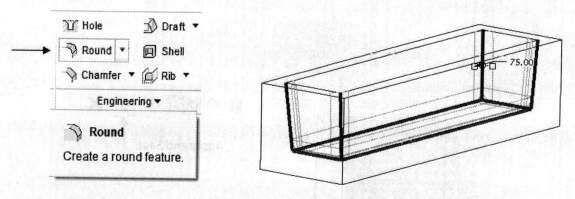

Step 6: Create rounds on the 4 edges on the top surface of the bath tub.

Pick the 4 edges around the cut feature on the top surface, as shown, and specify 37.5 as the radius dimension.

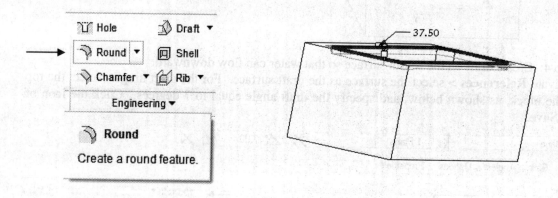

Step 7: Create a round along the edge on the top surface of the bath tub.

Pick the edge, as shown, and specify 37.5 as the radius dimension.

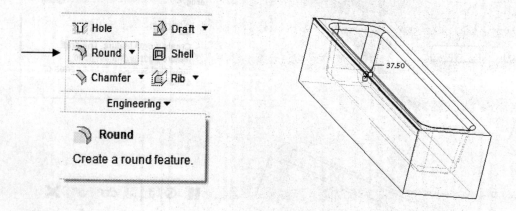

Step 8: Create a thin wall structure using **Shell**.

Click the icon of **Shell** from the Model tab. Pick the 4 surfaces shown in the following figure to remove the material in the shelling operation. Specify the thickness value to 12.5. Click the icon of **Apply and Save**.

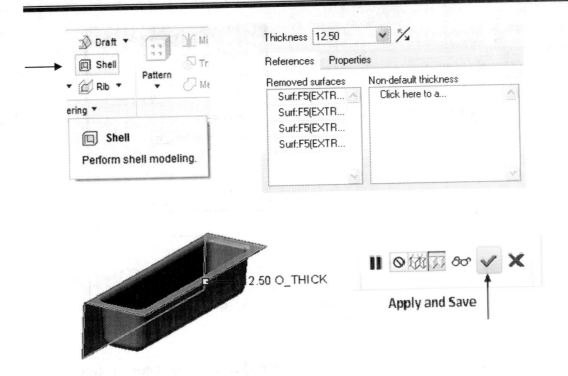

9.2 Creation of Sweep Features and Use of Sketcher Palette

As described in section 6.5, a sweep feature is created by defining 2 items. The first item is a datum curve used as the trajectory in the sweeping process. The second item is an area, which perpendicular to the datum curve for the sweeping process. In this example, we will use the Sketcher Palette to retrieve the I-shaped area from a database so that the modeling process can be greatly simplified.

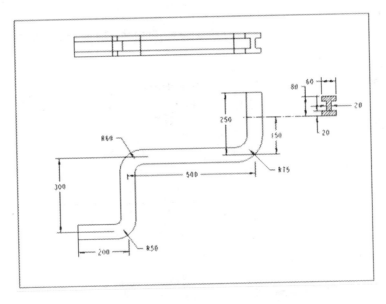

Step1: Create a datum curve to be used as a trajectory.

Click the icon of **Sketch**. Select **TOP** from the Model Tree as the sketching plane. In the Sketch window, click **Sketch** to accept the selection of the sketching plane, and click the icon of **Sketch View** to orient the sketching plane parallel to the screen. Click the icon of **Line** to make the following sketch. Click the icon of **Circular Fillet** to modify the corners.

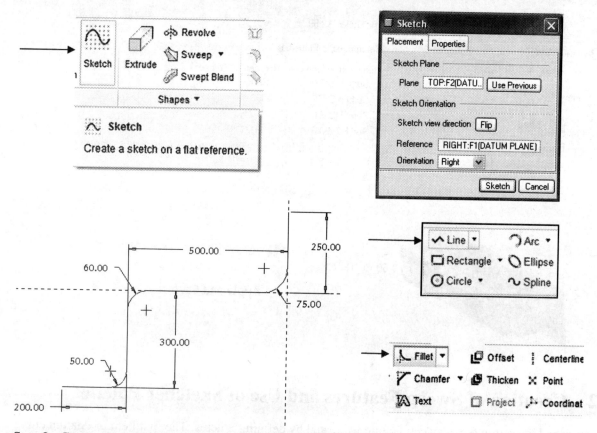

Step 2: Create the sweep feature with the use of sketcher palette.
Click the icon of **Sweep**. Click **References** and pick the sketched datum curve.

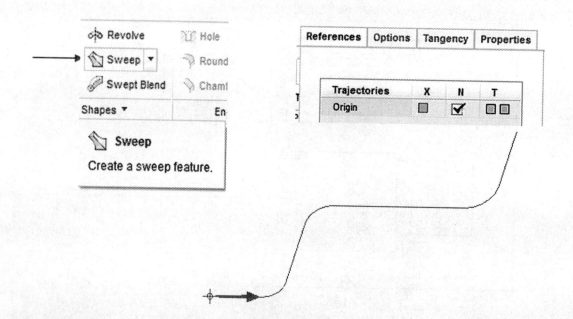

Click the icon of **Create sweep section**. Click Sketcher Palette > **Profiles** > select I-profile (double click I_profile). Move the I-shape to the sketch plane and align the bottom of the I-shape to the horizontal reference (The projection of the **FRONT** datum plane) and keep symmetry about the vertical reference (The projection of the RIGHT datum plane). Set the scale to 20.

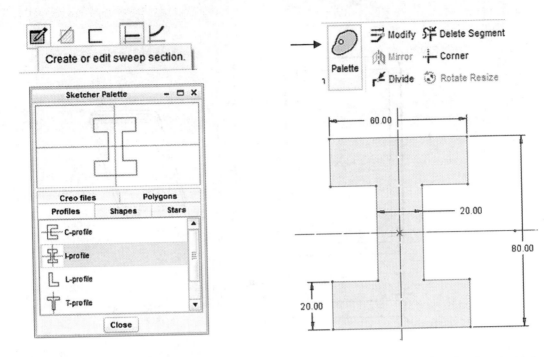

Click the icon of OK and the icon of **Apply and Save**. An engineering drawing is attached.

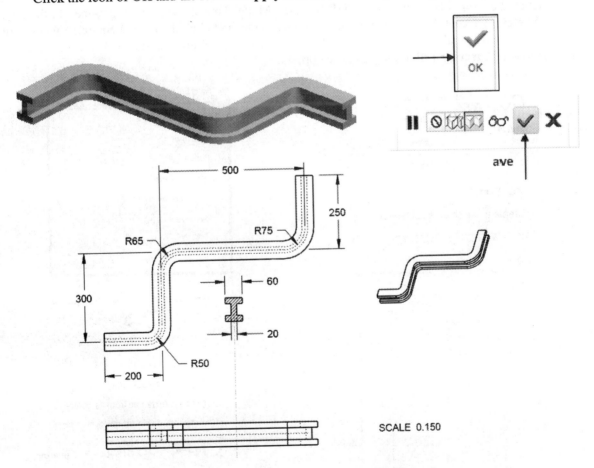

In the following example, we also use **Sweep** to create a plastic made cover, which is widely used in electronic devices such as cell phones.

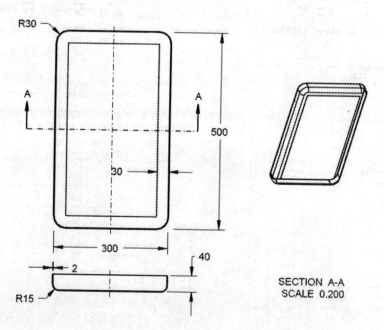

R30

A ← A

500

30

300

2

40

R15

SECTION A-A
SCALE 0.200

Step1: Create a datum curve to be used as a trajectory.
   Click the icon of **Sketch**. Select **TOP** from the Model Tree as the sketching plane. In the Sketch window **Sketch** to accept the selection of the sketching plane, and click the icon of **Sketch View** to orient the sketching plane parallel to the screen. Click the icon of **Rectangle** and sketch a center rectangle. Click the icon of **Circular Fillet** to modify the corners.

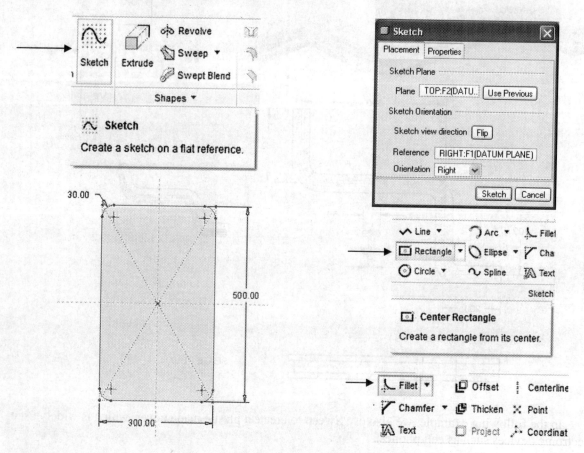

Step 2: Create the sweep feature using this closed curve as the trajectory.
Click the icon of **Sweep**. Click **References** and pick the sketched datum curve.

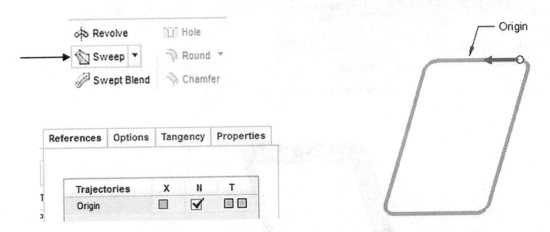

Click the icon of **Sweep as surface**. Click the icon of **Create sweep section**. Click the icon of Line to sketch 2 lines with the 2 dimensions equal to 40 and 30. Click the icon of **Circular Fillet** to modify the corner. The radius value is 15. Click **OK**. Click the icon of **Apply and Save**.

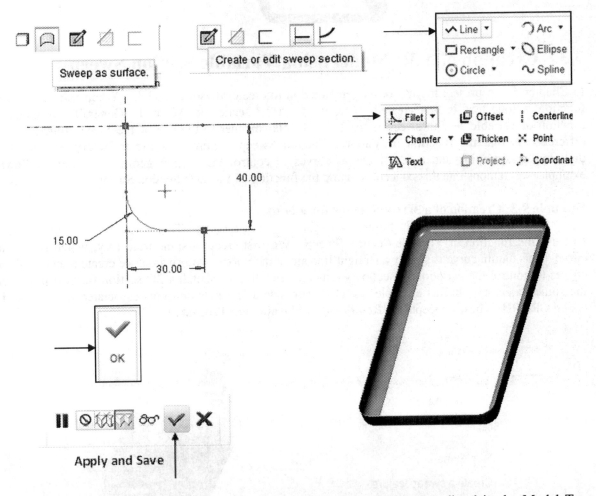

To add thickness to the surface feature, highlight the sweep feature listed in the Model Tree. Click the icon of Thicken.

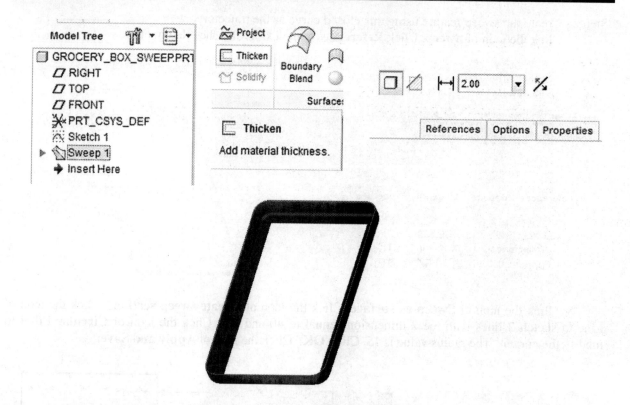

9.3 Creation of a 3D Model using Variable Section Sweep

In Chapter 6, we present the use of Sweep function to create 3D solid models. When using the Sweep function, a trajectory is first created. Afterwards, a 2D section is sketched. Generally speaking, the function of variable section sweep is used in a similar manner to the use of the Sweep function. The difference is that the function of Variable Section Sweep requires a spine trajectory to control the direction of sweeping and a set of datum curves to control the section geometry. In the following example, we demonstrate this concept of using the function of Variable Section Sweep.

Example 9-3: Creation of a 3D solid model for a bottle

The following figure illustrates a 3D solid model of a bottle. To create this 3D solid model, we will use the function of Variable Section Sweep. We first create a spine trajectory, which is a datum curve. This datum curve is simply a straight line along the y-axis. Afterwards, we create a set of 4 datum curves to control the variation of section geometry. Finally, we sketch a 2D section for sweeping along the spine trajectory. In this example, we also introduce a few new concepts associated with a function called GRAPH. These concepts are **Relations**, **Evalgraph** and **Trajpar**.

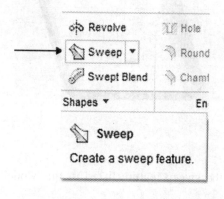

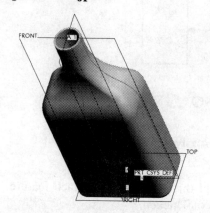

Step 1: Create a 3D solid model and sketch datum curves.

File > New > Part > type *bottle* as the file name and clear the icon of **Use default template > OK.**

Select mmns_part_solid (units: Millimeter, Newton, Second) and type *bottle* in **DESCRIPTION**, and *student* in **MODELED_BY**, then **OK.**

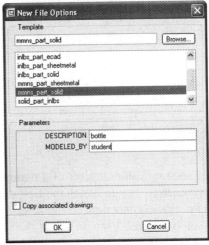

The first feature is a datum curve to be used as the spine trajectory. The datum curve is a straight line. The dimension length is 150 mm. Click the icon of **Sketch**. Select **FRONT** from the Model Tree as the sketching plane. In the Sketch window, click the box of **Sketch** to accept the selection of the sketching plane. Click the icon of **Sketch View** to orient the sketching plane parallel to the screen. Click the icon of **Line** and sketch a vertical line. Make sure that the starting point of this line is at the origin of the coordinate system such that the normal direction is upwards if this sketched line is viewed as a vector in a 2D space. Specify 150 as the length of this sketched line.

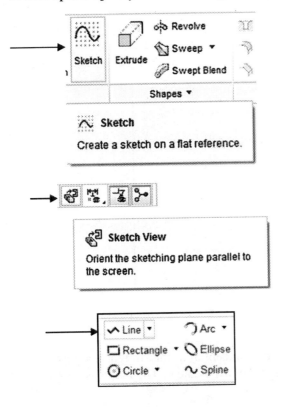
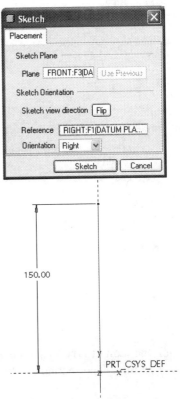

Upon completion, pick the icon of **OK**.

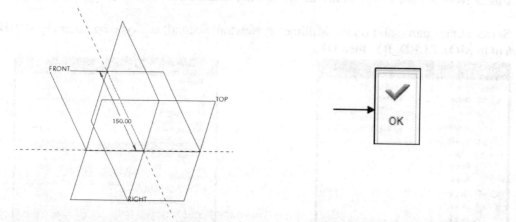

The second feature is a set of 4 datum curves to be used as the trajectories to control the variation of section geometry. Let us sketch the first datum curve. Click the icon of **Sketch**. In the Sketch window, select Use Previous (equivalent to the selection of **FRONT** from the Model Tree as the sketching plane. Click the icon of **Sketch View** to orient the sketching plane parallel to the screen. Click the icon of **Line** and sketch a vertical line. This vertical line is 35 mm distance from the y-axis. The dimension of length is 85.

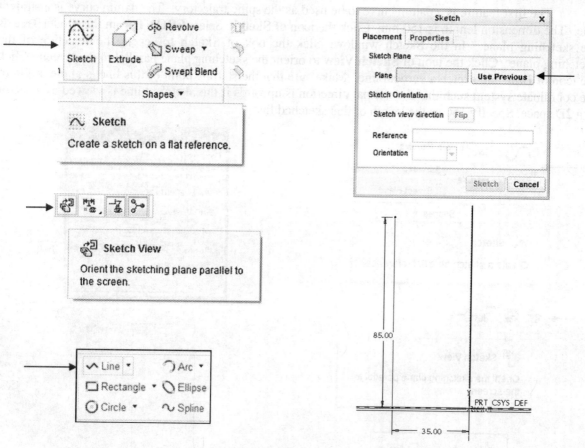

Click the icon of **Arc** to sketch 2 arcs. The first arc is tangential to the straight line just created. The radius is 25 mm. The second arc is tangential to the first arc just created. The radius is 35 mm. The other end of the second arc is tangential to a vertical line, which will be created at 10 mm distance from the y-axis.

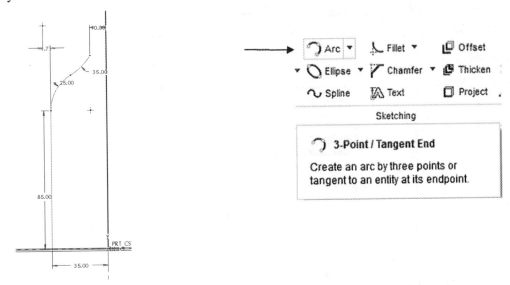

Finally, click the icon of **Line** to sketch a vertical line, which is tangential to the end of the second arc just created. The user may click the icon of **Constraint** and select the icon of Tangential to ensure that the tangency between the vertical line and the second arc. Modify the dimension of the total height of this sketch to 150 mm, as shown.

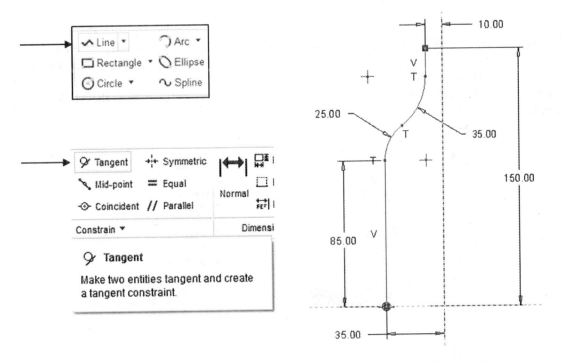

To create the second curve, we use **Copy** and **Mirror**, instead of sketching the datum curve. From the Model tab, expand Operations. Click Feature Operations.

In the pop up window, click Copy > Mirror > Select > Dependent > Done.

In the **Select** process, pick the datum curve just created or pick Sketch 2 from the Model Tree > **OK**.

In the process of mirroring the selected datum curve, we need to select a datum plane for mirroring. From the Model Tree, select the **Right** datum plane > **Done**.

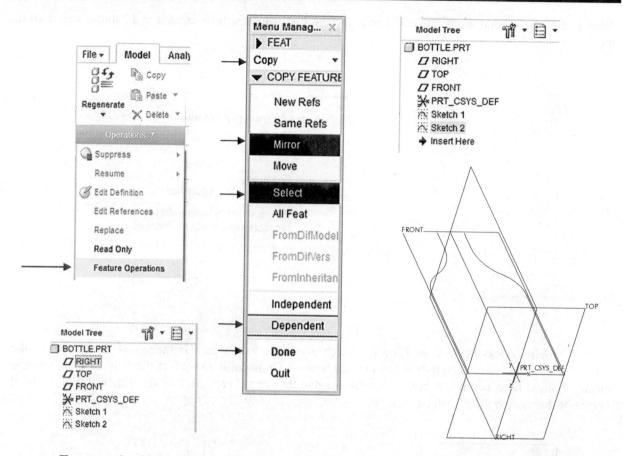

To create the third curve, we follow the previous procedure to use **Copy.** The only difference is to use **Move**, instead of using **Mirror**. From the Model tab, expand Operations and select **Feature Operations > Copy > Move > Select > Dependent > Done**.

In the **Select** process, pick the first created datum curve, or pick Sketch 2 from the Model Tree, and click OK to complete the selection.

In the pop up window or Move Feature window, select **Rotate**.

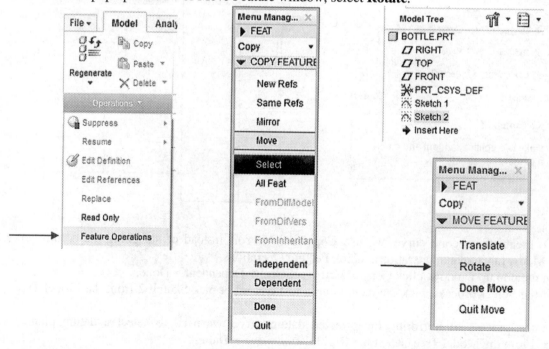

Rotate > Crv/Edg/Axis > pick the straight line datum curve > **Okay** to accept the default setting for angle manipulation > type *90* as the rotation angle and press Enter > Done Move.

There is a pop up window, showing Dim 1, Dim 2, ... Dim 6 > click Dim 2 and the dimension of 35 appears > **Done** and change the value from 35 to 20 and press Enter > **Done**.

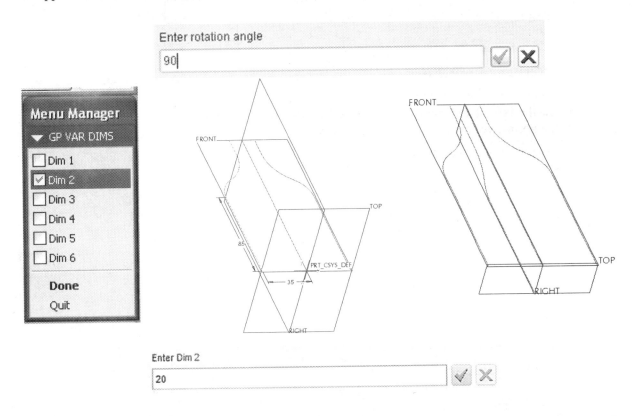

To create the 4th curve, we follow the previous procedure to use **Copy** and **Mirror.** From the Model tab, expand Operations and select **Copy > Mirror > Select > Dependent > Done.**

Select > pick the datum curve just created through Rotation > **OK.**

Plane > select the **Front** datum plane > **Done**.

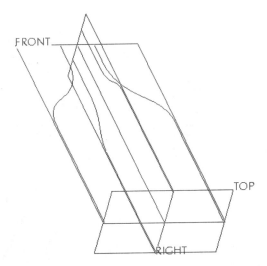

Step 2: Use the function of Variable Section Sweep to create the 3D solid model.
From the toolbar of feature creation, select the icon of **Variable Section Sweep.**

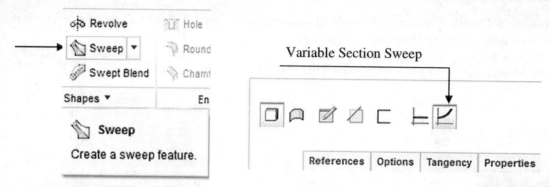

Click the box of **References** > Select the datum curve of straight line as the spline trajectory, serving as the normal vector along the sweeping direction.

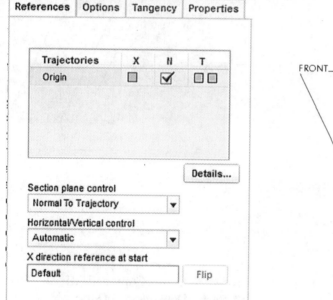

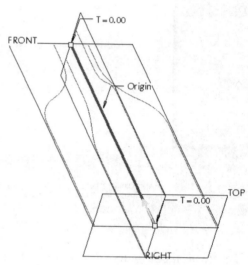

Holding down the **Ctrl** key, pick the set of 4 datum curves one by one.

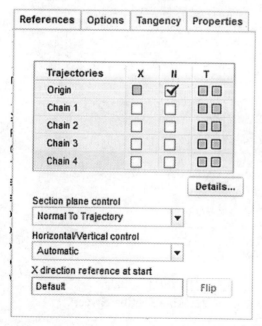

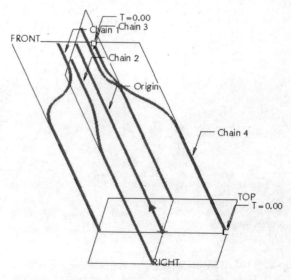

Click the icon of create sweep section and sketch a rectangle. Click the icon of **Sketch View** to orient the sketching plane parallel to the screen. Click the icon of **Rectangle** to sketch a rectangle passing through the 4 cross symbols (the ends of the 4 datum curves). Use the constraint of Coincident (points on entry) to make sure that the 4 sides of the rectangle passing through the 4 datum curves. As a result, there is no need for dimensioning for the sketched rectangle.

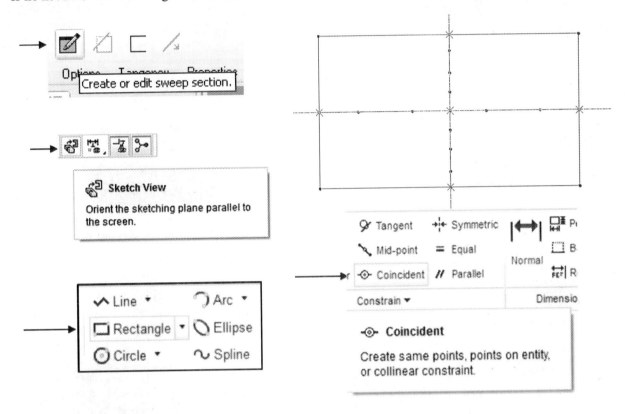

Create rounds at the 4 corners. Select the icon of **circular fillet** from the toolbar of sketcher, click two neighboring sides to form a round. Repeat this procedure 3 times. Use the constraint of equal to equalize the 4 radii to have a single dimension, which is 8, as shown. Make sure that the rectangle goes through the 4 datum curves. If not, use the coincident constraint to re-enforce.

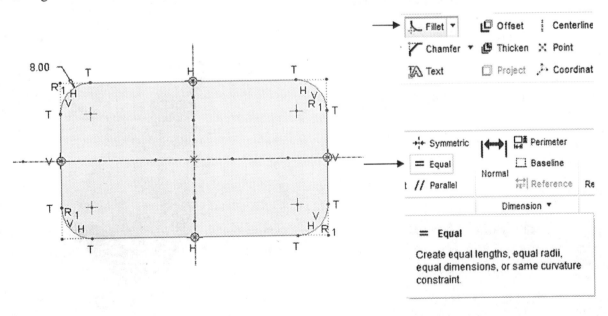

Upon completion, pick the icon of **OK** from the toolbar of sketcher. Make sure that the icon of Solid is checked, not the icon of Surface is checked. Click the icon of **Apply and Save** to complete the creation of the bottle feature.

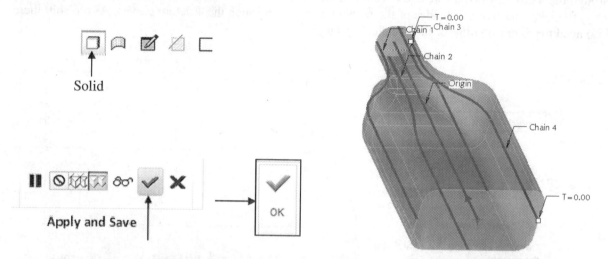

To create a thin wall structure, select the icon of **Shell** from the Model tab. Set the wall thickness value to 2, and select the top surface of the bottle.

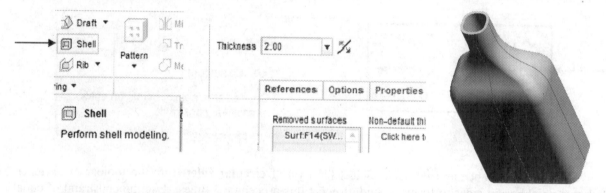

To control the wall thickness at the bottom, say setting the thickness equal to 3 instead of 2, click the box of Non-default thickness > change the value to 3 if the user wants to make such a change. Upon completion, click the icon of **Apply and Save**.

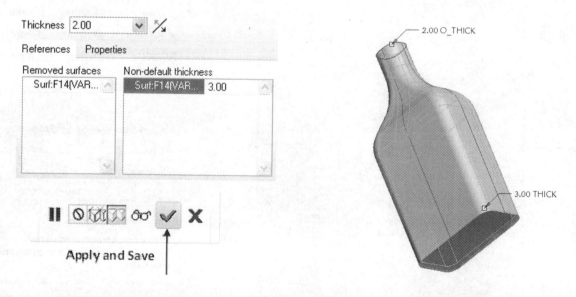

Now let us further improve the appropriateness of the geometry of the created 3D solid model. Let us change the constant corner radius equal to 8 to a set of variable radius values. This variable in terms of the radius value is controlled by use of a sketch, which will be created in the following.

From the Model tab, expand **Datum** and select **Graph**. Type corner radius as the name of the graph, and press **Enter**.

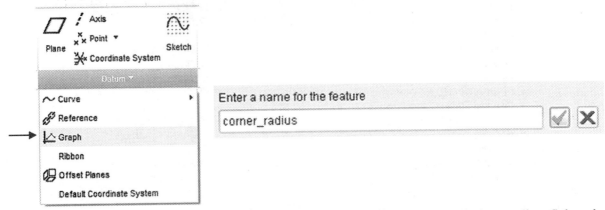

Click the icon of **Centerline** to sketch a horizontal centerline and a vertical centerline. Select the icon of coordinate system and position the origin to the intersection of the 2 centerlines. To make a sketch, click the icon of **Line** to sketch a horizontal line with the 2 dimensions equal to 40 and 85, respectively.

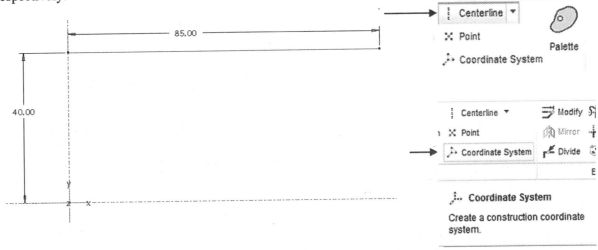

Afterwards, select the icon of **Spline** to sketch a free-lance curve and a straight horizontal line. Make sure that the sketch has the dimensions of 10, 12, and 150. Also keeping the tangential connections is important. Click OK to complete this sketch.

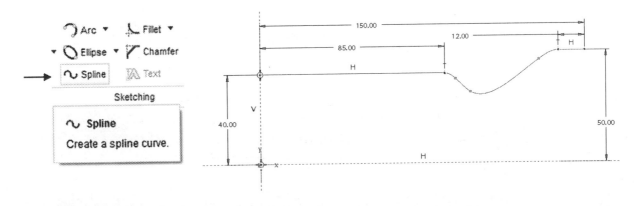

Now let us incorporate this sketch to the sweep feature of the bottle. From the Model Tree, move the position of graph CORNER_RADIU to a position above Sweep 1.

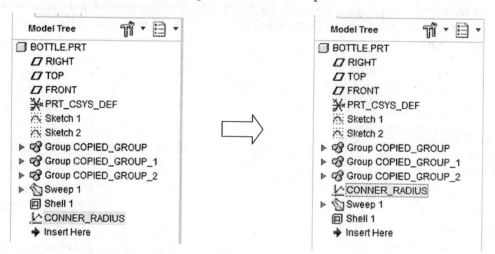

Now let us establish a relation between the graph CORNER_RADIUS and the radius dimension defined in the sketch of Sweep 1. Highlight Sweep 1 from the Model Tree, right-click and hold, select **Edit Definition**. Click the box of edit sweep section and click the icon of Sketch View. The dimension of 8 is on display, indicating the dimension of 8 is sd9 stored in the database.

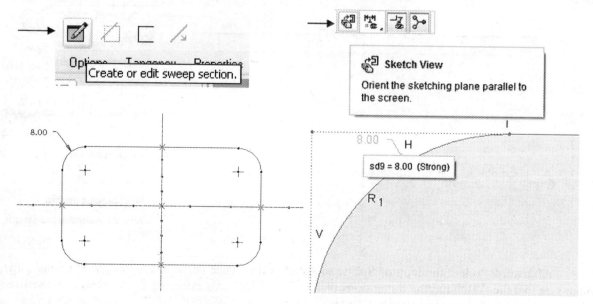

From the main toolbar, select the **Tools** tab > **Relations**.

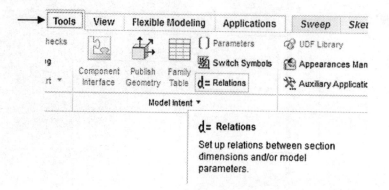

In the Relations window, type sd9 = evalgraph("corner radius", trajpar*150)/5 > **OK**.

Do the following clicks to go back to the sweep feature page. Click the **Model** tab > Click the icon of **Sketch** > Click **OK**. Click the icon of **Apply and Save** to complete the modification to the corner radius feature.

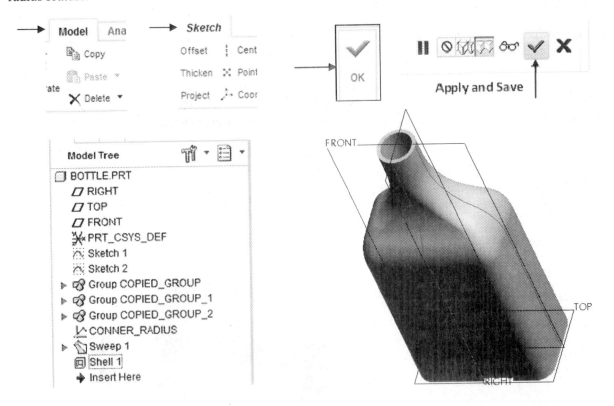

Note that the trajpar is a parameter, which varies between 0 and 1. There is a divider of 5 appeared in the defined relation. This divider is a scaling factor used to sketch the graph. The user may notice that the original dimension is 8, and the sketch value is 40, which is 5 times as large as the original one. The following is an engineering drawing of the designed bottle with the graph depicting the variation of the corner radius.

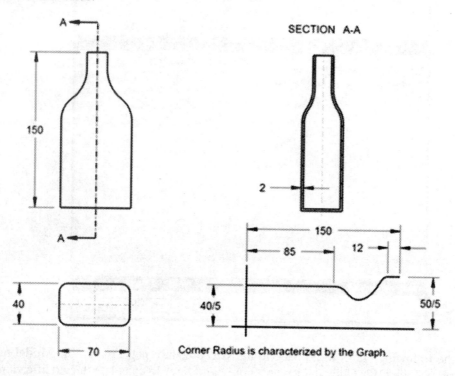

Corner Radius is characterized by the Graph.

9.4 Creation of Analytical Features

In the previous section, we created a bottle. Assume the bottle is used to contain lubrication oil, as illustrated in the following figure. In the design process, designers may concern about the weight of the bottle designed and the volume of oil, which the bottle is capable of having. It is desirable to establish a relation between those quantities and the design parameters, such as the maximum dimensions of the bottle, the wall thickness of the bottle and the mark to specify the oil level. Under the Creo Parametric design environment, we create analytical features to provide the designers with such needed information.

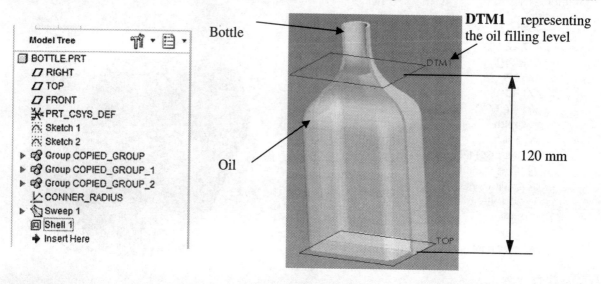

Step 1: Let us open the file: bottle.prt. Examine the information listed in the model tree. The 3D solid model was created first using **Sweep**. The **Shell** operation created a thin wall structure so that an empty space was available to be filled with the lubricating oil.

Let us first specify the mass density of the bottle material. Assume the value is 1.30 g/cm^3, which is equivalent to 1.30 x 10^{-9} tonne/mm3. One tonne equals to 10^6 gram. Select **File > Prepare > Model Properties.**

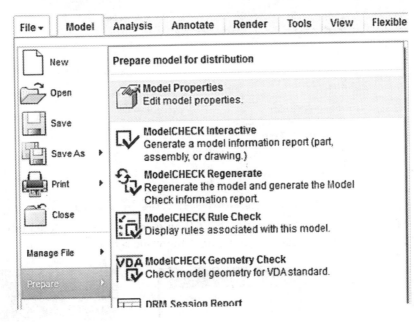

In the Model Properties window, in the material block, click the change listed in the Material block. Enter 1.3e-9 > **Ok**. Click **Close**.

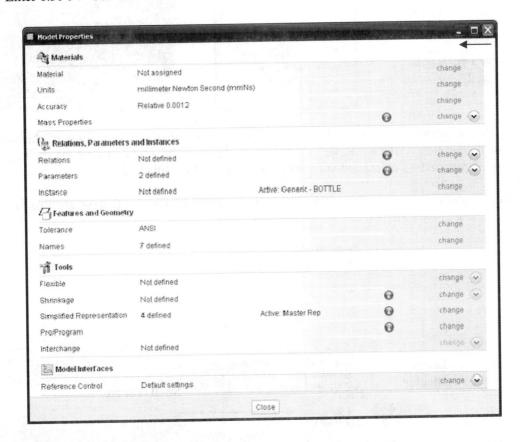

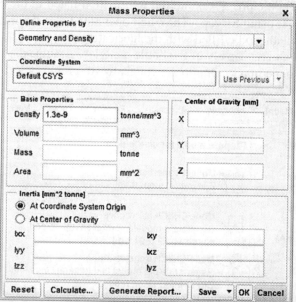

Step 2: Let us create a datum plane representing the filling level. From the Model tab, click the icon of Plane. Pick the **TOP** datum plane > enter 120 as the value > **OK**.

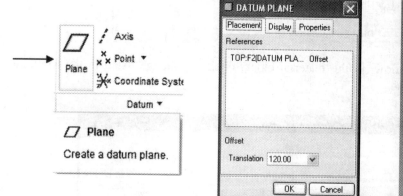

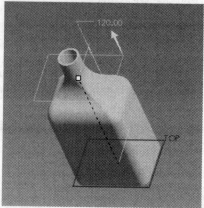

In order to obtain the volume of the filled oil, we first calculate the volume of the solid part before the shell operation. Afterwards, we calculate the volume of the solid part after the shell operation. The difference between the 2 calculated volumes is the volume of the filled oil.

Step 3: In the model tree, drag the **Insert** indicator before the shell feature so that we are able to evaluate the volume of the solid part before the shell operation.

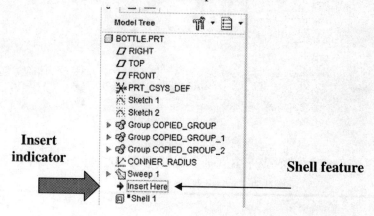

Step 4: Volume measurements

From the **Analysis** tab, click **Measure > Volume.** In the **Volume** window, pick **DTM1.** Select **Make Feature** and specify **VOL_SOLID** as the name of this analytical feature. In the **Feature** window, specify Volume as the parameter name to associate with the measured value. Note that the measured volume shown in the window is 288183 mm³.

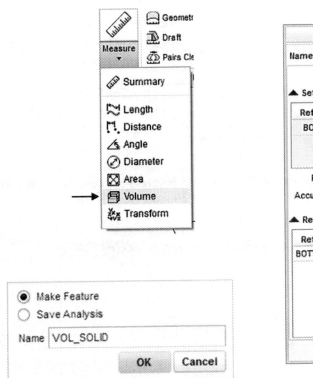

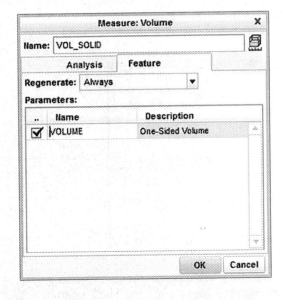

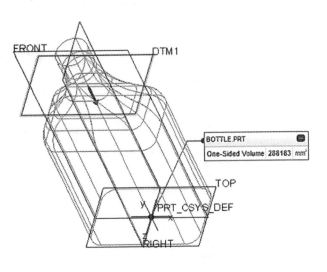

Step 5: Displace the measured value in the model tree.

Click **Settings > Tree Columns.**

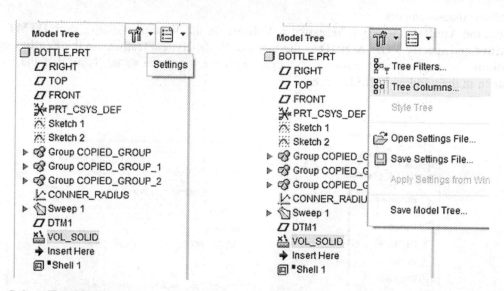

Select **Feat Parms** by expanding **Info** > type *VOLUME* as **Name** and press the **Enter** key > **Apply** > **OK**. There is a new column called VOLUME shown in the model tree and the measured value of 362012.557096 is listed.

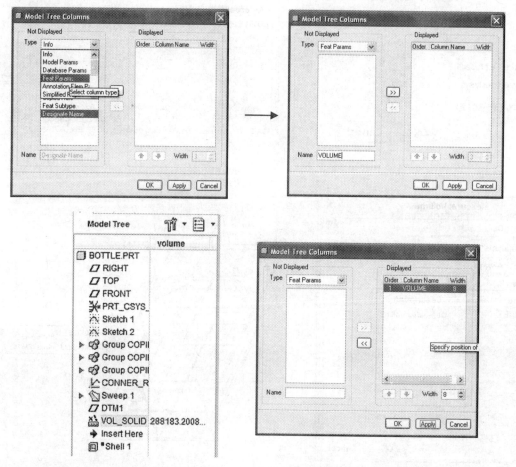

Step 6: Create a second Analysis Feature to measure the solid volume after the shell operation and display the measured volume in the **VOLUME** column of the model tree. We follow the procedure used in creating the first Analysis Feature.

Let us move the **Insert indicator** after the shell feature.

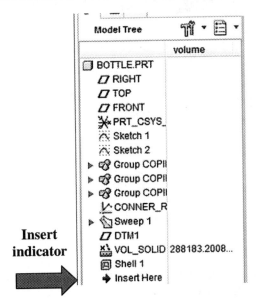

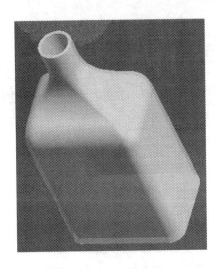

Follow the precious procedure to measure the volume. Click the **Analysis** tab. Click **Measure > Volume.** In the **Volume** window, pick **DTM1**. Select **Make Feature** and specify **VOL_SHELL** as the name of this analytical feature. In the Feature window, specify Volume as the parameter name to associate with the measured value. Note that the measured volume shown in the window is 288183 mm^3.

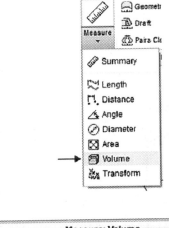

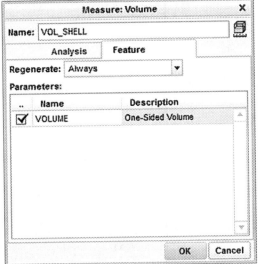

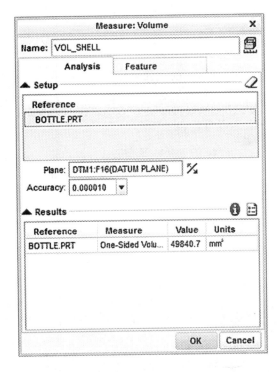

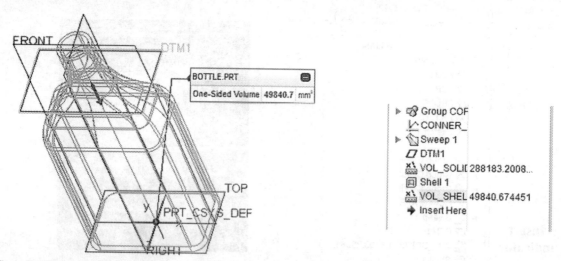

Step 7: Create a third Analysis Feature to calculate the difference between the two calculated volumes. The volume of oil can be easily calculated by the following:

$$
\begin{array}{rcl}
\text{VOL\_SOLID} & = & 288183 \\
\text{-)} \quad \text{VOL\_SHELL} & = & 49841 \\
\hline
\text{VOL\_SOLID} & = & 238342 \quad (\text{mm}^3)
\end{array}
$$

Users may create an analysis feature to do the above calculation. Click the icon of **Analysis**. In the **Analysis** window, specify the Analysis **Name**: type *VOL_OIL* and press the **Enter** key. Remember you must press the **Enter** key when entering a numerical value or a string of characters.

Select **Relation** as the Measurement Type > **Next** to start the establishment of a relation and the **Relation** window appears.

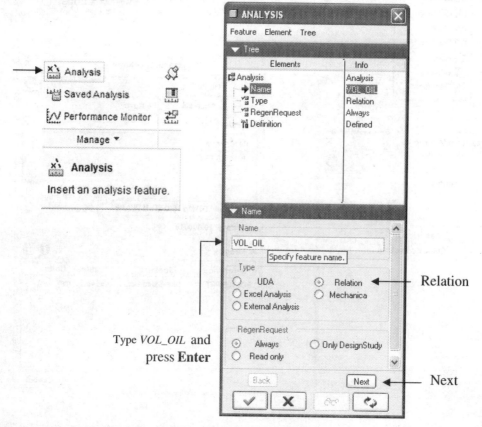

In the window of **Relation**, define the relation as follows:

VOLUME = VOLUME:FID_VOL_SOLID- VOLUME:FID_VOL_SHELL

Afterwards, click **OK**.

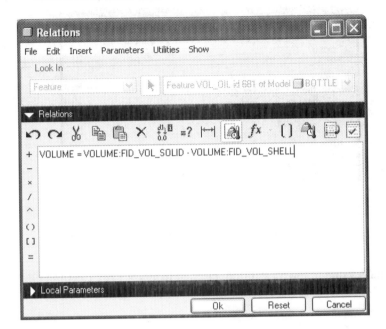

FID stands for Feature ID.

Click the check mark in the Analysis window to complete the process of defining the new analysis feature, which has established a relation. In the model tree, the calculated value is displayed.

Step 8: Evaluate the mass of the bottle component.
Calculating the amount of the bottle mass is equivalent to calculating the mass amount of the shell model.
From the **Analysis** tab, click the icon of **Mass Properties.** In the **Mass Properties** window, pick the coordinate system > select **Feature** > type *BOTTLE_MASS*.

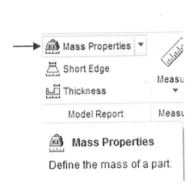

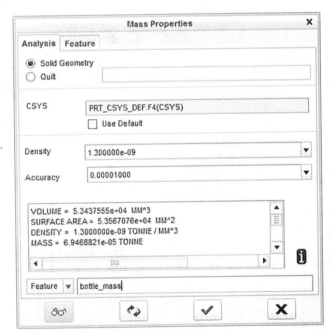

The measured value of $6.96e^{-5}$ (tonne) or 69 (gram) is listed in the window. Click the box called Feature, which is next to Analysis. Make sure MASS is checked and uncheck all other parameters > click the check mark to complete the definition of this analytical feature.

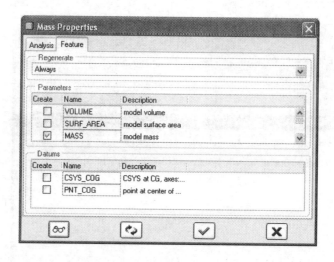

To display the calculated mass value in the model tree, click **Settings > Tree Columns**.

Select **Feat Prams** by expanding **Info** > type *MASS* as **Name** and press the **Enter** key > **Apply** > **OK**. There is a new column called MASS shown in the model tree and the measured value of 0.000069 (tonne) or 69 (gram) is listed.

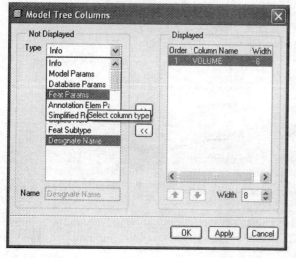
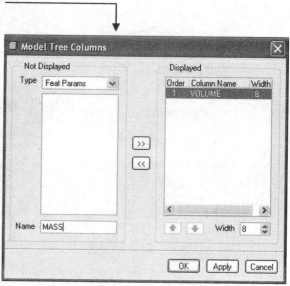

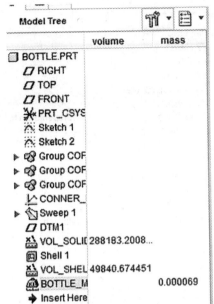

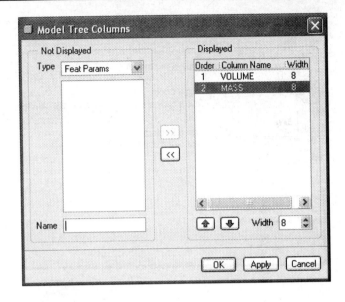

To calculate the mass of the filled oil, readers may do the following:

Mass of the filled oil = density x volume = (0.71 g/cm3)(238342 mm^3)=169.23 (gram)

The total mass of the bottle with the filled oil is given by 169.23 + 69 = 238.23 (gram).

9.5 Creation of a 3D Solid Model for the Filled Oil

In the above example, we worked with the geometry of a bottle. How to create a 3D solid model for an object, which is in a liquid state, such as the filled oil in the previous example? In this section, we use an operation called **Cut Out** to create a 3D solid model for the filled oil. Basically, there are 3 steps.

Step 1: Use Save a Copy to obtain a new file and let us call it oil_liquid.prt. Open the oil-liquid.prt and delete the so that the modified 3D solid model has a new name called oil_liquid.prt.

Step 2: Assemble this modified model and the bottle together.

Step 3: Use the operation called Cut Out to obtain a 3D solid model for the filled oil.

Step 1: Let us open the bottle file.

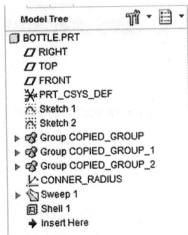

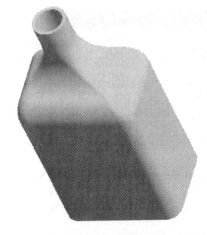

From File, use **Save a Copy** to save it to a new file. Call the new file oil_liquid.prt > **OK**.

Click Open and open the newly created oil_liquid.prt. Highlight Shell 1. Right-click to pick **Delete**. Afterwards, save the modified file.

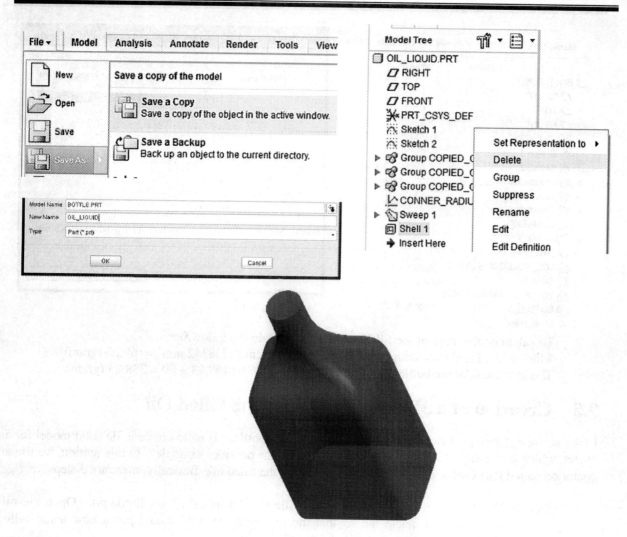

Step 2: Create an assembly to assemble the modified bottle and the original bottle.

File > New > Assembly > type *oil_bottle_together* as the file name > clear the box > **OK.** Select the mmns_asm_design system. Type *Oil Bottle Together* in the Description box and type *student* in the Modeled_by box > **OK.**

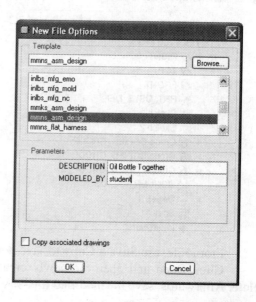

Select the icon of **Assemble** from the assembly icon list. From the local memory, or **In Session**, select oil_liquid.prt, and open it.

Activate **Placement**. Under the **Constraint Type**, pick the icon of **Default**, which means automatically placing PART_DEF_CSYS to the location of ASM_DEF_CSYS and the orientations of the 2 coordinate systems are identical > **Full Constrained** is indicated under **Status**> click the icon of **Apply and Save**.

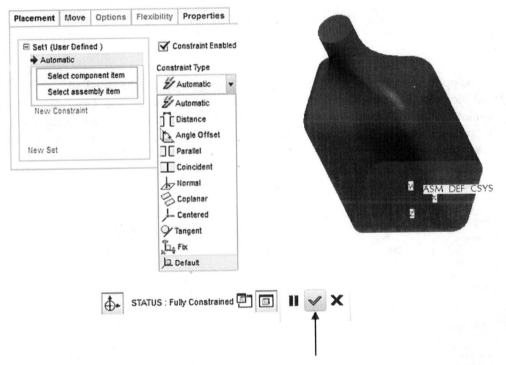

Now we bring *bottle.prt* to the assembly. Following the same procedure, pick the icon of **Assemble**, and open the file called *bottle.prt* from **In Session**.

Activate **Placement**. Under the **Constraint Type**, pick the icon of **Default**, which means automatically placing PART_DEF_CSYS to the location of ASM_DEF_CSYS and the orientations of the 2 coordinate systems are identical > **Full Constrained** is indicated under **Status**> click the icon of **Apply and Save**.

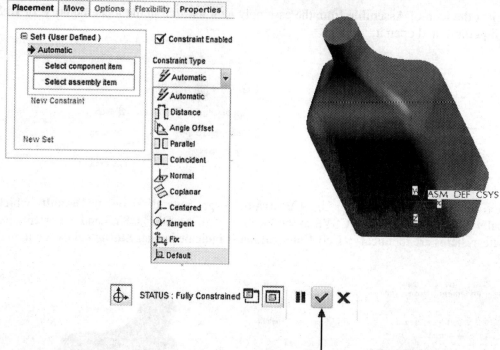

Step 3: Use the operation called **Cut Out** to obtain a 3D solid model for the filled oil.

From the Assembly group, expand Component and click **Component Operations**. In the Menu Manager window, select **Cut Out**. From the model tree, pick *OIL_LIQUID.PRT* as the part to perform **CUT OUT** process to > **OK**. From the model tree, pick *BOTTLE.PRT* as the reference part for **CUT OUT** process > **OK**. A confirmation window appears. Click Yes to complete the Cut Out operation.

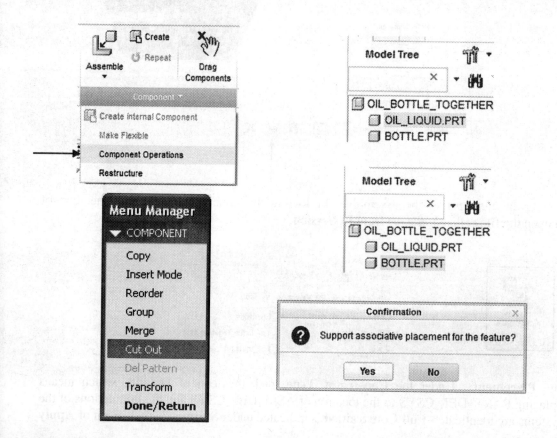

Oil Liquid

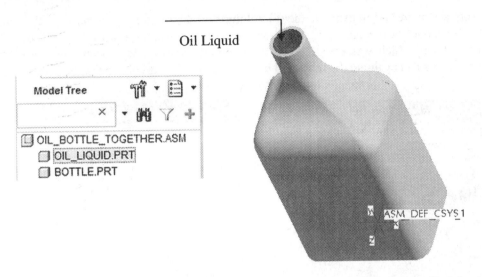

In the model tree, highlight OIL_LIQUID.PRT. Right-click and click **Open**. For the purpose of comparison, two (2) 3D solid models are on display. One is before CUT OUT and the other is after CUT OUT.

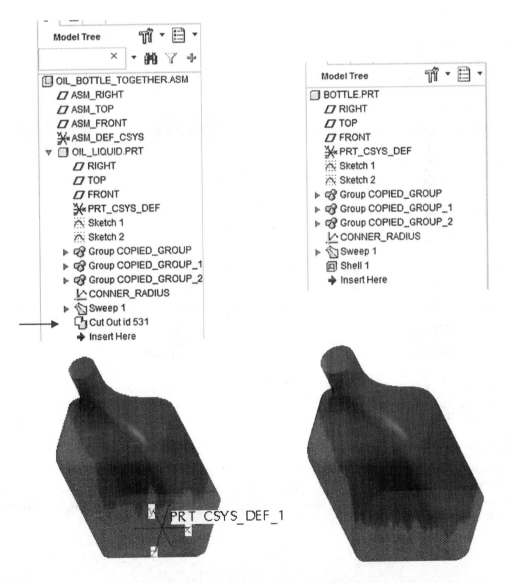

If users are interested in evaluate the oil volume and the mass properties of oil, they may use this created 3D solid model of the oil liquid. As shown below, a extrude cut operation can be performed to consider the oil level, which was set at 120 in the previous example. By specifying the oil density, say 0.71 gram/cm^3, users can evaluate the mass and oil volume of oil, as described in the previous section.

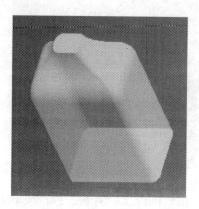

9.6   Creation of a Pendulum Model

In this section, we create a pendulum system. There are 2 components in this system, namely, a housing component and a pendulum component.

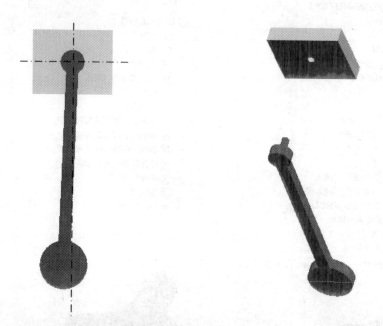

In the following, we create these 2 components first. When these 2 components are available, we create an assembly called clock_pendulum. Final, we perform a dynamic analysis to set the pendulum component in motion.

Let us start with creating a 3D solid model for the housing component.

File > New > Part > type *housing* as the file name and clear the icon of **Use default template**. Select mmns_part_solid (units: Millimeter, Newton, Second) and type Housing in **DESCRIPTION**, and *Student* in **MODELED_BY**, then **OK**.

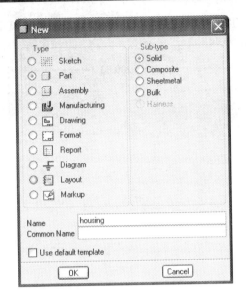

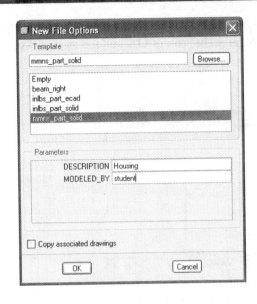

Click the icon of **Extrude** and specify 40 as the value of extrusion distance.

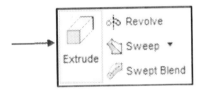

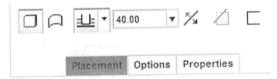

Select the **FRONT** datum plane from the Model Tree as the sketching plane, and click the icon of **Sketch View** to orient the sketching plane parallel to the screen.

Click the icon of **Center Rectangle** and sketch a rectangle with 2 dimensions set to 200 and 160.

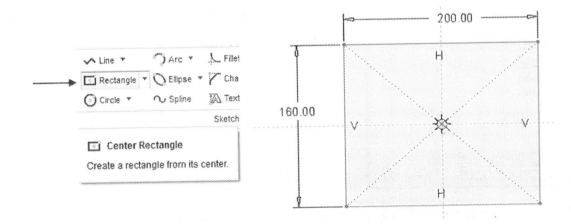

Select the icon of **Circle** and sketch a circle. The diameter dimension is 20 mm. Upon completion, click the icon of **OK** and the icon of **Apply and Save**.

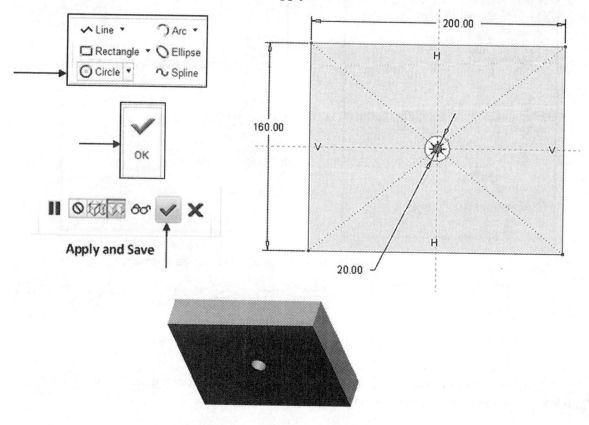

Now let us create the pendulum component.

File > New > Part > type pendulum as the file name and clear the icon of **Use default template > OK.** Select mmns_part_solid (units: Millimeter, Newton, Second) and type *pendulum* in **DESCRIPTION**, and s*tudent* in **MODELED_BY**, then **OK.**

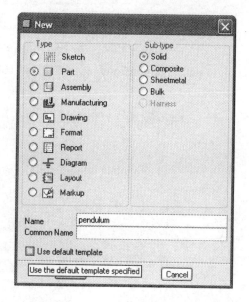

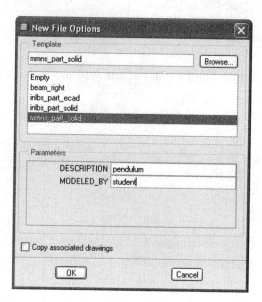

Select the icon of **Extrude.** Specify 30 as the value of extrusion distance.

From the Model Tree, click the **FRONT** datum plane as the sketching plane, and click the icon of Sketch View to orient the sketching plane parallel to the screen.

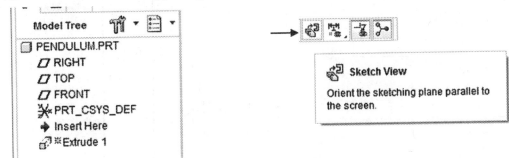

Select the icon of **Circle** and sketch 2 circles. The diameter dimensions are 60 and 120, respectively. The distance between the 2 circles is 500.

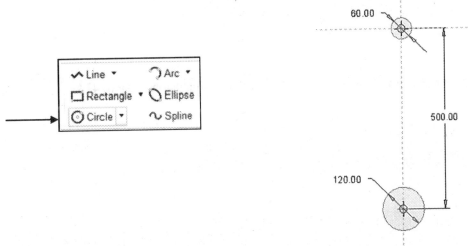

Click the icon of **Centerline** and sketch a vertical centerline.

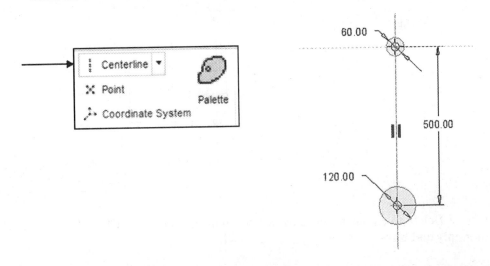

Click the icon of **Line** and sketch a vertical line. The dimension is 424.

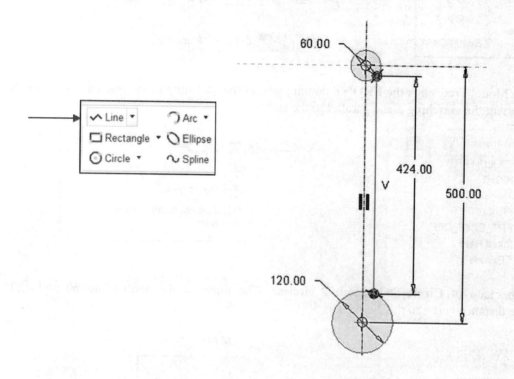

Click the icon of **Mirror** and obtain another line with the dimension equal to 424.

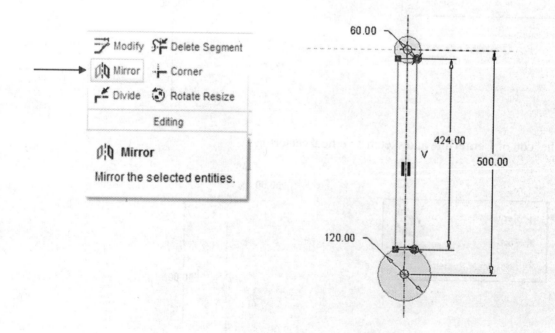

Click the icon of **Delete** to eliminate those extra line segments and arcs. Click the icon of **OK**, and click the icon of **Apply and Save**.

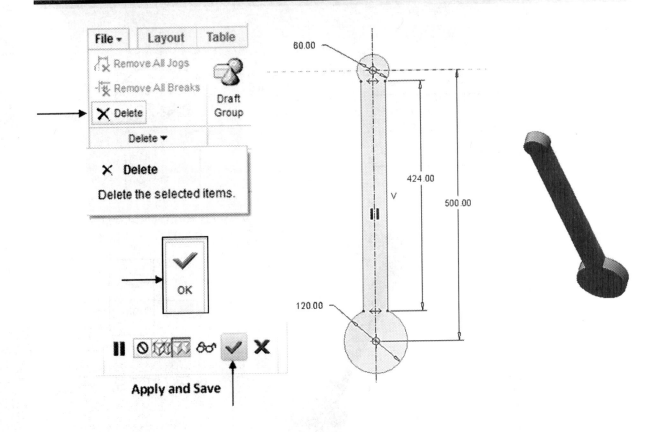

Select the icon of **Extrude.** Specify 30 as the value of extrusion distance.

From the Model Tree, click the **FRONT** datum plane as the sketching plane, and click the icon of Sketch View to orient the sketching plane parallel to the screen.

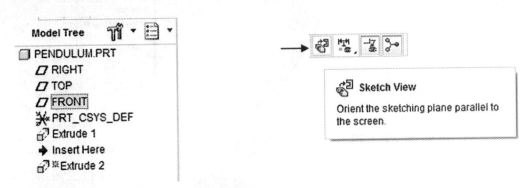

Click the icon of **Circle** and sketch a circle. The diameter value is 20. Click the icon of **OK**. Flip the extrusion direction and click the icon of **Apply and Save**.

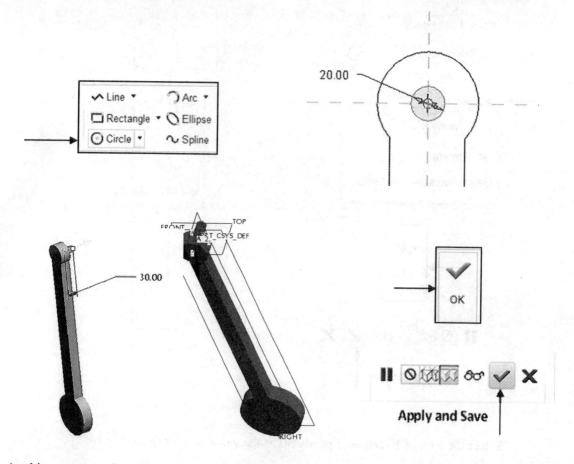

At this moment, the construction of pendulum is completed. Considering the need to set the pendulum into motion, we need to create a datum point at the center of the big circle. In this way, we will be able to define a set of initial conditions for starting the motion.

There are 3 steps to create such a datum point. Step 1 is to create a datum plane, which is parallel to the **TOP** datum plate. Click the icon of **Creating Datum Plane** > click **TOP** from the model tree > specify *500* as the offset distance > **OK**. DTM1 is created.

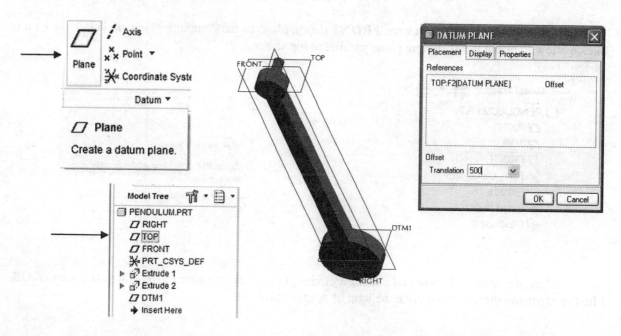

In Step 2, click **DTM1** so that **DTM1** is selected. From the Model tab, click **Intersect** > holding down the **Ctrl** key, pick the front surface of the pendulum so that a straight line is created. Click the icon of **Apply and Save**.

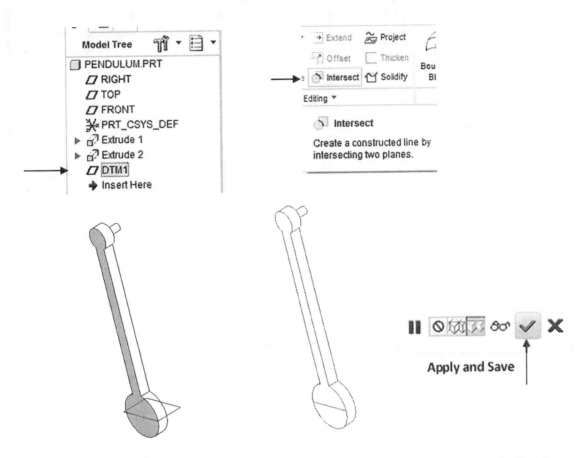

In Step 3, click the icon of **Creating Datum Point** > click the datum curve (straight line) just created > in the **DATUM POINT** window, type 0.50 as the offset value or the ratio of this datum curve > **OK**.

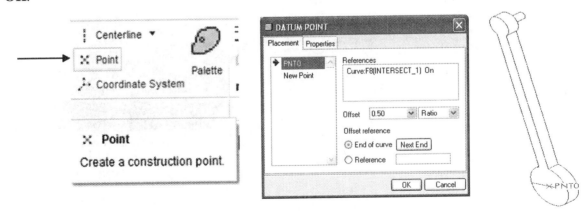

Create an assembly for the fan system.

File > New > Assembly > type *pendulum system* as the file name > clear the box > **OK**. Select the mmns_asm_design system. Type *Pendulum System* in the Description box and type *student* in the Modeled_by box > **OK**.

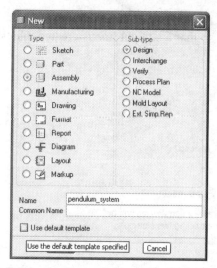
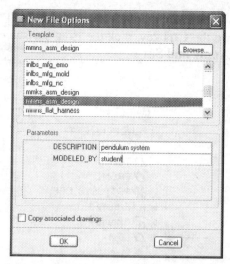

Select the icon of **Assemble** from the assembly icon list. From the local memory, or **In Session**, select housing.prt, and open it.

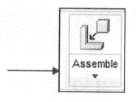
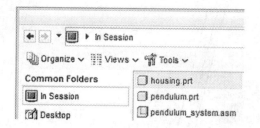

Activate **Placement**. Under the **Constraint Type**, pick the icon of **Default**, which means automatically placing PART_DEF_CSYS to the location of ASM_DEF_CSYS and the orientations of the 2 coordinate systems are identical > **Full Constrained** is indicated under **Status**> click the icon of **Apply and Save**.

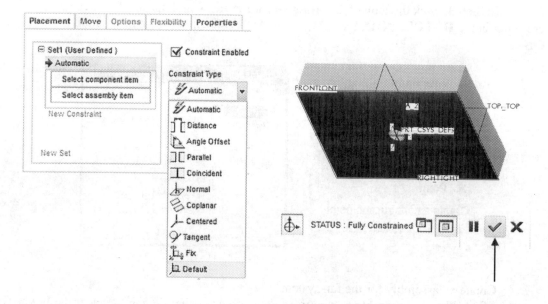

Now we bring *pendulum.prt* to the assembly. Following the same procedure, pick the icon of **Add**, and open the file called *pendulum.prt* from **In Session**.

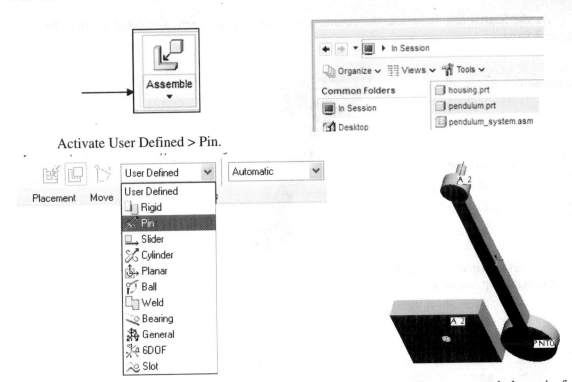

Activate User Defined > Pin.

For the **Axis alignment**, pick the axis from the housing component and the axis from the pendulum component.

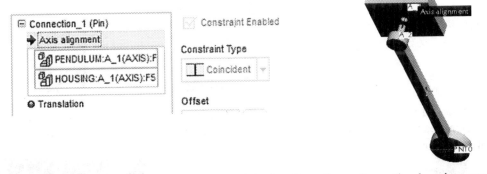

For the **Translation Constraint,** pick the 2 surfaces from the housing component and the pendulum component, respectively, as shown in the following figure.

As the **Status** box indicates, the connection definition has been completed > click the icon of **Apply and Save**.

Now let us simulate the motion of this pendulum system through mechanism.
From the top menu, click **Applications > Mechanism**. The Mechanism Tree is on display.

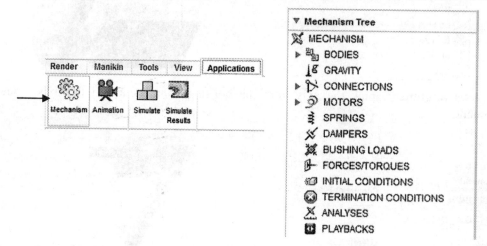

Let us first record the current position as the initial position of the pendulum system in motion. Click the icon **of Drag packaged components** from the main menu > click the icon of **Take a snapshot,** Snapshort1 is taken > **Close**.

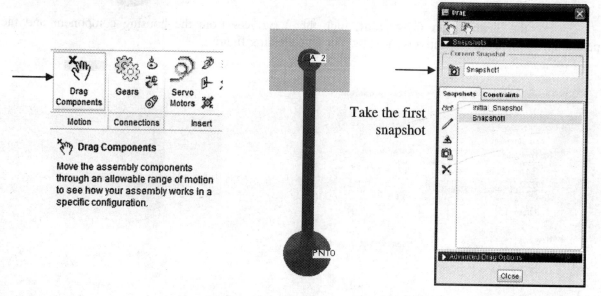

Take the first snapshot

To set the initial conditions, right-click on the **INITIAL CONDITIONS** listed in the model tree > **New**.

In the window of **Initial Condition Definition**, select **Snapshort1** > click the icon of **Define tangential slot velocity.** Specify the vector for velocity as [1, 0, 0] or along the X-direction.

From the display, pick the defined datum point associated with the pendulum component. Specify 120 (mm/sec) as the velocity value. Click **OK**.

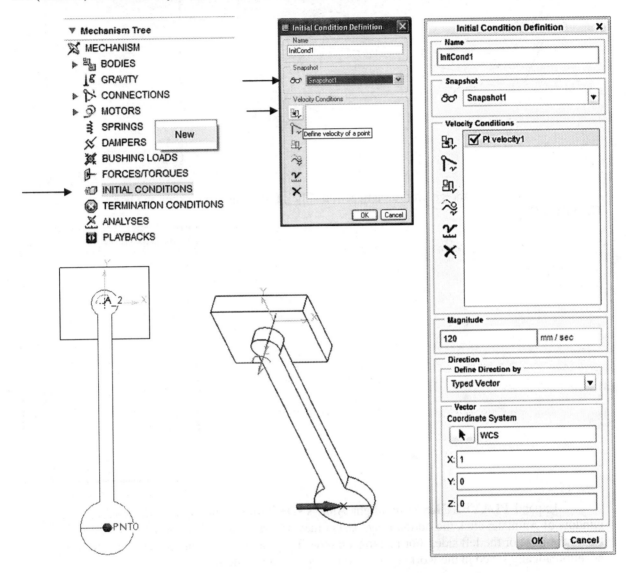

In the model tree, highlight **Analysis** and right-click > **New**. Set the analysis type to **Dynamic**. Specify *100* as the duration of the analysis. Set the Initial Configuration to **I.C. State**. Click the icon of **Run**. Readers may notice the motion is a circular motion. The reason is the gravity force is not entered to the simulation.

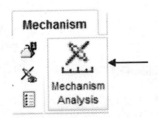

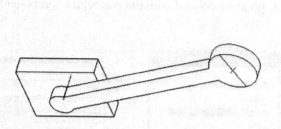

Now let us add the gravity force in action. Click **Ext Loads** and check the box called **Enable Gravity > Run**.

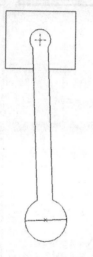

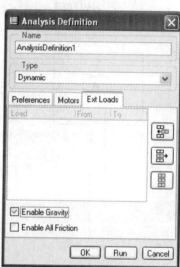

Expand **PLAYBACKS** > highlight AnalysisDefinition1 and right-click > select **Play**. In the window of Animate, click the button Play. Users may adjust the speed of animation by moving the speed bar to the right or the left side. For making a movie file, just click the button Capture. A movie file will be automatically saved in the working direction as pendulum_system.mpeg.

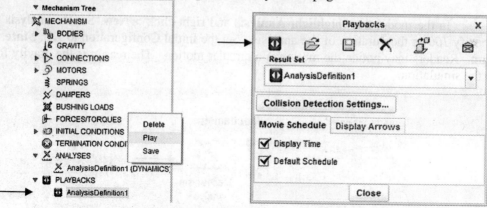

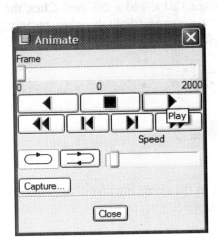

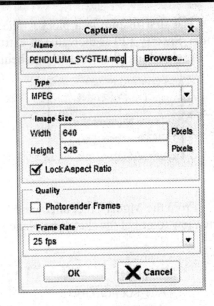

9.7   Creation of a Hovercraft Model

In this section, we create a hovercraft model first.   Afterwards, we perform simulation to set the hovercraft in motion through the use of Mechanism. Before getting on this journey, let us create a folder called hovercraft so that this folder will be the working directory when components of the hovercraft system are being created. In the following, we first create 2 components, namely, fan support and fan. When these 2 components are available, we create an assembly called fan system. Afterwards, we create the platform component. Then we create a new assembly file where we assemble 4 fan systems with the platform component to imitate the lift and propulsion actions. Final, we create the track component. At that time, we create a new assembly system where all the sub-assemblies are assembled together.

9.7.1   Creation of a Fan System

Step 1: Create a 3D solid model

   File > New > Part > type *fan_support* as the file name and clear the icon of **Use default template**. Select mmns_part_solid (units: Millimeter, Newton, Second) and type fan support in **DESCRIPTION**, and *Student* in **MODELED_BY**, then **OK.**

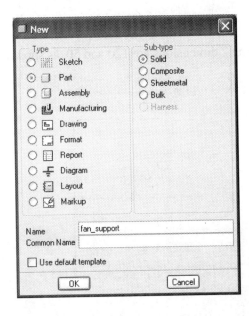

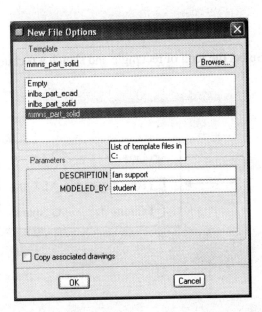

The first feature is a block. The three dimensions are 120 x 120 x 50 mm. Click the icon of **Extrude.** Specify 120 as the value of extrusion distance. We use symmetric in this case, meaning 60 mm before the sketching plane and 60 mm behind the sketching plane.

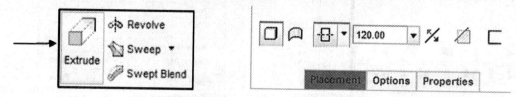

From the Model Tree, click the **FRONT** datum plane as the sketching plane, and click the icon of Sketch View to orient the sketching plane parallel to the screen.

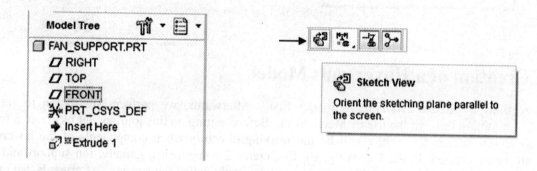

Click the icon of **Centerline** and sketch a horizontal centerline.

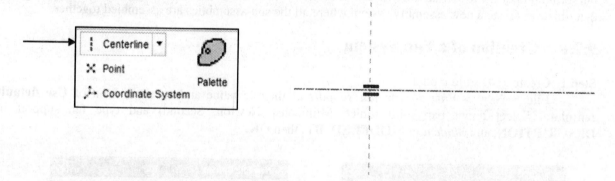

Select the icon of rectangle and sketch a rectangle. The 2 dimensions are 120 and 50, as shown.

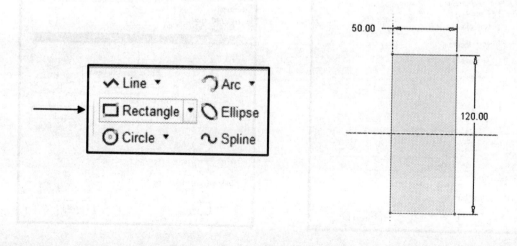

Upon completion, pick the icon of **OK**, and click the icon of **Apply and Save.**

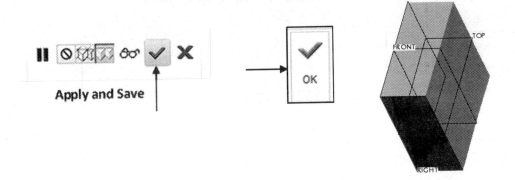

Step 2: Click the icon of **Extrude** and select **Cut** and the depth of cut is 45..

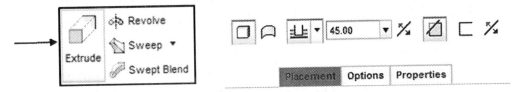

Select the surface of the block on the right side as the sketching plane, and click the icon of **Sketch View** to orient the sketching plane parallel to the screen.

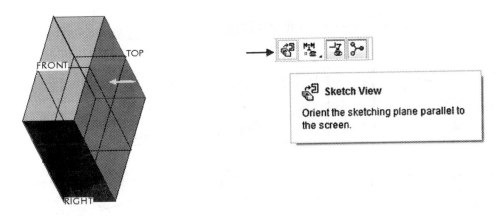

Click the icon of **References** and add **FRONT** as a new reference.

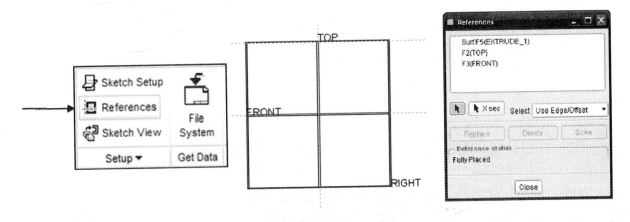

Click the icon of **Circle** to sketch 2 circles. The 2 diameter dimensions are 105 and 20, respectively. Upon completion, click the icon of OK, and the icon of **Apply and Save**.

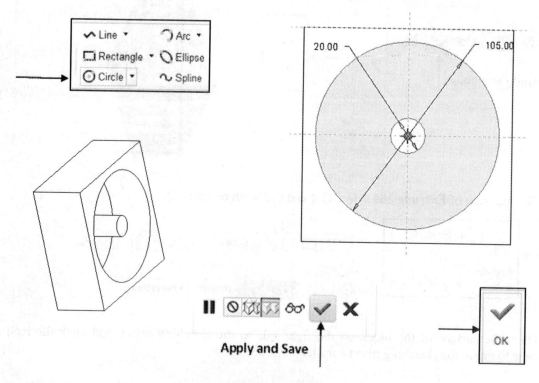

Apply and Save

OK

Step 3: Click the icon of Extrude and select Cut and Thru All.

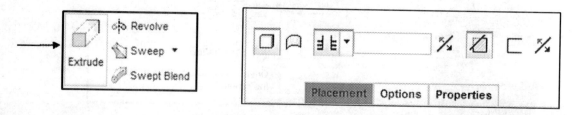

Select the inner surface of the block as the sketching plane, and click the icon of **Sketch View** to orient the sketching plane parallel to the screen.

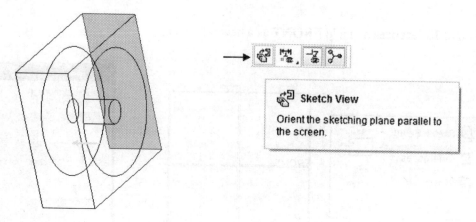

Sketch View

Orient the sketching plane parallel to the screen.

Click the icon of **References** and add **FRONT** as a new reference.

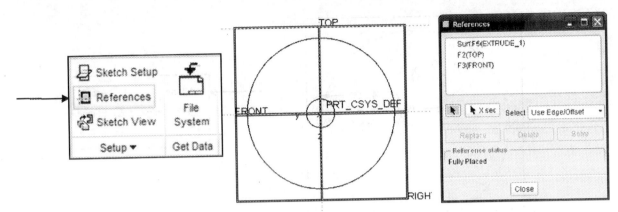

Click the icon of Centerline. Sketch a vertical centerline and a horizontal centerline.

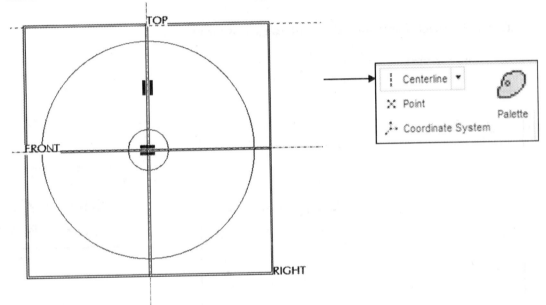

Click the icon of **References** and select the 2 circles as references.

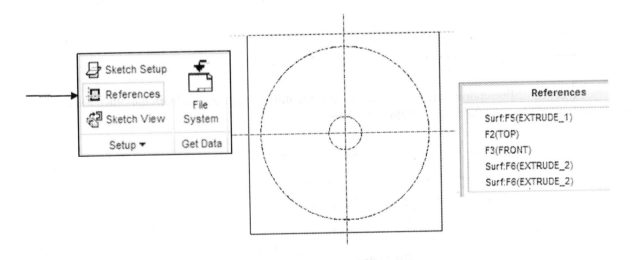

First, sketch a vertical line and a horizontal line. The dimension of length is 43, as shown.

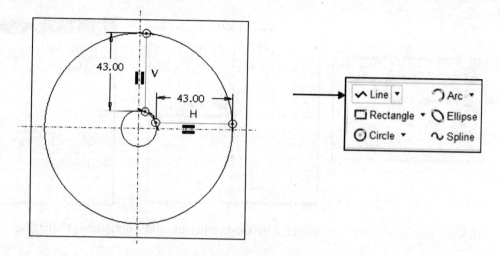

Afterwards, sketch 2 arcs along the 2 circles used as the references.

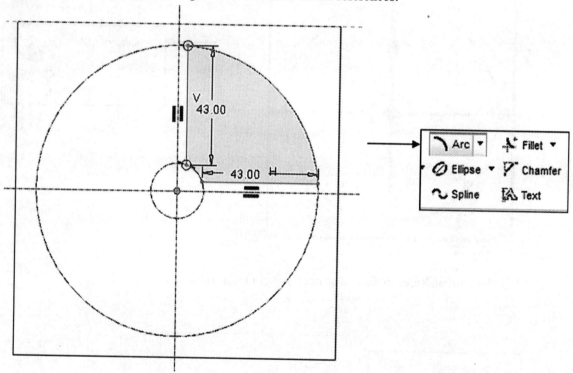

Select the 2 line entities and 2 arc entities. Use the mirror function to obtain the other 3 sketches. Click the icon of **OK**, and the icon of **Apply and Save**.

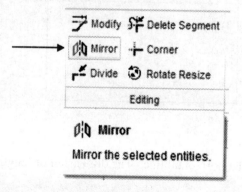

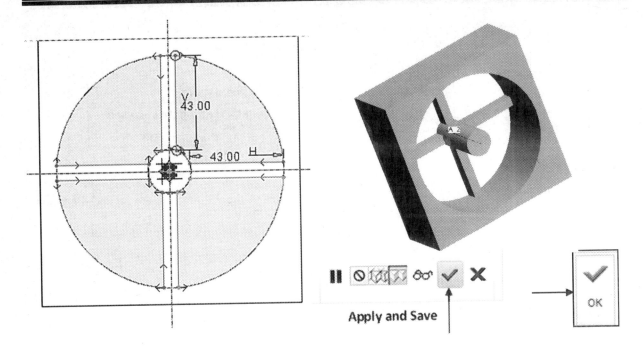

Apply and Save

To create the fan component,

Step 1: Create a 3D solid model, a cylinder feature and 2 datum curves.

File > New > Part > type fan as the file name and clear the icon of **Use default template > OK.**

Select mmns_part_solid (units: Millimeter, Newton, Second) and type *fan component* in **DESCRIPTION**, and *student* in **MODELED_BY**, then **OK.**

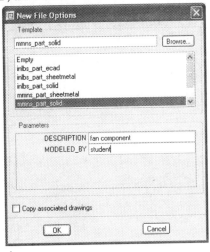

The first feature is a cylinder. Click the icon of **Extrude.** Select Symmetric and specify 42 as the value of extrude distance.

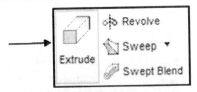

From the Model Tree, select the **FRONT** datum plane as the sketching plane, and click the icon of Sketch View to orient the sketching plane parallel to the screen.

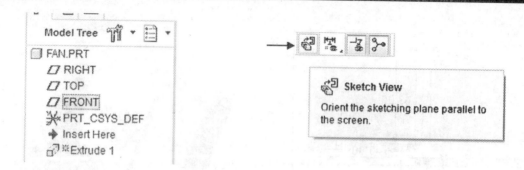

Click the icon of Circle and sketch 2 circles. The values of the 2 diameters are 20 and 40. Upon completion, click the icon of OK, and click the icon of Apply and Save.

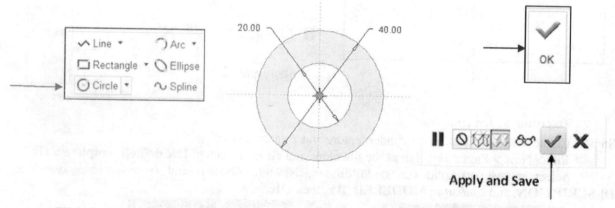

Click the icon of **Datum Plane Tool** to create 2 datum planes. The offset values are 10 and (-10) with respect to the **FRONT** datum plane.

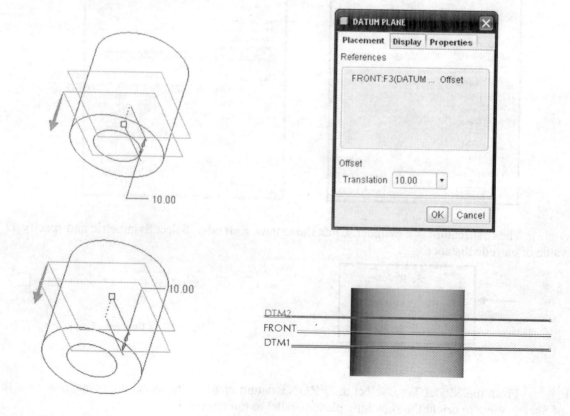

From the Model Tree, select FRONT. Click the icon of **Sketch Tool.** Click the icon of Sketch View to orient the sketching plane parallel to the screen.

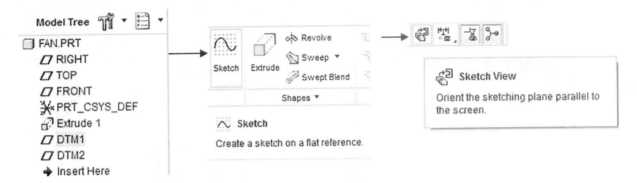

Click the icon of **Circle** and sketch a circle. The diameter value is 100.

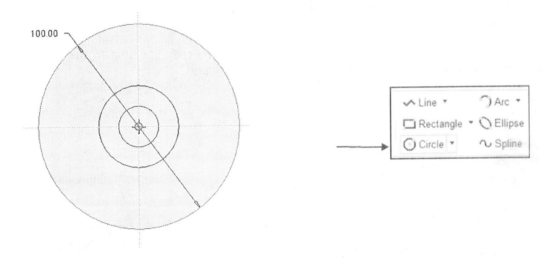

Repeat this procedure to sketch a circle on DTM2. The diameter value is 100.

Click the icon of Datum Point Tool to define a datum point, PNT0, on **DTM1**. The datum point is on the sketched circle. The length ratio value is 0.4, as shown.

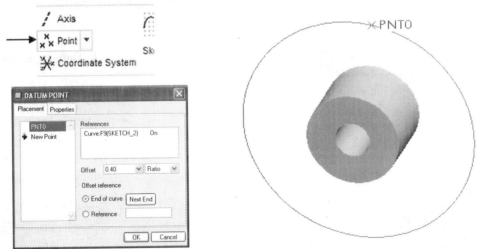

Click the icon of Datum Point Tool to define a datum point, PNT1, on **DTM2**. The datum point is on the sketched circle. The length ratio value is 0.1, as shown.

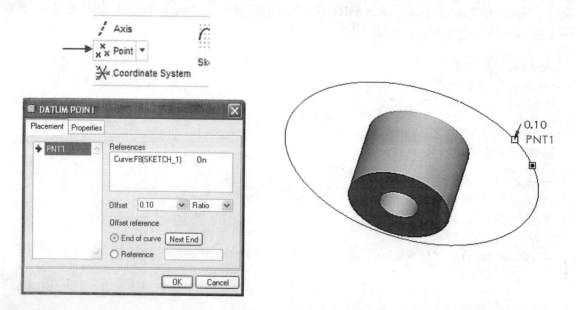

Create a datum curve going through PNT1 and PNT0 (pay attention to the Order). Expand Datum and click Curve. Pick PNT1 first and pick PNT0 afterwards.

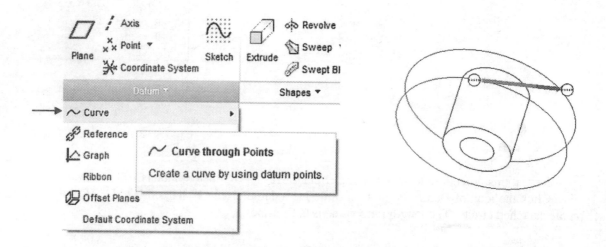

Activate Ends Condition. Click Start Point in the Curve side box. Click Tangent in the End condition box. Pick the sketched circle on DTM2.

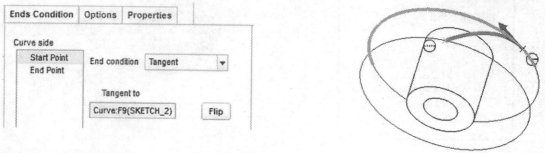

Click End Point in the Curve side box. Click Tangent in the End condition box. Pick the sketched circle on DTM1. Click the icon of **Apply and Save**.

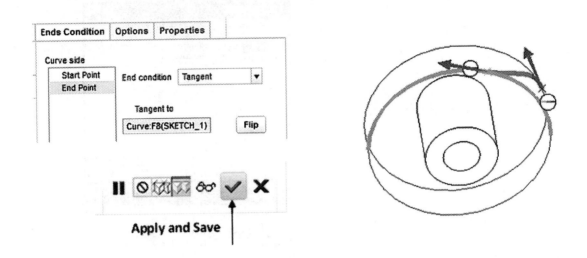

To project the created datum curve on to the cylindrical surface. Highlight the datum curve. Click the icon of Project. Select Normal to surface and pick the cylindrical surface. A projected curve is created. Click the icon **of Apply and Save**.

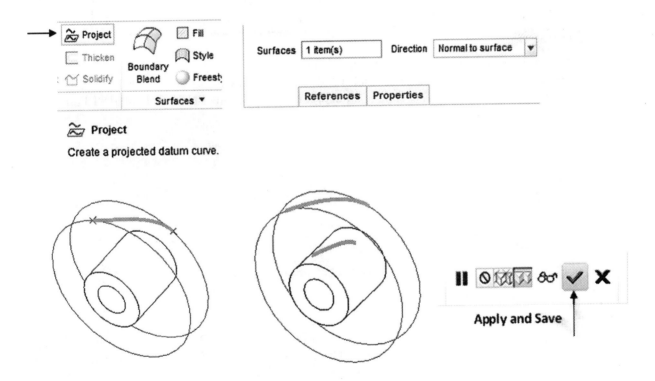

Step 2: Create 2 datum points, PNT2 and PNT3, at the 2 ends of the projected curve.

Click the icon of Datum Point. Pick the end of the projected curve to define PNT2. Repeat this process to define PNT3 at the other end of the projected curve.

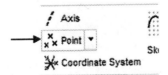

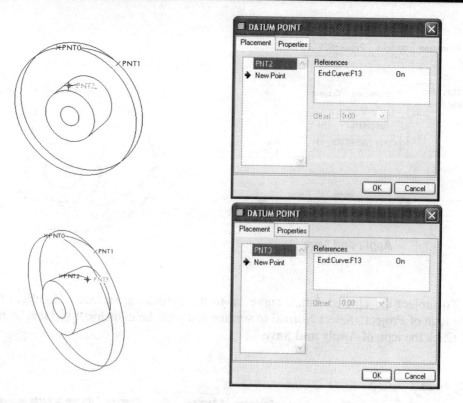

Step 3: Create 2 datum curves (actually 2 straight lines).

Expand Datum and click Curve. Pick PNT0 first and pick PNT2 afterwards. A straight line is created. Repeat this process to create another straight line by connecting PNT1 first and PNT3 afterwards.

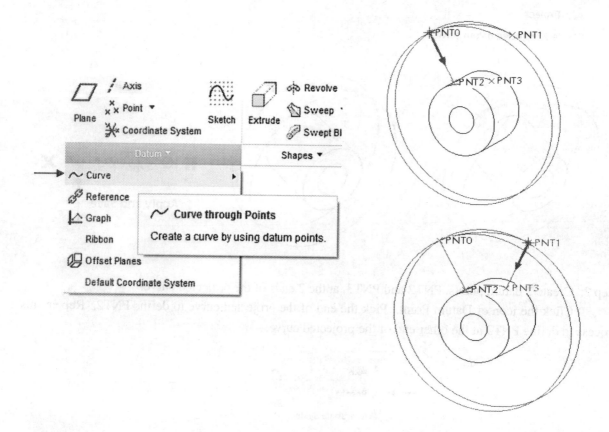

Step 4: Create a surface using the 4 datum curves created.
Click the icon of Boundary blend tool. For the first direction, pick the 2 straight lines.

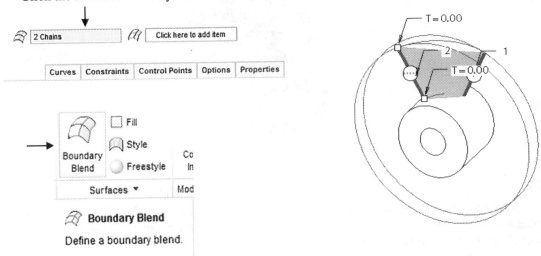

For the second direction, pick the 2 datum curves. Click the icon of Apply and Save to complete
the create a surface.

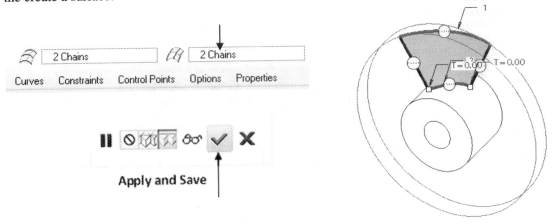

Step 5: Use the Thicken tool to convert the surface feature to a 3D solid feature.
Highlight the created surface. Click the icon of Thicken > specify 2 as the thickness value.
Select Automatic fit from the options box. Users may check a few times to set the thickness distribution
to Both Sides. Click the icon of **Apply and Save**.

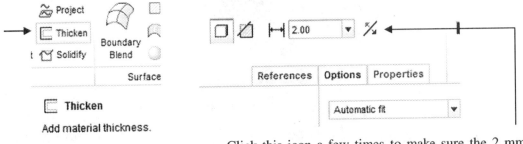

Click this icon a few times to make sure the 2 mm
thickness is added to BOTH SIDES

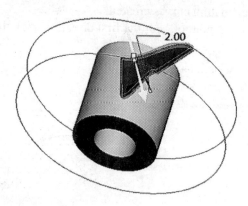

Step 6: Use Pattern and Reference Pattern to create the 3 other fan blades
From the model tree, highlight Boundary Blend 1 > right click and pick Pattern > Axis and pick the axis of the cylinder > set the number of copies including the current one to 4 and the increment to 90 > click the icon of **Apply and Save**.

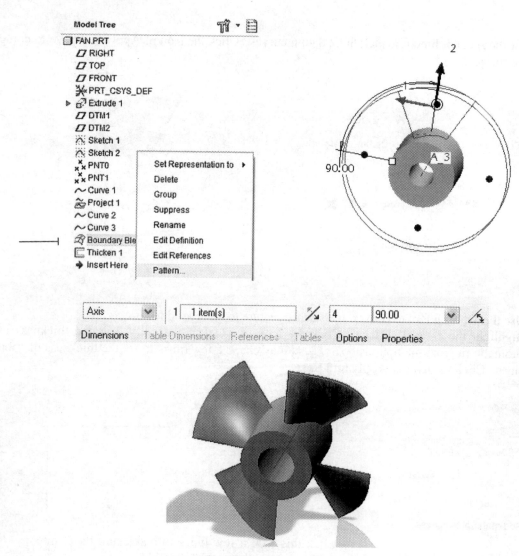

From the model tree, highlight **Thicken** > right click and pick **Pattern.** It is Reference pattern. Just click the icon of **Apply and Save**.

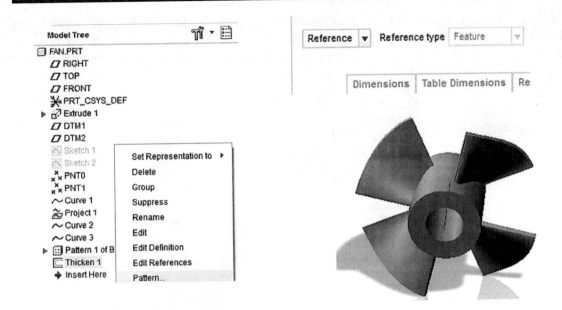

To create an assembly for the fan system:

Step 1: Create an assembly for the fan system.

File > New > Assembly > type *fan system* as the file name > clear the box > **OK.** Select the mmns_asm_design system. Type *Fan System* in the Description box and type *student* in the Modeled_by box > **OK**.

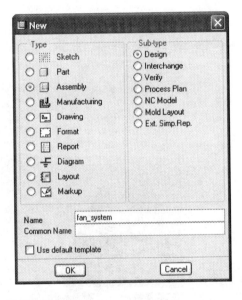

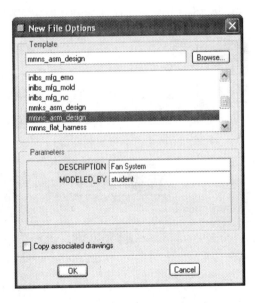

Select the icon of **Assemble** from the assembly icon list. From the local memory, or **In Session**, select fan_support.prt, and open it.

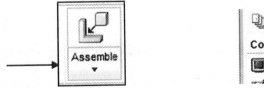

Activate **Placement**. Under the **Constraint Type**, pick the icon of **Default**, which means automatically placing PART_DEF_CSYS to the location of ASM_DEF_CSYS and the orientations of the 2 coordinate systems are identical > **Full Constrained** is indicated under **Status**> click the icon of **Apply and Save**.

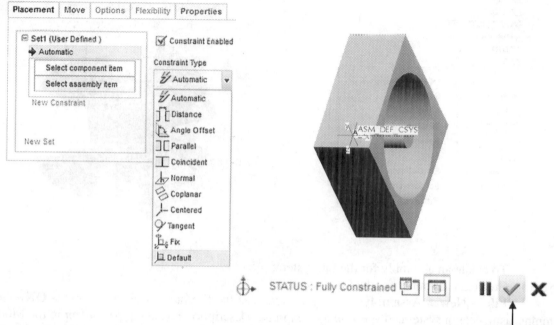

Now we bring *fan.prt* to the assembly. Following the same procedure, pick the icon of **Assemble**, and open the file called *fan.prt* from **In Session**.

Activate User Defined > Pin.

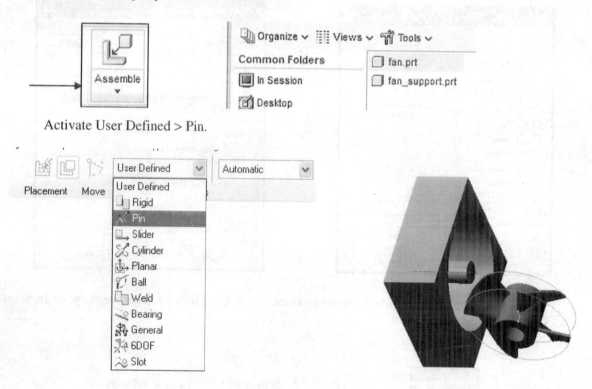

For the **Axis alignment**, pick the axis from the fan support component and the axis from the fan component.

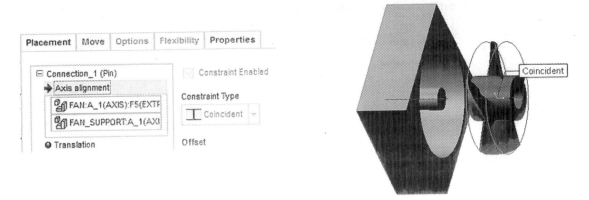

For the Translation **Constraint,** pick the 2 surfaces from the fan support component and the fan component, respectively, as shown in the following figure.

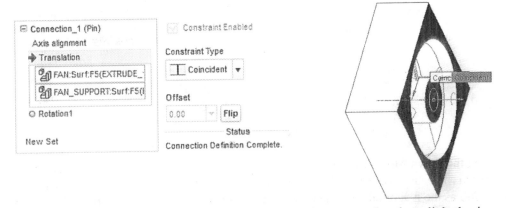

As the Status box indicates, the connection definition has been completed > click the icon of **Apply and Save**.

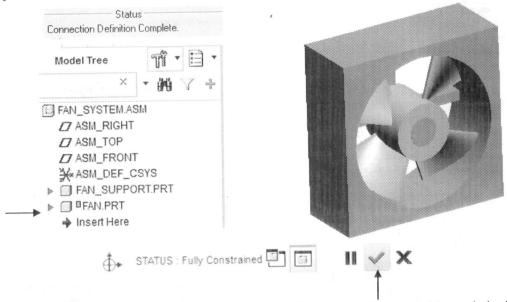

Form the main toolbar, select **Applications > Mechanism**. The assembly mode is shifted to the Mechanism mode. When examining the model tree, the model tree is expanded to include the functions of mechanism, such as CONNECTOINS, MOTORS, ANALYSES and PLAYBACKS. When expanding those functions further, for example, expanding CONNECTIONS leads to a list of JOINTS, CAMS, SLOTS and GEARS.

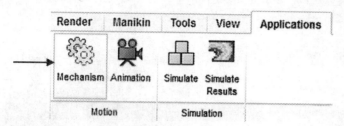

To add a servo motor, highlight ROTATIONAXIS. Make a right-click to select Servo Motor from the pop up menu.

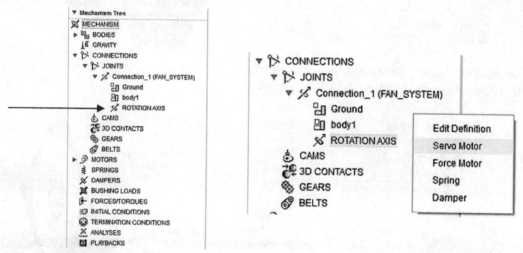

In the Servo Motor Definition window, the design system automatically selects the pin axis as the rotation axis because there is only one joint defined. Click **Profile**, select Velocity > Constraint, and specify 360 as the magnitude, or one revolution per second as the rotation speed. Click **OK**.

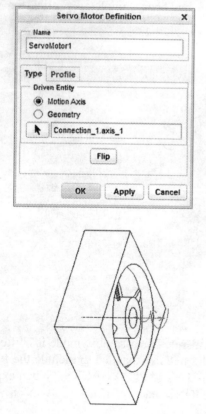

To perform an analysis, click the icon of **Mechanism Analysis**. Set the End Time to 10 (sec). Set the Frame rate to 10 so that we are able to catch the motion of rotation smoothly > **Run**.

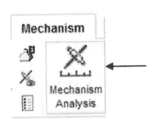

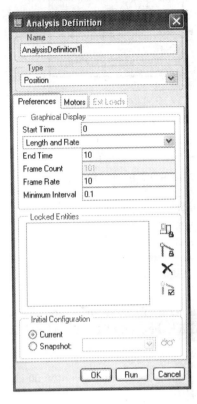

9.7.2 Creation of a Hovercraft Platform System

We first create the platform component. Afterwards, we create a new assembly file to assemble the fan system and the platform component.

Step 1: Create a 3D solid model for the platform component.

      File > **New** > **Part** > type hovercraft_platform as the file name and clear the icon of **Use default template** > **OK**. Select mmns_part_solid (units: Millimeter, Newton, Second) and type *Platform* in **DESCRIPTION**, and *student* in **MODELED_BY**, then **OK**.

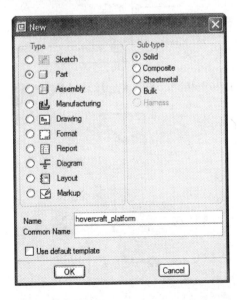

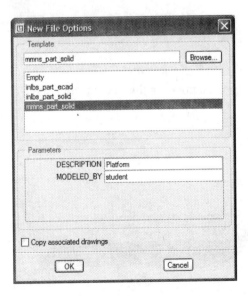

Click the icon of **Extrude.** Specify *86* as the height of the platform.

Pick the **TOP** datum plane as the sketching plane. Click the icon of **Sketch View** to orient the sketching plane parallel to the screen.

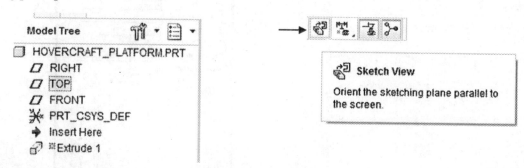

Click the icon of **Circle** and sketch a circle. Click the icon of **Delete** to delete the half circle on the right side. Click the icon of **Line** to sketch 3 lines, as shown.

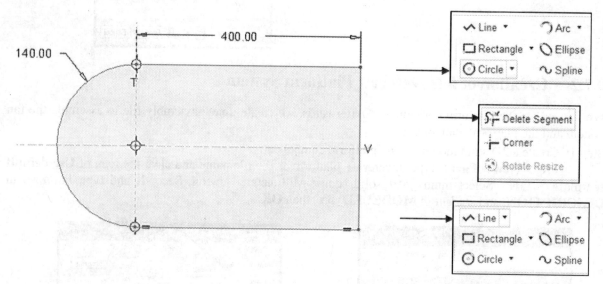

Upon completing this sketch, click the icon of **OK,** and click the icon of **Apply and Save**.

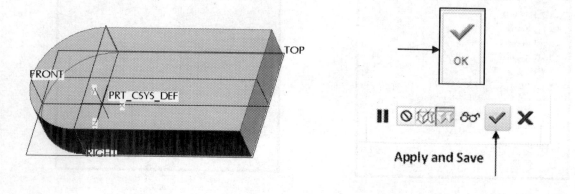

Create 2 datum planes. Click the icon of **Datum Plane**. Pick the **RIGHT** datum plane and set the offset value to 245 and 60, respectively.

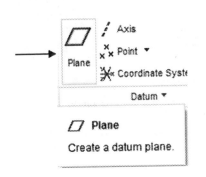  

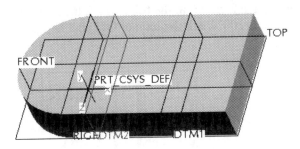

Now click the icon of **Shell** to create an air chamber for lifting the platform. Specify 4 as the thickness value. Pick the bottom surface. Click the icon of **Apply and Save**.

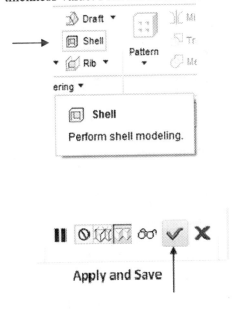 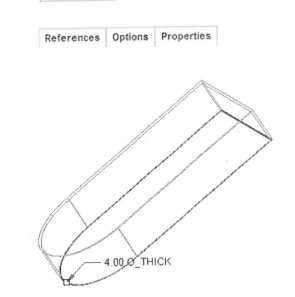

Click the icon of Extrude. Select Cut and specify Thru All as the choice of the depth of cut.

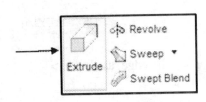 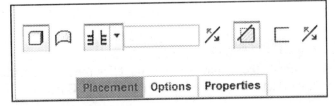

Click the top surface of the platform and click the icon of Sketch View to orient the sketching plane parallel to the screen.

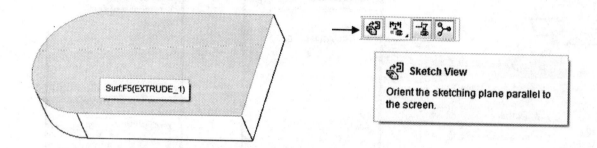

Click the icon of **Circle** and sketch 2 circles at the following 2 locations defined by the 2 datum planes just created. The diameter value is 100. Click the icon of **OK** and the icon of **Apply and Save**.

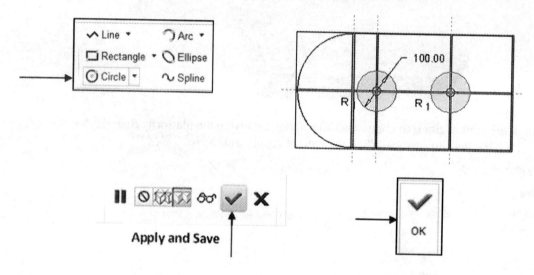

Let us create 2 datum points. First click the icon of **Datum Point**. Click the edge, as shown. Change the offset value to 0.5. Click **OK**. **PNT0** is created.

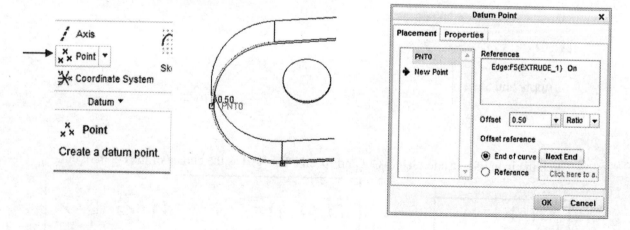

To create the second datum point, click the icon of **Datum Point.** Click the edge, as shown.> Change the offset value or the ratio value to *0.50* . Click **OK**. **PNT1** is created.

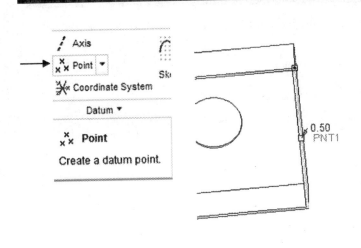

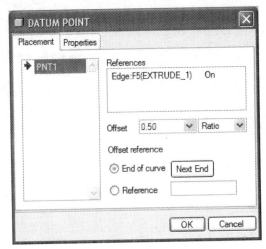

To create an assembly for the hovercraft system:

Step 1: Create an assembly to assemble the modified bottle and the original bottle.

File > New > Assembly > type *hovercraft_system* as the file name > clear the box > **OK.** Select the mmns_asm_design system. Type *Hovercraft System* in the Description box and type *student* in the Modeled_by box > **OK**.

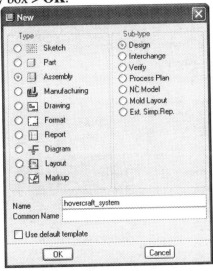

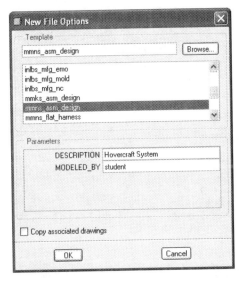

Select the icon of **Assemble**. From the local memory, or **In Session**, select hovercraft_platform, and open it.

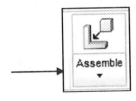

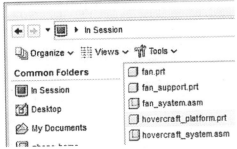

Activate **Placement**. Under the **Constraint Type**, pick the icon of **Default**. **Full Constrained** is indicated under **Status**> click the icon of **Apply and Save**.

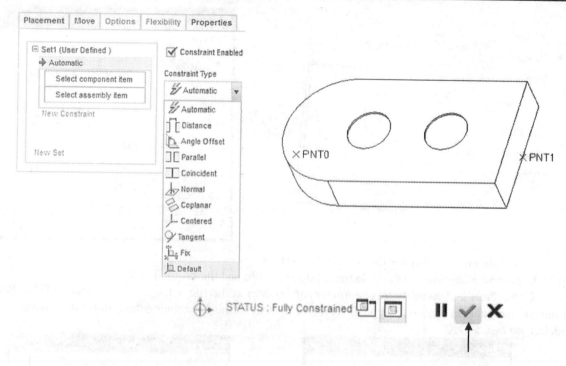

Now we bring *fan_system.asm* to the assembly. Following the same procedure, pick the icon of **Assemble**, and open the file called *fan_system.asm* from **In Session**.

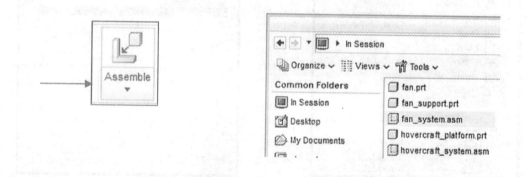

We use the Three-Click method discussed in Chapter 7 to assemble the 2 fan systems with the platform component to function as the propulsion fan system, as shown below.

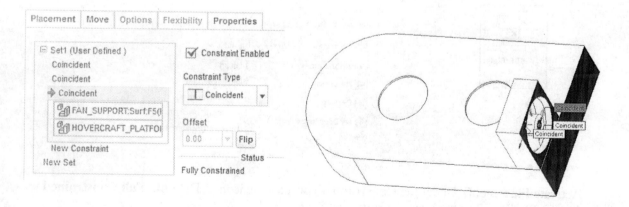

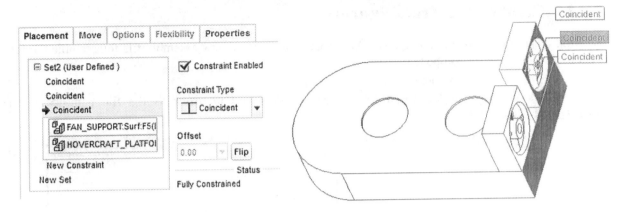

We use the Three-Click method discussed in Chapter 7 to assemble another 2 fan systems with the platform component to function as the lifting fan system, as shown below.

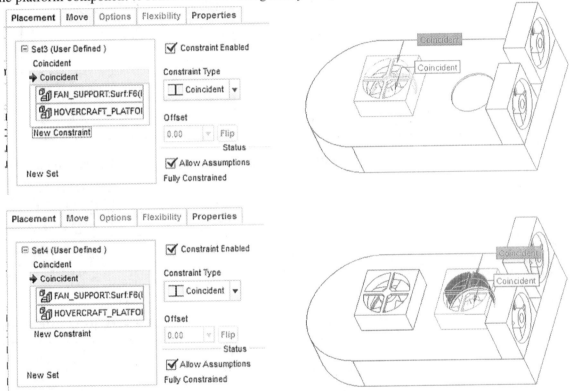

As shown, the hovercraft system assembly consists of the platform component and 4 fan system assemblies, serving as sub-assemblies.

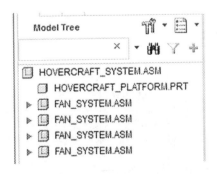

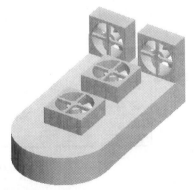

9.7.3 Creation of a Track System

We first create the platform component. Afterwards, we create a new assembly file to assemble the fan system and the platform component.

Step 1: Create a 3D solid model for the track component.

Click the icon of **Create a new object** > **Part** > type *track* as the file name > select **mmns_part_solid** > **OK**.

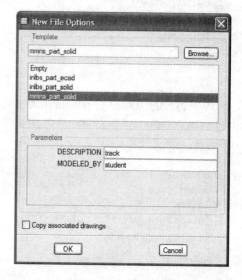

From the Model Tree, select the **TOP** datum plane (sketching plane). Click the icon of Sketch. Click the icon of Sketch View.

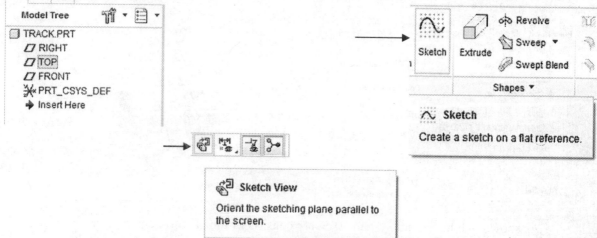

Click the icon of Centerline > make 2 clicks on the horizontal reference to create a horizontal centerline.

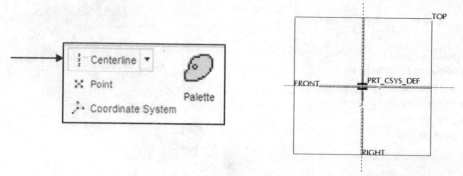

Click the icon of **Line** and sketch 5 lines, as shown. Modify the displayed dimensions to 4620, 1570.80, 1848, 1478.40 and 135°, respectively.

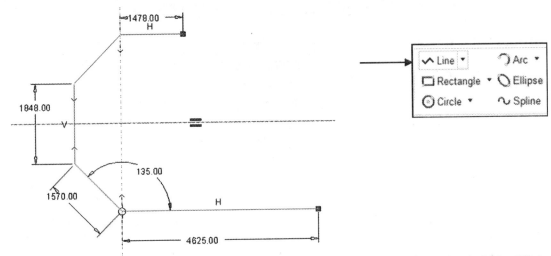

Click the icon of Circular Fillet to add rounds at the corners. The radius value is 300. Click the icon of **OK**.

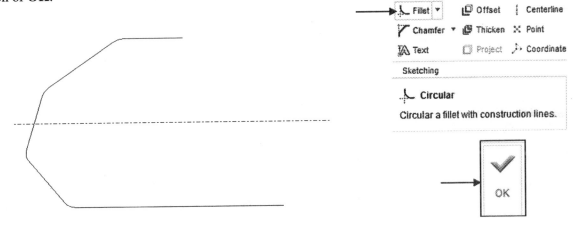

In order to simulate the motion of the 3D solid model of hovercraft, the hovercraft and track must be assembled in a special manner to allow for movement. Click the icon of **Create a new object** > **Assembly** > type *hovercraft_track* as the file name > select **mmns_asm_design** > type hovercraft and track as the description > type student as the author or modeled_by > **OK**.

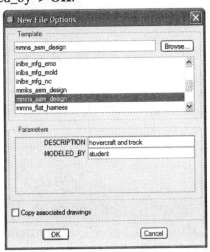

We begin the process of importing the track component first. The track should be set on the ground. Click the icon of **Assemble** > click **In Session** > select **Track** > **Open**.

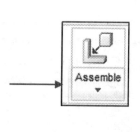

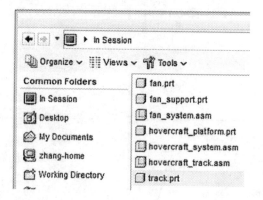

Activate **Placement**. Under the **Constraint Type**, pick the icon of **Default**. **Full Constrained** is indicated under **Status**> click the icon of **Apply and Save**.

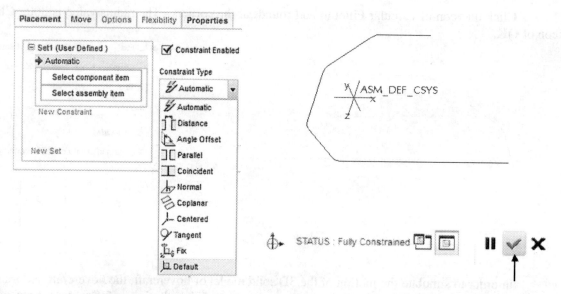

The next step is to assemble the hovercraft system. Click the icon of Assembly > click In Session > select hovercraft_system.asm.

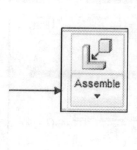

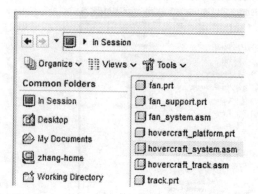

Expand the box called **User Defined** and select **Planar** because the idea is to allow the motion in the track plane only.

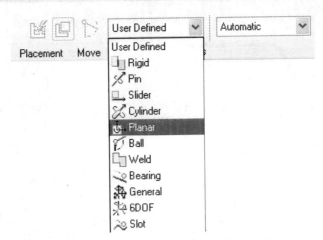

Click Placement > pick the **TOP** datum plane from the track component and pick the **TOP** plane from the hovercraft_platform component, thus completing the process of defining the planar constraint. Click **New Set** to start the process of defining the second constraint, which is a **Slot** connection.

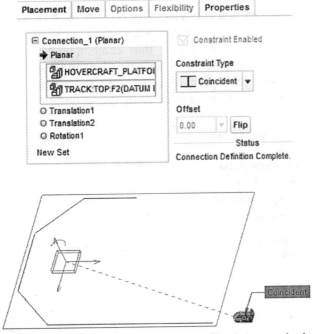

Expand the box called **User Defined** and select **Slot** because the hovercraft platform has to follow the track. Pick PNT0 from the hovercraft_platform component and pick all segments of the track from the track component while holding down the **Ctrl** key, thus completing the process of defining a slot connection. Click **New Set** to start the process of defining the third constraint, which is also a slot connection.

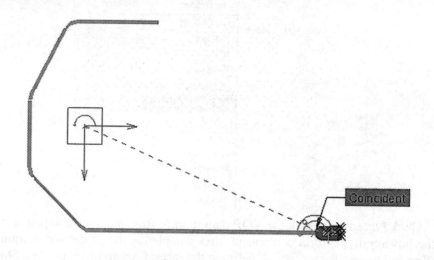

Expand the box called **User Defined** and select **Slot** because the hovercraft platform has to follow the track. Pick PNT1 from the hovercraft_platform component and pick all segments of the track from the track component while holding down the **Ctrl** key, thus completing the process of defining a slot connection. Click **New Set** to start the process of defining the third constraint, which is also a slot connection. Pick **PNT1** from the hovercraft_platform component and pick all segments of the track from the track component, thus completing the process of defining the second slot connection. Click the icon of **Apply and Save**.

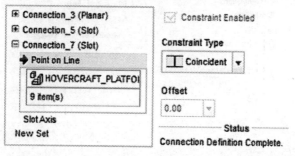

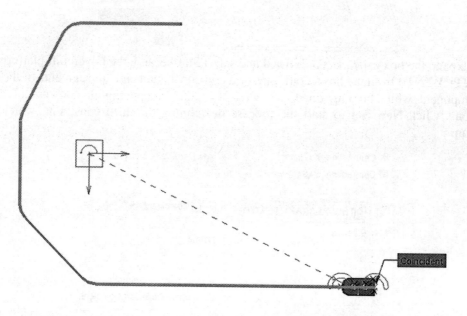

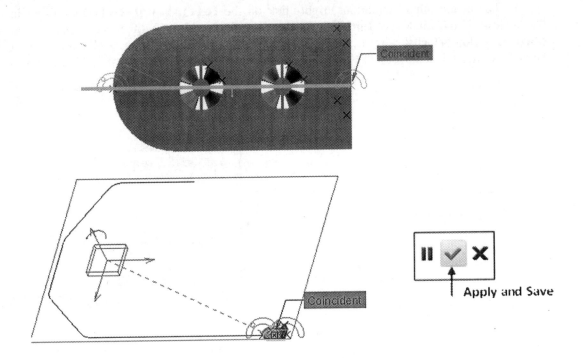

Form the main toolbar, select **Applications > Mechanism**. The Mechanism Model Tree is on display.

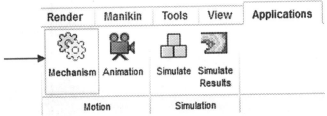

Let us first record the current position as the initial position of the hovercraft with respect to the track component. Click the icon **of Drag packaged components** from the main menu > click the icon of **Take a snapshot,** Snapshort1 is taken > **Close**.

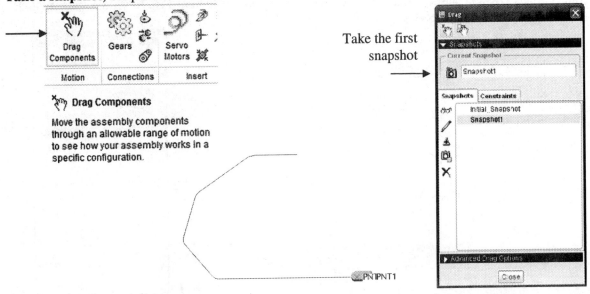

To set the initial conditions, right-click on the **INITIAL CONDITIONS** listed in the model tree > **New**. In the window of **Initial Condition Definition**, select **Snapshort1** > click the icon of **Define tangential slot velocity** > from the display, select the first connection > **OK** and specify 50 as the velocity value. Click the icon of **Flip** to set the velocity direction in the negative X direction.

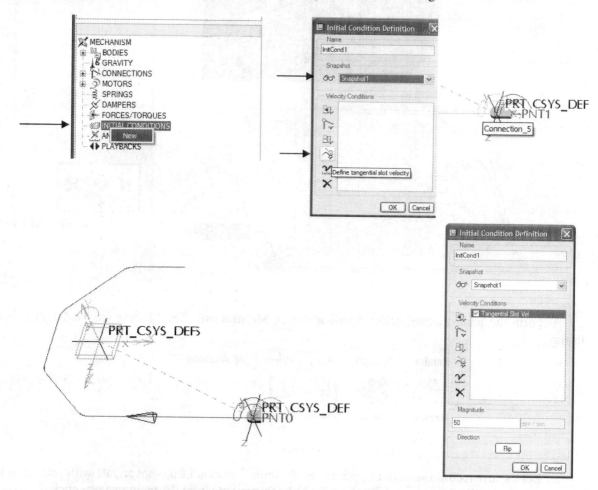

Click the icon of **Define tangential slot velocity**, again > from the display, select the second connection > **OK** and specify 50 as the velocity value. Click the icon of **Flip** to set the velocity direction in the negative X direction > **OK**.

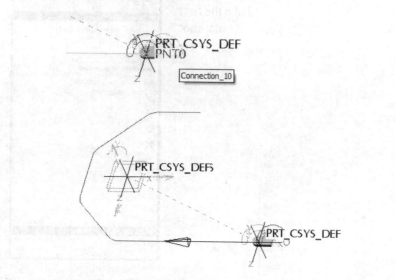

Click the icon of **Mechanism Analysis.** Set the analysis type to **Dynamic**. Specify *200* as the duration of the analysis. Set the Initial Configuration to **I.C. State**. Click the icon of **Run**.

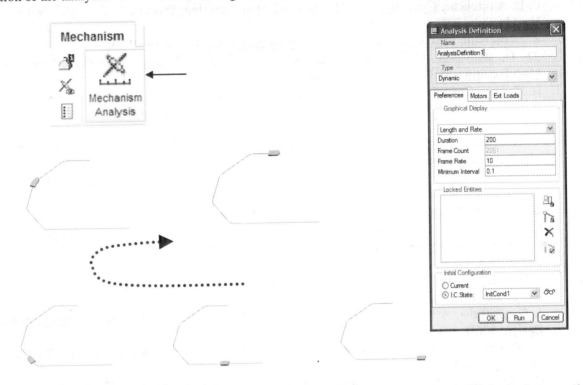

Click the icon of **PLAYBACKS.** AnalysisDefinition1 is already selected. Click the button of **Play** in the Paybacks window. Users may adjust the speed of animation by moving the speed bar to the right or the left side. For making a movie file, just click the button Capture. A movie file will be automatically saved in the working direction as pendulum_system.mpeg.

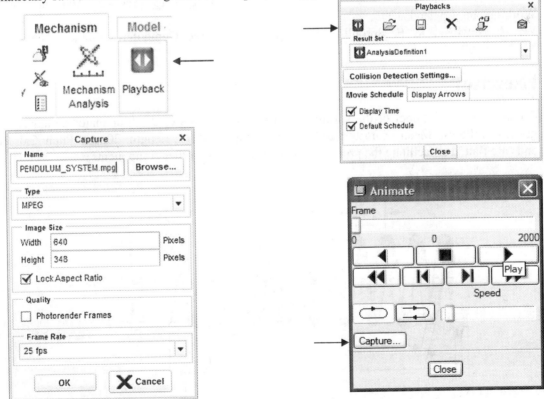

9.8 References

1. F. L. Amirouche, <u>Computer-aided Design and Manufacturing</u>, Prentice Hall, Englewood Cliffs, New Jersey, 1993.
2. R. E. Barnhill, <u>IEEE Computer-Graphics and Applications</u>, 3(7), 9-16, 1983.
3. D. D. Bedworth, M. R. Henderson, and P. M. Wolfe, <u>Computer-Integrated Design and Manufacturing</u>, McGraw-Hill, New York, NY, 1991.
4. H. R. Buhl, <u>Creative Engineering Design</u>, Iowa State University Press, Ames, Iowa, 1960.
5. B. L. Davids, A. J. Robotham and Yardwood A., <u>Computer-aided Drawing and Design</u>, London, 1991.
6. J. H. Earle, <u>Graphics for Engineers, AutoCAD Release 13</u>, Addison-Wesley, Reading, Massachusetts, 1996.
7. J. Encarnacao, E. G. Schlechtendahl, <u>Computer-aided Design: Fundamentals and System Architectures</u>, Springer-Verlag, New York, 1983.
8. G. Farin, <u>Curves and Surfaces for Computer-aided Geometric Design</u>, New York, 1988.
9. S. Fingers, J. R. Dixon, A review of research in mechanical engineering design, Part II: Representations, analysis, and design for the life cycle, <u>Research in Engineering Design</u>, 1(2), 121-38, 1989.
10. J. D. Foley, A. D. VanDam, <u>Fundamentals of Interactive Computer Graphics</u>, Addison-Wesley, San Francisco, 1982.
11. J. G. Griffiths, A bibliography of hidden-line and hidden-surface algorithms, <u>Computer-aided Design</u>, 10(3), 203-6. 1978.
12. M. P. Groover and E. W. Zimmers, <u>Computer-aided Design and Manufacturing</u>, Englewood Cliffs, NJ, 1984.
13. C.S. Krishnamoorthy, <u>Finite Element Analysis, Theory and Programming</u>, 2nd Ed., 1995.
14. D. Hearn, M. P. Baker, Computer Graphics, Englewood Cliffs, NJ, 1986
15. P. Ingham P. <u>CAD System in Mechanical and Production Engineering</u>, London, 1989.
16. M. Mantyla, <u>An introduction to Solid Modeling</u>, Rockville IN:Computer Science Press., 1988
17. C. McMahon and J. Browne, <u>CADCAM: from Principles to Practice</u>, Addison Wesley, Workingham, England, 1993.
18. W. M. Newman, R. F. Sproull, <u>Principles of Interactive Computer Graphics</u>, New York, McGraw-Hill, 1979.

9.9 Exercises

1. Create a 3D solid model of the spring shown below. Values of the four major parameters are given as follows: Mean Diameter: φ6.0, Wire Diameter: φ0.75, Length: 20, and Pitch: 2.0. Both ends are flatted to facilitate the process of assembling it with other components.

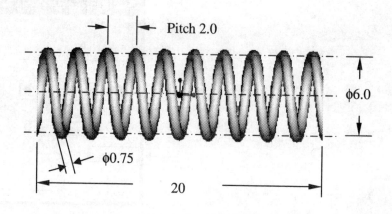

2.　　Create the component drawings and an assembly drawing for the pendulum system.

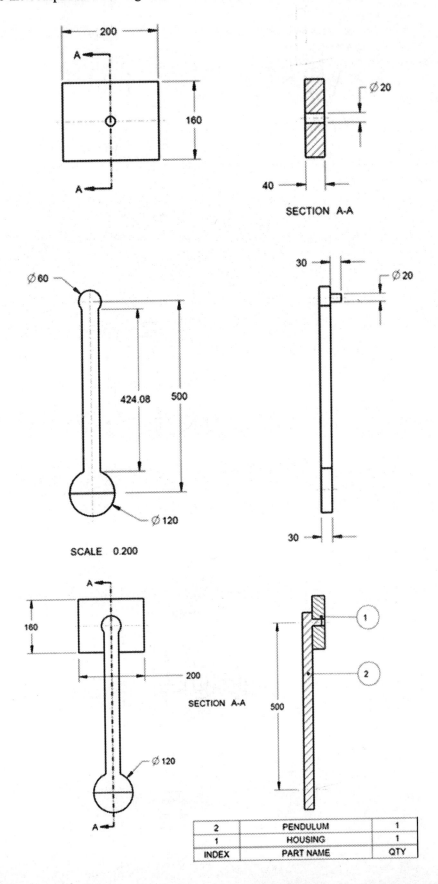

SCALE 0.200

SECTION A-A

2	PENDULUM	1
1	HOUSING	1
INDEX	PART NAME	QTY

3.   Create a 3D solid model of the component shown below. Prepare an engineering drawing.

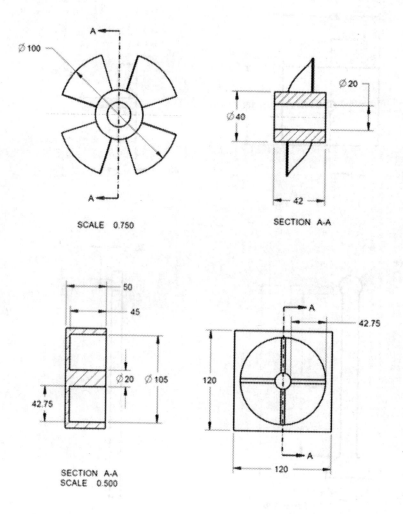

SCALE 0.750

SECTION A-A

SECTION A-A
SCALE 0.500

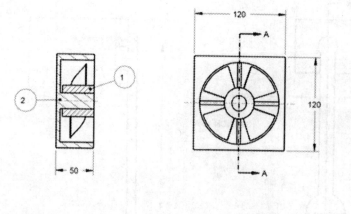

SECTION A-A
SCALE 0.500

2	FAN_SUPPORT	1
1	AXIAL_FAN	1
INDEX	PART NAME	QTY

CHAPTER 10

Creo Parametric Simulation and FEA

10.1 Introduction

Creo Parametric, like other CAD design software systems, provides users with design analysis tools through a system called Simulation. Creo Parametric Simulation is a multi-discipline computer aided engineering tool that enables users to model, analyze and optimize their designs. Creo Parametric Simulation by itself consists of two products. As illustrated in the following figure, they are STRUCTURE and THERMAL. Each product has its own focus and addresses a specific group of interests. In this chapter, we will provide the information related to modeling and analysis. In this chapter, our focus will be on learning how to use both STRUCTURE and THERMAL to perform finite element analysis.

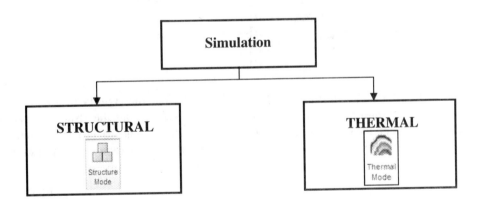

10.2   Structural Modeling

Let us take a simple cantilever beam as a case study to demonstrate the procedure for modeling structural systems. The following figure presents a cantilever beam. The left end of the beam is fixed and the right end is set free. Assume a load is acting on the free end of the cantilever beam. The over hanged length of the beam is L. The cross-section of the beam is marked as A.   Our concerns are related to deformation and stress distributions of the beam when subjected to the load.

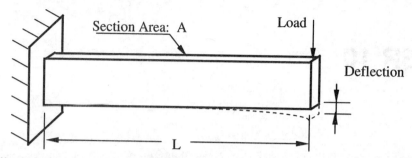

As described above, there are several factors, which have directly effects on the deformation and stress distributions when subjected to the loading. The first factor is the size and geometric shape of the beam. As illustrated, the over hanged length and the section area are two of those factors. For example, a large over hanged length induces a large amount of deflection at the free end of the beam.

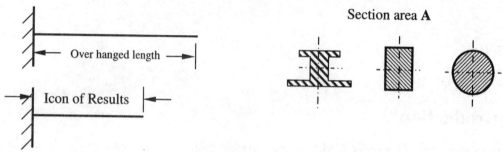

The load condition is also an important factor. When the magnitude of the load acting on a mechanical structure increases, the stress and strain distributions respond to the increase accordingly. For example, the maximum tensile stress developed at the fixed end of a cantilever beam could reach a critical value, or the maximum stress allowable. Under such circumstances, breakage can occur and the beam may fail to perform properly.

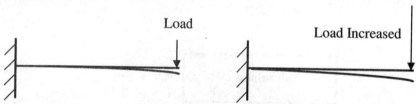

Material type is an important factor, too. It is well known that the rigidity of steel material is better than the rigidity of aluminum material. For example, while keeping all the structural parameters unchanged, replacement of steel material by aluminum material would lead to larger deflection. An appropriate selection of material type is a critical factor to sustain the safety factor which assures a safe operation during the service.

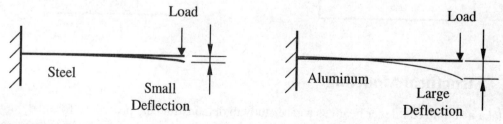

The constraint condition, to which the beam is subjected to, is an important factor. As shown below, the free end of a cantilever beam lacks support. As a result, the cantilever system is more susceptible to deflection than the beam with both ends supported, as shown. The boundary condition often plays a critical role in determining the system response when it is subjected to loading.

Modeling a mechanical structure for the analysis requires that the model used is an acceptable representation of the real physical system. It is important the model used in engineering analysis incorporates important factors, which are related to the system response under study. For this reason, Creo Parametric Simulation, like other FEA systems, requires users to follow a procedure. The procedure ensures that the problem formulation is appropriately carried out so that a unique solution obtained through the process of solving it is assured. The following figure is a block diagram illustrating the procedure used to perform engineering analysis of a mechanical structure, such as a cantilever beam.

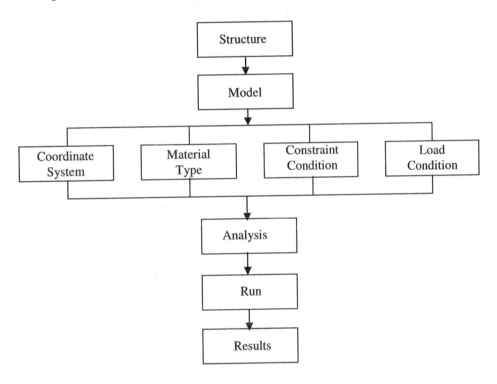

As illustrated, before getting on **Creo Parametric Simulation**, a user has to complete the construction of a 3D solid model. The model may need additional datum points, datum curves and surface regions so that loading and constraint conditions can be applied. **Simulation** by itself requires four (4) conditions specified. They are the coordinate system, material type, constraint condition and load condition. Upon completion of these conditions, an analysis package is prepared so that the converging criterion for numerical computation can be selected. Running FEA under **Simulation** requires a sufficient disk space to ensure its efficiency in computation. Creo Parametric Simulation also has a built-in graphical function to allow the user to review the results obtained from computer simulation.

10.3   Case Study 1: A cantilever beam

The geometry of a cantilever beam is shown below. There is a distributed load uniformly acting on the top surface of the beam. The magnitude is 200 N and the direction is downward or along the negative y direction. The material of the beam is steel. The fixed end is on the left side of the beam.

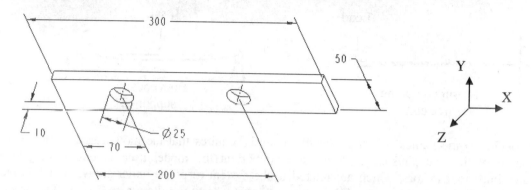

Now let us use **Simulation** to perform a static analysis and show the distribution of deformation and the distribution of the tensile stress in the x-direction.

Step 1: Create a file for the 3D solid model under Creo Parametric.

File > New > Part > type *ex10_1* as the file name and clear the icon of **Use default template > OK.** Select **mmns_part_solid** (units: Millimeter, Newton, Second) and type *Example 10-1* in **DESCRIPTION**, and *student* in **MODELED_BY**, then **OK.**

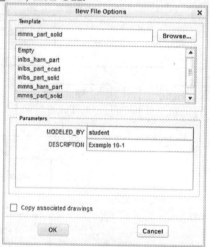

To create the first feature, a block with the 3 dimensions equal to 300x50x10 mm, click the icon of **Extrude**. Select **Symmetry** and specify *10* as the thickness value.

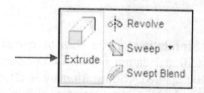
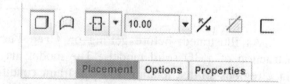

From the Model Tree, select the **FRONT** datum plane as the sketching plane. Click the icon of **Sketch** View to orient the sketching plane parallel to the screen.

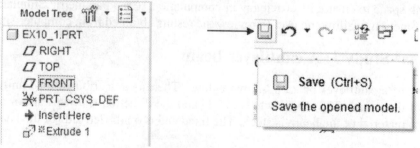

Click the icon of **Centerline** to sketch a horizontal centerline.

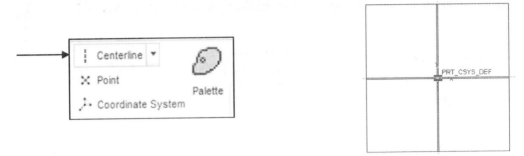

Click the icon of Rectangle to sketch a rectangle with the dimensions equal to 300 and 50, respectively. Keep the rectangle symmetric about the horizontal centerline.

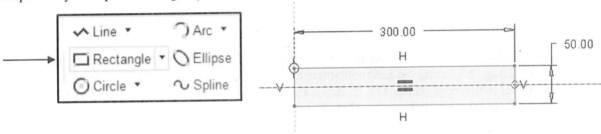

Click the icon of **Circle** to sketch 2 circles. The diameter value is 25. There are 2 position dimensions to specify the location of the 2 centers of the 2 circles. Click the icon of OK and click the icon of **Apply and Save**.

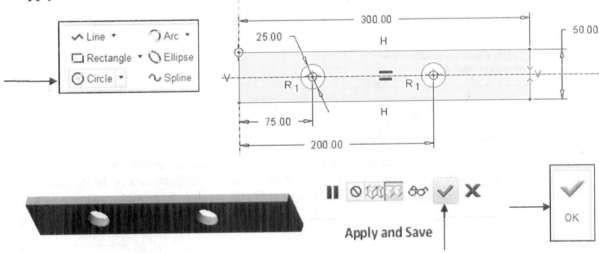

Step 2: Under the **Simulation** environment, specify the material type.
From the **Applications** tab, click **Simulation**. Click the icon of Structural Mode.

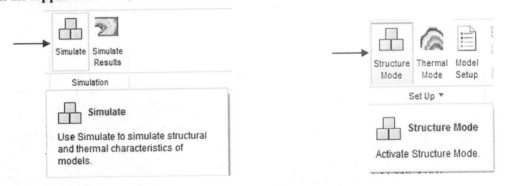

Click the icon of **Materials** > select **STEEL** from the list of Materials in Library > click the directional arrow to switch the selection to the list of Materials in Model > **OK**.

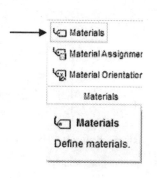

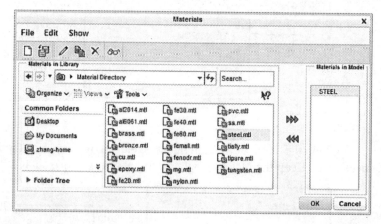

Click the icon of **Material Assignment** > in the Material Assignment window, the material type **STEEL** is already shown and the assignment has already been done because there is only one volume or one component in this case > click **OK** to accept the material assignment. In the model tree, the material type and the material assignment are also listed.

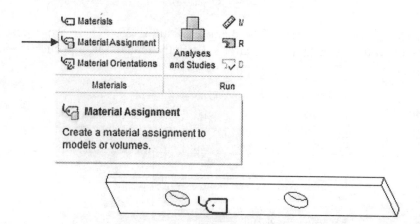

Step3: Under the Simulation environment, define the fixed end constraint condition.

Click the icon of Displacement to define a displacement constraint. Select the surface at the left end of the beam > **OK** > accept the default settings, namely, fixing all 6 degrees of freedom > **OK**.

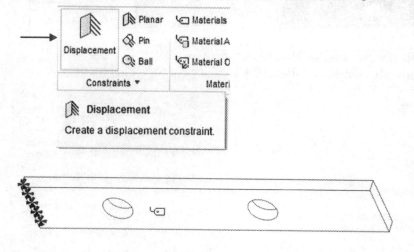

Step 4: Under the Simulation environment, define the load condition.
Click the icon of **Force/Moment Load > Surface(s) >** select the top surface of the beam > **OK**.
Type in –200 as the load component in the y direction > **OK**.

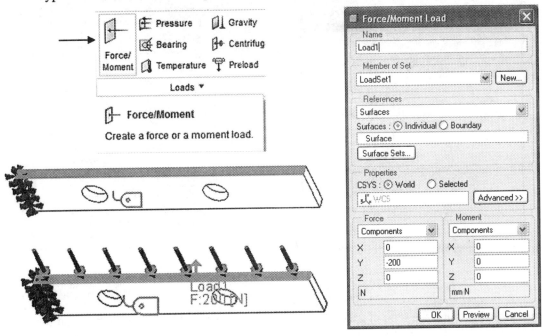

Step 5: Under the **Simulation** environment, set up **Analyses** and **Run** it
Click the icon of **Analyses and Studies > File > New Static >** type *beam_1* as the name of the
Design Study Folder > **OK**.

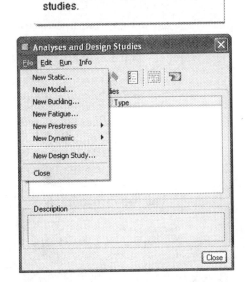

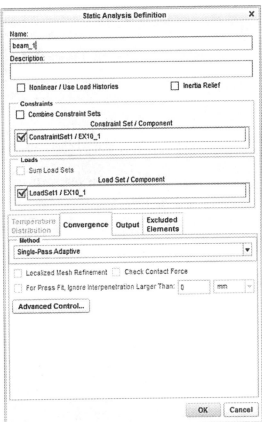

Before running the program, select the icon of Run Settings and specify a sufficient memory space, say 512 Megabytes for RAM Allocation, > **OK**. Afterwards, run the program.

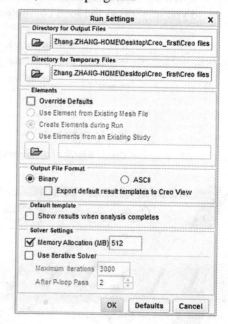

Afterwards, click the icon of green flat to run the program. There is a message on display. The message is about to run interactive diagnostics for detecting the occurrence of errors while running the program. Click **Yes**.

Yes
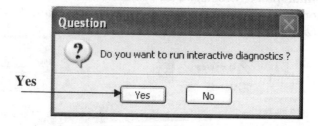

Users may click the icon of Display study status to check the running process. When the run is completed, users should check the results.

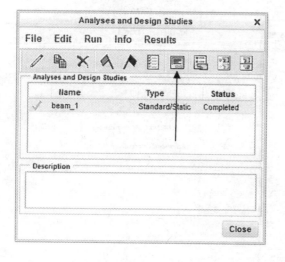
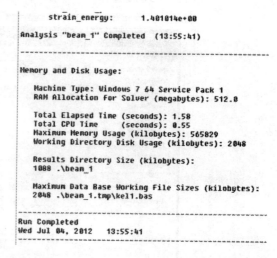

Step 7: Under the **Simulation** environment, show the **Results**

Select the icon of **Results.** Type *Beam Deflection* as the title > locate the Design Study folder called Beam_1.

Select Fringe > choose Displacement > Magnitude > OK and Show.

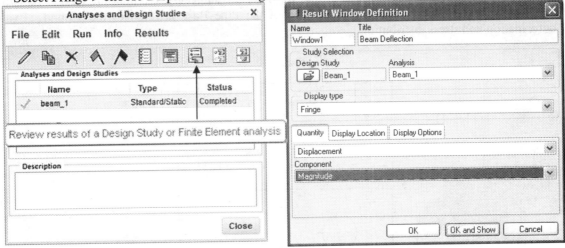

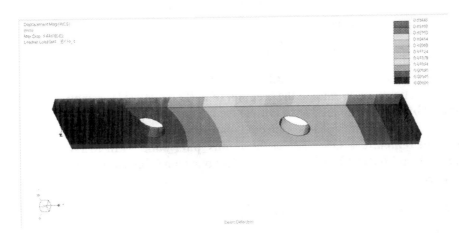

Click **Edit > Copy** > type *Stress distribution in the x direction* to view the normal (tensile and compressive) stress in the x direction.

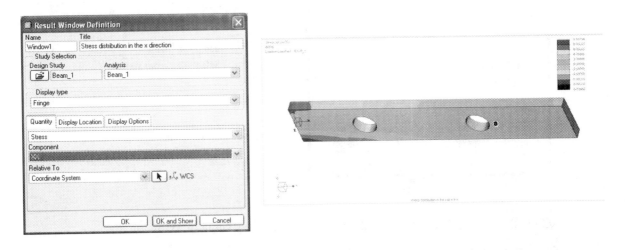

10.4   Case Study 2: Application of Pressure Loads

A component called Pipe Base is shown below. The mechanical structure is subjected to pressure loads. There are 2 through holes. The walls of the two holes are subjected to a pressure load of 20 N/mm^2, and 10 N/mm^2, respectively. The bottom surface of the Pipe Base is fixed to the ground. Evaluate the deformation and stress distribution.

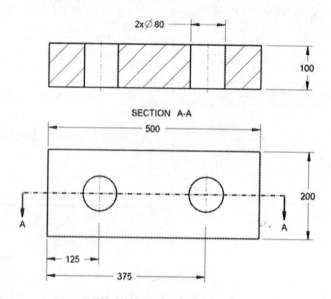

Step 1: Create a 3D solid model for the cantilever beam.

From **File**, click **New** to initiate the creation of a 3D model. Users may directly choose the icon of **Create a new object** from the toolbar to initiate the creation of a 3D model.

Make sure that the Part mode is selected, and type *pipe_base* as the file name. Clear the box called **Use default template > OK.** Select the **mmns_part_solid**. Fill in **DESCRIPTION** by typing *pressure loads*. Fill in **MODELED_BY** by typing in your name, say *student.*> **OK.** A Creo Parametric work screen appears.

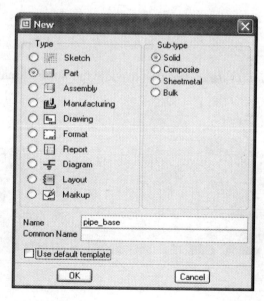

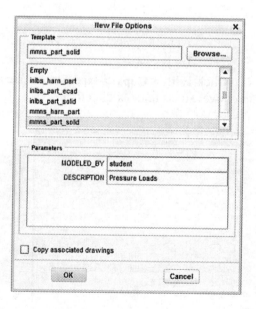

Click the icon of **Extrude.** Specify *100* as the thickness value of extrusion distance.

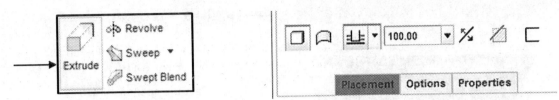

From the Model Tree, pick the **FRONT** datum plane as the sketching plane, and click the icon of **Sketch View** to orient the sketching plane parallel to the screen.

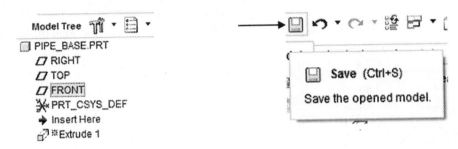

Select the icon of **Rectangle** to sketch a rectangle with the 2 dimensions equal to 500 and 200. Click the icon of OK, and the icon of Apply and Save.

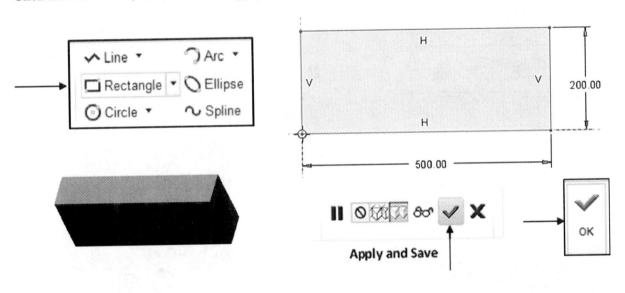

Step 2: Create a feature having 4 through holes using the **Cut** operation.
Click the icon of **Extrude.** Select Cut and select Thru All as the choice of depth of cut.

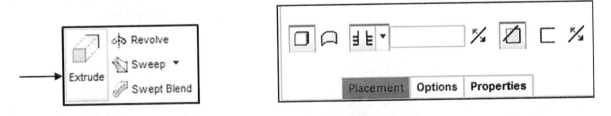

Pick the front surface of the block (not the FRONT datum plane) as the sketching plane. Click the icon of **Sketch View** to orient the sketching plane parallel to the screen.

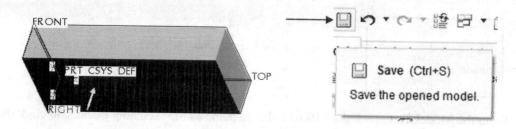

Select the icon of **Circle** to sketch 2 circles, which are equal to one another in diameter, as shown below. The diameter dimension is 80. Note the 3 position dimensions to locate the 2 centers of the 2 circles. They are 100, 125 and 375, respectively. Click the icon of **OK**, and the icon of **Apply and Save**.

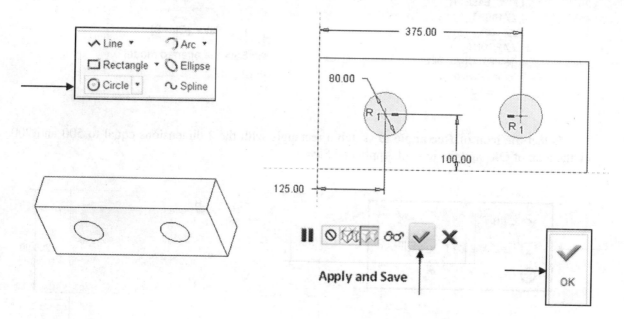

Step 3: FEA under Simulation.

From the Applications tab, click **Simulation** and **Structural**.

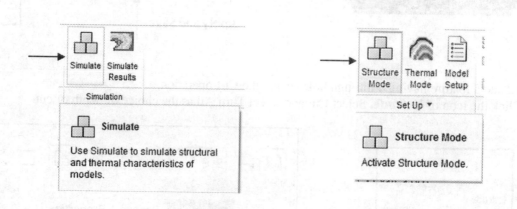

Click the icon of Materials. Select **STEEL** from the list of Materials in Library > click the directional arrow to switch the selection to the list of Materials in Model > **OK**.

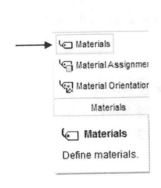

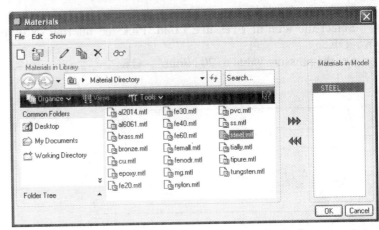

Click the icon of **Material Assignment** > in the Material Assignment window, the material type **STEEL** is already shown and the assignment has already been done because there is only one volume or one component in this case > click **OK** to accept the material assignment. In the model tree, the material type and the material assignment are also listed.

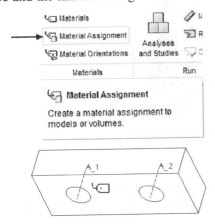

Step 4: Under the Simulation environment, define the fixed end constraint condition.

Select the icon of **Displacement** > select the surface at the bottom of the pipe base component as the fixed end, and accept the default settings, namely, fixing all six degrees of freedom.

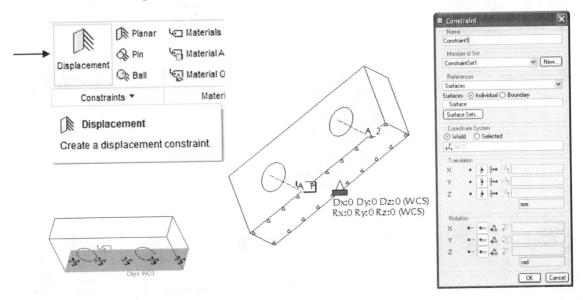

Step 5: Under the Simulation environment, define the load condition.

Select the icon of **Pressure Load.** Pick the internal cylindrical surface at the left position, as shown > **OK.**

Set the pressure value to 20 N/mm² > **OK.**

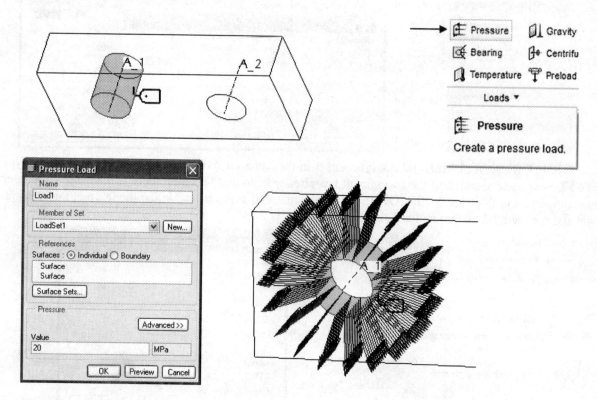

To define the second pressure load, select the icon of **New Pressure Load** from the toolbar of functions, again > activate the surface selection > pick the internal cylindrical surface at the right position, as shown > **OK.**

Set the pressure value to 10 N/mm² > **OK.**

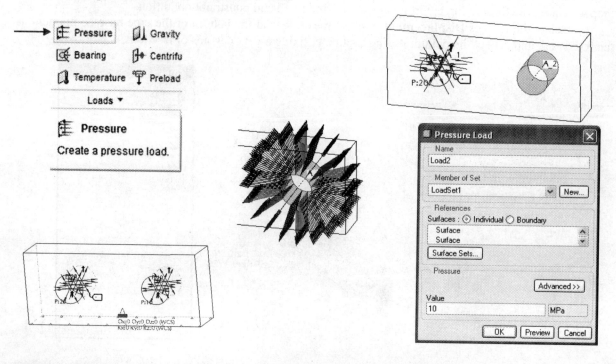

Step 6: Under the Simulation environment, set up **Analysis** and **Run** it
Click the icon of **Analysis and Studies** > **File** > **New Static** > type pipe_base > **OK**.

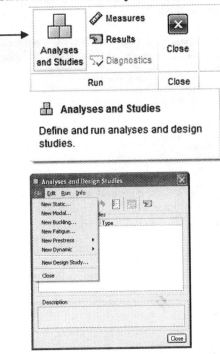

Click the icon of green flat to run the program. There is a message on display. The message is about to run interactive diagnostics for detecting the occurrence of errors while running the program. Click **Yes**.

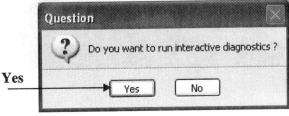

Users may click the icon of Display study status to check the running process. When the run is completed, users should check the results.

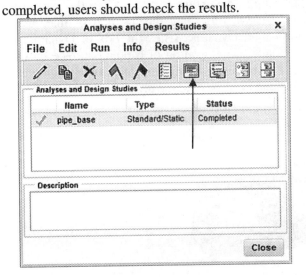
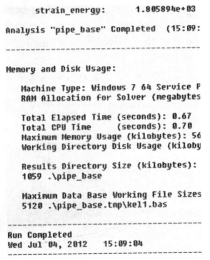

Step 8: Under the Simulation environment, study the **Results**

Select the icon of **Results.** Type *block deflection* as the title > locate the Design Study folder called pipe_base. Select **Fringe** > choose **Displacement** > **OK and Show**.

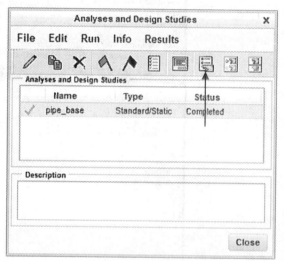
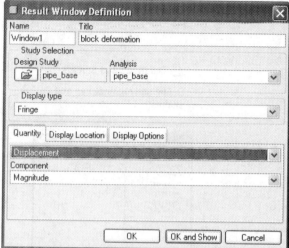

Plot of the displacement distribution.

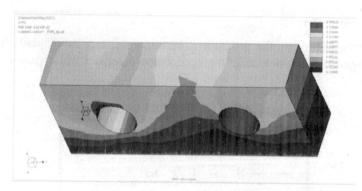

Plot of the displacement distribution with a capping surface crossing the 2 holes. From the main toolbar, select **Insert** > **Cutting/Capping Surfs** > select **Capping Surface** > select **XZ** > the user may need to adjust the value of the Depth percentage to *30* or *40* to show the location of maximum displacement > **Apply**. Users may also use the function called Dynamic. Click the box of Dynamic > locate your cursor to the cross-section and move your mouse. The position of capping surface moves following the movement of your mouse. This allows the user to dynamically view the stress distribution > click the middle button of mouse when it is done to go back to the main window.

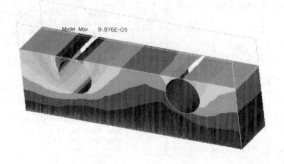

Plot of the maximum principal stress distribution. From the main toolbar, select **Copy** > change the selection of **Displacement** to **Stress** and pick **von Mises** > **OK and Show**.

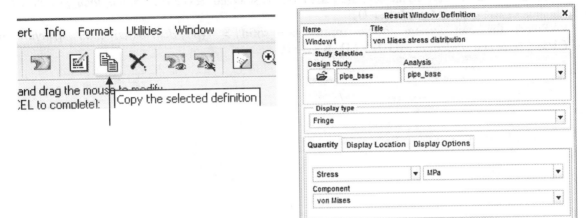

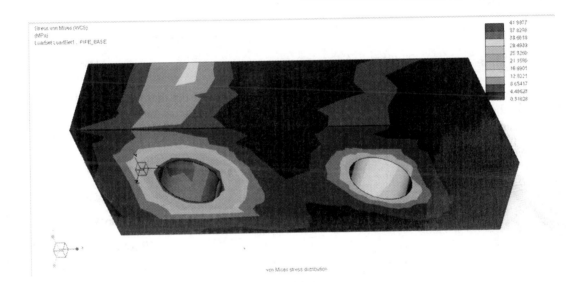

Section 10.5 Case Study 3: Study of a Beam Structure in 2D Space

The following figure illustrates a simple support beam. The cross-section area is a rectangle with the 2 dimensions equal to 50 and 25 mm. The load condition is a uniform distributed load. Its magnitude is 0.2 N.mm. The material type is steel. Let us perform an FEA analysis under the Creo Parametric Simulation environment.

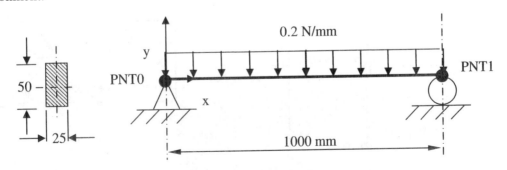

Step 1: Create a 2D model for the simple supported beam with a pin connection at the left side and with a simple support at the right side with a distributed load.

From **File**, click **New**. Make sure the **Part** mode is selected. Type *distributed_load_structure* and clear the box of **use default template > OK**

Select the unit system to be **mmns_part_solid** > type *distributed load structure* in **DESCRIPTION** and *student* in **MODELED_BY > OK**.

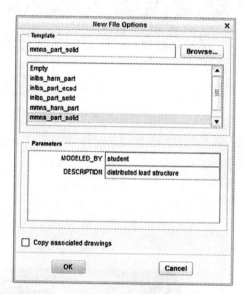

Define a datum curve, which is along the x-axis. The length of the datum curve is 1000 mm and it is symmetric about the y-axis. From the Model Tree, pick **FRONT** as the sketching plane. Click the icon of Sketch, and click the icon of Sketch View to orient the sketching plane parallel to the screen.

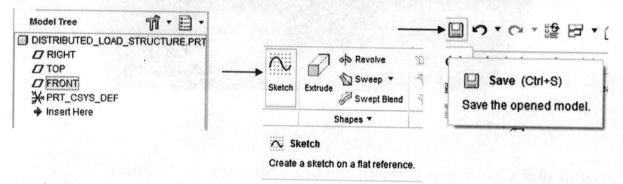

Click the icon of **Centerline** and sketch a centerline along the y-axis. This vertical centerline is used for symmetry.

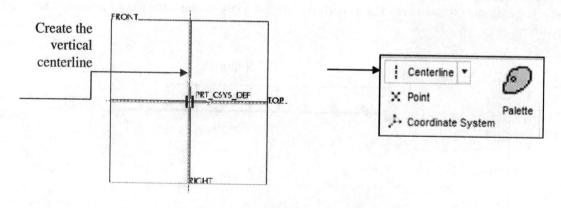

Click the icon of **Line** and sketch a line along the x-axis. The sketched line is symmetric about the vertical centerline. The dimension is 1000. Click the icon of **OK**.

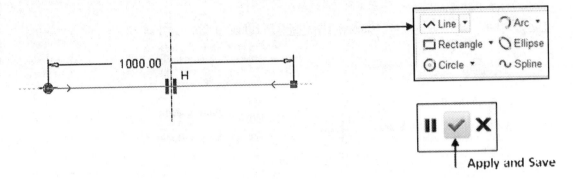

Apply and Save

Create two datum points. The first datum point is at the left end of the datum curve. Select the icon of **Datum Point**. Pick the point at the left end of the datum curve on display. Make sure the offset value is set at 0.00.

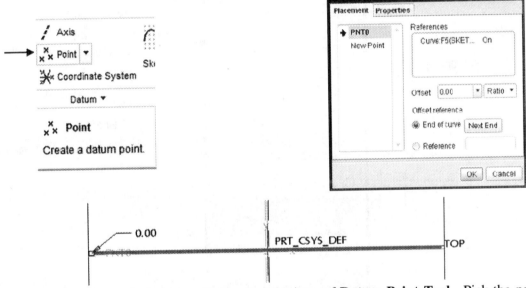

To define the second datum point, select the icon of **Datum Point Tool**. Pick the point at the right end of the datum curve. Make sure the offset value is set at 0.00.

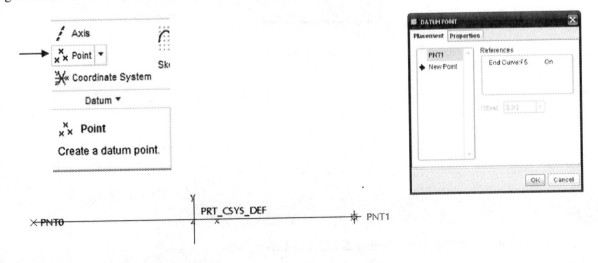

Step 2: Perform FEA under **Creo Parametric Simulation**
From the **Applications** tab, > **Simulation > Structure > OK.**

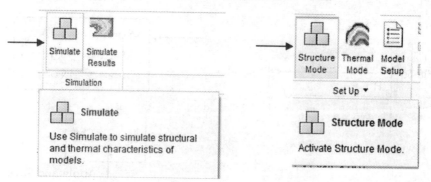

Click the **Refine Model** tab, click the icon of **Beam**. Accept Beam1 as the name.

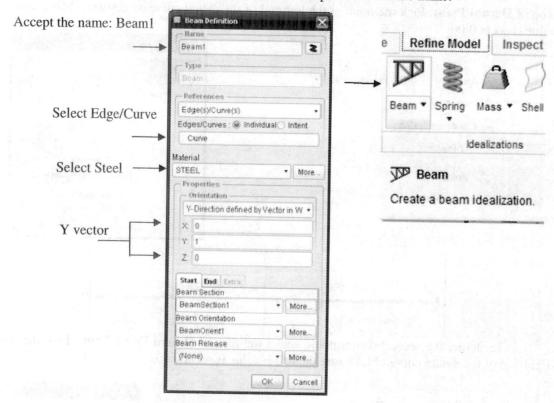

On the appeared **Beam Definition** window, do the followings:
Select **Edge/Curve** > pick the datum curve.

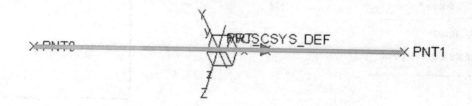

Select More from **Material** > Select **STEEL** > Close

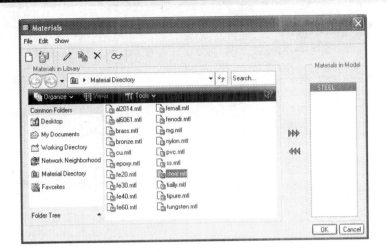

In the Properties field, set x = 0, y = 1 and z = 0 as the normal vector for orientation.

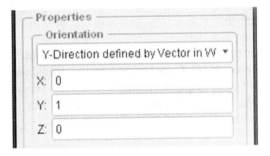

Select More from **Section** > **New** > select Rectangle > type *25* and *50* as b and d, respectively > **OK**.

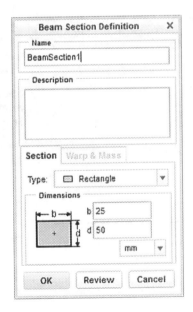

Define the Beam Orientation: click **More** > **New**, and make sure that DY=0 and DZ=0 to complete the process of defining the beam section > **OK**.

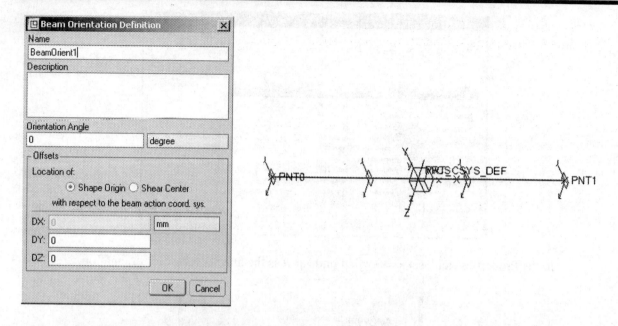

Step 3: Define a simple supported constraints at both ends of the beam.

Click the icon of **Displacement Constraints.** In the Constraint window, select **Point(s)** in the References box. Pick **PNT0** at the left end of the beam. Fix the 3 translation degrees of freedom. Fix the rotation about X and the rotation about Y. Set the rotation about z-axis to free. In this way, a pin structure is defined at the left end of the beam.

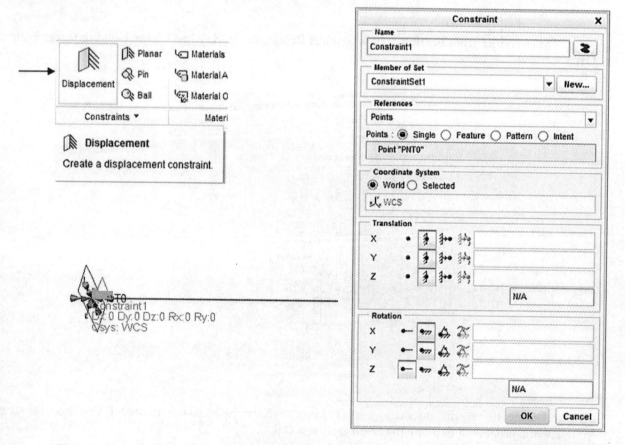

Click the icon of **Displacement Constraints.** In the Constraint window, select **Point(s)** in the References box. Pick **PNT1** at the right end of the beam. Fix the translation in Y and translation in Z. Set the translation in X free. Fix the rotation about X and the rotation about Y. Set the rotation about z-axis to free. In this way, a simple support structure is defined at the right end of the beam.

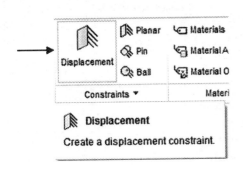

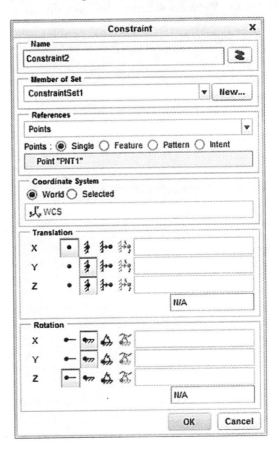

Step 4: Define the load condition.
Select the icon of **Force/Moment.**

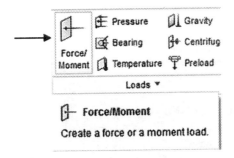

In the Force/Moment Load window, select Edges/Curves in the References box. Pick the datum curve. Select Force Per Unit Length in the Distribution box. Select Uniform in the Spatial Variation box. Type -0.2 in the Y direction before the force direction is downward. Click **OK**.

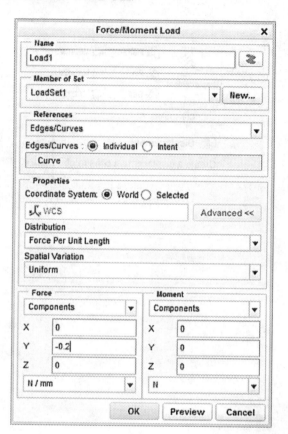

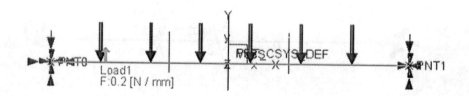

Step 5: Perform a static analysis
        Click the icon of **Analysis and Studies**.

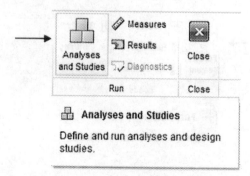

In the Analysis and Design Studies window, click **File > New Static**.

In the Static Analysis Definition window, both the defined constraint condition and the defined load condition are listed. Type *distributed_load_structure* as the file name. It is important for the user to check the Method box. Make sure Multi-Pass Adaptive is listed. Click **OK**.

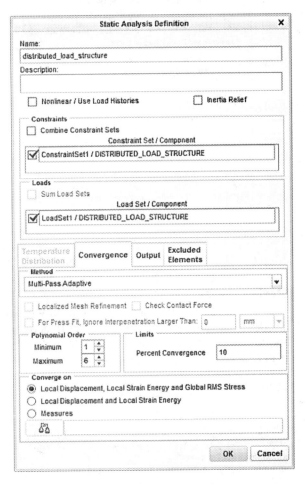

To run the analysis, click the icon of green flag. Just before the start of running the program, a message is on display. The message is asking the user "Do you want to run interactive diagnostics?" Click **Yes**. In this way a warning message will appear if an abnormal operation occurs.

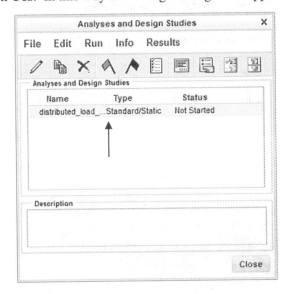

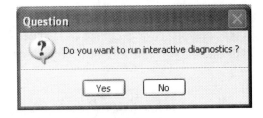

When running the FEA program is successful, the user may click the icon of Display study status, a report is on display, indicating the "Run Completed."

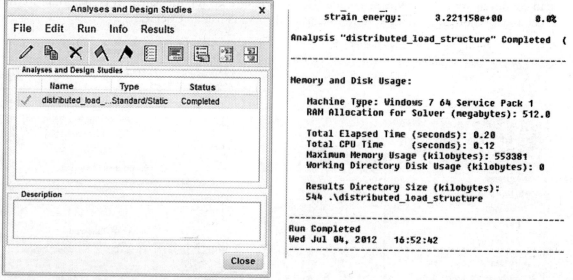

Step 6:   Show the results obtained from FEA by plotting the distribution of deflection.

To study the obtained result, say the reaction forces at the two support locations, click the icon of **Review results.**

In the Result Window Definition window, type Reaction forces at both ends as the name. Select Model in the Display type box. Select Reactions at Point Constraints in the Quantity box. Select Force in the Secondary Quantity box. Select Y in the Component box. Click **OK and Show.**   The magnitude is 100 N at each of the two supports, as shown.

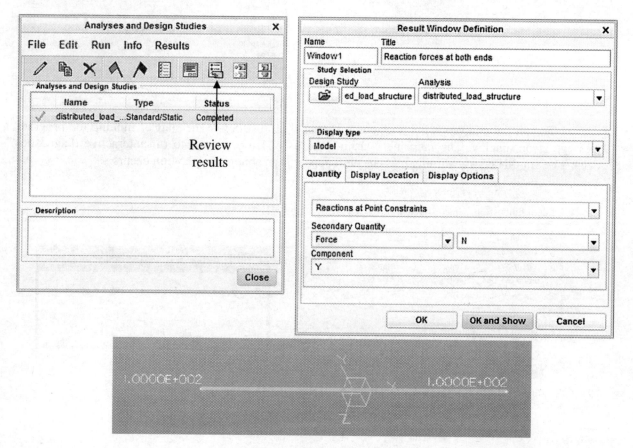

To construct the Shear and Moment diagrams, click the icon of Copy the selected definition. A new Result Window Definition appears.

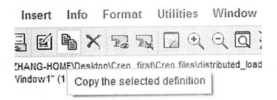

In this new window, we first change the name to Shear Diagram. Select Graph in the Display type box. Select Shear and Moment in the Quantity box. Select Vy in the Beam box. Select Curve Arc Length in the Relative To box. In the Graph Location box, click the pick box and pick the datum curve. Press the middle button of the mouse. Select **OK** to accept the default settings in the pop up window. Finally, click **OK and Show.**

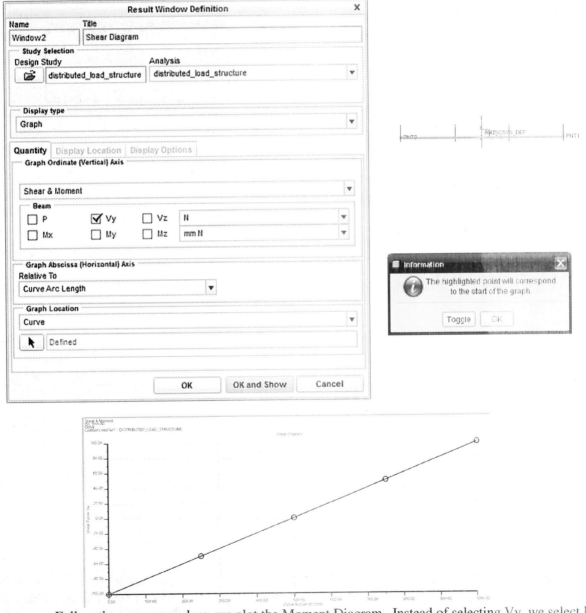

Follow the same procedure, we plot the Moment Diagram. Instead of selecting Vy, we select Mz.

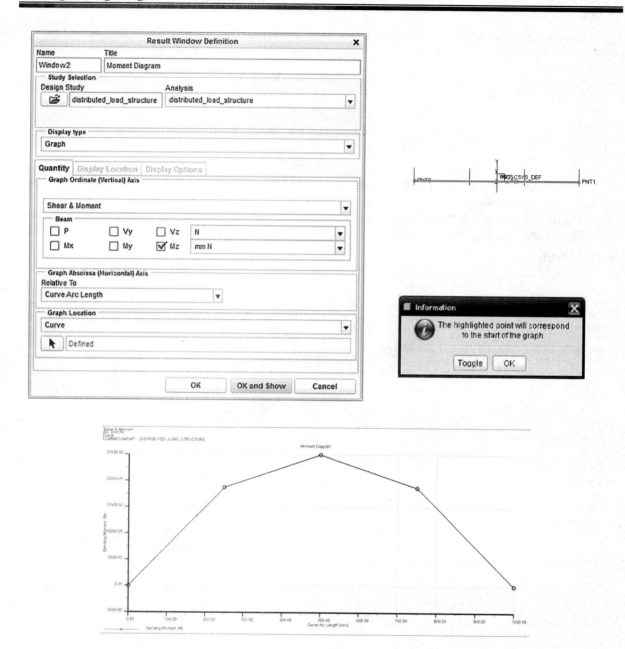

To plot the displacement distribution, click the icon of Copy the selected definition. A new Result Window Definition appears.

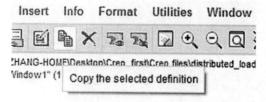

In this new window, we first change the name to Distribution of Displacement. Select Fringe in the Display type box. Select Displacement in the Quantity box. Select Magnitude in the Component box. click **OK and Show.** The maximum value of displacement is 0.05023 mm at the middle of the beam.

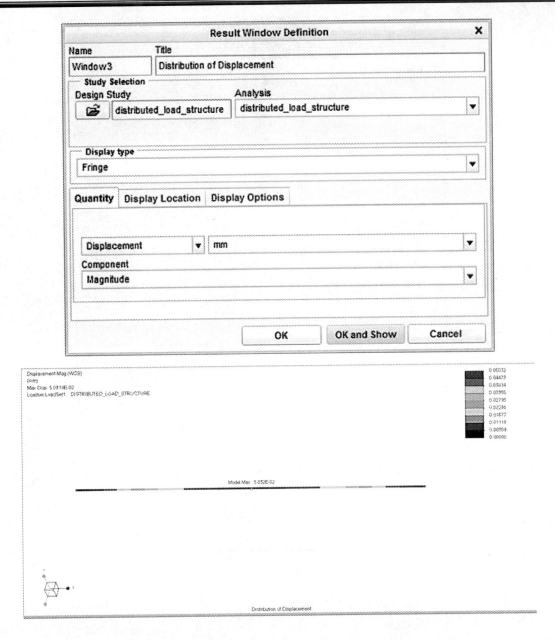

To plot the von Mises distribution, click the icon of Copy the selected definition. A new Result Window Definition appears.

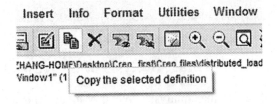

In this new window, we first change the name to Distribution of von Mises Stress. Select Fringe in the Display type box. Select Stress in the Quantity box. Select von Mises in the Component box. Click **OK and Show.** The maximum value of von Mises stress for the entire beam is 2.40 MPa acting at the middle of the beam.

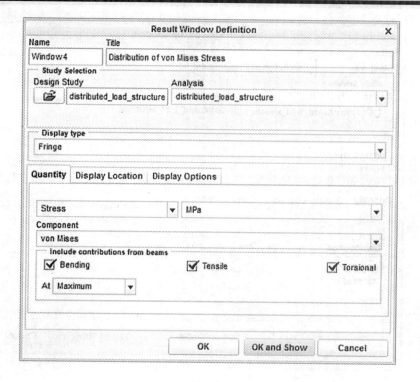

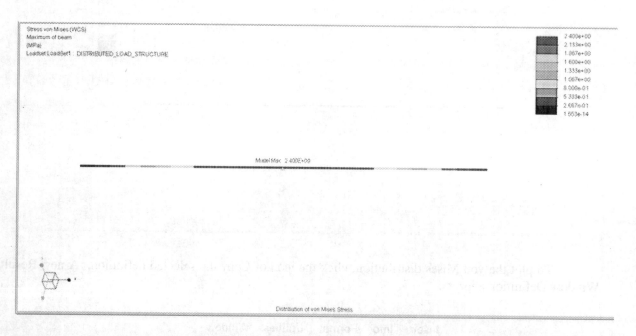

Section 10.6 Case Study 4: Thermal Analysis of a Firewall

In this case study, we deal with a thermal analysis. We investigate the temperature distribution of a firewall. The firewall is modeled as a solid block with the 3 dimensions equal to 1000 x 500 x 2000 mm. To control the temperature distribution, there are 2 water channels designed to disputed excessive heat confined within the firewall. The diameter is 200 mm. The convection boundary condition is 0.001 mV/(mm2C) and environment temperature is 20 $^{\circ}$C . The material type is brick. The material properties are listed below:

Properties	Values
Density	2.50 (g/cm^3)
Poisson's ratio	0.15
Young's modulus	40000 (MPa)
Coefficient of thermal expansion	1.20 E -05 (1/C^o)
Specific heat capacity	5.0 E +08 (mm^2/sec^2/C^o)
Thermal conductivity	0.008 (N/sec/C^o)

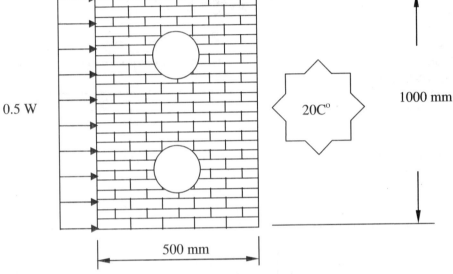

0.5 W

20C^o

1000 mm

500 mm

Step 1: Create a 3D solid model for the firewall structure.

From **File**, click the icon of **Create a new object** from the menu toolbar to initiate the creation of a 3D model. Type *firewall* as the file name, clear the box of **Use default template > OK**. Select the unit of **mmns_part_solid**, type *firewall* under the **description** of the model, and type *student* or *your name* under the **modeled_by > OK**.

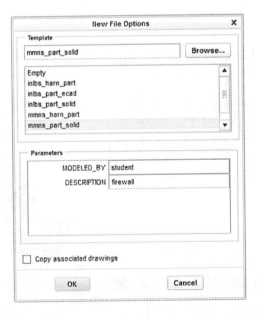

Click the icon of **Extrude**. Specify the depth value equal to 2000.

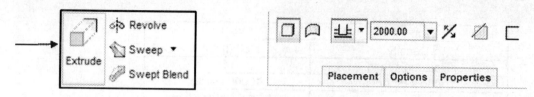

From the Model Tree, select the **FRONT** datum plane as the sketching plane. Click the icon of **Sketch View** to orient the sketching plane parallel to the screen.

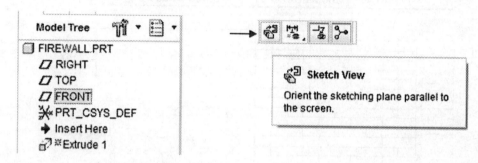

Click the icon of **Rectangle** and sketch a rectangle. The 2 dimensions of the rectangle are 500 and 1000, respectively.

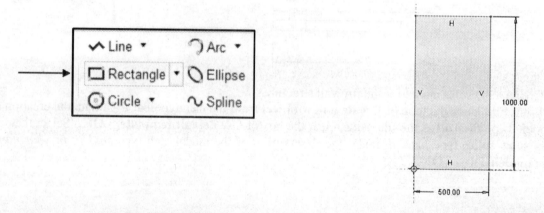

Click the icon of Circle. Sketch 2 circles. The diameter dimension is 150. The 3 position dimensions are 250, 250, and 250. Upon completion, click **OK** and click the icon of **Apply and Save**.

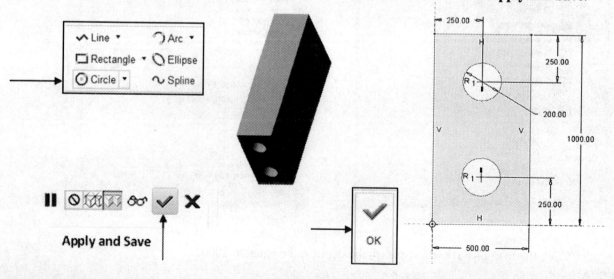

Step 2: Perform FEA under the Simulation environment.
In the Applications tab, click **Simulation > Thermal Mode**.

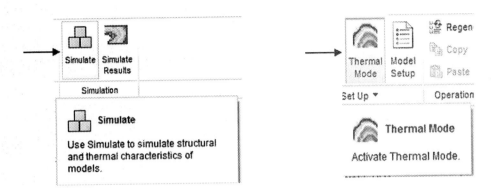

Click the icon of **Materials >** select **New** from the left side called **Materials in Model** because the material type of brick does not exist in the Simulation Library. We need to input and install this information related to the material properties based on the given information as listed.

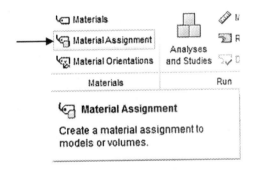

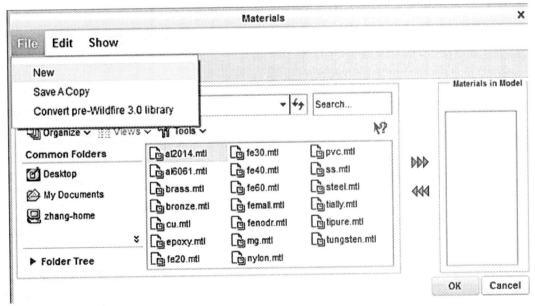

In the **Material Definition** window, type brick as the name of material. Change the scale to g/cm3 in the density box and specify 2.5 g/cm3 as the density value. In the **Structural** page, specify 0.15 as the Poisson's Ratio value. Specify 40000 MPa as the Young's Modulus value. Specify 1.2e-5 /C as the value of Coefficient of Thermal Expansion.

Turn to **Thermal** page, specify 5.0e+8 mm2/(sec2C) as the Specific Heat Capacity value, and 0.008 mW/(mmC) as the Thermal Conductivity value.

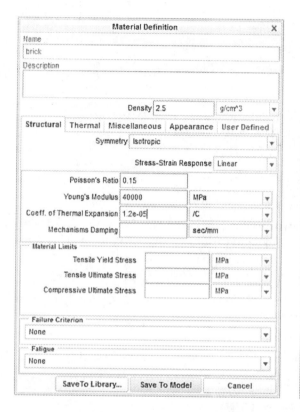
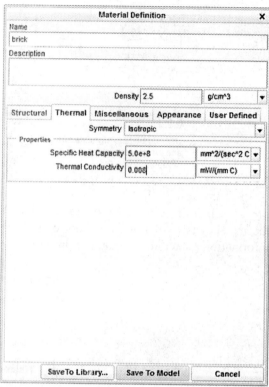

Upon completing the information > **Save to Model** > **OK.** We need to assign this set of material properties to the firewall component. Click the icon of **Material Assignments.** The software system has automatically completed the assignment because there is only one volume in the system > **OK.**

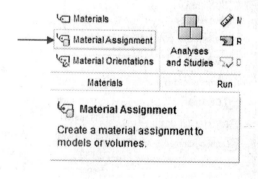

Step 3: Define the heat load condition.

Click the icon of Heat. Pick the surface on the left side of the firewall. Enter 500 as the heat load value. Note it is 500 mW. Click OK to complete the definition of a hear load.

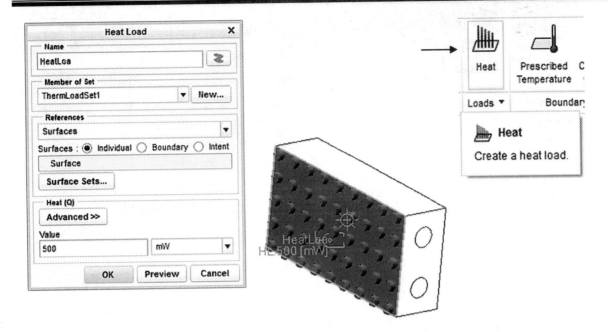

Step 3: Define the convection boundary condition.

Click the icon of Convection Condition. Pick the surface on the right side of the firewall. Specify 0.001 mW/(mm2C) as the value of the Convection Coefficient. Specify 20 °C as the Bulk Temperature. Click **OK**.

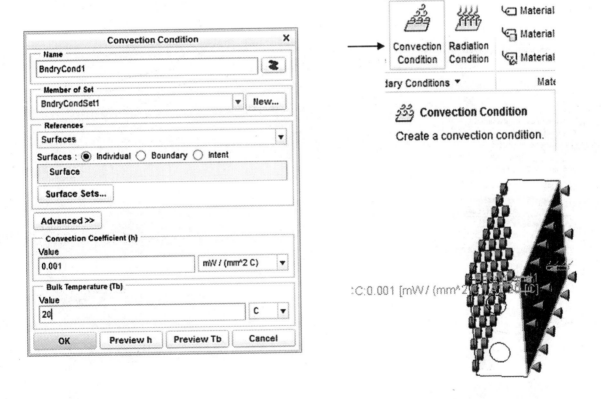

Step 4: Under the Simulation environment perform FEA

Click the icon of Analyses and Studies. In the Analyses and Design Studies window, click **File > New steady state thermal.**

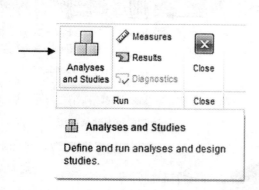

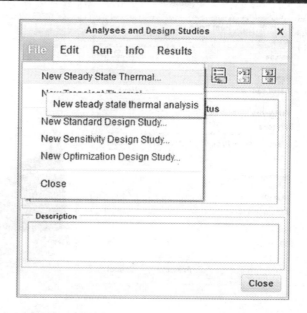

In the Steady Thermal Analysis Definition window, the defined thermal load condition is listed. The defined thermal convection condition is listed. Make sure that Single-Pass Adaptive is listed in the Method box. Click **OK.** In the Analyses and Design Studies window, Click the **Green Flag** to run the program. Just before the start of running the program, a message is on display. The message is asking the user "Do you want to run interactive diagnostics?" Click **Yes**. In this way a warning message will appear if an abnormal operation occurs.

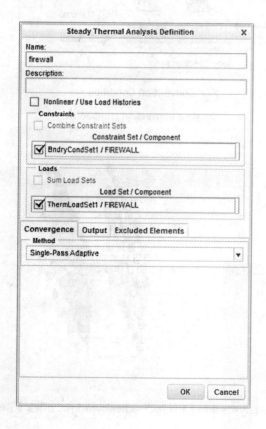

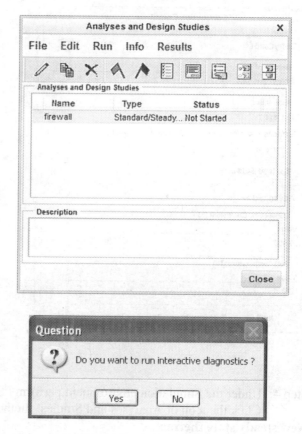

To monitor the computing process, users may click the icon of **Display study status**.

Step 5: Show the results obtained from FEA by plotting the distribution of temperature and heat flux.
   To study the obtained result, say the distribution of temperature, click the icon of **Review results.**
   In the Result Window Definition window, type distribution of temperature as the name. Fringe in the Displaytype box. Select Temperature in the Quantity box. Click **OK and Show.** The value of the maximum temperature is 40 °C on the left side of the firewall.

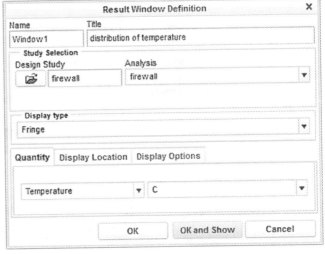

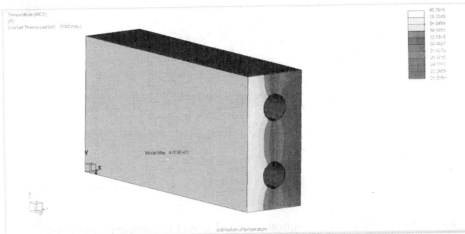

Step 6: Show the results obtained from FEA by plotting the heat flux distribution and animate the heat flux flow.

Click the icon of Copy the selected definition. A new Result Window Definition appears.

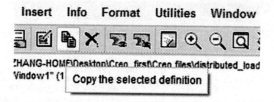

In this new window, we first change the name to distribution of heat flux. Select Vectors in the Display type box. Select Flux in the Quantity box. Select Magnitude in the Component box. Click **OK and Show.**

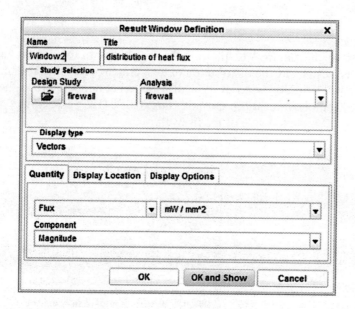

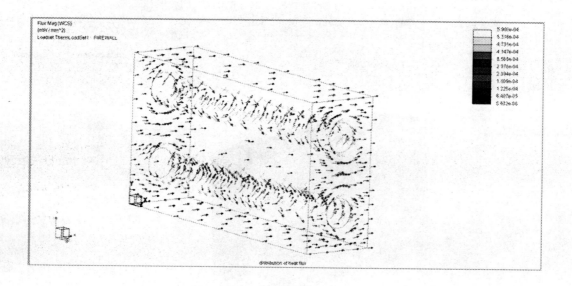

Step 6: Show the results of heat flux distribution obtained from FEA through animation.

Click the icon of Copy the selected definition. A new Result Window Definition appears.

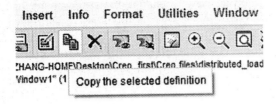

In this new window, we first change the name to animation of heat flux. Select Vectors in the Display type box. Select Flux in the Quantity box. Select Magnitude in the Component box. Click Display Options. Select Standard Vectors. Check the box of Animate and check the box of Auto Start. Click **OK and Show.** The heat flux flow is vividly displayed on the screen.

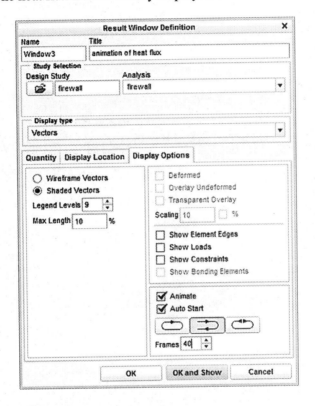

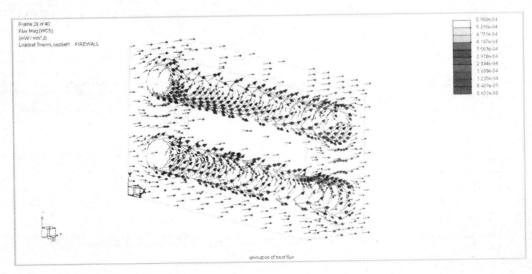

There are many options available in the Simulation package. Reader should explore those new features and new methods. For example, how to change the color of the background on the display so that the animation picture would be more appealing? Readers may just click Format > Renault Window. In the Visibilities window, there are several types of color are available for users to pick, such as black, blue, white, etc. The following plot was made by selecting the blue color.

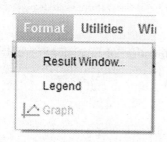

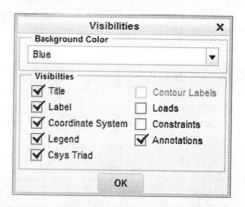

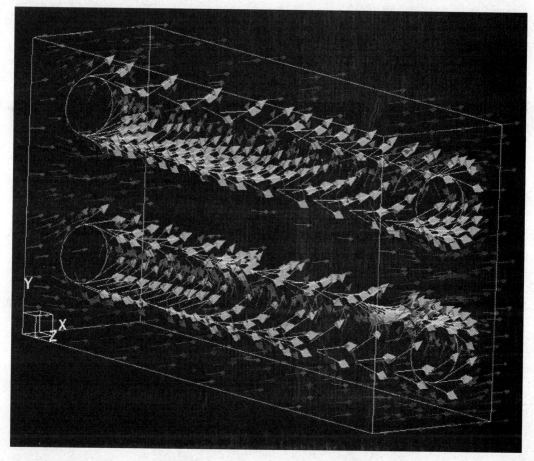

10.7 References

1.   F. L. Amirouche, <u>Computer-aided Design and Manufacturing</u>, Prentice Hall, Englewood Cliffs, New Jersey, 1993.

2.   D. D. Bedworth, M. R. Henderson, and P. M. Wolfe, <u>Computer-Integrated Design and Manufacturing</u>, McGraw-Hill, New York, NY, 1991.

3.   T. C. Chang, R. A. Wysk, and H. P. Wang, <u>Computer-aided Manufacturing</u>, , Prentice Hall, Englewood Cliffs, New Jersey, 1991.

4.   M. P. Groover and E. W. Zimmers, <u>Computer-aided Design and Manufacturing</u>, Englewood Cliffs, NJ, 1984.

5.   C. McMahon and J. Browne, <u>CADCAM: from Principles to Practice</u>, Addison Wesley, Workingham, England, 1993.

6.   Parametric Technology Corporation, Pro/MFG & Pro/NC-CHECK User's Guide, Release 20, 1998.

7.   J. Rehg, <u>Computer-Integrated Manufacturing</u>, Prentice Hall Career & Technology, Englewood Cliffs, New Jersey, 1994.

10.8 Exercises

1.   A block component is shown below. The material type is AL2014. The magnitude of load is 1000 Newton acting on the top surface of the block. The direction is upward. The bottom surface of this block is fixed to the ground. Simulate the displacement distribution of this block when it is subjected to this tensile load.

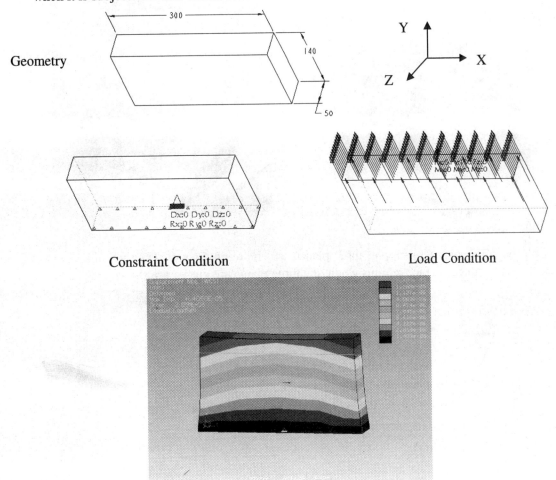

Geometry

Constraint Condition   Load Condition

2.   A spur gear component is shown below. Assume the material is steel. The force acting on the surface of tooth is 200 N in the direction normal to the surface of tooth. Set the fixed condition to the cylindrical surface of the hole as the constraint condition. Perform FEA to illustrate the displacement and stress distributions.

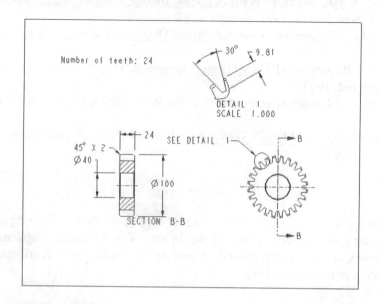

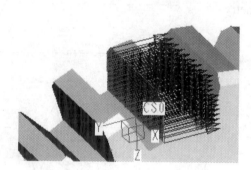

3. A plastic plate is used to support three plants, which are on display. The three dimensions of the plate and the three surface regions where the three plants are placed are shown below

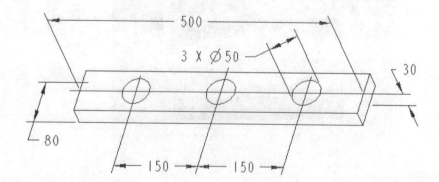

Assume that the weight of each plant is 200 N. The plate material is Nylon. Evaluate the deflection distribution and the distribution of the von Mises stress.

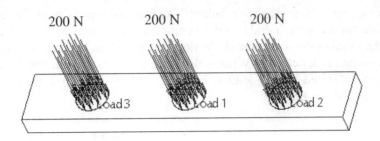

Assume the plate is fixed to the two supports. The dimensions of the two supports are shown in the figure.

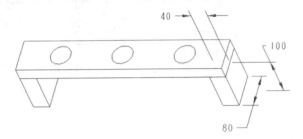

4.   A simple supported beam is shown below. The left end of the beam is a pin connection and the right end of the beam is supported by a roller connection. The material type of the beam structure is steel. The load is acting at the middle of the beam length. The magnitude of the load is 100 N and the direction of the load is downward. The cross section of the beam is a rectangle and the two dimensions are 25 mm and 50 mm, respectively. Perform FEA to determine the reaction forces at both ends, and construct a shear force diagram and a moment diagram.

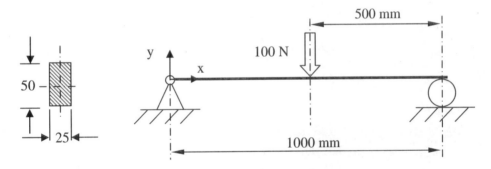

5.   A simple supported beam is shown below. The material type is steel. Perform FEA to determine the reaction forces at both ends, and construct a shear force diagram and a moment diagram. What is the value of the maximum deflection under the load? Where is such a location associated with the maximum deflection?

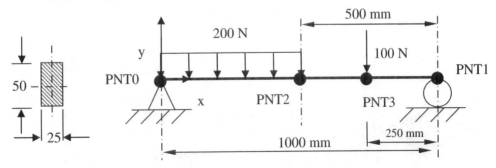

6. A simple supported beam is shown below. The material type is steel. Perform FEA to determine the reaction forces at both ends, and construct a shear force diagram and a moment diagram. What is the value of the maximum deflection under the load? Where is such a location associated with the maximum deflection? What is the value of the maximum von Mises stress for the entire beam when subjected to this load condition? Where is such a location associated with the maximum von Mises stress?

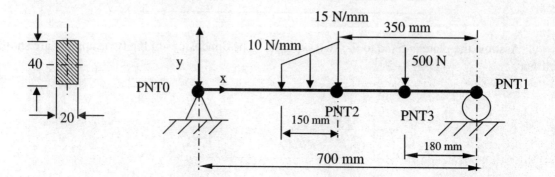

INDEX